The MICHELIN Guide

New York City

RESTAURANTS

2016

Michelin Travel Partner
Société par actions simplifiées au capital de 11 288 880 EUR
27 Cours de l'Ile Seguin - 92100 Boulogne Billancourt (France)
R.C.S. Nanterre 433 677 721

Dépôt légal septembre 2015

Printed in Canada - septembre 2015
Printed on paper from sustainably managed forests

Compogravure : Nord Compo à Villeneuve d'Ascq (France)
Impression et Finition : Transcontinental (Canada)

Our editorial team has taken the greatest care in writing this guide and checking the information in it. However, practical information (administrative formalities, prices, addresses, telephone numbers, Internet addresses, etc) is subject to frequent change and such information should therefore be used for guidance only. It is possible that some of the information in this guide may not be accurate or exhaustive as of the date of publication. Before taking action (in particular in regard to administrative and customs regulations and procedures), you should contact the appropriate official administration. We hereby accept no liability in regard to such information.

Dear Reader

It's been an exciting and formative year for the entire team at the MICHELIN guides in North America, and it is with great pride that we present you with our 2016 edition to New York City. Over the past year our dynamic inspectors have extended their reach to include a variety of establishments and multiplied their anonymous visits to restaurants in our selection in order to accurately reflect the rich culinary diversity this great city has to offer.

The Michelin Red Guides are an annual publication that recommends an assortment of delicious destinations and awards stars for excellence to a select few restaurants. Our company's founders, Édouard and André Michelin, published the first MICHELIN guide in 1900, to provide motorists with useful information about where they could service and repair their cars as well as find a good quality meal. Later in 1926, the star-rating system was introduced, whereby outstanding establishments are awarded for excellence in cuisine. Over the decades we have made many new enhancements to the Guide, and the local team here in New York City eagerly carries on these traditions. As part of the Guide's historic, highly confidential, and meticulous evaluation process, our inspectors have anonymously and methodically eaten their way through all five boroughs with a mission to marshal the finest in each category for your enjoyment. While they are expertly trained professionals in the food industry, the Guides remain consumer-driven and provide comprehensive choices to accommodate your every comfort, taste, and budget. By dining and drinking as "everyday" customers, our inspectors are able to experience and evaluate the same level of service and cuisine as any other guest. This past year has seen some unique advancements in the city's dining scene. Some of these can be found in each neighborhood introduction, complete with photography depicting our favored choices.

For more information and to get our inside scoop, you may follow the Inspectors on Twitter (@MichelinGuideNY) and Instagram (@ michelininspectors) as they chow their way around town and talk about unusual dining experiences, tell entertaining food stories, and detail other personal encounters. We thank you for your patronage and truly hope that the MICHELIN guide will remain your preferred reference to New York City's restaurants.

Contents

Dear Reader 3
The MICHELIN Guide 6
How to Use This Guide 8

Where to **Eat** 10

Manhattan 12

- Chelsea 14
- Chinatown & Little Italy 32
- East Village 46
- Financial District 88
- Gramercy, Flatiron & Union Square 98
- Greenwich & West Village 134
- Harlem, Morningside & Washington Heights 186
- Lower East Side 204
- Midtown East 222
- Midtown West 260
- SoHo & Nolita 314
- TriBeCa 340
- Upper East Side 360
- Upper West Side 392

The Bronx 414

Brooklyn 432

- ▶ Downtown 436
- ▶ Fort Greene & Bushwick 458
- ▶ Park Slope 480
- ▶ Sunset Park & Brighton Beach 496
- ▶ Williamsburg 512

Queens 542

Staten Island 594

Indexes 610

Alphabetical List of Restaurants 612
Restaurants by Cuisine 622
Cuisines by Neighborhood 633
Starred Restaurants 648
Bib Gourmand 651
Under $25 653
Brunch 655

Subway Map 672

The MICHELIN Guide

"This volume was created at the turn of the century and will last at least as long".

This foreword to the very first edition of the MICHELIN guide, written in 1900, has become famous over the years and the Guide has lived up to the prediction. It is read across the world and the key to its popularity is the consistency in its commitment to its readers, which is based on the following assurances.

→ Anonymous Inspections

Our inspectors make anonymous visits to restaurants to gauge the quality of cuisine offered to the everyday customer. They pay their own bill and make no indication of their presence. These visits are supplemented by comprehensive monitoring of information—our readers' comments are one valuable source, and are always taken into consideration.

→ Independence

Our choice of establishments is a completely independent one, made for the benefit of our readers alone. Decisions are discussed by the inspectors and editor, with the most important considered at the global level. Inclusion in the Guide is always free of charge.

→ The Selection

The Guide offers a selection of the best restaurants in each category of comfort and price. A recommendation in the Guides is an honor in itself, and defines the establishment among the "best of the best."

How the MICHELIN Guide Works

→ Annual Updates

All practical information, the classifications, and awards, are revised and updated every year to ensure the most reliable information possible.

→ Consistency & Classifications

The standards and criteria for the classifications are the same in all countries covered by the Michelin Guides. Our system is used worldwide and easy to apply when selecting a restaurant.

→ The Classifications

We classify our restaurants using XXXXX-X to indicate the level of comfort. A symbol in red suggests a particularly charming spot with unique décor or ambience. The ✿✿✿-✿ specifically designates an award for cuisine. They do not relate to a chef or establishment and are unique from the classification.

→ Our Aim

As part of Michelin's ongoing commitment to improving travel and mobility, we do everything possible to make vacations and eating out a pleasure.

How to Use This Guide

The Michelin Distinctions for Good Cuisine

Stars for good cuisine

- ✿✿✿ Exceptional cuisine, worth a special journey
- ✿✿ Excellent cuisine, worth a detour
- ✿ A very good restaurant in its category

Bib Gourmand

Inspectors' favorites for good value

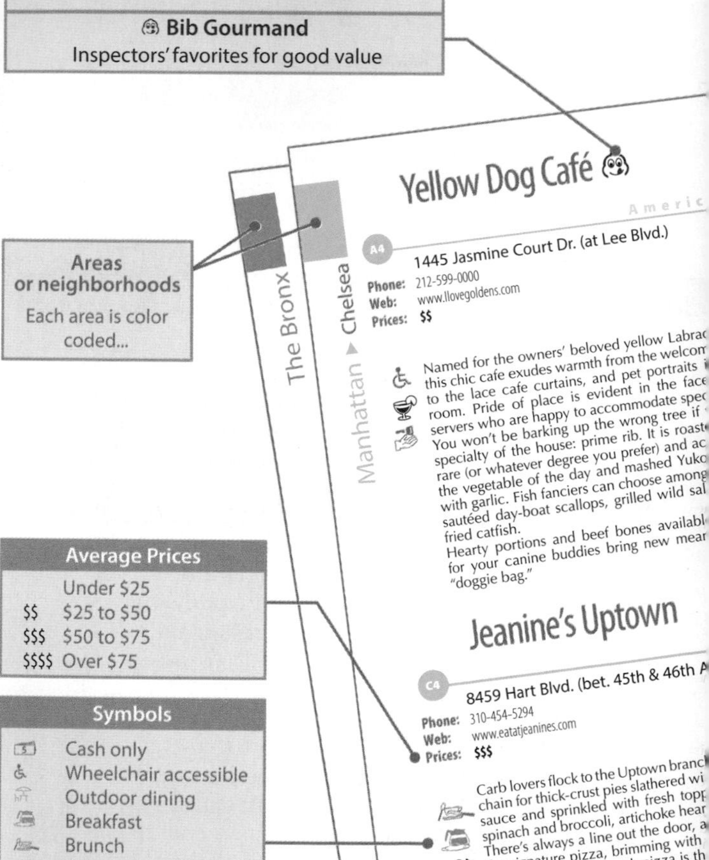

Areas or neighborhoods

Each area is color coded...

Average Prices

	Under $25
$$	$25 to $50
$$$	$50 to $75
$$$$	Over $75

Symbols

- Cash only
- Wheelchair accessible
- Outdoor dining
- Breakfast
- Brunch
- Dim sum
- Notable wine list
- Notable sake list
- Notable cocktail list
- Notable beer list
- Valet parking
- Private dining room

Restaurant Classifications by Comfort

More pleasant if in red

X	Comfortable
XX	Quite comfortable
XXX	Very comfortable
XXXX	Top class comfortable
XXXXX	Luxury in the traditional style
	Small plates

Map Coordinates

Sonya's Palace ✿✿

Italian XXXX

Manhattan ▶ Chelsea

A4 100 Reuther Pl. (at 30th Street)

Dinner daily

Phone: 415-867-5309
Subway: 14th St - 8 Av
Web: www.sonyasfabulouspalace.com
Prices: $$$

Home cooked Italian never tasted so good than at this unpretentious little place. The simple décor claims no big-name designers, and while the Murano glass light fixtures are chic and the velveteen-covered chairs are comfortable, this isn't a restaurant where millions of dollars were spent on the interior.

Instead, food is the focus here. The restaurant's name may not be Italian, but it nonetheless serves some of the best pasta in the city, made fresh in-house. Dishes follow the seasons, thus ravioli may be stuffed with fresh ricotta and herbs in summer, and pumpkin in fall. Most everything is liberally dusted with Parmigiano Reggiano, a favorite ingredient of the chef.

For dessert, you'll have to deliberate between the likes of creamy tiramisu, ricotta cheesecake, and homemade gelato. One thing's for sure: you'll never miss your nonna's cooking when you eat at Sonya's.

153

San Francisco ▶ Nob Hill

Lunch daily

107

Where to Eat

Manhattan 12
The Bronx 414
Brooklyn 432
Queens 542
Staten Island 594

Manhattan

DIVERSITY IN DINING

Chelsea is a charming residential neighborhood combining modern high-rises and sleek lofts with classic townhouses and retail stores aplenty. To that end, this nabe is a shopper's paradise, offering everything from computer marts and high fashion boutiques, to **Chelsea Market**—the city's culinary epicenter. And let's not forget the art: this neighborhood's once-dilapidated warehouses and abandoned lofts are currently home to over 200 prominent galleries as well as the artists who contribute to them. Naturally, find a burgeoning cultural scene. To feed its well-educated, art-enthusiastic residents, and out-of-towners on pilgrimage here, Chelsea teems with casual cafeterias. Those old-world Puerto Rican luncheonettes that used to dot Ninth Avenue have now given way to mega-hip temples of fusion cooking—where diners are accommodated in stylish digs and the cocktail menu packs a

potent punch. Carousers party until last call at such high-energy hangouts as **1 OAK**, launched by greenmarket-obsessed chef, Alex Guarnaschelli's Butter Group. Patrons of this hot spot may then jump ship to the likes of **Marquee**, but remain loyal to such late-night stalwarts as **Robert's Steakhouse @ Scores New York**. Nestled inside The Penthouse Executive Club, it's really all about the "meat" at this fortress of flesh, where gentlemen seem far more lured by char-rich steaks on plates than those ladies on their laps. These insomnious hordes can

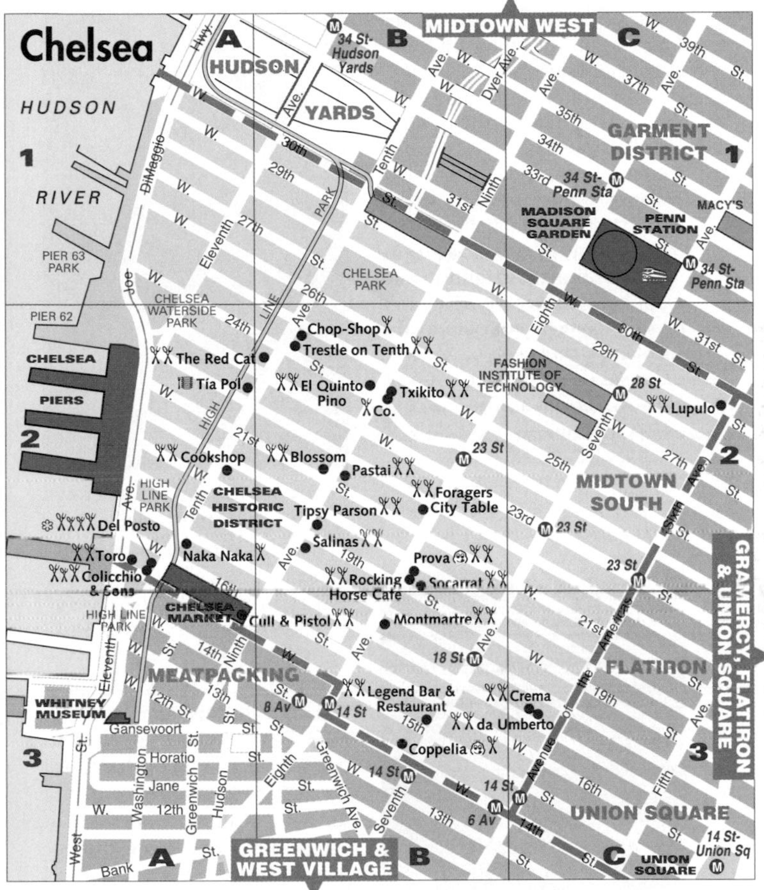

also be seen swinging to live salsa at **Son Cubano**, an Old Havana-inspired supper club whose superb mojitos and Spanish small plates will have you shouting *viva la Cubanos* before the night is out!

THE HIGH LINE

Located above Manhattan's mean streets and atop an elevated freight railroad, **The High Line** is a lengthy public space with a large presence in Chelsea. Populated by yuppies and young families, and punctuated by acres of indigenous greenery as well as surprisingly stunning views of the Hudson, this city-center oasis also offers unique respites for refreshment. **Bubby's High Line** is perpetually packed for its impressive repertoire of food and drink. Envision rambling locals ordering off a kid's menu; or late-night revelers devouring a "midnight brunch" and you will begin to understand what this neighborhood is all about. Too rushed to dwell over dessert? Their retail store sells pastries and ice cream sandwiches to-go, after which a shot of single-origin drip espresso at **Blue Bottle Coffee Café** is not just fitting, but first-class. As history would have it, the last functional freight train that passed through The High Line had cars filled with meat. It therefore seems only natural that **Delaney Barbecue's Smokeline** also boasts a station here. This down-home shack may only prepare simple, straightforward food, but it makes for a fantastic pit stop, perhaps en-route to **The Taco Truck** churning out Mexican street eats during the summer heat. Nearby, **Terroir at The Porch** is an open-air, full-service café with small plates, wine, and beer to boot. Seal such stellar sips with a cooling kiss from **L'Arte del Gelato**. Sound like bliss? It is.

In 1997, the 1898 Nabisco factory reopened as **Chelsea Market**, a fabled culinary bazaar whose brick-lined walkways are now cramped with stores selling everything—think lemons to lingerie. Carb-addicts begin their circuitous culinary excursion here at the now-expanded **Amy's Bread**, where artisan-crafted

loaves are as precious as crown jewels. Then they might linger over at **Bar Suzette** for scores of undeniably excellent, very fluffy crêpes. Meanwhile, the calorie-counters collect at **Beyond Sushi** for healthy, tasty renditions of the Japanese staple, wrapped here in black rice and topped with creamy tofu. From Asian signatures to everyday Italian, **Buon Italia** will not only help stock your pantry for a night in with *nonna*, but sates those inevitable hunger pangs while you're at it—a stand upfront sells cooked foods and sandwiches to crowds on the run. Other welcome members to this epicurean community include **Dickson's Farmstand** for house-made pâté; sweet sanctum **Sarabeth's** or **Fat Witch Bakery** for goodies and holiday gifts; as well as **Ronnybrook Milk Bar**, a milk and shake shop-turned-full service restaurant. Keep tossing your way north before sealing the deal at **The Grill at La Piscine** (on the stunning rooftop of Hôtel Americano) with a bite of any kind but sure sip of *vino*!

Blossom

Vegan XX

187 Ninth Ave. (bet. 21st & 22nd Sts.)

Subway: 23 St (Eighth Ave.)
Phone: 212-627-1144
Web: www.blossomnyc.com
Prices: **$$**

Lunch & dinner daily

Unpretentious and welcoming, this is a vegan favorite with spot-on spicing and delicious surprises. The cream-colored interior is dim with dark velvet curtains and votive candlelight reflected in round mirrors. The vibe may seem moody come evening, but the staff is always warm and affable.

Huge portions and the bold flavors of smoked tempeh, spinach, pine nuts, and cremini mushrooms prove the power of vegetables to dedicated carnivores. Follow this with meaty and woodsy grilled seitan, glazed with violet-mustard and served over a mélange of roasted salsify and sautéed kale surrounded by horseradish cream. Come dessert, try the hand-churned cashew ice cream or a lemony cheesecake with a mixed berry reduction and coconut-cookie crust.

Chop-Shop

Asian X

B2

254 Tenth Ave. (bet. 24th & 25th Sts.)

Subway: 23 St (Eighth Ave.)
Phone: 212-820-0333
Web: www.chop-shop.co
Prices: **$$**

Lunch Mon– Sat
Dinner nightly

Now an über-hip scene, this far west strip of Chelsea has been attracting its fair share of affluent locals and a flurry of dashing eateries; Chop-Shop is part of that evolution. Outfitted in reclaimed pine, vintage lights, and concrete floors, it has an industrial look but is awash with sunlight thanks to soaring windows.

The eclectic menu roams across Asia with deliciously balanced and infinitely varied plates. Subtlety reigns in an avocado-tofu summer roll paired with peanut curry sauce or salt-and-pepper shrimp, while Chinese water spinach with fermented tofu cream delivers an intense punch of flavor. Fried rice with salmon and peas is less than classic but more than popular. Rich tastes and silky textures meld beautifully in coconut crème caramel.

Co.

Pizza

B2

230 Ninth Ave. (at 24th St.)

Subway: 23 St (Eighth Ave.)
Phone: 212-243-1105
Web: www.co-pane.com
Prices: $$

Lunch Tue-Sun
Dinner Daily

Head to Co. for something other than those Naples-aping pizzerias that have come to monopolize the whole of New York. A serious destination for its dedicated take on pies, this carb haven pays equal attention to the dough and toppings, with outstanding results. These are the ways of celebrated baker and chef, Jim Lahey, who perfected his yeasty, smoky flavors at Sullivan Street Bakery (a few doors away) and is NYC's resident expert on bread-making.

Amid wood-paneled walls, wine racks, and modern-looking mirrors, crowds savor innovative combinations, such as spicy merguez with smoked pepper sauce, pecorino, and mint on a puffy crust. Nightly specials include a creamy leek and celeriac soup, finished with olive oil and freshly ground black pepper.

Colicchio & Sons

American

A2

85 Tenth Ave. (bet. 15th & 16th Sts.)

Subway: 14 St - 8 Av
Phone: 212-400-6699
Web: www.craftrestaurantsinc.com
Prices: $$$

Lunch Wed – Fri
Dinner nightly

In front, the Tap Room pours an impressive roster of beers to go with pricey small plates. Beyond this, a dining room mixes chrome and a glass wine wall with leather banquettes and a birds-eye mural of the neighborhood. This layout almost recalls namesake Chef Colicchio's stint behind the stoves at Gramercy Tavern.

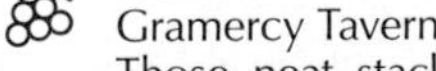

Those neat stacks of chopped wood resting on polished shelves out front are analogous to the menu's ambition: relaxed, rustic yet very contemporary. Warm Parker House rolls are an auspicious prelude to ivory-pink hamachi set over beets with smoked crème fraîche. Fusilli with wild boar ragù and pecorino is nothing short of excellent. Consider going for the fixed menu; it just may cost less than ordering à la carte by the time the check arrives.

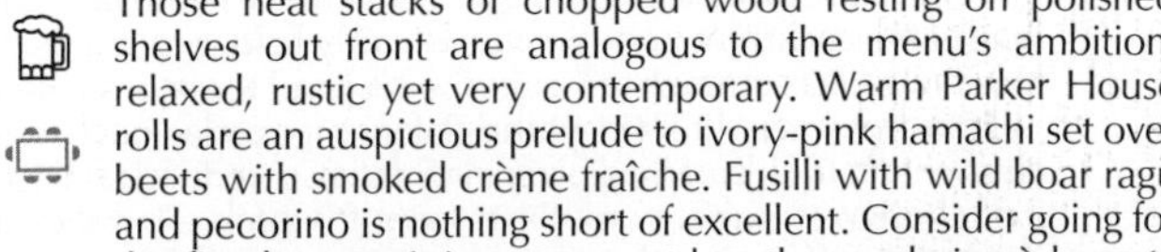

Cookshop

American

156 Tenth Ave. (at 20th St.)

Subway: 23 St (Eighth Ave.) Lunch & dinner daily
Phone: 212-924-4440
Web: www.cookshopny.com
Prices: $$

Airy, sun-flooded, and in a location that still manages to seem brand-spanking new, Cookshop brings highbrow dining to western Chelsea. The plant-filled dining room is furnished with ethically sourced American oak tables and spotlights a wall of banquettes. The bar is perfect for solo dining.

The kitchen drives this locavare philosophy with energy and skill. A cooling late-summer tomato soup is a smooth balance of sweet and tart flavors, enhanced with tangy lemon-basil and riesling. House-made *lasagnette* highlights the best of the season with high-minded Italian style, through tight, wavy ridges of pasta beautifully dressed in delicate pesto. Save room for sweet treats like a peanut butter Bavarian with Concord grape *granite* and milk ice cream.

Coppelia

Latin American

207 W. 14th St. (bet. Seventh & Eighth Aves.)

Subway: 14 St (Seventh Ave.) Lunch & dinner daily
Phone: 212-858-5001
Web: www.coppelianyc.com
Prices: $$

Think of ultra-casual Coppelia as a favorite anytime Latin-American diner, ready to please with its enormous menu served 24 hours a day, seven days a week. The space is long and narrow, including a counter for solo guests, checkerboard floors, and cheery yellow walls. Come midnight, the booths are hopping.

The Havana salad has nothing to do with its namesake city but is an unbeatable combination of curly kale, queso fresco, toasted pepitas, crunchy mustard seeds, and tomatoes tossed in lemony vinaigrette. Crisp and flaky empanadas have both classic and quirky fillings, ranging from shredded chicken and chorizo to sweet corn. Save room for a towering slice of carrot cake featuring the unique twist of Manchego cheese and zesty lime frosting.

Crema

Mexican XX

C3

111 W. 17th St. (bet. Sixth & Seventh Aves.)

Subway: 18 St
Lunch & dinner daily
Phone: 212-691-4477
Web: www.cremarestaurante.com
Prices: $$

Thanks to her perseverance, focus, and vision, Chef/owner Julieta Ballesteros has ensured that Crema remains ahead of the curve and at the top of her neighborhood. The long dining room is colorful, with a cactus garden, vibrant Latin music, and a semi-open kitchen for a peek inside the buzz, especially during happy hour when small plates are flying to the bar. Like the vibe, the cooking favors bold tastes over subtlety.

Daily soups showcase careful execution—the chicken and rice may look simple but is spiked with lime and topped with cilantro and grated *queso fresco* for superb comfort. *Alambres de filet mignon* pleases with lime-marinated and buttery skewered meat, served alongside beer-battered onion rings and bright lemon-basil *chimichurri*.

Cull & Pistol

Seafood XX

A3

75 Ninth Ave. (in Chelsea Market)

Subway: 14 St - 8 Av
Lunch & dinner daily
Phone: 646-568-1223
Web: www.cullandpistol.com
Prices: $$

Cull & Pistol is a sensational seafood spot. This breath of fresh salt-laden air is replete with reclaimed teak tables, brushed steel chairs, and a zinc-topped raw bar groaning with crimson-red crab claws, chilled lobster, shrimp cocktail, and clams from all shores.

It's an impressive start tailed by a vast oyster menu and deeply comforting classics that may be slurped up at two-tops inside the cozy space. Then, a whole fish salt-baked in a hefty cask is cracked open, teasing diners with plumes of thyme- and lemon-scented steam. At lunch, the clambake is a briny, heavenly mash-up of lobster, mussels, Dickson's sausage, corn on the cob and fingerling potatoes, served family-style in a rich shellfish broth. Dessert is pure and sweet bliss.

da Umberto

Italian XX

C3

107 W. 17th St. (bet. Sixth & Seventh Aves.)

Subway: 18 St — Lunch Mon – Fri
Phone: 212-989-0303 — Dinner Mon – Sat
Web: www.daumbertonyc.com
Prices: $$$$

There is a finely tuned harmony to dining at such classic New York restaurants as this one. The Italian menu is familiar and unpretentious, the kitchen is adept, and ingredients are superb. But, what truly sets it apart is an ability to serve exactly what you crave without seeming trite or predictable. Even the look is a perfectly conjured mix of warm neutrals with a sleek yet informal Northern Italian style and impeccably timed servers.

Start with the traditional antipasto and then proceed to one of the daily specials like veal Milanese or a lavish dish of *garganelli* with mushrooms and black truffles. When the dessert cart rolls around, expect an array of excellent house-made sweets like pristine berries under whisked-to-order *zabaglione*.

El Quinto Pino

Spanish XX

B2

401 W. 24th St. (bet. Ninth & Tenth Aves.)

Subway: 23 St (Eighth Ave.) — Lunch Tue – Sun
Phone: 212-206-6900 — Dinner nightly
Web: www.elquintopinonyc.com
Prices: $$

Blend Barcelona tapas with New York creativity and get this Chelsea baby from Alex Raij and Eder Montero. After tripling its footprint, it has made even more of an impression in the area's crowded landscape of small plates-style spots. Still packed, guests can now forgo balancing drinks on a skinny bar adorned with wool tapestries, and relax in a properly romantic dining room.

Choose a wine from the chalkboard and dive into the deconstructed yet sublime flavors. Supple and smoky calamari delivers surprise after surprise with squid jus, parmesan, and black garlic all perfectly balanced with umami. Intensely aromatic, earthy, and excellent, the *arroz brut de conejo* stuffs "dirty" rice and rabbit into tender cabbage beautifully braised in saffron broth.

Del Posto ✿

A2

85 Tenth Ave. (at 16th St.)

Subway: 14 St - 8 Av
Phone: 212-497-8090
Web: www.delposto.com
Prices: **$$$$**

Lunch Mon – Fri
Dinner nightly

In a city like ours, there should be room for all types of restaurants—and that includes those of a more traditional persuasion. The exquisitely attired Del Posto is unashamedly Old School and comes with an expanse of mahogany, acres of marble, and rows of immaculately set tables; you also get a pianist and a veritable army of servers holding down various ranks.

In surroundings of such grandeur, it's easy to assume the food will play second fiddle but that would be a mistake because the Italian food here is very good indeed. The menu layout and pricing can be a little bewildering at first but what becomes abundantly clear is that this is a well-orchestrated kitchen and one which demonstrates considerable skill and plenty of genuine care. Fish fin crudo is a great way to start; pasta dishes are surprisingly robust and generously proportioned; and entrées such as lamb with figs come with an awareness of contemporary tastes. Although pastry chef extraordinaire Brooks Headley has left, his signature desserts remain an immortal highlight on Del Posto's menu.

The only thing here you'll find difficult is in believing this place is barely over a decade old.

Foragers City Table

Contemporary 

300 W. 22nd St. (at Eighth Ave.)

Subway: 23 St (Eighth Ave.) — Lunch Sat – Sun
Phone: 212-243-8888 — Dinner Mon – Sat
Web: www.foragerscitygrocer.com
Prices: $$

Chef Nickolas Martinez flaunts his pedigree with intensity at this homage to all things local and organic. The restaurant-cum-market is an offshoot of an independent grocer in DUMBO, though its kitchen philosophy seems to have arrived via California.

Inside, the boxy dining room radiates functionality through large, unemcumbered windows and hardwood tables. It is staffed and patronized by the sort of local-loving sycophants who consider it an honor to dine here. And it actually is.

Begin with Sfoglini trumpets generously bathed in a luxurious lamb Bolognese with tender broccoli rabe and earthy brown beech mushrooms. Unabashed spice tingles with every slurp of clear sweet shrimp- chicken- and herb-filled dumpling soup.

Legend Bar & Restaurant

Chinese XX

B3

88 Seventh Ave. (bet. 15th & 16th Sts.)

Subway: 14 St (Seventh Ave.) — Lunch & Dinner daily
Phone: 212-929-1778
Web: www.legendrestaurant88.com
Prices: ◎

While Legend may offer a nice variety of Asian fare, just stick to the Sichuan specialties and be thoroughly rewarded. Find one of the many highlights in supremely flavorful and tender Chong Qing spicy chicken, loaded with viciously good dried chilies. The house duck is a traditional presentation of roasted and crisped meat with wraps as well as a host of accouterments, including crushed peanuts, fragrant herbs, scallions, and very tasty plum sauce. Bok choy with black mushrooms is a crunchy, simply delicious departure from the intensity of other dishes you may face here.

The dining room has a certain hip and chic feel that fosters a lively happy hour scene. Colorful fabrics, striped walls, and statues of deities make for an attractive space.

Lupulo

Portuguese XX

C2

835 Sixth Ave. (at 29th St.)

Subway: 28 St (Eighth Ave.) — Dinner nightly
Phone: 212-290-7600
Web: www.lupulonyc.com
Prices: $$

Located at the base of Eventi, a Kimpton Hotel, Chef George Mendes' elegant restaurant is a beautiful, industrial-chic ode to the casual home cooking of Portugal. Food voyeurs should vie for a seat at the bar, where they can eye fresh seafood lined up in plump, shimmering rows or enjoy the action behind the glass wall of the semi-open kitchen. Otherwise, a seat in the bustling dining room, decked out in gorgeous Portuguese tiles and hip lobster-trap lights, ought to do the trick.

Try the *espargos assados*, a dish of tender, spit-grilled spring asparagus topped with shaved dried sea urchin, sorrel, olive oil and a dust of sea salt; or the wickedly good *frango piri-piri*, grilled to perfection and served with its mouthwatering namesake pepper sauce.

Montmartre

French XX

B3

158 Eighth Ave. (bet. 17th & 18th Sts.)

Subway: 18 St — Lunch Fri – Sun
Phone: 646-596-8838 — Dinner nightly
Web: www.montmartrenyc.com
Prices: $$$

This dark, oh-so-Frenchy Chelsea charmer finds its culinary footing in Patrick McGrath's kitchen takeover—and the results are seriously delicious. Duck inside and you'll find a small, but sweet little spot to cool your heels in or, come summer, make your way back to the excellent (and intimate) covered back garden.

Any place you land, you'll be treated to McGrath's spot-on dishes like an excellent brandade, whipped to salty, creamy perfection and topped with a layer of silky red pepper-infused olive oil; a well-spiced *pâté de campagne* served with grilled sourdough and pickled veggies; or a wildly fresh piece of salmon laid over a bed of sugar snap peas, crumbled French feta, pickled ramps, and laced with saffron aïoli.

Naka Naka

Japanese

458 W. 17th St. (bet. Ninth & Tenth Aves.)

Subway: 14 St - 8 Av
Phone: 212-929-8544
Web: www.nakanakany.com
Prices: $$$

Dinner Tue – Sun

Like a graceful ballet, Naka Naka's kimono-draped servers, lustrous pearl-hued lanterns, and elegant calligraphy create a dance that instantly transports you from Chelsea to Japan. Housed in a timeworn tenement building amid gleaming high-rise condos, the soothing atmosphere draws a largely urban crowd, slung in the low wooden seats of this hidden gem.

There is a melody to the food as well, beginning with aged, unfiltered sake. Dishes include cold soba topped with flaky fish tempura and the signature Naka Naka box, an ever-changing selection of exceptional tempuras, rice, and miso-dressed tuna. Salty, briny, mouth-coating flavors soon climax with bites of the vibrant sea urchin and downright perfect salmon roe sushi, worthy of its own Kyoto temple.

Pastai

Italian

B2

186 Ninth Ave. (bet. 21st & 22nd Sts.)

Subway: 23 St (Eighth Ave.)
Phone: 646-688-3463
Web: www.pastainyc.com
Prices: $$

Lunch & dinner daily

To call it simply an "artisanal pasta bar" would be selling Pastai short. It also happens to be attractive and thoroughly likable, repurposing milk bottles as water pitchers and displaying bright flowers, pennytiles, and wainscoting beneath its vintage ceiling. Wooden communal tables enhance the very pleasant atmosphere.

The white-tiled kitchen and pasta station are front and center, keeping the menu's focus on everyone's mind. Tart and aromatic fresh-lemon pasta arrives twirled in a sort of broccoli rabe "pesto" with roasted tomatoes and creamy burrata. Handcrafted ravioli are so delicate and translucent that snips of asparagus and ricotta stuffing appear milky-green. Desserts like the lemon-olive oil cake are deliciously simple.

Prova

Italian XX

B2

184 Eighth Ave. (bet. 19th & 20th Sts.)

Subway: 18 St — Lunch & dinner daily
Phone: 212-641-0977
Web: www.provanyc.com
Prices: $$

Good looks run in the family, as this former Donatella space has been reimagined into the rustic, charming Prova. Donatella Arpaia proves there is still room for more pizza in New York, especially when sourcing superior ingredients and committing to Neapolitan pizza excellence. Distressed wood planks, brick walls, and a flaming red pizza oven set a cozy stay-a-while scene.

Ingredients steal the show, many D.O.P. straight from Italy. A meal could begin with a classic like silky *parmigiana di melanzane* or you could launch right into the pizza. Slow-kneaded dough with a long fermentation results in a luscious pie, with crisp, minimally charred edges. The darling *Romana* is topped with *fior di latte*, San Marzano tomatoes, meaty anchovies, olives, and torn basil.

The Red Cat

American XX

B2

227 Tenth Ave. (bet. 23rd & 24th Sts.)

Subway: 23 St (Eighth Ave.) — Lunch & Dinner daily
Phone: 212-242-1122
Web: www.theredcat.com
Prices: $$

If crowds indicate quality (and downtown they often do) then this clear favorite is still going strong after more than 15 years. Loyal customers as diverse as the city itself flood the long bar and richly colored room for lunch, dinner, or just for a finely mixed cocktail and snack. Flowers give the space a touch of luxury; Moorish lanterns add warmth.

The pleasures here are straightforward, beginning with a smoky bowl of charred eggplant dip, with a healthy splash of sherry vinegar, garlic, and herbs, served with fresh bread. Don't miss schmaltz-fried eggs on top of crispy potato rosti, piled with buttery sautéed spinach and tender brisket. Crunchy cinnamon churros with a spiced chocolate ganache and guava-caramel sauce are a decadent finish.

Rocking Horse Cafe

B2 — Mexican XX

182 Eighth Ave. (bet. 19th & 20th Sts.)

Subway: 14 St - 8 Av — Lunch & dinner daily
Phone: 212-463-9511
Web: www.rockinghorsecafe.com
Prices: $$

A Chelsea classic since 1988, this Mexican café has a split personality. The front room—with vibrant orange walls, glowing lanterns, bare tabletops, and a long bar—is a bright, casual place to sample tequila cocktails or crunch into handmade tortilla chips and smoky salsa. Beyond a blue mosaic wall, the back room is a down-to-earth dining spot with a relaxed feel.

The distinctive menu includes the likes of *cordero enchipotlado,* chipotle braised lamb shank with caramelized onions, roasted tomatoes, and epazote over a creamy bed of *cotija*-spiked polenta; or blue corn *crepas de pato* stuffed with duck confit. The wise diner who ventures beyond commonplace dishes here is rewarded with complex, from-scratch cooking with soul.

Salinas

B2 — Spanish XX

136 Ninth Ave. (bet. 18th & 19th Sts.)

Subway: 18 St — Dinner nightly
Phone: 212-776-1990
Web: www.salinasnyc.com
Prices: $$$

Salinas is undeniably sexy. Step beyond the wrought-iron gates and squeeze your way past the bar to find the dusky scene. The patio dining room is where fashionistas nestle like pretty young things on button-tufted banquettes amid bunches of pink roses and flickering votives. A retractable glass roof shields the attractive Brazilian walnut floors and limestone walls from outside elements.

The Spanish cuisine of Chef Luis Bollo, a native of San Sebastián, sparkles with coastal influences. Tapas are *muy* creative and include *boquerones* over delicate toast strips spread with smashed avocado. The *fideos negros y crujientes* is an ink-stained mound of toasted vermicelli, cuttlefish, and aïoli foam grandly stirred together upon presentation.

Socarrat

Spanish

B2

259 W. 19th St. (bet. Seventh & Eighth Aves.)

Subway: 18 St
Phone: 212-462-1000
Web: www.socarratrestaurants.com
Prices: $$

Lunch & dinner daily

True, Soccarat is named for that ridiculously tasty burnished rice crust at the bottom of the paella pan. And yes, this place serves one of the city's best. The *paella de la huerta* with chicken combines spicy house-made chorizo, chickpeas, artichokes, tomatoes, and more in one traditional hot flat-bottom pan built for two (or more). However, there is much more on the menu to explore, especially during their highly regarded brunch-time feast of steak *a la plancha* with eggs, or an *ensalada mixta* tossing greens, asparagus, boiled egg, tuna, and olives.

Glossy walls reflect the convivial room's gentle light, while mirrors and portraits lend depth and color. Communal tables are packed with your newest old friends and tapas-loving locals.

Tía Pol

A2

205 Tenth Ave. (bet. 22nd & 23rd Sts.)

Subway: 23 St (Eighth Ave.)
Phone: 212-675-8805
Web: www.tiapol.com
Prices: ⊜

Lunch Tue – Sun
Dinner nightly

Tapas may have taken over Chelsea's storefronts, but stepping into this small plates paradise, you'll do a double take and wonder if this is Barcelona. The dimly lit, narrow room packs in wine-guzzling guests awaiting just a few tables. Busy servers uncork bottles and stream in and out of the open kitchen with Spanish classics like hand-shaved *jamón* and piquillo peppers. It's entertainment for the waiting game, which is always part of the experience at this ten-year-old staple.

First bites say everything, and the fluffy wedge of tortilla, with its dab of garlicky aïoli, sets the standard for here and beyond. Don't miss the skirt steak, the most flavorful meat on the menu and a frequent special, served with potatoes and pickled red onions.

Tipsy Parson

B2 American XX

156 Ninth Ave. (bet. 19th & 20th Sts.)

Subway: 23 St (Eighth Ave.) Lunch & dinner daily
Phone: 212-620-4545
Web: www.tipsyparson.com
Prices: $$

The masculine bar shelved with books and premium spirits, dining room bric-a-brac, and French doors overlooking a garden clearly convey familiar, homey comfort. Dining here is like visting at an old friend's house, starting with drinks in the living room and ending on the back porch. But with much better food.

The chive buttermilk biscuit is a distinctive, flaky force to be reckoned with. Clear Southern flavors are further explored with sour pickles and thick slices of green tomatoes both dredged in cornmeal and deep-fried to piping hot perfection, served with buttermilk dressing, avocado salad, tomato jam, and hatch chile salsa. Small plates like "big damn shrimp" do not disappoint, but save room for the superb cornflake-topped crumble for two.

Toro

A2 Spanish XX

85 Tenth Ave. (entrance at 15th St. & Eleventh Ave.)

Subway: 14 St - 8 Av Dinner Mon – Sat
Phone: 212-691-2360
Web: www.toro-nyc.com
Prices: $$

Trendy location? Check. Sleek, warehouse-sized space? Check. Floor-to-ceiling windows filled with romantic sunsets? Check. In brief, Toro is a head-turner graced with intent service and extraordinary food. Begin with inventive (and strong) crowd-pleasing sips at the impressive bar before settling in to a comfy communal table.

The music gets louder at sundown, but find yourself fixated on such deeply flavorful *pinchos* as *sardina y mantequilla de cabra* (crusty bread spread with goat butter and preserved sardines) or aged duck ham kissed with olive oil, lemon zest, and sweet, delicious fat. Links of smoky, tender chorizo set over chickpea stew is a comforting creation, while inky-dark *sepia risotto en su tinta* made with orzo is rich, buttery, and perfect.

Trestle on Tenth

Austrian XX

B2

242 Tenth Ave. (at 24th St.)

Subway: 23 St (Eighth Ave.) Lunch & dinner daily
Phone: 212-645-5659
Web: www.trestleontenth.com
Prices: $$

West Chelsea's non-stop canteen is favored by a steady stream of gallerists, fashionistas, and tourists out for a jaunt along the High Line. Despite the glitz of this ascendant neighborhood, the look here is cozy, sociable, and downright humble.

Pastas may veer from the Austrian theme but are nonetheless delicious. Try the tagliatelle tossed in a buttery broth of clams, parsley, and garlic. Calf's liver here is outrageously funky and just as delicious, tender and supremely fresh beneath carmelized onions and a sweet wine reduction. The *Nusstorte* is a symphony of cruncy walnuts, sticky caramel, and Madagascan vanilla ice cream. Wash it all down with a Swiss wine or craft beer.

Rocket Pig is the restaurant's highly popular offshoot next door.

Txikito

Spanish XX

B2

240 Ninth Ave. (bet. 24th & 25th Sts.)

Subway: 23 St (Eighth Ave.) Dinner nightly
Phone: 212-242-4730
Web: www.txikitonyc.com
Prices: $$

Start off with a "gin tonic" and taste what the fuss is all about. Always packed, delicious, and passionate, this Basque spot conveys a world of regional cuisine, thanks to Chefs Alex Raij and Eder Montero. Colorful touches and a chalkboard of daily specials lend an informal Spanish feel. Closely spaced tables remind you that you're in New York.

The Basque menu offers both small and large plates that often seem simple but are rich, tasty, and downright special—don't miss the anchovies! Their worthy signature octopus carpaccio (*pulpo*) is cut into remarkably thin slices, dressed in lemon, marjoram, and *piment d'Espelette*. If the umami-rich *laminas de setas*—citrus-marinated king oyster mushrooms offset with salty Marcona almonds—is available, get it.

Chinatown & Little Italy

As different as chow mein and chicken cacciatore, these two neighborhoods are nonetheless neighbors and remain as tight as thieves. In recent years, their borders have become increasingly blurred, with Chinatown gulping up most of Little Italy. It is said that New York cradles the maximum number of Chinese immigrants in the country, and settlers from Hong Kong and mainland China each brought with them their own distinct regional cuisines.

EAT THE STREETS

Chowing in Chinatown can be delectable and delightfully affordable. Elbow your way through these cramped streets to find a flurry of markets, bubble tea cafés, bakeries, and more. Freshly steamed pouches of chicken, seafood, and pork are all the rage at **Vanessa's Dumpling House**, a neighborhood fixture with a long counter and longer queue of hungry visitors. There is lots ore deliciousness to be had in this 'hood—from feasting on freshly pulled noodles; ducking into a parlor for a scoop of black sesame ice cream; or breezing past a market window with crocodile meat on display—claws included! **New Kam Man** is a bustling bazaar offering everything from woks to wontons; and Vietnamese mecca, **Tan Tin-Hung**, is a mini but "super" market proffering the best selection of Vietnamese ingredients in town—red perilla, *rau ram*, and "*culantro*" are ready for your home kitchen. But, for more instant gratification, binge on the salty eats from **New Beef King**. Imagine a spicy blend of jerky and barbecue—this neat and mod spot has it all. Over on Mulberry Street, **Asia Market Corp.** is a sight for sore eyes as shelves spill over with Malaysian, Indonesian, and Thai specialties. The space is tight, but the range of imported goods is nothing less than thrilling. Find celebrity chefs at these Asian storefronts, haggling over the freshest fish and quality produce, before sneaking under

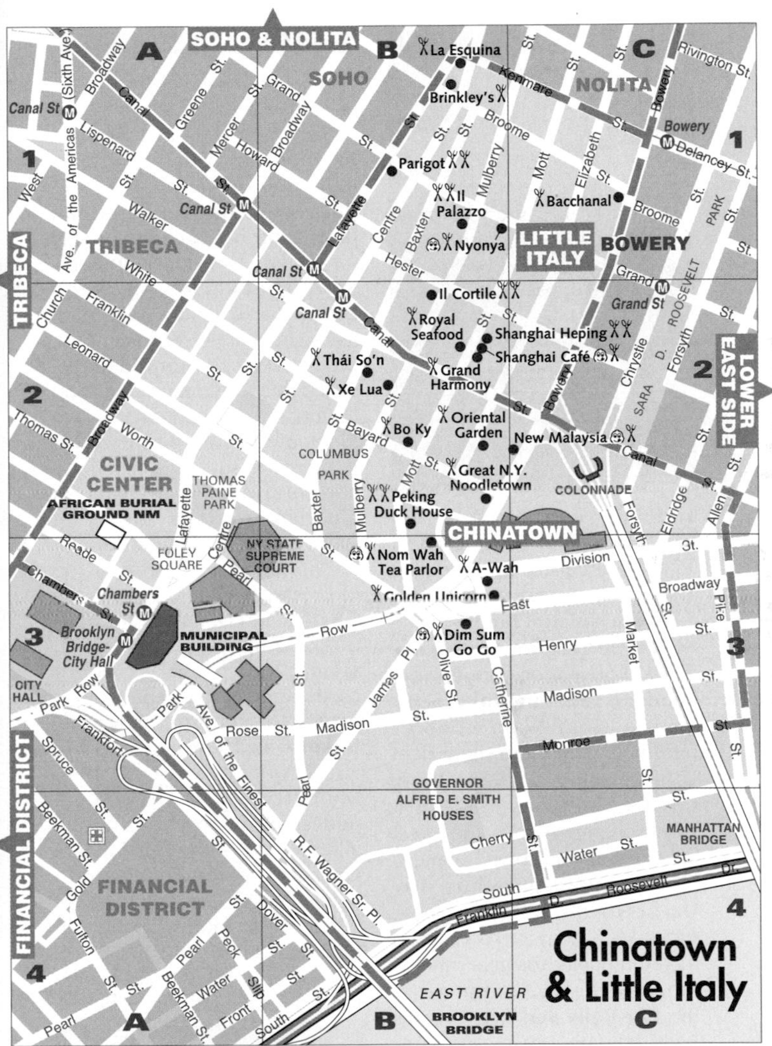

the Manhattan Bridge for a crusty *bánh mì*. From chilies to curry pastes, **Bangkok Center Grocery** boasts all ingredients necessary for a Thai-themed feast—not to mention their publications and friendly owner! Fans of Cantonese cuisine join the line outside **Big Wong King**, where comfort food classics (congee and roast duck) are as outstanding as the setting is ordinary. **Amazing 66** is a brightly lit, bi-level darling with two dining rooms. Here dishes arrive almost as swiftly as the crowds go in and out, naturally making it a spot where taste and efficiency are of superlative quality. Dim sum is obligatory

and weekend brunch is a longtime tradition at **Jing Fong**. Take the escalator up a floor to arrive at this mainstay, where the service is gruff but the Hong Kong-style treats are particularly good. For a more snug vibe, head to **Tai Pan Bakery** for pastries that keep couples returning. The exquisitely light sponge cake at **Kam Hing Coffee Shop** has made it a worthy competitor in the "Best bakeries around town" contest; just as artisan bakeshop, **Fay Da**, has been serving its Chinese treats with a modern twist to the community for near-infinity. Klezmer meets Cantonese at the **Egg Rolls and Egg Creams Festival**, an annual summer street celebration honoring the neighboring Chinese and Jewish communities of Chinatown and the Lower East Side. Every year during Chinese New Year, partygoers pack these streets, with dragons dancing down the avenues accompanied by costumed revelers and firecrackers.

LITTLE ITALY

The Little Italy of Scorsese's gritty *Mean Streets* is slowly vanishing into what may now be more aptly called Micro Italy. The onetime stronghold of a large Italian-American population has dwindled today to a mere corridor—Mulberry Street between Canal and Broome streets. But, the spirit of its origins still pulses in century-old markets, cramped delis, gelato shops, and mom-and-pop trattorias. Seasoned palates love **Piemonte Ravioli** for incredible homemade sauces amid dried and fresh pastas—available in all shapes with a variety of fillings. **Alleva Dairy** (known for homemade ricotta) is the oldest Italian cheese store in the country; and **Di Palo Fine Foods** boasts imported *sopressata, salumi,* and cheeses. Primo for pastries and espresso, fans never forget to frequent **Ferrara's Bakery and Café** on Grand Street. During warmer months, Mulberry Street becomes a pedestrian zone with one big alfresco party—the **Feast of San Gennaro** is particularly raucous. While these days you can get better Italian food elsewhere in the city, tourists and old-timers still gather to treasure and bathe in the nostalgia of this nabe.

A-Wah

Chinese

B3

5 Catherine St. (bet. Division St. & East Broadway)

Subway: Canal St (Lafayette St.) Lunch & dinner daily
Phone: 212-925-8308
Web: www.awahrestaurant.com
Prices: ⊜

An incredibly popular member of NYC's diverse culinary scene, simple, tiny, and singularly focused A-Wah fires up a vast array of Hong Kong-style comfort foods from ginger chicken feet to sautéed pea leaves. The region's tasty take on *lo mein* is a total departure from the familiar version. Here, find a platter of thin noodles topped with pork or duck, served with a side of delicate, consommé-like broth for dipping.

However, the biggest treat is the fantastic *bo zai fan*: rice cooked to crunchy perfection in a clay pot and crowned with ginger, scallions, and a mind-boggling choice of seventeen toppings like frog, pork, and preserved vegetables. These dishes and their tasty burnt-rice sides are made even better with a thick and sweet house-made soy sauce.

Bacchanal

Contemporary

C1

146 Bowery (at Broome St.)

Subway: Bowery Lunch Sat – Sun
Phone: 646-355-1840 Dinner Tue – Sun
Web: www.bacchanalnyc.com
Prices: **$$**

When you name your restaurant Bacchanal your customers can reasonably expect a decent bar—and here it's the centre of attention. The place is also suitably dark and moody, but it's not so much "distressed" as "mildly neurotic" because next to the bar is an open kitchen vying for your attention. It's a moot point as to whether this is a bar with a bistro attached or a bistro with a great bar; even those running it can't decide because the volume of the music goes up and down like a fiddler's elbow.

In the meantime, the kitchen keeps things fairly simple and does them well enough. Along with dishes from the grill like whole daurade, expect offerings like fresh octopus salad with plenty of arugula and succulent lamb chops with pea tapenade.

Bo Ky

Chinese

80 Bayard St. (bet. Mott and Mulberry Sts.)

Subway: Canal St (Lafayette St.) — Lunch & dinner daily
Phone: 212-406-2292
Web: N/A
Prices: ◎◎

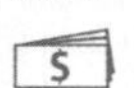

If you're drawn to those bare bones sort of places where food quality, beyond-warm service, and value speak for itself, this is your Chinatown slam dunk. Bo Ky's steamed-up windows (from the succulent meats roasting inside) are an invitation to come in and get cracking on a perfect bowl of wonton and noodle soup.

Crispy skinned and exquisitely juicy chicken drizzled with dark soy and served beside chili-studded *nuoc cham* may be the closet local sib to the Hong Kong classic, presented here with a Vietnamese touch. Its textural interplay is as first-rate as the house specialty itself— a crispy fried shrimp-and-scallion roll wrapped in bean curd skin. Spice fiends can turn up the heat at home—their secret-recipe addictive sauces are for sale by the jar!

Brinkley's

406 Broome St. (bet. Centre & Lafayette Sts.)

Subway: Spring St (Lafayette St.) — Lunch & dinner daily
Phone: 212-680-5600
Web: www.brinkleysnyc.com
Prices: $$

Brinkley's seems to be the provincial "pub" for everyone from students and hipsters to executives looking for a thirst quencher and bite after work. This easy and informal spot wears a boho-chic look with metallic stools lining a zinc-topped bar, a black-and-white checked floor, and burgundy leather booths. The team fits the casual, neighborhood feel of its vibrant yet rather noisy surroundings.

Find such straightforward delights as a grilled chicken salad with walnuts, grapes, and red onion in a shallot vinaigrette. Then, move on to a deliciously crusty lobster club filled with bacon and avocado, served with sweet potato fries. A taste of their moist bread pudding topped with whipped cream will ensure some very simple, homespun bliss.

Dim Sum Go Go

Chinese

5 East Broadway (at Chatham Sq.)

Subway: Canal St (Lafayette St.) Lunch & dinner daily
Phone: 212-732-0797
Web: N/A
Prices: **$$**

This wildly popular dim sum joint is still packed to the gills most days, and for good reason: the Cantonese fare and dim sum served up at this bright, contemporary spot is as good as the food you'll find trekking out to those super-authentic places in far-flung Queens. Even better, they take reservations—and dim sum orders are taken by the staff as opposed to rolled around on the traditional cart, helping ensure the food stays super fresh.

If the price seems a bit higher than its competitors, you'll find it's worth it for dishes like sweet shrimp, rolled in rice paper and laced with dark soy sauce; plump snow pea leaf dumplings spiked with vibrant ginger and garlic; rich, tender duck dumplings; or an irresistibly flaky baked roast pork pie.

Golden Unicorn

18 East Broadway (at Catherine St.)

Subway: Canal St (Lafayette St.) Lunch & dinner daily
Phone: 212-941-0911
Web: www.goldenunicornrestaurant.com
Prices: **$$**

This age-old dim sum parlor, spread over many floors in an office building, is one of the few Cantonese spots that actually has the space and volume to necessitate its parade of steaming carts brimming with treats. While Golden Unicorn's system is very efficient and part of the spectacle, arrive early to nab a seat by the kitchen for better variety and hotter items. A helpful brigade of suited men and women roam the space to offer the likes of exquisitely soft roast pork buns, or congee with preserved egg and shredded pork. Buzzing with locals and visitors, it is also a favorite among families who appreciate the kid-friendly scene as much as the delectable, steamed pea shoot and shrimp dumplings, pork *siu mai*, and rice rolls stuffed with shrimp.

Grand Harmony

Chinese

B2

98 Mott St. (bet. Canal & Hester Sts.)

Subway: Canal St (Lafayette St.) Lunch & dinner daily
Phone: 212-226-6603
Web: N/A
Prices: $$

With every seat filled before noon and dim sum carts roaming the sea of famished diners, Grand Harmony's expansive but rather run-down hall echoes the commotion of Chinatown. Naturally, they must be doing something right, so snag a seat upon arrival and flag those nimble women as they direct their carts through the labyrinth of tables.

Resting upon these coveted carts is a plethora of solid dim sum. Friendly servers parade the likes of beautifully crisp bean curd skin stuffed with vegetables, shrimp, and pork; congee studded with bits of dried fish and scallions; and juicy shrimp and chive dumplings all at an unbelievably good price. Leave room for what lies on the dessert cart, like fried sweet sesame balls or creamy coconut jelly to finish this feast.

Great N.Y. Noodletown

Chinese

B2

28 Bowery (at Bayard St.)

Subway: Canal St (Lafayette St.) Lunch & dinner daily
Phone: 212-349-0923
Web: N/A
Prices: $$

When heading to Great N.Y. Noodletown, invite plenty of dining companions to share those heaping plates of roasted meats and rice and noodle soups served at this bargain favorite. Locals stream in until the 4:00 A.M. closing bell for their great Cantonese fare—food is clearly the focus here, over the brusque service and unfussy atmosphere. Guests' gazes quickly pass over the imitation wooden chairs to rest on the crispy skin of suckling pig and ducks hanging in the window.

These dishes are huge, so forgo the rice and opt instead for deliciously chewy noodles and barbecue meats. Incredible shrimp wontons, so delicate and thin, and the complex, homemade *e-fu* noodles demonstrate technique and quality to a standout level that is rarely rivaled.

Il Cortile

Italian

125 Mulberry St. (bet. Canal & Hester Sts.)

Subway: Canal St (Lafayette St.) — Lunch & dinner daily
Phone: 212-226-6060
Web: www.ilcortile.com
Prices: $$

Beyond this quaint and charming façade lies one of Little Italy's famed mainstays, ever-popular with dreamy eyed dates seeking the stuff of Billy Joel lyrics. The expansive space does indeed suggest a nostalgic romance, with its series of Mediterranean-themed rooms, though the most celebrated is the pleasant garden atrium (*il cortile* is Italian for courtyard), with a glass-paneled ceiling and abundant greenery.

A skilled line of chefs present a wide array of familiar starters and entrées, from eggplant *rollatini* to chicken Francese; as well as a range of pastas, such as *spaghettini puttanesca* or *risotto con funghi*. Several decades of sharing family recipes and bringing men to one bent knee continues to earn Il Cortile a longtime following.

La Esquina

114 Kenmare St. (bet. Cleveland Pl. & Lafayette St.)

Subway: Spring St (Lafayette St.) — Lunch & dinner daily
Phone: 646-613-7100
Web: www.esquinanyc.com
Prices: $$

When La Esquina opened it was a breath of bright air, offering enjoyably fresh cuisine that stood tall among the paltry selection of Manhattan Mexican. Thankfully, the city's south-of-the-border dining scene has evolved since then. However, La Esquina remains a fun and worthy option. More playground than restaurant, this multi-faceted setting takes up an iconic downtown corner and draws a hip crowd to the grab and go taqueria, 30-seat café, and lively subterranean dining room and bar.

The spirit here is not just alive but kicking with classic renditions of tortilla soup; *mole negro enchiladas* filled with excellently seasoned chicken; as well the likes of *carne asada* starring black Angus sirloin with *mojo de ajo*.

New Malaysia

Malaysian

C2

46-48 Bowery (bet. Bayard & Canal Sts.)

Subway: Canal St (Lafayette St.) Lunch & dinner daily
Phone: 212-964-0284
Web: N/A
Prices: ⊜

Mad for Malaysian? Head to this lively dive, sequestered in a Chinatown arcade. Proffering some of the best Malaysian treats in town, including all the classics, New Malaysia sees a deluge of regulars who pour in for a massive offering of exceptional dishes. Round tables cram a room furnished with little more than a service counter. Still, the aromas wafting from flaky *roti canai* and Melaka crispy coconut shrimp keep you focused on the food.

Capturing the essence of this region are brusque servers who speedily deliver abundant and authentic bowls of spicy-sour *asam laksa* fragrant with lemongrass; *kang-kung belacan,* greens with dried shrimp and chili; and *nasi lemak*, the national treasure starring coconut rice, chicken curry, and dried anchovies.

Nom Wah Tea Parlor

Chinese

B3

13 Doyers St. (bet. Bowery & Pell St.)

Subway: Canal St (Lafayette St.) Lunch & dinner daily
Phone: 212-962-6047
Web: www.nomwah.com
Prices: ⊜

Even after a renovation, this "parlor" continues to thrive as a retro dive replete with truly awful service. But keep reading, because the supremely delicious food and unreal value more than make up for Nom Wah's many flaws.

Dim sum is the main draw at this busy neighborhood diner, where small groups fill the dining counter and pack into pleather booths for the likes of pan-fried dumplings stuffed with ground pork and sweet shrimp. Scallion pancakes flaunt outstanding texture; fried shrimp wrapped in bean curd unites top product with heavenly flavor; and noodles sautéed with superior soy is a salt fiends dream. Bring hungry friends and expect lots of leftovers, because the simple pleasures here have been known to thrill even the most ardent epicurean.

Nyonya

Malaysian

B1

199 Grand St. (bet. Mott & Mulberry Sts.)

Subway: Canal St (Lafayette St.) Lunch & dinner daily
Phone: 212-334-3669
Web: www.ilovenyonya.com
Prices: $$

Nyonya prides itself with a comfortable setting composed of brick walls and wood tables, but everyone's really here for their food, which is always on the money. Adept servers are eager to steer you through the varied menu—and sometimes even away from such delicious dishes as *asam laksa*, an exceptionally spiced and intensely sour broth floating with lemongrass, ground fish, and thick, round noodles.

Asians and other hungry locals pack this haunt for seemingly simple yet deeply satisfying items like *achat* (pickled vegetables tossed with turmeric and peanuts); *mee siam* (noodles stir-fried with tofu, eggs, and shrimp in a chili sauce); or pungent beef *rendang*. Crispy prawns garnished with curry-infused toasted coconut are nothing short of wow!

Oriental Garden

Chinese 

B2

14 Elizabeth St. (bet. Bayard & Canal Sts.)

Subway: Canal St (Lafayette St.) Lunch & dinner daily
Phone: 212-619-0085
Web: www.orientalgardenny.com
Prices: $$

A daily destination for dim sum, Oriental Garden is a treasure among tourists, foodies, and wealthy Chinese residents. The place is known to get packed as crowds pour in for top-notch dumplings, whose prices seem to escalate with its popularity. So, be sure to reserve ahead for a seat in this group-friendly den, decked with kitschy fish tanks and food photo-covered menus boasting delicious dim sum.

Set menus are widely appealing and have been known to unveil such tasty crowd-pleasers as steamed watercress and pork dumplings; crispy fried shrimp wontons; and crab claws. Equally worthy (read: safe) options include a duo of lettuce wraps with minced duck and pork served with hoisin; or one massive oyster cooked in its shell with classic black bean sauce.

Parigot

French XX

B1

155 Grand St. (at Lafayette St.)

Subway: Canal St (Lafayette St.) Lunch & dinner daily
Phone: 212-274-8859
Web: N/A
Prices: **$$**

Parigot is a *trés* charming bistro on (now mega trendy) Grand Street. Owned and operated by Chef Michel Pombet and partner, Catherine Amsellem, the French cooking is classic yet fine-tuned for its downtown crowd. However, the warm, time-worn décor stays true to its roots. Tables are topped with paper and crayons to entertain the kids in tow.

Service is adept, and locals seem to feel their *joie de vivre* as the place is always abuzz. The vast, straightforward, and hearty menu is an equal draw with exquisitely rich onion soup bobbing beneath sliced *croûtes* and melted cheese. The superb duck confit is set over a sautéed mushrooms, haricot verts, and salsify. Pâté is wonderously pork-y, rich, perfectly seasoned, and paired with grilled country bread.

Peking Duck House

Chinese XX

B2

28 Mott St. (bet. Chatham Sq. & Pell St.)

Subway: Canal St (Lafayette St.) Lunch & dinner daily
Phone: 212-227-1810
Web: www.pekingduckhousenyc.com
Prices: **$$**

It's worth your while to wend through Chinatown's teeming sidewalks to delight in the eponymous house specialty here. Once inside, however crowded, the neutral-toned interior adds a calming effect to the many tables gearing up for their bird's arrival, and the mode of transport is a linen-draped cart.

The duck is deftly carved and dramatically served by the chef himself, so push in your chair and prepare for a festive DIY feast of warm, soft pancakes, cool cucumbers, scallions, and sweet hoisin. Although the duck is what makes this a destination, there are several other entrées like sizzling sliced beef with scallops; and live lobster with ginger and scallions. To begin, the clear golden broth of the duck wonton soup is an appropriate prelude to the main event.

Royal Seafood

Chinese

B2

103 Mott St. (bet. Canal & Hester Sts.)

Subway: Canal St (Lafayette St.) Lunch & dinner daily
Phone: 212-219-2338
Web: N/A
Prices: ⓈⓈ

Bright, chaotic, and jam-packed with a multi-generational Chinese crowd, this well-priced favorite has dim sum lovers lined up and waiting in droves. Dinnertime brings a quieter vibe, along with an extensive Cantonese menu. The sizable room is decked with round tables draped in pink linens and kitschy Chinese touches. This communal scene has friends and strangers alike dining side by side.

Join the masses and feast on the likes of steamed dumplings, nicely crafted and filled with mushrooms, vegetables, ground pork and peanut, or seafood and greens. The shrimp wrapped in yellow bean curd skin are crisply fried, not at all greasy, and completely delicious. Pan-fried wontons are thin and delicate yet exploding with flavor from garlic and chives.

Shanghai Café

Chinese

B2

100 Mott St. (bet. Canal & Hester Sts.)

Subway: Canal St (Lafayette St.) Lunch & dinner daily
Phone: 212-966-3988
Web: N/A
Prices: ⓈⓈ

This quirky café is a Chinatown stalwart. Busy booths line one wall, while big round tables are popular for gathering families. Note the dumpling station upfront, where agile chefs assemble these mouthwatering parcels.

Regulars know to arrive early for lunch to make the most of their vast menu, appetizing to vegetarians and omnivores alike. Servers are remarkably capable, balancing trays of addictive steamed juicy buns and cold dried bean curd, or soft rice cakes stir-fried with chicken and shrimp. The "queen" mushroom is sized for a king; its thick slices cooked until tender and bathed in an umami-rich brown sauce. The salty pork slices and fresh, crunchy bamboo shoots arrive in a broth so nourishing that you will slurp to the last drop.

Shanghai Heping

B2 Chinese XX

104 Mott St. (bet. Canal and Hester Sts.)

Subway: Canal St (Lafayette St.) Lunch & dinner daily
Phone: 212-925-1118
Web: N/A
Prices: $$

When faced with the long, no-frills menu, there should read a caution sign to not miss out on the crab and pork soup dumplings. The plump juicy filling and flavorful broth held in each delicate wrapper with soy-ginger seasoning explain the afternoon crowd lunching out of takeout boxes on the entrance in.

Large bamboo steamer baskets line most tables, and the seared pan-fried pork dumplings are not to miss either. Cold appetizers shine like dark soy- and sugar-cooked bamboo shoots with wheat gluten; and thinly-sliced, earthy stir-fried eel with chives. There are larger, steaming hot plates to choose from like Shanghai rice cakes with beef. The sweet "Eight Jewel Rice" dessert matches a mound of sticky rice with red bean paste, red dates, and golden raisin "jewels."

Thái Sơn

B2 Vietnamese X

89 Baxter St. (bet. Bayard & Canal Sts.)

Subway: Canal St (Lafayette St.) Lunch & dinner daily
Phone: 212-732-2822
Web: N/A
Prices:

Thái So'n is by far the best of the bunch in this Vietnamese quarter of Chinatown. It's neither massive nor fancy, but it's bright, clean, and perpetually in business. One peek at the specials on the walls (maybe golden-fried squid strewn with sea salt) will have you begging for a seat in the crammed room.

Speedy servers scoot between groups of City Hall suits and Asian locals as they order the likes of *cha gio,* pork spring rolls with *nuoc cham*; or *goi cuon,* fantastic summer rolls filled with poached shrimp and vermicelli. Naturally, *pho* choices are abundant, but the real star of the show is *pho tai*—where raw beef shavings are cooked to tender perfection when combined with a scalding hot, savory broth replete with herbs, sprouts, and chewy noodles.

Xe Lua

Vietnamese

B2

86 Mulberry St. (bet. Bayard & Canal Sts.)

Subway: Canal St (Lafayette St.) Lunch & dinner daily
Phone: 212-577-8887
Web: N/A
Prices: ⊜

Fantastic food is the sole focus of this Vietnamese dive. The décor—albeit stark—highlights a semi-tropical theme and the crowd might be touristy, but don't let that deter you as the food is wonderfully authentic and very reasonable.

Condiments atop each table serve to enhance even the most humble *goi cuon* stuffed with grilled pork and vermicelli. *Muc chien don* is a plate of chewy, crisped squid tossed in salt, pepper, and tailed by cucumbers and red onion for ample tang; while the house special *pho xe lua* reveals a rich, savory broth full of noodles, brisket, and beef tendon. Combine this with sprouts, chilies, and herbs for a surefire delight.

Enjoy dessert with a Vietnamese iced coffee that will give even your great-aunt Grace the shakes.

Feast for under $25 at all restaurants with ⊜.

East Village

Long regarded as the capital of cool, the East Village was once a shadier incarnation of Tompkin's Square Park and second home to squatters and rioters. However, the neighborhood today is safer, cleaner, and far more habitable. And while cheap walk-ups filled with struggling artists or aspiring models may be a thing of the past, the area's marked gentrification hasn't led to any sort of dip in self-expression or creativity. In fact, reflecting the independent and outspoken spirit for which this nabe is known, the East Village flaunts a distinct personality and vibrant dining landscape.

CHEAP EATS

Budget-friendly bites abound in these parts. Family-run **Veselka**, located in the heart of this 'hood has been serving traditional Ukrainian specialties for over 60-years, and is a fitting homage to the area's former eastern European population. After a night of bar-hopping or other mischief, grab a restorative bite of salt and fat at **Crif Dogs**, where deep-fried hot dogs are doled out until 4:00 A.M. Along these streets, find a number of food-related endeavors that are the product of laser-focused culinary inspiration. **Porchetta** for instance is a smash for crackling-skinned pork sandwiches. **S'mac** is known for its lip-smacking variations of everyone's favorite comfort food—mac n cheese; and **Luke's Lobster** has expanded into a city-wide network presenting rolls stuffed with crustaceans fresh from Maine. For ramen, Japanese-import **Ippudo** churns out steaming bowlfuls to its boisterous patrons. Meanwhile, **Brodo** (the brainchild of Hearth Chef/owner Marco Canora) is a trendsetting storefront (window?) dispensing comforting bowls of

broths that are available in three sizes and types—the Hearth broth, Organic Chicken, and Gingered Grass-fed beef. Others may join the constant queue of students looking for a crusty slice of white from **Artichoke Basille's Pizza** on 14th Street. And while on the topic of cravings of all stripes, the sensory assault around St. Mark's Place offers an immersion in Asian savors that is delightfully kitschy and incredibly worthwhile. Discover a taste of Korea by way of **Korilla**, a food truck sensation brought stateside by Chef Edward Song. Located on the first floor of a brick structure just off Cooper Square, this mostly take-out barbecue spot is beloved for pearly-white tofu coated with crimson-red, fire-hot *gochujang* and crowned by leafy bok choy. If that doesn't have you salivating, duck into **Boka** for spicy Korean fried chicken. Or, follow the scent of *takoyaki* frying and sizzling *okonomiyaki* at **Otafuku**. Hungry hordes know to look for the red paper lanterns that hang outside raucous haunts like **Yakitori Taisho**; while taste buds are always tingling at divey *izakayas* such as **Village Yokocho**. But, among this area's sultry sake dens, none rival the outrageous offering at subterranean **Decibel**.

A SWEET SIDE

Badass attitude and savory dishes aside, the East Village also has an incredibly sweet side.

Moishe's Bake Shop is a Kosher treat where challah, rugelach, and light-as-air marble sponge cake have been on the menu since 1978. In operation since 1894, **Veniero's Pasticceria & Caffé** brings yet another taste of the Old World to these newly minted locals. This Italian idol draws long lines, especially around holiday time, for old-school baked goods. There can never be a dearth of caffeine

in the city, and chic-geeks love **Hi-Collar**—a nifty, Japanese-esque coffee house bedecked with a brass counter and back wall accented by rice paper screens. Stay late and you may even be served some sake. Chef-cum-celebrity, David Chang's dessert darling **Momofuku Milk Bar** also rents space here and serves clever variations on dessert. Pastrami pockets, "Compost" cookies, and luscious soft-serve have sweet teeth swooning (and returning). **Big Gay Ice Cream** may have started life as a modest truck on the move, but is now a top-seller for signatures like the Bea Arthur—a swirl of vanilla, *dulche de leche*, and crushed Nilla wafers.

The craft cocktail movement has taken firm root in this "village" of trend, where many subtly (sometimes even undisclosed) locations offer an epicurean approach to mixology. **Death & Co.** is a dimly lit, hot-as-hell spot that is perpetually packed to the gills. But, if in need of a more intimate scene, seek out the secret passageway inside **Crif Dogs** to access **PDT** or Please Don't Tell—where Benton's Old-Fashioned crafted from bacon-smoked Bourbon may just be every cocktail critic's dream. Cached behind a wall in a Japanese restaurant, **Angel's Share's** snazzy bartenders shake and stir for a civilized crowd, while **Mayahuel's** mescal- and tequila-based creations lead to loud, south-of-the-border-style fun. And finally, polished **Pouring Ribbons**, devoted solely to vintage Chartreuse, continues to be praised in the nabe as a sanctuary of sorts among savants.

VENIERO
SINCE 1894
PASTICCERIA
PASTICCERIA
ANNA

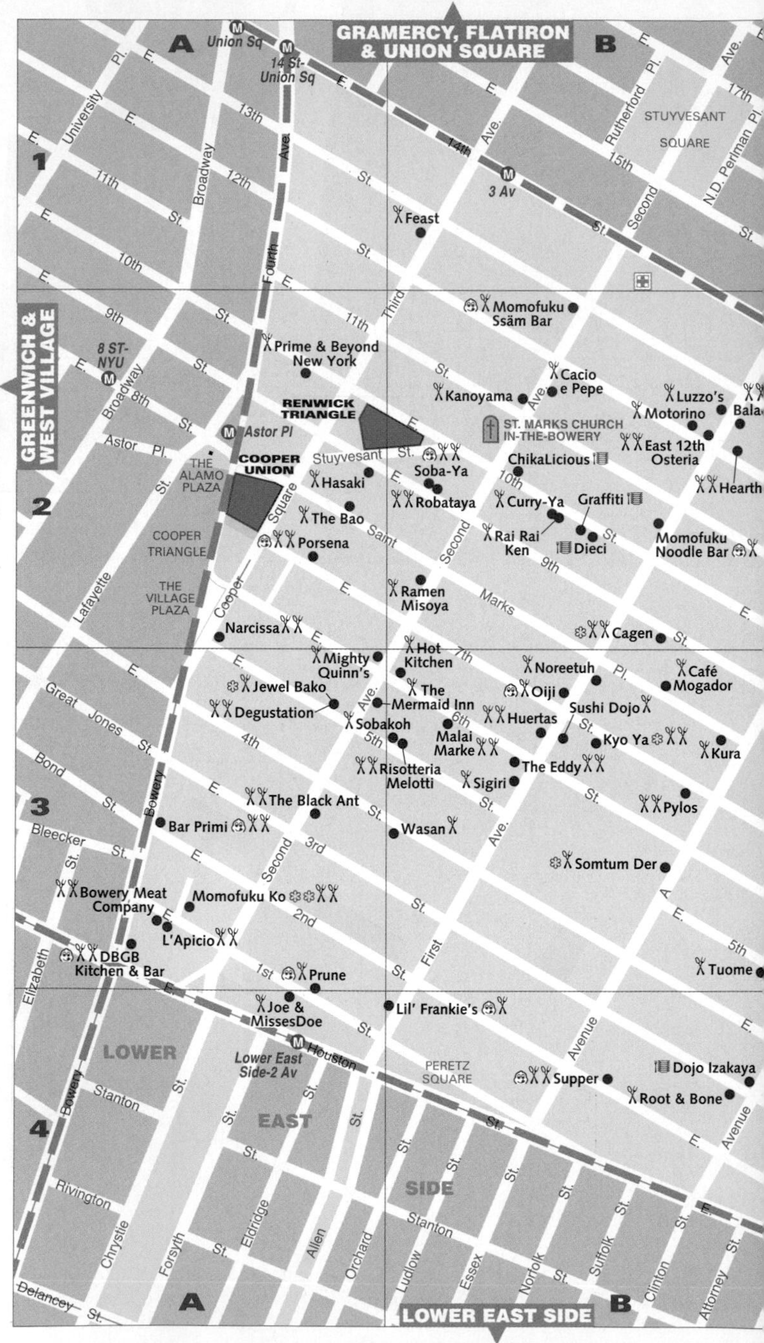
GRAMERCY, FLATIRON & UNION SQUARE
GREENWICH & WEST VILLAGE
LOWER EAST SIDE
Union Sq
14 St-Union Sq
8 ST-NYU
Astor Pl
3 Av
Lower East Side-2 Av
STUYVESANT SQUARE
RENWICK TRIANGLE
COOPER UNION
THE ALAMO PLAZA
COOPER TRIANGLE
THE VILLAGE PLAZA
ST. MARKS CHURCH IN-THE-BOWERY
PERETZ SQUARE
LOWER
EAST
SIDE
Feast
Momofuku Ssäm Bar
Prime & Beyond New York
Cacio e Pepe
Kanoyama
Luzzo's
Motorino
Bala
East 12th Osteria
Hearth
ChikaLicious
Soba-Ya
Hasaki
Robataya
Curry-Ya
Graffiti
The Bao
Rai Rai Ken
Dieci
Momofuku Noodle Bar
Porsena
Ramen Misoya
Cagen
Narcissa
Mighty Quinn's
Hot Kitchen
Noreetuh
Café Mogador
Jewel Bako
The Mermaid Inn
Oiji
Degustation
Sushi Dojo
Sobakoh
Huertas
Malai Marke
Kyo Ya
Kura
Risotteria Melotti
The Eddy
Sigiri
The Black Ant
Pylos
Bar Primi
Wasan
Somtum Der
Bowery Meat Company
Momofuku Ko
L'Apicio
DBGB Kitchen & Bar
Prune
Tuome
Joe & MissesDoe
Lil' Frankie's
Dojo Izakaya
Supper
Root & Bone
A
B
1
2
3
4

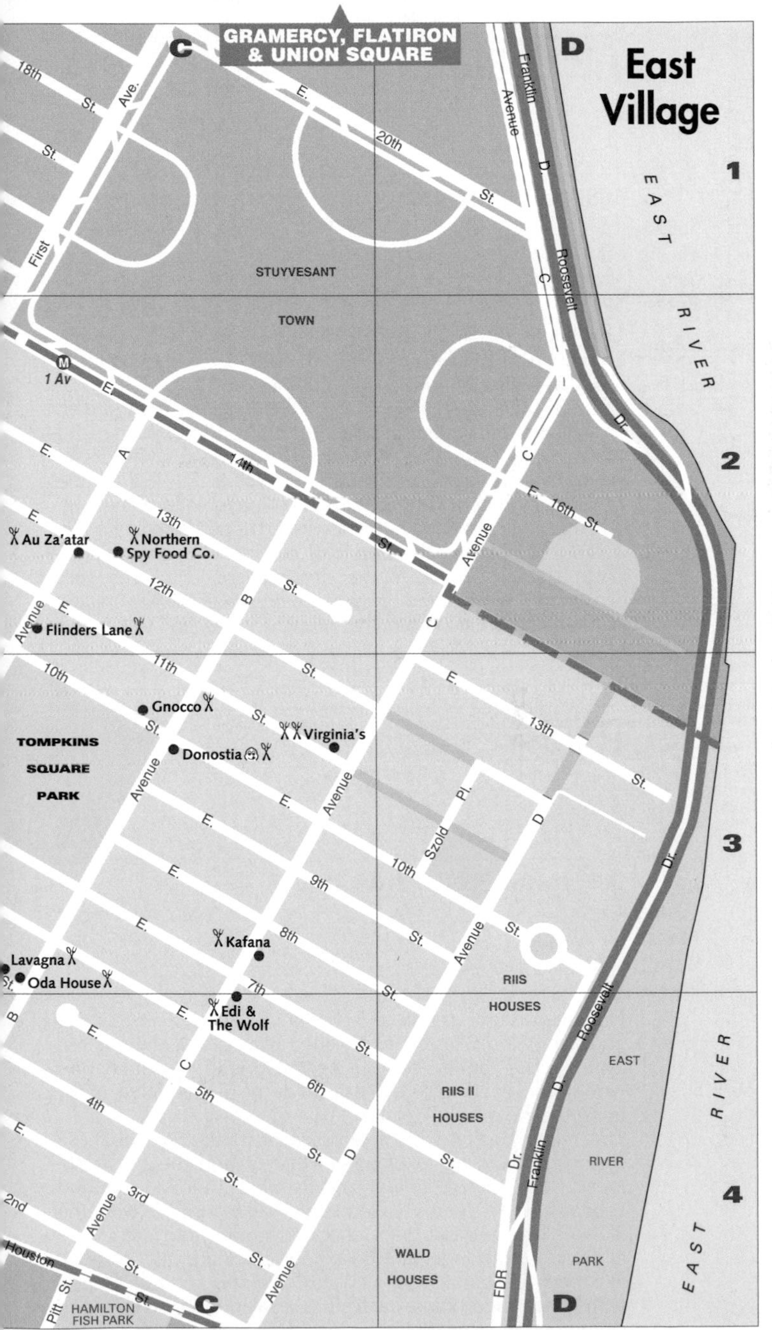
GRAMERCY, FLATIRON & UNION SQUARE
East Village
C
D
1
2
3
4
STUYVESANT
TOWN
TOMPKINS SQUARE PARK
RIIS HOUSES
RIIS II HOUSES
WALD HOUSES
EAST RIVER PARK
HAMILTON FISH PARK
EAST RIVER
1 Av
Au Za'atar
Northern Spy Food Co.
Flinders Lane
Gnocco
Donostia
Virginia's
Kafana
Lavagna
Oda House
Edi & The Wolf
E. 20th St.
E. 18th St.
E. 16th St.
E. 14th St.
E. 13th St.
E. 12th St.
E. 11th St.
E. 10th St.
E. 9th St.
E. 8th St.
E. 7th St.
E. 6th St.
E. 5th St.
E. 4th St.
E. 3rd St.
E. 2nd St.
Houston St.
Pitt St.
First Ave.
Avenue A
Avenue B
Avenue C
Avenue D
Szold Pl.
Franklin D. Roosevelt Dr.
FDR Dr.

Au Za'atar

Middle Eastern

C2

188 Ave. A (at 12th St.)

Subway: 1 Av — Lunch & dinner daily
Phone: 212-254-5660
Web: www.auzaatar.com
Prices: $$

Don't let the simple décor fool you—what this Arabian-French bistro lacks in ambience, it more than makes up for in mouthwatering Middle Eastern cuisine.

The menu features such delights as lamb shank braised with Armagnac and prunes, delicious char-grilled meats, and many meze. Of course, every meal here begins with fresh, piping hot pita. Hot, tender, and brushed with olive oil, the bread is sprinkled with the namesake spice blend along with a hearty dollop of labne. Pair it with an appetizer of *batin jan makdous*, pickled baby eggplants stuffed with garlic-walnut paste, then move on to the *kafta* kebab. Juicy and well-seasoned, this charred ground beef skewer arrives plated with grilled tomato and onion, crunchy salad, and rice pilaf.

Balade

208 First Ave. (bet. 12th & 13th Sts.)

Subway: 1 Av — Lunch & dinner daily
Phone: 212-529-6868
Web: www.baladerestaurants.com
Prices:

Honing in on the cuisine of Lebanon, Balade is a welcoming and tasty Middle Eastern experience fronted by a cheerful red awning. The spotless room is accented with tile, brick, and wood; and each table bears a bottle of private label herb-infused olive oil.

The menu begins with a glossary of traditional Lebanese ingredients and the explanation that *Balade* means "fresh, local." The meze; grilled meat-stuffed sandwiches; and Lebanese-style pizzas called *manakeesh* topped with the likes of lean ground beef, chopped onion, and spices are all fresh-tasting indeed. House specialties are also of note, like the *mujaddara crush*—a platter of lentils and rice topped with crispy fried onions as well as a salad of cool, chopped cucumber and tomato.

Bar Primi

Italian XX

325 Bowery (at 2nd St.)

Subway: Bleecker St — Lunch & dinner daily
Phone: 212-220-9100
Web: www.barprimi.com
Prices: **$$**

Chef Andrew Carmellini has added this pasta-centric trattoria to his clutch of inspired operations. A tomato-red awning highlights the two-floor space designed by Taavo Somer, which features whitewashed brick walls, tawny leather banquettes, and a communal table topped with terra-cotta pots of greenery.

Bensonhurst-native Chef Sal Lamboglia uses first rate ingredients to produce two categories of toothsome strands and shapes. Traditional preparations bring the likes of bucatini with lamb *all'Amatriciana*; while seasonal inspiration includes *fiore di carciofi*, a coiled tube of artichoke cream, dressed with diced fatty bacon and pecorino. The menu is bolstered by small plates like fontina-stuffed meatballs in a thick *sugo* as well as rotating daily specials.

The Bao

13 St. Marks Pl. (bet. Second & Third Aves.)

Subway: Astor Pl — Lunch & dinner daily
Phone: 212-388-9239
Web: N/A
Prices: **$$**

Trade the hustle and bustle of Chinatown for the equally boisterous St. Marks Place as a destination for excellent soup dumplings. This being the East Village, the dining room is chic but low-key with a pale earthy color scheme framing a communal table and metal chairs.

As for the menu, the restaurant's name says it all: the bao is absolute perfection. Presented in a bamboo steamer with soy and vinegar dipping sauce, each parcel is artfully dimpled, delightfully toothsome, and plumped with tasty broth and seasoned meat. Save room for sampling some of their other delicious specialties, including julienned celery stalks stir-fried with dried tofu; diced chives tossed with ground pork and fermented black beans; or XO sauce-fried rice.

The Black Ant

Mexican XX

A3

60 Second Ave. (bet. 3rd & 4th Sts.)

Subway: Astor Pl
Phone: 212-598-0300
Web: www.blackantnyc.com
Prices: $$

Lunch Sat – Sun
Dinner nightly

Bringing a dose of Mexico City chic to the East Village, this restaurant takes its name from the ancient Mesoamerican fable of an ant and incorporates that imagery throughout the setting. Black and white checkerboard flooring, blackboard wall tiles bearing white ants, and a very cool giant ant mural reinforce the theme.

The menu is an unrestricted look at Mexican cuisine. It is only fitting that specialties here include the Climbing Ant cocktail combining tequila, Aperol, and *mole* bitters; freshly-mashed guacamole seasoned with crushed ant salt; and grasshopper-crusted shrimp tacos. Insect-free creations are just as appealing, as in tacos stuffing tender masa tortillas with large chunks of battered and fried cod cheek, aïoli, and cabbage-mango slaw.

Bowery Meat Company

Steakhouse XX

A3

9 E. 1st St. (bet. Bowery & Second Ave.)

Subway: 2 Av
Phone: 212-460-5255
Web: www.bowerymeatcompany.com
Prices: $$$$

Dinner nightly

It's official: Chef Josh Capon, also of Lure Fishbar and El Toro Blanco, can now add sizzling steaks to his impressive wheelhouse. Cozy velvet booths, dusky blue floor-to-ceiling drapery, and dark wood details honor the swagger of the steakhouse archetype, but crowds of millennials lend a fresh face to this buzzy downtown address.

A list of specially selected oysters from the raw bar—like kumamotos from Washington State dressed with wasabi leaf and lemon—or zucchini carpaccio with feta and toasted pistachios prelude Bowery Meat Company's red-blooded roster. This may reveal a bone-in filet mignon au poivre, dry-aged NY strip, and grilled pork ribeye with Korean barbecue sauce. And, don't overlook those side dishes—the sour cream and onion hash brown is a must.

Cacio e Pepe

182 Second Ave. (bet. 11th & 12th Sts.)

Subway: 3 Av — Dinner nightly
Phone: 212-505-5931
Web: www.cacioepepe.com
Prices: $$

This charming Italian *gioia* has welcomed diners for more than a decade now. But in relaying its pleasures, one must begin with the eponymous house specialty. This fresh *tonnarelli* tossed with pasta water, olive oil, cracked black pepper, and a showering of pecorino is pure delight. Those willing to branch out will find other pasta dishes here as equally pleasing, like the *maltagliati* dressed with a savory monkfish ragù revved up with olives, capers, and an unexpected hit of ginger. Mussels in black pepper "soup" is a savory bowl of mollusks and broth with garlicky croutons for soaking up the enticingly salty liquid.

Exposed brick and wood furnishings complement the *zucca*-orange walls lined with wine bottles offered on the all-Italian list.

Café Mogador

Moroccan

101 St. Marks Pl. (bet. First Ave. & Ave. A)

Subway: 1 Av — Lunch & dinner daily
Phone: 212-677-2226
Web: www.cafemogador.com
Prices: 

The key to this beloved café's long-term success is its popular array of tasty, crowd-pleasing Moroccan favorites. A veritable landmark in the East Village, the decades-old hangout is as inviting as ever—and despite the constant crush of its brainy-hip set, it remains inexplicably fresh-faced.

Open from morning to night, breakfast offers the likes of eggs any style sided by hummus and tabouli, whereas afternoon fare may include tasty specials like *bastilla* or *harira*—the hearty and fragrant soup. Chicken tagine is excellent: try it with fluffy couscous and *charmoula*, a spicy green herb sauce, or order it Casablanca-style with chickpeas, raisins, and onions.

For a taste of Morocco across the East River, visit Mogador's flourishing Williamsburg outpost.

Cagen ✿

B2

414 E. 9th St. (bet. Ave. A & First Ave.)

Subway: Astor Pl — Dinner Tue – Sun
Phone: 212-358-8800
Web: www.cagenrestaurant.com
Prices: $$$$

Boasting soothing textured walls the color of sand, sturdy but comfortable furnishings, and cool slate flooring, this serene and serious space is just what one would expect of a high-end Japanese dining room. But, beyond this quotidian look is a kitchen that turns out very exciting—and quite unexpected—food. Tables are an available option, but a seat facing Chef Toshio Tomita at the pristine elm counter is the place to be.

While the menu offers both à la carte dining and a sushi-only omakase, the Chef's Counter omakase is by far the best experience to be had here. This meal begins with a playful platter of bites (envision smoked ham *katsu*) to break the ice and stimulate the palate for the kitchen's sparkling sashimi. Slices of Hokkaido octopus, marinated bonito, and snapper are a treat, dressed not only with freshly ground wasabi root and top-notch soy sauce, but also the chef's signature *chimichurri*—a touch of fusion that signals his decade-plus years of working at Nobu. Another highlight is the chilled handmade soba served with spicy buckwheat sprouts and a divine dipping sauce.

Cooked dishes, like fried soft-shell crab with watermelon salad, and impressive nigiri round out Cagen's *kappo*-style meal.

ChikaLicious

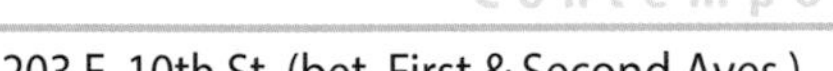

Contemporary

B2

203 E. 10th St. (bet. First & Second Aves.)

Subway: Astor Pl — Dinner Thu – Sun
Phone: 212-475-0929
Web: www.chikalicious.com
Prices: $$

Named for Pastry Chef/owner Chika Tillman, this sweet spot presents an all-encompassing dessert experience that somehow manages to impress without overkill. The chic white space offers counter seating overlooking a lab-clean kitchen, where the team prepares elegant jewels that start as butter, sugar, and chocolate. À la carte is offered, but the best way to appreciate this dessert bar is to select the prix-fixe. Feasts here may begin with an amuse-bouche of Darjeeling tea gelée with milk sorbet; followed by a mascarpone semifreddo topped with espresso granita. Then finish with pillowy cubes of coconut-marshmallow *petits fours*.

Dessert Club across the street tempts with delish cookies, cupcakes, and shaved ice for a grab-and-go fix.

Curry-Ya

Japanese

B2

214 E. 10th St. (bet. First & Second Aves.)

Subway: Astor Pl — Lunch & dinner daily
Phone: 866-602-8779
Web: www.nycurry-ya.com
Prices: $$

Complex, warming, and perfumed with fruity sweetness, slow-cooked *wafuu* (or Japanese-style) curry is a highly popular national treat. Tantalizingly draped over a mound of steamed short grain rice, each bowl calls for one of the kitchen's tasty embellishments such as panko-crusted fried shrimp, pan-fried hamburger steak, Berkshire pork, or chicken *katsu*. The brief menu also offers inspiring starters like flavor-packed tofu skin and green bean salad tossed with parmesan and a crushed-olive dressing.

Brought to you by Bon Yagi (also of Rai Rai Ken, a few doors away), this local jewel has 14-seats along a white marble counter lined with bowls of pickles and dried onion flakes. The space may seem simple but it's a spectacular destination to dig in and enjoy.

DBGB Kitchen & Bar 

French 

A3

299 Bowery (bet. First & Houston Sts.)

Subway: 2 Av
Phone: 212-933-5300
Web: www.dbgb.com
Prices: $$

Lunch Fri – Sun
Dinner nightly

Super chef, Daniel Boulud, shakes off some of his signature upmarket panache with this downtown favorite. The fun-for-all brasserie joins a lively bar area to a rear dining room, open kitchen, and chef's table. The space recalls the Bowery's history as a hub for restaurant supplies: dry goods are prominently shelved, bathroom walls are papered with vintage cookware catalogs, and gleaming copper pots (engraved with the names of famed French chefs) are on display.

Luxe burgers and a globally inspired lineup of house-made sausages are all popular. But go on to explore other dishes like the lunch prix-fixe offering decadent country pâté, ricotta and spinach ravioli in Vermont veal Bolognese, as well as a lemon bar with meringue bits and blueberry sorbet.

Degustation

Spanish 

A3

239 E. 5th St. (bet. Second & Third Aves.)

Subway: Astor Pl
Phone: 212-979-1012
Web: www.degustation-nyc.com
Prices: $$

Dinner nightly

With its slate-tiled walls and cozy lighting, this well-loved tapas bar is of the most elegant degree—and a romantic escape from the fray for couples on date night. Counter seating surrounds the spotless and very serious kitchen of Chef Nicholas Licata, and dapper proprietor Jack Lamb is a colorful presence.

The skillfully rendered and enticingly presented small plates are ever-evolving. Expect hot and crunchy *croquetas* oozing with mushroom-infused cream; or zesty *boquerones* dressed with yuzu peel and breadcrumbs. Sunchokes are roasted whole and sent forth with pumpernickel "soil" and an addictive mound of "funyons." For a fantastic finale, cubes of seared pineapple are composed with white chocolate sponge cake and intensely green lime granita.

Dieci

B2

228 E. 10th St. (bet. First & Second Aves.)

Subway: Astor Pl — Dinner nightly
Phone: 212-387-9545
Web: www.dieciny.com
Prices: $$

Dieci fuses Italian and Japanese cuisines for a successful marriage of taste and creativity. Springy ramen clutching spicy lamb Bolognese is a perfect example of this flavorful union. The tiny step-down setting is easy to miss but conquers its spatial challenge with comfortable seats. Find foodies centered around a dining counter that juts out from the kitchen—a handful of small tables also bolster the accommodations.

A unique array of small plates includes buffalo mozzarella with uni and yuzu foam, and steamed buns filled with Berkshire pork belly. Meanwhile, entrées go on to include miso-glazed cod set atop an appealing wild mushroom risotto fortified by a poached egg. Desserts are equally impressive, as in a silky Earl Grey crème brûlée.

Dojo Izakaya

38 Ave. B (bet. 3rd & 4th Sts.)

Subway: 2 Av — Dinner Mon – Sat
Phone: 212-253-5311
Web: www.dojoizakaya.com
Prices:

If dinner in Tokyo isn't in the cards, make your way to this Alphabet City nook for the next best thing. Inside the *izakaya,* just large enough to accommodate you and a small entourage, black walls produce a vibe that's cozy, not claustrophobic, and gentle prices give way to bold flavors.

The luscious array of pleasingly authentic cooked items on offer are best washed down by a cold beer or glass of sake. Highlights include *kani korokke,* temptingly gooey and creamy crabmeat-flecked croquettes; pork neck *kushiyaki,* slices of sweet, toothsome, fatty meat charred on a bamboo skewer and brushed with a savory glaze; as well as *mentaiko onigiri,* a grilled rice ball stuffed with spicy cod roe, dusted with sesame seeds, and wrapped in sheet of toasted nori.

Donostia 

Spanish 

C3

155 Ave. B (at 10th St.)

Subway: 1 Av
Phone: 646-256-9773
Web: www.donostianyc.com
Prices: ⊜

Lunch Sat – Sun
Dinner nightly

A little bite of Barcelona can be found just across from Tompkins Square Park at this bar *de conservas*. A mural depicting the Basque countryside frames the slender quarters. Most diners choose the marble counter seating, but there are also a handful of tables.

An array of small bites makes up Donostia's menu. Find Spanish cheeses and *charcuteria* of Iberico pork, but the true star here are the *conservas*. To refer to these as canned seafood would be technically correct but improper—digging into a few is obligatory. Among the temptations, expect a delicate miniature *tartalata* filled with smooth sea urchin and toothsome octopus. Also try meaty chunks of oil-cured bonito with spicy salsa *roja*, potato chips, and mini loaf-shaped crackers called *picos*.

East 12th Osteria

Italian 

B2

197 First Ave. (at 12th St.)

Subway: 1 Av
Phone: 212-432-1112
Web: www.east12osteria.com
Prices: $$

Lunch Sat – Sun
Dinner nightly

On the one hand, this is a straightforward little corner trattoria. On the other, Chef Roberto Deiaco's exciting cooking is a delicious presentation of Italian tastes and technique. The front of house is run by the chef's wife, who lends a personal and intimate air that's hard to fake and increasingly rare. The room glows with good vibes that radiate across the hardwood floor, marble bar, and tin ceiling.

Contemporary highlights accent the Northern Italian-focused menu of *fritto di mare* neatly piling hot and delicately crisp calamari, red mullet, jumbo shrimp and a zucchini blossom. *Tagliolini all'uovo* is twirled with basil pesto, *ricotta salata*, and black truffle; and slowly braised veal cheeks are coddled with *pinot bianco gremolata* sauce and polenta.

The Eddy

Contemporary XX

B3

342 E. 6th St. (bet First & Second Aves.)

Subway: 2 Av
Phone: 646-895-9884
Web: www.theeddynyc.com
Prices: $$

Dinner nightly

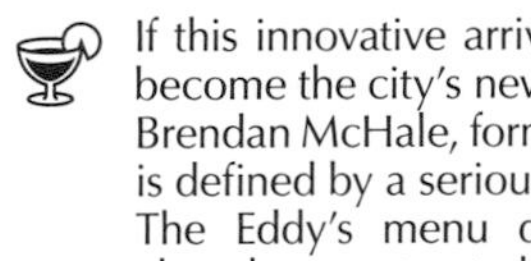

If this innovative arrival is any indication, Curry Row could become the city's newest restaurant strip. Headlined by Chef Brendan McHale, formerly of Jack's Oyster Bar, the wee bistro is defined by a serious bar and well-managed dining area.

The Eddy's menu defies easy categorization and offers cleverly constructed cooking. Fried beef tendons are a puffed and crunchy snack dabbed with charred onion cream and sweet trout roe. Delicate ricotta gnocchi with toasted hazelnuts showcases spring's sweet peas and pickled ramps, while golden spotted tile fish is seared and plated with squid ink Hollandaise, saffron broth, rice beans, and braised artichokes. Cardamom panna cotta with rhubarb granita and olive oil relays the menu's spirit to the finish line.

Edi & The Wolf

Austrian X

C4

102 Ave. C (bet. 6th & 7th Sts.)

Subway: 1 Av
Phone: 212-598-1040
Web: www.ediandthewolf.com
Prices: $$

Lunch Sat – Sun
Dinner nightly

Chefs Eduard Frauneder and Wolfgang Ban are the dynamic duo behind this downtown facsimile of a *heuriger*—basically a casual neighborhood wine tavern popular throughout Austria. The dark and earthy den is chock-full of reclaimed materials including a 40-foot rope salvaged from a church, now coiled above the tiny bar.

The crux of the offerings is comprised of small and shared plates such as cured and dried *landjäger* sausage, accompanied by house-made mustard and pickles. Entrées fall under the heading of "schnitzel & co." and offer a highly recommended wiener schnitzel, which starts with a pounded filet of heritage pork encased in an incredibly delicate and crunchy coating, finished with an Austrian-style potato salad and lingonberry jam.

Feast

Contemporary

102 Third Ave. (bet. 12th & 13th Sts.)

Subway: 3 Av — Lunch Sat – Sun
Phone: 212-529-8880 — Dinner Tue – Sun
Web: www.eatfeastnyc.com
Prices: $$

This recent arrival with the straightforward but promising moniker is a rustic, textbook amalgam of wood, brick, and tiles.

The kitchen is confidently led by an alum of Veritas who has devised several prix-fixe menus, served family-style. These might be based on the farmer's market or even a nose-to-tail meal of lamb, including merguez stew; and a lasagna layering shank, broccoli rabe, and goat cheese. If you're not up for a whole feast, dine à la carte on meaty, ocean-fresh oysters capped by cocktail sauce aspic; or a *nouveau* take on incredibly tender chicken and "dumplings" of liver-stuffed pan-fried gnocchi and wisps of crisped skin. End with the awesome Valrhona chocolate pudding—leaving a single dark chocolate cookie crumb behind is impossible.

Flinders Lane

International

162 Ave. A (bet. 10th & 11th Sts.)

Subway: 1 Av — Lunch & dinner daily
Phone: 212-228-6900
Web: www.flinderslane-nyc.com
Prices: $$

Two Melbourne natives bring Australian dining to the East Village with this whimsical bistro. Flinders Lane hosts a convivial set in a petite room that's trademark downtown, with its mix of industrial and rustic touches.

A strong Asian accent is woven throughout the menu, which also hails inspiration from Australia's Greek and Italian immigrants. Moist seaweed combined with avocado, snake beans, and roasted red pepper is a pop of flavors, brightened by a soy sauce- and toasted sesame oil-dressing. Grilled naan with *tandoori*-style rabbit is especially tasty thanks to its marinade of spiced yogurt and quick-pickled green mango garnish. And for as refreshing a dessert as you're likely to ever come across, order the coconut jelly with watermelon.

Gnocco

Italian

337 E. 10th St. (bet. Aves. A & B)

Subway: 1 Av
Phone: 212-677-1913
Web: www.gnocco.com
Prices: $$

Lunch & dinner daily

A casual cucina with a lovely back garden, Gnocco is a neighborhood staple with a homey touch. The restaurant charms with creaky wood floors and exposed brick walls accented by abstract paintings. The wood-burning oven at the entrance sets a warm tone, and greets guests with the heady aroma of freshly baked bread.

The signature *gnocco* (sweet, salty pillows of fried bread) can be ordered as an appetizer, side, or even as a dessert with Nutella. Pizzas shine on this carb-centric menu, thanks to that blistered thin crust hanging over the plate's edge. The *Amatriciana* layers tart tomato sauce with sweet red onion, shreds of pancetta, and a heavy-handed sprinkle of red pepper flakes. The *torta cioccolato* with chocolate mousse makes a fine dessert.

Graffiti

Contemporary

224 E. 10th St. (bet. First & Second Aves.)

Subway: 1 Av
Phone: 212-464-7743
Web: www.graffitinyc.com
Prices: $$

Dinner Tue – Sun

Credibly doted on since it's inception in 2007, this cub of Chef/owner Jehangir Mehta is still going strong and baby boy is quite the dreamboat. Dressed with tightly-packed square communal tables and beaded ceiling lights, petite Graffiti may be dimly lit, but an exposed brick wall glossed with a metallic finish and hugging framed mirrors is all brightness.

Feeding a pack of 20 on newspaper-wrapped tables are Indian-inspired sweet and savory small plates of watermelon and feta salad cooled by a vibrant mint sorbet; eggplant buns spiked with toasty cumin; green mango *paneer*; and a zucchini-hummus pizza. If you forget to order the addictive green chili shrimp, you can hit Mehtaphor in the Duane Street Hotel for a taste of this spicy delight.

Hasaki

Japanese

210 E. 9th St. (bet. Second & Third Aves.)

Subway: Astor Pl
Phone: 212-473-3327
Web: www.hasakinyc.com
Prices: **$$**

Lunch Wed – Sun
Dinner nightly

Since the mid-eighties, this local darling has been going strong thanks to its high quality ingredients, skilled kitchen, and excellent value. For under $20, the soba lunch set will warm the heart of any frugal fan of Japanese cuisine. This generous feast features a bowl of green tea noodles in hot, crystal-clear dashi stocked with wilted water spinach and fish cake, accompanied by lean tuna *chirashi*, yellowtail, and *kanpyo*. The *ten-don*, a jumbo shrimp tempura served over rice, is just as enticing. The à la carte offerings draw crowds seeking delish sushi as well as a host of tasty cooked preparations; a Twilight menu is nice for early birds.
The dining room has a clean and spare look, with seating available at a number of wood tables or sizable counter.

Hearth

Mediterranean 

403 E. 12th St. (at First Ave.)

Subway: 1 Av
Phone: 646-602-1300
Web: www.restauranthearth.com
Prices: **$$$**

Lunch Sat – Sun
Dinner nightly

After more than a decade delighting fans, Chef Marco Canora and his dining room still have what it takes to impress Manhattan's fickle diners. The space remains fresh and welcoming, and the chef has added an adjacent bone broth kiosk, Brodo, which has converts lining up for their daily fix. Italian classics given a creative reworking are the key to Hearth's longtime success.
Baccalà is used to compose roasted cod scattered with crisped bits of skin, silky chickpea purée, and garlic confit. Then veal-and-ricotta meatballs wrapped in slow-cooked tomato sauce are nestled in stone-ground polenta that is prepared *cacio e pepe*-style. And, desserts here are as enticing as the wines. Imagine a warm autumn fruit crisp, complete with pecan streusel and honey gelato.

Hot Kitchen

Chinese

B3

104 Second Ave. (bet. 6th & 7th Sts.)

Lunch & dinner daily

Subway: Astor Pl
Phone: 212-228-3090
Web: www.hotkitchenny.com
Prices: **$$**

True to its name, Hot Kitchen adds a dash of fiery Sichuan cooking to a neighborhood already rife with international delights. Whitewashed brick walls, chili-red beams, an orange accent wall, and ebony furnishings detail the tidy space.

Steer clear of the Chinese-American portion of the menu; instead, partake in the memorable house specialties featuring dried chilies, Sichuan peppercorns, and pickled peppers that singe with abandon. However, a handful of straightforward items do bring relief from the spicy onslaught, as in minced pork with pickled cabbage in a light, sour broth; chunks of dark and salty-sweet braised beef and potatoes; and myriad hotpots (a recent menu addition).

A second location can now be found in Midtown East on 53rd Street.

Huertas

Spanish XX

B3

107 First Ave. (bet. 6th & 7th Sts.)

Lunch Sat – Sun
Dinner nightly

Subway: Astor Pl
Phone: 212-228-4490
Web: www.huertasnyc.com
Prices: **$$$**

A festive spirit fronts this Basque country-inspired den, where *pintxos* are passed around in the bar. This is the kind of place that honors authentic sips like *kalimotxo* (red wine and cola), *vermut* (Catalan for vermouth), and sherry, so don't expect to see pitchers of sangria being bandied about.

The proper dining room in the back is where the highly recommended tasting menu is served. This reasonably priced prix-fixe stimulates with small bites like sardine *conserva* served on buttered crostini with shaved radish; and may be followed by softly scrambled eggs drizzled with ruby shrimp jus, or seared lamb loin with greenmarket produce and crushed black olives. A chocolate custard topped with whipped cream and crushed Marcona almonds is heaven on a plate.

Jewel Bako ✿

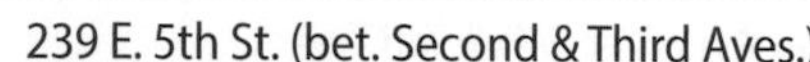

Japanese

A3

239 E. 5th St. (bet. Second & Third Aves.)

Subway: Astor Pl — Dinner Mon – Sat
Phone: 212-979-1012
Web: www.jewelbakosushi.com
Prices: **$$$**

Black walls surrounding two tiny windows form the façade of this surreptitious gem. Unlike the diverse neighborhood in which it resides, the décor inside the long room is simple and sleek, framed by low ceilings, curving bamboo slats, and close-knit tables. Servers are smartly attired if a little too-cool-for-school, but the passionate chefs here provide a wealth of culinary entertainment.

This is a place where painstaking detail is evident from start to finish. A large square plate, for instance, may feature the likes of ruby-red tuna set beside soy-mirin sauce; an edible cup filled with a spicy salmon mixture; densely packed roe topped with bonito flakes; and a peppery watercress salad. Then, a thick cut of salmon marinated in three types of miso and cooked *en papillote* is unwrapped to reveal the most tender, moist, and flaky meat. And finally, each grain of slightly sticky rice in the sushi omakase is cooked perfectly and combined with fluke, Tasmanian trout, and creamy otoro.

Young couples as well as die-hard downtowners idolize this "jewel" and for good reason—a dessert of green tea ice cream sandwiched between chocolate chip cookies is exemplary, delicious, and very, very special.

Joe & MissesDoe

Contemporary

A4

45 E. 1st St. (bet. First & Second Aves.)

Subway: 2 Av
Phone: 212-780-0262
Web: www.chefjoedoe.com
Prices: $$

Lunch Sat – Sun
Dinner Tue – Sun

Chef Joe and Jill Doe have revamped their earnest establishment with a tweaked menu and pared down interior look. Gone are the knickknacks that were previously sprinkled throughout this small room, which now seats about 30 at a single row of tables and long bar counter.

From his station in the open kitchen, the chef gives American cuisine a creative re-working. Broccoli meets *skordalia* in an appetizer of caramelized florets dressed with grated pecorino, sliced almonds, pistachios, and toasted garlic. Beef brisket is slow-braised then griddled, and plated with house-made steak sauce and spicy radish chow-chow. A sundae of chocolate chip banana bread with vanilla ice cream and bananas Foster sauce is yet another example of this enjoyable hybrid cuisine.

Kafana

Eastern European

C3

116 Ave. C (bet. 7th & 8th Sts.)

Subway: 1 Av
Phone: 212-353-8000
Web: www.kafananyc.com
Prices: $$

Lunch Sat-Sun
Dinner nightly

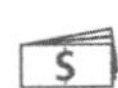

Traditional Serbian cuisine, a rarity in these parts, is the specialty at this heartwarming Alphabet City café. The intimate space is outfitted with exposed brick walls hung with mirrors and vintage photographs, rough-hewn wood tables, and boldly patterned banquettes. Carnations and votive candles pretty the room.

Begin a meal with an assortment of air-dried or smoked meats and tall slices of savory pies like the *gibanica* stuffed with tart feta layered in excellent phyllo. Other authentic and hearty treats include *ćevapi* (grilled minced meat kebabs) as well as wonderfully rustic stews combining lamb and wilted spinach, or beans with smoked baby back ribs. Kafana's regional wine list features a selection of orange wines from Slovenia and Croatia.

Kanoyama

Japanese 

175 Second Ave. (at 11th St.)

Subway: 3 Av — Dinner nightly
Phone: 212-777-5266
Web: www.kanoyama.com
Prices: **$$**

Offering an impressive lineup of excellent quality and deftly prepared fish, this popular and permanently packed sushi den is housed in a space that may be simply decorated but is spotless and well-maintained. The kitchen's focus here is on a parade of pristine cuts that are bolstered by a passage of daily items such as rich baby shad from Japan and tender, mild American white bonito. Also find a generous listing of plump, briny oysters; starters such as *wakasagi* tempura (fried baby smelts) sprinkled with green tea-salt; and a handful of cooked entrées. The value-conscious omakase is highly recommended.

Besides being tempting, the website is very informative: it presents diverse fish facts, photos, and recommendations for seasonality and preparation.

Kura

130 St. Marks Pl. (bet. Ave. A & First Ave.)

Subway: Astor Pl — Dinner Mon – Sat
Phone: 212-228-1010
Web: N/A
Prices: **$$$$**

Set among a stretch of storefronts is this plain white façade that is so discreet, it actually stands out and grabs your attention. Hidden within is a hangout favored by a predominantly Japanese clientele crowded at the counter.

Chef Norihiro Ishizuka runs the show, jovially engaging with his guests while slicing, forming, torching, and rolling. The only option here is omakase and diners choose their preference from three price points. Begin a meal here with sushi, which at times might be loosely formed, but the fish is of irreproachable quality and the experience absolutely special. Recent delights have included torched mackerel hako nigiri, a live prawn followed by its crispy deep-fried head, a heap of tiny raw *sakura ebi*, and a tuna hand roll to finish.

Kyo Ya ✿

Japanese

B3

94 E. 7th St. (bet First Ave. & Ave. A)

Subway: Astor Pl — Dinner Tue – Sat
Phone: 212-982-4140
Web: N/A
Prices: $$$

In the basement level of a classic walk-up smack in the midst of a hip-artsy downtown neighborhood, Kyo Ya looks and feels like a secret hideaway cloaked in undulating wood and dark slate. The height of professionalism and hospitality, the staff is not merely attentive but appreciative of your presence at their table—or perhaps at one of the prized chef's counter stools for kaiseki dining, where mesmerizing craft is exhibited.

This is a place where traditional cuisine is prepared with modern flair, and Japanese is the moneyed clientele's mother tongue.

Refinement pervades every element of every dish, like the delicate, slightly tart pickled cabbage potage with chewy tri-colored taro root-potato *dango* and pale green strips of simmered vegetables finished with a dab of miso. The sashimi of the day may feature a fresh oyster with sautéed onion and *yuzu kosho oroshi* swimming in ponzu; simmered firefly squid and celery topped with salty *karashi*-miso and pickled plum; or tender raw octopus. Clay pots reveal fragrant dashi cooked with woodear mushooms, carrots, turnips, and bobbing with a tiny melting ball of excellent mozzarella as well as the quenelle-like shrimp dumpling, *ebishinjo.*

L'Apicio

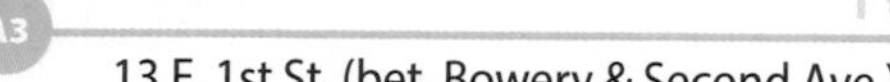

A3 Italian XX

13 E. 1st St. (bet. Bowery & Second Ave.)

Subway: 2 Av
Phone: 212-533-7400
Web: www.lapicio.com
Prices: $$

Lunch Sat – Sun
Dinner nightly

Despite being named for an 18th century Italian cookbook, this buzzy trattoria is a contemporary hit.

A downtown vibe courses throughout the swanky den that is slightly rustic and industrial—this setting is worth dressing up for. Half of the room is devoted to the bar, and the private dining room is best suited to exhibitionists who enjoy dining within glass walls in the center of the room.

Bright flavors and skilled creativity combine in their tailored selection of Italian plates designed for grazing. Start with dishes like fried green tomatoes capped with sweet basil pesto and milky mozzarella, or fresh agnolotti stuffed with sweetbreads. Finish with a wedge of moist olive oil cake sweetened with crème fraîche and *vin santo*-soaked raisins.

Lavagna

C3 Italian X

545 E. 5th St. (bet. Aves. A & B)

Subway: 2 Av
Phone: 212-979-1005
Web: www.lavagnanyc.com
Prices: $$

Lunch Sat – Sun
Dinner nightly

The little menu at this neighborhood fixture proves that quality trumps size. Lavagna's kitchen is snug but still manages to make ample use of a wood-burning oven to bake everything from delicate *pizette* to whole roasted fish. Pastas are always a treat, while other tasty options can include pan-fried smoked *scamorza* paired with a roasted red pepper crostini, juicy rack of lamb, or a slice of spot-on *crostata* filled with seasonal fruit and dressed with caramel sauce.

Framed mirrors, a pressed-tin ceiling, and candlelight produce a mood that is almost as warm as the genuinely gracious service, which ensures that regulars receive the royal treatment. That said, everyone who steps through these doors feels welcome and well taken care of.

Lil' Frankie's

Italian

19 First Ave. (bet. 1st & 2nd Sts.)

Subway: 2 Av
Phone: 212-420-4900
Web: www.lilfrankies.com
Prices:

Lunch Sat– Sun
Dinner nightly

Frank Prisinzano's pizzeria combines a series of intimate rooms for a laid-back vibe that's perfectly in step with the neighborhood. An open kitchen is in one room, a pizza oven in another, and a third boasts a wall of window panels that open for alfresco dining. Framed photos and colorful vinyl tablecloths add character.

The Neapolitan-style pizza is always a hit, perhaps topped with bright tomato sauce, fresh mozzarella, and slices of spicy salami. Also savor the likes of fava bean purée with dandelion greens for a thick and homey soup. Garlic bread, baked pasta of the day, and whole eggplant with *pepperoncino* oil are all flame-kissed creations from the wood-burning oven. Stop by during weekend brunch for "killer" pancakes made with buckwheat flour.

Luzzo's

211-13 First Ave. (bet. 12th & 13th Sts.)

Subway: 1 Av
Phone: 212-473-7447
Web: www.luzzospizza.com
Prices: $$

Lunch & dinner daily

A treasured century-old coal oven is the heart of this quirky Neapolitan-style pizza parlor, lined with exposed brick, mismatched chairs, and kitschy knickknacks. Italian music plays softly beneath the buzz of this ever-busy restaurant, as loyal crowds wait patiently outside for the piping hot pies topped with melting mozzarella.

A deep understanding of the art of bread baking is evident in every pie pulled from the coal-burning oven. The *diavola* features a tender, black-blistered crust topped with thin slices of spicy-salty salami, light and chunky tomato sauce beneath dollops of mozzarella. Round, square, and even puffy fried pies are all crafted with care at this convivial spot. For dessert, the *zeppole di Nutella* are an unabashed crowd-pleaser.

Malai Marke

Indian XX

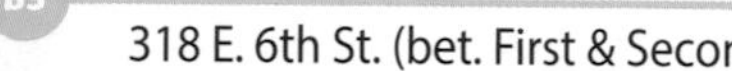

B3

318 E. 6th St. (bet. First & Second Aves.)

Subway: Astor Pl
Lunch & dinner daily
Phone: 212-777-7729
Web: www.malaimarke.com
Prices: $$

The name of this Curry Row resto translates to "extra cream" in Hindi tea stall slang, and rich and flavorful is indeed the order of the day. The clean, narrow space is bright and contemporary, with black tile walls and copper pots hanging from exposed brick.

From the kitchen, *tangra*-style Calcutta-Chinese specialties are a new offering, however it is best to focus your attention on the preparations originating from the Southwest coast. Seafood and coconut factor heavily in Latta Shetty's shrimp *ajadina,* a dry-gravy stir-fry rich with red chillies and myriad spices. Chicken *chutneywala* is simmered in a bright yellow cream sauce seasoned with tart-sweet green mango chutney; and pumpkin *sabji* is another fantastic offering that also happens to be vegetarian. Win win!

The Mermaid Inn

Seafood X

A3

96 Second Ave. (bet. 5th & 6th Sts.)

Subway: Astor Pl
Dinner nightly
Phone: 212-674-5870
Web: www.themermaidnyc.com
Prices: $$

This laid-back and inviting seafood spot has been a neighborhood favorite for over a decade now, spawning locations in Greenwich Village and the Upper West Side. A steady stream of guests lines the bar early in the week for Monday's all night happy hour with freshly shucked oysters, snack-sized fish tacos, and other specially priced bites. For a hearty plate after your nosh, try blackened catfish dotted with crawfish butter alongside hushpuppies, or the lobster roll with Old Bay fries. On Sunday nights, look out for lobsterpalooza—a whole lobster accompanied by grilled corn on the cob and steamed potatoes.

At the end of your meal there's no need to deliberate over dessert. A demitasse of perfect chocolate pudding is presented compliments of the house.

Mighty Quinn's

Barbecue

103 Second Ave. (at 6th St.)

Subway: Astor Pl — Lunch & dinner daily
Phone: 212-677-3733
Web: www.mightyquinnsbbq.com
Prices:

From its humble beginnings as a Smorgasburg favorite, Mighty Quinn's continues to impress with its "low and slow smoked barbecue." And, boasting permanent outposts at the Hudson Eats FiDi food hall and West Village, this rustic and casual wood-lined space feels young and energetic with crowds of hungry diners lined up to the door.

Cafeteria-like service features cleaver-wielding cooks proffering pulled pork, ribs, and more. Selections are sliced, weighed, and piled high before you even make it to the sides and vats of house pickles. Go for the baked beans, made with black-eyed peas and meaty burnt ends for plenty of umami. The best reason to come here may be the wonderfully wobbly-tender brisket, pink-tinged with smoke and thinly crusted in spice.

Momofuku Noodle Bar

Asian

171 First Ave. (bet. 10th & 11th Sts.)

Subway: 1 Av — Lunch & dinner daily
Phone: 212-777-7773
Web: www.momofuku.com
Prices: $$

This elder member of David Chang's culinary empire is hipper and hotter than ever. A honey-toned temple of updated comfort food, decked with blonde wood counters and a sparkling open kitchen, the service here may be brisk. But rest assured, as the menu is gutsy and molded with Asian street food in mind.

Those steamed buns have amassed a gargantuan following thanks to decadent fillings like moist pork loin kissed with Hollandaise and chives. Additionally, that bowl of springy noodles doused in a spicy ginger-scallion sauce is just one instance of the crew's signature work. Korean fried chicken with seasonal greens is fit for a king; while more modest items, including desserts like candy apple truffle, are beautifully crafted and rightfully elevated to global fame.

Momofuku Ko ✿✿

A3

8 Extra Pl. (at 1st St.)

Subway: 2 Av

Dinner Wed – Sun

Phone: 212-500-0831

Web: www.momofuku.com

Prices: **$$$$**

David Chang's beloved Ko has packed up its 600-square-foot tasting course concept and moved a few blocks south. Down a quiet alley and behind a door sporting his proverbial peach, you'll find the handsome new digs: a street-hip space sporting 40 seats, 22 of them surrounding the open kitchen via a U-shaped counter made of smooth black walnut.

Much else remains the same. Per the old rules, there is no à la carte—only the multicourse menu for the evening (which you're given in print before you go). Then, dishes are delivered by the chefs themselves, who briefly describe each ingredient; while servers slip seamlessly between guests, changing silver and filling drinks.

Chang is a veritable rock star chef by any standard (and his longtime lieutenant Sean Gray is the chef's equivalent of Keith Richards), so you're in expert hands from the start. Fresh, sweet sea bream is bound by translucent grated yam with fragrant shiso and pops of finger lime; and tender beef tartare is paired with cream of oyster as well as crushed popcorn. Delicate kabocha squash tortellini arrives with shaved parmesan and *agrodolce*; and a perfectly seared slice of venison is paired with silky potatoes and earthy Époisses.

Momofuku Ssäm Bar 

Contemporary

B2

207 Second Ave. (at 13th St.)

Subway: 3 Av — Lunch & dinner daily
Phone: 212-254-3500
Web: www.momofuku.com
Prices: $$

Trust us, you need Momofuku Ssäm Bar in your life. Inside David Chang's perennial favorite, you'll find a hip, young crowd rubbing elbows at the minimalist bar or sinking into low-slung tables to chat up their dinner companions. It's a fun, convivial ambience, no question—but the star of the show here is indisputably Chang's singular Korean and Japanese cooking style, which flirts with European and Californian influences.

There's perfectly sourced charcuterie and a lovely raw bar to kick things off, but don't leave without moving on to Chang's legendary pork buns—pillow-soft and laced with hoisin sauce, cucumber, and scallions. Or even a tender Flat Iron steak, grilled to perfection, and paired with *chicharrón* chips, ramps, and broiled asparagus tips.

Motorino

Pizza

B2

349 E. 12th St. (bet. First & Second Aves.)

Subway: 1 Av — Lunch & dinner daily
Phone: 212-777-2644
Web: www.motorinopizza.com
Prices: 

What started out as a Neapolitan-style pizzeria in Brooklyn has grown into a global chain with locations in Hong Kong and Manila. Cloaked in the scent of wood-fired pies, Motorino is praised as an all-day spot that's easy on the wallet. True, it may be smaller than the newer, slightly grander Williamsburg outpost, but these pizzas leave nothing to be desired.

Blackboard specials convey the product-focused sensibilities that begin with a lunchtime prix-fixe pairing a green salad of mint, beet greens, and red onion in balsamic vinaigrette with a perfectly charred and chewy pie. The foundation of each pizza is its outstanding crust spread with crushed tomatoes, gobs of melting fresh mozzarella, and perhaps a generous layering of spicy sausage slices.

Narcissa

A2

21 Cooper Sq. (at 5th St.)

Subway: Astor Pl — Lunch & dinner daily
Phone: 212-228-3344
Web: www.narcissarestaurant.com
Prices: $$

André Balaz's Standard East Village hotel is where you will find one of downtown's snazziest dining rooms. Richly stained wood furnishings in contrasting hues pair beautifully with tanned leather banquettes, sienna table linens, and perfectly calibrated lighting. The overall effect is warmer than a Malibu sunset.

Chef John Fraser (of Dovetail) has assembled a formidable team to realize his vision of polished farm-to-table dining, starring seasonal produce from the Hudson Valley. Beets take a turn in the rotisserie oven and arrive for your pleasure as a warm salad with hearty bulgur, pickled cucumber, and a pool of horseradish cream. Poussin is roasted whole and set atop steel cut oats slicked with jus, spicy sausage, and oven-wilted radicchio.

Noreetuh

Fusion

B3

128 First Ave. (bet. 7th St. & St. Marks Pl.)

Subway: Astor Pl — Dinner Tue – Sun
Phone: 646-892-3050
Web: www.noreetuh.com
Prices: $$

For a taste of something different, make a beeline to this worthwhile Hawaiian-flavored newcomer. Headed by a trio of Per Se veterans, Noreetuh features an intimate setting of two slender dining rooms adorned with hexagonal mirrors and shelving units used to store bottles from the impressive wine list.

Bigeye tuna poke strewn with seaweed, diced macadamia nuts, and pickled jalapeños is just one of the delicious highlights on offer, while plump shrimp seasoned with crushed garlic and arranged over a bed of sticky rice and baby romaine is another fine choice. For dessert, the signature take on bread pudding boasts caramelized slices of custard-soaked King's Hawaiian bread with rum raisins and a knockout scoop of pineapple ice cream.

Northern Spy Food Co.

American

C2

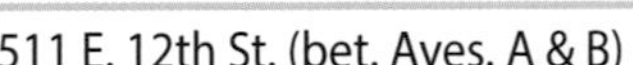

511 E. 12th St. (bet. Aves. A & B)

Subway: 1 Av — Lunch & dinner daily
Phone: 212-228-5100
Web: www.northernspyfoodco.com
Prices: $$

This enticing Alphabet City café beckons with its countrified setting and fiercely ingredient-driven comfort food. Reclaimed hickory flooring and salvaged wood tabletops fill the petite room dressed with framed mirrors, vintage wallpaper, and a banquette painted robin's egg blue. The look is unbeatably quaint.

The cuisine also happens to be innovative, as in a snack of pork sticky rolls swiped with parsnip glaze, or a first course of roasted sunchokes, fennel, and clementine sements pierced with dried black-garlic chips. The night's offering of organic-pastured local pork may reveal tender slices of pan-seared loin fanned over jalapeño cornbread that has been cooked down to "polenta." On Sunday nights, enjoy a three-course prix-fixe for under $30.00.

Oda House

Eastern European

C3

76 Ave. B (at 5th St.)

Subway: 2 Av — Lunch & dinner daily
Phone: 212-353-3838
Web: www.odahouse.com
Prices: $$

For a taste of something different, this inviting café serves intriguing specialties from Georgia. That country's proximity to Russia, Turkey, and Armenia results in a vibrant and enticingly diverse cuisine that Oda House does proud.

A liberal use of fragrant spices, cheese-filled breads, kebabs, and slow-cooked meats typify the kitchen's preparations. Classic dishes include *satsivi*, boiled chicken served cool in a creamy walnut sauce seasoned with warm spices, accompanied by *gomi*, hominy grits in a mini cauldron studded with morsels of rich, stretchy *sulgani* cheese. Balance out the hearty fare with a fresh, perfectly dressed garden salad.

The vibe is simple and rustic with pumpkin-stained stucco walls, exposed brick, and wood furnishings.

Oiji 

B3 Korean

119 First Ave. (bet. 7th St & St. Marks Pl.)

Subway: Astor Pl — Dinner Tue – Sun
Phone: 646-767-9050
Web: www.oijinyc.com
Prices: $$

Headed by a duo of young Korean-born chefs who met at the Culinary Institute of America and put their education to work in the stellar kitchens of Bouley and Gramercy Tavern, Oiji dishes out an updated take on Korean flavors. The intimate dining room is small and moodily lit, with an open kitchen that allows diners to see and hear the action as it takes place. Polished and refined yet familiar, the concise menu of small plates offers an appealing approach. Decadently rich and creamy, the wild sesame soup—a dairy-free sensation—is poured over wild mushrooms, chewy rice cake, and black truffle. Pine smoke-infused mackerel is served with a wedge of lemon and yuzu-soy sauce to brighten the fragrant and oily-rich fish. Of course, the kimchi is not to be missed.

Porsena 

A2 Italian 

21 E. 7th St. (bet. Second & Third Aves.)

Subway: Astor Pl — Lunch Sat-Sun
Phone: 212-228-4923 — Dinner nightly
Web: www.porsena.com
Prices: $$

Sophisticates of all ages flock to this neighborhood favorite to be enveloped by a warm, welcoming, and upbeat vibe. Euro-chic Porsena also boasts adept servers who can be seen strutting about with appetizing platters of aromatic food.

As always, Chef Sara Jenkins proves herself to be a talent and a pro through presentations that are unfussy yet remain uniquely flavorful and always special. The menu rotates with the seasons, but standbys cannot be missed, like wild escarole salad with crisp leaves wilting in hot anchovy dressing; or huge rounds of *anelloni* tossed with spicy lamb sausage, peppery mustard greens, and breadcrumbs. If offered, get the lasagna expertly layering pasta sheets with a creamy béchamel and hearty veal-prosciutto ragù.

Prime & Beyond New York

Steakhouse

90 E. 10th St. (bet. Third & Fourth Aves.)

Subway: Astor Pl
Phone: 212-505-0033
Web: www.primeandbeyond.com
Prices: $$$

Dinner nightly

This location of the Fort Lee, NJ original brings great steak to the East Village. Appropriate for this locale, the setting eschews the standard men's club swagger of most steakhouses for a look that's spare and cool. Despite the chillax vibe, expect to see suits; the meat is that good. In fact, it's procured from the same purveyor that supplies Peter Luger and Keens.

Aged in-house for six weeks, the USDA Prime Porterhouse is presented hot off the grill but well rested, richly flavored, tender, and juicy. Myriad cuts satisfy all preferences, while sides like kimchi, spicy scallion salad, and fermented cabbage stew are especially appealing and honor the owners' heritage. Heartwarming Korean style soups and stews are wonderful wintertime favorites.

Prune

American

54 E. 1st St. (bet. First & Second Aves.)

Subway: 2 Av
Phone: 212-677-6221
Web: www.prunerestaurant.com
Prices: $$

Lunch Sat-Sun
Dinner nightly

Chef Gabrielle Hamilton's sterling little bistro has long bewitched the city's foodies who cram its bar and row of tables. Unpretentious cooking in a room branded by pops of purple is Prune's hallmark, and a completely revised menu shines with newfound inspiration.

"Straw and hay" pasta—fresh strands of egg and herbed linguine—is sauced with chicken livers and diced green tomatoes, while deep-fried rabbit is seasoned with romesco salt, and sided with buttermilk dressing. For the most simple yet epic finale ever, the season's best peaches are lightly sugared and laid over warm buttered toast.

Prune's daiquiri (a zesty combination of three rums garnished with a vanilla bean swizzle stick that perfumes each sip) is proof of serious cocktail creativity.

Pylos

Greek XX

128 E. 7th St. (bet. First Ave. & Ave. A)

Subway: Astor Pl — Lunch Wed – Sun
Phone: 212-473-0220 — Dinner nightly
Web: www.pylosrestaurant.com
Prices: $$

Restaurateur Christos Valtzoglou has found the winning formula with this longstanding hideaway. Although his Heartbreak and Boukies may be faded memories, Pylos continues to sparkle as brightly as the Aegean Sea on a summer day. Taking its name from the Greek translation of "made from clay," this contemporary taverna features a ceiling canopy of suspended terra-cotta pots dressing up a room with whitewashed walls and lapis-blue insets.

Pale-green stemware and stark white crockery are used to serve Greek wines and a menu of rustic home-style cooking. *Gigantes* are baked in honey-scented tomato-dill sauce; grilled marinated octopus is drizzled with balsamic reduction; and *anginares* moussaka is a creamy vegetarian take on the classic made with artichokes.

Rai Rai Ken

218 E. 10th St. (bet. First & Second Aves.)

Subway: Astor Pl — Lunch & dinner daily
Phone: 212-477-7030
Web: N/A
Prices:

Rai Rai Ken isn't quite what it used to be—it's bigger and much more comfortable. Just a few doors east of its former location, this room boasts a fresh and tidy look with blonde wood seating plus signature red vinyl stools. An array of pots remain bubbling and steaming behind the counter.

Rest assured the menu's star attraction—those thin and toothsome ramen noodles—are just as delicious, served with four near-addictive, fantastically complex broth variations: *shio, shoyu,* miso, and curry. Each bowlful is chock-full of garnishes, like slices of roasted pork, boiled egg, nori, fishcake, and a nest of springy noodles. Grab a business card before leaving as loyal diners are rewarded with a complimentary bowl after ten visits.

Ramen Misoya

Japanese 

129 Second Ave. (bet. St. Marks Pl. & 7th St.)

Subway: Astor Pl — Lunch & dinner daily
Phone: 212-677-4825
Web: www.misoyanyc.com
Prices:

With 30 locations worldwide, Ramen Misoya brings its trademark ambrosial bowlfuls to New York City. The earthy dining area dons a bamboo-lined ceiling as well as a TV monitor that is internally looped to broadcast the kitchen's every move.

The ramen offering here differentiates itself by centering on a trio of miso-enriched broths: *shiro* is a white miso fermented with rice *koji* (starter); *kome-miso* is richer tasting; and *mame-miso* is a strictly soybean product. The mouth-coating soup is delicious alchemy. Each slurp is a multifaceted distillation of pork and chicken bones with savory-salty-sweet notes, stocked with excellent noodles, vegetables, and the likes of panko-crusted shrimp tempura, fried ginger chicken, or slices of house-made *cha-su*.

Risotteria Melotti

309 E. 5th St. (bet. First & Second Aves.)

Subway: Astor Pl — Lunch Sat – Sun
Phone: 646-755-8939 — Dinner nightly
Web: www.risotteriamelottinyc.com
Prices: $$

By specializing in risotto, this unique family-owned spot rises above the city's endless proliferation of Italian dining options. The Melotti family produces rice in Veneto and this stateside location is sister to Isola della Scala in Verona.

Scenes from the film *Riso Amaro* on a mounted television add atmosphere to the rustic surrounds, where the air is filled with the sounds of stirring as each order is prepared. A bread basket stuffed with rice cakes precedes plates of risotto *limone e gamberi* made with lemon juice and studded with morsels of pan-seared shrimp. More complex *risotti* may be presented in a crispy Monte Veronese cheese cup and showcase Amarone wine. Here, each creamy and toothsome grain displays impressive technique.

Robataya

231 E. 9th St. (bet. Second & Third Aves.)

Subway: Astor Pl — Lunch & dinner daily
Phone: 212-979-9674
Web: www.robataya-ny.com
Prices: $$

Irasshaimase! This is the kind of intensely authentic place where welcomes are shouted to guests upon entering. At peak times, wait among Japanese expats and young couples lining the sidewalk. Aim straight for the counter to appreciate the theatrics of it all, where orders are acknowledged with more shouts flying from Japanese servers to chefs. The energy is high, but so are the standards for their expertly grilled meats and vegetables.

Kneeling cooks use long wooden paddles to deliver dishes hot off the robata, like *gyu tataki*, seared beef filet topped with tobiko and scallions on a bed of red onions with ponzu. Technical mastery is clear in a salt-packed sea bream's subtle smoky flavors emphasizing the delicacy of such white, flaky fish.

Root & Bone

American X

B4

200 E. 3rd St. (bet. Aves. A & B)

Subway: 2 Av — Lunch Wed – Sun
Phone: 646-682-7080 — Dinner nightly
Web: www.rootnbone.com
Prices: $$

Down-home cooking, fried chicken, and a cocktail are just the thing at this cramped but cozy café. The packed room is difficult to take in during the dinner rush, but pretty touches include whitewashed brick walls, a pressed-tin ceiling, and glass-paned cabinets stocked with crockery.

You might even adopt a drawl while reading through Root & Bone's pleasing menu. Grandma Daisy's warm angel biscuits are incredibly light and fluffy—especially alongside that salty-sweet, dark chicken-maple jus for dipping. The signature sweet tea-brined fried chicken is prepared in a designated corner of the room, filling the space with tempting aromas. Shrimp and grits with Virginia country ham has a Yankee touch thanks to the addition of Brooklyn lager to the sauce.

Sigiri

B3

91 First Ave. (bet. 5th & 6th Sts.)

Subway: 1 Av
Phone: 212-614-9333
Web: www.sigirinyc.com
Prices: $$

Lunch & dinner daily

Just off of Curry Row, Sigiri offers a sweetly spiced taste of Sri Lanka in an area known for its Indian dining. This second-floor room may be plain, but is very tidy with tables dressed in colorful linens that pop against the brownish walls. Stir-fried and slow-cooked specialties are sought after here, as in the black pork curry featuring an ink-dark sauce of roasted spices, chilies, black pepper, ginger, and cloves. The string hopper *kotthu* is deliciously traditional, served as a fluffy heap of rice noodles sautéed with bits of white meat chicken and an array of fresh vegetables with a small dish of vibrant coconut curry.

Alcohol is not served, but a number of soft drinks are offered and guests are welcome to bring their own wine or beer.

Sobakoh

Japanese

B3

309 E. 5th St. (bet. First & Second Aves.)

Subway: 2 Av
Phone: 212-254-2244
Web: www.sobakoh-nyc.com
Prices: $$

Lunch & dinner daily

Before entering Sobakoh, stop for a minute to appreciate Chef/owner Hiromitsu Takahashi, sequestered in his temperature- and humidity-controlled glass booth, forming layers of organically grown buckwheat flour dough into first-rate noodles. This ritual is performed several times daily by the smiling chef and is the foundation of the seasonally arranged offerings at this Japan-meets-East Village soba spot. Service can be sluggish, so start with a classic snack, like the refreshing daikon salad dressed with yuzu, wasabi, and bonito flakes. Then dive into your bowlful of *uni ikura soba*—chilled buckwheat noodles heaped with creamy sea urchin and plump salmon roe.

The inexpensive prix-fixe offered nightly is even cheaper before 7:00 P.M.

Soba-Ya 

Japanese XX

B2

229 E. 9th St. (bet. Second & Third Aves.)

Subway: Astor Pl — Lunch & dinner daily
Phone: 212-533-6966
Web: www.sobaya-nyc.com
Prices: ⊜

In a neighborhood replete with tempting Japanese dining options, Soba-Ya has been sating noodle cravings with awesome buckwheat soba and hearty udon—all homemade daily—for more than a decade. Enterprising co-owner Bon Yagi, also of Curry-Ya, favors authenticity over flash in his establishments, and this popular spot fashioning a traditional aesthetic is no exception.

Sit among the largely Japanese lunchtime clientele to savor and slurp cold, refreshing soba attractively served in a red-black bento box. Find it neatly stocked with the likes of dashi-poached vegetables, fresh and deliciously glazed salmon, or crisp shrimp tempura. Complete this meal with a pot of hot broth added to your remaining soy-based dipping sauce for a warming finish.

Supper 

Italian XX

B4

156 E. 2nd St. (bet. Aves. A & B)

Subway: 1 Av — Lunch Sat – Sun
Phone: 212-477-7600 — Dinner nightly
Web: www.supperrestaurant.com
Prices: **$$**

Laid-back yet lively, this Italian paradise draws a refined crowd looking to while away a few lazy hours over great wine and even better bites. Seats up front offer prime views of an action-packed kitchen, while the back is best for intimacy and more sips from the impressive list.

Fresh, thinly sliced squid quickly tossed in garlic, olive oil, lemon, parsley, and chili flakes is a study in the powers of simplicity; while *strozzapretti* with "Dad's Sunday Marinara Sauce" is an elevated rendition of the classic—finished with a mound of luscious ricotta. Even the plainest of pastas are enviably enriched here—imagine twirls of *spaghetti al limone* with a mountain of parmesan and black pepper. If you can save room, the tiramisu is light, fluffy, and *molto buono*!

Somtum Der ✿

B3

85 Ave. A (bet. 5th & 6th Sts.)

Subway: 2 Av

Lunch & dinner daily

Phone: 212-260-8570

Web: www.somtumder.com

Prices: $$

Based in Bangkok, this concrete jungle outpost is doing a terrific job of presenting Thai cuisine that perfectly reflects the modern spirit of the Northeast Isaan region. Upon entering Somtum Der, a cozy enclave stylishly accented with bright pops of red, diners are greeted by a glimpse of the kitchen and its *somtum* station. There, contents from the large glass jars of nuts, dried red chilies, and spices are ground in a mortar and pestle to produce its eponymous dish—also referred to as the city's best green papaya salad(s).

Order big here, as the portions aren't massive and the food is plain terrific. The kitchen is happy to kick things up a notch spice-wise, so be aggressive and request the hotter end of the spectrum for greater authenticity.

The service staff here is both friendly and hospitable, so heed their advice and include in every meal an addictive skewer of Der's-style grilled sticky rice to go along with the likes of lip-smacking *larb tod*. Other highlights have included succulent deep-fried chicken thighs sprinkled with toasted garlic chips and accompanied by a pungent citrus-and-spice dipping sauce. Smoky-sweet *moo ping kati sod*—marinated, grilled, and coconut-glazed pork set over cool rice vermicelli—is gloriously succulent and particularly addictive.

Sushi Dojo

Japanese

B3

110 First Ave. (bet. 6th & 7th Sts.)

Subway: Astor Pl — Dinner Tue – Sat
Phone: 646-692-9398
Web: www.sushidojonyc.com
Prices: $$

Chef David Bouhadana follows up his stint at Sushi Uo and some time in Japan to head up this winning *sushi-ya*. A 14-seat counter and handful of tables outfit this pleasant room, where the congenial chef sends forth an impressive array of morsels.

The chef's choice menu is highly recommended and offers good value for the masterful skill and high quality of fish. This is immediately clear in the nigiri presentation that has included Tasmanian trout, cherry salmon from Japan, and a trio of *maguro* (lean, medium, and fatty). Beyond the sushi menu, sample dishes like house-made cold tofu served with yuzu salt; and *kaki-age*, a light and crisp tempura-fried combination of delicate *mizuna*, seaweed, squid, and shrimp with green-tea salt.

Tuome

Fusion

B3

536 E. 5th St. (bet. Aves. A & B)

Subway: 2 Av — Dinner Tue – Sun
Phone: 646-833-7811
Web: www.tuomenyc.com
Prices: $$

Chef Thomas Chen's intimate venue flaunts petite East Village bones, a warm glow cast over the hip crowd, and a too-loud playlist that may cause indigestion for anyone older than a Millenial.

Asian accents filtered through the mind of this chef (who spent time behind the line at Eleven Madison Park) reveal a playful lineup. Treviso spears are brushed with creamy Caesar dressing and plated with warm, buttery croutons, clementine segments, and toasted sunflower seeds. Black bass is expertly seared and sauced with New England-style clam chowder pocked with Chinese sausage and perfectly complemented by a side of banana leaf-wrapped sticky rice enriched with duck fat. If you still have room for dessert, order the hot, crisp, and mildly sweet Chinese beignets.

Virginia's

C3 Contemporary XX

647 E. 11 St. (bet. Aves. B & C)

Subway: 1 Av Dinner Mon – Sat
Phone: 212-658-0182
Web: www.virginiasnyc.com
Prices: $$

Perfectly East Village in scale, this intimate yet ambitious bistro is composed of two slender rooms unified by butterscotch-colored banquettes and whitewashed brick walls hung with framed vintage menus. Fine stemware and items presented on wooden boards lend an upscale manner to the experience.

Chef Christian Ramos takes risks while building upon a steady foundation from time spent as a sous chef at Per Se. A crostini of fava bean tapenade and shredded squash is a bright summertime treat—best paired with an icy glass of rosé. Pan-seared striped bass with new potato wedges is sauced with saffron-infused cockle broth; and the black-and-white sablé arranged with a taste of cocoa nib mousse and candied pistachios offers a sweet finish.

Wasan

B3 Japanese X

108 E. 4th St. (bet. First & Second Aves.)

Subway: 2 Av Dinner nightly
Phone: 212-777-1978
Web: www.wasan-ny.com
Prices: $$

The Tokyo-born team of Chef Ryota Kitagawa and Kakusaburo Sakurai both spent time in the kitchen of the Waldorf-Astoria's pioneering Inagiku. Their pedigree is evident in this intimate room, offering excellent food and service.

A unique rendition of Japanese cooking includes the house salad of lettuces, radish, seaweed and slivered chayote presented in a delicately crisp, edible bowl made from wheat and corn flour. The ingredients are tossed at the table, resulting in a lovely presentation that's strewn with crisped bits. Delightful house-pickled vegetables include salt-pickled Napa cabbage, sweet-and-sour shavings of watermelon radish, and Brussels sprouts in curry vinegar. And with its foundation of *hijiki* seaweed rice, the lush *unagi* bowl is a treat.

Financial District

New York City's Financial District is home to some of the world's largest companies. Previously cramped with suits of all stripes, this buzzing business center is becoming increasingly residential thanks to office buildings being converted into condos and a sprouting culinary scene. Every day like clockwork, Wall Street warriors head to such lunch-only stalwarts as **Delmonico's** for their signature Angus boneless ribeye. If that's too heavy on the heart (or expense account), change course to **Nixtamalito**, the popular lunch kiosk at 1 Centre Street that churns out authentic and inexpensive Mexican eats.

NOSTALGIC NIGHTS

At sundown, bring a picnic basket and catch the Shearwater for a memorable sail around Manhattan. Alternatively, step aboard **Honorable William Wall**, the floating clubhouse of the Manhattan Sailing Club, anchored in the New York harbor from May through October every year. Not only does this stunning platform let you get up, close, and personal with Lady Liberty herself, but it also proffers a perfect view of the evening sailboat races—don't forget to have a drink while you're at it! Although there are several other voyages showcasing Gotham City in all its glory, visitors to this district remain eternally impressed by the **Champagne City Lights Cruise** of Manhattan, where you can enjoy some bubbly (or beer) and take in the sights of beautiful and expansive Battery Park City. During the summer, weekend trips to Governor's Island—a lush parkland featuring playing fields and hills—are not just popular but make for wonderful escapes among families and friends alike. In fact, all of the

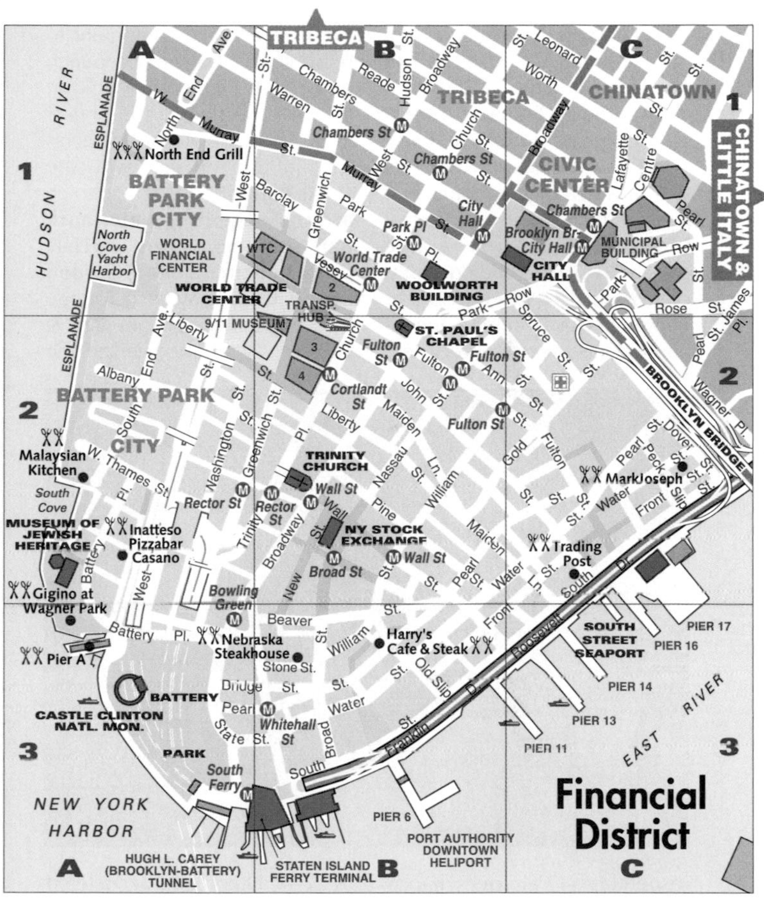

city's carnivores make sure to convene here every October for the hugely famous and always delicious festival **Meatopia**. Recently recuperated public markets also point to the residential boom in this quarter. Case in point: the burgeoning **Staten Island Ferry Whitehall Terminal Greenmarket** (open on Tuesdays and Fridays) is housed within the large and well-designed Staten Island Ferry Terminal, and deserves plenty of praise for sourcing local and farm-fresh produce to the community from a host of independent vendors.

BARS & BEVVIES GALORE

Despite the destruction wreaked by Superstorm Sandy, restaurants downtown seem to have bounced back into buzzing mode with finance whizzes drowning their worries in martinis, and reviewing portfolios over burgers and beer. One of the neighborhood's largest tourist draws, **South**

Street Seaport, is flanked by a collage of fantastic eateries and convivial, family-friendly bars. The legendary **Fraunces Tavern** is a fine specimen on Pearl Street that includes a restaurant and museum paying homage to early American history. While they proffer an impressive selection of brews and cocktails, crowds also gather here for comprehensive brunch- lunch- and dinner- specials. Every self-respecting NY'er loves happy hour, which is almost always buzzing here with over 130 craft beers and ciders to boot. Thanks to such flourishing destinations, buttoned-up suits have learned to loosen their ties and chill out with the locals over drinks at **The Dead Rabbit**. This delightful, multi-award-wining watering hole has been drawing city slickers to Water Street as much for specialty cocktails as for their well-conceived décor and small plates. If the ground floor's sawdust proves too rustic for your taste, head up to the Taproom for a whiff of elegance. While here, take a moment to relish some homemade punch before perusing the cocktail menu—a work of art in and of itself. Wash down this kitchen's Irish-influenced eats with the same nation's drink of choice at South Street's **Watermark Bar**. Speaking of bars, revelers from **Beekman Beer Garden Beach Club** may also lounge in style at **Livingroom Bar & Terrace**, accommodated in the sleek W Hotel, and accoutered with towering windows set above specially designed seats that afford unobstructed views of the glimmering skyline. By cooking up classic plates in conjunction with a litany of enticing martinis, this spot remains a coveted summer venue for concerts, corporate events, and other celebrations.

BITES ON-THE-GO

Jamaican food sensation **Veronica's Kitchen** carries on the food-cart craze in the FiDi with its spectrum of flavorful Caribbean classics. Locals never

seem to tire of the food from here, and return on the regular for the smoky and deliciously tender jerk chicken. Similarly, **Alan's Falafel Cart** on Cedar Street is an exquisite haunt for a mid day pick-me-up, minus the sticker shock. **Financier Patisserie** presents tantalizing sweets that have been known to leave a lasting impression on these cobbled streets. Top these off with a steaming cuppa' joe at one of the numerous vendors nearby and heave a satisfied sigh. Even food-focused events like the **Stone Street Oyster Festival** play to this district's strengths—what better way to lift your spirits and celebrate the local Blue Point harvest in September than by slurping up meaty and briny oysters, outdoors on narrow, sinuous, and very charming Stone Street? Located in the shadows of the monumental and glitzy World Trade Center is **Hudson Eats**—a substantial food court complete with an impressive lineup of nibbles and sips. If visions of a grilled cheese sammie scattered with chunks of fresh lobster come to mind, you have arrived in the right place. Custom cakes from **Mini Melanie** are prepared with extra care and deliver much decadence to the local palate by way of unique fillings, frostings, and toppings. Even waist-watchers are welcome to gorge here with over a multitude of gluten-free options on offer.

Gigino at Wagner Park

Italian 

20 Battery Pl. (in Wagner Park)

Subway: Bowling Green — Lunch & dinner daily
Phone: 212-528-2228
Web: www.gigino-wagnerpark.com
Prices: **$$**

Holed up in Battery Park is this culinary jewel that is routinely frequented by downtown residents. Its cave-like entrance leads to a quiet, serene area as well as an open terrace rife with incredible views that all New Yorkers would treasure. This is the sort of place to kick back and enjoy the calm in a bustling city, while sipping from an intelligent, well-priced wine list.

The food is just as precise and refined, thanks to a kitchen that understands the provenance of each dish. Find evidence of this in potato gnocchi bobbing in a slow-cooked tomato *sugo* dotted with tiny beef meatballs. Don't forget to give *spaghetti del Padrino* with *colatura*, anchovies, beets, and escarole a rightful whirl if only for its tempting garlic essence.

Harry's Cafe & Steak

B3

American 

1 Hanover Sq. (bet. Pearl & Stone Sts.)

Subway: Wall St (William St.) — Lunch & dinner Mon – Sat
Phone: 212-785-9200
Web: www.harrysnyc.com
Prices: **$$**

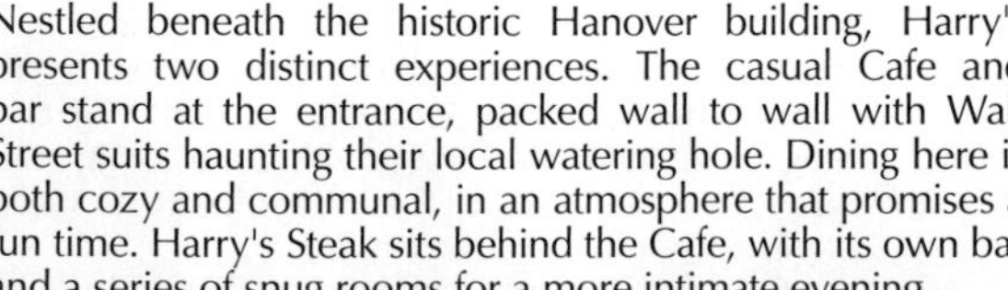

Nestled beneath the historic Hanover building, Harry's presents two distinct experiences. The casual Cafe and bar stand at the entrance, packed wall to wall with Wall Street suits haunting their local watering hole. Dining here is both cozy and communal, in an atmosphere that promises a fun time. Harry's Steak sits behind the Cafe, with its own bar and a series of snug rooms for a more intimate evening.

Begin with a classic starter, like mushrooms stuffed with sweet, succulent lobster; but everyone really comes for the steak. Here, a prime hanger steak is perfectly seared, juicy, and tender—impressive for this particular cut—served with homemade béarnaise. There is no room left for disappointment, but maybe enough for the pecan bread pudding.

Inatteso Pizzabar Casano

Italian XX

28 West St. (at 2nd Pl.)

Subway: South Ferry   Lunch & dinner daily
Phone: 212-267-8000
Web: www.inattesopizzabar.com
Prices: $$

Manhattan has no shortage of pizza. But shockingly, the touristy, banker-packed Battery Park City lacked a proper wood-fired pizza until the arrival of Inatteso. Tucked away, it features stunning views of the Statue of Liberty and Ellis Island from the south end of the bar. Any seat in the brightly lit, wood-paneled room provides a glimpse of the oven and scents of a blistering crust.

The 12-inch Margherita expresses pure pizza-making skill through soft, fluffy dough with a touch of semolina and knobs of *fior di latte*. It's not entirely traditional but completely enjoyable. The menu doesn't stop at pizza, and neither should you. Sample pasta like orechiette with broccoli rabe and pan-roasted mahi mahi with sweet and sour eggplant caponata.

Malaysian Kitchen

Malaysian

A2

21 South End Ave. (at Thames Place)

Subway: Rector St   Lunch & dinner daily
Phone: 212-786-1888
Web: www.malaysiakitchenusa.com
Prices: $$

New York Harbor views aren't always accompanied by delicious cooking, but this airy restaurant offers just that on one of the best promenades in Battery Park City. Walls of the dining room are draped with vivid scenes of life in Malaysia, while tables overlook the Statue of Liberty as well as boats that glide by on the Hudson River.

Skip the fusion items and stick to the robust Malaysian specialties. Flavorful renditions of classics include *nasi lemak* with coconut-perfumed rice, and *roti canai*, a flaky, elastic, fluffy bread with potato and chicken curry for dipping. Fork-tender and sensationally thick beef *rendang*—simmered in coconut milk, lemongrass, lime leaves, and fermented fish sauce—is pure slow-cooked comfort, served with a hefty portion of rice on the side.

MarkJoseph

Steakhouse

C2

261 Water St. (bet. Peck Slip & Dover St.)

Subway: Fulton St — Lunch Mon – Fri
Phone: 212-277-0020 — Dinner nightly
Web: www.markjosephsteakhouse.com
Prices: $$$

This smart and sleek steak haven continues to claim its rightful place among the faithful haunts of area residents, business types, and carnivores in town. Handsome in its dark wood-paneled glory, with a wine cellar display and white tablecloths, this traditional den exudes a clubby Wall Street scene. Expect to see a crowd of suits discussing stocks, shares, and sports scores, of course.

The quality of USDA Prime beef is paramount here, but the culinary technique is just another reason why this steakhouse succeeds. Steaks are perfect medium rare, brushed with sweet melting fat, seasoned with salt, and perhaps served with a gravy boat of béarnaise sauce. Finish off with a classic slice of pecan pie topped with swirls of whipped cream.

Nebraska Steakhouse

Steakhouse

B3

15 Stone St. (bet. Broad & Whitehall Sts.)

Subway: Bowling Green — Lunch & dinner Mon – Fri
Phone: 212-952-0620
Web: www.nebraskasteakhousenyc.com
Prices: $$$

Marked by a relatively modest and discreet façade, Nebraska Steakhouse remains a well-tread fixture in the FiDi. This classic watering hole with equally brazen diners hovering around a tiny, narrow, and well-soaked bar evokes that old-timey city tavern scene. Inside, the vibe is lively, drinks are strong, and their appetizing offerings are expertly handled.

Finding the door isn't a cakewalk and manipulating the crowd takes some negotiating, but rest assured that the end result is worth it. Yes, those steaks are on-point, but smoked trout salad followed by 22-ounces of tender and juicy grilled lamb Porterhouse chops never fails to sate.

In contrast with the gruff service, a pecan pie studded with chocolate chips and heavy cream is so sweet.

North End Grill

American XXX

A1

104 North End Ave. (at Murray St.)

Subway: Chambers St (West Broadway) Lunch & dinner daily
Phone: 646-747-1600
Web: www.northendgrillnyc.com
Prices: $$$

Its contemporary look features that same stunning combination of white umbrella-like fixtures, black-stained walls, and midnight blue banquettes. However, the reigning chef in the open kitchen reveals a menu shift towards grilled foods, updated comfort favorites, and charcuterie.

Start with an artfully arranged terrine layering strips of pig's ear topped with green beans and mustard vinaigrette. The flavors of wood infuse every element of a thick, blistered pizza decked with potatoes, pancetta, sweet onions, and gently poached eggs. French sensibilities shine in the simply grilled Colorado lamb chops with ribbons of zucchini, baby leeks, and carrots. For dessert, the creamsicle pie bursts with the taste of candied orange, whipped cream, and childhood.

Pier A

American XX

A3

22 Battery Pl. (inside Battery Park)

Subway: Rector St Lunch & dinner daily
Phone: 212-785-0153
Web: www.piera.com
Prices: $$$

Situated on a pier off the Hudson River, this three-story Victorian—a rambunctious New York landmark replete with a prominent clock tower and enormous promenade—is hardly your average watering hole. After all, where else can you slurp bivalves and sip craft beers among pressure gauges from 19th century steamships while taking in a view of the Statue of Liberty? The menu's tempting seafood options include a dozen types of fresh, plump oysters; lobster mac and cheese studded with greens and bacon and served in a cast iron skillet; as well as mini lobster rolls with a citrusy remoulade.

While the fare here begs for brews, grown-ups craving quiet conversation, a proper martini, and an ultra-hearty Tomahawk steak should head upstairs to Pier A Harborhouse.

Trading Post

American XX

C2

170 John St. (at South St.)

Subway: Fulton St — Lunch & dinner Mon – Sat
Phone: 646-370-3337
Web: www.tradingpostnyc.com
Prices: **$$**

A reprieve from the neighborhood's many pubs and quick-serve joints, this popular restaurant occupies three floors of a historic building across from the Rockwell-designed Imagination Playground. Stylish and eclectic with a maritime theme, the massive space boasts a rollicking bar and whiskey cellar plus an upscale second floor with water views and an elegant library.

The menu is just as wonderful and wide-ranging, with everything from flatbreads to skirt steak to lobster fried rice. Highlights include a healthy and delicious quinoa salad, studded with butternut squash, morsels of creamy feta, dried cranberries, and a drizzle of reduced balsamic vinegar. Jumbo shrimp plated with wilted kale, plump butter beans, and braised tomato is an impressive entrée.

Look for our symbol, spotlighting restaurants with a notable beer list.

Gramercy, Flatiron & Union Square

Anchored around the members-only Gramercy Park, this neighborhood of the same name is steeped in history, classic beauty, and tranquility. Even among thoroughbred NYers, most of whom haven't set foot on its private paths, the park's extreme exclusivity is the stuff of legends—because outside of the residents whose homes face the square, Gramercy Park Hotel guests are among the few permitted entrance.

Bounded by tourist-y Union Square and the fashionably edgy Flatiron District, this quiet enclave also boasts of beautiful brownstones, effortlessly chic cafés, and haute hotels. Channel your inner Dowager Countess of Grantham as you nibble on dainty finger sandwiches at the refreshed **Lady Mendl's Tea Salon**, a Victorian-style parlor tucked inside the Inn at Irving Place. Stroll a few blocks only to discover assorted pleasures at **Maury Rubin's City Bakery**, a popular haunt for fresh-baked pastries and—in true New York City style—pretzel croissants. Old-timers love the warm chocolate *babka* from **Breads Bakery**, but for those who like a little spice, **Curry Hill** is only a few blocks north. This exotic stretch brings Indian flavors to the big city by way of authentic, budget-friendly restaurants. While some of these *desi* diners are focused on the greasy takeout formula, foodies and home cooks know to comb the shelves at **Foods of India** for choice ingredients. Nearby, **Kalustyan's** is an equally celebrated spice emporium showcasing exceptional products like orange blossom water and thirty-plus varieties of dried whole chilies. Similarly, **Desi Galli** is a quick-serve spot for street food faves—think delicious stuffed bread. One can choose white or wheat paratha or roomali roti, also a griddled flatbread, to be filled with the likes of lamb keema, spicy channa and potato curry, or chicken tikka. The vibrant green, mint chutney is absolutely delicious.

FLATIRON DISTRICT

Named after one of the city's most notable buildings, the Flatiron District is a commercial center-turned-residential mecca. Engulfed with trendy clothing stores and chic restaurants, the area today is a colorful explosion of culture and shopping. A few blocks to the west is the welcoming Madison Square Park with its own unique history and vibe. Ergo, it is only fitting that visitors are greeted by the original outpost of burger flagship, **Shake Shack**, serving its signature fast food from an ivy-covered kiosk. While burgers and Chicago-style dogs are all the rage, it is their house-made custard that has patrons fixated and checking the online "custard calendar" weekly for favored flavors.

Tourists looking to trend it up should hang with the cool kids at the Ace Hotel, who take their sip from **Stumptown Coffee Roasters** to savor in the hipster-reigning lobby. The equally nifty NoMad hotel is home to Gotham's first **sweetgreen** and socialites watching their waistline along with "Silicon Alley" staffers can't get enough of their cold-pressed juices and frozen yogurt. A long way from clean tastes, barbecue addicts remain committed to the **Big Apple Barbecue Block Party** held every June. This weekend-long extravaganza features celebrity pit masters showing off their "smoke" skills to hungry aficionados. Another frequented spectacle is **Eataly NY**, founded by Oscar Farinetti but brought stateside by Mario Batali and Joe Bastianich. This *molto* glam marketplace incorporates everything Italiano under one

roof, including a dining hall with delicious eats, regional specialties, and aromatic food stalls.

UNION SQUARE

Nearby Union Square is a formidable historic landmark characterized by a park with tiered plazas that host political protests plus rallies. Today it may be best known for its **Greenmarket**—held on Mondays, Wednesdays, Fridays, and Saturdays—and heaving with seasonal produce. Beyond the market, find some fine wine to complement your farm-to-table meal from **Union Square Wines and Spirits**, or **Italian Wine Merchants**. Further evidence of this *piazza*'s reputation as the center of Manhattan's culinary scene, is the flourishing presence of **Whole Foods** as well as the city's very first **Trader Joe's**—within just blocks of one another.

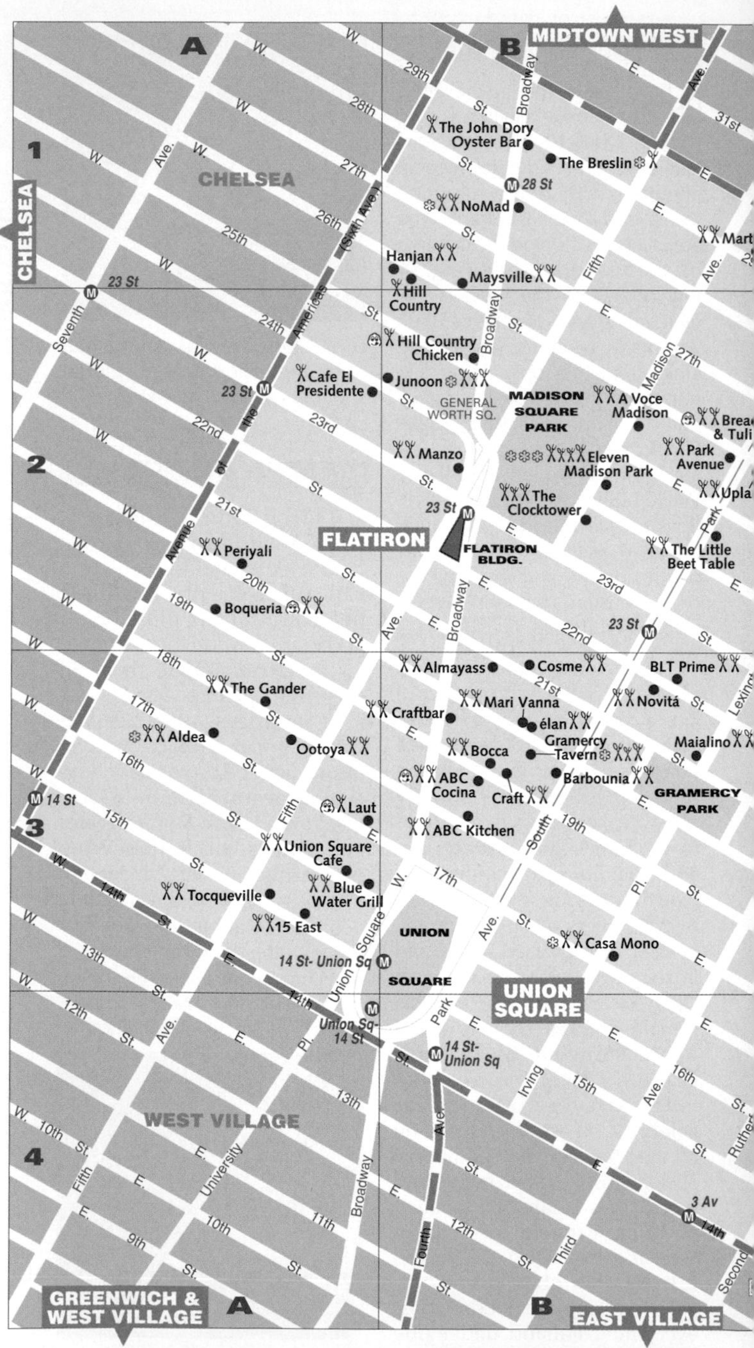
MIDTOWN WEST
CHELSEA
FLATIRON
UNION SQUARE
WEST VILLAGE
GREENWICH & WEST VILLAGE
EAST VILLAGE
MADISON SQUARE PARK
GENERAL WORTH SQ.
FLATIRON BLDG.
GRAMERCY PARK
UNION SQUARE
The John Dory Oyster Bar
The Breslin
NoMad
Hanjan
Hill Country
Maysville
Hill Country Chicken
Cafe El Presidente
Junoon
A Voce Madison
Manzo
Eleven Madison Park
Park Avenue
The Clocktower
Periyali
The Little Beet Table
Boqueria
Almayass
Cosme
BLT Prime
The Gander
Mari Vanna
Novitá
Craftbar
élan
Aldea
Ootoya
Bocca
Gramercy Tavern
Maialino
ABC Cocina
Craft
Barbounia
Laut
ABC Kitchen
Union Square Cafe
Blue Water Grill
Tocqueville
15 East
Casa Mono
28 St
23 St
14 St
14 St- Union Sq
Union Sq-14 St
14 St-Union Sq
3 Av

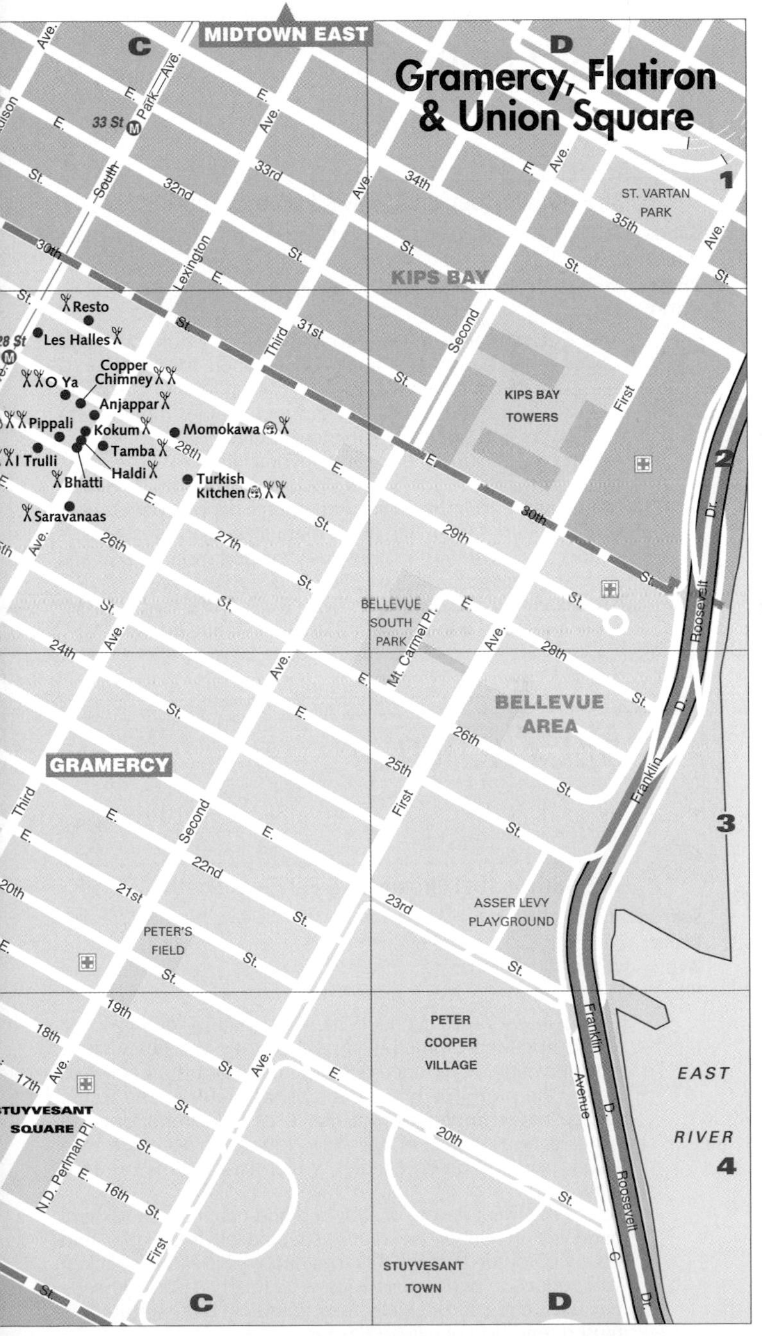

Gramercy, Flatiron & Union Square
MIDTOWN EAST
KIPS BAY
GRAMERCY
BELLEVUE AREA
ST. VARTAN PARK
KIPS BAY TOWERS
BELLEVUE SOUTH PARK
ASSER LEVY PLAYGROUND
PETER'S FIELD
PETER COOPER VILLAGE
STUYVESANT TOWN
STUYVESANT SQUARE
EAST RIVER
Resto
Les Halles
O Ya
Copper Chimney
Anjappar
Pippali
Kokum
Momokawa
Tamba
I Trulli
Haldi
Bhatti
Turkish Kitchen
Saravanaas
33 St
Park Ave. South
Lexington Ave.
Third Ave.
Second Ave.
First Ave.
Mt. Carmel Pl.
N.D. Perlman Pl.
Franklin D. Roosevelt Dr.
Avenue C

ABC Cocina

International XX

B3

38 E. 19th St. (bet. Broadway & Park Ave. South)

Subway: 23 St (Park Ave. South)
Lunch & dinner daily
Phone: 212-677-2233
Web: www.abccocinanyc.com
Prices: $$

ABC Cocina stands in stark contrast to her wholesome and whitewashed cousin next door, ABC Kitchen. Markedly sexy, this space favors a vampy backdrop furnished with black and magenta lacquered café chairs and metal tables topped with red flowers and bottles of habanero sauce.

Accents from Latin America and beyond lilt the menu of small plates, perhaps including sweet potato empanadas delicately crafted and imbued with smoked cherry pepper, paired with lemon yogurt sauce. Tamarind-marinated black sea bass is slender and neat with its lusciously crisped mottled skin still attached, dressed with tart juice and smoky-sweet chipotle barbecue sauce. The *tres leches* cake coddled with green apple foam and gooey *cajeta* is an illuminating finish.

ABC Kitchen

Contemporary XX

B3

35 E. 18th St. (bet. Broadway & Park Ave. South)

Subway: 23 St (Park Ave. South)
Lunch & dinner daily
Phone: 212-475-5829
Web: www.abckitchennyc.com
Prices: $$

Chef Jean-Georges Vongerichten's signature dining chez ABC Carpet and Home began at this rustic yet glossy farm-to-table venue. A hit since opening, the room is an absolute scene. The pretty people are almost as pretty as the room. Service never impresses, but that is of little importance to this gregarious gaggle of devotees. Tables are accented with flowers and soy-based candles, which cast a glow on each plate.

Expect the fresh flavors of ruby-red line-caught tuna sashimi marinated in ginger-soy sauce, sparked by fresh mint and red chili. Bowtie pasta with kasha and veal meatballs slicked with reduced, herb-infused jus is a hearty treat. Desserts may elicit cheers, especially the creamsicle tart—an orange-infused rendition of *gâteau Basque*.

Aldea ✿

Mediterranean XX

A3

31 W. 17th St. (bet. Fifth & Sixth Aves.)

Subway: 14 St - 6 Av
Phone: 212-675-7223
Web: www.aldearestaurant.com
Prices: **$$$**

Lunch Mon – Fri
Dinner Mon – Sat

A perfect climate and great scenery—it's easy to see the appeal of life on the Mediterranean. George Mendes' cheerfully run restaurant may not necessarily transport you there but you will leave here feeling as though your serotonin levels have received a timely boost.

Those who like to eat whilst deciding what to eat should head straight for the appealing Portuguese selection of *petiscos*, or snacks—the *croquetas de bacalhau* and the Serrano ham are good. The main menu is seasonally pertinent and full of dishes to match that southern European climate: they are bright, sunny, and you feel they are doing you good. Nothing says the Med more than sardines—and here they come expertly filleted and dressed with dill and bronzed fennel. But even when the sun's gone down, the kitchen is equally adept at more warming, comforting dishes—try the venison with Swiss chard and chestnuts.

The restaurant comes decorated with birch wood and shades of blue and is spread over two narrow rooms. Thanks to the open kitchen, the first floor has more buzz but if you're on a date, ask for the mezzanine level which is a little more intimate.

Almayass

Lebanese XX

24 E. 21st St. (bet. Broadway & Park Ave. South)

Subway: 23 St (Park Ave. South) — Lunch & dinner daily
Phone: 212-473-3100
Web: www.almayassnyc.com
Prices: $$

Armenian influences steer the Lebanese cuisine here to a unique and rather elegant place. While this family-run operation has numerous Middle Eastern locations, this is their sole U.S. outpost. Polished service befits the upscale room, installed with vivid artwork and tables generously sized for feasting.

Beginning with a selection of fresh and flavorful meze is absolutely necessary. Cold options include *kabiss*, an assortment of spicy pickled vegetables; and *moutabbal* Almayass, a magenta-colored spread of mashed beets seasoned with sesame paste, lemon, and garlic. Or opt for hot, succulent, and traditional *mantee*—little pockets stuffed with beef, earthenware-baked, and doused with tart yogurt. A selection of Lebanese producers headlines the wine list.

Anjappar

Indian X

116 Lexington Ave. (at 28th St.)

Subway: 28 St (Park Ave. South) — Lunch & dinner daily
Phone: 212-265-3663
Web: www.anjapparusa.com
Prices: $$

Step inside this Curry Hill standout to unearth a dining room that is festive without being kitschy. Carved woodwork and a palette of red and ivory embolden the tasteful setting.

Specializing in the cuisine of the Chettinad region, this South Indian kitchen showcases freshly ground spice blends and a particular fondness for eggs. This is clear in items like *nattukozi* (country chicken) *biryani* featuring a fluffy mound of fragrant basmati studded with a hard-boiled egg and pieces of bone-in chicken, sided by onion gravy, chopped fresh onion, and tomato-studded *raita*. Also sample the *meen kolambu* or chunks of kingfish in a brick-red curry redolent with mustard seeds, coarse ground black peppercorns, red chilies, and bits of fresh and aromatic curry leaf.

A Voce Madison

Italian XX

B2

41 Madison Ave. (entrance on 26th St.)

Subway: 28 St (Park Ave. South) — Lunch Mon – Fri
Phone: 212-545-8555 — Dinner Mon-Sat
Web: www.avocerestaurant.com
Prices: **$$$**

Sporting that perfect confluence of casual ease and upscale elegance, this modern beacon of *Italia* in the city is the preferred table for the Flatiron's stylish set. The chic, sleek interior boasts walnut floors, cognac leather chairs and abstract art, while a greenery dressed sidewalk seating area offers alfresco dining overlooking Madison Square Park.

A Voce Madison's kitchen has been steadied of late, and its contemporary spirit remains intact. Handmade pastas can feature ricotta and nettle-filled *cappellacci* drizzled with brown butter, while heartier options include a grilled pork chop with pickled rhubarb and kale three ways. For the uptown crowd, sister restaurant A Voce Columbus presents a similarly themed menu in the Time Warner Center.

Barbounia

Mediterranean XX

B3

250 Park Ave. South (at 20th St.)

Subway: 23 St (Park Ave. South) — Lunch & dinner daily
Phone: 212-995-0242
Web: www.barbounia.com
Prices: **$$**

Barbounia brings the pleasures of the Mediterranean to a primo locale. The welcome is warm, the ceilings are notably high, and the floor-to-ceiling bar is considerably stocked (note the wine list and its surprisingly large selection from Greece). The dining room is crowded with tables, so go for the cozy corner banquettes overlooking the action.

The rustic, satiating fare is ideal for sharing. Thick pieces of octopus are grilled to a buttery softness and served over marinated chickpeas with olives, oregano, and a slick of *labneh*. In the *shakshuka* with merguez, a cast iron skillet arrives bursting with flavor and bubbling at the table with a piquant paprika-spiked tomato sauce topped with baked eggs and studded with roasted peppers and sausage.

Bhatti

C2 Indian

100 Lexington Ave. (at 27th St.)

Subway: 28 St (Park Ave. South) Lunch & dinner daily
Phone: 212-683-4228
Web: www.bhattinyc.com
Prices:

This Northern Indian eatery is praised for its array of tasty grilled meats and kebabs that emerge from the *bhatti* (open-fire grill). Quality ingredients and a skilled kitchen combine with delicious results as in *haryali choza,* nuggets of white meat chicken marinated in an herbaceous blend of mint, cilantro, green fenugreek, chilies, and hung curd; or the unique house specialty *gilauti kebab,* made from fragrantly spiced lamb ground so fine and incredibly tender that it's almost pâté-smooth. Hearty dishes such as *khatte baigan,* silky chunks of eggplant stewed in a tangy onion-tomato masala and garnished with pickled ginger root, wrap up temptations.

The room is kitsch-free and tastefully done with dark wood furnishings set against red-and-gold wallpaper.

BLT Prime

B3 Steakhouse

111 E. 22nd St. (bet. Lexington Ave. & Park Ave. South)

Subway: 23 St (Park Ave. South) Dinner nightly
Phone: 212-995-8500
Web: www.bltprime.com
Prices: **$$$**

Prime Angus beef broiled at 1700 degrees fahrenheit, dabbed with herb butter, and presented on sizzling hot cast iron is the reason this Gramercy steakhouse continues to bask in unbridled success. Power brokers are found unwinding at the bar and downing classic cocktails before settling into taupe banquettes trimmed with gleaming zebrawood tables. The menu is printed on brown craft paper, but is also grandly displayed on a huge wall-mounted board.

Steak may be the most popular option, but this kitchen's talent runs deep. Sautéed Dover sole with soy-caper brown butter is a favorite among seafood fans. The nightly prix-fixe has included beautifully done wild Scottish partridge, wrapped in pancetta and plated with melted Savoy cabbage and apple cider jus.

Blue Water Grill

Seafood XX

A3

31 Union Sq. West (at 16th St.)

Subway: 14 St - Union Sq — Lunch & dinner daily
Phone: 212-675-9500
Web: www.bluewatergrillnyc.com
Prices: $$

This New York institution has become an iconic part of the Union Square landscape. The stately building is a former bank, with century-old architectural details and marble aplenty.

As the name would suggest, the menu leans heavily on seafaring classics with an ample raw bar and sushi counter. But more than anything, this kitchen aims to please, with starters like pork belly sliders topped with tangy fennel-lettuce slaw on a brioche bun. Octopus tentacles are crisp yet perfectly tender inside, served resting atop chickpeas with a deep-red tomato and roasted pepper ragout infused with smoked paprika. Fish is always perfectly handled and often rises well above its accompaniments on the plate.

Live jazz is a nightly draw to the downstairs lounge.

Bocca

Italian XX

B3

39 E. 19th St. (bet. Broadway & Park Ave. South)

Subway: 23 St (Park Ave. South) — Lunch Mon – Fri
Phone: 212-387-1200 — Dinner nightly
Web: www.boccanyc.com
Prices: $$

This trattoria hits all the right notes—and throws in a few novel riffs—to make it as a neighborhood favorite. The Roman cuisine has few faults, and the comfortable setting feels genuine with its parchment-lacquered walls, displayed wine storage, and framed posters of Federico Fellini's classics. Bocca is owned by the team behind Cacio e Pepe in the East Village, so you can expect delicious and dramatically presented *tonnarelli cacio e pepe*. However, the talented kitchen offers temptations aplenty, such as a bowl of fresh, rich-tasting *spaghetti alla chitarra* brilliantly dressed with cherry tomato sauce and 'nduja. Twice-cooked pork belly with braised cabbage and celery mostarda is another fine example of their hearty, regional flavors.

Boqueria

Spanish XX

53 W. 19th St. (bet. Fifth & Sixth Aves.)

Subway: 18 St (Seventh Ave.) — Lunch & dinner daily
Phone: 212-255-4160
Web: www.boquerianyc.com
Prices: $$

Named after Barcelona's famed market, Boqueria does that vibrant emporium proud with an array of ingredient-driven tapas. Their tortilla Española is a true classic, served as a towering wedge of organic eggs, tender potatoes, and sweet onions. Kale reaches new heights as a sweet and earthy salad tossed with a rainbow of cumin-roasted carrots, toasted sunflower seeds, pomegranate arils, and a lush swipe of tangy *labne*. Bombas *de la Barceloneta* are crunchy, beef-stuffed potato croquettes plated with salsa verde and silken, garlicky aïoli.

Envision high banquettes amid creamy hues, a white marble bar area filled with wooden boards of Spanish cheeses, olives in terra-cotta bowls, and crowds cooing over classic tapas like *pan con tomate. Delicioso.*

Bread & Tulips

Italian XX

B2

365 Park Ave. South (at 26th St.)

Subway: 28 St (Park Ave. South) — Lunch Mon – Fri
Phone: 212-532-9100 — Dinner Mon – Sat
Web: www.breadandtulipsnyc.com
Prices: $$

A cordial greeting and personal escort down to this lower level Hotel Giraffe dining room is a promising start to an inspired meal. Exposed brick, darkly polished wood, and smart arrangements create an air of seclusion to match the room's contemporary good looks (never mind the low ceiling and lack of windows).

The menu offers an array of brick oven-baked pizzas as well as small plates of au courant Mediterranean cooking like homemade organic ricotta and grilled octopus. A chilled beet salad mixes creamy goat cheese, young watercress, pink grapefruit, and toasted pistachios. Freshly made pastas are known to gratify, especially the pristine squid ink tagliatelle with tender calamari, diced chorizo, herbed breadcrumbs, and white wine *salsa bianco*.

The Breslin ✿

Gastropub

B1

16 W. 29th St. (bet. Broadway & Fifth Ave.)

Subway: 28 St (Broadway) Lunch & dinner daily
Phone: 212-679-1939
Web: www.thebreslin.com
Prices: **$$$**

Not sure you've come to the right place? Just look for those new media hotties climbing out of black cars, and know that you've arrived at The Breslin. Attached to the markedly hip Ace Hotel, this uber-stylish gastropub, known for its pretty patrons and perpetual buzz, is a place to see and be seen.

Booths tucked into nooks on one side of the room are by far the best seats in the house, but all is not lost if you can't nab one. Close-knit tables adorned with white china and rustic wooden boards are equally inviting, with views of the open kitchen. If your welcome was a bit...well lukewarm... you'll find that the tee- and tattoo-donning staff warms up as service progresses—not unlike one's appreciation for the chef's outstanding creations.

Parmesan and fried parsley leaves gild the romaine in a delicious, very garlicky Caesar salad; just as a coiled link of terrifically flavored merguez is perfectly finished with smoky Marcona almond aïoli. Meanwhile, warm and milky burrata gains great flavor and texture when kissed by nutty hazelnut pesto. Clementine cake frosted with mascarpone and dates is a sweet example of how this kitchen elevates seemingly simple eats to thoroughly stellar treats.

Cafe El Presidente

Mexican

30 W. 24th St. (bet. Fifth & Sixth Aves.)

Subway: 23 St (Sixth Ave.) — Lunch & dinner daily
Phone: 212-242-3491
Web: www.cafeelpresidente.com
Prices:

With its colorful interior signage and indoor/outdoor aesthetic, this tasty taqueria near Madison Square Park could easily pass for a Mexico City hot spot. Soaring ceilings cover an open kitchen and tortilla-production station where disks of masa—the foundation for an enticing lineup of tacos—are turned out at a steady clip.

Cafe El Presidente's attention to both quality and creativity is impressive, and proof is in the tacos *especiales*: wilted Swiss chard combined with roasted poblano chiles and sautéed yellow onion; or a spread of black bean purée topped with diced roasted sweet potato and dusting of *cotija*. For the ultimate conclusion, go for *Gringa Madison*, a rich pairing of pork *al pastor* and melted Chiuhuahua spiked with freshly chopped cilantro.

The Clocktower

Contemporary 

5 Madison Ave. (bet. 23rd & 24th Sts.)

Subway: 23 St (Park Ave South) — Lunch & dinner daily
Phone: 212-413-4300
Web: www.theclocktowernyc.com
Prices: **$$$**

British celebrity chef Jason Atherton and restaurateur Stephen Starr are the power players behind this swank space inside the Edition hotel. Housed in a tower built in 1909 for the former Metropolitan Life Insurance Co., it has the buzz and polish of a sleek English club—picture dark wood paneling, jewel-toned velvet furnishings, and vintage celebrity portraits. The cuisine follows suit, with the globe-hopping chef serving up skilled dishes like a foie gras-stuffed pigeon pie in perfect pastry dressed with spiced jus and plated with a light version of the Waldorf salad. Cornish fish stew is sided by decadent garlic mashed potatoes; and a dessert of strawberries and cream features gelée-crowned vanilla custard, olive oil cake, and strawberry verjus sorbet.

Casa Mono 

Spanish XX

B3

52 Irving Pl. (at 17th St.)

Subway: 14 St - Union Sq

Lunch & dinner daily

Phone: 212-253-2773

Web: www.casamononyc.com

Prices: $$$

Casa Mono is tiny, jammed, and totally New York. Furnished with a few closely packed tables that moan under the excess of mouthwatering plates as well as that mighty counter framed by a handful of seats, this grotto-like wine bar is loud, communal—and an absolute thrill.

Then consider the service, which moves like clockwork and confirms that this is no slipshod show. The staff may be brisk in their presentation of the kitchen's ambitious renditions of tapas, but with flavors so delicious and concepts inventive, so be it. A faithful mix of locals and hungry out-of-towners convene for fantastic bite-sized eats like buttery bone marrow with smoked caper chermoulah—a house signature that is rich, flavorful, and entirely unmissable. Even the humble *bacalao* fritter attains new heights here as a deep-fried, fluffy delight coupled with sweet-citrusy *alioli*. Lastly, fallback plates like razor clams *a la plancha* in garlic-parsley sauce remain outstanding, consistent, and full of Spanish soul. This kitchen isn't frightened to explore, so skill and innovation are at the forefront of every morsel, including the thick, creamy, and luscious *crema catalana con buñuelos*. One word comes to mind: bliss.

Oenophiles may head next door to drinking-focused sidekick, Bar Jamón.

Copper Chimney

Indian XX

C2

126 E. 28th St. (bet. Lexington Ave. & Park Ave. South)

Subway: 28 St (Park Ave. South) — Lunch & dinner daily
Phone: 212-213-5742
Web: www.copperchimneynyc.com
Prices: $$

Copper Chimney is a pleasing and tasteful retreat from Curry Hill's sassier options. Polite service and a dining room of pale gray walls and buff-colored banquettes soothe the spirit. But, one peek at the expansive menu is sure to entice your palate. The regional offerings bring extensive choice, with myriad vegetarian and *tandoori* specialties. Mild but flavorful curries like *dalchi machi* feature salmon in a pale orange sauce that is thick as *dal* and seasoned with mustard seeds, curry leaves, and whole dried red chilies. *Baingan bartha* is a sumptuous blend of roasted and mashed eggplant cooked with onions, tomatoes, and spices. Breads served hot off the *tawa* are a must, like the *aloo paratha* which is pillowy soft and stuffed with spiced potatoes.

Cosme

Mexican XX

B3

35 E. 21st St. (bet. Broadway & Park Ave. South)

Subway: 28 St (Park Ave South) — Lunch Sun
Phone: 212-913-9659 — Dinner nightly
Web: www.cosmenyc.com
Prices: $$$$

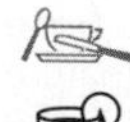

Mexico's world-renowned celebrity chef, Enrique Olvera, has finally landed stateside, and the food world is justifiably abuzz. Tucked into a sleek, urbane space with warm light and concrete floors, Cosme's menu features small and large plates for sharing—and enough raw seafood to make Le Bernardin blush.

Chef de cuisine Mariana Villegas oversees the execution with an eagle eye: a silky scallop *aguachile* is fanned out and topped with cool, poached jicama, serrano chiles, and fresh wasabi root; while a tender eggplant tamal arrives smoky-sweet and topped with house-made ricotta and a bright green herb sauce. Lastly, steak tacos are rubbed with black garlic and paired with chile slivers, blistered shisito peppers, and a smooth avocado-tarragon purée.

Craft

American XX

B3

43 E. 19th St. (bet. Broadway & Park Ave. South)

Subway: 14 St - Union Sq

Dinner nightly

Phone: 212-780-0880

Web: www.craftrestaurantsinc.com

Prices: **$$$$**

It's been many years since super-celebrity chef and TV personality Tom Colicchio opened Craft to great acclaim. Its popularity hasn't waned and the room is filled nightly with casually affluent New Yorkers. Good looks and a committed service team are the top assets and the décor is timeless yet cozy, aerial yet intimate. Bare bulbs emit a glow over wood tables and that smug, handsome bar should be drawing more diners.

The menu's forte lies in its meandering conceit, allowing guests to "craft" their own meal. Prices are aggressive and these pristine ingredients often plead for a bit more salt or a bit less cooking, but pastas and desserts are where this kitchen shines. A fall tagliatelle with a bath of white truffles is a stunning example of what's possible.

Craftbar

Contemporary XX

B3

900 Broadway (bet. 19th & 20th Sts.)

Subway: 14 St - Union Sq

Lunch & dinner daily

Phone: 212-461-4300

Web: www.craftrestaurantsinc.com

Prices: **$$**

Its ersatz industrial aesthetic and the rumble of the subway below combine to create a sense of energy and toil—although the service team can sometimes fail to embrace these concepts with any great vigor. But never mind because, as the name suggests, there's a big bar here, and a menu that has something for everyone.

There is quite a pronounced Asian flavor in many of the dishes, such as the big bowl of PEI mussels with Kaffir lime, chili paste, and Sichuan pepper. Those, however, who prefer their culinary influences a little more homegrown, will find much comfort in the "double stack" burger. Anyone mindful of the heart—its health, not its emotional state—will be reassured by the presence of ingredients like kale on the menu.

élan

B3 — Contemporary XX

43 E. 20th St. (bet. Broadway & Park Ave. South)

Subway: 23 St (Park Ave. South) — Dinner nightly
Phone: 646-682-7105
Web: www.elannyc.com
Prices: $$$

Diners of a certain age will remember Chef David Waltuck's trailblazing Chanterelle, which closed in 2009 after a commendable 30 years on the NYC restaurant scene. His new residence, housed in the former Veritas space has been tweaked to feature a gallery-style bar that showcases the works of emerging artists, plus a dining room of silver-striped banquettes and walls hung with foxed mirrors.

Global accents influence much of the cooking, as in duck breast paired with crispy vegetable spring rolls and sauced with smoky jus. The pine nut-studded seafood sausage is a classic, plated with sauerkraut and grainy mustard beurre blanc, and a sundae of cherry pit-infused ice cream—complete with cherry sorbet and almond cake—is a shining example of seasonality.

15 East

A3 — Japanese XX

15 E. 15th St. (bet. Fifth Ave. & Union Sq. West)

Subway: 14 St - Union Sq — Lunch & dinner Mon – Sat
Phone: 212-647-0015
Web: www.15eastrestaurant.com
Prices: $$$

A Japanese restaurant divided in two: you can perch at the counter and watch the sushi chefs in action or you can go next door and sit at a table in a slickly run, narrow room decked out in earthy tones. Either way, you'll be well looked after by an attentive team.

The menu is also divided—between sushi and sashimi from the bar, and hot dishes from the kitchen. There is an impressive selection of the former, with the sashimi being particularly worthy. The hot dishes range from the traditional to the more innovative and adapted. Avoid the over-generously battered tempura and go instead for the soba noodles, made in house and served with a choice of topping such as uni or *ikura*, or the rich squid ink risotto with spear squid.

Eleven Madison Park ✿✿✿

Contemporary XXXX

B2

11 Madison Ave. (at 24th St.)

Subway: 23 St (Park Ave. South)
Phone: 212-889-0905
Web: www.elevenmadisonpark.com
Prices: $$$$

Lunch Thu – Sat
Dinner nightly

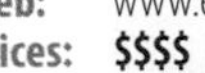

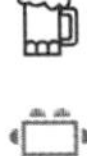

Chef Daniel Humm's cooking is clever, innovative and at times even a little whimsical; it is robust when it needs to be but also delicate at times and it is this variety and depth that really sets it apart. No menu is presented; instead, you're merely asked to relay your list of allergies as though talking to your pharmacist and your work is done.

The 15 or so courses that subsequently appear could be playful, like the carrot tartare made at the table, or display extraordinary understanding of technique, such as the dry-aged veal with bone marrow.

The restaurant is housed within the sort of grandeur that could only ever have belonged to a financial institution. It's a hard space to fill—conversations don't so much hang in the air as float up to the vast ceiling and never return. But somehow the room's sheer scale and the well-spaced tables allow you to feel cocooned in your own world. Considerable help comes courtesy of the engaging staff as they explain each dish in loving terms but without ever sounding too virtuous. They also know when to talk and when to leave you to get on with enjoying yourself.

The Gander

Contemporary

15 W. 18th St. (bet. Fifth & Sixth Aves.)

Subway: 14 St - Union Sq
Phone: 212-229-9500
Web: www.thegandernyc.com
Prices: **$$**

Lunch daily
Dinner Mon – Sat

This elegant companion to Chef Jesse Schenker's West Village hit, Recette, imbues each dish with distinct originality. The space flows from an inviting front lounge to a cozy back dining room, dressed with burlap ceiling pendants and ivory terrazzo flooring.

Go for the four-course prix-fixe dinner to experience this clever and delightful cuisine. Creamy anchovy dressing and meaty bacon join in the chef's take on this classic reinterpretation of a wedge salad. Risotto-style beluga lentils balance intense mushroom stock with a subtle hit of jalapeños. Many dishes highlight delicious restraint, like the pan-roasted branzino with foamy and mild foie-gras veloute. Finish with the slender bar of chocolate torte with white chocolate-miso ganache and fennel ice cream.

Haldi

102 Lexington Ave. (bet. 27th & 28th Sts.)

Subway: 28 St (Park Ave. South)
Phone: 212-213-9615
Web: www.haldinyc.com
Prices: **$$**

Lunch & dinner daily

It takes serious effort for an Indian restaurant to stand out from the crowd in jam-packed Curry Hill, but by highlighting the cuisine of Calcutta and its faction of Jewish immigrants, this arrival does just that. Haldi translates to turmeric in Hindi, and the space is rightfully decorated by the liberal use of yellow throughout.

Executive Chef Hemant Mathur heads up this operation along with the other members in restaurateur Shiva Natarajan's empire. Discover unique tastes like *mangshor* chop, a crunchy ground lamb-and-potato patty served with cilantro chutney; fish-fry Calcutta-style served with mustard-and-onion relish; or chicken *makmura* featuring minced chicken meatballs cooked in a rich creamy curry made from almonds and cashews.

Gramercy Tavern ✿

Contemporary XXX

B3

42 E. 20th St. (bet. Broadway & Park Ave. South)

Subway: 23 St (Park Ave. South) Lunch & dinner daily
Phone: 212-477-0777
Web: www.gramercytavern.com
Prices: $$$$

In a roll-call of New York's most beloved restaurants of the last couple of decades, Gramercy Tavern would be high on many people's list. It is one of those places that manage the rare trick of being so confident in its abilities that it can be all things to all people. You'll probably leave happy whether you've come on a date or are here to impress the in-laws; whether you're closing a deal or simply lubricating the thought processes behind a deal.

The "Tavern" side is the better one for lunch, especially if there are only two of you and you can sit at the bar—it doesn't take bookings so get here early and join in the grown-up "I'm not really queuing, I'm just standing here" queue outside. The "Dining Room" is for those who like a little more pomp with their pappardelle, and really comes into its own in the evening.

The cooking is the perfect match for the warm and woody surroundings: this is American food sure of its footing and unthreatening in its vocabulary. The main component, be it sea bass or pork loin, is allowed to shine and there is a refreshing lack of over-elaboration on the plate that demonstrates the confidence of the kitchen.

Hanjan

B1 **Korean** XX

36 W. 26th St. (bet. Broadway & Sixth Ave.)

Subway: 28 St (Broadway)
Phone: 212-206-7226
Web: www.hanjan26.com
Prices: $$

Lunch Mon-Fri
Dinner Mon – Sat

This contemporary take on Korean cuisine mimics the theme of Chef Hooni Kim's Hell's Kitchen trailblazer, Danji. A convivial crowd gathers along a cluster of tables in the petite space where ivory ceramic pieces are set against grey walls. Small plates arranged as "traditional" and "modern" highlight quality ingredients and stimulating presentations. The signature house-made tofu is unmissable: these chilled scoops of quivering soybean curd are a toasty shade of brown, sprinkled with slivered green onion and sesame seeds, and accompanied by soy sauce and perilla vinaigrette. Lunch is limited to a handful of starters, *bi bim bap,* and popular noodle dishes, perhaps mixing pork belly and vegetables doused in black bean sauce. Dinner is a better bet.

Hill Country

B1 **Barbecue** X

30 W. 26th St. (bet. Broadway & Sixth Ave.)

Subway: 28 St (Broadway)
Phone: 212-255-4544
Web: www.hillcountryny.com
Prices: $$

Lunch & dinner daily

Manhattan's Hill Country offers as succulent a barbecue experience as one can hope for without actually stepping onto the rolling hills of central Texas. This rollicking roadhouse proudly displays its Lone Star heritage throughout; the lower level doubles as a live country music venue and the ground floor is arranged with counters dispensing the mouthwatering victuals.

Consider your meat options, but don't fret 'cause it's all good, whether you choose lean (or moist) brisket, pork ribs, or smoked chicken to name just a few of the treats. Have your meal ticket stamped, then pick from a plethora of sides and sweets to complete your meal.

Downtown Brooklyn recently welcomed its own Hill Country Barbecue, adjacent to the Hill Country Chicken offshoot.

Hill Country Chicken

American

B2

1123 Broadway (at 25th St.)

Subway: 23 St (Broadway) — Lunch & dinner daily
Phone: 212-257-6446
Web: www.hillcountrychicken.com
Prices:

Gussied up in a happy palette of sunny yellow and sky blue, this 100-seat homage to deep-fried down-home country cooking serves exemplary fried chicken offered in two varieties. The "classic" sports a seasoned, golden-brown skin; "Mama El's" is skinless and cracker-crusted. Both are available by the piece or as part of whimsically named meals, like the "white meat solo coop."

Step up to the counter and feast your eyes on cast-iron skillets of chicken, as well as sides like creamy mashed potatoes, pimento macaroni and cheese, or grilled corn salad with red peppers and green onion. And then there's pie. More than 12 assortments, baked in-house and available by the slice, whole, or blended into a milkshake for a drinkable take on "à la mode."

I Trulli

Italian

C2

122 E. 27th St. (bet. Lexington Ave. & Park Ave. South)

Subway: 28 St (Park Ave. South) — Lunch Mon – Fri
Phone: 212-481-7372 — Dinner nightly
Web: www.itrulli.com
Prices: $$$

Warm, ambient, and widely appealing, this precious restaurant is known for crafting Italian food with a light touch. Neither young nor hip, it's a neighborhood stalwart that still lures locals with its sublime covered garden, fantastic (and affordable) wine list, and charming dining room of white walls and flickering candles. Their enoteca next door is perfect for a glass of *vino* with friends.

Then there's the menu, which is unabashedly pleasing, beginning with the *panelle*, chickpea fritters with goat cheese and a Sicilian-style caponata. House "musts" include *panzerotti* or mini-Apulian crispy calzones with tomato and mozzarella. Stuffed pastas are a huge draw—think of *ravioli per Olivia* oozing with ricotta and tossed in a light pistachio sauce.

The John Dory Oyster Bar

1196 Broadway (at 29th St.)

Subway: 28 St (Broadway)
Lunch & dinner daily
Phone: 212-792-9000
Web: www.thejohndory.com
Prices: $$

Brought to you by Chef April Bloomfield and company, this oyster bar occupies a blue-chip, corner spot in the untouchably cool Ace Hotel. The style is vintage with aquatic accents: floor-to-ceiling windows flood the space with light, while black-tiled columns, copper tables, and crayon-bright green and blue bar stools complete the look.

The unpretentious and modern menu showcases impeccable seafood. An assortment from the raw bar may feature whelks with parsley and garlic butter; east- and west-coast oysters shucked before your very eyes; and top quality shellfish with a lemon-and-shallot sauce. On the menu, find semolina soup with Nantucket bay scallops, or Spanish mackerel with crunchy cilantro-squid crackers.

Sadly, service can be indifferent.

Kokum

106 Lexington Ave. (bet. 27th & 28th Sts.)

Subway: 28 St (Park Ave. South)
Lunch & dinner daily
Phone: 212-684-6842
Web: www.kokumny.com
Prices: $$

The specialties of India's southern coastline are the focus at this gratifying Shiva Natarajan venue. Named after the tart tropical fruit, Kokum is prettified by a mural of fishing boats on a sandy stretch and exposed filament bulbs reflecting warmly off bronzed mirror panels.

Delights from Kerala, Chennai, and Mangalore anchor the menu. Roasted in a banana leaf with diced tomato and spices, the fish *pollichathu* is infused with sweetness and accompanied by fried tapioca root. *Kori gassi* is chicken in a rich curry containing plenty of dried red chilies but tempered by coconut milk and flecked with curry leaf. Carb fans can't resist the fragrant mound of vegetable biryani, drizzled with saffron butter, topped with fried onions and crushed *papadum*.

Junoon ✿

B2 Indian

27 W. 24th St. (bet. Fifth & Sixth Aves.)

Subway: 23 St (Sixth Ave.) Lunch & dinner daily
Phone: 212-490-2100
Web: www.junoonnyc.com
Prices: **$$$**

Attention to detail is what sets Junoon far apart from its *desi* brethren. The façade is dramatic, but once through those ebony doors, the cavernous setting is welcoming and plush with treasures from the subcontinent. The large bar exudes class and fun, with two antique *jhoolas* (swings) crafted from Burmese teak. Then, walk through a 200-year-old wooden arch and carved panels beyond, seemingly afloat in a reflecting pool, to enter the amber-tinted dining room where tables are luxuriously spaced.

The kitchen is patently ambitious and quite successful in presenting a contemporary vision of Indian cuisine. Every dish is thoughtfully composed and highlights only products of top quality. Begin with a thick octopus tentacle sent to the tandoor, emerging crisped, charred, incredibly tender, and served with pickled purple potato as well as herb oil. *Murg lababdar* tastes of pure elegance in seared and braised deboned chicken drenched in a sweetly spiced, deeply flavored tomato-onion gravy.

The creamy and exceedingly juicy *shahi* lamb shank is enriched with rose petal-*garam masala*, cumin, and coriander; while stout cake coddled with orange- and pink peppercorn-meringue is as unexpected as it is divine.

Laut

Asian

A3

15 E. 17th St. (bet. Broadway & Fifth Ave.)

Subway: 14 St - Union Sq

Lunch & dinner daily

Phone: 212-206-8989

Web: www.lautnyc.com

Prices: $$

Laut is a unique Malaysian restaurant that is at once cheerful and authentic yet never challenging or inaccessible. It is likewise true to its downtown spirit, in a room that features dim lighting and exposed brick prettied with chalk drawings of orchids and water lilies.

The personable staff and menu of Southeast Asian delights are as steady as the constant crowd. Popular choices include *roti telur,* a thin and slightly crisped yet pliable pancake stuffed with scrambled eggs, onions, and peppers, paired with fragrant chicken curry and coconut dipping sauce. The *nasi lemak* is a dome of coconut rice surrounded with sweet chili shrimp, hard-boiled egg, roasted peanuts, and dried anchovies for mixing into an outrageously good mélange of Malaysian flavors.

Les Halles

French

C2

411 Park Ave. South (bet. 28th & 29th Sts.)

Subway: 28 St (Park Ave. South)

Lunch & dinner daily

Phone: 212-679-4111

Web: www.leshalles.net

Prices: $$

Named for the famed Parisian marketplace, this Les Halles is better known locally for birthing New York's *enfant terrible,* Tony Bourdain. The writer and chef-turned-TV personality may be globe-trotting, but his legend remains part of the fabric here. Gaze up those worn wooden columns to sense this brasserie's storied history and age. Tightly knit tables generate competing conversations; checkered terrazzo floors and hardwood do little to buffer the hums.

Expect many *ooh-la-las* over very tasty *gratinée des Halles,* a French onion soup with melted cheese capping croutons soaked in a rich beef broth. Waiters are courteous yet quick in delivering timeless dishes like *steak au poivre* crusted with black peppercorns and coupled with deliciously crisp frites.

The Little Beet Table

B2 — American XX

333 Park Ave. South (bet. 24th & 25th Sts.)

Subway: 23 St (Park Ave South) — Lunch & dinner daily
Phone: 212-466-3330
Web: www.thelittlebeettable.com
Prices: **$$**

The product-focused, gluten-free food popularized by the fast-casual Little Beet now has a more elegant home in this Gramercy dining room outfitted with potted greenery and bold pieces of artwork.

It should come as no surprise that the beets are divine, whether in a salad of tender grilled wedges plated with strained yogurt, savory pumpkin seed granola, and young arugula; or used to brightly tint a creamy risotto topped with carrot purée and whipped ricotta. But while lovingly prepared vegetables make a strong showing on the menu, it's not all rabbit food here. Other recommendations include tuna tataki dressed with a charred jalapeño vinaigrette; and salmon, cooked so gently it's positively silken, plated with a creative interpretation of caponata.

Maialino

Italian 

2 Lexington Ave. (at 21st St.)

Subway: 23 St (Park Ave South) — Lunch & dinner daily
Phone: 212-777-2410
Web: www.maialinonyc.com
Prices: **$$**

Maialino is a trattoria, but only in theory. As the dining room of the Gramercy Park Hotel designed by the Rockwell Group, and overseen by service maestro Danny Meyer, there's nothing rustic or humble about it. The setting buzzes from day to night, and has established itself as a preferred watering hole for every sort of influencer.

Chef Nick Anderer's menu of Roman-inspired delights brings the upscale scene down to earth with an assortment of hearty preparations, like unctuous honeycomb *trippa alla Trastaverina* braised in a spicy tomato sauce. Enticing pastas include fat tubes of *paccheri* dressed with silky white beans, pleasantly bitter escarole, and a touch of rosemary. Come dessert, the curiously light ricotta-based panna cotta cannot be missed.

Manzo

Italian XX

B2

200 Fifth Ave. (at 23rd St.)

Subway: 23 St (Broadway) Lunch & dinner daily
Phone: 212-229-2180
Web: www.eataly.com
Prices: $$$

Wine-red walls and a mural of the pastoral countryside bring serenity to this corner of bustling Eataly—that quintessential emporium for all things Italian and edible.

As expected of a restaurant named for "beef" in Italian, Manzo serves up a meaty take on its country's cuisine. A plate of *carne cruda* is a fine opener and features paper-thin slices of raw (and domestically reared) *Piedmontese* beef topped with shards of nutty parmesan. House-made tagliatelle is twirled with olive oil-poached goat shoulder and black-truffle butter. The grilled dry-aged ribeye for two is enticingly fragrant, tender, juicy, and ample enough to have you proclaiming *basta*! If not, there's always dessert—like the dome of *cioccolato* with a quenelle of very nice hazelnut gelato.

Mari Vanna

Russian XX

B3

41 E. 20th St. (bet. Broadway & Park Ave. South)

Subway: 23 St (Park Ave South) Lunch & dinner daily
Phone: 212-777-1955
Web: www.marivanna.ru/ny
Prices: $$

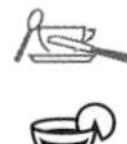

The bar is stocked with urns of house-infused vodka (apricot, seaberry, and cucumber-dill to name just a few) and the main dining room is often fully occupied by large groups. Despite the revelry, the ambience at Mari Vanna persuades its occupants to sit back and enjoy themselves in the shabby-chic room, done in a bleached palette complemented by embroidered seat backs and glowing chandeliers.

Traditional Russian specialties abound with an Olivier salad, *salo* (house-smoked fatback), borscht, and plump *pelmeni* served with herbed butter and sour cream. The kitchen's serious effort shines through in entrées like *golubtzi*, featuring two neat bundles of braised cabbage stuffed with fragrant ground beef and rice, then draped with a lush coat of tomato cream.

Marta

Italian

29 E. 29th St. (bet. Madison Ave. & Park Ave. So.)

Subway: 28 St (Park Ave. South) — Lunch & dinner daily
Phone: 212-651-3800
Web: www.martamanhattan.com
Prices: $$

Channeling the success of boutique hotel-style Italian dining, Danny Meyer and his team apply a similar mindset to this latest venture located at the Martha Washington hotel. A former woman's lodging, the space was recently given a dramatic makeover to accommodate the lobby level restaurant—a sharp-looking open layout complete with a dining counter overlooking wood-fired pizza ovens.

Like Maialino, Marta is helmed by Chef Nick Anderer and boasts a Roman accent. But, that's where the similarities end. Crispy, thin-crust pizza is the main attraction on this pasta-free menu: the margherita, for instance, is a crackling delight from the *pizze rosse* listing, while the *anatra* combining duck confit, fennel, and golden raisins is a novel *pizze bianche*.

Maysville

American

17 W. 26th St. (bet. Broadway & Sixth Ave.)

Subway: 23 St (Sixth Ave.) — Lunch & dinner daily
Phone: 646-490-8240
Web: www.maysvillenyc.com
Prices: $$

Just as the Ohio River that ran through Maysville, KY, allowed for the town's Bourbon to be relished by the rest of the world, this NYC namesake is a mecca for sips and celebrations. An amber-hued glow bathes the American whiskey temple, pivoted around an imposing, marble-topped bar. Gilt-edged mirrors offer a glimpse into the dining room, framed by vibrant ceilings. Inventive cooking is the name of this skilled kitchen's game and may include roasted squash served with fresh ricotta and garlic-infused cilantro pistou. Whole smoked trout is grilled to crisp perfection before being garnished with red onion, pickled mushrooms, and watercress.

Service is engaged all through dessert—a tart goat milk cheesecake with buttermilk granite is a combo to die for.

Momokawa

Japanese

157 E. 28th St. (bet. Lexington & Third Aves.)

Subway: 28 St (Park Ave. South) — Lunch & dinner daily
Phone: 212-684-7830
Web: www.momokawanyc.com
Prices: $$

By offering the comforting tastes of authentic Japanese cooking (the kind that people yearn for on a daily basis), Momokawa reminds us that sushi is for special occasions. Favored by expats and area residents, it's the type of place Tokyo salarymen might frequent before the long commute home. Ascend the winding staircase to discover a tidy room with counter seats and booths that can become private thanks to ceiling-mounted bamboo shades.

The range of tasty plates reveal *goma*-tofu, a dimpled round of sesame tofu topped with a bit of uni and freshly grated wasabi; as well as *satsuma-age*, tasty pan-fried fish cakes. Other satisfying courses include *ochazuke-mentai*, rice topped with spicy cod roe and nori, over which guests pour a savory green tea broth.

Novitá

Italian

102 E. 22nd St. (bet. Lexington Ave. & Park Ave. South)

Subway: 23 St (Park Ave South) — Lunch Mon – Fri
Phone: 212-677-2222 — Dinner nightly
Web: www.novitanyc.com
Prices: $$

This delightfully unpretentious trattoria is located on the ground floor of an art deco residential building that dates back to 1928. Novitá may have only opened in 1994, but elegant touches honor its tony Gramercy locale, with flowers dressing up the interior and canvas umbrella-topped tables outside. The dining room combines large, bright windows with pale yellow walls and a warm, autumnal-hued banquette. The staff's air of friendly formality suits the room. Enjoyable house-made pastas might feature *strozzapreti* tossed in fragrant basil pesto. Equally pleasing is a salad of *rucola*, avocado, and warm calamari. Other options include entrées like the black pepper-crusted tuna with lemon sauce, or a bittersweet chocolate-speckled semifreddo for dessert.

NoMad ✿

B1

1170 Broadway (at 28th St.)

Subway: 28 St (Broadway) Lunch & dinner daily
Phone: 347-472-5660
Web: www.thenomadhotel.com
Prices: $$$$

The reputation of the seductively louche NoMad hotel, housed within a strikingly bohemian beaux-arts building, owes much to the considerable talents of Will Guidara and Chef Daniel Humm of Eleven Madison Park, as they look after all things relating to food and drink.

The glass-roofed Atrium is the chief pleasure dome but a meal in NoMad's land is a moveable feast and some prefer eating in the more languid surroundings of the Parlour, where there's a little less head swiveling and competitive dressing. Wherever you sit, you'll find the service confident and engaging and the menu hugely appealing.

Don't come expecting the culinary pyrotechnics of Eleven Madison Park: here it's about familiar flavors in more approachable, less intricate dishes, but with the same care and understanding of ingredients. Chicken—which, if we're honest, would be the final meal of choice of many of us—is the undoubted star; they roast a whole bird, pimp it up with foie gras and black truffle and serve it for two. Bone marrow adds depth to beef, while asparagus with bread sauce shows the kitchen is equally adept when subtlety is required. For dessert, look no further than the aptly named "Milk & Honey."

Ootoya

8 W. 18th St. (bet. Fifth & Sixth Aves.)

Subway: 14 St (Sixth Ave.) — Lunch & dinner daily
Phone: 212-255-0018
Web: www.ootoya.us
Prices: **$$**

This Japanese chain boasts more than 300 locations throughout Asia, and now claims three more here in the Big Apple. Thankfully the chic interior does nothing to convey chain dining. Instead, the look is understated with wood slats, ikebana, and muted tones. Ootoya's budget-friendly pricing ensures a full house.

Hearty, home-style fare is the hallmark of their expansive menu of (mostly) cooked specialties. House-made tofu, rice bowls, fried free-range chicken with sweet-and-sour sauce, and pork *katsu* are but just a few of the product-focused items on offer. The lunch sets are an excellent value, built around fine quality fish such as *saikyo* miso-marinated grilled salmon with *chawan mushi*, steamed brown rice, and grains, accompanied by a heartwarming miso soup.

O Ya

Seafood XX

120 E. 28th St. (bet. Lexington Ave. & Park Ave. South)

Subway: 28 St (Park Ave. South) — Dinner Tue – Sat
Phone: 212-204-0200
Web: www.o-ya.restaurant
Prices: **$$$$**

The team here doles out seafood that defies the constraints of sushi and sashimi, as the primping each creation undergoes yields plates that can be stunning. And about those plates: O Ya's seemingly endless array of service pieces are beautiful, almost to the point of distraction.

Seafood, treated with an *itamae's* reverence and modern day ingenuity, is the foundation of a strictly set-menu experience. Tables are a comfortable seating option, but the best place to be is at the counter. From there, a view of what's about to be set before you builds much anticipation: torched hamachi is crowned by banana pepper purée; lightly grilled lobster sits atop shiso tempura; and a turkey egg-chive omelet is sprinkled with powdered Wagyu beef schmaltz.

Park Avenue

Contemporary 

360 Park Ave. South (at 26th St.)

Subway: 28 St (Park Ave. South) Lunch & dinner daily
Phone: 212-951-7111
Web: www.parkavenyc.com
Prices: **$$$**

This Flatiron corner with an identity crisis is now the latest incarnation of the uptown stalwart known for changing inspiration with each season. Larger than its previous digs, Park Avenue is a sprawling canvas on which design firm AvroKO works its magic.

The restaurant remains a family affair, with father and son Alan and Michael Stillman steadily steering the concept alongside Chef/partner Craig Koketsu. Just like the décor, the menu fully celebrates the seasons. Hearty wintertime flavors have featured mustard seed vinaigrette, Manchego, and chestnut honey-drizzled kale-and-chorizo salad. The whimsical "everything" crusted branzino is set on a smear of smoked cream cheese; while sticky toffee pudding is graced with brûléed bananas.

Periyali

35 W. 20th St. (bet. Fifth & Sixth Aves.)

Subway: 23 St (Sixth Ave.) Lunch Mon – Fri
Phone: 212-463-7890 Dinner nightly
Web: www.periyali.com
Prices: **$$$**

Aegean sensibilities and vibrant Mediterranean flavors are dished out with panache at this Greek mainstay, in operation and thriving since 1978. A glinting school of abstract metal fish artfully commands one wall, while an intimate rear seating area glows like a pale pink sunset in the room's evening light. The petite space can get packed with a dressy, European crowd.

First-rate cooking may begin with fresh and crisp *horiatiki salata* sporting creamy feta and powerfully fragrant dried oregano; or the small but pleasingly robust *sikotakia me fakes,* chicken livers sautéed with rosemary laid over a bed of lentils. The reliably decadent moussaka layers crisped potato slices, ground lamb, roasted eggplant, and béchamel so creamy that it verges on fluffy.

Pippali 

Indian 

C2

129 E. 27th St. (bet. Lexington Ave. & Park Ave. South)

Subway: 28 St (Park Ave. South) Lunch & dinner daily
Phone: 212-689-1999
Web: www.pippalinyc.com
Prices: $$

Named for the Ayurvedic healing herb, Pippali is a vibrant rookie in Curry Hill. On-point service makes it a dream destination for date night or dinner with friends. And, a natural color palette provides a striking backdrop for the kitchen's rout of delicious, brightly seasoned dishes.

Indian standards are done right here, but focus on regional fare for a distinct perspective: *kekada thokku* is a mound of crabmeat dressed in a spicy blend of mustard seeds and cumin; and *tawa* scallops sautéed in tomato relish are enhanced with curried avocado chutney. Presentations are clean, careful and unfussy as seen in Bihari *gosht* or braised lamb shanks; while Konkan shrimp curry, augmented with coconut and coriander, makes for an aromatic and deeply flavorful feast.

Resto

Contemporary

C2

111 E. 29th St. (bet. Lexington Ave. & Park Ave. South)

Subway: 28 St (Park Ave. South) Lunch & dinner daily
Phone: 212-685-5585
Web: www.restonyc.com
Prices: $$

Vibrant cooking, a winning ambience, and an inviting marble bar have made this brasserie a perpetual neighborhood favorite. Despite numerous kitchen shakeups, the talented team behind the line always lands on its feet and continues to turn out a roster of worthwhile temptations. Moules frites are a hold-over from when Belgian cooking dominated the menu, but contemporary plates have included charred squid salad with citrus segments and shaved sunchokes; *cavatelli* with creamy fontina cheese, shaved Brussels sprouts, and toasted pine nuts; and pork shoulder steak with fava bean *gribiche*.

For an array of meaty treats washed down by global brews, head next door to sister spot The Cannibal, which has a second, thriving outpost in midtown's Gotham Market West.

Saravanaas

Indian 

81 Lexington Ave. (at 26th St.)

Subway: 28 St (Park Ave. South)
Lunch & dinner daily
Phone: 212-679-0204
Web: www.saravanabhavan.com
Prices:

This Curry Hill branch of the international chain Saravana Bhavan is one of the neighborhood's most popular dining spots. The monochromatic white interior has taken a beating over the years, but that's easy to look past when the eats are as cheap and tasty as these.

The completely vegetarian menu is an authentic array of curries, breads, and weekend-only biryani, but the real head-turners are those table-long *dosas*. They arrive as crisp, tactile favorites on a metal tray ready to be picked apart and dunked into luscious *sambar* and fresh-tasting chutneys.

The *milagaipodi* onion *dosa*, a crispy rice-and lentil-flour crêpe spread with dried spices and a deliciously offensive amount of chopped red onion, is just one of many worthwhile treats.

Tamba

103 Lexington Ave. (bet. 27th & 28th Sts.)

Subway: 28 St (Park Ave. South)
Lunch & dinner daily
Phone: 212-481-9100
Web: www.tambagrillandbar.com
Prices: $$

Tamba's food may be very good, but the genuine hospitality delivered by owner Mr. Malik and his team of servers is memorable. These are the touches that set it well above its Curry Hill brethren.

Billed as an Indian grill, many dishes are char-kissed and arrive fresh from the tandoor like succulent *jalpari* (jumbo shrimp); mint *paneer tikka*; or *haryali* kebab, skewered chunks of white meat chicken marinated in an herbaceous coriander-mint purée served over a bed of salad greens and browned onions. Other favorites include *channa saag*, toothsome chickpeas and finely chopped spinach simmered in onion, tomato, ginger, and fragrant spices. Tamba's special naan is studded with bits of *tandoori* chicken and is a delicious complement to everything on the menu.

Tocqueville

Contemporary XX

1 E. 15th St. (bet. Fifth Ave. & Union Sq. West)

Subway: 14 St - Union Sq — Lunch & dinner Mon – Sat
Phone: 212-647-1515
Web: www.tocquevillerestaurant.com
Prices: $$

Be it lunch or dinner, few New York restaurants convey the civility found at Tocqueville, courtesy of Chef Marco Moreira and his wife Joann Makovitzky. The serene, butterscotch-colored room features spaciously arranged tables draped with starched linen and laden with sparkling cutlery and stemware.

Tocqueville's location, just steps away from the Union Square Greenmarket, influences its seasonally driven menu. A salad of frisée, shaved celery, and roasted local pear arranged with slices of nutty Cato Farm cheddar is a delightful starting point. House-made silken tofu presented with ginger-infused mushroom broth demonstrates the kitchen's global inspiration. Excellent desserts may offer a candied chestnut Napolean garnished with brandy sorbet.

Turkish Kitchen

Turkish XX

C2

386 Third Ave. (bet. 27th & 28th Sts.)

Subway: 28 St (Park Ave. South) — Lunch Sun – Fri
Phone: 212-679-6633 — Dinner nightly
Web: www.turkishkitchen.com
Prices: $$

Turkish Kitchen showcases all the classics but excels in the preparation of grilled meats. Indulge in *yogurtlu karisik*, a dish of moist and smoky char-grilled lamb, chicken, and spicy kebabs on a cooling bed of garlic-scented yogurt sauce and pita bread. Pillowy beef dumplings also wade in a pool of that signature garlicky yogurt sauce topped with paprika-infused oil and a dusting of sumac, oregano, and mint. A wide selection of Turkish wines makes a fine accompaniment to a hearty meal.

Dangling globe light fixtures give the entrance to this cavernous, multi-level restaurant with floor-to-ceiling windows a modern glow. Tables are topped with pristine white cloths and set between black and white striped chairs; cherry-red walls lend a pop of color.

Union Square Cafe

A3 — American XX

21 E. 16th St. (bet. Fifth Ave. & Union Sq. West)

Subway: 14 St - Union Sq — Lunch & dinner daily
Phone: 212-243-4020
Web: www.unionsquarecafe.com
Prices: **$$$**

Sadly Danny Meyer's first born, which opened back in 1985 is due to close at the end of 2015, but thankfully it will relocate blocks away. With that in mind, this institution is sure to be mobbed until the end. Despite the usual crush, there are few other service teams better at making every diner feel like a cherished guest and there are few other bars more comfortable for solo dining.

The menu is hailed for its broad appeal. Salads are seasonal and starters include the fried calamari, while signature items like the yellowfin tuna burger are an all-time fave. Pastas are expertly prepared, as in the spaghetti Siciliano with swordfish meatballs and spicy tomato sauce. Memorable entrées reveval sea scallops wrapped in thin sheets of crisped and salty prosciutto.

Upland

B2 — Contemporary XX

345 Park Ave. South (at 26th St.)

Subway: 28 St (Park Ave. South) — Lunch & dinner daily
Phone: 212-686-1006
Web: www.uplandnyc.com
Prices: **$$$**

An *Avengers*-like lineup unites Chef Justin Smillie, restaurateur Stephen Starr, and design firm Roman Williams to bring fabulous California-style dining to this stretch of Park Avenue South. Upland positively glows from its burnished wood furnishings, glossy cream-colored walls, and polished copper pipe shelving stocked with backlit jars of preserved lemons.

The kitchen sends out much to love, with Mediterranean and Italian accents to keep it all very interesting and delicious. *Estrella* pasta, star-shaped rigatoni dressed with crushed chicken liver, herbs, and pecorino, is a savory delight; crackling skin pork belly is seasonally plated with kale, blistered shisito peppers, and fuyu persimmon; and the yuzu soufflé with kalamansi curd is phenomenal.

Greenwich & West Village

Once occupied by struggling artists, poets, and edgy bohemia, Greenwich Village today continues to thrive as one of New York City's most artsy hubs. With Washington Square Park and NYU at its core, this area's typically named (not numbered) streets wear an intellectual spirit as seen in its many cafés, indie theaters, and music venues.

ASSORTED PLEASURES

Mamoun's has been feeding students for decades with some of the best falafel in town. Area residents however have been known to experience similar gratification at **Taïm**, which features updated renditions of this fried delight. Chase down the savory feast with one of their smoothies or opt for a creamy concoction from the humble **Peanut Butter & Co.** for a taste of sweet bliss. Whether in the mood to linger or pick up a jar to-go, find yourself rubbing shoulders with natives craving authentic Spanish flavors at nearby **100 Montaditos**. Also captivating the culinary elite are those delicate, very satisfying rice- and lentil-flour crêpes served with character and flair at food truck sensation, **N.Y. Dosas**. For crêpes in their original, faithful form along with other excellent French goodies, stop by **Patisserie Claude**, or unearth a slice of Italy by way of old-time bakeries and butchers also settled here. **Faicco's Pork Store** as well as **Ottomanelli & Sons Meat Market** have been tendering their treats for over 100 years now. Take home a round of parsley and cheese sausage or tray of arancini—even though the staff insist that one

must be eaten warm, before leaving the store. Setting aside the dusty floors and minimal décor, **Florence Prime Meat Market** in operation for over 70 years, is every gourmand's go-to spot for Christmas goose, Newport steak, and so much more. And really, what goes best with meat? Cheese, of course, with **Murray's Cheese Shop** initiating hungry neophytes into the art and understanding of their countless varieties. Completing Italy's culinary terrain in Greenwich Village is **Raffetto's**, whose fresh, handmade pastas never cease to please. Then hop countries and experience a smack of London at **A Salt & Battery**. Here, fish and chips are crafted from the finest ingredients and served with some first-rate sides. Think: curry sauce, Heinz baked beans, and mushy peas. Of course, no Village jaunt is complete without pizza, with

some of the finest to be found coal-fired and crisp, only by the pie, at **John's of Bleecker Street**. **Joe's** is another local delight dishing up thin-crust selections that promise to leave you with a lifetime addiction. Finish this carb and cheese extravaganza with a uniquely textured scoop from **Cones**, available in surprisingly tasty flavor combinations...even watermelon!

WEST VILLAGE

Located along the Hudson River and extending all the way down to Hudson Square, the West Village is predominately residential, marked by angular streets, quaint shops, and charming eateries. Once known as "Little Bohemia," numerous old-fashioned but resilient food favorites continue to thrive here and offer a taste of old New York. For a nearly royal treat, stop by **Tea & Sympathy** for high tea, followed by a full Sunday supper of roast beef and Yorkshire pudding. **Press Tea** serves up global flavors topped with Big Apple flair—pair the Mont Blanc Wild Himalayan with an Earl Grey cupcake to understand what all the fuss is about. Over on Commerce Street, fans are swooning over **Milk & Cookies**' unapologetically sinful goodies. These are reputedly as sensational as the breakfast and burgers always on offer at **Elephant & Castle**. The influential **James Beard Foundation** is also situated steps away, in a historic 12th Street townhouse that was once home to the illustrious food writer. If Tex-Mex is more your speed, then join the raucous twenty-something's at **Tortilla Flats**. Known as much for Bingo Tuesdays as for their potent house margaritas, it's a guaranteed good time.

Manhattan's love for brunch is a time-tested affair that continues to thrive in this far west stretch. Find evidence of this at **La Bonbonniere**, a pleasant little diner whose brazen and beautiful creations are excelled only by their absurdly cheap prices. Pack a basket of egg specialties and enjoy a picnic among the urban vista of roller skaters and runners at Hudson River Park. While strolling back across bustling Bleecker, let the overpowering aromas of butter and sugar lead you to the original **Magnolia Bakery**. Proffering over 128 handmade treats, this official sweet spot is a darling among tourists and date-night duos. **Li-Lac** is one of the city's oldest chocolate houses dispensing the best hand-crafted treats and chocolate-covered pretzels in town—take your pick between dark and milk! Beyond bakeries, the bar scene in the West Village is always abuzz. Night owls pound through an assortment of pints at the **Rusty**

Knot, while relishing cheap eats and fantastic live talent. Equally expert mixologists can be found pouring "long drinks and fancy cocktails" at **Employees Only**; just as bartenders reach inventive heights at **Little Branch**—where an encyclopedic understanding of the craft ensures dizzying results. At the foot of Christopher Street and atop the Hudson River waterfront, **Pier 45** is a particularly lovely destination for icy cold drinks, hot dogs, and sunbathing.

MEPA

Everyone from fashionistas, curious locals, families, and stiletto-clad socialites make the pilgrimage further north to the notoriously chic Meatpacking District. Once home to slaughterhouses, prostitution services, and drug dens, today MePa is packed with moneyed locals and savvy tourists looking to get their snack, sip, and groove on. Thanks to the huge success of the High Line—an abandoned 1934 elevated railway that is now a 19-block long park—these once-desolate streets now cradle some of the city's coolest restaurants and hottest nightclubs. As if in defiance of these cautious times, luxury hotels, "starchitect" high-rises, and festive bistros have risen—and these modish minions cannot imagine being elsewhere. But, in the midst of all this glitz find **Gansevoort Market**, a minimally publicized but very precious gem hounded by gastronomes.

The Standard hotel is of course the social hub with beer and bratwursts running the show every summer at **The Biergarten**. Come fall, hipsters soak up the scene at **Kaffeeklatsch**, a pop-up shop preparing hot beverages for freezing skaters doing the rounds at Standard Plaza—a public square-turned-ice skating rink. Finally, obfuscated by this haute hotel, **Hector's Café** is a modest holdout that continues to feed the few remaining meatpackers—usually all day, everyday.

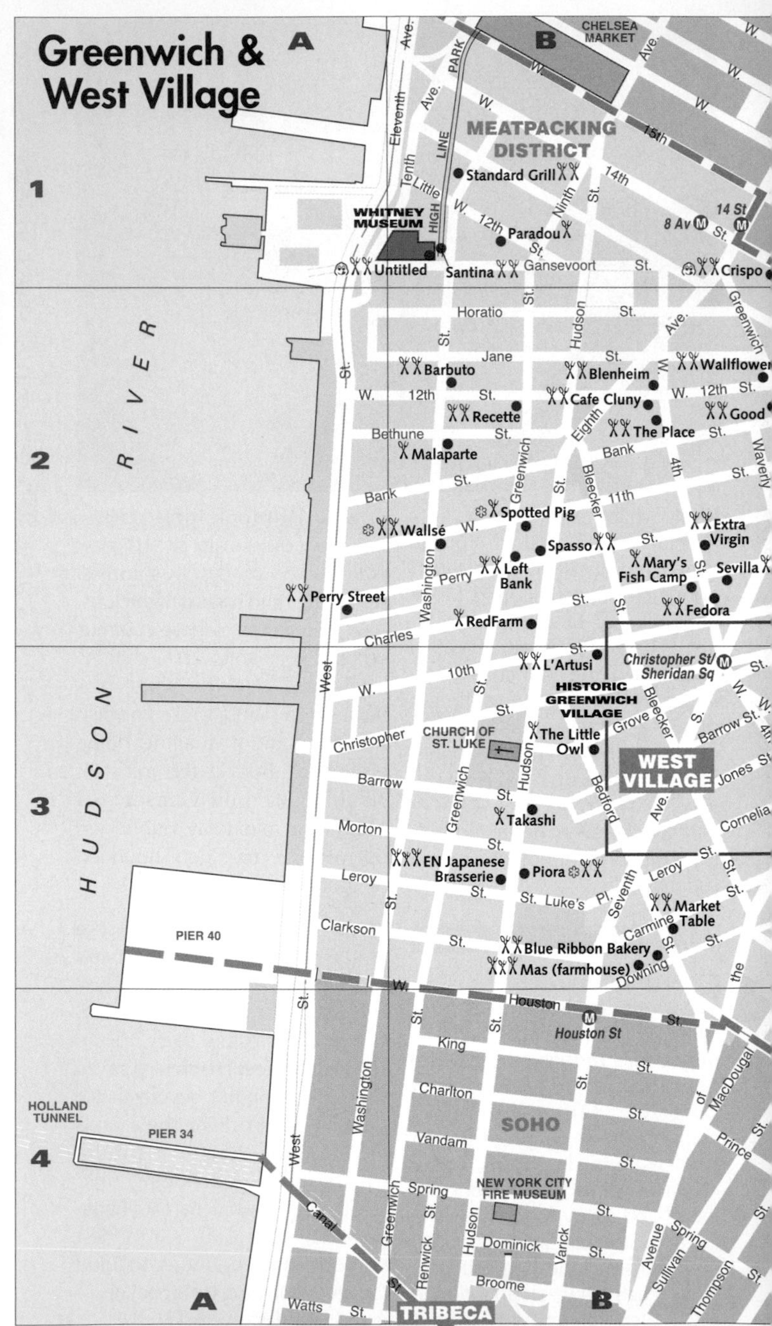
Greenwich &
West Village
A
B
1
2
3
4
HUDSON RIVER
CHELSEA MARKET
MEATPACKING DISTRICT
HIGH LINE
PARK
WHITNEY MUSEUM
Standard Grill
Paradou
Untitled
Santina
Crispo
14 St
8 Av
Barbuto
Blenheim
Wallflower
Cafe Cluny
Recette
Good
The Place
Malaparte
Spotted Pig
Wallsé
Extra Virgin
Spasso
Mary's Fish Camp
Sevilla
Left Bank
Perry Street
Fedora
RedFarm
L'Artusi
Christopher St/ Sheridan Sq
HISTORIC GREENWICH VILLAGE
CHURCH OF ST. LUKE
The Little Owl
WEST VILLAGE
Takashi
EN Japanese Brasserie
Piora
Market Table
Blue Ribbon Bakery
Mas (farmhouse)
PIER 40
Houston St
SOHO
HOLLAND TUNNEL
PIER 34
NEW YORK CITY FIRE MUSEUM
TRIBECA
Eleventh Ave.
Tenth Ave.
Little W. 12th St.
Ninth Ave.
W. 14th St.
W. 15th St.
Gansevoort St.
Horatio St.
Jane St.
W. 12th St.
Bethune St.
Bank St.
W. 11th St.
Perry St.
Charles St.
W. 10th St.
Christopher St.
Barrow St.
Morton St.
Leroy St.
Clarkson St.
W. Houston St.
King St.
Charlton St.
Vandam St.
Spring St.
Dominick St.
Broome St.
Watts St.
Canal St.
West St.
Washington St.
Greenwich St.
Hudson St.
Eighth Ave.
Greenwich Ave.
Bleecker St.
W. 4th St.
Waverly
Grove St.
Bedford St.
Seventh Ave.
St. Luke's Pl.
Carmine St.
Downing St.
Jones St.
Cornelia St.
Avenue of the Americas
MacDougal St.
Prince St.
Sullivan St.
Thompson St.
Renwick St.
Varick St.

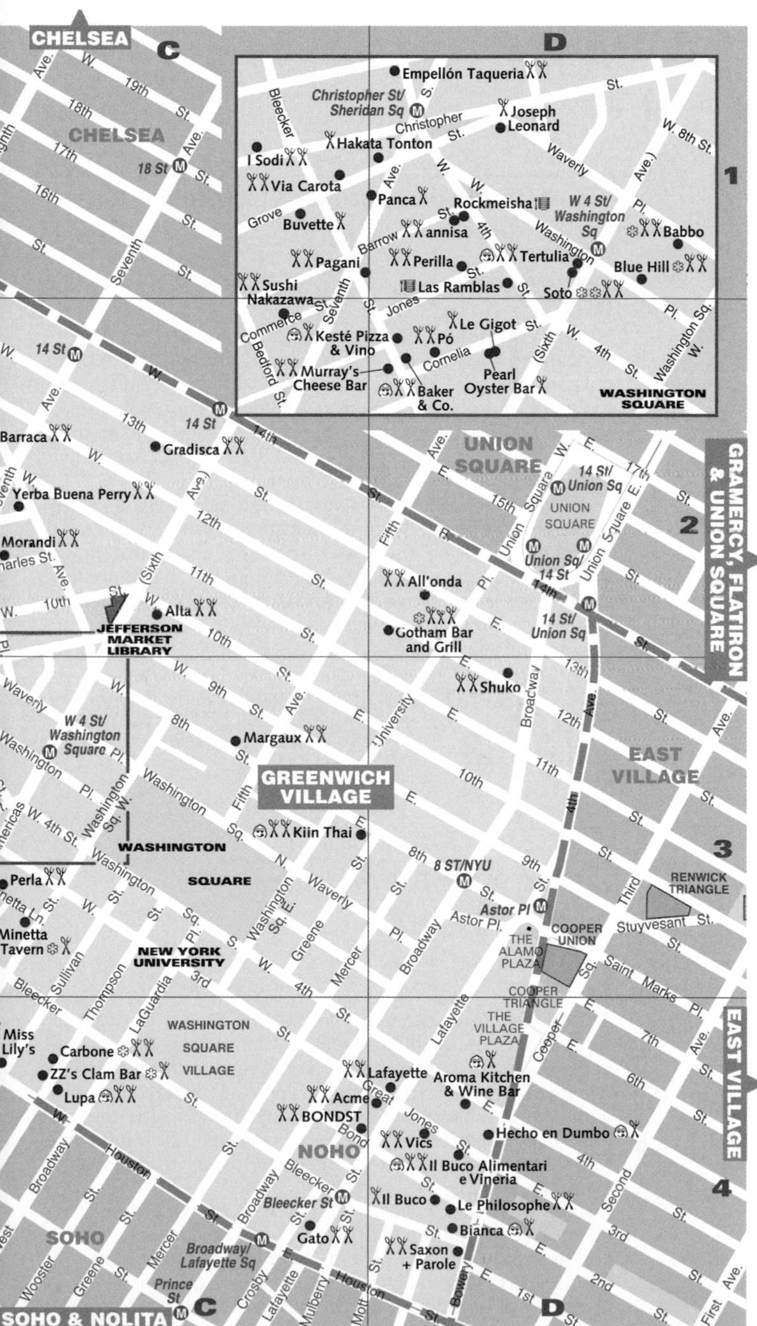
CHELSEA
C
D
CHELSEA
18 St
14 St
Empellón Taqueria
Christopher St/ Sheridan Sq
Joseph Leonard
Hakata Tonton
I Sodi
Via Carota
Panca
Rockmeisha
W 4 St/ Washington Sq
Buvette
annisa
Babbo
Pagani
Perilla
Tertulia
Blue Hill
Sushi Nakazawa
Las Ramblas
Soto
Le Gigot
Kesté Pizza & Vino
Pó
Murray's Cheese Bar
Baker & Co.
Pearl Oyster Bar
WASHINGTON SQUARE
Barraca
Gradisca
UNION SQUARE
Yerba Buena Perry
14 St/ Union Sq
Morandi
Union Sq/ 14 St
All'onda
Alta
Gotham Bar and Grill
14 St/ Union Sq
JEFFERSON MARKET LIBRARY
Shuko
W 4 St/ Washington Square
Margaux
EAST VILLAGE
GREENWICH VILLAGE
Kiin Thai
WASHINGTON
SQUARE
8 ST/NYU
Astor Pl
RENWICK TRIANGLE
Perla
Minetta Tavern
NEW YORK UNIVERSITY
COOPER UNION
THE ALAMO PLAZA
COOPER TRIANGLE
THE VILLAGE PLAZA
Miss Lily's
Carbone
WASHINGTON SQUARE VILLAGE
ZZ's Clam Bar
Lupa
Lafayette
Aroma Kitchen & Wine Bar
Acme
BONDST
Hecho en Dumbo
Vics
NOHO
Il Buco Alimentari e Vineria
Bleecker St
Il Buco
Le Philosophe
Gato
Bianca
Saxon + Parole
SOHO
Broadway/ Lafayette Sq
Prince St
SOHO & NOLITA
GRAMERCY, FLATIRON & UNION SQUARE
EAST VILLAGE
1
2
3
4

Acme

Contemporary XX

D4

9 Great Jones St. (bet. Broadway & Lafayette St.)

Subway: Broadway - Lafayette St — Lunch Sat – Sun
Phone: 212-203-2121 — Dinner nightly
Web: www.acmenyc.com
Prices: $$

NoHo is no stranger to *Vogue*-ready waitresses, but Acme's reincarnation two years ago produced an inventive Nordic culinary nirvana, equal parts rustic brasserie and sultry lounge. Naturally, the crowds came and never left its metal-topped bar and pine-green banquettes. One could stare at the gorgeously lit backdrop of bottles, but grab a Foxy Brown and contemplate the innovative menu.

Chef Mads Refslund brings his Danish sensibility to many dishes, including lightly cured mackerel finished with grated horseradish. But he also leaves room for comforting fusion dishes like Johnny Cakes—an American classic-turned-fun ensemble of thin cornbread flapjacks, accompanied by sweet, porky confit, as well as an assortment of crispy pig ears and pickled veggies.

All'onda

Italian XX

D2

22 E. 13th St. (bet. Fifth Ave. & University Pl.)

Train: 14 St (Seventh Ave.) — Lunch & dinner Tue – Sun
Phone: 212-231-2236
Web: www.allondanyc.com
Prices: $$$

All'onda cuts a dramatic impression from the outset, especially come nightfall, when its narrow, all-glass façade lights up like a dream. Inside, you'll find a décor swept in whitewashed brick, rich walnut paneling, honeycomb tiles and lovely, whimsical flower arrangements. Also the co-founder of Uma Temakeria, Chef Chris Jaeckle pulls influence from all sorts of lands far and near, surprising customers with every new visit.

Dinner might kick off with creamy hamachi crudo, sporting curls of crispy carrot and a fresh kick of *peperoncino* oil; and then move on to a nest of al dente bucatini twirled with uni, spicy breadcrumbs, and tarragon. Curly ramen—yes ramen—bobbing in parmesan broth with a soft egg, pork belly, and Brussels sprouts is a welcome surprise.

Alta

Contemporary 

64 W. 10th St (bet. Fifth & Sixth Aves.)

Subway: Christopher St - Sheridan Sq — Dinner nightly
Phone: 212-505-7777
Web: www.altarestaurant.com
Prices: **$$**

From an ivy-cloaked façade to the complex menu items, Alta seems to imply mystery. Inside its brick townhouse, this attractive and comforting scene mixes antique Moorish floors, splashes of yellow, and a cozy wood-burning fireplace. The second level looks like a balcony but is just as packed thanks to the kitchen's excellent menu selection.

These small plates have featured pillowy lamb meatballs in a pool of charred red-pepper sauce, or uni draped over crostini covered with a shimmering sheet of Ibèrico bacon. Wok-seared *taglierini* reveals cuttlefish slivers sautéed with crispy garlic chips.

First-rate ingredients are surpassed only by thoughtful combinations in desserts like silky *pot de crème* capped in pistachio powder—a midsummer night's dream.

annisa

Fusion 

13 Barrow St. (bet. Seventh Ave. South & W. 4th St.)

Subway: Christopher St - Sheridan Sq — Dinner nightly
Phone: 212-741-6699
Web: www.annisarestaurant.com
Prices: **$$$**

Anita Lo's menu is informed by her heritage and her peregrinations, and she clearly puts much effort into seeking out the best seasonal produce available. The Asian element of the fusion equation is quite pronounced yet there is also plenty of choice for those who prefer their influences to come from more Westerly cuisines. As a result, one can start with black sea bass sashimi with trout roe and follow it up, by way of contrast, with a "tasting of lamb" with cauliflower. Dishes are quite delicate creations and come with some flavor combinations that will certainly perk up your taste buds. The dining room exudes warmth; the service is self-assured and, given that annisa means "women" in Arabic, it is fitting that the wine list makes a point of featuring many female wine growers.

Aroma Kitchen & Wine Bar

Italian

36 E. 4th St. (bet. Bowery & Lafayette St.)

Subway: Bleecker St — Lun Sun
Phone: 212-375-0100 — Dinner Tue – Sim
Web: www.aromanyc.com
Prices: $$

When dolled-up crowds pack this cobblestoned street, the staff rises to the occasion with true Italian hospitality. Despite the trendy surrounds, authenticity is paramount as orange-framed doors are flung open to reveal lovely rustic rooms and a quiet, contemporary aura. The front area presents mirrors, a wood bar, and hefty shelves of interesting wines.

Beyond brick archways, a communal table in the dining room is ideal for savoring summer's bounty beautifully showcased in *scafata di verdure*, a *zuppa* bobbing with *quadrettini* dressed in a bright vegetable ragù. Flavorful bites of *strascinati* are tossed with sublime Moliterno cheese, lamb sausage, and smoky red peppers. A scoop of *stracciatella* gelato or the daily *sorbetto* ensures an exalted finish.

Baker & Co.

Italian

D2

259 Bleecker St. (bet. Cornelia & Jones Sts.)

Subway: W 4 St - Wash Sq — Lunch & dinner daily
Phone: 212-255-1234
Web: www.bakernco.com
Prices: $$

The latest brainchild of the team behind the wildly popular Emporio, brand-new Baker & Co. makes a big mark on NYC's Italian-American scene. From the exposed brick walls and wood-lined banquettes to the backyard garden and Faema espresso machine, the rustic, honest restaurant feels comfortable enough to spread out pappardelle with veal cheek ragù and seasonal daily specials like watermelon gazpacho. A rich, sweet soup spiked with tomatoes, it bobs with lumps of crabmeat and cooling cucumber.

The menu, though, leans more toward traditional Italian dishes. Dig into the braised rabbit meatballs, paired with shaved ricotta and *tonnato*-style aïoli, as well as *garganelli* bathed in a saffron *brodetto* and topped with peekytoe crab accompanied by *bottarga*.

Babbo ✿

Italian XX

D1

110 Waverly Pl. (bet. MacDougal St. & Sixth Ave.)

Subway: W 4 St - Wash Sq — Lunch Tue – Sat
Phone: 212-777-0303 — Dinner nightly
Web: www.babbonyc.com
Prices: $$$

Is Mario Batali's beloved wild child of the fine dining scene mellowing a bit with age? Only in the best possible way. This warm, inviting mainstay still likes to keep its elegant good looks edgy with a little thumping music, but the general vibe inside seems to have settled into a sweeter, calmer version of its rambunctious youth.

Nestled into quaint Waverly Place, Babbo's bi-level dining room fits right in: think shuttered windows and wrought-iron railings alongside thick wooden armchairs, white tablecloths, and the kind of dreamy low lighting made for late night rendezvous.

The food itself is always artful and precise, and the menu more than delivers on its promise: creative, rustic Italian fare made with stellar skill and extraordinary ingredients. Mainstays like a delicate lamb's tongue vinaigrette arrives humming with tender beech mushrooms and topped with a 3-minute egg and mâche; while soft beef cheek ravioli bathed in a Castelmagno cheese- and black truffle-reduction is subtle but wow-inducing.

Don't skip dessert: when this hot spot takes a swing on a classic semifreddo, drenching it in dark chocolate and a dusting of crushed pistachio, it hits it out of the park.

Barbuto

American XX

B2

775 Washington St. (at 12th St.)

Subway: 14 St - 8 Av — Lunch & dinner daily
Phone: 212-924-9700
Web: www.barbutonyc.com
Prices: $$

When New Yorkers dream of living in the West Village, Barbuto has a place in that dream, too. Springtime lunches with garage doors open to the sidewalk, and a feast of refined, simple dishes have earned Jonathan Waxman a devoted following in a neighborhood already full of charming restaurants. Casually professional service and the dimly lit dining room's dose of California cool enhance the experience. Barbuto's roast chicken deserves its legendary status, but other dishes tempt too. A *cavolo nero* salad of thinly sliced black kale and crunchy breadcrumbs tossed in a creamy dressing of anchovies and pecorino puts the average kale salad to shame. Linguini is coated with black pepper, egg, pancetta, and cheese in one indelible plate of carbonara.

Barraca

Spanish XX

C2

81 Greenwich Ave. (at Bank St.)

Subway: 14 St - 8 Av — Lunch & dinner daily
Phone: 212-462-0080
Web: www. barracanyc.com
Prices: $$

Spanish for "shack," rustic Barraca charms with timber ceilings and vats of sangria behind the bar. Blue chairs pop against all the wood and brick, bringing a Mediterranean feel to the intimate space. Banquettes line one side of the restaurant, suggesting cozy evenings of sharing *coca de atùn* (flatbread pizza) or *pan tomate*.

Empanadas are flaky and crusty, filled with thyme-laced beef, spring onion, allspice, and cheese. Classic *croquetas* are crackling outside and creamy within, resting on a dab of aïoli. But such snacks are just a prelude to the excellent paella; choose one version studded with shellfish and sweet peppers, or mix and match two or three different "flavors."

Crusty churros finish off an evening of pure Spanish pleasure.

Bianca

Italian

5 Bleecker St. (bet. Bowery & Elizabeth St.)

Subway: Bleecker St — Dinner nightly
Phone: 212-260-4666
Web: www.biancanyc.com
Prices: $$

There's a reason diners from all over the city clamor to squeeze into Bianca's low-lit and lovely little dining room, despite its no reservations policy. This is home-style Italian fare with finesse—where the pasta is cooked by someone accomplished in the understanding of what Italian pasta is and is not.

Bianca's intimate and sultry atmosphere makes it a great date night spot, with couples knocking elbows over dishes like the *lasagnette di verdure*, a delicate eggplant, zucchini and tomato tart of sorts. Others delight in the soft *tagliolini ai frutti di mare*, tossed with wildly fresh seafood and a long-simmered tomato sauce; or plump, fennel studded Italian sausage (*salsiccie e fagioli*), paired with a hearty and savory cannellini bean stew.

Blenheim

American

283 W. 12th St. (at W. 4th St.)

Subway: 14 St (Seventh Ave.) — Lunch & dinner daily
Phone: 212-243-7073
Web: www.blenheimhill.com
Prices: $$$

When a restaurant sources ingredients from its own farm in the Catskills, it clearly takes its farm-to-table ethos to heart. Even the décor here at Blenheim reflects this philosophy by way of distressed wood paneling and a style that is far more country-cool than precious. Service is eager and just as committed to the chef's mission of presenting pure ingredients with progressive elegance.

There may be no more genuine expression of this kitchen than the farm eggs, their yolk bright orange and fresh, set beside gently charred slices of hangar steak and fork-tender fingerlings. Silky foie gras torchon is finished tableside with refreshing tomato water; and dense, creamy *quadrello di bufala* with pistachio sable is a welcome stand-in for an arid bread pudding.

Blue Hill ✿

American XX

D1

75 Washington Pl. (bet. Sixth Ave. & Washington Sq. Park)

Subway: W 4 St - Wash Sq — Dinner nightly
Phone: 212-539-1776
Web: www.bluehillfarm.com
Prices: $$

Chef Dan Barber's iconic venue remains the paragon of farm-to-table dining in Manhattan by virtue of its seasonal lineup of pampered product. Everything on the menu is sourced from the Stone Barns Center (home to Blue Hill's Westchester farm) as well as a number of local producers.

Blue Hill's intimate space has been hosting a devoted foodie following for an impressive 15-some years, and service in this former speakeasy—where fresh flowers and candlelight cast a romantic spell—is nothing less than excellent.

The adept kitchen turns out contemporary cuisine, which in turn showcases the astounding quality stocked in the larder and allows vegetables to shine at all times. Asparagus spears are gently roasted to preserve their natural earthiness and coupled with vibrant beet yogurt as well as stinging nettles cream for a perfect balance in flavor. Then, moist striped bass draped atop fennel purée is decked with soft, sweet currants and toasted salty pine nuts to form a succulent and satisfying entrée. Familiar desserts highlight still more of the kitchen's best, as is the case with light and custard-y brioche bread pudding coupled with a quenelle of pleasantly bitter cocoa nib cream.

Blue Ribbon Bakery

Contemporary

B3

35 Downing St. (at Bedford St.)

Subway: Houston St — Lunch & dinner daily
Phone: 212-337-0404
Web: www.blueribbonrestaurants.com
Prices: $$$

The origin of this very New York bistro begins with brothers Eric and Bruce Bromberg discovering an abandoned brick oven in the basement of a bodega. This sparked the idea for a bakery, and in 1998 Blue Ribbon Bakery joined the duo's restaurant family. The sunny corner location is an inviting space, from the creaky wood-plank flooring to the heady aroma of freshly baked bread downstairs. Seats at the bar are a hot commodity for solo diners.

Opt for a dish that showcases the bakery's bread, such as the beef marrow with bacon bread and onion marmalade, a decadent appetizer that is just the right amount of sweet, salty, tart, and rich. Fried chicken with silky mashed potatoes and the matzoh ball soup both show Blue Ribbon's skill with comforting classics.

BONDST

XX

Japanese

C4

6 Bond St. (bet. Broadway & Lafayette St.)

Subway: Bleecker St — Dinner nightly
Phone: 212-777-2500
Web: www.bondstrestaurant.com
Prices: $$$

There's no denying that BONDST is still trendy after all these years; it even manages to stay sexy with sheer fabric panels, wispy tree branches, dark leathers, and private spaces. The three-story interior fills nightly with a very European crowd. (Romantics head downstairs; Bacchanalians go up.)

High quality fusion dishes may seem more crowd-pleasing than inventive, but are nonetheless delicious. Behind the wood sushi bar, the buzzing kitchen rolls mountains of maki, like paper-thin slices of pristine scallops balanced with a thick soy-jalapeño sauce and *yuzu kosho*. The *soba nomi* "risotto" is a wickedly rich and unmissable dish of glistening buckwheat soba folded with trout butter, king crab, and shrimp beneath a thatch of bonito flakes and gold paper.

Buvette

French

42 Grove St. (bet. Bedford & Bleecker Sts.)

Subway: Christopher St - Sheridan Sq — Lunch & dinner daily
Phone: 212-255-3590
Web: www.buvette.com
Prices: $$

Charming and proudly French, Buvette serves delicious Gallic plates to a notably svelte set. While carb addicts can barely fit into these wee seats, it's worth the squeeze for Chef Jody Williams' famously rustic cooking. Inside, everything comes alive with jazz and chatter. Instagrammable dishes take their cue from French classics and may feature crusty olive oil-drizzled country bread slathered with fluffy scrambled eggs, salty prosciutto, and nutty parmesan. Then await croissants—fresh, buttery, and flaky—served with sweet fruit preserves for a typically French and very decadent treat.

If not up the block at her other spot or across the pond in Paris, you may even find the chef herself holding meetings over a potent, frothy, and flawless cappuccino.

Cafe Cluny

Contemporary

284 W. 12th St. (at W. 4th St.)

Subway: 14 St - 8 Av — Lunch & dinner daily
Phone: 212-255-6900
Web: www.cafecluny.com
Prices: $$

This warm and cozy café flaunts its feminine persona with more than a touch of Village cool (and some occasional aloofness). There are ample windows for people-watching, or let your eyes wander to the botany drawings along the walls and bird sculptures decorating nooks.

The Cluny burger accompanied by golden fries is a sure-fire hit; it arrives topless to showcase the perfectly charred and glistening meat. Once fully dressed with your choice of bib lettuce, tomato, and red onion slices, it literally drips with goodness—maybe right onto those beautifully crisped fries. Come dessert, go for a simple and outrageously good plate of biscotti, served in a "jenga" arrangement of bittersweet chocolate and walnut or pistachio and anise flavors.

Carbone ✿

Italian XX

C4

181 Thompson St. (bet. Bleecker & Houston Sts.)

Subway: Houston St — Lunch Mon-Fri
Phone: 212-254-3000 — Dinner nightly
Web: www.carbonenewyork.com
Prices: $$$$

With nostalgia at the forefront, Carbone is plain gorgeous. While this big, bold, and beautiful ode to Italian-Americana comes alive at night under the low lights, lunch is equally admired among brash bankers with big appetites and Valentino-donning divas. That same sense of history pervades the entire space, which highlights plush banquettes, impressive ceramics, and glittering chandeliers. Was the striking tiled-floor inspired from a certain restaurant scene in *The Godfather*? Probably.

Mid-century classics are what this menu is all about, but exalted ingredients, skill, and presentations will excite even the most cynical savant. Stylish servers—who work the floor with a little flirt and lot of flair—remain in character while presenting top antipasti like crusty garlic bread, *soppressata*, and fresh, particularly divine olive oil-dunked mozzarella. A Caesar salad tossed tableside with carb-worthy croutons and gently pickled white anchovies hits the ball out of the park, while pale-yellow, ricotta-filled tortellini over an intensely rich and meaty ragù is a laudable delight.

Desserts like a proper cheesecake set atop a cookie-crumb base and laced with lemon curd is New York in all its old-school glory.

Crispo

Italian XX

B1

240 W. 14th St. (bet. Seventh & Eighth Aves.)

Subway: 14 St (Seventh Ave.) Dinner nightly
Phone: 212-229-1818
Web: www.crisporestaurant.com
Prices: $$

Convivial Crispo is a breath of fresh, rustic air. A protruding façade shelters its terrazza, while the back garden decked in smooth river stones feels warmer. The inside is dark and low-slung with brick walls, mosaic floors, and wrought-iron seats set around tiny, round tables. A plating station and kitchen reside in the back, as the full bar hums up front.

Courteous waiters attend to neatly arranged tables groaning beneath refined yet peasant-hearty food. Angel hair pasta is twirled around fresh seafood and then tossed in a fresh cherry tomato-cream sauce. Three tender lamb chops *scottaditto* (glistening with an herb-olive oil marinade) and served beside a goat cheese-polenta cake, could be sealed with a kiss of passion fruit or coconut sorbet.

Empellón Taqueria

Mexican XX

D1

230 W. 4th St. (at 10th St.)

Subway: Christopher St - Sheridan Sq Lunch Thu-Sat
Phone: 212-367-0999 Dinner nightly
Web: www.empellon.com
Prices: $$

Owning a primo Village corner, Alex Stupak has turned this casual taqueria into a totally happening spot—on Saturdays, the small place bursts with night owls from all over the city. Along with upbeat tunes and ever-flowing Mezcal, this restaurant has as much spirit as it does spice.

Of course, the flavor is abundant in dishes that can be terrifically delicious (if equally messy to eat). The *sopes* are a must, perhaps filled with enticingly salty and tasty refried black beans and a poached quail egg. Outrageously good queso melts Chihuahua cheese with any of the four toppings, especially the green chorizo, for pure gooey pleasure. Don't miss house salsas like smoked cashew or tomatillo-chipotle, even if it means paying extra as they're worth every penny!

EN Japanese Brasserie

Japanese XxX

B3

435 Hudson St. (at Leroy St.)

Subway: Houston St — Lunch & dinner daily
Phone: 212-647-9196
Web: www.enjb.com
Prices: $$$

EN doesn't pander to the spicy tuna-loving set, but effectively pays homage to highly seasonal Japanese cooking. In such simple and delicate food, flawless execution is a must so don't be hesitant to ask for a recommendation. The knowledgeable and genuine servers are happy to offer their opinion on items, be it the ground Kurobuta pork mixed with *natto*; or gently fried *agedashi* tofu floating in a thick, glossy dashi with mushrooms. Silken *chawanmushi* in a glazed stone cup is paired with kernels of charred corn for a delightful bit of bite, while Aburi sea trout is fanned sashimi-style across a striking onyx plate.

Lofty ceilings, large windows, and a glass wall lined with shelves of sake attract a young, professional, and fashionable clientele.

Extra Virgin

Mediterranean 

B2

259 W. 4th St. (at Perry St.)

Subway: Christopher St - Sheridan Sq — Lunch Tue – Sun, Dinner nightly
Phone: 212-691-9359
Web: www.extravirginrestaurant.com
Prices: $$

Consistently good with an easygoing attitude, this longstanding neighborhood gem is a hit with everyone from young families and ladies-who-brunch, to dog-owners enjoying sidewalk seating. Fresh flowers, blue-velvet barstools, and canvas paintings make it the perfect fusion of casual and classy; rock music lightens the mood.

Pristine olive oils march from the kitchen as if to whet the appetite for a parade of Mediterranean classics to pair with food-friendly Italian wines. Start with butternut squash ravioli bathed in brown butter-mascarpone sauce, or the beautifully textured halibut on herbed tomato carpaccio for an instant return to summer. Roasted Brussels sprouts combine with caramelized apples to cut the enticing richness of fatty pancetta.

Fedora

Contemporary XX

239 W. 4th St. (bet. Charles & 10th Sts.)

Subway: Christopher St - Sheridan Sq — Dinner nightly
Phone: 646-449-9336
Web: www.fedoranyc.com
Prices: $$

An ode to the New York old guard, Fedora still attracts the creative, the moneyed and the young. It's a sort of dreamlike supper club where well-crafted cocktails flow into endless conversations, the words absorbed into the crevices of the original carved wooden bar as they have for generations. No longer a renowned literati haunt, Fedora remains an attractive homage to the Village of yore.

Tuck your bag and coat into the cubby above the banquette and set off on an adventure in contemporary cuisine, one that mixes barbecue cream with smoked salmon and highlights the distinctive wines of Jura. This builds to the excellent and gargantuan crispy duck with perfectly lacquered skin accented by a date-barbecue sauce that's pure hedonistic inspiration.

Gato

Mediterranean 

324 Lafayette St. (bet. Bleecker & Houston Sts.)

Subway: Bleecker St. — Dinner nightly
Phone: 212-334-6400
Web: www.gatonyc.com
Prices: $$

It's been nearly a decade since Bobby Flay opened a restaurant in NY, and Gato has the famed chef's recipe down. With soaring arched brick ceilings, exposed brass fixtures, and views of Lafayette Street, this hip hangout exudes a slick downtown sensibility.

In fact, the cozy lounge and massive wooden bar are so cool, you may never make it to the dining room—which is fine, because the beautifully composed small plates pack plenty of flavor. Case in point: quail egg and creamy uni atop a tender artichoke on a plate dressed up with dots of oils and shellfish reduction. Lamb tenderloin needs hardly any marinade thanks to the top-quality meat, a rich pink center, and salsa verde; while smoky eggplant balances earthy and sweet with Manchego and balsamic vinegar.

Good

American XX

B2

89 Greenwich Ave. (bet. Bank & 12th Sts.)

Subway: 14 St - 8 Av
Phone: 212-691-8080
Web: www.goodrestaurantnyc.com
Prices: $$

Lunch Tue – Sun
Dinner nightly

Creamy walls and lime green wainscoting frame this cozy and comfortable little slice of Americana that has been pleasing Greenwich Village residents since 2000. Good also happens to be great for date night—the intimate bar pours top-shelf spirits and the muted dining room is dressed with crisp white linens. Everything has a certain serenity, even when it's bubbling at happy hour.

Chef/owner Steven J. Picker's menu puts his own signature on tempting seasonal cooking. Beautifully seared squid and Japanese eggplant grilled until silky are adorned with summer beans, cherry tomatoes, and mint. Turkey scallopini is crisp and light, set atop a bed of frisée, shaved celery, and *ricotta salata*. Long live the tortilla-crusted, jalapeño-kicked mac and cheese!

Gradisca

Italian XX

C2

126 W. 13th St. (bet. Sixth & Seventh Aves.)

Subway: 14 St (Seventh Ave.)
Phone: 212-691-4886
Web: www.gradiscanyc.com
Prices: $$

Dinner nightly

If one could choose an Italian mother, it would be *"mamma,"* the pasta maker at Gradisca. Walking into this quaint brownstone is like taking a step into a trattoria in Emila Romagna, complete with Fellini posters, napkin-covered bread baskets, and a smiling bartender pouring a glass of violet-scented Sangiovese.

Pasta plays front and center here and is luckily always handmade. Gorgeous, rose-shaped tortellini are stuffed with mounds of *prosciutto* and spinach, before being finished by a perfect plum tomato sauce. *Secondi* are also a must and may include the sublime *cotoletta alla Bolognese*, a perfectly breaded and pan-fried free-range chicken cutlet topped with a creamy truffle-béchamel sauce and served with a warm spinach *budino*.

Gotham Bar and Grill ✿

American XXX

D2

12 E. 12th St. (bet. Fifth Ave. & University Pl.)

Subway: 14 St - Union Sq
Phone: 212-620-4020
Web: www.gothambarandgrill.com
Prices: **$$$**

Lunch Mon – Fri
Dinner nightly

Warm, personable, and genuine, Gotham Bar and Grill has everything a New York restaurant needs to stand the test of time. Inside, find towering floral arrangements and lofty ceilings hung with massive fabric-draped fixtures, which soften the room's appearance. The interior is vast, but the sunken dining area, elevated bar, and smartly divided room feel more classic than overdone. The service team exemplifies on-the-ball excellence.

This kitchen's distinctive American seasonal cooking is in clear balance from start to finish. Begin with the simple-sounding tuna tartare combining chopped yellowfin and shiso surrounded by Japanese cucumber, enlivened with miso-ginger vinaigrette. Move on to explore seasonal risotto, showcasing wintery mushrooms or perhaps a summery feast of sweet shrimp, chives, and touch of tomato. Batter-fried soft-shell crabs are a feat of technical perfection, with body and crisped legs set over sautéed vegetables and a light citrus-soy reduction. Desserts alone are worth a visit, especially to indulge in the famously dense chocolate cake, served warm with a scoop of luscious salted-almond ice cream and cracked cocoa nibs.

The "greenmarket" prix-fixe lunch offers great value and quality.

Hakata Tonton

Japanese

61 Grove St. (bet. Bleecker St. & Seventh Ave. South)

Subway: Christopher St - Sheridan Sq — Dinner nightly
Phone: 212-242-3699
Web: N/A
Prices: $$

The food at this delicious West Village hot spot is specific to the Hakata region of Japan, an area that specializes in all kinds of pork parts like ears, feet, and tongue—and to secure a spot in the popular dining room, you should really call in a reservation or be prepared to wait. If the unusual menu and bland interior have you second-guessing yourself, have faith as the food will put those fears to rest soon enough.

Kick things off with their spicy namesake hot pot, bubbling with plump ramen noodles, tender dumplings, bright vegetables, rich Berkshire pork belly and pigs feet. Then move on to mouthwatering grilled pig ears and foot served with thinly sliced scallions and ginger; or (for the bravest souls) their signature *motsu* (intestine) hot pot.

Hecho en Dumbo

Mexican

354 Bowery (bet. 4th & Great Jones Sts.)

Subway: Bleecker St — Lunch Sat – Sun
Phone: 212-937-4245 — Dinner nightly
Web: www.hechoendumbo.com
Prices: $$

Sitting towards the top of NYC's rapidly improving Mexican food scene is Chef and Mexico City native Daniel Mena's spirited cantina. Venture through the exposed brick, salvaged wood, classically downtown dining room to peek at the open kitchen and counter where the tasting menu is offered (to those who reserve in advance).

A trio of excellent salsas and warm tortilla chips is a mouthwatering beginning to this authentic cooking. Indulge in a hearty, alder wood-smoked feast for two in the *parillada Yucateca,* featuring a gnaw-worthy Berkshire pork chop and 14-day dry-aged NY strip with warm Edam cheese topped in olives, capers, and puréed almonds. Mexican traditions shine in cinnamon-infused *capirotada* bread pudding with coconut crème anglaise.

Il Buco

Italian 

D4

47 Bond St. (bet. Bowery & Lafayette St.)

Subway: Bleecker St — Lunch Mon – Sat
Phone: 212-533-1932 — Dinner nightly
Web: www.ilbuco.com
Prices: $$

Il Buco is a *molto* charming amalgam of antique knickknacks, porcelain dishes, and polished copper pots. The hardest seats to nab are found downstairs, but the rustic dining room remains as inviting as ever, with tables full of vittles and *vino*. The kitchen showcases meticulously sourced ingredients that sing the praises of regional Italian know-how, like a mound of arugula, petite mustards, and chrysanthemum greens that top a rather tiny veal Milanese cooked to moist perfection. Thick ribbons of toothsome homemade tagliatelle tossed with myriad mushrooms, melted leeks, and pecorino emits a lovely aroma, befitting this unique and pretty pearl. Meanwhile, the porchetta—served once a year as a sort of sidewalk celebration—is still one of the best in town.

Il Buco Alimentari e Vineria

D4

53 Great Jones St. (bet. Bowery & Lafayette St.)

Subway: Bleecker St — Lunch & dinner daily
Phone: 212-837-2622
Web: www.ilbucovineria.com
Prices: $$

This is the kind of cooking and scene that makes us all wish we were Italian. Start with a stroll through the *alimentari* (located up front) to grab some pickled beans and serious cheeses. Then move on to the rustic dining area upstairs, which oozes warmth and comfort. Note the meticulously conceived copper roof, open kitchen, and other decorative accents that set a picturesque backdrop for a delicious meal.

The food here is authoritative and tasty, with a nice representation of Italian cooking from breakfast through dinner. The porchetta *panino* is timeless, amazing, and vies to be the finest around. Skillfully crafted homemade pasta includes textbook-perfect *bucatini cacio e pepe*. Finish with an *affogato*, topping a scoop of vanilla gelato with hot espresso.

I Sodi

Italian XX

105 Christopher St. (bet. Bleecker & Hudson Sts.)

Subway: Christopher St - Sheridan Sq — Dinner nightly
Phone: 212-414-5774
Web: www.isodinyc.com
Prices: $$

Manhattan has classic Italian and new Italian, but not many *thoughtful* Italian restaurants. Tuscan native Rita Sodi is out to change that with this trattoria. She consciously selected every aspect of the design, from the heavy linen napkins to the thick, striated glass windows that hide the modern space from the marauding groups of young people on Bleecker.

Inside this oasis, Negronis prep palates for al dente rigatoni and hearty, meat-focused dishes like the *coniglio in porchetta*. This exceptional rabbit preparation combines bacon-wrapped loin with a sweet wine- rosemary- and garlic-sauce. The herbal quality of such savoriness brings out the almost austere nature of the lean rabbit, showing how truly intuitive and innovative Italian cooking can be.

Joseph Leonard

170 Waverly Pl. (at Grove St.)

Subway: Christopher St - Sheridan Sq — Lunch & dinner daily
Phone: 646-429-8383
Web: www.josephleonard.com
Prices: $$

No bigger than your average studio apartment, Joseph Leonard has a big personality and is insanely popular for good reason. From the antique mirrors to the nightly crowds, this contemporary American has nailed the heart and soul of Greenwich Village to become a regular spot for sipping well-sourced wines with friends and chomping down on wonderfully crisp rock shrimp fritters.

The recognizable dishes are expertly prepared, fueled by top-notch ingredients and a kitchen that knows how to handle a pan-roasted chicken—arriving crisp-skinned and deliciously tender. Even humble Brussels sprouts get special treatment with a kick of *sriracha*. Finish it all off with monkey bread made with eggy-buttery brioche and a brilliantly subtle hint of maple.

Kesté Pizza & Vino

Pizza

D2

271 Bleecker St. (bet. Cornelia & Jones Sts.)

Subway: W 4 St - Wash Sq
Lunch & dinner daily
Phone: 212-243-1500
Web: www.kestepizzeria.com
Prices:

A runaway success since day one, Kesté takes the craft of making Neapolitan-style pizza to epic heights. *Pizzaiolo* Roberto Caporuscio first opened and established Kesté's reputation, even though he has now handed over this custom-built, wood-fired, volcanic stone *forno* to his very capable daughter, Giorgia.

Pizzas may be listed under two headings, but every pie (including gluten-free) is built upon a nicely salted, faintly tangy, gorgeously puffy crust with a delicately charred *cornicione*. Pizza *speciale* feature creative ingredients like pistachio pesto or butternut squash purée; while *pizze rosse* are topped with excellent homemade mozzarella, imported tomatoes, and an array of meat or vegetables. Weekday lunches showcase panini.

Kiin Thai

Thai

C3

36 E. 8th St. (bet. Greene St. & University Pl.)

Subway: 8 St - NYC
Lunch & dinner daily
Phone: 212-529-2363
Web: www.kiinthaieatery.com
Prices: $$

This sleek new Thai spot arrives on the heels of its popular sister restaurant, Somtum Der. Kiin Thai cuts an impressive figure design-wise, with its lofty ceilings, whitewashed walls and light-filled interior. Meanwhile, its equally impressive kitchen pushes out precise renditions of central and northern Thai dishes.

Don't miss the *khao soi,* a gorgeous orange-hued curry featuring chewy noodles, tender braised chicken, hard-boiled egg, and the requisite condiments ready to amp the dish up to an incendiary level. Fish *hor mok,* a custardy curry tucked with striped sea bass, coconut milk, and duck eggs, topped with herbs and Kaffir lime is silky, while the excellent *hor nueng gai* with chicken, Thai eggplant, rice, and herbs is tenderly steamed in banana leaf.

Lafayette

French XX

D4

380 Lafayette St. (at Great Jones St.)

Subway: Bleecker St
Lunch & dinner daily
Phone: 212-533-3000
Web: www.lafayetteny.com
Prices: $$

Chef Andrew Carmellini's homage to French cuisine lures patrons inside with its attractive baked-goods counter up front lined with organic breads and tempting pastries. From here, the room unfolds into a series of seductive spaces where one finds a rotisserie oven spinning bronzed birds, a backlit bar with an amber glow, and columns clad in warm honey and blue tile.

The cooking is nothing short of stellar, right from that Niçoise salad with thick slices of rare tuna, briny black olives, barely poached green beans, soft potatoes, and hard-boiled egg, to a local fillet of trout finished with mustard sauce and well-dressed frisée salad. Desserts are borderline irresistible, especially the mille-feuille Lafayette with chocolate cremeux and caramel-poached pear.

L'Artusi

Italian XX

B3

228 W. 10th St. (bet. Bleecker & Hudson Sts.)

Subway: Christopher St - Sheridan Sq
Lunch Sun
Phone: 212-255-5757
Dinner nightly
Web: www.lartusi.com
Prices: $$

This polished, airy West Village charmer is a magnet for beautiful people—or maybe it's just that everyone looks gorgeous in L'Artusi's romantically lit room, divvied up into three dining options and a quiet mezzanine, alongside its more traditional dining area. A semi-open kitchen, polished and gleaming with stainless steel, pushes out wickedly good Italian dishes like tender potato gnocchi in a rabbit cacciatore, laced with garlic, sweet tomato, rosemary and sage; or perfectly charred octopus paired with creamy potatoes spiked with chilies, olives and savory pancetta.

Polish that off with a drink from their generous list of *aperitivi* or fantastic selection of wines by the glass, and you'll be feeling quite beautiful yourself by dinner's end.

Las Ramblas

D1

170 W. 4th St. (bet. Cornelia & Jones Sts.)

Subway: Christopher St - Sheridan Sq
Phone: 646-415-7924
Web: N/A
Prices: ⚭

Lunch Sat – Sun
Dinner nightly

Sandwiched among a throng of attention-seeking storefronts, mighty little Las Ramblas is easy to spot, just look for the crowd of happy, munching faces. The scene spills out onto the sidewalk when the weather allows.

Named for Barcelona's historic commercial thoroughfare, Las Ramblas is a tapas treat. A copper-plated bar and collection of tiny tables provide a perch for snacking on an array of earnestly prepared items. Check out the wall-mounted blackboard for *especiales*. Bring friends (it's that kind of place) to fully explore the menu which serves up delights such as succulent head-on prawns roasted in a terra-cotta dish and sauced with cava vinegar, ginger, and basil; or béchamel creamed spinach topped by a molten cap of Mahón cheese.

Left Bank

B2 — Contemporary

117 Perry St. (at Greenwich St.)

Subway: Christopher St - Sheridan Sq
Phone: 212-727-1170
Web: www.leftbanknewyork.com
Prices: $$

Dinner nightly

Left Bank may have plenty of local competition, but few have the attentive and considerate service combined with such a lively bar scene. With its faux-farmhouse décor and rather bucolic corner location, it is a go-to neighborhood haunt. Happy hour specials bring them in, but the bar bites make them stay.

Every dish on the menu is pleasing, from the buttery lobster puffs perched on champagne cream to the perfectly crafted Mongolian dumplings, full of spicy lamb, cabbage, and onion with a cool soy-lime dipping sauce. The lovely farfalle with fresh favas, sunchoke, spring onion, and chili is bound by a sprinkling of nutty *Parmigiano*. Top it off with deliciously simple desserts, like a wedge of ricotta cheesecake and a properly poached Bosc pear.

Le Gigot

French

D2

18 Cornelia St. (bet. Bleecker & W. 4th Sts.)

Subway: W 4 St - Wash Sq
Phone: 212-627-3737
Web: www.legigotrestaurant.com
Prices: **$$**

Lunch & dinner Tue – Sun

As classically beautiful and intricate as the *Metro* signs of Paris, this *petit resto* is dedicated to honoring The City of Light. Modeled after the Left Bank bistro Polidor, the iconic interior features parquet floors, zinc-topped tables, and antique mirrored walls. The room fills quickly with regulars; the dedicated staff graciously greets most by name.

The food is equally beloved, with such classics as generous charcuterie platters that include sausage, duck rillettes, silky smooth chicken liver, and hearty country pâtés. The excellent boeuf Bourguignon is a comforting dish of braised beef cubes, carrots, potatoes, button mushrooms, sweet shallots, and plenty of bacon. Come dessert, tarte Tatin smells of apples and heaven (but with extra butter).

Le Philosophe

French 

D4

55 Bond St. (bet. Bowery & Lafayette St.)

Subway: Bleecker St
Phone: 212-388-0038
Web: www.lephilosophe.us
Prices: **$$**

Lunch Sat – Sun
Dinner nightly

With its bustling open kitchen and Parisian den good looks—think polished wood banquettes, bistro chalkboards and walls lined with black-and-white portraits of philosophers—Le Philosophe cuts a stylish figure. It's the kind of wonderful, low-key spot that begs you to become a regular: vibrant, casual and polished, with the kind of beer list you get excited about and a menu that (true to the restaurant's moniker) stops to make you think.

Dinner might begin with *blanquette de veau*, tender, perfectly cooked veal in a mouthwatering white sauce, surrounded by a lovely *jardinière* of vegetables and served with fragrant white rice. And then finish with a luscious crêpe Suzette, laced with a delicious caramel-orange drizzle and scoop of creamy vanilla ice cream.

The Little Owl

American

90 Bedford St. (at Grove St.)

Subway: Christopher St - Sheridan Sq
Lunch & dinner daily
Phone: 212-741-4695
Web: www.thelittleowlnyc.com
Prices: $$

Perched on a winsome corner of the West Village, Chef Joey Campanaro's The Little Owl continues to hold a dear place in the hearts of diners near and far who appreciate that simple food and great food can be one and the same. The broccoli soup (a pure, silky purée enriched with a trace of cream and crowned by a crouton of bubbling, aged cheddar) is among the best examples of this.

The small corner room is quaint and despite this establishment's popularity, the service team is completely attitude-free. The wee kitchen is on display, and the focused crew turns out a rousing roster of preparations that may bear an affinity for Mediterranean cuisine such as seared cod with *bagna cauda* vinaigrette, and gravy meatball sliders, a hands-down house specialty.

Lupa

Italian

170 Thompson St. (bet. Bleecker & Houston Sts.)

Subway: W 4 St - Wash Sq
Lunch & dinner daily
Phone: 212-982-5089
Web: www.luparestaurant.com
Prices: $$

One of the best places for a solid plate of pasta, Lupa fits in snugly between the fire escape-clad walk-ups and charming boutiques along these streets. A modestly decorated spot named for the she-wolf who raised Romulus and Remus, this gem carries an air of relaxed sophistication. It's where neighbors can gather for polite conversation over quartinos of Ligurian wine or the massive collection of *amari*.

If it's a lovely place to sit, it's a stellar place to dine. Textbook-perfect pasta shines here, with luscious *bucatini all' amatriciana* earning its mark among Lazio classics as well as the beguilingly simple yet stunning *cacio e pepe*. Entrées may sometimes miss the mark, but dessert more than makes up for it—try the unique cardamom panna cotta.

Malaparte

Italian

753 Washington St. (at Bethune St.)

Subway: 14 St - 8 Av
Lunch & dinner daily
Phone: 212-255-2122
Web: www.malapartenyc.com
Prices: $$

Tucked into one of those idyllic, tree-lined West Village corners that looks straight off a movie set, Malaparte is the kind of cozy, romantic spot you need in your date night rolodex. Bare wood tables; large, framed windows for people-watching; low lighting; and exposed brick walls all lend a hand in creating that perfect *osteria* vibe.

As if that weren't enough to sustain a loyal following, Malaparte takes its home-style Italian cooking to the next level. Try one of the excellent pizza specials; the *dadi di tonno scottato*, a dish of wildly fresh seared tuna tossed in avocado-sesame dressing; the bang-on lasagna Bolognese, a silky version of this classic dish boasting an exquisitely good veal and pork ragù; or the melt-in-your-mouth chocolate mousse.

Margaux

Mediterranean

5 W. 8th St. (bet. Fifth & Sixth Aves.)

Subway: W 4 St - Wash Sq
Lunch & dinner daily
Phone: 212-321-0111
Web: www.margauxnyc.com
Prices: $$

Calling all pretty young things: the fashionable Marlton Hotel is now home to one of the best bar-cum-restaurants around Washington Sq. Park. Walk through its posh lobby, past the sleek espresso station and massive wooden bar (complete with brass footrests—it's that kind of place), to enter Margaux, a 20th century-inspired Parisian bistro. The elegant, well-curated décor includes molded ceilings and floral tiles imported from Argentina, but you'll want to make a beeline for the dreamy, skylight-covered garden room.

Settle in and order an innovative cocktail like the Artichoke Tea, a blend of Cynar, tea syrup, lemon, and cava, as well as a plate of juicy rotisserie chicken with smashed sweet potatoes, tangy *urfa biber* pepper, and powerful green *harissa*.

Market Table

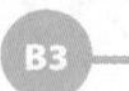

American XX

B3

54 Carmine St. (at Bedford St.)

Subway: W 4 St - Wash Sq

Phone: 212-255-2100

Web: www.markettablenyc.com

Prices: $$

Lunch & dinner daily

Think of this bright little corner as the template for a perfect neighborhood restaurant—one that everyone dreams of having nearby. The vibe is unpretentious yet cool, with a young, attentive service staff. The windowed room feels barnyard-chic, with a chalkboard wall listing wine and cheese offerings beneath reclaimed ceiling beams.

The menu is stocked with the kind of dishes that never disappoint—think bucatini tossed with fried eggplant and creamy burrata in a chunky tomato sauce. The kitchen's knack for making simple food vivid is clear in the impeccably cooked strip loin, served with carrots, haricots verts, and shishitos brought together with smoked chili "pesto."

The Clam, an equally delicious and seafood-focused sibling, is located a few blocks away.

Mary's Fish Camp

Seafood X

B2

64 Charles St. (at W. 4th St.)

Subway: Christopher St - Sheridan Sq

Phone: 646-486-2185

Web: www.marysfishcamp.com

Prices: $$

Lunch daily
Dinner Mon – Sat

This West Village seafood shack is much more than just a destination for lobster rolls. Located on an irresistibly cute corner with large windows, Mary's Fish Camp tempts with creative daily specials scrawled on a chalkboard, sweet and briny raw offerings, and nostalgic desserts like hot fudge sundaes. Crowds pack into the curving stainless steel counter while white, lazy fans spin overhead.

The summery space offers lots of choice, but the lobster roll should not be overlooked. A toasted bun is overflowing with hunks of tender, sweet meat dressed in the perfect proportion of mayonnaise and lemon juice, with a mountain of shoestring fries on the side. Begin the meal with spicy Key West conch chowder and then end with a slice of Americana—banana cream pie.

Mas (farmhouse)

Contemporary XxX

39 Downing St. (bet. Bedford & Varick Sts.)

Subway: Houston St
Phone: 212-255-1790
Web: www.masfarmhouse.com
Prices: $$$

Dinner nightly

Tucked away on Bedford Street, Mas (farmhouse) proves why restaurant design matters as much as the menu when creating a complete sensory experience. Carefully selected accents—weathered wood beams, hand-stitched pillows, antique mother-of-pearl napkin rings—bring to life a modern Provençal farmhouse, where rusticity, hospitality and sophistication play in perfect harmony with the culinary arts.

Poached shrimp floats in an apple-ginger bath topped with radish, for a cooling yet spicy amuse-bouche to arouse the appetite. This may be followed by delicate fillets of Long Island fluke served over hearts of palm with smoky and earthy shiitake mushrooms. That attention to detail and mouth-filling flavor keeps you engaged, charmed, and absolutely satisfied.

Miss Lily's

Jamaican

132 W. Houston St. (at Sullivan St.)

Subway: Houston St
Phone: 646-588-5375
Web: www.misslilysnyc.com
Prices: $$

Lunch Sat – Sun
Dinner nightly

Authentic Jamaican flavors and thumping reggae go hand-in-hand amid Miss Lily's bright orange booths, retro artifacts, and Formica-topped tables. Wide-open windows overlooking buzzy Houston Street merely add to the allure. A well-stocked bar and bins filled with produce set the mood for enjoyable classics brought to you at the hands of glam servers.

Start with jerk chicken that is insanely moist yet nearly black with intense spices, served with Scotch bonnet sauce that will have your mouth tingling for hours. Then cool down with Melvin's "body good" salad tossing kale, radish, celery, and apples in a citrus-ginger vinaigrette. From the Jamaican Sampler—think curry coat, oxtail stew, and callaloo—to a boozy rum cake, this Caribbean queen reigns supreme.

Minetta Tavern

Gastropub

113 MacDougal St. (at Minetta Ln.)

Subway: W 4 St - Wash Sq
Phone: 212-475-3850
Web: www.minettatavernny.com
Prices: **$$$**

Lunch Wed – Sun
Dinner nightly

While this 1937 setting has been restored and refreshed, nothing here changes and that is its beauty. This quintessential New York tavern is still surrounded by dark wood, checkerboard tiled floors, and those framed caricatures. The astute service team handles the crowds and energy as well as ever—they even don the same white-aproned livery seen in *Mad Men*. It's that kind of place.

The menu's dedication to bistro classics and New York steakhouse fare ensure its continued longevity. A thick slice of their mosaic-like terrine of oxtail, poached leek, and carrot surrounding a foie gras center is timelessly good. Those warm platters of juicy, tender, appetizingly charred New York strip steaks propped up against a bouquet of peppery watercress shine with simple, perfect flavor. An oval cast-iron pan of slow-cooked pork shank is rendered tender, luscious, and dark as a prune. Piping-hot *pommes aligot* are just what mashed potatoes were always meant to be: cheesy, creamy, and obscenely decadent.

Velvety bittersweet chocolate soufflés and towering wedges of bright white coconut cakes stacked with three layers of pastry cream, tart crème fraîche, and coconut shavings are brazen crowd-pleasers.

Morandi

Italian XX

211 Waverly Pl. (bet. Charles St. & Seventh Ave. South)

Subway: 14 St (Seventh Ave.)
Lunch & dinner daily
Phone: 212-627-7575
Web: www.morandiny.com
Prices: **$$$**

From first sight, this prominent West Village location does much to resemble a farmhouse or cantina. Wood panels, antique tiles, tin ceilings, and shelves displaying straw-covered bottles of Chianti conjure an American's idyllic dream of Italy. The food is a more genuine reflection.

Decadent beginnings might include tart and very crisp fried olives stuffed with meat. Plates of fried artichokes brightened with preserved lemon are unmissable, especially when paired with a choice of hand-stretched focaccia. Long twists of *busiate al ragù di pesce spada* are tossed with swordfish and excellent spicy almond pesto. Nightly specials showcase the likes of *vitello alla Milanese* with a crust so perfect and piping-hot, that it threatens to shatter with a fork.

Murray's Cheese Bar

American XX

264 Bleecker St. (bet. Leroy & Morton Sts.)

Subway: W 4 St - Wash Sq
Lunch Tue – Sun
Dinner nightly
Phone: 646-476-8882
Web: www.murrayscheesebar.com
Prices: **$$**

A turophile's dream come true, this cheese bar is built for people who just want to eat really amazing cheese. The upscale space, decked with subway tiles, whitewashed wood tables, and lacquered chairs, is a natural extension of neighboring Murray's Cheese, the famed Greenwich Village purveyor of phenomenal dairy products.

With a category to suit every craving (fresh, soft-ripened, washed-rind, semi-firm, and blue) the bar's extensive menu has it all, from buttery Pyrénéese Brebis to funky and heady gorgonzola *cremificato*. For a truly indulgent meal, add a glass of wine (*nebbiolo* with that rich gorgonzola), *salumi* (from American purveyors like D'Artagnan and Olli), slow-simmered lamb meatballs, and phenomenal cheeses served with sweet apricot compote.

Pagani

Italian

289 Bleecker St. (at Seventh Ave. South)

Subway: Christopher St - Sheridan Sq — Lunch & dinner daily
Phone: 212-488-5800
Web: www.paganinyc.com
Prices: $$

With witty cocktails, cured meats, and *rustico nuovo* décor, Pagani brings an extra dose of Italian charm to Bleecker Street, and a good one at that. Flauting a vibrant scene of locals guzzling indigenous Italian wines and Averna-steeped drinks, this brainchild of Massimo Lusardi targets a younger brood where authenticity and creativity go hand-in-hand.

His family may own several other restaurants, but sizeable portions of house-made pasta with updated embellishments (think: *montasio* cheese topping a decadent ragù of veal and pork) highlight balance and excellence. Just as veal shoulder arrives unbelievably fragrant and tender with herb-rubbed, toasted bread; rigatoni with braised rabbit and sweet carrots feel like a match made in culinary heaven.

Panca

92 Seventh Ave. South (bet. Bleecker & Grove Sts.)

Subway: Christopher St - Sheridan Sq — Lunch & dinner daily
Phone: 212-488-3900
Web: www.pancany.com
Prices: $$

First thing's first: go to the impressive wood bar lined with bottles of pisco and grab a handful of the wickedly good roasted Peruvian corn. Then settle into the rather lively and colorful dining room, or just ogle at the many *cebiche* options on the menu, another hallmark of the cuisine. If you choose to sit outside, be prepared to give up the interior's cantina-like vibe.

Explore the *tiradito* (think of it like *cebiche's* cousin), which highlight sashimi-like cuts of seafood like fluke, shrimp, and octopus served on a duo of peppery *aji amarillo* or *rocoto* sauces. Panca gives equal honor to those other pillars of its national cuisine, serving a cilantro-stewed chicken with pitch-perfect garlic rice and potatoes topped with salsa *criolla*.

Paradou

French

B1

8 Little W. 12th St. (bet. Greenwich & Washington Sts.)

Subway: 14 St - 8 Av — Lunch Sat – Sun
Phone: 212-463-8345 — Dinner Tue – Sun
Web: www.paradounyc.com
Prices: $$

For a restaurant that refuses to take itself too seriously, the crowd-pleasing bistro cuisine here is no joke. At home along a cobblestoned street in the clubby Meatpacking District, Paradou offers a handful of tables and a stocked bar. Move past the vintage French liquor ads and down a brick-lined hallway to find a year-round back garden outfitted with chandeliers, a high glass roof, and tables crafted from vintage wine crates.

The menu's foundation is Provençal cooking, but its lighthearted spirit feels free to stray. Begin with Amish bacon "crack"—chili-spiked bacon jerky made from Pennsylvania Amish pigs. The duck breast is expertly seared, with crisp skin and a pink center. Don't skip the springy crêpes, filled with Nutella and ripe bananas.

Pearl Oyster Bar

Seafood

D2

18 Cornelia St. (bet. Bleecker & W. 4th Sts.)

Subway: W 4 St - Wash Sq — Lunch Mon – Fri
Phone: 212-691-8211 — Dinner Mon – Sat
Web: www.pearloysterbar.com
Prices: $$

It's not hard to find a lobster roll in this city, and for that we can thank Rebecca Charles. This seafood institution—inspired by Charles' childhood summers spent in Maine—has been stuffing sweet lobster meat into split-top rolls since 1997. The two-room setting offers a choice: counter seating or table service. Wood furnishings and white walls are low-key; beachy memorabilia perks up the space.

Start the meal by slurping your way through a classic chilled shellfish platter before tucking into that signature lobster roll, served alongside a tower of shoestring fries. The kitchen shines in daily specials, too, such as the grilled lobster served with corn pudding or pan-roasted wild bass. A hot fudge sundae is an appropriately nostalgic finish.

Perilla

Contemporary XX

D1

9 Jones St. (bet. Bleecker & W. 4th Sts.)

Subway: W 4 St - Wash Sq
Phone: 212-929-6868
Web: www.perillanyc.com
Prices: $$

Lunch Sat – Sun
Dinner nightly

Low-key, casual, and classic, Perilla is simply a comfortable place to be—solo diners seek out the welcoming bar. Observe that the designer zebrawood tables are signed on the edge and then understand this place's level of care and dedication to detail. The subdued lighting, plush banquettes, and cream-colored walls lend a calm vibe despite the clubby music.

The kitchen combines quality ingredients with experimental flair, resulting in dishes that are pleasing but sometimes overly complex. Sample pastas like house-made *garganelli* with smoky *guanciale*, paprika, spring onion, piney-crunchy fiddlehead fern, and sweet octopus. The Long Island duck breast is cooked to gorgeous pink and served with roasted beets and savory baklava layering duck confit and greens.

Perla

Italian 

C3

24 Minetta Ln. (bet. MacDougal St. & Sixth Ave.)

Subway: W 4 St - Wash Sq
Phone: 212-933-1824
Web: www.perlanyc.com
Prices: $$

Dinner nightly

This rustic little Minetta Lane charmer is packed to the gills most nights of the week, but it comes by its popularity honestly. The ingredients are all in place: a stylish interior; a genuinely likable staff; an unfussy menu with well-sourced ingredients and detailed execution. What's not to love here?

Fresh from a face-lift, Perla now offers four different family-style dishes, serving multiple people at reasonable price points. Other menu highlights include plump Mediterranean sardines in a tomato sauce, pocked with tender braised tripe, salty black olives and fennel; a near-perfect rendition of *bucatini cacio e pepe*; and a succulent roast pork sandwich, fragrant with fennel seeds, and served with layers of garlicky broccoli rabe, *giardiniera*, and provolone.

Perry Street

Contemporary 

176 Perry St. (at West St.)

Subway: Christopher St - Sheridan Sq — Lunch & dinner daily
Phone: 212-352-1900
Web: www.perrystrestaurant.com
Prices: $$

All New York gastronauts will be familiar with the Vongerichten name but it's actually Jean-Georges' son Cédric who heads up the kitchen here.

The restaurant is on the first floor of the Richard Meier Towers and, if you stretch, you can just about see the Hudson outside. The room is bright, open, and contemporary although the anodyne muzak suggests a lack of faith in their customers' ability to create their own atmosphere or an acknowledgment of the room's lack of warmth.

The influences on the food are largely French and American with the occasional Asian note. The combinations on the plate are nothing too challenging; dishes are colourful; and the flavors pronounced. The great value lunch menu should make it far busier during the day than it is.

The Place

American 

310 W. 4th St. (bet. Bank & 12th Sts.)

Subway: 14 St - 8 Av — Lunch Sat – Sun
Phone: 212-924-2711 — Dinner nightly
Web: www.theplaceny.com
Prices: $$

Set deep within the West Village, The Place is the kind of cozy, grotto-style den that makes you feel all grown-up. Rendezvous-like, guests climb below street level to find a bar aglow with flickering votive candles. Wander back a bit, and you'll find rustic beams and white tablecloth seating; two outdoor terraces beckon when the sun shines.

The guileless name of this "place" and timeless look of its century-old setting is nicely juxtaposed by a wholly American menu that roams from east to west: duck confit-filled parcels with grain mustard and braised red cabbage is a lovely autumnal treat, while entrées please year-round with dishes like a cheddar-capped Shepherd's pie; Long Island duck breast with tamarind sauce; and Cuban-style pork chops.

Piora ✿

B3 — Contemporary XX

430 Hudson St. (bet. Morton St. & St. Luke's Pl.)

Subway: Christopher St - Sheridan Sq — Dinner nightly
Phone: 212-960-3801
Web: www.pioranyc.com
Prices: $$$

The West Village's impossibly quaint charm gets even more charming with an elegant dinner for two at beautiful Piora. The setting is polished, upscale and cozy, with a marble bar up front teeming with well-heeled beauties sipping cocktails; and a sleek white dining room in the back, featuring a stunning wall of glass overlooking a lush urban garden.

It's a soothing experience from the start, a chance to sit back and sink into a perfectly prepared drink (don't miss the creative libations) and let the hustle of the city slough off as you consider the neighborhood's manicured charms. The polished staff together with elegantly prepared and very contemporary cuisine—carefully presented and borrowing from the many influences of Piora's Korean-born owner and Italian-American chef—only seal the deal.

Take the perfectly al dente rigatoni, plated with savory crumbles of ground lamb-and-pork sausage and laced with dollops of bright green nettle pesto, jalapeño slivers, and shaved pecorino; or a beautifully prepared Four Story Hill Farm poularde, rendered to juicy, crispy perfection, and garnished with tawny sweet potato, pickled mustard seeds, tender Brussels sprouts, and foie gras foam.

Pó

Italian XX

D2

31 Cornelia St. (bet. Bleecker & W. 4th Sts.)

Subway: W 4 St - Wash Sq — Lunch Wed – Sun
Phone: 212-645-2189 — Dinner nightly
Web: www.porestaurant.com
Prices: $$

Sometimes the best design begins with a simple and humble concept. Case in point: Po', a lovely spot with a cozy ambience; good wine list; charming staff; and excellent Italian food. By day, the narrow space feels open and airy—especially in summer, when they prop the windows open and ceiling fans swirl lazily overhead. Come nightfall, it's a date night dream, with low lighting and an old-fashioned romantic vibe.

Get your night started with *polpette di carne*, a trio of silky meatballs braised in tomato sauce with *caciocavallo* and a thatch of fresh herbs. And then move on to a tangle of spinach tagliatelle with a rich *ragù alla bolognese*; or a succulent grilled pork chop, served over tender braised cabbage, with a pear-and-cranberry mostarda.

Recette

Contemporary XX

B2

328 W. 12th St. (at Greenwich St.)

Subway: 14 St - 8 Av — Lunch Sun
Phone: 212-414-3000 — Dinner Tue – Sun
Web: www.recettenyc.com
Prices: $$$

A consummate pleaser, this corner restaurant mimics the character of the neighborhood—intimate, quaint, and sophisticated. Inside and out, a buzzy vibe seems to extend from the semi-open kitchen to the small bar. Service is genuine and warm; decorative mirrors make the most of the diminutive space, accented with tall wood-framed windows.

Dishes are inventive, often deliciously riffing on the familiar. For a fun twist on wings, try the crispy, soft-centered "Buffalo" sweetbreads with a *blue di bufala* dip and pickled celery. Raw snapper is topped with grated *bottarga* and pickled onion, served alongside crispy oyster fritters. Heartier dishes include fresh-cut spaghetti with sweet shrimp, tomato, chili, and sea urchin or venison loin-stuffed cabbage.

RedFarm

Asian

529 Hudson St. (bet. Charles & 10th Sts.)

Subway: Christopher St - Sheridan Sq — Lunch Sat – Sun
Phone: 212-792-9700 — Dinner nightly
Web: www.redfarmnyc.com
Prices: $$

The hot spot for upscale (and of the moment) Chinese food, RedFarm packs in the flavor, the noise, as well as the people. On any given night, the line will snake out the door, and a wait is inevitable to score a seat at their communal table in this industrial space. It's worth any hassle, though, when you sit down to experience the farm-to-table, Asian-fusion concept from big names in the business like Joe Ng & Ed Schoenfeld.

The freewheeling kitchen relishes experimenting with local ingredients. Try the bright green pea-leaf and shrimp dumplings, which stand out beautifully in their near-translucent casing; or wok-fried Dungeness crab and crawfish in a thick and spicy basil-ginger sauce.

For some Peking duck fun, head downstairs to Decoy.

Rockmeisha

Japanese

11 Barrow St. (bet. Seventh Ave. South & W. 4th St.)

Subway: Christopher St - Sheridan Sq — Dinner Tue-Sun
Phone: 212-675-7775
Web: N/A
Prices: ⊜

Tightly-packed bar height tables fill this tiny *izakaya*-style restaurant, a quirky canteen with a menu designed for fun. The young crowd sips Sapporo or sake against a soundtrack of old school rock; and the décor, not far behind, ranges from vinyl records to a framed beer ad featuring Japanese women in bathing suits. The space is cramped yet fun, the atmosphere lively and loose.

An appropriately moist leek omelet shows the kitchen's deft execution of simple dishes. Meaty, deep-fried chicken wings coated in a nose-tingling vinegar-based buffalo sauce are an optimal drinking accompaniment, as is a bowl of *chashu* ramen with milky pork bone broth, delicate noodles, pork belly, pickled ginger, sliced scallions, and a generous sprinkling of sesame seeds.

Santina

Seafood XX

820 Washington St. (at Gansevoort St.)

Subway: 14 St - 8 Av — Lunch & dinner daily
Phone: 212-254-3000
Web: www.santinanyc.com
Prices: $$$$

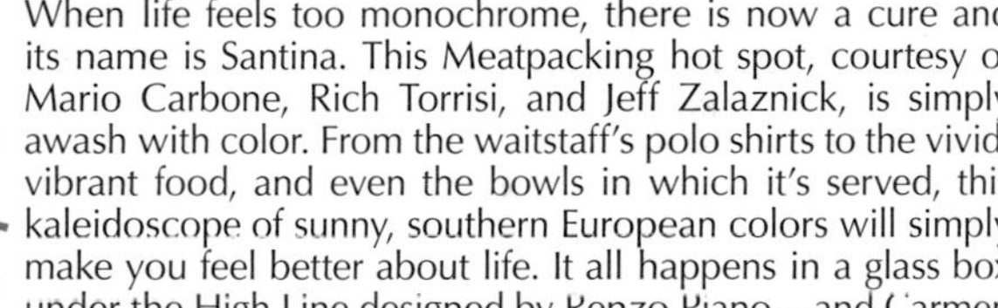

When life feels too monochrome, there is now a cure and its name is Santina. This Meatpacking hot spot, courtesy of Mario Carbone, Rich Torrisi, and Jeff Zalaznick, is simply awash with color. From the waitstaff's polo shirts to the vivid, vibrant food, and even the bowls in which it's served, this kaleidoscope of sunny, southern European colors will simply make you feel better about life. It all happens in a glass box under the High Line designed by Renzo Piano—and Carmen Miranda would love the bar.

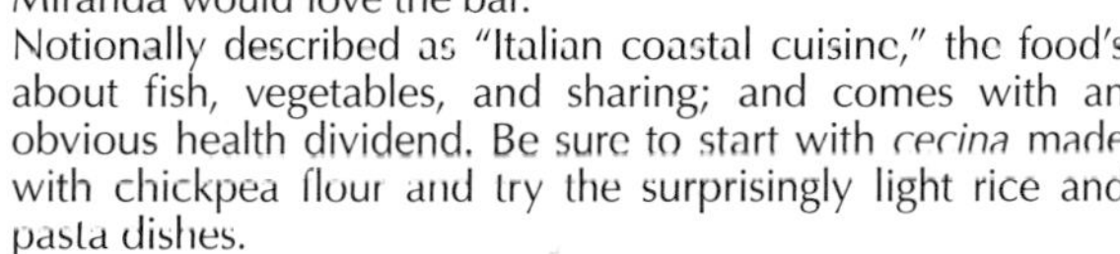

Notionally described as "Italian coastal cuisine," the food's about fish, vegetables, and sharing; and comes with an obvious health dividend. Be sure to start with *cecina* made with chickpea flour and try the surprisingly light rice and pasta dishes.

Saxon + Parole

Contemporary XX

316 Bowery (at Bleecker St.)

Subway: Bleecker St — Lunch Fri – Sun, Dinner nightly
Phone: 212-254-0350
Web: www.saxonandparole.com
Prices: $$$

Named after two 19th century racehorses, this spirited hipster-magnet is the creation of Executive Chef Brad Farmerie and the AvroKO Hospitality Group. Rich wood tones and warm lighting achieve a clubby atmosphere, from the buzzing long bar and communal table to the intimate, serene dining room's banquettes dressed with pristine linens.

Begin with a palate-pleasing surprise in cocktails like the celery gimlet. Then, sample rotating house-made "pots" filled with mousses like eggplant topped with sweet-sour relish and taro chips, or chicken liver with port and pepper jelly served with grilled sourdough bread. Seared branzino over cranberry bean and kale stew with tomato-caper broth and shaved fennel highlights wonderfully complementary flavors.

Sevilla

Spanish X

B2

62 Charles St. (at W. 4th St.)

Subway: Christopher St - Sheridan Sq
Lunch & dinner daily
Phone: 212-929-3189
Web: www.sevillarestaurantandbar.com
Prices: $$

Yellowed menus that haven't changed in decades make this old-school Spanish stalwart seem like a relic. Still, no one comes here to be surprised. Rather, they are plowing through their favorite renditions of paella, ranging from vegetable to seafood with chicken and chorizo. The paella Valenciana also adds clams, mussels, and lobster claws. Prices are low, portions are large, and lively crowds are always happy.

Dishes are made to order, so if that *arroz con pollo* takes 30 minutes to get to your table, know that it will be worthy of the wait. It arrives as a massive amount of saffron-tinged rice and tender bone-in chicken dotted with green onions, pepper strips, lots of garlic, chorizo, and peas. Come dessert, you cannot go wrong with the flan.

Shuko

Japanese XX

D3

47 E. 12th St. (bet. Broadway & University Pl.)

Subway: 14 St - Union Sq
Dinner Mon – Sat
Phone: 212-228-6088
Web: www.shukonyc.com
Prices: $$$$

Chefs Nick Kim and Jimmy Lau, the dynamic duo of the city's sushi scene, have reemerged to take residency behind this U-shaped ash counter. Every seat is filled nightly, surrounding the large team at work. Soft lighting highlights the texture of exposed brick walls to moody effect, and a thumping playlist says downtown—albeit too loudly.

A sushi tasting and sushi kaiseki are the only options offered yet diners will not be left wanting. While the latter is a fuller experience working in an abundance of flavors like pan-seared squab breast, the tasting is a slightly streamlined and more rewarding choice. Regardless of your decision, a morsel of toothsome house-made mochi, dabbed with toasty pistachio miso, is a delightfully enticing opener.

Soto ✿✿

Japanese XX

D1

357 Sixth Ave. (bet. Washington Pl. & W. 4th St.)

Subway: W 4 St - Wash Sq Dinner Mon – Sat
Phone: 212-414-3088
Web: N/A
Prices: $$$

Culinary dominance, unmistakable skill, and absolute discipline permeate every angle of this modest storefront. This is not some flashy temple to sushi, but rather an authentic and visually restrained rendering of a traditional Japanese restaurant. If the sterile look (with just blonde wood and bright lights to embellish) seems too antiseptic, then remember that Soto prides itself on precise preparations of luxurious raw seafood.

While operational issues combined with lackluster service may have impacted guests' experiences of late, the cuisine of Chef Sotohiro Kosugi remains extraordinary—as long as you can tune out the flaws.

Knife skills are paramount and every element is at its precise temperature, as these adept cooks coax each morsel of impossibly rich uni, served simply with uni powder, into a single bite that leaves a lasting impression. Composed dishes are not only strikingly beautiful, but an outright hit—imagine finely chopped and exceedingly silken toro tartare with avocado coulis, caviar, and chives accompanied by a sesame-ponzu sauce. And, unctuous fresh water eel combined with Tosa vinegar, smoky bonito flakes, and crisp Japanese cucumbers come together to form a neat but umami-rich finish.

Spasso

Italian XX

551 Hudson St. (at Perry St.)

Subway: Christopher St - Sheridan Sq — Lunch & dinner daily
Phone: 212-858-3838
Web: www.spassonyc.com
Prices: $$

The quaint far West Village has no dearth of Italian restaurants, and Spasso distinguishes itself not only with its ornate, white wood-framed windows, but an inviting ambience and stellar service. It's the friendly corner spot with a marble bar where you can sip a glass of *Nebbiolo* and chat with the chefs, or simply dine solo on bowls of fresh pasta.

The bells and whistles are here with squid ink *spaghettini* with *mosciame* or air-dried tuna (a specialty of Sardinia); and tripe ragù over tagliatelle. But creative dishes, like giardiniera-laced beef tartare also star, as a tangy twist on the traditional. Speaking of twists, *affogato* offers quite the kick with ice cream that is "choked" with sherry, amaro, or rye whiskey and then drizzled with a shot of espresso.

Standard Grill

Contemporary XX

848 Washington St. (bet. Little W. 12th & 13th Sts.)

Subway: 14 St - 8 Av — Lunch & dinner daily
Phone: 212-645-4100
Web: www.thestandardgrill.com
Prices: $$

Calling the Standard Grill a scene is an understatement. Tucked beneath the High Line in the hugely popular Standard Hotel, this clubby-chic grill blends black-and-white tiles, wood-framed windows overlooking Washington Street, and sidewalk seating with classic New York style. Modern downtown esthetics are reflected in their cadre of beautiful servers donning 1970s vintage plaid uniforms.

Given its prime location, hip crowd, and sprawling layout, one might expect the food to falter but the culinary team doesn't disappoint. Baked macaroni hits a home run with its creamy blend of trumpet mushrooms, smoky roasted cauliflower, and tangy *taggiasca* olives; as does the Southern-style Atlantic swordfish, grilled and topped with a lemon- and green olive-salsa.

Spotted Pig ✿

Gastropub

314 W. 11th St. (at Greenwich St.)

Subway: Christopher St - Sheridan Sq

Lunch & dinner daily

Phone: 212-620-0393

Web: www.thespottedpig.com

Prices: $$$

It's impossible to tell if the famously talented April Bloomfield ever imagined the celebrity draw her restaurant would have over the likes of, say, Kanye West (who reputedly tweeted a drinks invite here to his followers). But many years ago, when Spotted Pig sashayed its way onto an adorable corner of the West Village, New York City was more than ready to meet—and fall completely in love with—the gastropub.

But as popular as the restaurant (and now the gastropub trend itself) has grown, Bloomfield's cooking has always been the real draw. And, it doesn't matter if you are teetering on a wooden stool, knocking elbows with pencil-thin hipsters all night in this cozy, bi-level space. With food like this, you might as well be on the moon.

Bloomfield has made her name on those outstanding burgers, pan-seared mackerel, and legendary gnudi (feather-light orbs of ricotta "gnocchi" laced with brown butter, crispy sage, and nutty parmesan) but you really can't miss on this menu. Kick things off with a small plate of fresh, creamy burrata and grilled sourdough, spread with fava, mint, and a few chili flakes; and then move on to a perfectly roasted *poussin*, served with Sherry vinegar, grilled ramps, and delicate spring onions.

Sushi Nakazawa

Japanese XX

C2

23 Commerce St. (bet. Bedford St. & Seventh Ave. South)

Subway: Christopher St - Sheridan Sq
Dinner Mon – Sat
Phone: 212-924-2212
Web: www.sushinakazawa.com
Prices: **$$$$**

This is a typical NY destination, right down to the tough reservation. The calm setting contrasts the buzz surrounding Chef Daisuke Nakazawa. That hype means the place operates at its own pace; and your meal depends on where you sit—the counter offers fresh, meticulously prepared sushi and engaging chefs, while the dining room is steerage with apathetic servers doling out mediocre pieces of sushi all at once.

But, this kitchen is stocked with the best of America's waters. Uni from Maine is beautifully prepared and notable thanks to hay-smoked bonito. Then, expect a live scallop, pearly and sweet, with just a hint of yuzu pepper paste. And, that Florida tiger prawn could not be more fresh or enjoyable as it is knifed and shelled. For dessert, the lychee sorbet is ace.

Takashi

Japanese X

B3

456 Hudson St. (bet. Barrow & Morton Sts.)

Subway: Christopher St - Sheridan Sq
Dinner nightly
Phone: 212-414-2929
Web: www.takashinyc.com
Prices: **$$**

Tremendous care, planning, and sourcing of specialty cuts went into cozy Takashi before it ever opened its doors to acclaim. Chef/owner Takashi Inoue honors his Korean ancestry and Osaka upbringing with an array of shamelessly carnivorous *yakiniku* favorites. Walls display cutesy cartoons to clarify exactly what you are eating—like "testicargot."

Creative starters might include the Fashion Week Special, served as a cuffed paper bag of devilishly good collagen chips scented with hibiscus and blood orange. Tables are equipped with gas grills for searing platters of rare cuts, from tender beef cheek to large intestines and every stomach in between. Don't miss homemade desserts, like Madagascar vanilla soft-serve with rice dumplings and salted caramel sauce.

Tertulia

Spanish XX

D1

359 Sixth Ave. (bet. Washington Pl. & W. 4th St.)

Subway: W 4 St - Wash Sq — Lunch & dinner daily
Phone: 646-559-9909
Web: www.tertulianyc.com
Prices: **$$**

With a Spanish soul and tastefully raw space, Chef Seamus Mullen's Tertulia is big-hearted and boasts a surprisingly healthy side to its menu. The narrow room decked with a long wood bar and colorful tiles evokes those casual eateries in Spain, rife with a buzzing open kitchen and chalkboards scribbled with cheeses. The bites here are healthy but equally bright with flavor. *Tosta matrimonio* is a flax and quinoa crisp topped with black and white anchovies, slow-roasted tomato, and sharp sheep's milk cheese. Also, try *bocata de delicata*, a satisfying sandwich of slices of charred delicata squash, roasted red peppers, Swiss chard, and cheddar cheese.
For rotisserie fun or a perfect rib eye to grill on your rooftop, visit El Colmado Butchery in MePa.

Untitled

American XX

B1

99 Gansevoort St. (at Washington St.)

Subway: 14 St - 8 Av — Lunch & dinner daily
Phone: 212-570-3670
Web: www.untitledatthewhitney.com
Prices: **$$**

Who can outshine a world-renowned museum like the Whitney? Danny Meyer can—especially when his new restaurant, Untitled, is housed on site. Located by the entry to the popular High Line, the stunning, modern restaurant is a work of art itself, with floor-to-ceiling windows, sleek red chairs, and a beautiful semi-open kitchen.
Talented Chef Michael Anthony oversees the operations here (chef de cuisine is Suzanne Cupps), and the results are anything but ordinary: witness a bright starter of marinated mussels with crisp fava, yellow eye beans and edible flowers; or a tangle of *stradette* tossed with broccoli rabe pesto, French beans, tender sweet mushrooms, and fresh cheese. Close with an ultra-decadent triple-layer peanut butter and blueberry crunch cake.

Via Carota

Italian XX

51 Grove St. (bet. Bleecker St. & Seventh Ave. South)

Subway: Christopher St - Sheridan Sq — Dinner nightly
Phone: 212-255-1962
Web: www.viacarota.com
Prices: $$

An Italian eye for style and polished rusticity sit center stage at this sure-footed and fuss-free local favorite. From the warm dining room with whitewashed exposed brick walls and farmhouse tables to the marble bar, the artistic sensibility of Chefs/co-owners Rita Sodi and Jody Williams is evident before the meal even begins.

Crostini are deceptively simple and flavorful, such as chicken livers folded with caramelized onions and sage generously spread over grilled sourdough bread. Fried green olives, pitted and stuffed with pork sausage arrive piping-hot and pleasing. Thick ribbons of pappardelle are a satisfying, chewy base for a hearty wild boar ragù. Bone-in fried rabbit is served with whole cloves of sweet and spreadable roasted garlic.

Vics

Italian XX

31 Great Jones St. (bet. Bowery & Lafayette St.)

Subway: Bleecker St — Lunch & dinner daily
Phone: 212-253-5700
Web: www.vicsnewyork.com
Prices: $$

The eatery formerly known as Five Points has been reinvented as an Italian-leaning restaurant complete with exposed brick walls and the requisite red pizza oven. Though the dining room is bright and airy, a notable bar program—especially in Italian inflections such as homemade limoncello—prove there's more to this joint than meets the eye.

The best bites are unfussy updates of familiar dishes, such as rye rigatoni with rich braised lamb, fragrant torn oregano, and a sprinkling of sharp cheese. A silky, satisfying nest of *cacio e pepe* is heavy on the black pepper and nutty pecorino, and that red pizza oven produces thin, crisp pies topped with tomato, basil, and sharp pecorino. For dessert, a *bomboloni* of ricotta and chocolate is worth the splurge.

Wallflower

French

235 W. 12th St. (bet. Greenwich Ave. & W. 4th St.)

Subway: 14 St (Seventh Ave.)
Dinner nightly
Phone: N/A
Web: www.wallflowernyc.com
Prices: $$

When a Daniel restaurant veteran opens a casual little cocktail lounge and dining room, the locals will come and never leave. Xavier Herit spent seven years as head bartender at the renowned spot, and his expertise clearly shows in the impressive wine list and complex cocktails—he even crafts a house-made pinot noir syrup for the Scotch-based Père Pinard.

The prix-fixe is a true deal in this neighborhood, especially with choices from the raw bar and charcuterie. For heartier fare, try the country pâté or rabbit terrine, both classically prepared and perfectly seasoned. Silky beef short ribs are deeply comforting, garnished with bacon, mushroom, cipollini, and just the right amount of brawny sauce. The coffee-chocolate *pot de crème* is deliciously intense.

Yerba Buena Perry

Latin American

1 Perry St. (at Greenwich Ave.)

Subway: 14 St (Seventh Ave.)
Lunch Sat – Sun
Dinner nightly
Phone: 212-620-0808
Web: www.ybnyc.com
Prices: $$

As vivacious as a samba, Yerba Buena Perry transports you to a South American paradise, where Latin-inspired dishes cover each table, the bartender never stops shaking celebrated drinks, and loud laughter and music fill the tight space. A longtime favorite, this staff and the kitchen have their choreography down.

Of course the smoky chipotle-laced guacamole is a necessary way to start the meal. Some dishes show Peruvian twists, like jalapeño-soy dressed tuna ceviche with pickled watermelon; as well as Thai basil-jalapeño *ocopa* sauce, a Peruvian tradition, to accompany those thin and crisp butternut squash-and-Manchego empanadas. Don't leave without trying the wow-inducing panko-coated watermelon fries and poblano-infused tomato ketchup.

Wallsé ✿

Austrian XX

B2

344 W. 11th St. (at Washington St.)

Subway: Christopher St - Sheridan Sq — Dinner nightly
Phone: 212-352-2300
Web: www.kg-ny.com
Prices: $$$

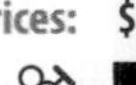

There are some foods that just feel right at certain times of the year. When the nights draw in and there's a little chill in the air, there are certain words whose very presence on a menu summon feelings of comfort and warmth—and those words surely include spaetzle, schnitzel, and strudel.

Austrian cuisine is known for being hearty and immeasurably satisfying, but the great strength of Wallsé is that you don't have to have spent the day skiing in Innsbruck to appreciate its cuisine because the adept kitchen has a lightness of touch and is not rigidly tied to tradition. Whether you've chosen the loin of venison with bone marrow or have gone for the *tafelspitz*, you'll find the dishes are nicely balanced and effortlessly easy to eat.

The restaurant is divided into two rooms, both dominated by striking paintings, some of which are of the chef himself. The clientele is a largely sophisticated bunch with an inherent understanding of how restaurants work which, in turn, creates an easy, relaxing atmosphere. The wine list also merits examination, if only to discover there's more to Austrian wine than Grüner Veltliner.

ZZ's Clam Bar ✿

169 Thompson St. (bet. Bleecker & Houston Sts.)

Subway: Spring St (Sixth Ave.) Dinner Tue – Sat
Phone: 212-254-3000
Web: www.zzsclambar.com
Prices: $$$$

A bouncer greets you at the door of this sexy little seafood nook, where you're ushered into a tiny, beautifully appointed dining room lined with just five white marble tables and sleek dark wood paneling. For a hot second, you might feel like you're the only one in the know about this secret lair, until the hip diners rubbing elbows at every table disabuse you of this notion.

But really, once you get past the silly bouncer, you will never want to leave this den. And although you'll pay a handsome price for small portions here, when each bite sings with this much freshness and flavor, who's counting? Kick things off with anything from the amazing raw bar, where you'll find wildly fresh goodies like creamy oysters bursting with briny flavor. Then move on to delicate, salty trout roe laced with truffle honey and set over a thick slice of buttery toast; otherworldly uni toast, perfectly sweet and laid over malty pretzel with mustard oil and chopped chives; or melt-in-your-mouth Chianina beef carpaccio with luxurious Santa Barbara uni and caviar.

And finally, this sleek, contoured, and sexy bar puts out some of the most sublime cocktails in town.

Harlem, Morningside & Washington Heights

This upper Manhattan pocket is best known for its 1920s jazz clubs that put musicians like Charlie Parker and Miles Davis on the map. Home to Columbia University, this capital of African-American, Hispanic, and Caribbean culture lives up to its world-renowned reputation as an incubator of artistic and academic greats. Having officially cast off the age-old stigma of urban blight, these streets are now scattered with terrific soul food joints and authentic African markets that make Harlem a vibrant and enormously desired destination.

MORNINGSIDE HEIGHTS

Considered an extension of the Upper West Side, park-lined Morningside Heights is frequented for its big and bold breakfasts. Inexpensive eateries are set between quaint brownstones and commercial buildings. When they're not darting to and from classes, resident scholars and ivy-leaguers from Columbia University can be found lounging at the **Hungarian Pastry Shop** with a sweet treat and cup of tea. Special occasions may call for an evening gathering at **Lee Lee's Baked Goods**. Rather than be misled by its plain-Jane façade, prepare yourself for gratification here by way of the most delicious and decadent rugelach in town. When spring approaches, stroll out onto the terrace and enjoy an apricot-filled treat in the breeze.

WEST HARLEM

Further north lies Harlem, a sanctuary for the soul and stomach. Fifth Avenue divides this region into two very unique sections: West Harlem, a hub for African-American culture; and East Harlem, a pulsating Spanish

district also referred to as "El Barrio." Beloved for its sass and edge, West Harlem is constantly making way for booming gentrification and socio-cultural evolution. One of its most visible borders is **Fairway**, a Tri-State area staple that draws shoppers of all stripes. Pick up one of their goodies to-go or simply savor the same while sifting through the extensive literary collection over at the historic Schomburg Center for Research in Black Culture. When the sun sets over the Hudson River, find locals and savvy tourists slipping into **Patisserie des Ambassades**, where a modern, chic décor does much to lure—for breakfast, lunch, and dinner. Not only do the aromas from fresh-baked croissants, *éclairs au chocolat*, and cream-filled beignets waft down the block, but they also ensure long lines at all times. Every August, **Harlem Week** brings the community together for art, music, and food. Join the fun and take in some of the most soulful tunes in town. Both east and west of Central Harlem, food has always factored heavily into everyday routine, and the choices are as varied as the neighborhood itself. From Mexican and Caribbean, to West African cuisine, there are rich culinary delights to be had. **Lolo's Seafood Shack** cooks up Caribbean-infused steampots and serves them out of a counter; while **Manna's** on Frederick Douglass Boulevard attracts diners to its soul food steam table, where church groups rub shoulders and share stories with backpacking visitors. Fried food junkies fantasize over Chef Charles Gabriel's acclaimed buffet and amazing fried chicken at **Charles Country Pan Fried Chicken**, but for an evening at home, comb the shelves at **Darou Salam Market** for wide-ranging West African groceries that never fail to sate. Seal this spree at **Harlem Shambles**, a true-blue butcher shop specializing in quality cuts of meat and poultry that promise to enhance every meal.

EAST HARLEM

Over in East Harlem, Spanish food enthusiasts and culture pundits never miss a trip to **Amor Cubano** for home-style faves. If smoked and piggy *lechón* served with a side of sultry, live

Cuban beats isn't your idea of a good time, there's always that counter of divine Caribbean eats at **Sisters**; or juicy jerk chicken at **Winston & Tee Express**. Not pressed for time? Choose to scope the tempting taco truck and taqueria scene along "Little Mexico" on East 116th Street—otherwise known as the nucleus of New York City's Mexican communities.

Almost like a vestige of the Italian population that was once dominant in this district, **Rao's** remains a culinary landmark. Operated from a poky basement and patronized by bigwigs like Donald Trump or Nicole Kidman, it is one of the city's most difficult tables to secure. The original benefactors have exclusive rights to a seat here and hand off reservations like rent-controlled apartments. But, rest assured as there is other enticing Italian to be enjoyed at **Patsy's Pizzeria**, another stronghold in East Harlem, famous for its hot coal oven (and occasionally its pizza); while **Hot Bread Kitchen**, a tenant of **La Marqueta marketplace**, offers a global selection at both breakfast and lunch, and is reputed to be quite the holy havens among carb addicts.

WASHINGTON HEIGHTS

Set along the northern reaches of Uptown, Washington Heights offers ample food choices along its steep streets. From Venezuelan food truck sensation **Patacon Pisao**, to restaurants like **Malecon** preparing authentic *morir soñando*, *mangu*, and *mofongo*, this colorful and lively neighborhood keeps dishing it out. In fact, the Tony award-winning musical *In The Heights* is a tribute to the ebullient district, where Dominican and Puerto Rican communities have taken root. Late-nighters never tire of the Latin beats blasting through the air here, after which a visit to Puerto Rican *piragua* carts selling shaved ice in a rainbow of tropical flavors seems not only nourishing, but necessary. Locals queue up in lines around the block outside **Elsa La Reina del Chicharrón** for crunchy, deep-fried *chicharrónes*, after which palates may be quenched with *jugos naturales* or natural juices made from cane sugar and fresh fruits for a healthy treat. Need some sweet after this abundant savory feast? **Carrot Top Pastries** continues to entice passersby with assorted cookies, colorful cakes, and deliciously moist sweet potato pies.

Amazing fish markets and butcher shops also dot these hilly blocks, and less than ten bucks will get you a plate of traditional pernil with rice and beans at any number of diners nearby. Hungry, in-the-know hordes can be found ducking into **La Rosa Fine Foods** for fish, meat, and vegetables; or **Nelly's Bakery** for a caffeine boost from the creamy *café con leche*. Nearby in Inwood, **Piper's Kilt** is a standing relic among German and Irish settlers for accurate renditions of their country's cuisines. Settle into a booth and order a perfect pint to go with "Irish nachos" or "Kilt burgers." It's just like continental Europe here, only minus the jet lag!

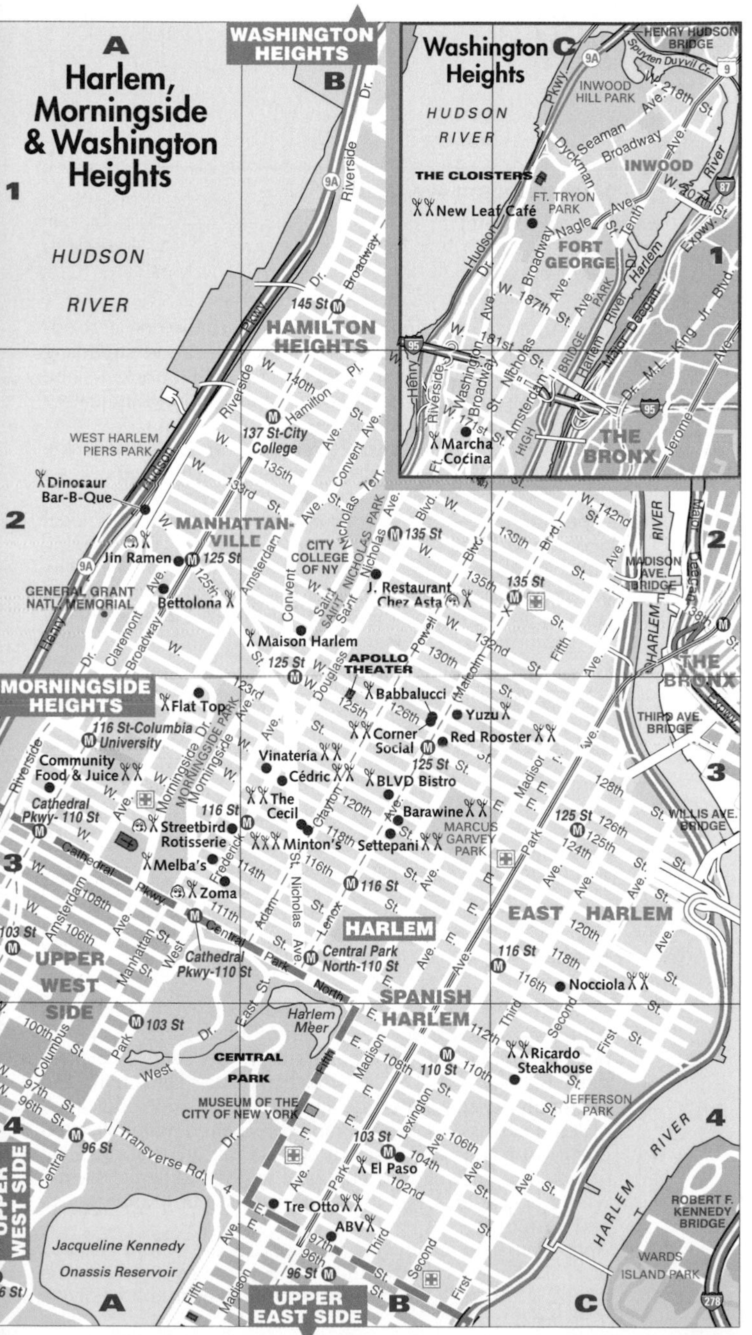
Harlem, Morningside & Washington Heights
WASHINGTON HEIGHTS
Washington Heights
HUDSON RIVER
THE CLOISTERS
New Leaf Café
Marcha Cocina
INWOOD HILL PARK
INWOOD
FT. TRYON PARK
FORT GEORGE
THE BRONX
HENRY HUDSON BRIDGE
145 St
HAMILTON HEIGHTS
137 St-City College
WEST HARLEM PIERS PARK
Dinosaur Bar-B-Que
MANHATTAN-VILLE
Jin Ramen
125 St
CITY COLLEGE OF NY
135 St
J. Restaurant
Chez Asta
GENERAL GRANT NATL. MEMORIAL
Bettolona
Maison Harlem
APOLLO THEATER
MADISON AVE. BRIDGE
MORNINGSIDE HEIGHTS
Flat Top
116 St-Columbia University
Community Food & Juice
Babbalucci
Yuzu
Corner Social
Red Rooster
Vinatería
Cédric
BLVD Bistro
The Cecil
Barawine
Minton's
Settepani
Streetbird Rotisserie
Melba's
Zoma
Cathedral Pkwy-110 St
116 St
MARCUS GARVEY PARK
THIRD AVE. BRIDGE
WILLIS AVE. BRIDGE
HARLEM
EAST HARLEM
Central Park North-110 St
103 St
UPPER WEST SIDE
SPANISH HARLEM
Nocciola
Harlem Meer
CENTRAL PARK
MUSEUM OF THE CITY OF NEW YORK
110 St
Ricardo Steakhouse
JEFFERSON PARK
96 St
El Paso
Tre Otto
ABV
Jacqueline Kennedy Onassis Reservoir
UPPER EAST SIDE
HARLEM RIVER
ROBERT F. KENNEDY BRIDGE
WARDS ISLAND PARK

ABV

B4

1504 Lexington Ave. (at 97th St.)

Subway: 96 St (Lexington Ave.) — Lunch Sat – Sun
Phone: 212-722-8959 — Dinner nightly
Web: www.abvny.com
Prices: $$

This Americana gastropub's sophisticated cooking and no-nonsense mien are a perfect fit for its location straddling Carnegie Hill and East Harlem. Residents flock to the welcoming surrounds outfitted with tufted honey-tan leather banquettes and an open kitchen.

Craft beers and small-producer wines comprise the beverage selection at ABV (alcohol by volume) and the menu is an impressively prepared lineup of seasonally skewed creations. Expect autumnal butternut squash cannelloni boasting local ricotta and pumpkin seed-marjoram pesto, or lip-smacking buttermilk-brined fried chicken with kimchi-cabbage slaw and crumbly cornbread topped with a melting pat of butter. A summertime offering of Frog Hollow peach sorbet headlines the short but sweet dessert choices.

Babbalucci

Italian

B3

331 Lenox Ave. (bet. 126th & 127th Sts.)

Subway: 125 St (Lenox Ave.) — Lunch & dinner daily
Phone: 646-918-6572
Web: www.babbalucci.com
Prices: $$

A wood-fired pizzeria named after a snail? Yes—and there's actually a snail pizza on the menu. But, regardless of your preferred choice of topping, say *salame piccante* or Sicilian tuna, Babbalucci's 12- or 16-inch pies are light, thin, and pleasantly crisp. Other delicious offerings include small plates such as wood-fired radicchio paired with blistered cherry tomatoes and luscious burrata, all given a drizzling of *vin cotto,* as well as exceptional pastas like penne slicked with a ricotta-enriched tomato sauce hit with *pepperoncini* and fresh mint.

And, thanks to an inviting location set back from the fray of 125th Street and a beautiful brick pizza oven within, the setting at this rustic Harlem newcomer is every bit as divine as its food.

Barawine

Contemporary XX

B3

200 Lenox Ave. (at 120th St.)

Subway: 116 St (Lenox Ave.) Lunch Sat – Sun
Phone: 646-756-4154 Dinner nightly
Web: www.barawine.com
Prices: $$

Amid the leafy, brownstone-lined Mount Morris Park Historic District, Barawine is an inviting dining room overseen by Fabrice Warin (formerly the sommelier at Orsay). This eye-catching space emanates a warm glow, enticing Lenox Avenue passersby to step in for a drink, snack, and much more. The bar area's communal table is a convivial perch, in addition to the quieter seating in back. Throughout, whitewashed walls attractively double as wine storage.

The crowd-pleasing menu defies classification but offers something for everyone. Expect to enjoy béchamel-enriched macaroni and cheese with diced ham and melted Gruyère; chicken breast with ratatouille and feta, as well as vegan options such as quinoa and grilled tofu salad, and dairy-free chocolate mousse.

Bettolona

Italian X

A2

3143 Broadway (bet. LaSalle St. & Tiemann Pl.)

Subway: 125 St (Broadway) Lunch & dinner daily
Phone: 212-749-1125
Web: N/A
Prices: $$

Morningside Heights' darling gets high marks from Columbia University students for pasta and pizza. The little room is crowded with locals fueling up on delightful lasagna *verdi*, meaty linguine Bolognese, or the puffy, crusty delights that emerge from the wood-burning oven. The succulent array includes pizza *affumicata* spread with crushed tomato, fresh cherry tomatoes, smoked fresh mozzarella, and crumbles of sausage. The chicken breast Marsala is stuffed with spinach, fontina, mushrooms, and is a tasty example of their heartier cooking.

Lodged under the elevated 1 train, Bettolona is inviting nonetheless with its closely arranged wood tables, brick walls, and rustic vibe. Baby sibling Coccola brings their signature pizza and *panuozzo* up to West Harlem.

BLVD Bistro

Southern

B3

239 Lenox Ave. (at 122nd St.)

Subway: 125 St (Lenox Ave.)
Phone: 212-678-6200
Web: www.boulevardbistrony.com
Prices: $$

Lunch Tue – Sun
Dinner Tue – Sat

Tucked into the base of a corner brownstone, this southern restaurant delivers the best of old Harlem: warm hospitality, a feel-good, soulful soundtrack, and flaky biscuits slathered with apple butter. Filled with dark leather booths and high wood tables, the intimate dining room boasts a convivial atmosphere that's only enhanced by the chef's presence as he greets his devoted customers.

After those buttery biscuits, a decadent meal might continue with rich seven cheese macaroni, topped with crumbled bacon and parsley. Cornmeal-crusted grouper receives careful execution, resulting in flaky flesh and a crunchy crust. The sides shine, too, including red beans and rice with a hint of thyme and a smoky stew of black eyed peas with Andouille sausage.

The Cecil

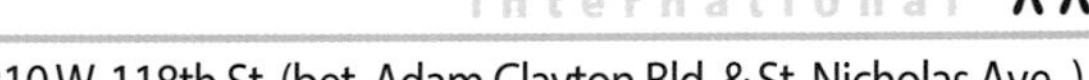

B3

210 W. 118th St. (bet. Adam Clayton Bld. & St. Nicholas Ave.)

Subway: 116 St (Frederick Douglass Blvd.)
Phone: 212-866-1262
Web: www.thececilharlem.com
Prices: $$

Lunch Sat – Sun
Dinner nightly

As evidenced by this buzzing hot spot, Harlem continues to prove it's a destination-worthy enclave for serious eats. Neon signage out front marks The Cecil's entrance and the lounge's provocative artwork gets things off to a sexy start once diners step inside.

Dinner here is a trip around the globe, guided by a menu that spotlights Africa, Asia, South America, and the US South. Skillet-fried salmon, dusted with cornmeal for a satisfying crunch, comes plated atop spicy kimchi-inspired slaw; and the *feijoada* is a stoneware pot full of black beans, braised oxtail, and merguez garnished with slivered collard greens and orange segments. Even the wine list has a passport, with an impressive selection from black producers under the heading African Diaspora.

Cédric

French XX

B3

185 St. Nicholas Ave. (at 119th St.)

Subway: 116 St (Frederick Douglass Blvd.) — Lunch Sat – Sun
Phone: 212-866-7766 — Dinner nightly
Web: www.cedricbistro.com
Prices: $$

Cédric Lecendre's great little bistro is as cool and jubilant as Harlem itself. Marked by red awnings outside, the room is snug and cheerfully adorned with etched mirrors, gold accents, and splashes of rouge. The staff's French accents might hint of Paris, but the black-and-white prints on the walls return you to the landmarks of Manhattan.

This kitchen's updated French bistro classics are universally pleasing. Enjoy thinly sliced endive tossed with walnuts and Roquefort cheese; followed by pan-seared duck breast with a cherry sauce and *gratin Dauphinois*; or hot and juicy grilled hanger steak with caramelized shallots, red wine reduction, and a heap of crispy shoestring frites. Desserts like the *île flottante* are traditional and spot-on.

Community Food & Juice

American XX

A3

2893 Broadway (bet. 112th & 113th Sts.)

Subway: Cathedral Pkwy/110 St (Broadway) — Lunch & dinner daily
Phone: 212-665-2800
Web: www.communityrestaurant.com
Prices: $$

As part of Columbia University's sprawl, this address is a godsend for students, faculty, and locals from morning to night. Although it's spacious with plenty of outdoor options, the popular spot doesn't accept reservations—and has the lines to prove it. Executive Chef/partner Neil Kleinberg (also of downtown fave Clinton St. Baking Company) turns out joyful fare, and the weekly blueberry pancake special is just one reason why this place gets so much love.

For lunch, a kale salad with artichoke hearts, pickled carrots, and crispy chickpeas is anything but rote. Come dinnertime, the fish or steak of the day has revealed pan-seared mahi-mahi with roasted cauliflower and black truffle beurre blanc, or grilled strip steak brushed with glistening teriyaki.

Corner Social

American XX

321 Lenox Ave. (at 126th St.)

Subway: 125 St (Lenox Ave.) Lunch & dinner daily
Phone: 212-510-8552
Web: www.cornersocialnyc.com
Prices: $$

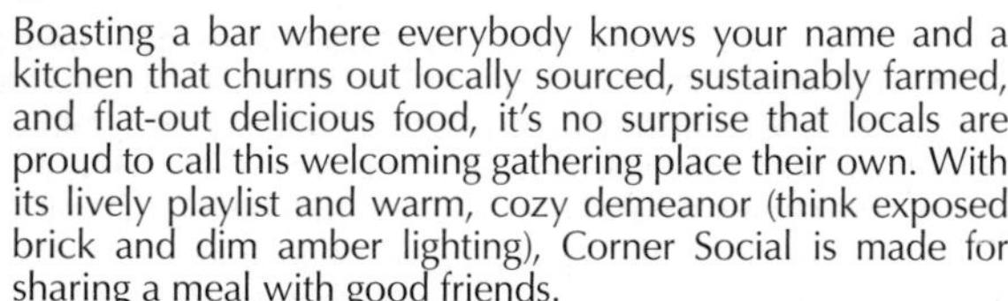

Boasting a bar where everybody knows your name and a kitchen that churns out locally sourced, sustainably farmed, and flat-out delicious food, it's no surprise that locals are proud to call this welcoming gathering place their own. With its lively playlist and warm, cozy demeanor (think exposed brick and dim amber lighting), Corner Social is made for sharing a meal with good friends.

Start with the guacamole, which comes with thick, crispy tortillas from Hot Bread Kitchen, a nearby incubator whose mission is to train and employ immigrant women. Entrée options abound, from a buttermilk-fried chicken sandwich, to hanger steak drizzled with warm, house-made steak sauce and propped up by crispy potato wedges dusted with parmesan and white truffle salt.

Dinosaur Bar-B-Que

Barbecue 

A2

700 W. 125th St. (at Twelfth Ave.)

Subway: 125 St (Broadway) Lunch & dinner daily
Phone: 212-694-1777
Web: www.dinosaurbarbque.com
Prices: $$

Huge, loud, and perpetually packed, this way west Harlem barbecue hall draws crowds from near and far. The bar area is rollicking, and for that reason kept separate from the dining quarters. There, wood beams and slats, swirling ceiling fans, and oxblood leather booths fashion a comfortable—and quieter—setting.

The scent of wood smoke wafting through the red brick structure (which coincidentally once served as a meatpacking warehouse) only heightens the diners' carnivorous cravings. Minimize decision-making and order the Extreme Sampler: a heaping feast of apple cider-brined smoked chicken, dry-rubbed slow-smoked pork ribs, and lean Creekstone Farms brisket. Add on a creative side or two—perhaps the barbecue fried rice studded with bits of pulled pork?

El Paso

Mexican

1643 Lexington Ave. (at 104th St.)

Subway: 103 St (Lexington Ave.) Lunch & dinner daily
Phone: 212-831-9831
Web: www.elpasony.com
Prices: $$

El Paso is an East Harlem cantina that serves some of the most gratifying south-of-the-border fare in town. True-blue residents as well as those new to this evolving neighborhood crowd its affable rooms, where margaritas, ice-cold cerveza, and smiles flow freely. Stucco walls and decorative metal work grace the interior, while the covered back patio has a breezy mien.

Tacos, quesadillas, and ceviche kick off cooking that hits all the right notes. Zesty guacamole is freshly mashed and served up in a *molcajete* with warm tortilla chips. Bold citrus- and tequila-braised *carnitas Michoacanás* are kissed by green chilies and crowningly paired with a bowl of hearty black beans and tender tortillas for wrapping. The silken flan offers a sweet finish.

Flat Top

Contemporary

1241 Amsterdam Ave. (at 121st St.)

Subway: 116 St (Broadway) Lunch & dinner daily
Phone: 646-820-7735
Web: www.flattopnyc.com
Prices: $$

Morningside Heights' scholarly set, already familiar with Jin Ramen, has been quick to adopt this bistro from the same team of partners. A mural of the Harlem Viaduct gives the low-key setting a sense of place, while friendly service accentuates the neighborly vibe.

Global accents mark Flat Top's cuisine in starters like a caprese salad with burrata, or shrimp ceviche. Meanwhile entrées have included black pepper-flecked roasted chicken breast. The latter is presented sliced over steamed Yukon gold potatoes and a mouthwatering herb sauce made from puréed cilantro, roasted jalapeños, and hint of cream. For dessert, a dressed-up chocolate cake is layered with whipped ganache, crispy bits of *feuilletine*, and presented with a side of Guinness ice cream.

Jin Ramen

Japanese

3183 Broadway (bet. 125th St. & Tiemann Pl.)

Subway: 125 St (Broadway) — Lunch & dinner daily
Phone: 646-559-2862
Web: www.jinramen.com
Prices: $$

All you really need to know is that this is the hands-down best ramen above 59th Street. Sure, decorative elements are simple, and it hardly matters that this little gem is hidden behind the 125th Street station's brick escalator. What comes from the kitchen deserves kudos.

The menu is concise, offering a few items such as house-made *gyoza* for starters. These pan-fried shrimp dumplings have a delicate, crisped wrapper and arrive with sesame-seed flecked dipping sauce. *Shio*, *shoyu*, and miso ramen are all delightful, but the *tonkatsu* ramen is a special treat. The piping hot, almost creamy, mouthcoating distillation of pork bones is deliciously rich and stocked with fragrant *chasu*, pickled bamboo shoots, slivered green onion, and a soft-boiled egg.

J. Restaurant Chez Asta

Senegalese

2479 Frederick Douglass Blvd. (bet. 132nd & 133rd Sts.)

Subway: 135 St (Frederick Douglass Blvd.) — Lunch & dinner daily
Phone: 212-862-3663
Web: www.chezjacob.com
Prices: $$

Impressive in its authenticity, this Senegalese café is a rare bird in a neighborhood of vibrant dining choices. Meals here are exquisitely prepared and brim with unique flavors and scents, resulting in a truly transporting experience.

Spotless and comfy, the dining room offers a clutch of wood tables sturdy enough to support the heaping portions of chicken *yassa* or lemon-marinated chicken cooked with onions; as well as *souloukhou*, fish and vegetables in a peanut sauce. For a true taste of the country's flavors, go with the *thiebou djeun*, a one pot wonder of broken rice infused with tomato and Scotch bonnet pepper. It's cooked with fish, cabbage, okra, and cassava, and speckled with *xóoñ* (those crusty, toothsome bits scraped from the bottom of the pan).

Maison Harlem

French

341 St. Nicholas Ave. (at 127th St.)

Subway: 125 St (St. Nicholas Ave.)
Phone: 212-222-9224
Web: www.maisonharlem.com
Prices: $$

Lunch & dinner daily

A steady stream of locals, phone-toting tourists and City College academics filling these well-worn wooden tables proves that this bistro has little trouble attracting a crowd. Floor-to-ceiling windows, dark red banquettes, and quirky touches like vintage Gallic posters or football jerseys tacked to the walls lend a whiff of whimsy.

Maison Harlem's menu plays around with culinary traditions, with results that may include a classic rendition of coq au vin with smoky lardons, browned button mushrooms, and fresh noodles to garnish the wine-braised chicken pieces. Sticking to tradition, ratatouille is a sunny bowlful of diced and stewed summer vegetables. The tarte Tatin layers thick but spoon tender caramelized apple wedges over outrageously buttery pastry.

Marcha Cocina

Latin American

4055 Broadway (at 171st St.)

Subway: 168 St
Phone: 212-928-8272
Web: www.marchanyc.com
Prices: $$

Lunch Fri – Sun
Dinner nightly

Colors evoke the Caribbean at Marcha, a narrow restaurant known for authentic Spanish tapas. A long bar dominates the sea-blue and sunny-yellow room filled with high tables and a convivial crowd. The music is a touch loud, the service is refreshingly down-to-earth, and the food impresses beyond what its neighborhood bar-vibe might suggest.

The menu is broad and affordable, which makes a perfect excuse to sample widely. Staples from tender *tortilla Espanola* to *gambas al ajillo* are delicious executions of classic tapas. Ribbons of luscious Spanish ham are on handsome display in the *hongos e higos coca*, a chewy flatbread also topped with mushrooms, figs, and buttery almonds. It would be blasphemy to skip the dates wrapped in bacon or the thick-cut yucca fries.

Melba's

300 W. 114th St. (at Frederick Douglass Blvd.)

Subway: 116 St (Frederick Douglass Blvd.) — Lunch Sat – Sun
Phone: 212-864-7777 — Dinner nightly
Web: www.melbasrestaurant.com
Prices: **$$**

A colorful spirit and Southern classics do much to remind guests of this quickly gentrifying area's flavor, culture, and past. Quaint and lovely Melba's is a place to gather and relax over good food and drinks, from Auntie B's mini-burgers slathered in smoky-sweet sauce to an absolutely perfect fruit cobbler—a golden-brown and berry-licious height of the pantheon.

Equally important is the swoon-inducing Southern-fried chicken: darkly bronzed, salty-sweet, and tender. Thick fillets of fresh flakey tilapia may be densely crusted with crushed pecans and topped with white gravy. Expect surprises here, from the spring rolls with black-eyed peas, collards, and red rice, to a complex Italian *semillion* (ideal for pairing with that fried chicken and waffles).

Minton's

American 

B3

206 W. 118th St. (bet. Adam Clayton Powell Jr. Blvd. & St. Nicholas Ave.)

Subway: 116 St (Lexington Ave.) — Dinner Tue – Sun
Phone: 212-243-2222
Web: www.mintonsharlem.com
Prices: **$$$$**

This grand jazz club is the sister act to The Cecil, located next door. Don a jacket (as recommended for men) and settle into its throwback surroundings to feast and listen to the sweet sounds of live jazz. The art deco interior references Minton's 1938 opening, and black-and-white portraits pay homage to the legendary figures who have graced this stage.

The only distraction from the music is the cooking: an updated take on Southern cuisine that's perfectly suited to this neighborhood haunt's debonair crowd. Smothered lobster and shrimp casserole is richly dressed with pimento cheese grits and crawfish gravy; while hoppin' John pilau, made with Carolina gold rice, fried black-eyed peas, and roasted red pepper purée, is like risotto with a down-home twist.

New Leaf Café

American XX

C1

1 Margaret Corbin Dr. (in Fort Tryon Park)

Subway: 190 St Lunch & dinner Tue – Sun
Phone: 212-568-5323
Web: www.newleafrestaurant.com
Prices: $$

Located in a 1930s mansion designed by the Olmstead brothers, New Leaf Café was opened as part of the New York Restoration Project. The inside feels like a large cottage with stone walls and arched windows. Alfresco lunch on the flagstone terrace showcases this high, hilly setting with unparalleled views of the Palisades (squint to find the George Washington Bridge).

The American menu features a fried risotto cake with gooey mozzarella over Tokyo turnips and sweet pea coulis; or a hunk of seared tuna with tiny mushroom-filled ravioli. Profiteroles are a particular treat, filled with vanilla ice cream and drizzled with luscious chocolate sauce.

The gorgeous surrounds and jazz concerts make this a sought-after spot for private events after sun down.

Nocciola

Italian XX

C3

237 E. 116th St. (bet. Second & Third Aves.)

Subway: 116 St (Lexington Ave.) Lunch & dinner daily
Phone: 646-559-5304
Web: www.nocciolanyc.com
Prices: $$

The transformation of this East Harlem address into a pleasing trattoria is a breath of fresh air for the neighborhood. Run by the team behind El Paso, the slender space has been minimally re-touched but nevertheless feels cozy and inviting with its dark-stained wood furnishings and warm brown-shaded walls.

The menu boasts house-made pastas like silken fettuccine treated to a soaking of *Domenico* sugo—a hearty amalgam of sweet fennel sausage, pan-fried spicy meatballs, and pork ragù in a bright tomato sauce. A roasted whole fish is beautifully done, expertly de-boned and dressed with a touch of *salmoriglio*, charred lemon and young arugula. Top off this confident cooking with a block of classic tiramisu that boasts an ample dusting of cocoa powder.

Red Rooster

American XX

310 Lenox Ave. (bet. 125 & 126th Sts.)

Subway: 125 St (Lenox Ave.) Lunch & dinner daily
Phone: 212-792-9001
Web: www.redroosterharlem.com
Prices: $$$

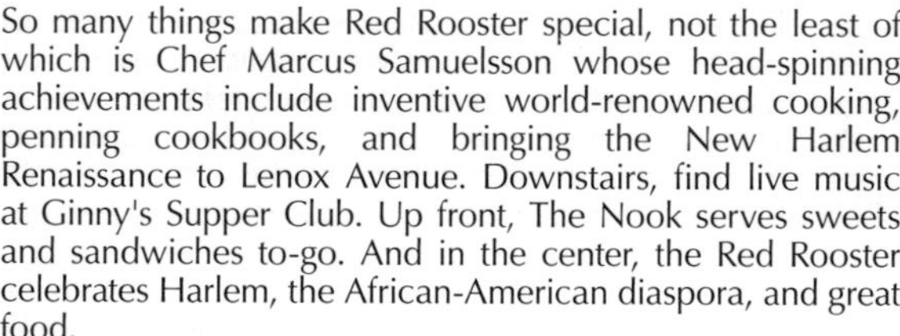

So many things make Red Rooster special, not the least of which is Chef Marcus Samuelsson whose head-spinning achievements include inventive world-renowned cooking, penning cookbooks, and bringing the New Harlem Renaissance to Lenox Avenue. Downstairs, find live music at Ginny's Supper Club. Up front, The Nook serves sweets and sandwiches to-go. And in the center, the Red Rooster celebrates Harlem, the African-American diaspora, and great food.

Start with a brilliantly simple wedge of crumbly, buttery corn bread. Then, move on to the likes of highly spiced and "dirty" basmati rice with sweet shrimp and swirls of lemon aïoli; or try their interpretation of South African "bunny chow" served as lamb stew on a sesame bun with fried egg and fresh ricotta.

Ricardo Steakhouse

Steakhouse XX

2145 Second Ave. (bet. 110th & 111th Sts.)

Subway: 110 St (Lexington Ave.) Lunch Fri – Sun
Phone: 212-289-5895 Dinner nightly
Web: www.ricardosteakhouse.com
Prices: $$

Walk up to the entrance of Ricardo Steakhouse on a Saturday night and don't be surprised to see imposing doormen focused on crowd control. Beloved by longtime locals, this place remains very popular for its genuine, ungentrified East Harlem vibe. Beyond its polished façade and wood-framed doors find small tables, eye-catching artwork, and on occasion, a formidable DJ. The menu combines whimsical wording and Latin influences with starters that range from empanadas or fried calamari to raw bar offerings. Heaping entrées (listed under "Da Meats") include the Ricardo Special, a grilled platter pairing tender skirt steak and a juicy pork chop with black beans, rice, and fried plantains.

A few blocks north, Ricardo Ocean Grill is also satisfying crowds.

Settepani

Italian XX

B3

196 Lenox Ave. (at 120th St.)

Subway: 125 St (Lenox Ave.) — Lunch & dinner daily
Phone: 917-492-4806
Web: www.settepani.com
Prices: $$

Poised within the charming enclave of the Mount Morris Park Historic District, this worthy *ristorante* offers Italian cuisine that is a testament to the ascending quality of Harlem dining. The elegant, cream-colored space flaunts art dressed walls, a marble bar, and towering windows draped with silk.

Looking to the north and to the south, the menu here delivers all-around gratification. Begin with *insalata conca d'oro* for a sparkling combination of shaved fennel, red onion, orange segments, and crushed black olives; perhaps followed by *spaghetti di mare* baked in parchment paper, loaded with squid, shrimp, and chopped tomato, plated tableside. The spoon-tender osso buco is garnished with *fregola*, drizzled with lush veal jus, and absolutely delicious.

Streetbird Rotisserie

Fusion 

2149 Frederick Douglass Blvd. (at 116th St.)

Subway: 116 St (Frederick Douglass Blvd.) — Lunch & dinner daily
Phone: 212-206-2557
Web: www.streetbirdnyc.com
Prices: $$

Chef Marcus Samuelsson's latest Harlem hot spot is a funky corner devoted to slow-roasted chicken and old-school street-style. Wade through the boisterous, rum punch-fueled crowd and enter this party to find splashes of custom graffiti, eye-popping murals, and lighting fixtures made from cassette tapes, drum sets, and bicycle tires.

Despite all this sensory overload, it is impossible not to notice the plump, auburn birds spinning in the glass-fronted oven. Tender, juicy, and exceptionally flavorful, they steal the show and are supported by the chef's signature mash-up of global flavors: green papaya salad, jasmine fried rice, and cornbread. Not feeling the poultry? Opt for the spicy *piri-piri* catfish with crispy shallots and avocado.

Tre Otto

Italian XX

B4

1410 Madison Ave. (bet. 97th & 98th Sts.)

Subway: 96 St (Lexington Ave.) — Lunch & dinner daily
Phone: 212-860-8880
Web: www.treotto.com
Prices: $$

East Harlem's favorite neighborhood trattoria has triumphantly returned following a move next door. Thanks to proprietors Louis and Lauren Cangiano, the popular surrounds—complete with cheery red walls, exposed brick, and penny-tile floors—are as cozy and welcoming as ever.

Tre Otto's mouthwatering menu boasts home-style dishes made from recipes gathered over time. Antipasti include a luscious salad of shaved fennel and orange segments crowned by tender-grilled octopus drizzled with zesty *salmoriglio* sauce. Freshly made trenette pasta is twirled with pesto *Trapanese*, a divinely rich combination of tomatoes, almonds, garlic, and basil; while the flavors of pizza, topped with red onions, capers, and tuna, call Sicily's sparkling coastline to mind.

Vinatería

Italian XX

B3

2211 Frederick Douglass Blvd. (at 119th St.)

Subway: 116 St (Frederick Douglass Blvd.) — Lunch Sat – Sun
Phone: 212-662-8462 — Dinner nightly
Web: www.vinaterianyc.com
Prices: $$

Adding to Harlem and its hidden charms is Vinatería, an Italian darling brimming with wines to accompany each sublime bite. Not only is it cozy, but the attractive slate-toned room etched in chalk with scenes of decanters and menu specials will augment your appetite.

The semi-open kitchen in the back unveils such treasures as house-cured sardines with fiery piquillo peppers and crunchy croutons; or a salad of earthy golden and red beets mingled with yogurt, oranges, arugula, crunchy pistachios and tossed with a lemon vinaigrette. Herbs plucked from their copper planters may be featured in an impeccably grilled rosemary-marinated pork blade served with rich mashed potatoes; or desserts like citrus-glazed rosemary panna cotta bathed in chamomile grappa.

Yuzu

Japanese

B3

350 Lenox Ave. (bet. 127th & 128th Sts.)

Subway: 125 St (Lenox Ave.) Lunch & dinner Tue – Sun
Phone: 646-861-3883
Web: www.yuzunewyork.com
Prices: **$$**

Add sushi to Harlem's burgeoning lineup of eateries that are delighting residents and luring curious foodies uptown. The space is spare but fits in well within the *sushi-ya* archetype. An L-shaped counter and numerous tables compose the seating options in the room, which is painted pale yellow to reference the namesake citrus fruit. Yuzu's personable staff lends an amiable tone to the vibe.

Chef Tomoyuki Hayashi has worked at the venerable Sushi Azabu, so expect to be pleased from start to finish. Sushi platters are a good show of skill, and may be composed of lean tuna, torched salmon, and unagi nigiri, plus well-constructed maki. Cooked options include cold and hot small plates such as yuzu- and miso-marinated seafood or grilled Bluefin tuna belly.

Zoma

Ethiopian

A3

2084 Frederick Douglass Blvd. (at 113th St.)

Subway: 116 St (Frederick Douglass Blvd.) Lunch Sat – Sun
Phone: 212-662-0620 Dinner nightly
Web: www.zomanyc.com
Prices:

Smart, cool, modern, and always welcoming, Zoma may well be this city's most serious Ethiopian restaurant. The crowded bar emits a golden light from below to showcase its premium spirits, and the ambient dining room is filled with locals from this thriving community.

Attention to detail is clear from the steaming hot towel for cleaning your hands to the carefully folded *injera* used for scooping up their chopped salads, chunky stews, and saucy vegetables. Unusual starters might include green lentils with a cold and crunchy mix of onions, jalapeños, ginger, white pepper, and mustard seeds. The *doro watt*—a chicken dish of the Amhara people—is a very traditional stew with a berbere sauce of sun-dried hot peppers and ground spices.

Lower East Side

The Lower East Side is one of New York City's most energetic, stylish, and fast-evolving neighborhoods. Bragging a plethora of shopping, eating, and nightlife, this high-energy hub proudly retains the personality of its first wave of hard-working immigrants. But, thanks to a steady stream of artists and entrepreneurs over the last few decades as well as a real estate uprising, the area faces constant transformation with an influx of high-rises breaking through trendy boutiques and galleries. And yet, some nooks remain straight up dodgy as if in defiance of such rapid development; while others feel downright Village-like in stature and spirit.

AROUND THE WORLD

Visit the Lower East Side Tenement Museum for a glimpse of the past before trekking its enticing, ethnically diverse streets. Then for a taste of yore, traipse into **Russ & Daughters** for delectable Kosher including smoked, cured fish and hearty bagels. This nosher's delight was instituted in 1914 but continues to be mobbed even today, especially during

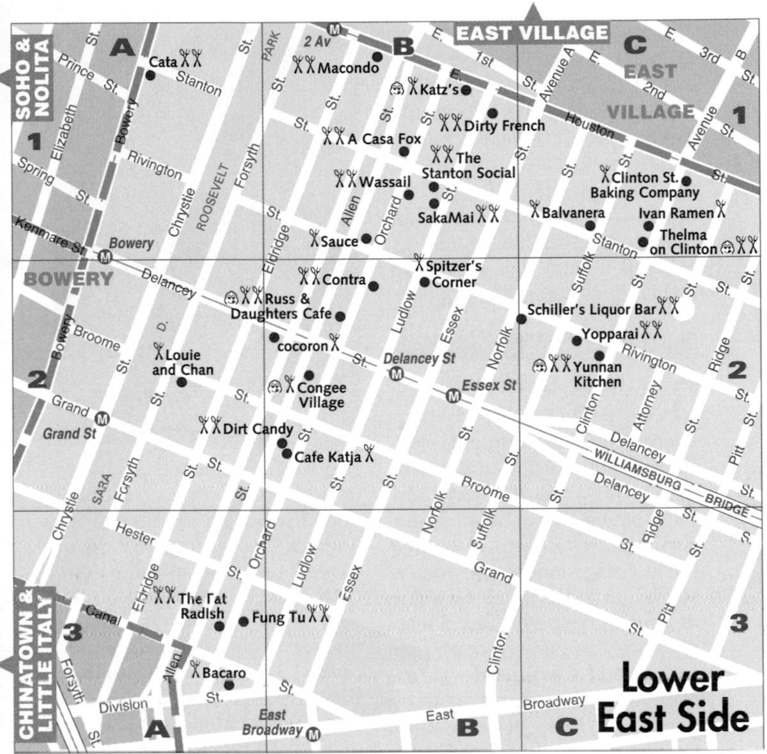

the holidays when that "ultimate salmon and caviar" package is nothing short of...you guessed it...ultimate! Also inhabiting these streets are German, Italian, and Chinese residents, whose apposite cultures have triggered a host of diverse and tasty eats 'n treats. Find signs of this at **Nonna's LES Pizza** where the red, white, and green squares are known to tug at all the right nostalgic strings. **Palà**, which boasts a vast list of gluten-free and vegan selections, is not far behind with homesick hordes craving a host of heart-warming pies. Meanwhile, an afternoon spent at **Gaia Italian Cafè** breezing through magazines and biting into delicious *dolci* or perfect biscotti will take you back to Rome on a dime. This toasty spot may be mini in size, but cooks up flavors that are big and bright. **Tiny's Giant Sandwich Shop** is yet another unpretentious but wholly irresistible gem where sandwiches rule the roost and are slung at all times. Ground zero for partygoers, punk rockers, and scholars, this Rivington Street paragon is a rare treat highlighting fresh ingredients and creative presentations. While on the topic of a spirited scene, **New Beer Distributors** is a warehouse-y beer shop in operation since 1968. Housing numerous bottles and cans from the globe over, craft beer aficionados will adore perusing its metal racks for rare (read exotic) varietals. Then, if sweet is what you need, **Economy Candy** is a flourishing emporium of old-time confections. Moving from timeless pleasures to new-fangled pastries, **Bisous Ciao Macarons** gives Stanton Street a hit of French flair thanks to its luxurious namesake goodies.

ETHNIC FUN

By the 1950s, the ethnic mosaic that defined this district intensified with a surge of new settlers, but this time they were mainly from Puerto Rico and the Dominican Republic. These communities continue to dot the culinary landscape today, so come to savor such favorites as *mofongo* or *pernil*. Domincan *especiales* and creamy *café con leche* at **El Castillo de Jagua** keep the party pumping from dawn till dusk, while sugar junkies find their fix at **Tache Artisan Chocolate**—launched by pastry chef, Aditi Malhotra. Try the tequila-infused dark chocolate ganache, which stays for a moment in your mouth but leaves an impression that will last a lifetime. Rivington Street is a perfect hybrid of the Old World and New Order. During the day, the mood here is chill with locals looking to linger at cozy coffee houses. For a wholesome pick-me-up, head to **TeaNY** specializing in all things wonderful (and vegan) including "the cup that cheers," usually served with brunch on weekends. Come sunset, these streets start to fill with raucous carousers looking to land upon a scene-y restaurant or popular party spot. Further

south, Grand Street is home to well-manicured residential complexes scattered amid shops and catering to a cadre of deep-rooted residents. While here, carb-addicts should be afraid, very afraid, of **Kossar's Bialys** flooded with bagels, *bialy*, and *bulkas*. Then there's **Doughnut Plant** proffering inventive selections crafted from age-old recipes. To replicate that classic deli experience at home, pick up pickles to-go from **The Pickle Guys**—settled on Essex and stocked with barrel-upon-barrel of these briny treats.

Fire escape-fronted Orchard Street is venerated as the original hub of the 'hood. Once dominated by the garment trade with stores selling fabrics and notions, it tells a different tale today with sleek eateries set amid trendy boutiques selling handmade jewelry and designer skateboards. Even tailors remain a cult favorite here, offering cheap, while-you-wait service. At lunchtime, find them at sandwich-slinging hot spots like **Black Tree**. Concurrently, **Cup & Saucer** is a teatime treasure serving everything under the sun, while **Dimes** (the café that exudes Cali-cool on Canal Street) is a reliable resource for three square meals a day. It's packed to the rafters during peak hours, so shoppers looking to cool their heels may drop by **Il Laboratorio del Gelato**, located on Ludlow.

ESSEX STREET MARKET

Every self-respecting foodie makes the pilgrimage to **Essex Street Market**, a treasure trove of gourmet food. Frequented for its top-notch produce merchants, butchers, bakers, and fishmongers all housed under one roof, this public bazaar expounds on their expertise by way of cooking demonstrations and wine tastings that keep crowds coming back for more. Burned-out browsers however may rest their feet and calm a craving at **Essex**, or even **Shopsin's General Store** notorious for its encyclopedic carte of goodies (and cranky owner). Finally, everything from chocolate (at **Roni-Sue's**); ice cream (at **Luca & Bosco**); or cheese (at **Saxelby Cheesemongers**) make this pleasure palace an enticing destination for gastronomes and curious palates alike.

A Casa Fox

B1 Latin American XX

173 Orchard St. (bet. Houston & Stanton Sts.)

Subway: 2 Av — Lunch Fri – Sat
Phone: 212-253-1900 — Dinner Tue – Sun
Web: www.acasafox.com
Prices: $$

This bold and bright darling serves superlative Latin fare with fantastic authenticity and a whole lotta love. This is largely thanks to Chef/owner Melissa Fox, who can be seen in the open kitchen or checking on guests in the snug space, filled with Mexican tiles, wide plank floors, and a warming fireplace.

Be sure to begin any meal with a selection of empanadas, as in pulled pork with caramelized onion, chorizo and aged manchego, or the outstanding *carne enchorizada* (seasoned ground beef with onions, tomatoes, yucca, chayote, and potatoes). Other dishes might include the *camarones a las brazes*, grilled shrimp in a sour-orange marinade wrapped in smoky bacon; or chicken *tostones*, its pulled meat on a well-grilled round of masa with *crema* and mango salsa.

Bacaro

A3 Italian X

136 Division St. (bet. Ludlow & Orchard Sts.)

Subway: East Broadway — Dinner Tue – Sun
Phone: 212-941-5060
Web: www.bacaronyc.com
Prices: $$

Heavy iron candelabras, crumbling stone walls, and communal wooden tables lend a sultry vibe to this underground labyrinth, named for a Venetian *bacaro* (or counter for casual grazing of snacks and wine). The first floor's marble-topped bar beckons for small bites and a glass of wine, while nooks beneath low stone ceilings in the downstairs dining room call for a romantic evening over candlelight.

Crafted by the same chef/owner of Peasant in NoLita, Bacaro's menu highlights the best of Venetian cuisine. *Bigoli con sugo d'anatra* brings together whole-wheat pasta with tender, pulled duck, a tomato-cream sauce, and shavings of salty parmesan. For dessert, the velvety flourless chocolate cake, topped with dried apricots, is as decadent as the setting.

Balvanera

Argentinian

152 Stanton St. (at Suffolk St.)

Subway: Delancey St
Phone: 212-533-3348
Web: www.balvaneranyc.com
Prices: $$

Dinner nightly

A balanced taste of Argentina is the centerpiece of this lively bistro, which is a destination for beautifully marbled, expertly grilled meats and super-fresh veggies. Service is attentive and free of attitude in a neighborhood where this is all too common, and whitewashed brick walls alongside tightly packed wooden tables highlight the low key, welcoming scene.

Balvanera's versatile menu is designed for sharing, from the authentically flaky empanadas with a zippy *chimichurri* to succulent house-made chorizo, served simply with a slice of smoky roasted red pepper. Meats are a must, including the dry-aged, grilled bone-in rib eye, garnished with crisp watercress. To balance all that meat, dig into sweet roasted carrots with frisée, orange, and pepitas.

Cafe Katja

Austrian 

79 Orchard St. (bet. Broome & Grand Sts.)

Subway: Delancey St
Phone: 212-219-9545
Web: www.cafekatja.com
Prices: $$

Lunch Tue – Sun
Dinner nightly

Beer mugs are clinking and schnapps is flowing at the rustic Cafe Katja. After slowly expanding to neighboring storefronts over the past few years, the owners have now realized its much-deserved grandeur without losing its charm. Expats plus locals are de rigueur here, and routinely stop in for incredibly delicious and unbelievably hearty eats.

Co-chef and owner Erwin Schrottner (who hails from outside Graz) keeps everything authentic, from house-made bratwurst platters to the mustard sour cream. The pretzels arrive straight from Europe as divine carbo-bombs served with *liptauer* cheese and butter. The idea of warm chocolate cake may seem passé, but this rendition with terrifically bittersweet orange marmalade is a treat for all the senses.

Cata

Spanish 

245 Bowery (at Stanton St.)

Subway: 2 Av
Phone: 212-505-2282
Web: www.catarestaurant.com
Prices: $$

Dinner nightly

Blue plaid and jean-clad waiters set the casual tone for Cata, a downtown-cool restaurant with a long bar and glass case displaying the day's fresh seafood. Distressed mirrors, vaulted ceilings, and iron accents fill the dark, cavernous space with a certain broody, old-world vibe. Long communal tables are ideal for groups lingering over small plates and a long list of gin-based cocktails.

Nibbling should be the strategy here, starting with whole deviled eggs stuffed with tangy-sweet *gribiche* beneath a single crunchy fried oyster. Crispy bite-sized bombas filled with creamy potato, Manchego, and Serrano ham sit in a very nice, mildly spicy tomato sauce. Paella is ever-pleasing with head-on shrimp, chorizo, and a satisfying *socarrat* at the bottom of the pan.

Clinton St. Baking Company

American 

4 Clinton St. (bet. Houston & Stanton Sts.)

Subway: 2 Av
Phone: 646-602-6263
Web: www.clintonstreetbaking.com
Prices:

Lunch daily
Dinner Mon – Sat

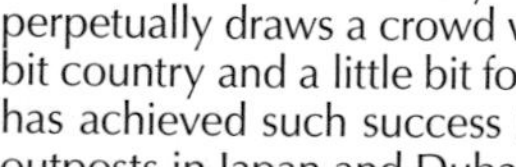

What started as a bakery has become a legend—one that perpetually draws a crowd waiting for ample rewards. A little bit country and a little bit food lab, this brunch-focused bijou has achieved such success in NY that the owners now have outposts in Japan and Dubai. Service can struggle to keep up with the crowds, but the loud and lively dining room doesn't seem to notice.

Breakfast for dinner is always a treat, especially when golden brown Belgian waffles are served with warm maple butter and topped with buttermilk-brined fried chicken for a flawless marriage of sweet and savory. Lighter but still lovely, chicken tortilla soup sees a pile of crunchy fried tortilla strips over hearty broth bobbing with carrots, celery, and shredded chicken.

cocoron

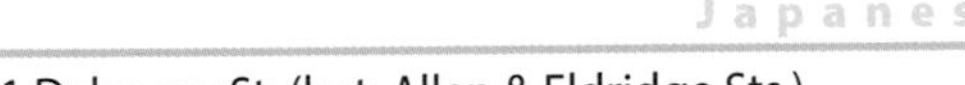

Japanese

B2

61 Delancey St. (bet. Allen & Eldridge Sts.)

Subway: Delancey St — Lunch & dinner Tue – Sun
Phone: 212-925-5220
Web: www.cocoron-soba.com
Prices: ⚭

Don't mind the manga posters or the menu's colorful cartoons; this is a serious destination for all things soba. The room is cramped and the furniture flimsy, yet a seat at the counter facing the open kitchen promises excellent cold, warm, and dip soba noodles. Service underwhelms and the scene is quirky, but the focus here is solely on the noodles and noodles alone.

Curry dip soba arrives as a shallow bamboo basket of firm, chilled noodles just as a heavily spiced sauce with pork, ginger, and green onion bubbles away in a clay pot set atop a small flame. Dunk these strands of cold soba into the hot broth and let the slurping begin. Then rest assured that when you're done, the curry is fortified with hot soba water to form a delicious and drinkable soup.

Congee Village

Chinese

B2

100 Allen St. (bet. Broome & Delancey Sts.)

Subway: Delancey St — Lunch & dinner daily
Phone: 212-941-1818
Web: www.congeevillagerestaurants.com
Prices: ⚭

From the edge of Chinatown comes Congee Village, with its neon-etched sign that shines bright at night. Coveted for its fantastic cooking (check the front window for a slew of accolades), the menu also has a Cantonese focus. Service is basic and the décor kitschy at best, but it's clean, tidy, and tons of fun.

This soothing namesake porridge comes in myriad forms—ladled into a clay pot with bits of crispy roasted duck skin, or mingled with pork liver and white fish to form an intense and rich flavor combination. Pair it with dunkable sticks of puffy deep-fried Chinese crullers for a satisfying contrast in texture. Less adventurous palates may deviate into such solid standards as sautéed short ribs and sweet onions tossed in a smoky black pepper sauce.

Contra

B2 Contemporary XX

138 Orchard St. (bet. Delancey & Rivington Sts.)

Subway: 2 Av Dinner Tue – Sat
Phone: 212-466-4633
Web: www.contranyc.com
Prices: $$

Avant-garde Contra brims with a youthful vibe, from the music overhead to the chefs' creativity. Beyond the entrance's neon sign is a small, lamp-lit space with exposed brick and inviting banquettes. At the bar, patrons can sample the forward-thinking fare or fully indulge in an affordable five-course menu.

An experimental spirit is clear from the first bite of a warm poppy- and sesame seed-loaf brushed with pork fat and served with sweet-cream butter. Mackerel arrives with blistered skin, tender peas, favas, and charred Padron peppers. Superlative desserts show glimmers of genius, as in the loosely whipped cloud of sunchoke purée with warm toffee caramel and icy apple granita.

Visit Wildair a few doors down for like-minded cuisine in a more casual setting by the same team.

Dirt Candy

B2 Vegetarian XX

86 Allen St. (bet. Broome & Grand Sts.)

Subway: Grand St Dinner Tue – Sat
Phone: 212-228-7732
Web: www.dirtcandynyc.com
Prices: $$

Fans of this vegetarian temple were heartbroken when the original East Village location closed, but thankfully their grief was short-lived. Chef Amanda Cohen and team quickly transplanted themselves to bigger, bolder digs, where industrial elements meld with bright white walls and a chic bar proffers both cocktails and consolation seating.

Dirt Candy's menu is best described as a bounty of creativity, with options like "Fennel," a hearty salad of raw and pickled shavings with black bean cake and caramelized yogurt spread *carta di musica*; as well as "Carrots," the orange veggies roasted with jerk spices and served over a carrot waffle with peanut *mole* sauce. Desserts are every bit as inspired, like a chocolate tart peppered with caramelized onions.

Dirty French

French XX

180 Ludlow St. (bet. Houston & Stanton Sts.)

Lunch & dinner daily

Subway: 2 Av
Phone: 212-254-3000
Web: www.dirtyfrench.com
Prices: $$$

Dirty French is Major Food Group's stab at a hotel restaurant—and what a theatrical, charismatic stab it is. Settled in the Ludlow Hotel, this space shares the neighborhood's irreverent attitude, from the pink neon signs at the door to the casual kicks on the hipster waiters. Tables are tightly packed and lively conversations drown out funky music.

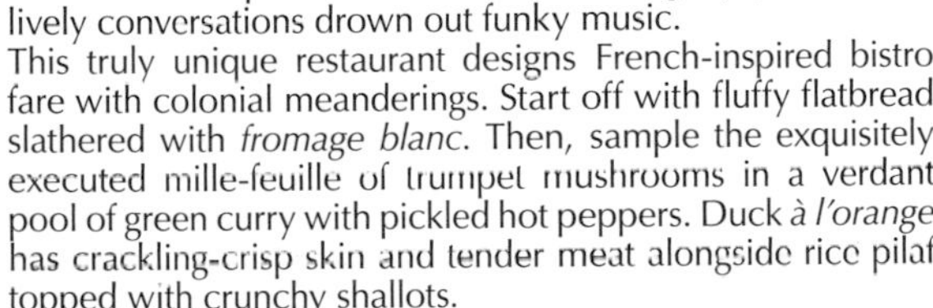

This truly unique restaurant designs French-inspired bistro fare with colonial meanderings. Start off with fluffy flatbread slathered with *fromage blanc*. Then, sample the exquisitely executed mille-feuille of trumpet mushrooms in a verdant pool of green curry with pickled hot peppers. Duck *à l'orange* has crackling-crisp skin and tender meat alongside rice pilaf topped with crunchy shallots.

The Fat Radish

Contemporary XX

17 Orchard St. (bet. Canal & Hester Sts.)

Lunch Tue – Sun
Dinner nightly

Subway: East Broadway
Phone: 212-300-4053
Web: www.thefatradishnyc.com
Prices: $$

British-leaning yet focused on local and seasonal cooking, this kitchen showcases two ways to indulge—choose between creative vegetarian dishes or old-world classics that are always worth the splurge. The farmhouse-style interior is a nice contrast to the Lower East Side setting, with exposed brick walls, charmingly mismatched wooden seats, and a distressed mirror listing daily specials.

Guests may be torn between the hearty Scotch egg or macrobiotic plate. Yet the casual-cool servers will be quick to point out that just as much detail goes into the burger as the roasted cauliflower over braised lentils with sheep's milk yogurt. Finish the meal in British style with a slice of banoffee pie, with layers of banana, caramel toffee, and fluffy whipped cream.

Fung Tu

Asian XX

A3

22 Orchard St. (bet. Canal & Hester Sts.)

Subway: East Broadway Dinner Tue – Sun
Phone: 212-219-8785
Web: www.fungtu.com
Prices: $$

It's a cool crowd that flocks to Fung Tu, tucked away in an up-and-coming Lower East Side pocket between the Manhattan and Williamsburg Bridge. Inside, you'll find a long, narrow dining space where chatty millennials and thirty-something parents with toddlers in tow dine with equal ease; and a cool bar upfront is designed with plate-sharing and lingering in mind.

The Chinese-influenced menu cleverly mines its home continent for deliciously exotic accents, but the ambitious dishes can be hit or miss. Surefire items include the springy egg noodles tossed with tender chopped clams, then laced with scallions, ginger, garlic, and chili oil; or fresh, perfectly-cooked sea bream served with fennel, tangerine peel, chili oil, and fermented black beans.

Ivan Ramen

Japanese

C1

25 Clinton St. (bet. Houston & Stanton Sts.)

Subway: Delancey St Lunch & dinner daily
Phone: 646-678-3859
Web: www.ivanramen.com
Prices: $$

This delicious little *ramen-ya* couldn't have landed on a more fitting spot. It may appear rough around the edges, but the ultra-hip 'hood and its affinity for indie rock beats fit Ivan's scene to a tee. Then consider their sweet staff gliding within the snug space filled with packed seats and realize how serious a treat this is.

Solo diners head to the counter for a view of the action-packed kitchen, while others look for a seat from which to admire that mural of manga cutouts. Find them launching into pickled daikon with XO sauce and sesame seeds for a 'lil crunch and whole 'lotta flavor. Displaying a flare for non-traditional ingredients, *paitan* ramen with tender chicken confit in a chicken-and-kombu broth makes for a singular, savory, and tasty highlight.

Katz's

205 E. Houston St. (at Ludlow St.)

Subway: 2 Av
Phone: 212-254-2246
Web: www.katzsdelicatessen.com
Prices: 

Lunch & dinner daily

One of the last-standing, old-time Eastern European spots on the Lower East Side, Katz's is a true NY institution. It's crowded, crazy, and packed with a panoply of characters weirder than a jury duty pool. Tourists, hipsters, blue hairs, and everybody in between flock here, so come on off-hours. Because it's really *that* good.

Walk inside, get a ticket, and don't lose it (those guys at the front aren't hosts—upset their system and you'll get a verbal beating). Then get your food at the counter and bring it to a first-come first-get table; or opt for a slightly less dizzying experience at a waitress-served table.

Nothing's changed in the looks or taste. Matzo ball soup, pastrami sandwiches, potato latkes—everything is what you'd expect, only better.

Louie and Chan

303 Broome St. (bet. Eldridge & Forsyth Sts.)

Subway: Grand St
Phone: 212-837-2816
Web: www.louieandchan.com
Prices: $$

Lunch Sat – Sun
Dinner nightly

With a name that nods to the convergence of Chinese and Italian immigrants in this part of lower Manhattan, Louie and Chan is a dimly lit, tightly packed restaurant with inspired cooking. The main space feels more bar than dining room, with intentionally scruffy walls decorated with distressed mirrors. Service is friendly and a young crowd keeps things lively.

Cocktails are Asian-inspired while the menu uses Italy as its muse. Delicate gnudi arrive in a rustic bowl of tender lamb ragù topped with a dollop of smoked ricotta. A wood-burning oven is responsible for the blistered crust pizzas, including the *bacio del diavolo,* decked with tart tomato sauce, chunks of 'nduja, house-made mozzarella, and spicy whole Calabrese peppers.

Macondo

Latin American XX

B1

157 E. Houston St. (bet. Allen & Eldridge Sts.)

Subway: 2 Av — Lunch Sat – Sun
Phone: 212-473-9900 — Dinner nightly
Web: www.macondonyc.com
Prices: **$$**

Readers of Gabriel Garcia Marquez will be familiar with this Latin American restaurant's name—Macondo is the fictional setting of *100 Years of Solitude*. Here on the Lower East Side (and at the West Village outpost), it is an intimate small plates restaurant with a long bar of counter seating, semi-open kitchen, and exposed brick walls with stocked shelves of Latin pantry ingredients.

Sharing is the strategy here, from the crispy chicken croquettes to the raw kale and manchego salad with crunchy roasted pumpkin seeds and a sweet kick from sticky dried dates, topped with a lemon-chipotle dressing. Be prepared to battle over the last bite of *arroz con pollo*, a piping-hot cast iron pan of plump bomba rice, piquant chorizo, tender chicken, and cherry tomatoes.

Russ & Daughters Cafe

Deli XX

B2

127 Orchard St. (bet. Delancey & Rivington Sts.)

Subway: Delancey St — Lunch & dinner daily
Phone: 212-475-4881
Web: www.russanddaughterscafe.com
Prices: **$$**

From white-jacketed servers to that pristine counter, this updated yet model LES café channels the very spirit and charm of its mothership, set only blocks away. The adept kitchen follows suit, taking the original, appetizing classics and turning them on their heads to form an array of proper and profoundly flavorful dishes.

Regulars perch at the bar to watch the 'tender whip up a cocktail or classic egg cream, while serious diners find a seat and get noshing on hot- and cold-smoked Scottish salmon teamed with potato crisps. The result? A thrilling contrast in flavor and texture. Caramelized chocolate babka French toast is crowned with strawberries for a sweet-savory treat; and "eggs Benny" with salmon, spinach, and challah never fails to peg a bruncher.

SakaMai

Japanese XX

157 Ludlow St. (bet. Rivington & Stanton Sts.)

Subway: Delancey St — Dinner nightly
Phone: 646-590-0684
Web: www.sakamai.com
Prices: $$$

A modern *izakaya* like no other, SakaMai sets a new standard for downtown cuisine. With its chic urban style, a curated sake- *shochu-* and whiskey-list, and creative dishes, this authentic haunt draws a food- and drink-focused crowd that's more interested in Japanese sips than pints of beer.

Plates are meant to be shared, sashimi are top-notch, and flavors simply impress: a well-seasoned Waygu steak arrives with roasted vegetables and tasty sauces; while a porcelain sea urchin shell, filled with gently scrambled eggs, caviar, and more sea urchin, is as decadent as it sounds. For an exceptional balance between flavor and texture, try the kanpachi dressed with a chiffonade of shiso, *myoga*, yuzu juice, freshly ground wasabi, and *shoyu* glaze.

Sauce

78-84 Rivington St. (at Allen St.)

Subway: 2 Av — Lunch Sat – Sun
Phone: 212-420-7700 — Dinner nightly
Web: www.saucerestaurant.com

What would you expect from a spot called Sauce? Some serious and very delicious red sauce—naturally! Serving Italian-American comfort food with a nostalgic décor to match, Sauce stays modern with its local, hipster-friendly playlist, and quirky ambience—the attractive crowd doesn't hurt either. It's a fun meal to say the least.

Pasta is made in-house daily, with specials that feature potato-kale gnocchi or the signature ricotta *cavatelli* showered with pecorino. The menu highlights regional specialties from Little Italys across the country, including SF's cioppino and classic *Nuyorkese* tomato gravy like *nonna* used to make. Try the robust Sergio Leone steak smothered in tomato sauce and topped with a fried heritage egg for tons of fun and flavor.

Schiller's Liquor Bar

American

131 Rivington St. (at Norfolk St.)

Subway: Delancey St — Lunch & dinner daily
Phone: 212-260-4555
Web: www.schillersny.com
Prices: $$

In business for over a decade, this fantastically retro city favorite still buzzes with cool crowds and tasty American comfort food—thanks to a focused and skilled kitchen. Plunked on prime Lower East Side real estate, the commanding bistro's white-tile exterior, black- and white-tiled floor, and wrought-iron doors invite groups of friends for cocktails and $1 oyster happy hour at the curved bar.

While the libations aren't standout, they are a nice complement to tried-and-true classics like braised pork tacos folded with pineapple, tomatillos, pickled red onion, and lime crema with a devilish salsa habanera. A braised brisket patty melt with a decadent blend of pepper jack, mustard, and balsamic onions is as faultless as a tart and refreshing Key lime pie.

Spitzer's Corner

Gastropub 

B2

101 Rivington St. (at Ludlow St.)

Subway: Delancey St — Lunch & dinner daily
Phone: 212-228-0027
Web: www.spitzerscorner.com
Prices: $$

Spitzer's is a spirited corner eatery dedicated to craft brews and gastropub fare in a buzzing locale. Large glass windows overlook the heart of the neighborhood, providing an entertaining vantage point for people-watching over pints of nutty Bronx Pale Ale. There are large communal tables made of reclaimed wood and chalkboards listing comfort food classics.

This is a cozy drinking den, and its kitchen focuses on food that pairs well with suds. Tables are laden with quality renditions of burgers and mac 'n cheese. Spinach and artichoke dip is equally comforting, topped with broiled cheese and served with chargrilled pita. A fried chicken sandwich sees generous chunks of crunchy thigh meat stuffed into potato rolls with butter lettuce and a pickle.

The Stanton Social

Fusion XX

99 Stanton St. (bet. Ludlow & Orchard Sts.)

Subway: 2 Av — Lunch Sat – Sun
Phone: 212-995-0099 — Dinner nightly
Web: www.thestantonsocial.com
Prices: $$

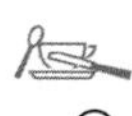

This hugely favored haunt's low lighting, thumping beats, and beautiful crowd clearly say nightlife lounge, but its roster of pleasing creations establish the kitchen as an expert in flavors and textures. The multi-level room is sexy yet remains timeless despite its age. Those chic, dark leather banquettes provide plenty of space for large groups to kick back to whatever the DJ spins in the second-floor lounge.

This isn't a place for conversation between friends, but rather a large group destination for delicious small plates like crisp red snapper tacos with creamy avocado and zesty mango salsa. Tasty Asian flavors combine seamlessly with chunks of skewered salmon cooked rare and coated in crunchy *sriracha*-infused peas over cold soba and earthy beets.

Thelma on Clinton 

American XX

29A Clinton St. (bet. Houston & Stanton Sts.)

Subway: Essex St — Lunch Sat – Sun
Phone: 212-979-8471 — Dinner Mon – Sat
Web: www.thelmaonclinton.com
Prices: $$

With its cozy bistro décor and sincere, down-to-earth service, Thelma on Clinton is the kind of unpretentious restaurant everyone wants around the corner from home.

Owner Melissa O'Donnell is a longtime fixture on New York's restaurant scene, and Thelma is her latest contribution—this time, in her old Salt Bar space. Does she kill it? She kills it: and she might just get double credit for producing such delicious fare in a kitchen smaller than some local apartment kitchens. Kick things off with the scrumptious bacon-wrapped dates, laced in a irresistible, sticky maple sauce. Then move on to tender spring pea and asparagus risotto with plump peas, crunchy asparagus and Grana Padano cheese; or olive oil-poached codfish in a lovely citrus sauce.

Wassail

Gastropub XX

B1

162 Orchard St. (bet. Rivington & Stanton Sts.)

Subway: 2 Av Dinner nightly
Phone: 646-918-6835
Web: www.wassailnyc.com
Prices: $$

Everyone's buzzing about Wassail's awesome list of 90+ ciders from around the world, but there are a few delectable reasons to check out this Lower East Side gem. Chef Joseph Buenconsejo's vegetable- and grain-focused menu is initially a surprise, but the technique, seasonality, and personality he brings to each dish will sway even the most adamant carnivore.

Witness peas done three ways—mashed, julienned, sliced in their pods, and plated with creamy ricotta, pea broth, and mini *parathas*; or a glossy, slow-cooked egg served over salty broccolini and shredded Brussels sprouts with a lemony sorrel Hollandaise. Rebecca Eichenbaum's savory-leaning desserts, like a frozen spruce soufflé topped with buttermilk granita and pistachio crumble, are pure bliss.

Yopparai

Japanese XX

C2

151 Rivington St. (bet. Clinton & Suffolk Sts.)

Subway: Delancey St Dinner Mon – Sat
Phone: 212-777-7253
Web: www.yopparainyc.com
Prices: $$$

Buzzing into Yopparai is like waltzing into culinary wonder. Secluded above street level, the attentive staff and cozy vibe alone make this Japanese haven a must. Same for the food, which adds immense thrill to the equation.

From the homemade *natto* or amazing, artisanal udon, to the unparalleled flavor from tofu, each dish features a plethora of intricately prepared parts that unite perfectly. While their items are consistently appealing, standouts include *inaniwa* udon, set in a shallow pool of cool dashi topped with thin slices of chicken, tomato, cucumber, and nori accompanied by peanut sauce. The smooth and custardy *yodoufu* is a revelation served warm in a wooden box.

For extra sake fun, drop by Azasu, a group-friendly delight from the same team.

Yunnan Kitchen

Chinese XX

79 Clinton St. (bet. Delancey & Rivington Sts.)

Subway: Delancey St — Dinner Tue-Sun
Phone: 212-253-2527
Web: www.yunnankitchen.com
Prices: **$$**

The Lower East Side is awash in delicious Asian food, but Yunnan Kitchen, which aims its sights on the delicate, refreshingly diverse cuisine of the Yunnan region, sets itself apart from the pack. Beautiful trinkets like heirloom necklaces and tiger print rugs, carefully gathered from owner Erika Chou's travels, line the walls of this communal eatery and provide the perfect exotic backdrop for the kitchen's subtle, unique dishes.

A pomelo salad arrives in juicy little clusters over chrysanthemum greens with deep-fried shallots; while impossibly moist *shao kao* lamb is skewered, then barbecued to spicy perfection with red chili pepper. Fresh red snapper served over a springy pile of sweet potato noodles laced in Sichuan peppercorn oil makes for a fine finale.

Sunday brunch plans?
Look for the !

Midtown East

An interesting mix of office buildings, hotels, high-rises, and townhouses, Midtown East is one of the city's most industrious areas. Home to the iconic Chrysler Building and United Nations Headquarters, the vibe here is buzzing with suits, students, and old-timers wandering its streets. Whether it's that reliable diner on the corner, a gourmet supermarket, or fine dining gem, this neighborhood flaunts it all. Close on the heels of its global theme, **Adana Grill** is a highly enjoyable Turkish takeout spot, where items are grilled to order. The wait is long and entirely worth it. Residents of neighboring Beekman and Sutton Place are proud of their very own top fishmonger (**Pisacane Seafood**); cheese shop (**Ideal Cheese**); butcher (**L. Simchick Meats**); bagel and lox shop (**Tal Bagels**); and to complete any dinner party—renowned florist (**Zeze**). While **Dag Hammarskjöld Plaza Greenmarket** may by dwarfed by Union Square, come Wednesdays it presents just the right amount of everything to feed hungry locals. Then sample a bit of chic at Paris-based café **Rose Bakery**, housed inside the very haute and very hip Dover Street Market. It may be tucked behind a soaring cement column sheathed in colorful macramé, but turn a corner to find display cases filled with fresh salads and tempting sweets.

GRAND CENTRAL TERMINAL

Built by the Vanderbilt family in the 19th century, **Grand Central Terminal** is a 21st century food sanctuary. An ideal day

at this titanic and particularly gorgeous train station may begin with a coffee from **Joe's**. Later, stop by one of Manhattan's historic sites, the **Grand Central Oyster Bar & Restaurant**, nestled into the cavernous lower level. This gorgeous seafood respite presents everything from shellfish stews and fresh fish, to an incredible raw bar and more. Then take a turn—of taste—and head to **Neuhaus**, venerable chocolatiers who craft their delicacies from exceptional ingredients. Some may stop by family-owned and renowned **Li-Lac Chocolates** for such nostalgic confections as dark chocolate-covered pretzels or beautifully packaged holiday gift boxes. But, those who meet the dress code may end the affair at **Campbell Apartment**, the restored private office of 1920s railroad mogul John W. Campbell, and one of the area's swankier stops for a famously dry martini. Of course, no trip to this Terminal is complete without a visit to the "whispering gallery" where low, ceramic-tiled arches allow whispers to sound like more like shouts. Just beyond, the loud dining concourse hums with lunch stalls ranging from **Café Spice** for Indian or **Eata Pita** for Middle Eastern. **Mendy's** is midtown's go-to for everything kosher—think pastrami and brisket mingled in with some Mid-Eastern eats. Then, finish with the sweetest treats—maybe red velvet cupcakes at the terminal's very own **Magnolia Bakery** outpost. Moving on to the market, Eli Zabar has expanded his empire, and continues to proffer the freshest fruits and vegetables at **Eli Zabar's Farm to Table**. But, for an impressive assortment of pastries and cakes, **Eli Zabar's Bread & Pastry** is your best bet. In addition to its

myriad fishmongers, butchers, and bakers, home cooks and top chefs are likely to find the best selection of spices here—at one of the market's better-kept secrets, **Spices and Tease**, specializing exotic blends and...you guessed it...unique teas. But, if you're among truly hungry hordes with time to spare, make sure to visit one of the several prized restaurants situated beneath Grand Central's celestial ceiling mural for a stellar night.

JAPANTOWN

Trek a few blocks east of Lexington to find a very sophisticated Japantown, where scores of *izakaya* and restaurants are scattered among hostess clubs. Salarymen frequent old-world hangouts like **Riki**, **Ariyoshi**, and **Tsukushi**, or rookies like **Lucky Cat**. Favored **BentOn Cafe** may be a retail outpost of a bento delivery service, but tenders excellent, daily changing bentos at terrific value. Japanese expats with ladies in tow linger over the psuedo-Italian spread at **Aya**, just as the yuppy crews may opt for a light bite from **Cafe Zaiya** or **Dainobu** (both bustling deli-cum-markets). **Nishida Shoten** is cherished for comforting noodles soups; **Hinata Ramen** is an all-time gem for steaming bowls of

ramen; while **Nikai** is beloved for its vast selection. Red meat fiends join the lines outside **Katsu-Hama** or **Yakiniku Gen** for delicious grilled meats. Looking to impress your out-of-town guests? Plan a Japanese-themed evening by stocking up on gleaming ceramics, cookware, and authentic produce from specialty emporium, **MTC Kitchen**. A few blocks south, younger and quieter Murray Hill has its own distinct vibe. Here, fast-casual finds thrive thanks to thirty-somethings sating late-night cravings. Meanwhile, The Kitano, one among a handful of Gotham's Japanese-owned boutique hotels, continues to lure thanks to its sleek vibe, live tunes at **JAZZ at Kitano**, and traditional kaiseki cuisine served at their subterranean hot spot, **Hakubai**.

SWEETS AND SPIRITS

Slightly north, owner and pastry chef, Stephane Pourrez, brings French flair and baked treats to **Éclair** on 53rd Street. Showcasing a lineup of pastries, cakes, macarons, and of course, those eponymous eclairs, this sweet midtown spot also houses some of *the* flakiest croissants in town. Steps away, savor some bubbly and cool beats at **Flute**, or indulge in wine at petite **Pierre Loti**.

MetLife

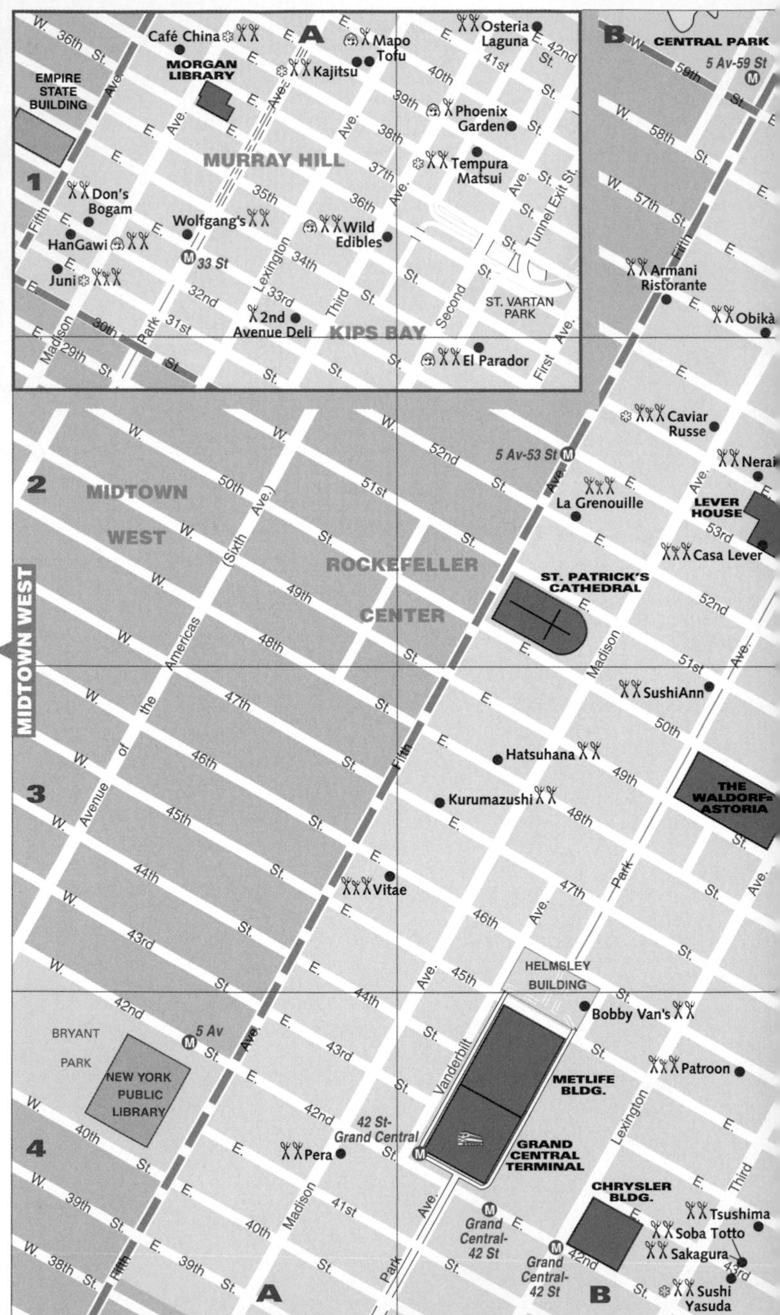
MIDTOWN WEST
MURRAY HILL
KIPS BAY
MIDTOWN WEST
ROCKEFELLER CENTER
CENTRAL PARK
EMPIRE STATE BUILDING
MORGAN LIBRARY
ST. VARTAN PARK
ST. PATRICK'S CATHEDRAL
LEVER HOUSE
THE WALDORF=ASTORIA
HELMSLEY BUILDING
METLIFE BLDG.
GRAND CENTRAL TERMINAL
CHRYSLER BLDG.
BRYANT PARK
NEW YORK PUBLIC LIBRARY
Café China
Mapo Tofu
Kajitsu
Osteria Laguna
Phoenix Garden
Tempura Matsui
Don's Bogam
Wolfgang's
Wild Edibles
HanGawi
Juni
2nd Avenue Deli
El Parador
Armani Ristorante
Obikà
Caviar Russe
Nerai
La Grenouille
Casa Lever
SushiAnn
Hatsuhana
Kurumazushi
Vitae
Bobby Van's
Patroon
Pera
Tsushima
Soba Totto
Sakagura
Sushi Yasuda
33 St
5 Av-59 St
5 Av-53 St
5 Av
42 St-Grand Central
Grand Central-42 St
Grand Central-42 St

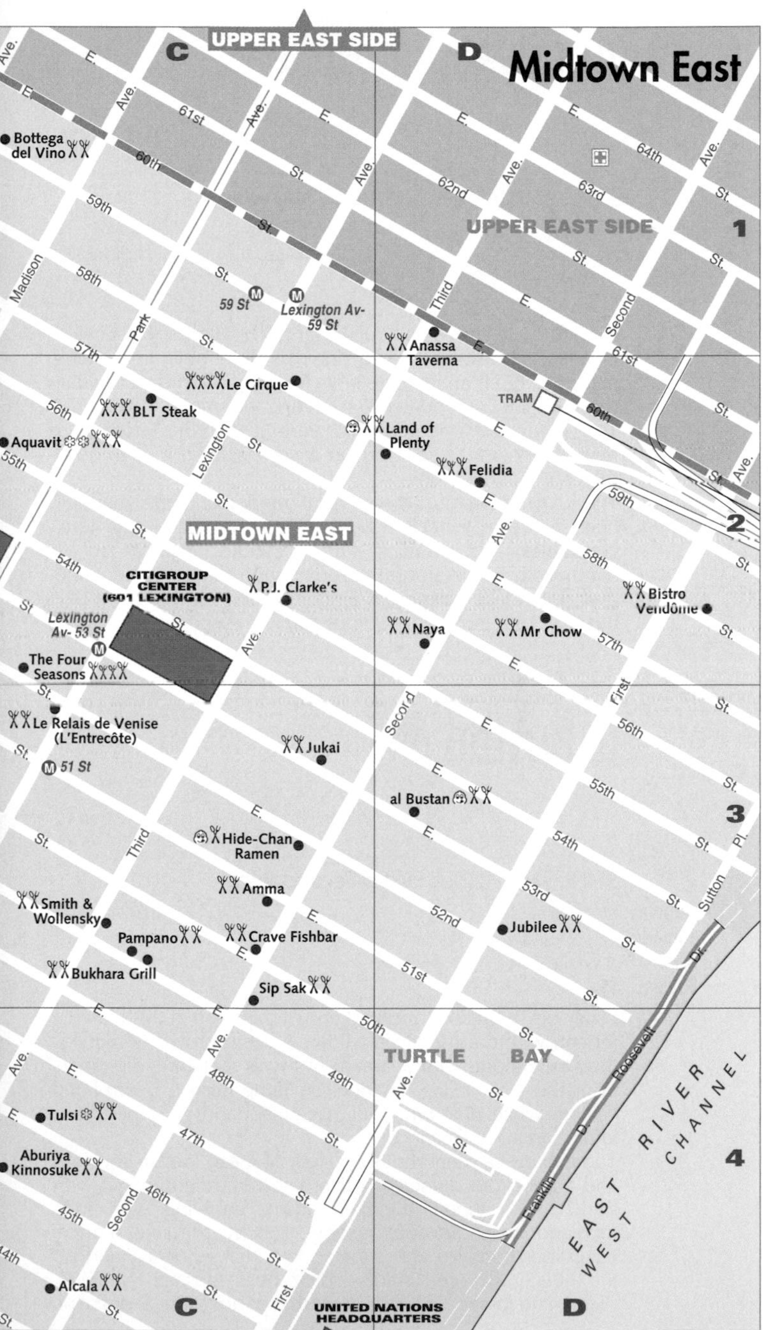
Midtown East
UPPER EAST SIDE
MIDTOWN EAST
TURTLE BAY
UNITED NATIONS HEADQUARTERS
CITIGROUP CENTER (601 LEXINGTON)
Bottega del Vino
Le Cirque
BLT Steak
Aquavit
Anassa Taverna
Land of Plenty
Felidia
P.J. Clarke's
Naya
Mr Chow
Bistro Vendôme
The Four Seasons
Le Relais de Venise (L'Entrecôte)
Jukai
al Bustan
Hide-Chan Ramen
Amma
Smith & Wollensky
Pampano
Crave Fishbar
Bukhara Grill
Sip Sak
Jubilee
Tulsi
Aburiya Kinnosuke
Alcala
59 St
Lexington Av-59 St
Lexington Av-53 St
51 St
TRAM
EAST RIVER
WEST CHANNEL
Franklin D. Roosevelt Dr.
Sutton Pl.

Aburiya Kinnosuke

Japanese XX

C4

213 E. 45th St. (bet. Second & Third Aves.)

Subway: Grand Central - 42 St — Lunch Mon – Fri
Phone: 212-867-5454 — Dinner nightly
Web: www.aburiyakinnosuke.com
Prices: $$$

Call it a trip to Tokyo without the tariff. This dark, sophisticated Japanese *izakaya* is tucked down a side street in bustling midtown. Grab an intimate table for two or join the crowd at the open kitchen counter surrounding the smoky *robata* grill. The waiters talk up the omakase, but it's worth trusting your own instincts to guide you on a personalized tour through their authentic offerings.

The *sukiyaki* is a must-try seasonal offering of tender marbled beef served in a hot pot bobbing with a beaten egg, tofu, vegetables, and noodles. Other favorites include smoky bamboo shoots fresh off the *robata* with shaved bonito; and their legendary *tsukune*, a tender ground chicken meatball brushed with teriyaki and dipped in raw egg.

al Bustan

Lebanese XX

D3

319 E. 53rd St. (bet. First & Second Aves.)

Subway: Lexington Av - 53 St — Lunch & dinner daily
Phone: 212-759-5933
Web: www.albustanny.com
Prices: $$

Lebanese specialties are fired up with aplomb at this enticing retreat, where a moneyed Middle Eastern crowd dominates the space along with a stream of locals including diplomats from the UN. Inside, chandeliers hang from a beam-lined ceiling, while neat white leather chairs and glass partitions impart an air of elegance.

The expansive menu boasts a slew of meze, house specials, and a knockout dinner prix-fixe. Let the feasting begin with *samboussek jibneh*, a baked pastry bubbling with salty feta and crisp *fattoush*, tossing crunchy romaine lettuce, cucumber, tomato, and sumac. And that's not all: add on the hugely flavored *sujuk*—spicy beef sausage—sautéed, sliced, and kissed with lemon for that perfect smack of flavor.

Alcala

Spanish XX

246 E. 44th St. (bet. Second and Third Aves.)

Subway: Grand Central - 42 St
Lunch Mon – Fri
Dinner nightly
Phone: 212-370-1866
Web: www.alcalarestaurant.com
Prices: $$$

This cozy Spanish eatery is a stone's throw from the United Nations, drawing a lively evening mix of sophisticated international clientele and neighborhood regulars. With its buttery yellow walls and homey little bar stocked with delicious Spanish wines, Alcala might remind you of an old Spanish *finca*, but at heart its also one of those old school New York haunts, where the waiters and cooks have been in place forever and you wouldn't dream of kicking your meal off without a drink.

The dishes are delicious, well-prepared, and ample. Try the *sardinas a la parrilla*, laced with hot pimiento oil; fresh, grilled branzino in a bright tomato coulis; or the *tarta de aresse*, a rich custard pie with mouthwatering crème anglaise and strawberry coulis.

Amma

Indian XX

246 E. 51st St. (bet. Second & Third Aves.)

Subway: 51 St
Lunch & dinner daily
Phone: 212-644-8330
Web: www.ammanyc.com
Prices: $$

Vibrant family-style South Asian cooking is appropriately set within this former townhouse, as *amma* is the word for mother in several South Indian languages. And manners are a must, as this "home" is adjacent to the UN, and service is attentively buttoned-up.

Find generously-portioned options from both the north and south subcontinent. Street snack Bombay *bhel puri* is colorfully seasoned with tamarind water and mango powder-laced *chaat masala*. Hard-to-find menu items such as *bagharey baingan* or eggplants simmered in a thick, rich peanut curry, make you feel like you've been let in on a little secret and invited to the neighbor's party. Pistachio *kulfi* is a satisfyingly sweet, cardamom-spiced finale which makes another neighborly visit inevitable.

Anassa Taverna

Greek XX

D1

200 E. 60th St. (at Third Ave.)

Subway: 59 St — Lunch & dinner daily
Phone: 212-371-5200
Web: www.anassataverna.com
Prices: $$

Two floors of whitewashed brick walls and large windows dressed with sheer drapery provide a respite for weary shoppers and a sociable clientele at this contemporary taverna. The upstairs dining room is sedate, but remains your best bet when crowds pack the ground-level bar area.

Anassa's menu is an honest presentation of Greek specialties, including a platter of spreads, sushi-quality charcoal-broiled octopus, and a selection of Mediterranean and North Atlantic fish to be grilled and dressed with extra virgin olive oil, fresh lemon, and capers. Nightly specials add further variety to the extensive menu. Don't miss Wednesday's luscious slow-roasted pork shoulder served fork-tender in a parchment bundle with fresh herbs and wedges of lemon potatoes.

Armani Ristorante

Italian XX

B1

717 5th Ave. (at 56th St.)

Subway: 5 Av - 53 St — Lunch daily
Phone: 212-207-1902 — Dinner Mon – Sat
Web: www.armanirestaurants.com
Prices: $$$

At Giorgio Armani's Fifth Avenue restaurant what you're wearing is as important as what you're eating. Overlooking the famous street, models serve as (distracted) staff members and bartenders are pure showstoppers—to no one's surprise. Would you expect anything less of the man whose luxurious Armani Casa furniture lines the space?

His streamlined and modern aesthetic prevails, right down to the glistening, ruby-red tuna tartare. Each cube cut by hand, the sea-fresh fish rolls in truffle oil and chives with briny sea beans and trout roe for a fantastic play on texture. Equally precise, the pan-seared spring flounder is infused with a coriander reduction, fresh porcini, and fennel with an airy foam that looks so good it may as well be Photoshopped.

Aquavit ✿✿

Scandinavian XXX

C2

65 E. 55th St. (bet. Madison & Park Aves.)

Subway: 5 Av - 53 St
Phone: 212-307-7311
Web: www.aquavit.org
Prices: $$$$

Lunch Mon – Fri
Dinner Mon – Sat

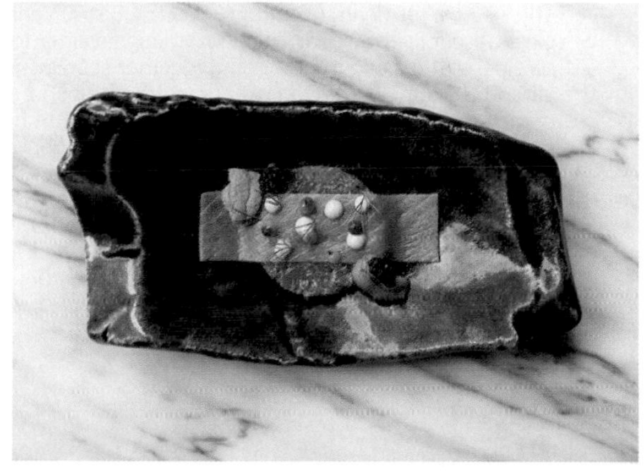

Gorgeously Scandinavian yet pleasantly corporate, Aquavit is a tribute to the Nordic culinary movement with more midtown-friendly appeal. The décor flaunts a bit of playfulness thanks to a mossy green carpet, fur-covered bag stools, and retro lighting. The ambience is quiet and waiters a tad imperious.

Evening tasting menus and a wonderful three-course prix-fixe with overlapping options mean that an array of appetites and budgets can be readily accommodated. The dinner hour is when the chef's true style shines most brightly, through clean and unfussy cooking that is a lovely blend of European techniques and Scandinavian flavors.

Klädesholmen Matjes herring is reinvented for the modern palate, encrusted in seeds and rye cubes served on a piece of slate, alongside soft-boiled quail eggs, Västerbotten cheese, and a swipe of horseradish. Follow this with a springtime composition of crisp-skinned Arctic char over pea purée, nettles, sweet and snap peas, and a few halved shrimp. Desserts that feature a textural composition of chocolates are a contemporary highlight.

Lunch is a low-key, business-like gathering of Swedish meatballs and *skagen*, but the service is thankfully far less uptight.

Bistro Vendôme

French XX

D2

405 E. 58th St. (bet. First Ave. & Sutton Pl.)

Subway: 59 St — Lunch & dinner daily
Phone: 212-935-9100
Web: www.bistrovendomenyc.com
Prices: $$

The nearby residents of Sutton Place fit Bistro Vendôme, a classic sort of spot where three cozy dining rooms, top-notch service, and excellent food come together seamlessly. Often glimpsed gliding across the restaurant, the husband-and-wife owners warmly cater to locals during pleasant but humming dinner hours. The space makes everyone feel lucky—such solid dining options don't typically exist this far east.

Familiar and well-done classics may include an enjoyably but never over-whelmingly flavorful fish soup sided with Gruyère cheese, *rouille*, and croûtes. The well-executed striped bass arrives with a bed of zucchini cooked in a fragrant tomato-saffron broth; while an *ile flottante* with caramel sauce is like an ode to a Parisian bistro.

BLT Steak

Steakhouse XXX

C2

106 E. 57th St. (bet. Lexington & Park Aves.)

Subway: 59 St — Lunch Mon – Fri
Phone: 212-752-7470 — Dinner nightly
Web: www.bltsteak.com
Prices: $$$$

The best steakhouse in New York City is hotly contested among many contenders, but this handsome retreat sets itself apart with genuine hospitality, great management, and Sunday nights filled with hungry families and friends.

This spot nails crowd-pleasing dishes like addictively hot popovers the size of softballs served to every table, which are extra delicious when slathered with butter and sea salt. Steaks are good, but sides truly excel, from inch-thick and perfectly crunchy onion rings to umami-rich and salty roasted mushrooms. Even crispy potato skins get the special treatment here—first baked, then deep-fried, and finally topped with bacon, cheese, sour cream, and chives. It may be a precursor to a heart attack, but it's worth every bite.

Bobby Van's

American XX

B4

230 Park Ave. (in East Walkway & 46th St.)

Subway: Grand Central - 42 St
Phone: 212-867-5490
Web: www.bobbyvans.com
Prices: $$$$

Lunch Mon – Fri
Dinner Mon – Sat

Nestled at the base of The Helmsley building near Grand Central lies Bobby Van's, a perennial favorite of the expense-account set. Its classic steakhouse atmosphere—gruff but prompt service, noisy post-work bar scene, and gargantuan portions—is met with commendable dishes that reach beyond the normal chop shop fare.

While the beef speaks for itself, the kitchen's execution takes common combos to the next level: mozzarella and tomatoes are drizzled in flavorful balsamic and olive oil with a chiffonade of basil and shallots; while soft-shell crabs arrive perfectly battered and tempura fried. This massive special, with crisp asparagus and bed of sautéed spinach, showcases great culinary technique and seasonality not expected from a midtown lunch hangout.

Bottega del Vino

Italian XX

C1

7 E. 59th St. (bet. Fifth & Madison Aves.)

Subway: 5 Av - 59 St
Phone: 212-223-2724
Web: www.bottegadelvinonyc.com
Prices: $$$$

Lunch & dinner daily

For true Northern Italian elegance, Bottega del Vino is divine, no matter the time of day. In front, casual Bar Quadronno caters to local business people looking to meet for a European-style breakfast, light lunch, or unbeatable cappuccino. Head to the more formal, rear dining room with tables dressed in white to savor a very authentic Italian meal.

Veronese influence is clear from the start, with dishes like whole grilled calamari served simply over a bed of arugula drizzled in excellent olive oil with a splash of lemon. The pillowy spinach and potato gnocchi swimming in a creamy sauce with crisp prosciutto and pecorino outdoes most other plates like it in the city. Finish with warm Nutella-filled crêpes served with vanilla ice cream.

Bukhara Grill

Indian XX

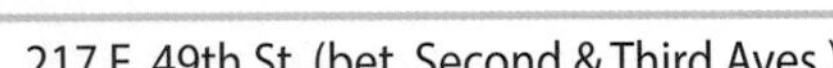

C3

217 E. 49th St. (bet. Second & Third Aves.)

Subway: 51 St — Lunch & dinner daily
Phone: 212-888-2839
Web: www.bukharany.com
Prices: $$$

In NYC's ever-expanding realm of Indian dining, Bukhara Grill has stood the test of time with excellence. Glimpse their expert chefs who seem contentedly trapped behind a glass kitchen wall. Featuring a noisy and yuppie set, this tri-level space is decorated (albeit oddly) with clunky wooden booths, closely set tables, and private rooms.

Peek into the kitchen for a whiff of *tandoori* treats and Mughlai specialties. *Dahi aloo papri* or spicy potatoes and chickpeas tossed in yogurt and tamarind is a predictably perfect starter. The signature, wickedly creamy *dal* Bukhara will have you coming back for more (tomorrow). Even if the service may range from sweet to clumsy, hand-crafted breads meant to sop up the likes of *sarson ka saag* remain a crowning glory.

Casa Lever

Italian XXX

B2

390 Park Ave. (entrance on 53rd St.)

Subway: Lexington Av - 53 St — Lunch Mon – Fri
Phone: 212-888-2700 — Dinner Mon – Sat
Web: www.casalever.com
Prices: $$$$

The modernist design and crowds of corporate denizens give this loud, lively favorite a *Mad Men* feel. Housed in the basement of the iconic Lever House, this sexy, low-lit space is decked with tufted charcoal bucket seats circling red cocktail tables, wood panels, honeycomb-shaped wine racks, and Warhol-esque artwork. The gracious staff is top-notch.

An elegant, Northern Italian menu offers the likes of perfectly roasted, thinly sliced *vitello tonnato* in that unlikely yet incredibly delicious sauce of tuna, capers, and mayonnaise. Linguine with sea urchin, crab meat, crushed tomato, and *peperoncino* is generous and beautifully calibrated. To finish, the contemporary *millefoglie* layers delicate pastry, vanilla Chantilly cream, and raspberry *granite*.

Café China ✿

Chinese XX

A1

13 E. 37th St. (bet. Fifth & Madison Aves.)

Subway: 34 St - Herald Sq
Phone: 212-213-2810
Web: www.cafechinanyc.com
Prices: $$

Lunch & dinner daily

An inconspicuous façade lost in midtown masks this striking restaurant, decorated with seductive portraits of 1930s Shanghai starlets, bright red chairs, lush bamboo planters, and a dominating marble-and-dark wood bar.

The kitchen continues to struggle with popularity, yet on each table find balanced and elegant expressions of Sichuan cuisine that can stand above most in the city—one that avoids the easy umami of monosodium glutamate and egg rolls for composed, elegant expressions of this region's dishes.

The almost overwhelming menu features dozens of cold and hot appetizers, noodles, entrées, and desserts. From refreshing pieces of cold-poached chicken tossed with a generous mound of chili-oil and peanuts, to aromatic smoked tofu mingled with silky batons of celery stalk, flavors here often bring more complexity than straight heat and the presentations are more genteel than brute.

But that's not to say the kitchen doesn't conduct a fiery arrangement—try crisp, meaty, and double-cooked pork belly harmonized with hot Sichuan peppercorns, green bell peppers, leeks, and fermented black beans. It's a face-melting experience that is more New York authentic, but still, devilishly delicious.

Caviar Russe ✿

B2 Contemporary XXX

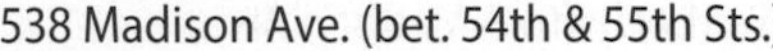

538 Madison Ave. (bet. 54th & 55th Sts.)

Subway: 5 Av - 53 St — Lunch daily
Phone: 212-980-5908 — Dinner Mon – Sat
Web: www.caviarrusse.com
Prices: $$$$

No playful pun, no name-check for grandma, no oblique reference to a geographical landmark—whoever christened this restaurant clearly wanted to attract a certain type of customer.

This is not the place when you should order by pointing vaguely at the menu—that way lies trouble because you may find yourself having to re-mortgage your apartment to pay for the 250 grams of Oscetra caviar you've just inadvertently requested. Best leave that section of the carte to the oligarchs and retired dictators and concentrate on the main menu. Here you will find contemporary dishes of surprising delicacy and precision, with a pleasing bias towards wonderful seafood and shellfish, such as scallops with ricotta gnudi, or delicious bluefin tuna with uni and asparagus.

You get buzzed in at street level, which adds a bit of mystery to proceedings. Up the stairs and you'll find yourself in a lavish little jewel box, with colorful murals on the wall, Murano chandeliers hanging from an ornate ceiling, and semi-circular booths. The only thing missing is James Bond's nemesis drumming his fingers on the table in the corner.

Crave Fishbar

Seafood

945 Second Ave. (bet. 50th & 51st Sts.)

Subway: 51 St — Lunch Sun – Fri

Phone: 646-895-9585 — Dinner nightly

Web: www.cravefishbar.com

Prices: $$

Just like the raucous bars that populate the neighborhood, this spot is filled to the brim with an exuberant crowd. However this coveted fish bar's sophisticated following aren't interested in bottomless pitchers of beer; they're here to dive into Chef Todd Mitgang's skillfully rendered seafood preparations. Local sea scallops are presented raw and chopped atop slices of roasted sweet potato and dressed with spicy mayonnaise, nori powder, and crumbled house-made oyster crackers. Meanwhile, John Dory has an Indian accent—marinated in spiced yogurt, then roasted and plated with a *chana masala* of green garbanzo beans.

Chow down at the 25-foot marble bar, or head to the back room—a pretty clash of reclaimed timber, floral wallpaper, and plaid upholstery.

Don's Bogam

Korean

17 E. 32nd St. (bet. Fifth & Madison Aves.)

Subway: 33 St — Lunch & dinner daily

Phone: 212-683-2200

Web: www.donsbogam.com

Prices: $$

At Don's Bogam, the food is fantastic and service indulgent. So, reserve ahead as every seat is filled—from the festive bar up front right down to those fun two-tops sporting blazing grills. Make no mistake—this is no average K-town joint. Inside, a top-notch venting system lets diners enjoy a smoke-free evening of exceptional grilled meats. Start wtih deep-fried pork *mandu*, which are crisp, on-point, and extra divine. Wonderfully flaky *buchu gochu pajeon* is studded with chives for perfect flavor; while pork belly marinated in red wine is smoky and supremely tender.

For the ultimate payoff, opt for the memorable beef platter featuring thinly sliced *macun* and *yangneuym galbi* set beside king trumpet mushrooms—meaty and mouthwatering in their own right.

El Parador

Mexican

B2

325 E. 34th St. (bet. First & Second Aves.)

Subway: 33 St
Phone: 212-679-6812
Web: www.elparadorcafe.com
Prices: $$

Lunch & dinner daily

This neighborhood mainstay boasts over fifty years of success. With their fantastic menu, killer margaritas, and dedication to hospitality, El Parador is worthy of its status as a beloved destination. The intimate space is decked with ornate wood chairs, red banquettes, and wood plank ceilings, while white brick walls are hung with artwork and artifacts.

The bountiful menu offers favorites like taco trays and nachos in three varieties, as well as a rotating menu of daily specials (be sure to try the fish of the day). Fill up on *aguachile de camaron*, deliciously classic shrimp ceviche in lime juice and jalapeño; or tender, falling-off-the-bone baby-back ribs served with tequila-chili *guajillo* salsa, cabbage slaw, and braised *camote*.

Margaritas are a must, but of course.

Felidia

D2

243 E. 58th St. (bet. Second & Third Aves.)

Subway: Lexington Av - 59 St
Phone: 212-758-1479
Web: www.felidia-nyc.com
Prices: $$$$

Lunch Mon – Fri
Dinner nightly

Cookbook author, television series host, and restaurateur Lidia Bastianich has been behind this flagship restaurant and greeting customers since 1981. Service could use a little finesse and some of Bastianich's charm, but the elegant décor inspires dressing up for dinner and the exceptional wine list offers a vast collection of Italian choices.

Signature *paste* sparkle here, such as *cacio e pere* ravioli stuffed with delicate pear and bathed in black pepper and pecorino. Massive portions of scallops, squid, a split langoustine, and lobster star in the *grigliata* drizzled with lemon vinaigrette. Rely on Lidia to deliver a cannoli that lives up to its true potential—envision narrow tubes filled with lemony ricotta cream spilling into the center of the plate.

The Four Seasons

American XXXX

C2

99 E. 52nd St. (bet. Lexington & Park Aves.)

Subway: 51 St — Lunch Mon – Fri
Phone: 212-754-9494 — Dinner Mon – Sat
Web: www.fourseasonsrestaurant.com
Prices: $$$$

The name alone invokes an image straight out of *Mad Men*—with beautiful sophisticates and well-dressed men rubbing elbows in a posh, mid-century room with mile-high ceilings, breathtaking flower arrangements, and intimate tables circling a center fountain. In real life, The Four Seasons is all that and more, with a rollicking fun seating chart that's a see-and-be-seen affair; excellent (if no longer particularly groundbreaking) food; an impeccable wait staff; and ultra-glamorous décor.

Kick things off with exquisitely fresh steak tartare, expertly prepared tableside. Then move on to tender and flaky Dover sole kissed with Hollandaise; followed by a near-perfect soufflé with Grand Marnier. Speaking of alcohol, go on and order that martini—Don Draper would.

HanGawi

Korean XX

A1

12 E. 32nd St. (bet. Fifth & Madison Aves.)

Subway: 33 St — Lunch Mon – Sat
Phone: 212-213-0077 — Dinner nightly
Web: www.hangawirestaurant.com
Prices: $$

Beyond an ordinary façade lies this serene, shoes-off retreat with traditional low tables, Korean artifacts, and meditative music. Said footwear is stored in cubbies, seating is the color of bamboo, and clay teapots adorn the back wall. The setting is soothing, but the atmosphere is surprisingly convivial, with groups gabbing over stuffed shiitake mushrooms and green tea.

The *ssam bap* offers a fun DIY experience with a long platter of fillings. Dark leafy lettuce and thin, herbaceous sesame leaves are topped with creamy slices of avocado, crunchy bean sprouts, pickled daikon, carrot, cucumber, radish, and three rice options—white, brown, and a nutty, purple-tinged multigrain. Topped with miso *ssam* sauce, each bite is a fresh burst of uplifting textures.

Hatsuhana

Japanese XX

B3

17 E. 48th St. (bet. Fifth & Madison Aves.)

Subway: 47-50 Sts - Rockefeller Ctr — Lunch Mon – Fri
Phone: 212-355-3345 — Dinner Mon – Sat
Web: www.hatsuhana.com
Prices: $$$

It's been around since the beginning of time (in NYC Japanese restaurant years) but this is no lesser a destination for excellent sushi. With a retro décor that spans two floors and a business that's run like a machine, Hatsuhana is a go-to for corporate dining.

Though the rave reviews came decades ago, their traditional *Edomae* sushi still holds its own. Fish is top quality, the army of chefs have solid knife skills, and rice is properly prepared. This reliability draws a host of regulars who develop relationships with the *itamae*. Stick to the counter and go omakase: the sushi will be surprisingly impressive with accommodations for the spicy tuna-set. Table service can be bumbling with reduced quality, but there is the menu of cooked items on offer to cool frustrations.

Hide-Chan Ramen

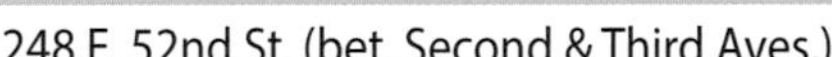

Japanese X

C3

248 E. 52nd St. (bet. Second & Third Aves.)

Subway: Lexington Av - 53 St — Lunch Mon– Sat
Phone: 212-813-1800 — Dinner nightly
Web: N/A
Prices: ¢¢

There is a meticulous science and culture to this *ramen-ya* that has seemingly perfected the customized noodle experience. Two suggestions to novices: dine during off-hours to avoid their mile-long line; and ponder *exactly* how firm you like your ramen cooked and rich you like your broth before even stepping afoot.

The décor may not say much, but the food speaks volumes in terms of authenticity and flavor. Start with steamed buns of succulent pork or pan-fried *gyoza*, before moving on to enticing mains centered around unbeatable renditions of ramen. *Kuro* ramen features an intensely nourishing and garlicky *tonkotsu* broth bobbing with bits of *char siu*. Meanwhile, health-conscious NYers are in luck, as both vegetable and chicken broth are also on offer here.

Jubilee

French XX

D3

948 First Ave. (bet. 52nd & 53rd Sts.)

Subway: Lexington Av - 53 St — Lunch & dinner daily
Phone: 212-888-3569
Web: www.jubileeny.net
Prices: $$

Settled into sleek Sutton Place, Jubilee is New York City's very own version of *Cheers*. Affluent families are in full force here, while friends gather on weeknights to mingle over wine and fine French-Belgian cuisine. The European-inflected nautical décor screams quaint coastal elegance with perpetually packed tables and a bar where everybody knows your name. A silky, saffron-scented fish soup, accompanied by grated Gruyère, a few croûtes, and pot of *rouille* is deliciously classic and incredibly sumptuous. But before filling up, be sure to sample the sole *meuniere*—a delicate fish seared perfectly and served with sautéed spinach leaves. If that doesn't sound like the best way to end a long day, their popular crème brûlée offers the ultimate fix.

Jukai

C3

237 E. 53rd St. (bet. Second & Third Aves.)

Subway: Lexington Av - 53 St — Dinner Mon – Sat
Phone: 212-588-9788
Web: www.jukainyc.com
Prices: $$$

If you can't make it to Tokyo by dinnertime, this subterranean den is the next best thing. Smartly styled in wood and bamboo, it's packed with expats lingering over elaborate meals attended to by an amicable staff.

The menu is traditional, though the chef's unique influences are well expressed in a massive oyster "sashimi" that's sliced in half on the shell and served with a mirin-soy dip and grated radish. To allow for a wide sampling of their top quality sashimi—from fluke and scallop to uni—opt for the tasting menu, and be sure to request the premium shabu-shabu. Thinly sliced Washu is swished in a bubbling dashi and coupled with noodles, bok choy, tofu, mushrooms, and two drinkable dipping sauces—ponzu as well as a signature sesame shabu-shabu sauce.

Juni ✿

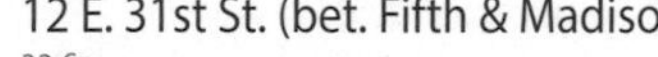

A1

12 E. 31st St. (bet. Fifth & Madison Aves.)

Subway: 33 St — Lunch Mon – Fri
Phone: 212-995-8599 — Dinner Mon – Sat
Web: www.juninyc.com
Prices: $$$$

Australian exports don't just include beef and precious metals—these days its chefs also seem highly prized by various countries around the world. Being largely unhindered by an allegiance to a particular culinary tradition seemingly allows them to freely embrace innovation and creativity, and they all arrive with a healthy international outlook.

Cairns-born Shaun Hergatt's cooking is certainly original. Whether you're having the squab with salsify or the "rabbit and the carrot," you'll know you're in the hands of a kitchen with a mastery of modern cooking techniques. His dishes are all artfully presented creations and the combinations of superlative ingredients and well-defined flavors display far greater depth than the somewhat terse three-word menu descriptions would suggest.

The dining room, within the Hotel Chandler, is a touch anodyne and tables are ridiculously far apart, but the atmosphere remains far from solemn thanks, in no small part, to the personality and genuine care shown by the well-informed and helpful service team.

Kajitsu ✿

Japanese XX

A1

125 E. 39th St. (bet. Lexington & Park Aves.)

Subway: Grand Central - 42 St — Dinner Tue – Sun
Phone: 212-228-4873
Web: www.kajitsunyc.com
Prices: **$$$**

It's the way of the modern world that we think of the changing of the seasons more in terms of our wardrobe rather than our food—but a meal at Kajitsu could change that. This Japanese vegan restaurant serves shojin cuisine based on the precepts of Buddhism—if you're in search of an antidote to the plethora of steakhouses in the city, this is it. The second floor, traditionally decorated space is a sanctuary of peace and tranquility and offers table or counter seating and service that is as charming as it is earnest.

Such is the skill of the kitchen you'll forget in no time about the absence of fish or meat. It's all about balance, harmony and simplicity—and allowing the ingredients' natural flavors to shine, whether it's the delicate onion soup with mizuna and potato, or the visually arresting *hassun* which could include everything from mountain yam to burdock root.

Your period of contemplation and newfound respect for your fellow man may come to a juddering halt when you find yourself back on Lexington but, for a few moments at least, you'll feel you connected with nature.

Kurumazushi

Japanese XX

B3

7 E. 47th St., 2nd fl. (bet. Fifth & Madison Aves.)

Subway: 47-50 Sts - Rockefeller Ctr Lunch & dinner Mon – Sat
Phone: 212-317-2802
Web: www.kurumazushi.com
Prices: **$$$$**

Mimicking Tokyo's tucked-away restaurant style, this sushi destination is located up a dark staircase in a midtown building and through a sliding door. The focal point of the room is the sushi bar, where Chef/owner Toshihiro Uezu meticulously prepares each morsel in a minimal space.

For the full theatrical experience, brace your wallet and settle into the omakase. The undeniable quality of each ingredient is center stage, displayed simply on stone glazed pottery.

Take a cue from the Japanese and limit conversation: the succession of sashimi and sushi is quick, and all senses should work together without distraction to savor the smooth, buttery fatty tuna, Spanish mackerel (with its lightly blistered skin), pearly white sea bream, and rich *unagi*.

La Grenouille

French XXX

B2

3 E. 52nd St. (bet. Fifth & Madison Aves.)

Subway: 5 Av - 53 St Lunch & dinner Tue – Sat
Phone: 212-752-1495
Web: www.la-grenouille.com
Prices: **$$$$**

La Grenouille is a bastion of old-world glamor and manners with an exorbitant budget for floral arrangements. Although this storied enclave still attracts a devoted following, there's always room for local newbies and blinged-out tourists. Everyone looks good in this lavish space, where red velvet banquettes, polished wood veneer, and softly lit tables bathe the room in rose and apricot hues.

Classic and classy, this French cuisine deserves high praise. Delicate ravioli is stuffed with chopped lobster hinting of tarragon and dressed with creamy, tart beurre blanc; an exquisitely tender-seared beef filet arrives with *pommes Darphin* and a lick of perfect sauce *au poivre*; and for dessert, the *île flottante* is heaven under a cloud of spun caramel.

Land of Plenty

Chinese XX

204 E. 58th St. (bet. Second & Third Aves.)

Subway: 59 St — Lunch Mon – Fri
Phone: 212-308-8788 — Dinner nightly
Web: www.landofplenty58.com
Prices: $$

A sleek, clean, and subterranean space attended to by adept servers, this Chinese haven feels far more nice and elegant than the other Sichuan spots in midtown. Instead of sweet-and-sour pork, crowds of lively, food-savvy diners come for authentic lunchtime specials prepared by a cadre of talented chefs.

The food is just plain stellar, featuring excellent versions of this cuisine's classics, which may start with addictive pickled vegetables or soft pork dumplings paired with sweet soy. While some settle on crunchy conch bathed in roasted chili oil, others opt for smoked duck fried rice to pair with sautéed crispy chicken tossed with chilies and sesame seeds. String beans stir-fried with minced pork and bamboo shoots is a revelatory way to end the affair.

Le Cirque

European XXXX

151 E. 58th St. (bet. Lexington & Third Aves.)

Subway: 59 St — Lunch Mon – Fri
Phone: 212-644-0202 — Dinner Mon – Sat
Web: www.lecirque.com
Prices: $$$$

This legendary Sirio Maccioni restaurant opened its doors over 40 years ago to a very different Manhattan, but its timeless cuisine still packs the house. The dramatic interior alone warrants a visit: a beautiful semi-circular dining room boasting arching banquettes; a soaring wall of windows; and draping overhead canopies.

Chef Raphael Francois is currently holding court in Le Cirque's kitchen, effortlessly blending time-honored recipes with delicious new additions. Don't miss the grilled octopus salad, with tender rainbow potatoes, cherry tomatoes, taggiasca olives, and fresh herbs; or the (Daniel Boulud-created) paupiette of black bass, wrapped in thin sheets of potato, laced with a lovely red wine sauce and served over melted leeks.

Le Relais de Venise (L'Entrecôte)

C3 Steakhouse XX

590 Lexington Ave. (at 52nd St.)

Subway: 51 St — Lunch & dinner daily
Phone: 212-758-3989
Web: www.relaisdevenise.com
Prices: $$

Sibling to the Paris original, this midtown outpost boasts a prime location and exceptional value. Inside, it's no amateur show and there's just one menu option—but what an impressive one it is. Start with green salad tossed in a light mustard vinaigrette before slicing into a juicy steak, dressed with the kitchen's mouthwatering (and top secret!) sauce. Of course, it is only upon the arrival of salty, crunchy frites when your meal will truly start to sing. Desserts aren't a highlight; so opt instead for another glass of *vin* from their judicious and vast list.

The décor is classic and the staff, dressed in sassy outfits, are the very image of Paris-chic. So sit back, relax, and take it all in—and find that for a moment, you'd forgotten you were in Manhattan.

Mapo Tofu

A1 Chinese X

338 Lexington Ave. (bet. 39th & 40th Sts.)

Subway: Grand Central - 42 St — Lunch & dinner daily
Phone: 212-867-8118
Web: N/A
Prices: ©©

"How many?" That's the greeting at this temple of "ma la," where enticing aromas are sure to lure you in. Find yourself among executives and locals slurping up a host of chili oil specialties (don't wear white!). This is the kind of place where dragons go to recharge their breath.

Some may peruse the menu—rife with typos—for daily specials, but most blaze their tongues with Sichuan pickles or chilled noodles tossed in an intense sesame vinaigrette. The place is named after a humble dish, but many items surprise with bold flavors like silky fish fillets swimming in a spicy broth with Napa cabbage, or camphor tea-smoked duck. Peppercorns in stir-fried chicken unite subtle sweetness with intense heat, while sponge squash offers a cooling, textural finale.

Mr Chow

D2 Chinese XX

324 E. 57th St. (bet. First & Second Aves.)

Subway: 59 St — Dinner nightly
Phone: 212-751-9030
Web: www.mrchow.com
Prices: $$$$

Oh Mr Chow, how you hook the hordes with your flavorful fusion and fancy prices! Perhaps it's the retro scene decked in black-and-white, lacquered Asian-accented chairs, and glinting mirrors. Or, maybe it's the noodle guy's theatrical display of hand-pulling? Whatever the hype, Mr Chow still has it and Sutton suits along with their wealthy wives party here like it's 1999.

Attentive service and flowing drinks keep everything moving as fans nibble away on the well-priced Beijing duck prix-fixe with four starters along with entrées. Tender orange chicken satay and water dumplings with seafood are tasty, but Dungeness crab sautéed with egg whites, and *ma mignon*, cubes of tender fried beef tossed in a sweet-spicy sauce laced with scallions truly get the crowd going.

Naya

D2 Lebanese XX

1057 Second Ave. (bet. 55th & 56th Sts.)

Subway: Lexington Av - 53 St — Lunch & dinner daily
Phone: 212-319-7777
Web: www.nayarestaurants.com
Prices: $$

Amid this bland stretch of cheap booze and loud beats lies Naya, a tiny and mod neighborhood spot with tasty Lebanese fare. Inside, the streamlined décor feels smart and attractive, with white pleather booths contrasting against shiny dark tables. This sleek aesthetic runs to the back where a large table is best for suit-donning groups.

Most love Naya for its vast choice of Lebanese meze and daily specials featuring home-style food with modern flair. It is clear that this is a professional operation, as obliging waiters present you with the likes of a "quick Naya" lunch special unveiling generous portions of *fattoush*, *labne*, and *baba ghannouj*. A chicken shawarma sandwich reaches epic scopes when paired with their deliciously tangy homemade pickles.

Nerai

Greek XX

55 E. 54th St. (bet. Madison & Park Aves.)

Subway: 5 Av - 53 St — Lunch Mon – Fri
Phone: 212-759-5554 — Dinner nightly
Web: www.nerainyc.com
Prices: **$$$**

Nerai endeavors to transport diners to Santorini, creating a stark contrast to its rather stiff midtown surrounds. A resort-chic vibe echoes through the whitewashed walls, sea-blue accents, and lots of cool marble. But the holiday ends there, as this crowd is all about business—especially at lunch.

The fresh, light cuisine begins with beautifully prepared starters like tender, enticingly charred octopus atop chickpeas, roasted pepper, and quick-pickled onions drizzled with lemon and olive oil. Grilled sea bass is a flawless shade of white, salty and crisp-skinned alongside seasonal vegetables like zucchini and buttery pea purée. Finish with the lovely *portokalopita* topped with a scoop of bittersweet chocolate sorbet boldly flavored with orange.

Obikà

Italian XX

590 Madison Ave. (at 56th St.)

Subway: 59 St — Lunch daily
Phone: 212-355-2217
Web: www.obika.it
Prices: **$$**

Conveniently located in the glass atrium of the IBM building, Obikà exudes an elegant yet casual style that attracts slim suits and sleek shoppers alike. Plentiful sunlight lends an airy feel to the space, which offers counter dining and table seating, smartly separated from the building's lobby with planters.

The focus here is the truly exceptional mozzarella—fresh *bufala*, hauntingly smoked, or tangy *burrata*—which can be paired with a *tagliere* of cured meats and/or grilled vegetables for a perfectly light lunch. The menu ventures on to offer an exceptional rendition of lasagna *tradizionale*, made with delicate layers of pasta, hearty beef ragù, béchamel, and a showering of parmesan. Come dessert, the tiramisu is another classic.

Osteria Laguna

B1 Italian XX

209 E. 42nd St. (bet. Second & Third Aves.)

Subway: Grand Central - 42 St Lunch & dinner daily
Phone: 212-557-0001
Web: www.osteria-laguna.com
Prices: **$$**

A little bit corporate (it is midtown, after all) and a little bit casual (daytrippers from nearby Grand Central), Osteria Laguna has nailed its audience and delivers a perfect blend to suit both worlds. Inside, it's delightfully rustic, complete with the requisite Italian ceramic plates and wooden chairs with rush seating.

Crowd-pleasers like pastas, pizzas from the wood-burning oven, *antipasti*, salads, and nicely done fish, starch, and vegetables comprise the menu at this better-than-average gem. The friendly service can be spotty, but the perfectly crisped wood-fired pizzas are always spot on. The portions are abundant, perhaps even too much given the tiny tables, but the prices aren't, so you can treat your out-of-town friend and keep the change.

Pampano

C3 Mexican XX

209 E. 49th St. (bet. Second & Third Aves.)

Subway: 51 St Lunch & dinner daily
Phone: 212-751-4545
Web: www.richardsandoval.com
Prices: **$$$**

Nothing screams you need a trip to Acapulco like a stressful day in midtown, and we've got your remedy. Pampano, a popular Mexican seafood restaurant, offers two types of oases for the weary worker: downstairs, you'll find a lively bar (especially come happy hour) with a few small tables to enjoy their *botanas* menu; upstairs, you'll find a transporting, beachy dining space with whitewashed ceilings, wicker chairs, lazy ceiling fans, and an outdoor patio.

Don't miss the fresh guacamole; excellent rotating list of ceviches, plump with off-the-boat fish and humming with bright lime; or grilled grouper, marinated in *achiote* and wrapped in banana leaf.

Next door, Pampano Taqueria keeps the hungry lunch crowds at bay with delicious tacos on the fly.

Patroon

B4 — American XXX

160 E. 46th St. (bet. Lexington & Third Aves.)

Subway: Grand Central - 42 St — Lunch & dinner Mon – Fri
Phone: 212-883-7373
Web: www.aretskyspatroon.com
Prices: $$$$

For those in the know, this elegant canteen needs no introduction. Patroon exudes the air of a private club—one where suited professionals huddle over drinks at the sleek bar; and dining rooms fill with power lunchers who smoke cigars on the rooftop.

That this restaurant draws a devoted crowd of regulars should come as no surprise; the maître d' and his gracious servers are top-notch and the kitchen team is highly competent. Come dinnertime, the classic cooking is especially impressive: bracing ceviche may feature Long Island fluke; then Dover sole is plated tableside; and light yet satisfying leek gratin caters to diners who would rather invest the calories elsewhere—say a fine pour from the well-curated wine list or a perfect crème brulée for dessert.

Pera

A4 — Turkish XX

303 Madison Ave. (bet. 41st & 42nd Sts.)

Subway: Grand Central - 42 St — Lunch & dinner daily
Phone: 212-878-6301
Web: www.peranyc.com
Prices: $$

For fantastically flavorful Turkish food mingled with modern influences, Pera never fails to please. Lunch does big business in this attractive dining room, layered in a chocolate-brown color scheme and packed with corporate groups and visitors looking for a sleek place to roost.

Though dinner is more low-key, the menu always boasts simple and exceptional plates like warm hummus with *pastirma*; lentil and bulgur tartare; as well as watermelon chunks tossed with feta, fresh tomatoes, and a perfect trickle of olive oil. While service can verge on disorganized, all will be forgiven after a forkful of their classic and tender chicken *adana* or lamb burger—a juicy bunful of ground lamb coupled with garlic spread, homemade pickles, and addictively crispy fries.

Phoenix Garden

Chinese

242 E. 40th St. (bet. Second & Third Aves.)

Subway: Grand Central - 42 St — Lunch & dinner daily
Phone: 212-983-6666
Web: www.phoenixgardennyc.com
Prices: $$

This fuss-free and no-frills basement joint shows Chinatown that delicious Chinese food for a great value can exist outside of its borders. Forgo ho-hum lunch deals and pop in at dinnertime for a delectable selection of Cantonese cooking.

The vast menu can take some navigating, so chat up the servers for their expert advice in order to get the goods. Highlights include exquisite salt-and-pepper shrimp, shell-on, butterflied, flash-fried and tossed with sliced chilies and garlic; sautéed snow pea leaves in an egg-white sauce of sweet crabmeat, carrots, and snow peas; sizzling eggplant casserole studded with minced pork and ham; and crispy Peking duck sliced tableside, rolled up in pancakes, and layered with hoisin, cucumber, and scallions.

P.J. Clarke's

Gastropub

915 Third Ave. (at 55th St.)

Subway: Lexington Av - 53 St — Lunch & dinner daily
Phone: 212-317-1616
Web: www.pjclarkes.com
Prices: $$

Old time and on the ball, P.J. Clarke's drips with New York history—ad men and business execs have patronized this pour house for generations, and with good reason. Besides a dazzling medley of drinks, the kitchen sends out a crowd-pleasing menu showcasing solid technique. Following its repute, the distinct décor spotlights notable artifacts, worn floors, and smartly dressed tables.

Weekends draw a touristy set, but who's complaining with an amazing Bloody Mary so close at hand? Highlights include potato chips with an outrageously gooey blue cheese gratin; braised short rib spring rolls with horseradish-tinged sour cream; and tuna tartare tacos filled with scallion and sesame seeds. The cheeseburger is as classic and on-point as the staff itself.

Sakagura

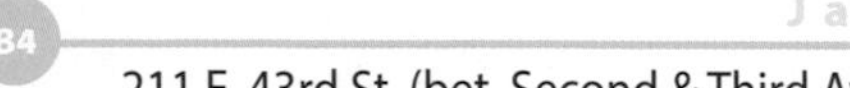

Japanese

B4

211 E. 43rd St. (bet. Second & Third Aves.)

Subway: Grand Central - 42 St — Lunch Mon – Fri
Phone: 212-953-7253 — Dinner nightly
Web: www.sakagura.com
Prices: $$$

Got sake on the brain? You'll need to book in advance, but tucked away in the basement of a midtown office building, Sakagura is an amazing little hideaway with a phenomenal sake list (including seasonal selections) and a smattering of delicious small plates for pairing. All this fabulousness may have gone to their head a bit as the service seems a bit lacking these days, but it's worth it for that flash of authentic Tokyo by way of midtown.
A couple of gems off the massive menu include the *uzaku*, grilled eel with cucumbers and seaweed in vinaigrette; perfectly chewy soba noodles presented in a traditional basket with dipping sauce, scallion, and wasabi; and tender *tori karaage*, a delicious Japanese fried chicken marinated in sake, soy, and ginger.

2nd Avenue Deli

Deli

A1

162 E. 33rd St. (bet. Lexington & Third Aves.)

Subway: 33 St — Lunch & dinner daily
Phone: 212-689-9000
Web: www.2ndavedeli.com
Prices:

While the décor may be more deli-meets-deco and there's a tad less attitude, this food is every bit as good as it was on Second Avenue. Ignore the kvetching and know that this is a true Jewish deli filled with personality, and one of the best around by far.
The menu remains as it should: kosher, meat-loving, and non-dairy with phenomenal pastrami, pillowy rye, tangy mustard, perfect potato pancakes, and fluffy matzoh balls in comforting broth. Have the best of both worlds with the soup and half-sandwich combination.
Carve a nook during midday rush, when in pour the crowds. The deli also does takeout (popular with the midtown lunch bunch), and delivery (grandma's pancakes at your door). Giant platters go equally well to a bris or brunch.

Sip Sak

Turkish XX

928 Second Ave. (bet. 49th & 50th Sts.)

Subway: 51 St
Phone: 212-583-1900
Web: www.sip-sak.com
Prices: $$

Lunch & dinner daily

The celadon façade of this tiny Turkish treasure with its frosted glass awning and art nouveau look holds its own in mundane midtown. Walls lined with large mirrors and a shiny pressed-tin ceiling stand over an armada of cool white marble-topped tables and bentwood bistro chairs.

The décor seems French, but the cuisine leads to the Eastern Mediterranean with a definite stop in Turkey. A central, fully stocked bar serves as the launching point for Chef Orhan Yegen, who can be seen (and heard) directing his staff as they entice diners with a meze of citrusy olives, delicious hummus, garlicky *cacik*, and creamy *tarama*. House specials like rustic braised lamb chunks set atop a smooth eggplant purée seem straightforward but are deeply comforting.

Smith & Wollensky

Steakhouse 

C3

797 Third Ave. (at 49th St.)

Subway: 51 St
Phone: 212-753-1530
Web: www.smithandwollensky.com
Prices: $$$$

Lunch Mon – Fri
Dinner nightly

Sitting proudly on the corner of Third Avenue for nearly 40 years, Smith & Wollensky is a veritable New York institution. This is the kind of clubby steakhouse where stellar martinis are still poured tableside and the regulars get their names engraved on a plaque. It's where business deals go down and old-time Manhattanites live it up.

Begin with beloved classics, including a beefsteak tomato-and-onion salad finished with house dressing and crumbled blue cheese; or spoon-licking sides like creamed spinach, crispy hash browns, and crunchy onion rings. Then, allow the adept servers to steer you towards the in-house favorite—namely, a beautifully marbled, deliciously fatty, and perfectly tender Colorado rib steak, bone-on and big enough for three.

Soba Totto

Japanese XX

B4

211 E. 43rd St. (bet. Second & Third Aves.)

Subway: Grand Central - 42 St
Phone: 212-557-8200
Web: www.sobatotto.com
Prices: $$

Lunch Mon – Fri
Dinner nightly

It's a jam-packed lunchtime operation here at Soba Totto, where business folks gather and quickly fill the popular space. As the name suggests, everyone arrives in droves for the tasty homemade soba. Dinnertime brings a mellower vibe, and a crowd of beer- and sake-sipping patrons ordering tasty plates of spicy fried chicken and *yakitori* galore.

Midday features several varieties of lunch sets. Tasty appetizers may unveil a salad of assorted pickles and simmered daikon in a sweet ginger dressing. Skip over the fried seafood in favor of the *soba totto gozen* set, which includes the wonderful soba in fragrant *dashi*; or try one of the many delicious *dons* topped with tasty tidbits like sea urchin and salmon roe or soy-marinated tuna, grated yam, and egg.

SushiAnn

Japanese XX

B3

38 E. 51st St. (bet. Madison & Park Aves.)

Subway: 51 St
Phone: 212-755-1780
Web: www.sushiann.net
Prices: $$

Lunch Mon – Fri
Dinner Mon – Sat

Step through the serene, bamboo-filled entrance and into this dedicated sushi den. The mood is respectfully formal yet friendly, thanks to the focused kitchen staff who are happily interacting with guests. Just arrive with a sense of what (and how much) you'd like to eat and insist upon omakase.

Let the day's catch dictate your meal and take a seat at the counter, where only the glassed-in display of fish and mollusks separates you from this team of skilled, disciplined chefs. The omakase may be wildly varied depending on the day (and your chef), but high standards are always maintained and each crunchy morsel is treated with integrity. A ceramic dish of sashimi may reveal a glistening array of mild giant clam, firm *tai*, and tuna that melts in the mouth.

Sushi Yasuda ✿

Japanese XX

B4

204 E. 43rd St. (bet. Second & Third Aves.)

Subway: Grand Central - 42 St
Phone: 212-972-1001
Web: www.sushiyasuda.com
Prices: $$$$

Lunch Mon – Fri
Dinner Mon – Sat

Efficiency trumps hospitality at this sushi temple, where warm honey-toned bamboo slats are by far the warmest feature. Reservations are managed with little coddling, arrivals lack any greeting, tardiness is not accepted, and loitering at the counter is not an option. But to sushi-loving diehards, this is just the cost of admission.

Tables packed with suits (this is midtown, after all) should be avoided in favor of the sleek counter attended to by a pristinely attired staff as this is where the magic happens. And, your experience here depends entirely on the *itamae* enlisted in front of you. Their mission is to ensure that each diner receives fish that has just been cut, formed, and dressed moments before it is eaten.

After years of buildup, this kitchen is finally living up to its hype—with a wealth of classically assembled and spectacularly fresh sushi on offer. Every item is handled with such care and is truly memorable: a sparkling combo of sea scallop and oyster is sprinkled with soy sauce, sea salt, and lemon; a duo of uni lets the palate compare specimens from Santa Barbara and Hokkaido; and a trio of King, Alaskan white, and wild New Zealand salmon nigiri makes for a fantastic treat.

Tempura Matsui ✿

B1 Japanese XX

222 E. 39th St. (bet. Second & Third Aves.)

Subway: Grand Central - 42 St — Dinner Mon – Sat
Phone: 212-986-8885
Web: www.tempuramatsui.com
Prices: **$$$$**

With a whopping 40 years of experience in Japan under his belt, tempura master Chef Masao Matsui requires just three ingredients—flour, water, and egg—to transform a larder of exceptionally fresh seafood and vegetables into a feast unlike any other in New York City.

Tempura Matsui is tucked into the corner of a non-descript residential tower, lending an air of Japanese authenticity from its location that's amplified by a luxuriously old-world interior. A counter surrounding the chef's station seats a row of Matsui aficionados set comfortably with lacquer trays, handmade ceramic platters, and gorgeous implements, while a handful of booths offer a much more limited view of the virtuoso proceedings.

Diners hoping for fare with American flair will be disappointed, as the food here caters to students of traditional Japanese cuisine. Chef Matsui is a watchful presence, guiding his sous-chefs to produce pieces that are pale gold, delicately crisp, and perfectly cooked. House-made *goma dofu, chawan mushi,* and sashimi begin the feast, but as lovely as these bites are, they are merely the opening act for the divine tempura—mouthwatering shrimp head, sweet hunk of King crabmeat, and seaweed-wrapped scallop.

Tsushima

Japanese XX

B4

210 E. 44th St. (bet. Second & Third Aves.)

Subway: Grand Central - 42 St
Phone: 212-207-1938
Web: N/A
Prices: **$$**

Lunch & dinner daily

A shiny black awning marks the entrance to this slightly antiseptic yet considerably authentic sushi bar. A few rooms done in traditional Japanese style provide seating choices at this den, which hums with business groups on the run as well as neighborhood dwellers seeking fantastic value lunches and terrific quality sushi in the evening.

Choose to dine at their sushi counter or at a table in the well-lit dining room, attended to by speedy servers. Then, dive into generously sized lunch specials featuring perhaps a colorful *chirashi*, headlining yellowtail, salmon, *tamago*, and amberjack set deftly over well-seasoned sushi rice. Sticky-glazed eel, nicely grilled and plenty fatty, is an absolute must as is the impressive omakase for dinner.

Vitae

Contemporary XXX

A3

4 E. 46th St. (bet. Fifth & Madison Aves.)

Subway: Grand Central - 42 St
Phone: 212-682-3562
Web: www.vitaenyc.com
Prices: **$$$**

Lunch Mon – Fri
Dinner Mon – Sat

Ordering an Old Fashioned at lunchtime is fraught with all sorts of social implications so praise be to restaurants like Vitae, which are grown up enough to ensure that no eyebrows are raised when someone decides they want lunch the old fashioned way.

This is a sophisticated and elegant midtown restaurant with an appealing self-confidence. Even the soundtrack appears to have been chosen by someone who actually knows what good music sounds like. Service is snappy, assured, and well-organised.

The menu is contemporary without being faddish. Flavor combinations, such as the sesame salmon with soy, are recognizable and complementary and dishes pass that most basic of tests: they are very easy to eat. And those cocktails are pretty good too.

Tulsi ✿

C4 — Indian XX

211 E. 46th St. (bet. Second & Third Aves.)

Subway: Grand Central - 42 St — Lunch Mon – Sat
Phone: 212-888-0820 — Dinner nightly
Web: www.tulsinyc.com
Prices: $$

Anyone who loves their Indian food but got jaded by the generic ghee-heavy menus of Curry Hill should head along to Tulsi. In place of the seizure-inducing colored lighting, this midtown favorite offers billowing muslin and neutral tones; and instead of the usual Bollywood clichés, it provides tranquil, sophisticated surroundings, and attentive, sweet natured service.

The menu is also markedly different from the norm. For the appetizers, the kitchen takes the sort of snacks you can find streetside on Chaupati and, by putting its own spin on them (and using primary ingredients), raises them to new heights—such as with the white beans of *ragda chaat*, which is a great way to start your meal. You can also go Goan for some Portuguese influence with the succulent shrimp *balchao*. But, be sure to leave room for authentic goat biryani served on the bone, or something from the tandoor like those tender lamb chops.

As a nod to local tastes, spicing can be a little timid but those who are familiar with India—and anyone who knows their silly mid-on from their backward point—will still find much to savor.

Wild Edibles

535 Third Ave. (bet. 35th & 36th Sts.)

Subway: 33 St — Lunch & dinner daily
Phone: 212-213-8552
Web: www.wildedibles.com
Prices: $$

A small, sleepy sign hides this particularly spare room outfitted with a counter and tightly spaced tables, and yet, this is every seafood fan's dream. Thanks to amiable service and one refreshingly uncomplicated objective—to prepare its catch simply but expertly—Wild Edibles has amassed a loyal following and quite rightly so.

Start with locally sourced tuna tartare coupled with a light vinaigrette, garlic chips, and olive oil; or dig into clam chowder, a creamy, dreamy bowlful of plump bivalves, celery, potatoes, and smoky bacon. While the raw bar items are inviting and entrées delicious, you'll want to make like a regular here, and order a whole fish, sauce, as well as a side. Then wash it all down with a beer or glass of wine from the thoughtfully curated list.

Wolfgang's

Steakhouse XX

4 Park Ave. (at 33rd St.)

Subway: 33 St — Lunch & dinner daily
Phone: 212-889-3369
Web: www.wolfgangssteakhouse.net
Prices: $$$$

Wolfgang's is no stranger to the bustling New York steakhouse scene. From the lunch hour business crowd to the lively, post-work bar scene, Wolfgang's jams in locals and tourists alike—each coming for the classic fare and precise Manhattans. The service can be gruff at times, but they have a good track record of squeezing you into a table or perch at the bar without a reservation.

Once seated, the bone-in Porterhouse, cooked rare, is the only way to go. It arrives sizzling in its own liquid fat and topped with butter. Save space for a slice of bacon—a must-order appetizer—creamed spinach, and crispy German potatoes with yet more salt and fat (at this point, why not?). Just beware: while dishes are sized to share, they're priced like Maseratis.

Midtown West

More diverse than its counterpart (Midtown East) but still grim in parts, Midtown West presents a unique mix of tree-lined streets and ethnic enclaves amid glitzy glass-walled towers. It is also home to numerous iconic sights, including now well-known **Restaurant Row**—the only street in all five boroughs to be proudly advertised as such. The fact that it resides in an area called Hell's Kitchen and highlights an impressive range of global cuisines, is sealing evidence of this nabe's devotion to good food.

EAT THE STREETS

Also referred to as "Clinton," Hell's Kitchen is a colorful mosaic of workaday immigrants, old-timey residents, and young families. Gone are the Prohibition-era dens, which are now replaced by swanky restaurants, boutique hotels, and hip bars. **Little Brazil**, set only steps from bustling Sixth Avenue, showcases samba and street food every summer on Brazilian Day. And, speaking of the same nation, tourist-centric **Churrascaria Plataforma** is an all-you-can-eat Brazilian steakhouse showing off their wares via waiters, armed with skewers of succulent roasted meat. Midtown may be choked by cabs and corporate types on the go, but in true NY-style the residents demand (and streets oblige with) outstanding eats in varying venues. Under the guidance of the Vendy Awards and the blog Midtown Lunch, discover a changing lineup of speedy but satisfying street food faves as well as delis stocked with everything including Mexican specialties, dried chilies, and farm-fresh produce. Those in a hurry hustle over to **Tehuitzingo** for over 17 types of tacos, but if seeking a more reliable scene, find a seat at **Tulcingo del Valle** where tortas are turned out alongside burritos and burgers. Carnivores also revel over those perfectly pink patties laced with crispy fries at Le Parker Meridien's **burger joint**, but if barbecue

is what floats your boat, trek to the wilds of Eleventh Avenue and into **Daisy May's** for some smoky, succulent 'cue. For a more rare treat, **K-town** is a dark horse-like quarter that has been known to sneak up and surprise. Its instant and unapologetically authentic vibe owes largely to the prominence of aromatic barbecue joints, karaoke bars, and of course, grocers hawking everything from fresh tofu to handmade dumplings.

Macy's is across the street and may sport a frenzied scene, but tucked into its quiet crypt is **De Gustibus**, a cooking school and stage for culinary legends. Trek further along these midtown streets and find that equal attention is tendered to cooking as to arranging storybook mannequins behind the velvet ropes of glossy department stores. Shop till you drop at Bergdorf; then cool your heels over caviar and croissants at the *très* French and fancy **Petrossian**. Otherwise, stir things up with a potent martini and tasty small plate served out of the stately **Charlie Palmer at the Knick**, comfortably situated in the Knickerbocker Hotel in Times Square.

Switching gears from specialty spots to mega markets, **Gotham West** is one of Manhattan's most favored gourmet feats. Settled along Eleventh Avenue, this culinary complex cradles a number of chef-driven stalls and artisanal purveyors offering tapas, charcuterie, sammies, and everything in between. Of special note is the first stateside outpost of **Ivan Ramen**, where the rockstar chef's global fan base slurp down bowlfuls of these wispy rye noodles bobbing in a sumptuous broth. **City Kitchen** is another formidable bazaar featuring a rustic-industrial setting and outfitted with kiosks from **ilili Box**, **Gabriela's Taqueria**, **Luke's Lobster**, **Dough**, and more. And of course, cached beneath the graceful Plaza hotel is the traditional and tastefully done **Plaza Food Hall**. Here,

a dizzying array of comestibles is on full-display and makes for a marvelous attraction—distraction? Curated by mega-watt personality, Todd English, this 32,000-square-foot space is a perfect meeting spot if you're looking to sip, savor, and shop. Beginning with caviar, lobster rolls, or sushi; and closing with coffee or cupcakes, this veritable tour de force perfectly typifies the city's culinary elite.

FOOD FIXES

A few steps west and Gotham City's eclectic identity reveals yet another facet, where

Ninth Avenue unearths a wealth of eats. A wonderful start to any day is practically certified at **Amy's Bread**, where fresh-baked baguettes lend countless restaurant kitchens that extra crumb of culture. But, it is their famously colorful cakes and cookies that tempt passersby off the streets and into the store. Across the way, **Poseidon Bakery** is a winner for Greek sweets. It is also the last place in town that still crafts their own phyllo dough by hand—a taste of the spanakopita will prove it. Its moniker may depict another district, but **Sullivan Street Bakery's** one and only retail outlet is also housed along this stretch—a location so perilously far west in the Manhattan mindset that its success is worth its weight in gold. Just as Jim Lahey's luxurious loaves claim a cult-like following, so do the fantastic components (a warm Portuguese-style roll?) at **City Sandwich**. Meanwhile, theater-lovers and Lincoln Tunnel-bound commuters know to drive by **The Counter** and place an order for hand-crafted burgers, proclaimed to be a "must try before you die." New Yorkers in the know never tire of the lure behind **La Boîte**'s spice blends, or the sumptuous cured meats and *formaggi* found at **Sergimmo Salumeria**. Find more such salty goodness at veteran butcher, **Esposito Meat Market**, proudly purveying every part of the pig alongside piles of offal. Thirsty travelers should keep trekking further south of Port Authority Bus Terminal to unearth an enclave rich with restaurants and food marts. Here, foodies start their feasting at **Ninth Avenue International Foods** proffering such pleasures as olives, spices, and spreads. But, among their outstanding produce, find the renowned *taramosalata* (as if prepared by the gods atop Mount Olympus themselves). Then consider that it also stars on the menu of many fine dining destinations nearby and know that it must be truly something special.

TIME WARNER CENTER

Finally, no visit to this district is complete without paying homage to the epicurean feat that is the **Time Warner Center**. Presiding and preening over Columbus Circle, high-flying chefs indulge both themselves and their pretty patrons here with ground-breaking success. Discover a range of savory and sweet delights indoors—from **Bouchon Bakery's** colorful French macarons, to the eye-popping style and sass of **Stone Rose Lounge**. Located on the fourth floor, **Center Bar** (brought to you by Michael Lomonaco) is a sophisticated perch for enjoying a champagne cocktail while taking in the views of lush Central Park. This is classic New York—only more glossy and glamorous than usual.

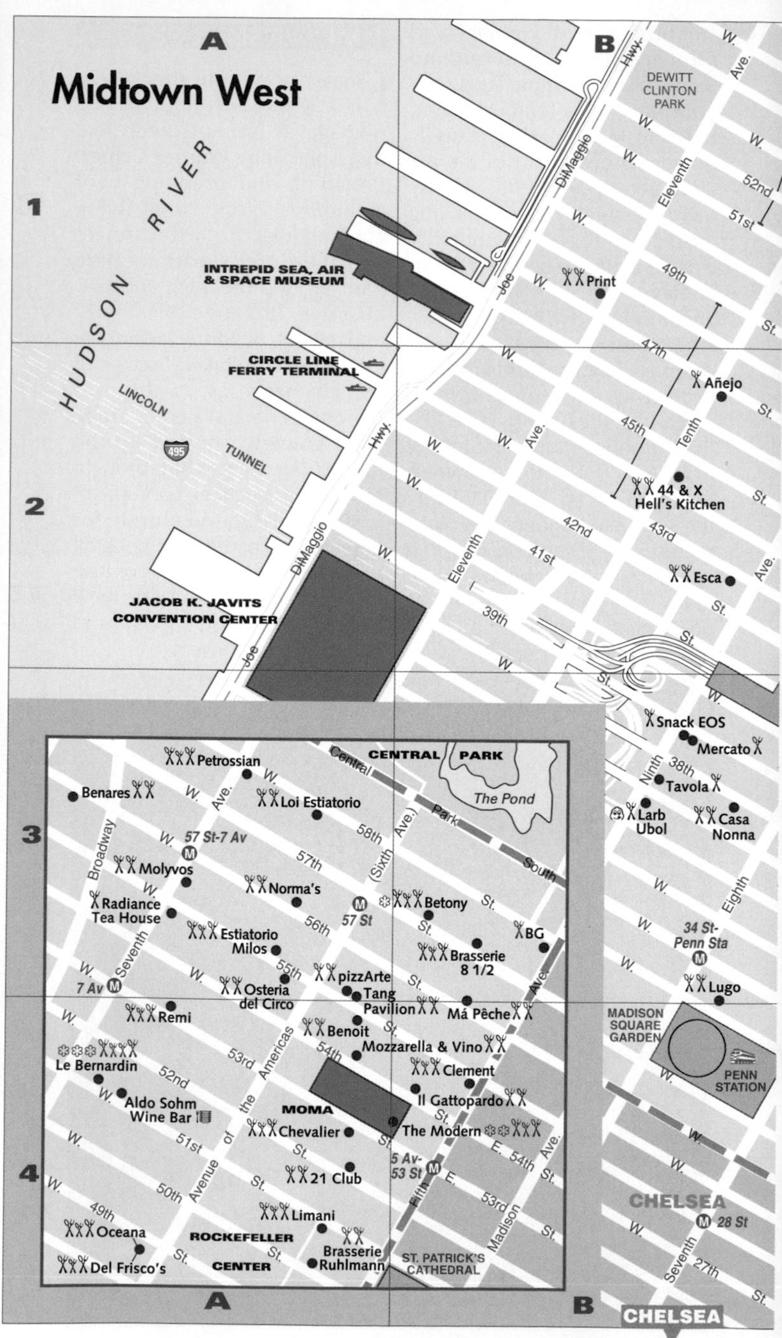
Midtown West
A
B
1
2
3
4
HUDSON RIVER
INTREPID SEA, AIR & SPACE MUSEUM
CIRCLE LINE FERRY TERMINAL
LINCOLN TUNNEL
495
JACOB K. JAVITS CONVENTION CENTER
Joe DiMaggio Hwy.
DEWITT CLINTON PARK
Print
Añejo
44 & X Hell's Kitchen
Esca
Snack EOS
Mercato
Tavola
Larb Ubol
Casa Nonna
34 St-Penn Sta
Lugo
MADISON SQUARE GARDEN
PENN STATION
CHELSEA
28 St
CENTRAL PARK
The Pond
Petrossian
Benares
Loi Estiatorio
57 St-7 Av
Molyvos
Norma's
57 St
Betony
Radiance Tea House
Estiatorio Milos
BG
Brasserie 8 1/2
7 Av
Osteria del Circo
pizzArte
Tang Pavilion
Má Pêche
Remi
Benoit
Le Bernardin
Mozzarella & Vino
Clement
Aldo Sohm Wine Bar
MOMA
Il Gattopardo
Chevalier
The Modern
5 Av-53 St
21 Club
Limani
Oceana
ROCKEFELLER CENTER
Brasserie Ruhlmann
Del Frisco's
ST. PATRICK'S CATHEDRAL
CHELSEA

UPPER WEST SIDE
C
D
Bar Masa
Porter House
Masa
TIME WARNER CENTER
59 St-Columbus Circle
Per Se
Marea
CENTRAL PARK
UPPER EAST SIDE
The Pond
1
Central Park South
Taboon
Ardesia
Casellula
Tori Shin
Yakitori Totto
CARNEGIE HALL
57 St-7 Av
5 Av-59 St
HELL'S KITCHEN
Danji
Braai
57 St
MIDTOWN
Chez Napoléon
Russian Samovar
Gallagher's
7 Av
WEST
Don Antonio by Starita
Toloache
50 St
Hell's Kitchen
Kung Fu Little Steamed Buns Ramen
50 St
MOMA
La Masseria
Becco
49 St
RADIO CITY MUSIC HALL
5 Av-53 St
2
Barbetta
Sake Bar Hagi
Scarlatto
ROCKEFELLER CENTER
THEATER DISTRICT
Hakkasan
47-50 Sts-Rockefeller Ctr
The Sea Grill
42 St- Port Authority Bus Terminal
Utsav
ST. PATRICK'S CATHEDRAL
PORT AUTHORITY BUS TERMINAL
Osteria al Doge
The Lambs Club
TIMES SQUARE
Times Sq
Sushi Zen
db Bistro Moderne
MIDTOWN EAST
Times Sq-42 St
Aureole
Gabriel Kreuther
42 St-Bryant Pk
Times Sq-42 St
5 Av
BRYANT PARK
METLIFE BLDG.
3
GRAND CENTRAL TERMINAL
GARMENT DISTRICT
Szechuan Gourmet
NY PUBLIC LIBRARY
Grand Central-42 St
Lan Sheng
42 St-Grand Central
MIDTOWN EAST
Frankie & Johnnie's
MACY'S
Stella 34
Keens
42 St-Grand Central
CHRYSLER BUILDING
34 St-Penn Sta
HERALD SQUARE
Cho Dang Gol
Ai Fiori
34 St-Herald Sq
Madangsui
Kristalbelli
MURRAY HILL
EMPIRE STATE BUILDING
New Wonjo
Kang Suh
4
Kunjip
Miss Korea
Kirakuya
Mandoo Bar
33 St
28 St

Ai Fiori ✿

Italian XXX

C4

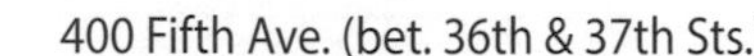

400 Fifth Ave. (bet. 36th & 37th Sts.)

Subway: 34 St - Herald Sq
Phone: 212-613-8660
Web: www.aifiorinyc.com
Prices: $$$$

Lunch Mon – Fri
Dinner nightly

Elegantly accessed either by a sweeping spiral staircase or the Langham Place hotel elevator, Ai Fiori stands proudly above its busy Fifth Avenue address. Walls of windows and espresso-dark polished wood dominate the space. The Carrara marble bar and lounge furnished with silvery tufted banquettes are ideal for solo diners; large florals, brown leather chairs, and square columns adorn the formal dining room. No matter where you sit, the servers are attentive, the linens are thick, chargers are monogrammed with a goldleaf "F" and every last detail is very, very lovely.

As one might expect of a Michael White restaurant, pastas here are masterful. Begin with perfectly al dente spaghetti evenly coated in subtly sweet tomato sauce with flakey crabmeat, gently spiced red chilies, and grated *bottarga*. Fish courses can be even more enticing. Dine on some of the brightest, freshest halibut known to this city, served on an excellent mix of smoky butter beans, chopped pancetta, artichokes, crispy golden croutons, and wonderfully minerally *cavolo nero*.

Finish your meal on a tasty note with a passion fruit curd and mango jelly tartlet along with a crunchy cookie to accompany your cup of strong, hot coffee.

Aldo Sohm Wine Bar

Contemporary

151 W. 51st St. (bet. Sixth & Seventh Aves.)

Subway: 50 St (Broadway) Lunch Mon – Fri
Phone: 212-554-1143 Dinner Mon – Sat
Web: www. aldosohmwinebar.com
Prices: $$

Step through this buffed metal doorway to find an oenophile's fantasy where Zalto stemware is stacked high and each polished glass is ready to be filled by one of the 200 selections brilliantly curated by Le Bernardin's super-star sommelier, Aldo Sohm. Over 40 wines on the list are offered by the glass.

A tailored crowd sits and sips—perhaps on an oversized U-shaped sofa, a comfy counter, or handful of tall tables. The scene is luxe but also comfortable, featuring crystal fixtures, vivid artwork, and a stylish array of bric-a-brac stacked high to the soaring ceiling. Tapas-sized snacks are designed for sharing with wine consumption in mind and include a plate of cheeses, charcuterie, harissa-roasted carrots, or chicken drumstick prepared coq au vin-style.

Añejo

Mexican

668 Tenth Ave. (at 47th St.)

Subway: 50 St (Eighth Ave.) Lunch Sat – Sun
Phone: 212-920-4770 Dinner nightly
Web: www.anejonyc.com
Prices: $$

This tasty *cocina* set in Hell's Kitchen is unpretentious and intimate. The house is always full and crowds are convivial, especially while sipping one of Añejo's beloved cocktails. The namesake margarita is an upscale, top-shelf refresher made with fresh lime juice and agave nectar that pairs perfectly with just about anything from the kitchen.

Ceviche, small plates, and tacos are all to be enjoyed with gusto. Start with the guacamole trio featuring traditional, pineapple-chipotle, and tomatillo-charred poblano variations. Then move on to a warm mushroom salad with wilted watercress, brown butter, and Berkshire pork chorizo. Pumpkin tamale is an outstanding deconstructed square of smashed kabocha squash, lamb *barbacoa,* and *crema* inside a banana leaf.

Ardesia

Contemporary 

C1

510 W. 52nd St. (bet. Tenth & Eleventh Aves.)

Subway: 50 St (Eighth Ave.) Dinner nightly
Phone: 212-247-9191
Web: www.ardesia-ny.com
Prices: $$

This is one of the area's best spots for grabbing an *aperitivo* and bite after work. Service is young, friendly, and knowledgeable, so make sure to ask for a recommendation as it can yield tasty rewards. Towering ceilings and a wall of windows seem to augment the rather petite space; and a chalkboard wall lists wines available by the glass, even if the most impressive selections are only offered by the bottle on the menu.

Contemporary small plates begin with notable cheese offerings like ricotta Ginepro, cold-smoked sheep's milk, and pale yellow Ossau Iraty accompanied by a walnut covered in date-coconut jam and thick, crusty bread from Amy's. Sample skewers lined with garlicky shrimp or spiced lamb. Then finish with a sweet and earnest take on homemade s'mores.

Barbetta

Italian XXX

C2

321 W. 46th St. (bet. Eighth & Ninth Aves.)

Subway: 50 St (Eighth Ave.) Lunch & dinner Tue – Sat
Phone: 212-246-9171
Web: www.barbettarestaurant.com
Prices: $$$

It doesn't get more old-world New York than this iconic Restaurant Row institution. Opened in 1906, Barbetta is a testament to proper dining out: men are required to don dinner jackets, outerwear is mandatorily checked, and a brigade of starched servers flit about the hushed and gilded surrounds. Perhaps unsurprisingly, the impossibly romantic patio has been the backdrop for countless marriage proposals. The kitchen's Northern-influenced specialties are listed on thick cardstock, and each selection is highlighted by the year of its addition to the menu. Linguine with *pesto alla Genovese* is as scrumptious today as it was in 1914; while luscious rabbit *alla Piemontese*, dating back to the Clinton era and braised in white wine and lemon, is equally divine.

Aureole ✿

XXX

Contemporary

C3

135 W. 42nd St. (bet. Broadway & Sixth Ave.)

Subway: 42 St - Bryant Pk
Phone: 212-319-1660
Web: www.charliepalmer.com
Prices: $$$$

Lunch Mon – Fri
Dinner nightly

Nestled smack dab in the middle of the melee that constitutes modern-day Times Square, Aureole's message is clear from the moment you enter its serene glass façade: drop your bags (and perhaps your shoulders) and relax—it's time to be pampered by a truly exquisite seafood-centric meal in a luxurious setting.

Up front, you'll find the Liberty Room, home to a lively bar that's ideal for an after-work drink or pre-dinner cocktail; and a small collection of handsome, walnut-topped tables comprising a more casual dining area. Toward the back of the restaurant, the formal dining room cuts an impressive, elegant figure with sexy low lighting; crisp white tablecloths; and polished table settings.

Dinner might begin with a beautifully composed peekytoe crab salad, sporting vibrant green avocado panna cotta, juicy watermelon and sea beans; and then move on to a gorgeous slice of fresh Alaskan black cod in a sweet and savory marinade, paired with crisp snap peas, bok choy, and *choy sum*. End with a stunning finale like the elegantly prepared Saint Honoré, a flaky tuille topped with a flower-shaped pinwheel piped with silky Manjari chocolate mousse and dotted with light-as-air *choux* puffs.

Bar Masa

Japanese XX

10 Columbus Circle (in the Time Warner Center)

Subway: 59 St - Columbus Circle — Lunch & dinner Mon – Sat
Phone: 212-823-9800
Web: www.barmasanyc.com
Prices: **$$$**

Make no mistake: Masa's adjacent lounge is by no means a bargain substitute for the stunner next door. Bar Masa remains as hopping as when it first opened, and on any given night every tightly packed seat is perpetually filled—thanks in part to a no-reservations policy. Despite the crowds, softly lit Japanese limestone walls give the room an air of serenity.

The long list of creative sips are excellent, so lay your lips on a cucumber mint gimlet while eagerly awaiting selections off the extensive menu. Serious effort is blatantly apparent: raw petals of *sakura* trout are tantalizingly dressed; pudding-soft tofu and perfectly ripe avocado are a heavenly pairing for an *uramaki*; and fluffy wild mushroom fried rice is sprinkled with wasabi salt.

Becco

Italian XX

355 W. 46th St. (bet. Eighth & Ninth Aves.)

Subway: 50 St (Eighth Ave.) — Lunch & dinner daily
Phone: 212-397-7597
Web: www.becco-nyc.com
Prices: **$$**

This Restaurant Row stalwart has no shortage of competition, but remains unrivaled when it comes to pleasing diners and theater-goers with reliable and hearty Italian fare. This is all thanks to culinary authority Lidia Bastianich, her impresario son Joe, and longtime Executive Chef William Gallagher.

Becco's pleasing vision of Italian cuisine includes house-made mozzarella *en carozza* sandwiched between fried bread with pesto and tomato sauces; and Belgian-ale roasted pulled pork with salsa verde. The *sarma* (Croatian for stuffed cabbage) honors the family's Istrian heritage with meat-stuffed cabbage in tomato sauce over pan-fried spinach spaetzle.

The wine list features bottles priced at $29, with selections from their own highly regarded label.

Benares

240 W. 56th St. (bet. Broadway & Eighth Ave.)

Subway: 59 St - Columbus Circle — Lunch & dinner daily
Phone: 212-397-0707
Web: www.benaresnyc.com
Prices: $$

Unassuming inside and out, Benares serves solid Northern Indian fare in a casual setting. The South Asian clientele is testament to its authenticity. The décor may seem a bit limited, but thoughtful touches include a colorful glass chandelier and a framed painting of women washing clothes along the Ganges (in the restaurant's namesake city).

Fragrant spice mixtures abound as seen in succulent and crunchy shrimp marinated with *ajwain*, garlic, and ginger, then grilled in the tandoor. Curry offerings showcase boldly satisfying comfort food, such as bowls of fork-tender *rezala*, the goat served bone-in with fragrant saffron and creamy yogurt. Any meal here should be accompanied by pillow-soft naan, and thick cucumber raita dotted with a pungent masala.

Benoit

60 W. 55th St. (bet. Fifth & Sixth Aves.)

Subway: 57 St — Lunch & dinner daily
Phone: 646-943-7373
Web: www.benoitny.com
Prices: $$

In the former home of the venerated La Côte Basque, Alain Ducasse's Benoit brings a hint of fame to this address. The casual bistro is rife with elegance through oak-paneled walls, polished brass, and red velvet seating, all set off by art nouveau lighting fixtures reclaimed from the previous tenants. Peugeot pepper grinders, bread presented in linen sacks, and espresso served in custom-made Pillivuyt cups add to the overall experience.

Chef Philippe Bertineau heads the kitchen, bringing a skilled hand to the likes of *foie de veau*, seared calf's liver paired with potatoes Lyonnaise. Pan-seared monkfish tail is prepared *coq au vin*-style with red wine sauce, lardons, pearl onions, and sautéed mushrooms. Desserts are categorically *magnifique*.

Betony ✿

B3 Contemporary

41 W. 57th St. (bet. Fifth & Sixth Aves.)

Subway: 57 St
Phone: 212-465-2400
Web: www.betony-nyc.com
Prices: $$$$

Lunch Mon – Fri
Dinner nightly

Midtown and Betony go together like caviar and blinis. Serious funds have been invested to create this smart, grown-up restaurant and its gilded features, wood paneling, and well-spaced tables provide very comfortable surroundings in which to do business or impress friends. The experienced service team, though, do a good job in ensuring the atmosphere never veers into the terminal seriousness that blights many a formal restaurant.

When one surveys this luxurious backdrop and the impeccably manicured clientele, it is perhaps something of a surprise to find that the food is adventurous and creative. Chef Bryce Shuman and his kitchen team know all the latest cooking techniques and are not afraid to use them. Ravioli with smoked potato shows off their delicate touch but the grilled short rib demonstrates that they also know how to create layers of flavor.

The menu comes in four sections and one is gently encouraged to have all four, although the hors d'oeuvres are meant more for sharing with a drink. Speaking of drinks, make sure you start by ordering a milk punch—the kitchen isn't the only team here who has some clever ideas and the ability to see them through.

BG

American

B3

754 Fifth Ave. (at 58th St.)

Subway: 5 Av - 59 St
Phone: 212-872-8977
Web: www.bergdorfgoodman.com
Prices: **$$$**

Lunch daily
Dinner Mon – Sat

On the 7th floor of Bergdorf Goodman, BG offers ladylike posh to the label-conscious clientele of this fashion emporium. The Kelly Wearstler-designed brasserie combines springtime hues with hand-printed Chinoiserie wallpaper, gilded fixtures, and lacquered accents.

Large windows frame killer Central Park vistas and highlight the well-coiffed crowd savoring a number of fine salads. However, the carte du jour offers more vibrant dining with decadent renditions of American comfort favorites, like lobster mac and cheese. The silken tomato basil soup is enriched with just the slightest hint of cream; and Israeli couscous is infused with smoked paprika and stocked with seared black bass and shellfish.

Afternoon tea is a suitably refined affair.

Braai

South African

C1

329 W. 51st St. (bet. Eighth & Ninth Aves.)

Subway: 50 St (Eighth Ave.)
Phone: 212-315-3315
Web: www.braainyc.com
Prices: **$$**

Dinner nightly

From its ground floor townhouse home, Braai is adored for tantalizing South African cuisine. Two tables sit up front in a snug patio, which dovetails into a long and slender dark wood space. Drawing inspiration from its region, wide planks make up the floors while the arched ceiling is thatched with straw. Yet the African-inspired décor in the dining room, set with marble-topped communal tables, is anything but cliché. The menu is resplendent with new and balanced flavors that are at once evident in *frikkadel,* a classic dish of baked meatballs in broth; or calamari drenched in a lovely wine-lemon emulsion. Speaking of mainstays, *bunny chow,* a street treat of lamb curry ladled into a bread bowl, is a favorite here as well as at nearby sib, Xai Xai.

Brasserie 8 1/2

French XXX

B3

9 W. 57th St. (bet. Fifth & Sixth Aves.)

Subway: 57 St — Lunch Sun – Fri
Phone: 212-829-0812 — Dinner nightly
Web: www.patinagroup.com
Prices: $$$

Dress-up, descend that sweeping staircase, and make a grand entrance upon stepping into this well-lit, spacious, grown-up canteen. The serene lounge, with just a handful of tables and walls boasting original works by Henri Matisse and Pablo Picasso, is a rarefied gift that feels worlds away from midtown's cacophony. The masculine, clubby aura of the dining room showcases ivory terrazzo floors, exotic wood veneer-lined walls, polished metal columns, and more artwork.

Talented Chef Franck Deletrain brings a traditional vision of brasserie cooking in items such as coq au vin; or *saucisson chaud*, braised pork sausage nestled in a bed of *lentils du Puy*. Finish with pear poached in spiced red wine, with mascarpone and pistachio financiers.

Brasserie Ruhlmann

French XX

A4

45 Rockefeller Plaza (bet. Fifth & Sixth Aves.)

Subway: 47-50 Sts - Rockefeller Ctr — Lunch & dinner daily
Phone: 212-974-2020
Web: www.brasserieruhlmann.com
Prices: $$$

True, some New Yorkers may think of this place as kind of touristy, but this is quintessential brasserie cooking in an equally quintessential Manhattan setting at the base of Rockefeller Center, overlooking its plaza. There is little debate that this French *bijou* offers some of the best people-watching around. The décor pays homage to its art deco namesake, Émile-Jacques Ruhlmann, through edgy lines and geometric prints.

Some dishes may be on the menu more for pleasing the crowds than reflecting tradition (hence the sushi rolls). Still, the *croque monsieur* is everything you dream it to be—impossibly rich with paper-thin and salty *jambon de Paris*, creamy béchamel, and a dangerously good layering of melted Gruyère over thick slices of brioche.

Casa Nonna

310 W. 38th St. (bet. Eighth & Ninth Aves.)

Subway: Times Sq - 42 St
Phone: 212-736-3000
Web: www.casanonna.com
Prices: $$

Lunch Mon – Fri
Dinner nightly

Quaint sounding Casa Nonna is actually a behemoth of a restaurant run by an international dining group. A boon to garment district workers and suburban commuters, this sprawling, multi-room space is just a few blocks away from bustling Penn Station and the Port Authority bus terminal.

There is a dish for every taste at Casa Nonna, whose attractive menu is replete with satisfying and well-prepared Roman and Tuscan fare. Panini and Neapolitan-style pizza are popular during lunchtime, while dinner serves a hearty lineup of *primi* such as *tagliolini frutti di mare*, with fine breadcrumbs clinging the vibrant tomato sauce to the pasta. Entrées feature grilled Cornish hen, spiced *alla diavola*-style with garlic, lemon, and hot pepper.

Casellula

401 W. 52nd St. (bet. Ninth & Tenth Aves.)

Subway: 50 St (Eighth Ave.)
Phone: 212-247-8137
Web: www.casellula.com
Prices: $$

Dinner nightly

Casellula oozes with warmth in both look and feel. Dark wood tables, exposed brick, and flickering votives are a sight for sore eyes, while the delightful staff is so attentive and friendly, that you may never want to leave.

Small plates are big here, while medium plates feature tasty sandwiches (crunchy *muffulettas* stuffed with fontina and cured meats) and shrimp tacos splashed with *salsa verde*. Pity the lactose intolerant, as cheese (and lots of it) followed by dessert (maybe a pumpkin ice cream "sandwich" pecked with brown butter caramel?) are part and parcel of the special experience at this petite place. Feeling blue? They've got that and much more with over 50 different varieties, perfectly complemented by an excellent and vast wine list.

Chevalier

Contemporary XXX

A4

28 W. 53rd St. (bet. Fifth & Sixth Aves.)

Subway: 5 Av - 53 St — Lunch Mon – Fri
Phone: 212-790-8869 — Dinner Mon – Sat
Web: www.baccarathotels.com
Prices: **$$$$**

Bearded hipsters are not the target market for every new opening. This glamorous brasserie within the Baccarat Hotel is unashamedly geared to the more grown-up members of the city's social scene—those for whom 53rd Street is downtown. The space exudes old-school charm as the dapper waitstaff coddles those Manhattan powerbrokers and their mink-trimmed cohorts.

The menu offers a modern re-working of classic French dishes. The clientele are not the sort to be too concerned by prices but at least one can see where the money goes. The scallops, served with comté and morels, are huge and the veal loin with sweetbreads is not for the fainthearted.

And as you would expect from a hotel called Baccarat, the glassware is pretty impressive too.

Chez Napoléon

French X

C2

365 W. 50th St. (bet. Eighth & Ninth Aves.)

Subway: 50 St (Eighth Ave.) — Lunch Mon – Fri
Phone: 212-265-6980 — Dinner Mon – Sat
Web: www.cheznapoleon.com
Prices: **$$**

Oh so popular and family-run by the Brunos since 1982, this atmospheric *bijou* is not to be missed for its unapologetically creamy and butter-dreamy plates of traditional French cuisine. It's not polite to discuss age, but let's just say that Chef/*grandmère*, Marguerite Bruno, has steadily commanded this kitchen for an impressive tenure.

The scene is *magnifique*. Take in the creaky wood floors and parchment-colored walls hung with French-themed jigsaw puzzles, then indulge in chilled silky leeks dressed with the famous house vinaigrette; sautéed veal kidneys in mustard-cream sauce; and steak *au poivre* with black or green peppercorn sauce. Plan ahead when ordering so you have time (and space) for a classic dessert soufflé sided with crème anglaise.

Cho Dang Gol 

Korean

55 W. 35th St. (bet. Fifth & Sixth Aves.)

Subway: 34 St - Herald Sq — Lunch & dinner daily
Phone: 212-695-8222
Web: www.chodanggolny.com
Prices:

Among the delicious offerings that comprise the *banchan* welcoming diners to this hopping K-town spot, take note of the tofu. Warm, fluffy, and house-made, it's just one of the reasons why Cho Dang Gol is a standout for Korean cuisine. In fact, the restaurant is named for a South Korean village famous for its soybean curd. Next in line for your attention is a listing of bubbling-hot *jjigaes* featuring the likes of short rib, taro, and glass noodles. House specials like a wild sesame-and-mushroom casserole are also a hit.

Though the staff can be brusquely efficient—a product of the high business volume—Korean artifacts and rustic wooden tables lend a sweet sentimentality to the place that, combined with the fresh, high-quality food, make it well worth a visit.

Clement

Contemporary 

700 Fifth Ave. (at 55th St.)

Subway: 5 Av - 53 St — Lunch daily
Phone: 212-956-2888 — Dinner Tue – Sat
Web: www.peninsula.com/NewYork
Prices: $$$

This particularly elegant bar and dining room is one of the lucky few to call the Peninsula New York home. Created by design firm Yabu Pushelberg, the posh setting includes a series of rooms, each with their own striking touches that sprawl from a thickly carpeted staircase off the lobby. Worth a mention is the book room, with its stacks of bound-linen rag paper, mauve fabrics, and fresh flowers in mercury glasses.

So too is the kitchen, whose talented team sends out ambitious preparations like the locally sourced scallop composition pairing carpaccio zested by pink grapefruit and yuzu with seared specimens swiped by sunchoke foam. Another winner is crisp-skinned black bass set beside maitake mushrooms and gussied up tableside with roasted duck broth.

Danji

Korean

346 W. 52nd St. (bet. Eighth & Ninth Aves.)

Subway: 50 St (Eighth Ave.) Lunch Mon – Fri
Phone: 212-586-2880 Dinner Mon – Sat
Web: www.danjinyc.com
Prices: $$

Thanks to tall communal tables that practically fill the dining room, Chef Hooni Kim's Hell's Kitchen hot spot is both festive and bustling. Attractive and smartly designed, its silk panels, pottery, and striking display of spoons are further enhanced by a flattering lighting scheme.

Equally impressive are the menu's myriad small plates, each of them a refreshing take on Korean specialties. Blocks of soft tofu are quickly deep-fried and boldly dressed with *gochujang* and a ginger-scallion vinaigrette. Poached daikon rings accompanied by bok choy, are glazed with a dark and spicy sauce and stacked high for dramatic presentation. Vegetarian highlights include spicy, crispy dumplings filled with tofu, vegetables, and cellophane noodles.

db Bistro Moderne

Contemporary

55 W. 44th St. (bet. Fifth & Sixth Aves.)

Subway: 5 Av Lunch & dinner daily
Phone: 212-391-2400
Web: www.dbbistro.com
Prices: $$$

Chef Daniel Boulud's midtown canteen is fashioned by Jeffrey Beers and dons a contemporary demeanor. The front lounge is abuzz with post-work and pre-theater gaggles, while well-behaved crowds in the back are seated in a walnut-paneled space dressed with mirrors and black-and-white photography.

Like its setting, the menu is inventive and unites classic bistro cooking with market-inspired creations. That lush *pâté en croute* is a buttery pastry encasing layers of creamy country pâté, guinea hen, and foie gras, dressed with huckleberry compote, toasted pine nuts, and pickled enoki mushrooms. Wild rice-crusted fluke presented with Hawaiian blue prawn and sauce *Américaine* further demonstrate the kitchen's contemporary leanings.

Del Frisco's

Steakhouse

A4

1221 Sixth Ave. (at 49th St.)

Subway: 47-50 Sts - Rockefeller Ctr
Phone: 212-575-5129
Web: www.delfriscos.com
Prices: $$$

Lunch Mon – Fri
Dinner nightly

Prime, aged, corn-fed beef is the main attraction at this sprawling, outrageously successful outpost of the Dallas-based steakhouse chain. Portions range from the petite filet to a 24-ounce Porterhouse that will make any Texan proud. The menu begins with a suitably rich feast of cheesesteak egg rolls or white clam flatbread; but then does an about face with a knife-and-fork Caesar salad. Lunch is an affordable way to sample their classics.

Complementing its McGraw-Hill Building home, Del Frisco's flaunts a masculine look with a large L-shaped bar, dramatic wrought-iron balcony, wood accents, and towering windows. The mezzanine dining area, accessible by a sweeping staircase, enjoys a quieter ambience.

Del Frisco's Grille in Rockefeller Plaza is another option.

Don Antonio by Starita

Pizza

C2

309 W. 50th St. (bet. Eighth & Ninth Aves.)

Subway: 50 St (Eighth Ave.)
Phone: 646-719-1043
Web: www.donantoniopizza.com
Prices: $$

Lunch & dinner daily

Hell's Kitchen's best pizzeria boasts serious street cred. The namesake original in Naples has been in operation since 1901, while this outpost is run by pizza maestros, Antonio Starita and Roberto Caporuscio. Always busy, the setting features a red-tiled domed pizza oven and walls lined with art depicting volcanoes—this calls to mind the logo of Caporuscio's other pizza hot spot, Kesté.

The lightly fried, wood-fire finished *montanara Starita* is a house specialty. An array of other fried and filled pies feature a first-rate listing of *pizze rosse, pizze bianchi,* and even gluten-free options. The *speciale* has included the Guiseppe spread with earthy artichoke purée beneath gobs of melted house-made mozzarella, and drizzles of olive oil.

Esca

Seafood

B2

402 W. 43rd St. (bet. Ninth & Tenth Aves.)

Subway: 42 St - Port Authority Bus Terminal — Lunch Mon – Sat
Phone: 212-564-7272 — Dinner nightly
Web: www.esca-nyc.com
Prices: **$$$**

Chef David Pasternack's Italian-style seafood has kept this Theater District mainstay hopping for fifteen years now. The two-room space is cozy and boasts a rustic charm with its lemon-yellow walls and displayed wine storage.

The steady kitchen turns out consistently impressive cuisine that starts off with a listing of crudo, such as petals of pale pink seabream simply but impeccably dressed with Meyer lemon-infused olive oil, Amagansett sea salt, and black pepper. Other plates reveal seared monkfish liver, custard-soft within, served atop radicchio, organic grains, and candied citrus. The house-made *bucatini* with Rita's spicy octopus sauce is deliciously zesty. Dessert may highlight a semolina pudding with caramel sauce and vanilla yogurt.

Estiatorio Milos

Greek

A3

125 W. 55th St. (bet. Sixth & Seventh Aves.)

Subway: 57 St — Lunch & dinner daily
Phone: 212-245-7400
Web: www.milos.ca
Prices: **$$$**

This Greek restaurant offers such a deliciously singular focus on the sea that dinner here feels like a relaxing jaunt to the Mediterranean coast. Feast your eyes on the ever-present bounty of iced fish, flown in fresh and displayed in the back of the cavernous room where a well-dressed, business-minded crowd gathers.

Oregano plants atop each table are snipped into bowls of olive oil to accompany the fine bread that precedes the selection of raw bar specialties and grilled fish. The day's bounty may reveal charred *barbouni*, or red mullet, dressed with olive oil, capers, and a sprig of flat leaf parsley. Side dishes unveil *chtipiti*—a mouthwatering spread made from roasted red peppers and barrel-aged feta that you'll want to slather on everything.

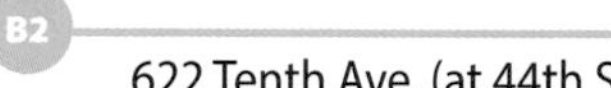

44 & X Hell's Kitchen

B2

American XX

622 Tenth Ave. (at 44th St.)

Subway: 42 St - Port Authority Bus Terminal — Lunch & dinner daily
Phone: 212-977-1170
Web: www.44andx.com
Prices: $$

The moniker is a mouthful, but this modern bistro's endearing appeal has attracted eclectic crowds since opening on a block west of no-man's land. Today, this corner of Hell's Kitchen is a solid, mature venue that offers plenty of reason to swing by. Cute servers in black t-shirts are gracious and attentive, presenting updated renditions of spirited comfort food. Lobster tacos with charred tomato salsa, crunchy buttermilk fried chicken accompanied by a chive waffle and maple syrup jus, as well as pan-roasted mahi mahi with lobster and scallop risotto emerge from the skilled kitchen. House-baked apple pie was a lovely sweet special to ward off the chill of an autumn evening.
Sister spot 44 ½ boasts a menu of Asian and Mediterranean influences.

Frankie & Johnnie's

C4

Steakhouse XX

32 W. 37th St. (bet. Fifth & Sixth Aves.)

Subway: 34 St - Herald Sq — Lunch Mon – Fri
Phone: 212-947-8940 — Dinner Mon – Sat
Web: www.frankieandjohnnies.com
Prices: $$$

No surprise that this is a former speakeasy. The first floor is dedicated to drinking at the bar and booths filled with people sipping martinis before heading to Penn Station. Head upstairs, beyond an artistically assembled mound of wax over the vestibule, to enter this classic dining room. Spacious tables, crisp linens, and swift service ensure a steady business clientele.
All in all, Frankie & Johnnie's is the kind of place where you shouldn't have to look at the menu. Just go with a nicely marbled, medium rare Porterhouse steak sliced tableside and served with the bone for gnawing. Traditional sides like whipped potatoes or creamed spinach push the limits with butter and cream. For dessert, the cheesecake is prepared with solid New York know-how.

Gabriel Kreuther ✿

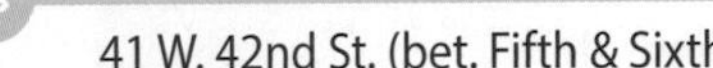

Contemporary XXX

C3

41 W. 42nd St. (bet. Fifth & Sixth Aves.)

Subway: 42 St - Bryant Pk
Phone: 212-257-5826
Web: www.gknyc.com
Prices: **$$$$**

Lunch Mon – Fri
Dinner Mon – Sat

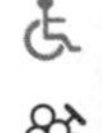

The Grace Building's swooping white travertine façade is a bulwark for the spacious and serene treasure within, a familiar name that has once again brightened Manhattan's dining scene. Don't let the oasis of nearby Bryant Park distract you from this new destination, where cream leather seating, reclaimed timber columns, and a glass-walled display kitchen combine for a uniquely pulled together enclave boasting a luxe lounge area.

Chef Gabriel Kreuther's Alsatian heritage provides a distinctive mark here, evinced by the stork imagery throughout and by his exciting cuisine espousing regional pride. His elegantly composed sturgeon and sauerkraut tart is a delightful signature creation adorned with American caviar and infused with smoke. Frilly cones of nori-enriched pasta are presented with meaty slices of Alaskan king crab and parsnip purée; while lusciously tender Maine lobster poached in Mangalitsa *lardo* is dressed with *jamón* emulsion.

Kreuther has brought back the palate cleanser, updated and perfectly executed, to prepare you for the finale which may be titled "Contemporary" and reveal pistachio genoise and vanilla cream encased in dark cherry gelée topped with lime-vanilla sorbet.

Gallagher's

C2 — Steakhouse XX

228 W. 52nd St. (bet. Broadway & Eighth Ave.)

Subway: 50 St (Broadway) — Lunch & dinner daily
Phone: 212-586-5000
Web: www.gallaghersnysteakhouse.com
Prices: $$$

A multi-million dollar renovation hasn't glossed over any of Gallagher's iconic character. Walls covered with photos of horses and jockeys harken back to the 85-year-old stallion's former proximity to the old Madison Square Garden. The menu's "other soup" is a sly reference held over from Prohibition days; and diners still walk past the window-fronted meat locker where slabs of USDA Prime beef are dry-aged.

Gallagher's fresh sparkle is exhibited by the display kitchen, set behind glass panes. The chefs here turn out contemporary-minded fare like hamachi crudo with a yuzu-jalapeño vinaigrette to go with choice cuts of meat grilled over hickory. The rib steak is a bone-in ribeye that arrives mouthwateringly tender with a side of warm and savory house sauce.

Hakkasan

C2 — Chinese XXX

311 W. 43rd St. (bet. Eighth & Ninth Aves.)

Subway: 42 St - Port Authority Bus Terminal — Lunch Sat – Sun
Phone: 212-776-1818 — Dinner nightly
Web: www.hakkasan.com
Prices: $$$$

When you fancy eating somewhere sensual and sophisticated, then going to the Theater District is unlikely to be your first thought. At least this sleek, moodily-lit Chinese restaurant comes with an 80-foot corridor behind its front door, allowing you time to adjust from tourist town to sexy sanctum.

Cobalt-blue glass, marble and mirrors help create a striking space that feels surprisingly intimate considering its size. Service may need the occasional prompt but the Cantonese food is good and the cocktails terrific. Standouts are stir-fried sugar pea shoots with crabmeat and scallops, and jasmine tea-smoked chicken. And if you're wondering how they charge what they do for sesame prawn toast, order it and you'll see (clue: it's the foie gras).

Hell's Kitchen

Mexican XX

C2

679 Ninth Ave. (bet. 46th & 47th Sts.)

Subway: 50 St (Eighth Ave.) Dinner nightly
Phone: 212-977-1588
Web: www.hellskitchen-nyc.com
Prices: $$

Effortlessly cozy and always friendly, Hell's Kitchen is loved for its bold, satisfying meals. Bare-wood tables, exposed bricks, and chandeliers cleverly made of wine bottles enhance the undeniably jovial space. An orange-tiled bar, wall of banquettes, and spacious booths ensure seating for any size group.

Start with a martini glass filled with slices of tender raw steak ceviche in limey marinade with red onion, tomato, and chopped cilantro, served with ancho chili-dusted house chips. Then, move on to the agave-marinated pork loin, moist and glistening over a mound of buttery white rice and grilled vegetables—though the star of that dish (and many others) is the rust-colored *mole*. Sauces here are flavor-forward, incredibly complex, and a clear highlight.

Il Gattopardo

Italian XX

B4

13 W. 54th St. (bet. Fifth & Sixth Aves.)

Subway: 5 Av - 53 St Lunch & dinner daily
Phone: 212-246-0412
Web: www.ilgattopardonyc.com
Prices: $$$

This *leopard's* take on Italian dining favors elegance over rusticity. Set within two Beaux Arts townhouses (once home to a Rockefeller family member), the restaurant is an understated sprawl of ivory walls contrasting dark-stained floors and smoky mirrors.

The smartly attired staff attends to a buttoned-up crowd digging into pricey but pleasing fare like shaved artichoke salad with organic frisée, lemon, olive oil, and *bottarga di muggine*. Here, veal scaloppini is a pounded filet layered with grilled eggplant and smoked provolone, alongside braised escarole studded with black olives. Like everything else at Il Gattopardo, the *cassata Siciliana*—with its candied fruit and bright green almond paste—is a dressed-up take on the classic.

Kang Suh

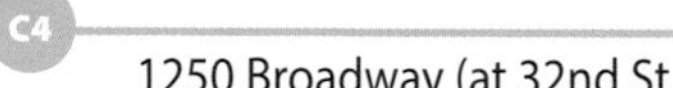

Korean XX

C4

1250 Broadway (at 32nd St.)

Subway: 33 St
Phone: 212-564-6845
Web: N/A
Prices: $$

Lunch & dinner daily

A longtime favorite of Korean barbecue fans, this lively yet homey joint delivers an authentic and charming experience. Donning an old-school vibe, the room may seem trapped in time, but be assured as there is delish food and free-flowing soju on deck here. Bypass the first floor and find a roost on the second level, where warm, almost maternal servers with a sense of humor present an array of fragrant grilled meats.

The *haemool pa jeon* is a flaky seafood pancake and excellent starter that may be trailed by delicate slices of *galbi* sizzling on the grill. Further indulge this meat feast with *jaeyook gui* or marinated pork grilled to pink perfection. Yet still be sure to save room for *boodae chongol*—a bubbling stew of kimchi, pork, vegetables, and noodles.

Keens

Steakhouse XX

C4

72 W. 36th St. (bet. Fifth & Sixth Aves.)

Subway: 34 St - Herald Sq
Phone: 212-947-3636
Web: www.keens.com
Prices: $$$

Lunch Mon – Fri
Dinner nightly

When it comes to steakhouses, Keens is a New York original. Dating back to 1885, these rooms (the Lincoln, Lamb's, and Lillie Langtry) are imbued with Gilded Age charisma. Large tables are closely arranged under low ceilings lined with clay churchwarden pipes—a vestige of Keens' men-only, smoker's club days.

Every night brings a full house of big appetites for belly-busting cuts of meat. Signature favorites include the mutton chop and Porterhouse sized for two or more, dry-aged in-house to achieve nutty perfection. For the complete experience, cover your table with fantastic sides like creamed spinach and hashbrowns.

The Pub Room pours one of the most extensive selections of single malt Scotch around—happy hour brings complimentary nibbles.

Kirakuya

Japanese

C4

2 W. 32nd St. (bet. Broadway & Fifth Ave.)

Subway: 34 St - Herald Sq
Phone: 212-695-7272
Web: www.sakebarkirakuya.com
Prices: **$$**

Lunch Mon – Fri
Dinner Mon – Sat

Located on the second floor of a nondescript building, this authentic *izakaya* buried in K-town feels exotic and unexpected. Out the elevator and beyond the dim (even dingy) hallway, your welcome will be warm and energetic. The long room is clad in dark brown wood, but bright with large windows and very good service. Take it as an auspicious sign that Japanese is spoken at many of the tables.

Midday is limited to the budget-friendly lunch set, as in a tasty *shio saba* meal of grilled mackerel with a salad, miso soup, and pickles. The wide-ranging evening menu includes overnight dried squid, Berkshire pork belly in a sweet soy sauce, *tsukune* (grilled chicken meatball), and a few Western-influenced snacks like French fries with rosemary salt.

Kristalbelli

Korean

C4

8 W. 36th St. (bet. Fifth & Sixth Aves.)

Subway: 34 St - Herald Sq
Phone: 212-290-2211
Web: www.kristalbelli.com
Prices: **$$$**

Lunch Mon – Fri
Dinner nightly

Turning up the heat in the dreary Garment District, Kristalbelli is a sexy harbinger of this fast-changing neighborhood. Outside, a gray slate- and marble-façade plus an impressive wooden door imply opulence; inside, crystal barbecue grills set on grey marble framed by a jolly gold monk make table-top dining over-the-top. The fun and bling continues upstairs in the young, hip, and hopping lounge.

Yet amid all this glitz and glam is a well-trained service team and very talented kitchen. *Banchan* opens with a superlative assortment that might include green chilies with fermented bean paste, marinated mushrooms, cold egg custard with scallions, and kimchi. A sparkling signature crystal bowl does not distract from the deeply flavored, almost buttery ribeye.

Kung Fu Little Steamed Buns Ramen 

Chinese 

811 Eighth Ave. (bet. 48th & 49th Sts.)

Subway: 50 St (Eighth Ave.) Lunch & dinner daily
Phone: 917-388-2555
Web: www.nykungfuramen.com
Prices: ⊜

With its lineup of traditionally prepared comfort food, this steamy joint kicks Hell's Kitchen's Chinese competitors to the curb. Set among the bright lights of the Theater District yet more indicative of the noodle houses found south of Canal Street or along Flushing Avenue, the perpetually packed gem offers a so-so ambience but very friendly service.

Hand-pulled and hand-cut noodles are stir fried with a number of mouthwatering accompaniments; while the dumpling variety is so great it's almost impossible to focus. Herb-spiked pork and shrimp wonton soup is well worth the 20-minute wait, allowing diners plenty of time to devour pan-fried Peking duck bundles and scallion pancakes stuffed with sliced beef; or steamed buns full of mushroom and bok choy.

Kunjip

Korean

9 W 32nd St. (bet. Broadway & Fifth Ave.)

Subway: 34 St - Herald Sq Lunch & dinner daily
Phone: 212-216-9487
Web: www.kunjip.com
Prices: ⊜

One of K-town's better recommendations, this ever-bustling restaurant is open 24-hours a day, seven days a week. Prepare yourself to be immersed in a noisy setting, wafting with food aromas, where orange-shirted servers whiz by, balancing trays heaped with plates of *banchan*, sizzling stone bowls of *bibimbap*, or empty dishes from instantly re-set tables.

You may feel compelled to order right away as the line out the door makes for a less than leisurely ambience, but relax. The staff is pleasant and the vast menu is worth perusing. Find specialties like *mae woon dduk boki*—a saucy stew of pan-fried rice cake tossed with softened white onion, plenty of scallions, mung bean noodles, and fish cake all tossed with spicy, sweet, and rich *gochujang*.

La Masseria

Italian XX

C2

235 W. 48th St. (bet. Broadway & Eighth Ave.)

Subway: 50 St (Eighth Ave.) Lunch & dinner daily
Phone: 212-582-2111
Web: www.lamasserianyc.com
Prices: $$

Stone, stucco walls, and exposed wood beams warm this bright and popular Theater District standby. The convenient location ensures that every large white-clothed table in the dining room is routinely full, and spot-on service delivered by smartly attired team keeps the mood upbeat.

When it comes to the food, the menu chooses homey Italian comforts over theatrics. Homemade stuffed fresh mozzarella allows the character of each ingredient—peppery arugula, roasted eggplant—to shine. Don't miss a selection of pasta *fatta in casa*. Entrées include a tender, juicy, expertly pounded veal chop with wedges of crisply roasted potatoes and a zippy chopped tomato and black olive salad. Finish with a warm and buttery inverted apple tart topped by vanilla ice cream.

The Lambs Club

American XX

C3

132 W. 44th St. (bet. Broadway & Sixth Ave.)

Subway: Times Sq - 42 St Lunch & dinner daily
Phone: 212-997-5262
Web: www.thelambsclub.com
Prices: $$$

On a storied stretch dotted by blue-blooded social institutions and boutique hotels (like the Chatwal which also happens to be its home) find The Lamb's Club, named for the theater group that once resided here. Helmed by Chef/restaurateur Geoffrey Zakarian and reimagined by designer Thierry Despont, this handsome retreat is a glamorous art deco backdrop of ebonized walls and red leather seating set aglow by stainless steel torchieres and a fireplace.

It's a fitting scene for the novel American food that follows. Try slow-poached halibut with crispy frog's legs and licorice herbs, paired with seasonal sides like roasted carrots with prune purée and pecan granola. End with apple crisp "tatin" sandwiching flaky pastry, roasted apples, and caramel mousse.

Lan Sheng

60 W. 39th St. (bet. Fifth & Sixth Aves.)

Subway: 42 St - Bryant Pk — Lunch & dinner daily
Phone: 212-575-8899
Web: N/A
Prices: $$

Midday hordes gathered outside its plain-Jane façade evidences the popularity of this midtown Sichuan stop. The pleasant and comfy interior fashioned from high-backed banquettes, wood-carved wall hangings, and colorful accent lights provides a respite once you make it through the doors. Recent experiences have indicated inconsistent cooking, but the fiery and smoky specialties here are still praiseworthy. Nibble on a crispy pile of camphor tea-smoked duck while waiting for the standout items to arrive. These may include miso- and chili-simmered whole fish showered with green onion; strips of bitter melon dressed with black bean sauce; as well as shredded potatoes shined with oil, vinegar, and hit with dried red plus thinly sliced green chilies.

Larb Ubol

480 Ninth Ave. (bet. 36th & 37th Sts.)

Subway: 34 St - Penn Station — Lunch & dinner daily
Phone: 212-564-1822
Web: www.larbubol.com
Prices:

Chef Ratchanee Sumpatboon is cooking up her own delicious Isaan-Thai storm in Hell's Kitchen. Inconspicuously lodged between Penn Station and Port Authority, Larb Ubol is tidy, cheerful, and dressed with colorful fabrics.

The *som tom kort muar* is cool and limey yet very spicy with green and red chilies dotting the crunchy mound of lettuce, green papaya, rice noodles, and fried pork rind. Savory and satisfying *pla dook larb,* a spicy ground catfish salad, combines wild ginger, fresh mint, and lime. The deep-fried pork belly, *pad ped moo krob,* is rendered crisp yet wonderfully chewy, then stir-fried with chopped eggplant, sweet red pepper, and red curry paste. Cool off with a scoop of coconut ice cream garnished with preserved palm seeds.

Le Bernardin ✿✿✿

A4 Seafood XXXX

155 W. 51st St. (bet. Sixth & Seventh Aves.)

Subway: 50 St (Broadway) Lunch Mon – Fri
Phone: 212-554-1515 Dinner Mon – Sat
Web: www.le-bernardin.com
Prices: $$$$

Eric Ripert's paean to all things piscatorial is unquestionably one of the daddies of the New York dining scene. No one gets to occupy this amount of prime midtown real estate for this long without knowing exactly what they're doing—and doing it supremely well. Run with consummate ease by a well-organized team, its influence stretches beyond merely the entertaining of big-hitters and even bigger spenders.

But however celebrated, the sine qua non of any self-respecting seafood restaurant must be the ability to cook a piece of fish absolutely perfectly and, in this, Le Bernardin displays deftness and consistency. Just try the luxuriantly buttery wild striped bass and you'll get the idea.

"Almost Raw," "Barely Touched," and "Lightly Cooked" are the headings under which you'll find an impressive array of dishes. The influences are global but the cooking is underpinned by a mastery of technique; ingredients are of unimpeachable quality and the kitchen has the confidence to never overcrowd a plate so that the fish always remains the star of the show.

Limani

Greek XXX

A4

45 Rockefeller Plaza (entrance on 50th St.)

Subway: 47-50 Sts - Rockefeller Ctr — Lunch & dinner daily
Phone: 212-858-9200
Web: www.limani.com
Prices: **$$$**

Rockefeller Center's splashy new canteen has quickly positioned itself as a top contender for formal Greek dining. The ethereal space is all gleaming white surfaces and colorful mood lighting; whole fish are displayed on ice, and an onyx reflecting pool sits in the center of it all.

Limani's dressed-up crowd nibbles on contemporary Hellenic delights executed with aplomb. The raw bar offers icy treats—oysters, sashimi, and ceviche—and globally sourced catch is the foundation of cooked preparations, like grilled Canadian halibut dressed with olive oil and capers. *Gigantes* cooked in a tomato sauce redolent of dill and anise are a worthy side dish; while *karidopita*, spiced walnut cake soaked with honey, makes for a sweet Greek finish.

Loi Estiatorio

A3

132 W. 58th St. (bet. Sixth & Seventh Aves.)

Subway: 57 St — Lunch Sun – Fri
Phone: 212-713-0015 — Dinner nightly
Web: www.loiestiatorio.com
Prices: **$$**

Chef, cookbook authority, and restaurateur Marisa Loi has moved her refined take on traditional Greek cuisine to this new address, formerly the home of Seäsonal. The room is minimally revamped, with dark leather furnishings and panoramic photos of sun-bleached coastline that hang on the pale walls.

Lovers of Greek cuisine will revel in the cooking's familiar scents and flavors, while marveling at the kitchen's unique, inspired spin. It's possible to feast on starters alone like *ladolemono*-dressed grilled octopus with fava bean purée, or *papoutsakia* (stuffed eggplant topped with caramelized béchamel sauce). But, don't overlook the entrées—rooster, braised in red wine as well as spiced tomato sauce and served over Greek pasta, is especially decadent.

Lugo

Italian XX

1 Penn Plaza (entrance on 33rd St.)

Subway: 34 St - Penn Station — Lunch & dinner Mon – Fri
Phone: 212-760-2700
Web: www.ldvhospitality.com
Prices: **$$**

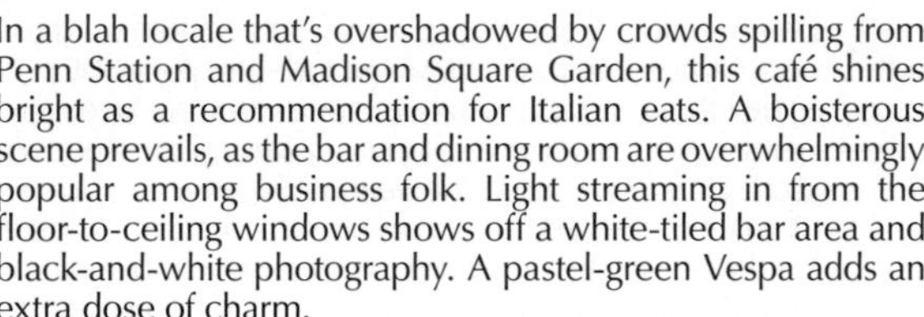

In a blah locale that's overshadowed by crowds spilling from Penn Station and Madison Square Garden, this café shines bright as a recommendation for Italian eats. A boisterous scene prevails, as the bar and dining room are overwhelmingly popular among business folk. Light streaming in from the floor-to-ceiling windows shows off a white-tiled bar area and black-and-white photography. A pastel-green Vespa adds an extra dose of charm.

Tables receive a satisfying array of items like warm hand-pulled mozzarella, Neapolitan-style pizza, and zesty entrées like Mediterranean branzino with spicy *puttanesca*. Pasta is deftly prepared and certainly a worthy indulgence, especially the tiny ridged tubes of *rigatoncini* coated with slow-cooked, meaty Bolognese.

Madangsui

Korean XX

C4

35 W. 35th St. (bet. Fifth & Sixth Aves.)

Subway: 34 St - Herald Sq — Lunch & dinner daily
Phone: 212-564-9333
Web: www.madangsui.com
Prices: **$$**

With a menu that reads like a who's who list of Korean all-star dishes, Madangsui is one of those old-school joints that regulars and first-timers seem to enjoy equally well—most likely because when they do any one of their classic Korean dishes, they hit it out of the park.

The setting is clean and simple (think Korean barbecue hall) and the staff genuinely warm and friendly, but the lip-smacking roster of classics is the real draw here. Past the lineup of terrific *bi bim baps*, don't miss the excellent *mandu*, fried to perfection and piped with tender pork and vegetables; or *japchae*, a sweet potato noodle stir fry; or one of the restaurant's increasingly popular lunch specials—imagine a refreshing bowl of *naengmyeon* served in icy cold broth.

Mandoo Bar

2 W. 32nd St. (bet. Broadway & Fifth Ave.)

Subway: 34 St - Herald Sq — Lunch & dinner daily
Phone: 212-279-3075
Web: N/A
Prices: ¢¢

Tasty, cheap, quick, and clean, Mandoo Bar knows exactly who it is and what it does well. A neon pink "M" lights up the front window, through which passersby can glimpse a sort of grandmotherly chef folding dumplings with myriad fillings. Each wrapper color indicates what is tucked within, with green for vegetable, white for pork, and pink for seafood.

True to its name, these *mandoo* can be found on every table. Crisp fried pork *goon mandoo* are half-moon shaped and seared until brown and blistered, stuffed with minced pork seasoned with Chinese chives. Simple flavors are the hallmarks of their boiled vegetable dumplings—enticingly plump and chewy. The full kitchen also offers an array of larger dishes, like *jap chae* and *bi bim bap.*

Má Pêche

15 W. 56th St. (bet. Fifth & Sixth Aves.)

Subway: 57 St — Lunch Mon – Sat
Phone: 212-757-5878 — Dinner nightly
Web: www.momofuku.com
Prices: $$

Midtown's version of Momofuku is a soaring space furnished in sleek blonde wood and located on the lower level of the Chambers hotel. Like all siblings, this "Lucky Peach" family member strives to make its own voice heard—and it does so successfully.

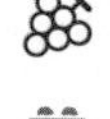

Dim sum Momofuku-style is the name of the game here, and stimulating small plates are wheeled around the canvas-wrapped expanse. The gastro chain's iconic pork buns are presented on their own cart in mini bamboo steamers. A raw bar wagon is stocked with torched sea scallop crudo dressed with yuzu and olive oil; and hot treats include succulent jerk chicken wings. Be sure to save room for dessert, as goodies from Milk Bar star and may include birthday cake truffles, or blueberry-miso soft-serve.

Marea ✿✿

Seafood XXX

D1

240 Central Park South (bet. Broadway & Seventh Ave.)

Subway: 59 St - Columbus Circle
Lunch & dinner daily

Phone: 212-582-5100

Web: www.marea-nyc.com

Prices: $$$$

There are some restaurants that have a discernible pulse that makes you immediately aware you've arrived somewhere a little special. At this elegant and refined Italian restaurant you aren't so much as welcomed in as taken in hand and enveloped in a sort of benevolent bubble of care. It's a grown up establishment with a suitably urbane clientele who all look at home in this part of town. Sit in the main dining room where all the action happens, rather than in the alcove off the bar—which is undoubtedly—Siberia.

As the name suggests, seafood and shellfish lie at the heart of the menu. And needless to say, the ingredients are not only of irreproachable quality but are also treated with respect and deftness by the kitchen, whether it's the brilliant white halibut or the salt-baked wild bass. Start with the crudo, and then head for a generous bowl of homemade pasta such as tagliolini with clams and calamari, followed by a whole fish or a classic entrée.

It's not of course compulsory to stick to fish—the lamb chops make a worthy alternative. The wine list is a deserving tome and along with the big names are some lesser known growers who merit investigation.

Masa ✿✿✿

C1 Japanese XX

10 Columbus Circle (in the Time Warner Center)

Subway: 59 St - Columbus Circle
Phone: 212-823-9807
Web: www.masanyc.com
Prices: $$$$

Lunch Tue – Fri
Dinner Mon – Sat

To taste what may be the continent's best sushi, experience the quiet, contemplative, and very exclusive ceremony of Chef Masa Takayama's omakase. Through the heavy wooden door, discover a room that is as unchanging and calming as a river stone, set amid blonde *hinoki* wood and a gargantuan forsythia tree. Yes, you'll forget it's on the fourth floor of a mall.

Attention to detail is unsurpassed; that bespoke Japanese porcelain seems designed specifically for the sweet shrimp it holds. Service displays the same smooth grace, unobtrusive yet at-the-ready with their hot towels, fingerbowls, tea, and touches of pedagogy or insight. Don't let their tendency to upsell extra courses mar your pleasure.

A seaweed salad of vinegar-seasoned jellyfish awakens the palate to the subtle progression of courses that follow. Masterful proportion and elemental balance is unparalleled in the mind-melting toro tartare with salty grains of Californian osetra caviar and toasted bread for crunch. Yet Masa truly distinguishes itself with its parade of sushi showcasing the best of Tokyo's Tsukiji market. Expect phenomenal aji mackerel with grated yuzu, traditional *unagi*, and an indelible finish of toro *temaki*.

Mercato

352 W. 39th St. (bet. Eighth & Ninth Aves.)

Subway: 42 St - Port Authority Bus Terminal — Lunch & dinner daily
Phone: 212-643-2000
Web: www.mercatonyc.com
Prices: $$

Italian hospitality with a Pugliese accent is on display at Mercato, a rustic trattoria in the western midtown hinterlands. The space is country-chic, with distressed wood tables, soft, exposed bulbs, and vintage signs. The atmosphere is inviting and the menu is inspired by the classic dishes of Puglia, the birthplace of owner Fabio Camardi.

First get a drink in your hand, then start with *fave e cicoria*, a straightforward purée of fava beans and garlicky chicory greens. A well-rounded Italian meal must have pasta, so be sure to indulge in the likes of orecchiette with broccoli rabe and garlic, enhanced with anchovies and breadcrumbs. For something deeply satisfying, try the fennel-dusted porchetta with a hearty side of potato and green cabbage mash.

Miss Korea

Korean

10 W. 32nd St. (bet. Broadway & Fifth Ave.)

Subway: 34 St - Herald Sq — Lunch & dinner daily
Phone: 212-594-4963
Web: www.misskoreabbq.com
Prices: $$

If K-Town were a music arena, Miss Korea would be the headliner. Window-lined and perched above the crowded street level with an ambience that feels equally elevated, it has a unique personality that outshines the competition. Settle into the ground floor or head up a labyrinth of stairs to enter yet another pleasant dining room filled with tropical accents, tabletop grills, and cozy dining nooks.

This lady is loved by many, so go with a group to really explore the menu and indulge in authentic *japchae* stir-fried with beef and veggies, or flaky seafood pancakes. *Dolsot bibimbap* highlights crusty rice spiced with kimchi and *gochujang*, while those pork *mandoo* are extra divine when dunked in light soy. Barbecue pork belly could be prize-winning.

The Modern ✿✿

Contemporary XXX

B4

9 W. 53rd St. (bet. Fifth & Sixth Aves.)

Subway: 5 Av - 53 St
Phone: 212-333-1220
Web: www.themodernnyc.com
Prices: **$$$$**

Lunch Mon – Fri
Dinner Mon – Sat

It goes without saying that The Modern has one of the city's most prized locations, designed to capture the iconic feel of the MoMA in which it is seamlessly housed. Art enthusiasts appreciate these modernist surrounds, which are timeless and particularly glorious. The bar-cum-lounge up front is all buzz, while the dining room's view of the lush sculpture garden lends tranquility that is conducive to intimacy and quiet conversation.

Chef Abram Bissell and team have settled in and are truly wowing these fine, globe-trotting patrons with excellent food complete with a palpably unique personality. Meanwhile, service remains well-timed and always warm. Appealing dishes showcase neat, clean flavors and may include roasted cauliflower florets composed with perfectly creamy crab butter, almond-cauliflower purée, and sweet, fleshy crabmeat. Delicate balance and top quality ingredients are at the height of an exceedingly tender lobster "marinated with truffles" and served in a luscious sauce with shaved radishes and bright herbs.

And, for dessert, rhubarb bread pudding is topped with vanilla mascarpone mousse and a scoop of Greek yogurt sorbet for a bit of flourish and a whole lot of pleasure.

Molyvos

Greek XX

A3

871 Seventh Ave. (bet. 55th & 56th Sts.)

Subway: 57 St - 7 Av — Lunch & dinner daily
Phone: 212-582-7500
Web: www.molyvos.com
Prices: $$

Enter this popular home to Greek gourmands and Carnegie Hall patrons to find a stacked display of Chef/partner Jim Botsacos' cookbook *New Greek Cuisine*—a confident yet auspicious welcome to Molyvos's laudable cooking. The upscale dining room basks in a creamy palette with touches of warm orange and black-and-white photography. The bar area is more casual, with bare tables and woven placemats

The menu boasts *mezedes* like lamb pie with *vlahotiri* cheese, and classic *piperies yemistes* that stuff roasted red peppers with a zesty mixture of rice, tomato, dill and *manouri* cheese. Strained yogurt with quince compote and toasted almonds is a sweet finish. An interesting list of Greek wines, Mediterranean beers, and ouzo is deliciously suited to the cooking.

Mozzarella & Vino

Italian XX

A4

33 W. 54th St. (bet. Fifth & Sixth Aves.)

Subway: 57 St — Lunch & dinner daily
Phone: 646-692-8849
Web: www.mozzarellaevino.com
Prices: $$

Spoiler alert: as the moniker of this midtown treasure implies, the star of the show here is *mozzarella di bufala*. Bring your appetite to the pretty, narrow space, which features whitewashed brick and taupe walls lined with mirrors and brown leather banquettes, and attempt to choose a version (there are many) of the milky cheese.

Can't decide? Our favorites saw it rolled with grilled sweet peppers hinting of anchovies and presented sliced over arugula; as well as diced and stuffed into a trio of golden-brown, crumb-coated *arancini* filled with sweet pea-studded creamy rice. A salad of avocado and shaved fennel with citrus segments and fresh mint is a refreshing starter, and the short list of entrées indulges with a hearty, oven-baked pasta of the day.

New Wonjo

Korean XX

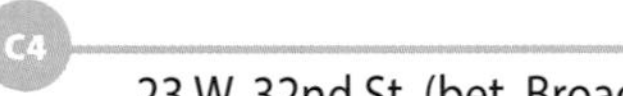

C4

23 W. 32nd St. (bet. Broadway & Fifth Ave.)

Subway: 34 St - Herald Sq — Lunch & dinner daily
Phone: 212-695-5815
Web: www.newwonjo.com
Prices: $$

Smack in the middle of Koreatown, New Wonjo offers a savory respite among the sensory overload of this jam-packed quarter. The simple, well-maintained space offers seating for small parties on the ground level, and a second floor reserved for barbecue-seeking groups to huddle around platters of marinated slices of beef brisket (*chadol baeki*) or spicy squid with pork belly (*o sam bul goki*) sizzling on table top grills.

Non-barbecue options feature tasty Korean favorites, with starters like *mandoo, japche*, and *pajun*. Sample satisfying stews like *gamba tang*—a bubbling red chili-spiked broth floating slowly simmered and very meaty pork bones with chunks of potato, cabbage, greens, and onions that is wonderfully flavorful but never incendiary.

Norma's

American XX

A3

119 W. 56th St. (bet. Sixth & Seventh Aves.)

Subway: 57 St — Lunch daily
Phone: 212-708-7460
Web: www.parkermeridien.com
Prices: $$

Serving heaping platters of breakfast well into the afternoon, Norma's may have been inspired by the humble diner but rest assured that she is no greasy spoon. Tables at this Le Parker Meridien dining room are bound to be filled with business types already dealing over the first meal of the day. Upscale touches include tables wide enough to accommodate a laptop beside your plate, a polished staff, and gratis smoothie shots.

The menu adds personality with whimsically titled dishes like "bing popping waffles" or "Normalita's huevos rancheros." The crunchy French toast's outrageously good sweetness begins with a marshmallow-y layering of crisped rice, gilded with a sprinkling of powdered sugar, ramekin of caramel sauce, and individual bottle of maple syrup.

Oceana

Seafood

120 W. 49th St. (at Sixth Ave.)

Subway: 47-50 Sts - Rockefeller Ctr — Lunch Mon – Fri
Phone: 212-759-5941 — Dinner nightly
Web: www.oceanarestaurant.com
Prices: **$$$**

A more apposite name would be hard to imagine and that's not just because this restaurant serves the bounty of the sea; it also stretches out as far as the eye can see. Get a table in the far corner and you may feel you've sailed to distant shores, while the sheer scale of the room may leave you feeling mildly Lilliputian. Come during the day and you'll witness Corporate America at lunch—and they clearly appreciate the efficiency with which it's run.

The menu offers enough choice to satisfy the most demanding of sea dogs: there are oysters and lobsters, classics and more contemporary offerings; there are dishes for two like salt-baked mackerel or paella and, for those who fancy themselves as hunter-gatherers, whole fish.

Osteria al Doge

Italian

142 W. 44th St. (bet. Broadway & Sixth Ave.)

Subway: Times Sq - 42 St — Lunch & dinner daily
Phone: 212-944-3643
Web: www.osteria-doge.com
Prices: **$$**

Theater District dining can seem uninspired next to Osteria al Doge. Here, sunny yellow walls, rustic farmhouse tables topped with fresh flowers, and a staff that's genuinely gracious even while attending to the lunchtime throngs make up a completely charming package. As if in defiance of its bustling locale, this authentic *osteria* gives much cause to sit and savor.

The menu offers a taste of Venice in a range of specialties that include risotto *nero*, pan-roasted calf's livers in an onion gravy, and grilled prawns over soft polenta with sweet paprika sauce. Daily specials are another enjoyable way to go, as in the velvet-smooth, dairy-free spinach soup buoyed by a fontina crostini; or *cavatelli* tossed with sausage, sweet peas, and creamy tomato sauce.

Osteria del Circo

Italian XX

A3

120 W. 55th St. (bet. Sixth & Seventh Aves.)

Subway: 57 St — Lunch Mon – Fri
Phone: 212-265-3636 — Dinner nightly
Web: www.circonyc.com
Prices: $$$

Step right up to this bold and buzzy midtown destination for a tasteful take on the Big Top, courtesy of the Maccioni family. The setting is a riot of theme and color: a trapeze hangs figurines above the entrance, red-and-white fabrics billow from the tent-like ceiling, harlequin-upholstered seating surrounds tables set with cobalt goblets, and animal sculptures are stationed throughout.

The crackerjack menu highlights thin-crust pizza, Tuscan fish soup (*cacciucco alla Livornese*); as well as wonderful handmade pastas like silky *tortelli* stuffed with finely chopped radicchio and taleggio, dressed with an earthy mushroom purée and salty speck. Italian-American classics like clams casino, eggplant *Parmigiana*, and chicken Marsala punctuate the lineup.

Petrossian

A3

182 W. 58th St. (at Seventh Ave.)

Subway: 57 St - 7 Av — Lunch & dinner daily
Phone: 212-245-2214
Web: www.petrossian.com
Prices: $$$

With such exemplary attributes—location, historic setting, and a refined staff—this French bastion smacks of old-world indulgence. The exterior's detailed stonework features frolicking cherubs and griffins, while a wrought-iron door guards the entrance. Inside, the dining room harkens back to the 80s with its mirrored bar and pink-and-black granite. Lalique crystal fixtures add a touch of timeless bling.

The best way to begin a meal at Petrossian is to partake in some caviar, smoked salmon, or foie gras (all available for purchase next door in the boutique). Then dive into a bowl of borscht, served with tiny meat-filled pastries, before treating your palate to seared diver sea scallops with sweet English peas, plump morels, *bottarga*, and parmesan nage.

Per Se ✿✿✿

C1

Contemporary XXXXX

10 Columbus Circle (in the Time Warner Center)

Subway: 59 St - Columbus Circle
Phone: 212-823-9335
Web: www.perseny.com
Prices: **$$$$**

Lunch Fri – Sun
Dinner nightly

There is no more dramatic departure from the soulless Time Warner Center than entering through the iconic blue doors to Per Se. An upscale sense of calm—the kind that only money can buy—instantly soaks the atmosphere. The words *posh* and *exclusive* come to mind when admiring the spacious tables, corner banquettes, and stunning views.

Chef Thomas Keller continues to raise the bar with meals that express artistry and seasonality right down to the moment. A classic since day one, the "oysters and pearls" still swim in that bath of luxurious caviar. Summery flavors reach their peak in the beautiful roulade of veal breast *en persillade*. The extraordinary vegetable tasting menu will threaten to convert the most die-hard omnivore with chestnut- and mascarpone-filled agnolotti dressed with julienned Tuscan kale and pickled Swiss chard stems. Flavors and textures may temporarily veer off into strange (and slow) territory during cheese and dessert courses. While this innovative and creative vision may delight some, it will confound others. No matter. The celebrated "coffee and doughnuts" is a grand finale.

Those without reservations can stop at the opulent Salon, where much of the menu is available à la carte.

pizzArte

Italian XX

A3

69 W. 55th St. (bet. Fifth & Sixth Aves.)

Subway: 57 St Lunch & dinner daily
Phone: 212-247-3936
Web: www.pizzarteny.com
Prices: $$

The serene, slender, bi-level dining room that is pizzaArte stands in stark contrast to the workaday bustle outside its doors. A bar and a domed wood-burning pizza oven populate the first floor, while the upstairs is filled with closely set tables and gallery-white walls displaying original art.

Expect the room to be packed with a chic, Italian-accented clientele who flock here for blissfully authentic Neapolitan-style pizzas. These are baked to perfect pliability with a bit of char, topped with impeccable ingredients like creamy *mozzarella di bufala*, broccoli rabe, and sausage. Fine cooking skills are displayed in the *paccheri al baccala*, tossing pasta tubes with cherry tomatoes, plump Sicilian capers, intense Gaeta olives, and firm fillets of cod.

Porter House

Steakhouse XXX

C1

10 Columbus Circle (in the Time Warner Center)

Subway: 59 St - Columbus Circle Lunch & dinner daily
Phone: 212-823-9500
Web: www.porterhousenewyork.com
Prices: $$$$

Michael Lomonaco's flagship steakhouse offers unparalleled views of Central Park from its Time Warner Center perch. Here, tables are well-spaced and allow for fine dining, but look for those few intimate booths located in the front bar area—they make for a great escape on busy nights.

The views certainly distinguish this handsome retreat from the pack, as do its carefully selected aged meats, quality fish, and expert sides. The kitchen puts out a tasty helping of sweet and spicy onion rings, buttermilk-battered and deep-fried in portions designed for linebackers. The beautifully marbled ribeye is aged for more than 45 days and would be delicious simply seared, though a chili rub adds an aggressive spice. Cool down with a lightly dressed purslane salad.

Print

American

653 Eleventh Ave. (at 48th St.)

Subway: 50 St (Eighth Ave.) Lunch & dinner daily
Phone: 212-757-2224
Web: www.printrestaurant.com
Prices: $$

Travel to these western hinterlands and breath a whiff of Californian sensibility. Print's home, off the lobby of the Ink48 hotel, has an easy-breezy layout that unites lounging and supping in a space that is pleasantly moody and particularly cozy.

The talented team behind this locavore kitchen takes its mission seriously: there is a full time forager on payroll, water is poured into recycled glasses, the kitchen composts, and the menu highlights the provenance of ingredients. Seasonality and simplicity are shown in creations like a wintertime salad of watercress, blood orange, Medjool dates, crushed Marcona almonds, and sherry vinaigrette.

During the summer, ride up to the 16th-floor Press lounge for drinks, small plates, and killer views.

Radiance Tea House

Asian

158 W. 55th St. (bet. Sixth & Seventh Aves.)

Subway: 57 St - 7 Av Lunch & dinner daily
Phone: 212-217-0442
Web: www.radiancetea.com
Prices: $$

Radiance Tea House is a delicious midtown curiosity. The ordinary locale obscures its presence, but one step inside reveals an unexpected world of green tea and tranquility. Walls are shelved with books about tea and wellness to peruse or purchase, as well as a selection of tea tins and ceramic ware.

Arrive during the lunchtime peak and the scent of rice wine vinegar wafts through the air from tables loaded with dumplings and dipping sauce. A vast selection of loose-leaf blends is offered to be enjoyed alongside chicken wontons with house-made chili oil, green tea soba noodles with sesame sauce, and shrimp-stuffed baby bok choy.

Tea lovers note that a traditional Chinese tea ceremony can be booked one day in advance for a minimum of two persons.

Remi

Italian XXX

A4

145 W. 53rd St. (bet. Sixth & Seventh Aves.)

Subway: 7 Av — Lunch Mon – Fri
Phone: 212-581-4242 — Dinner nightly
Web: www.remi-nyc.com
Prices: $$

This well-orchestrated production delights every sense. Designed by Adam Tihany, Remi's slim interior captivates with inlaid wood floors, a striped banquette evoking a gondolier's shirt, Venetian mural, and trio of blown glass chandeliers. A glass wall overlooks a courtyard where seating is offered in warmer weather.

The lengthy menu of Northern Italian specialties is perfectly at home, starting with *carciofi alla Veneziana*—roasted baby artichoke hearts atop a vibrant herb purée, garnished with pitted black olives, roasted garlic cloves, and pecorino. Then, move on to beautifully served *tortelli di zucca* stuffed with roasted squash and *mostarda alla Mantovana*, dressed with drizzles of browned butter, grated cheese, and fried sage.

Russian Samovar

Russian XX

C2

256 W. 52nd St. (bet. Broadway & Eighth Ave.)

Subway: 50 St (Broadway) — Lunch & dinner daily
Phone: 212-757-0168
Web: www.russiansamovar.com
Prices: $$

Which came first: the vodka or the celebs? It's hard to say when it comes to this hot spot, which caters to hockey players, Russian intelligentsia, and vodka aficionados alike. Our bets are on that beautiful vodka selection, available in all kinds of flavors, qualities, and sizes (shot, carafe, or bottle). Nestled into the bustling Theater District, Russian Samovar is both quirky and elegant—with low lighting, glass panels, and musicians tickling the piano and violin. The staff, both attentive and sweet, can walk you through delicious fare like fresh salmon-caviar blini, prepared tableside; *pelmeni*, tender veal dumplings served with sour cream and honey mustard; or milk-cured Baltic herring, paired with pickled onions, potatoes, and carrots.

Sake Bar Hagi

Japanese

152 W. 49th St., B1F (bet. Sixth & Seventh Aves.)

Subway: 50 St (Broadway) — Dinner nightly
Phone: 212-764-8549
Web: N/A
Prices: ⓈⓈ

This basement *izakaya* can be a challenge to locate—its name is slyly marked on a door that opens to a flight of stairs. Descend to find an unremarkable, brightly lit, and boisterous room tightly packed with wood furnishings and a strong Japanese following.

The space may be small but the menu is vast, so bring friends to ensure a fulfilling experience. Their spot-on small plates are designed to be washed down by beer, sake, or distinctly Japanese cocktails like cassis with oolong tea or soda, or a Calpico sour. Be sure to include wasabi-spiked *shu mai* stuffed with ground pork; or *takoyaki,* deep-fried octopus croquettes with daikon and grated ginger root. Spicy cod roe fried rice and grilled hamachi collar with a light squeeze of lemon are other standouts.

Scarlatto

C2

Italian

250 W. 47th St. (bet. Broadway & Eighth Ave.)

Subway: 50 St (Eighth Ave.) — Lunch & dinner daily
Phone: 212-730-4535
Web: www.scarlattonyc.com
Prices: $$

Dip down below street level to find a lovely exposed brick interior displaying rows of wine bottles and glass beaded wall sconces to match the sparkly tiara crowning Audrey Hepburn in a framed still from *Roman Holiday*.

The menu doesn't offer many surprises but this is cooking that—just like a little black dress—never goes out of style. Among the array, search out *polpette al pomodoro,* house-made meatballs in a tomato ragù, or bean soup with fresh pasta. Their *pollo Parmigiana* is a "red sauce" classic, made with breaded and fried chicken breast draped in a bright tomato sugo beneath a bounty of grated and caramelized parmesan, served atop a mound of al dente spaghetti.

Theater-goers take note: a prix-fixe dinner is offered throughout the evening.

The Sea Grill

Seafood

19 W. 49th St. (bet. Fifth & Sixth Aves.)

Subway: 47-50 Sts - Rockefeller Ctr
Phone: 212-332-7610
Web: www.patinagroup.com
Prices: **$$$**

Lunch Mon – Fri
Dinner Mon – Sat

This seafood-centric grill looks onto the iconic Rockefeller Center ice-skating rink and is framed by a wall of windows. Inside, find a cool aqua-accented space that inspires dressing up. Yes, tourists flock here after a spin on the ice, but it is also popular among business crowds—especially at lunch when the bar is bustling with sharp suits munching on lobster tail with a martini on the side.

The food itself is light and fresh. In-season you may find soft-shelled crab, served alongside a seaweed salad with citrus-marinated hearts of palm. The Northeast supplies many local seafood choices, such as the Block Island golden snapper *a la plancha*, with tangy cherry-tomato vinaigrette. Dependable and familiar classics like jumbo lump crab cakes are also on offer.

Snack EOS

Greek

522 Ninth Ave. (at 39th St.)

Subway: 42 St - Port Authority Bus Terminal
Phone: 646-964-4964
Web: www.snackeos.com
Prices: **$$**

Lunch & dinner daily

Found just steps away from traffic-clogged Port Authority is this boon to the dining landscape of a workaday quarter of Hell's Kitchen. Come for lunch and find corporate types enjoying a respite in the small cheerful room as they dig into cool salads and hot grilled skewers washed down with mint lemonade.

Mediterranean flavors frame the cooking here, so expect to enjoy vibrant items like *melitzanosalata* scooped up with pita chips from the meze selection—a spread of roasted eggplant seasoned with plenty of fresh garlic, red wine vinegar, diced red pepper, and chopped parsley. Delicious *kalamaki* (skewers) of chicken breast, thigh meat confit, and onions are grilled, brushed with lemon-honey vinaigrette, and set over a farro salad studded with sun-dried tomatoes.

Stella 34

Italian

151 W. 34th St. (entrance at 35th St. & Broadway)

Subway: 34 St - Herald Sq — Lunch & dinner daily
Phone: 212-967-9251
Web: www.patinagroup.com
Prices: **$$**

Windows overlook the Empire State Building at the long and light-filled Stella 34, located on the sixth floor of Macy's. The space is contemporary—with mosaic tile floors, bare tabletops, and coffee-colored banquettes—but the food is pure comfort, with three wood-burning ovens churning out Neapolitan-style pizzas.

A meal at the curvaceous bar would best begin with some *salumi* and *formaggi*, or *pappa al pomodoro* thick with bread, tomato, Tuscan kale, white beans, and Pecorino Romano. Pasta is as enticing as the crispy pizzas—*cresta di gallo* satisfies with escarole *maccheroni* (in the shape of a rooster's crest) tossed with tomatoes, red onion, chilies, *guanciale*, and pecorino. For dessert, the renowned Vivoli gelato arrives here straight from Florence.

Sushi Zen

Japanese

C3

108 W. 44th St. (bet. Broadway & Sixth Ave.)

Subway: 42 St - Bryant Pk — Lunch Mon – Fri
Phone: 212-302-0707 — Dinner Mon – Sat
Web: www.sushizen-ny.com
Prices: **$$$**

Sushi Zen's peaceful interior and intimate scale is a welcomed contrast to its high-traffic location. Tall ceilings and pale earthy hues combine for a soothing look that is accentuated by wood flooring, stone, and an artful tangle of bamboo stalks.

The counter is bright, comfortable, and puts you in view of Chef Toshio Suzuki in action. Lunchtime brings crowds who come for the excellent value set sushi menu. A salad with ginger-based dressing and delicately crisp tempura of shrimp, seasonal vegetables, and yuba precede excellent quality Edomae-sushi, featuring rice seasoned with the chef's own vinegar. Bite-sized pieces can include translucent fluke spiked with wasabi; Spanish mackerel sprinkled with grated ginger and chopped green onion; or warm *unagi*.

Szechuan Gourmet

Chinese

21 W. 39th St. (bet. Fifth & Sixth Aves.)

Subway: 42 St - Bryant Pk
Phone: 212-921-0233
Web: N/A
Prices: **$$**

Lunch Mon – Fri
Dinner nightly

Come lunchtime, midtown office workers with a jones for the tingly heat of Sichuan peppercorns or the burn of bright red chili oil know exactly where to go. A queue for tables is nearly obligatory, but the pace settles down in the evening and on weekends. Inside, red lanterns and pink linens accent the bustling room and servers attend to tables where specialties are piled high.

Though the menu is vast, you can't go wrong by tearing into the best scallion pancakes in town; or cool, hand-shredded chicken draped in a creamy sesame paste and chili oil. Smoked tofu shreds tossed with Asian celery and toasted sesame oil; or wok-tossed jumbo prawns with a crispy shell of peppercorns and spiced salt are the reason for those long lines.

Taboon

Middle Eastern 

773 Tenth Ave. (at 52nd St.)

Subway: 50 St (Eighth Ave.)
Phone: 212-713-0271
Web: www.taboononline.com
Prices: **$$**

Lunch Sun
Dinner nightly

Taboon's namesake brick-walled, wood-fired oven is burning a bit brighter these days since Chef Efi Nahon has returned to Hell's Kitchen's finest Middle Eastern dining room. That oven not only provides a heartwarming welcome and sets the whitewashed interior aglow, but it is also responsible for baking the incredible plank of bread that is alone worth a trip here.

Bring friends because this midtown marvel's recently revised menu is best enjoyed by grazing the list of zesty meze like house-made scallop and crab sausage *shakshooka* with poached quail egg, or wild mushroom bread pudding with creamy talleggio and romesco. Vegetables aren't spared the flames, as in a luscious and healthy pile of roasted broccolini splashed with orange oil.

Tang Pavilion

Chinese 

65 W. 55th St. (bet. Fifth & Sixth Aves.)

Subway: 57 St — Lunch & dinner daily
Phone: 212-956-6888
Web: www.tangpavilionchinese.com
Prices: $$

This longstanding, elegant Chinese favorite is a delightful contrast to its brassy midtown location. Set foot inside the hushed dining room featuring pale peach walls dressed with black lacquer trim. Jacketed servers dote on a dressy crowd savoring Shanghainese specialties.

The kitchen offers countless delectable house delicacies emphasizing the regional focus. Honey ham Shanghai-style is a sweet and salty treat dressed with dates and lotus seeds. The "eight jewels with hot paste" is a mouthwateringly spiced stir-fry of mushrooms, bamboo shoots, wheat gluten, scallops, chicken, and shrimp. Green beans with tofu sheets is a gorgeously simple combo of soybeans and paper-thin ribbons of bean curd skin judiciously bathed in a light, broth-based sauce.

Tavola

488 Ninth Ave. (bet. 37th & 38th Sts.)

Subway: 42 St - Port Authority Bus Terminal — Lunch & dinner daily
Phone: 212-273-1181
Web: www.tavolahellskitchen.com
Prices: $$

This Hell's Kitchen pizzeria is housed in the former Manganaro's Grosseria Italiano, a family-run emporium dating back to 1893. Bright and clean but boasting the patina of its long existence, the dining room now greets guests with a wall of Italian products and a sky-lit double pizza oven.

The wood-burning dome crafted of volcanic clay from Mt. Vesuvius produces an array of blistered, chewy, quality-topped pies such as the *Baresa*, bearing sweet fennel sausage, broccoli rabe, and roasted breadcrumbs. Grilled local calamari with lemon-caper *salmoriglio* can be found among the starters. The pastas are also an excellent choice, especially *lasagna della casa*, stacking fresh sheets with bright and saucy veal ragù, ricotta, and *mozzarella di bufala*.

Toloache

Mexican XX

251 W. 50th St. (bet. Broadway & Eighth Ave.)

Subway: 50 St (Broadway) Lunch & dinner daily
Phone: 212-581-1818
Web: www.toloachenyc.com
Prices: **$$**

This first location of midtown's Mexican hot spot (with outposts in SoHo and the Upper East Side) remains immensely popular for ample reason. An extensive selection of tequilas flow freely from the spirited bar, chunky guacamole is endlessly mashed from mounds of ripe avocados, and *antojitos* emerge from the brick oven in this two-story dining room decked with Talavera tiles, wood-beam ceilings, and stunning copper lanterns.

Toloache puts a contemporary spin on each of its zesty dishes. Tacos begin with tender, excellent masa tortillas amply stuffed with beer-braised beef brisket (*suadero*), tomatillo salsa, and horseradish *crema*. The signature *camarones* Toloache showcase a handful of large, fresh shrimp draped with a vibrant dried *cascabel* salsa.

21 Club

American XX

21 W. 52nd St. (bet. Fifth & Sixth Aves.)

Subway: 5 Av - 53 St Lunch & dinner Mon – Sat
Phone: 212-582-7200
Web: www.21club.com
Prices: **$$$**

Fabled 21 Club has been in business for over 85 years, but there's nothing slowing it down. Opened originally as a speakeasy, this New York institution has wined and dined everyone from movie stars and moguls to moneyed city folk. From its lantern-holding jockeys and townhouse exterior, to the leather- and wood-paneled dining room that feels like a step back in time, this is a classic through and through.

The menu is a perfect accompaniment to the setting with choices like seared foie gras tinged with mango chutney and spread atop toasted brioche; or a splendid and classic rendition of steak tartare paired with a green salad. Upstairs and in the back, the feel is formal—so for a casual bite with prettier prices, head off the main entrance to Bar 21.

Tori Shin ✿

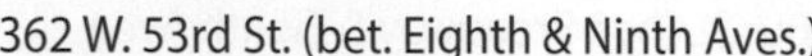

C1 Japanese XX

362 W. 53rd St. (bet. Eighth & Ninth Aves.)

Subway: 50 St (Eighth Ave.) Dinner nightly
Phone: 212-757-0108
Web: www.torishinny.com
Prices: **$$$**

When the city's best *yakitori* decided to up and relocate, its Upper East Side neighborhood suffered a crushing culinary loss—one that would soon become midtown's gain. And after a long construction, Tori Shin is finally welcoming both fresh and familiar faces to its brand-new Hell's Kitchen home.

A small bar pouring sake, shochu, and Japanese whiskey welcomes patrons into a multi-level dining room where table seating is now offered in abundance—including a clutch of options in a mezzanine room with gorgeous gold leaf walls. Boasting 500-year old hinoki and a serene palette of sand and stone, this is an upscale, sophisticated spin on the original location.

What hasn't changed, however, is the quality of the organically raised chicken parts and the expert skill in which they are sizzled over the *binchotan*-fired grill. Skewers of crisped wing, seared heart, and creamy liver need nothing more than a few grains of salt to express true flavor. Ordering à la carte is a fun way to explore the menu, which offers grilled vegetables and items like chicken *cha-shu* in addition to omakase—a succulent onslaught of *kara-age*, chicken and duck *tsukune*, blistered shisito peppers, and *soboro don*.

Utsav

Indian XX

C2

1185 Sixth Ave. (entrance on 46th St.)

Subway: 47-50 Sts - Rockefeller Ctr
Lunch & dinner daily
Phone: 212-575-2525
Web: www.utsavny.com
Prices: $$

Meaning "festival" in Sanskrit, Utsav is an upscale hideaway perched on a suspended corridor between two office buildings. The ground floor features a bar and small plaza with outdoor seating, while the upstairs dining room is swathed in gold fabric and spacious with floor-to-ceiling windows. Orchid-topped tables look even prettier once the food arrives.

The wallet-friendly and over-flowing lunch buffet brings office workers in by droves, while the early evening prix-fixe is popular with the pre-theater crowd. Delights include tandoori chicken *kali mirch* liberally seasoned with crushed black pepper, as well as Hyderabadi shrimp curry with a bright red tamarind and chili sauce so tasty it begs to be sopped up by hot wedges of *aloo paratha*.

Yakitori Totto

Japanese X

C1

251 W. 55th St. (bet. Broadway & Eighth Ave.)

Subway: 57 St - 7 Av
Lunch Mon – Fri
Dinner nightly
Phone: 212-245-4555
Web: www.tottonyc.com
Prices: $$

To say that this *yakitori-ya* nails authenticity is an epic understatement. Its discreet signage and second floor location feels more Tokyo than Manhattan, J-pop dominates the playlist, and the crowd is a reassuring mix of Japanese-speakers and in-the-know foodies.

Best of all is the aroma of sizzling skewers that are deftly prepared over a charcoal fire. It's all about grilled meats here, like *buta karashi*—pork loin with sweet onion and spicy mustard—but that doesn't mean you should skip *yakumi zaru* tofu, soft cubes dressed with slivered green onion, bonito flakes, ginger, and *ume* salt. At lunch, go for *yakitori don* with skewers of chicken breast and green onion (*negima*) over rice, paired with pickled cucumbers and licked by a sweet *yakitori* sauce.

SoHo & Nolita

SoHo (or the area South of Houston) and Nolita (North of Little Italy) prove not only that New York City has a penchant for prime shopping and divine dining, but that the downtown scene lives on now more than ever.

SHOPPING CENTRAL

Halfway through the 20th century, SoHo's cast iron structures gave way to grand hotels, large theaters, and commercial establishments. Thanks to this large-scale development, housing costs

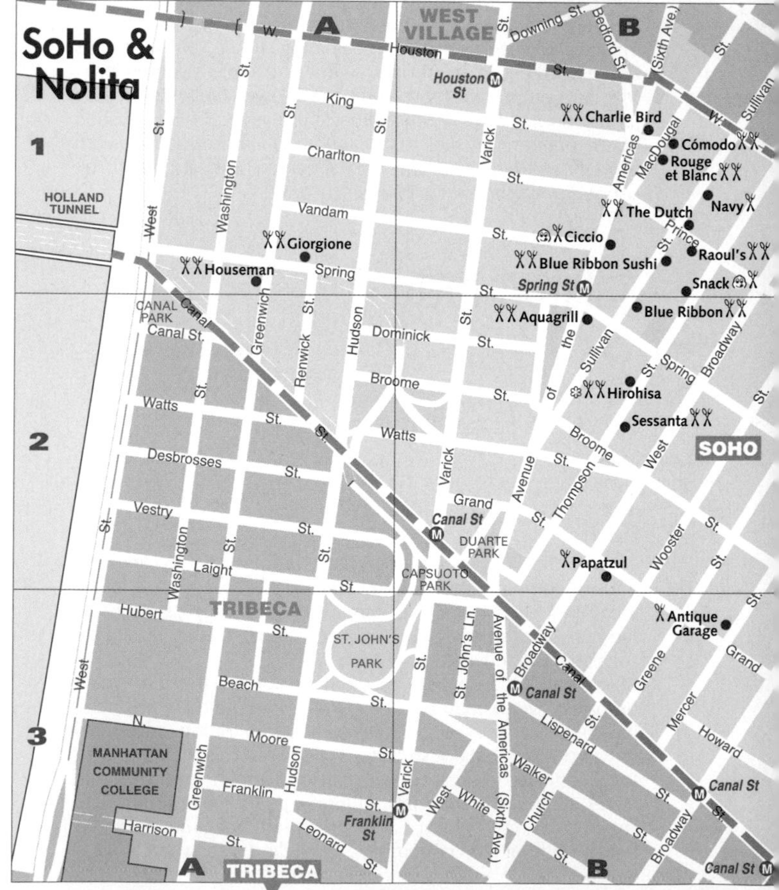

soared and artists absconded to adjoining Chelsea. And yet, these streets south of Houston remain true to their promise of sun-drenched restaurants and sleek cafés filled with wine-sipping sophisticates, supermodels, and scores of tourists. Locals fortunate enough to live in SoHo's pricey condos, know to stock up on cheese and meats from **Despaña Tapas Café**—they may even prepare a traditional tortilla Española or octopus platter for you with advance notice. Follow this with a fantastic selection of sips at **Despaña Vinos y Mas**, the wine boutique next door. Scatttered with fancy boutiques, these residents are here to stay. Entertaining guests for dinner is bound to be a breeze after a visit to **Pino's Prime Meat Market** complete with quality options. The butchers here know the drill and are happy to engage rookies as they break down some of the best game in town. On the flip side,

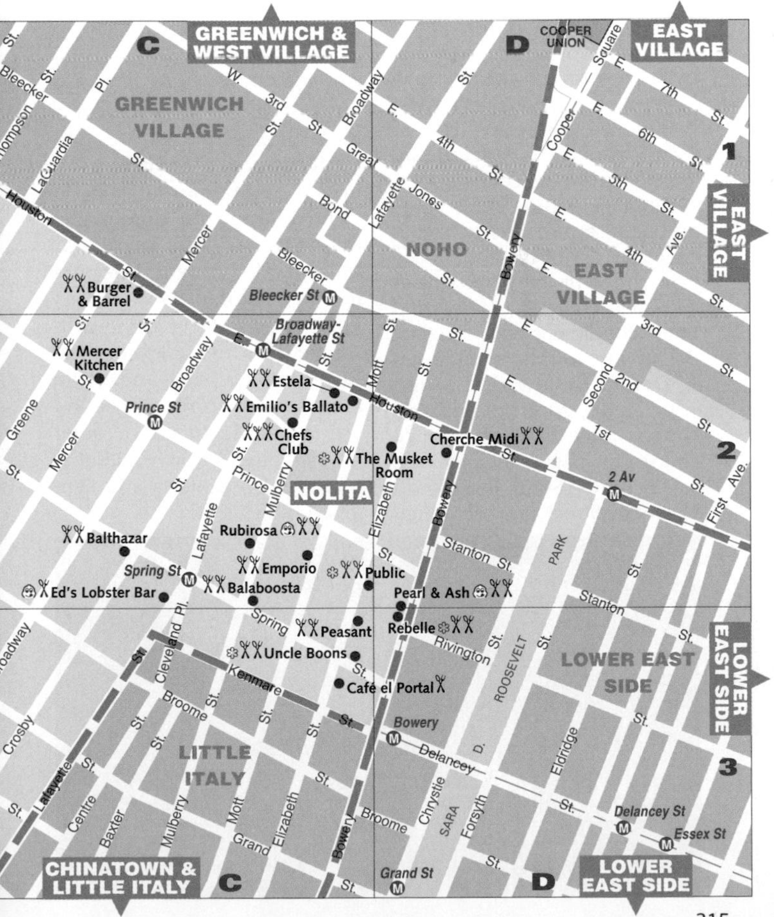

vegetarians take great pride in **The Butcher's Daughter**, a meat-free emporium with the sole purpose of treating, cutting, and carving regionally sourced and sustainable produce.

If yearning for Italian specialties, sample the brick oven-baked prosciutto rolls at old-time treasure, **Parisi Bakery**; or, the signature square pizza along with Sicilian arancini at **Prince St. Pizza**. Sugar junkies find their fix at **Vosges Haut Chocolat**, where sweets reach new heights of innovation. Try "The Goose's Golden Eggs" featuring real bacon caramel in half-shelled chocolate eggs for a truly exquisite and decadent experience, before heading over to **MarieBelle**, another renowned cocoa queen, combining exotic ingredients and precise methods to create precious "chocolate jewels." For the Big Apple's most cherished cheeses, coffees, and other condiments, the original Broadway location of **Dean & Deluca** is always packed with locals, food lovers, and hungry office workers. And of course, for bagels in their best form, **Black Seed Bagels** on Elizabeth Street is a perpetual dream. Others may wait till the clock strikes happy hour, before sampling the sips at **Astor Wines & Spirits**, whose selection displays amazing variety and is every barkeep's creed. Weekly tastings and wine-related events here are exemplary and focused on unique varietals, so book ahead. Packed with some of the finest Chilean wines, **Puro Wines** is another precious gem, while **City Winery** over on Hudson Square (equipped with grapes, barrels, storage, and expertise) is a legit place for oenophiles to make their own private-label wine. If sweet is your favorite way to seal a meal, then follow your nose to **Little Cupcake Bakeshop** on Prince or **Maman** (a café on Center Street) for comforting French baked goodies. Meanwhile, home shoppers frequent **Global Table** for its international accessories with simple lines and vivid finishes. Avoid hunger pangs inevitable after a shopping spree by visiting **Smile to Go**, a quiet spot set blocks from Canal that serves big breakfasts and light lunch bites.

NIGHTS OUT IN NOLITA

Nolita may have been an integral part of Little Italy back in the day, but today it is its own, distinctive district and explodes with swanky boutiques, sleek restaurants, and hip bars. Located farther east than tourist-heavy SoHo, this neighborhood is also home to slightly cooler (read cosmopolitan) groups. Not unlike its name, Nolita's eclectic residents shun the typical nine-to-five drill and reject SoHo's scene-y hangouts in favor of more intimate spots that invariably begin with the word "café." At the top of this list is **Café Habana**, offering that ubiquitous diner vibe and four square meals a day—breakfasts may include sunny-side-up eggs topped with *salsa verde* and *salsa ranchera*. Amazing Mexico City-style corn on the cob is also available for takeout next door at **Café Habana To Go**; while **Cafe Gitane** is an exquisite hipster hangout, well-tread at all times for wonderful French-Moroccan food served with stellar cocktails. The ethos in Nolita is simple yet resolute—to do a single thing very well. This may have been inspired by **Lombardi's** on Spring Street, which claims to be America's very first pizzeria (founded in 1905). The fact that they still serve these coal oven-fired delicacies by the pie (not the slice) clearly hasn't been bad for business, and lines continue to snake out the door if not the block. Hopping cuisines from Italy to Israel, **Hoomoos Asli** draws a trail of twenty- and thirty-somethings for fluffy pitas packed with crispy falafel and outstanding hummus. The décor and service may be rudimentary at best, but serious effort goes into the food as well as that refreshing side of tart lemonade.

Top off this plethora of eats at the aromatic and ever so alluring **Dominique Ansel Bakery**. Formerly an executive pastry chef at Daniel, the chef here is now fulfilling his own dessert dreams with a spectrum of specialty cakes, tarts, cookies, and pastries. For a taste of dessert bliss, follow instructions and eat the made-to-order "Magic Soufflé" piping hot. Desserts are best matched with coffee, perhaps at **La Colombe**—a Philadelphia-based roaster located nearby on Lafayette. If date-night duos aren't closing the deal over one of their exquisite and eco-friendly blends, then find them sweetening things up at **Papabubble**, a stylish spot showcasing candies created with eye-popping design and detail. Flaunting equal parts creative and classic flair, **Rice to Riches** brings comfort food to this edgy nook in bowls of creamy rice pudding. The fact that these are appended with

quirky names like "Sex Drugs and Rocky Road" or "Fluent in French Toast" only adds to this sugar den's supreme appeal. For more of this rich and creamy goodness, **A.B. Biagi** brings the craft of traditional Italian gelato-making infused with a taste of Brazil to the core of Nolita. Their wide range of light yet very luscious gelatos and sorbets highlights exotic flavors including passion fruit as well as goat cheese with orange peel and anise. Cheesecake addicts take note that **Eileen's Special Cheesecake** bears the moniker "special" for good reason. Embellished with fruit toppings and fun flavors like amaretto or coconut custard, Eileen's divine creations continue to control the downtown scene, chasing those Junior's fans back to Brooklyn.

One of the greater challenges this neighborhood poses is the decision of where to end the day or night. However, savvy locals know that tucked into these vibrant streets are scores of snug bars, each with its own sleek city feel. Originally a speakeasy during the Prohibition era, today **Fanelli Café** is one of the city's oldest establishments offering an array of Italian-inspired eats at all times of day. Date-night duos can never forget about **Pravda**, a pretty lounge which presents a tantalizing array of vodkas, while **Sweet & Vicious** pours concoctions that have been said to leave you starry-eyed. And between these countless dinners and drinks, Nolita also caters to New York City's culinary elite by virtue of its numerous wholesale kitchen supply stores, all settled and thriving along the Bowery.

Antique Garage

Turkish

B3

41 Mercer St. (bet. Broome & Grand Sts.)

Subway: Canal St (Broadway) Lunch & dinner daily
Phone: 212-219-1019
Web: www.antiquegaragesoho.com
Prices: $$

Bohemian-chic Antique Garage makes for a perfectly discreet rendezvous. Complete with high ceilings and the beat-up bones of a former garage, this sultry spot combines vintage furniture, pendant-like chandeliers, and mirrors galore to create the quintessentially cool hangout. Insanely talented jazz musicians jam in the corner, while gin martinis and Turkish white wines flow as freely as the conversation.

Ottoman cuisine rules here with well-made, welcoming, and wonderful bites—after hitting SoHo's boutiques and galleries, those bowls of spicy olives are the ideal snack for sharing. For heartier fare, try a grilled *halloumi* salad tossed with briny artichoke hearts, or smoky lamb shish kabobs, traditional in presentation and deeply satisfying in flavor.

Aquagrill

Seafood

B2

210 Spring St. (at Sixth Ave.)

Subway: Spring St (Sixth Ave.) Lunch & dinner daily
Phone: 212-274-0505
Web: www.aquagrill.com
Prices: $$

New York is no stranger to oysters but Aquagrill is an institution that puts the other shuckers to shame. A destination for all-things seafood since the 1990s, the menu features as many as 27 types of oysters each day, with patrons holing up at the bar to ingest dozens upon dozens of these bivalves with pitch-perfect wines to match.

As always, the kitchen serves a fine lineup of heartier fish dishes including the downright sensual wild *toro* tartare with shiitakes, peppercress, and truffle-soy sauce. Pan-seared red snapper over crispy jasmine rice cakes and sautéed vegetables in ginger-peanut sauce is a show of well-balanced textures and bracing flavors; but a handmade chocolate sampler remains the true starlet, with each morsel as decadent as the next.

Balaboosta

C2 Mediterranean XX

214 Mulberry St. (bet. Prince & Spring Sts.)

Subway: Spring St (Lafayette St.) Lunch Tue – Sun
Phone: 212-966-7366 Dinner nightly
Web: www.balaboostanyc.com
Prices: $$

It's hard to walk by and avoid falling in love with this thoroughly charming Mediterranean favorite and its keen (if wandering) eye on Sephardic cuisine.

A small bar serves cocktails and organic wines while the dining room is full of bare tables, exposed brick walls, and shelves lined with bottles and books. Like the main arena, this kitchen bears a bright, friendly vibe. Here, smoke and fire take center stage in the shrimp cazuela, a tagine of plump shrimp, chickpeas, preserved lemons, and fiery jalapeño. Tender striped bass with crispy skin is a thoroughly comforting dish, served on a bed of sautéed mushrooms with buttery spinach and chewy black gnocchi, drizzled with crab bisque. Linger over *kanafeh,* syrup-soaked shredded filo dough stuffed with cheese.

Balthazar

C2 French XX

80 Spring St. (bet. Broadway & Crosby St.)

Subway: Spring St (Lafayette St.) Lunch & dinner daily
Phone: 212-965-1414
Web: www.balthazarny.com
Prices: $$$

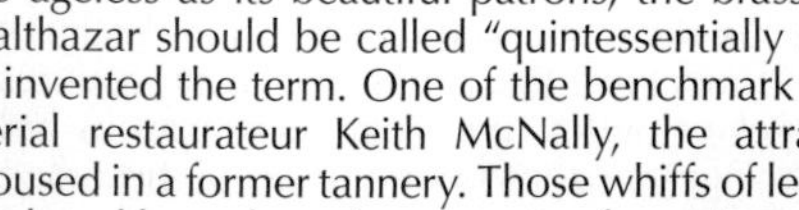

As ageless as its beautiful patrons, the brassy and mirrored Balthazar should be called "quintessentially SoHo" because it invented the term. One of the benchmark brasseries from serial restaurateur Keith McNally, the attractive space is housed in a former tannery. Those whiffs of leather have been replaced by red awnings, scents of pastries, and an excellent oyster-filled raw bar completing its Parisian transformation.

It seems as though every other table is topped with their bestselling steak frites—hardly a value but expertly prepared and served with a heaping side of fries. On the delicate side, sautéed skate is served with sweet raisins and tart capers; while silky beef tartare with shallots, herbs, and Worcestershire spreads just like butta.

Blue Ribbon

Contemporary XX

B2

97 Sullivan St. (bet. Prince & Spring Sts.)

Subway: Spring St (Sixth Ave.) Dinner nightly
Phone: 212-274-0404
Web: www.blueribbonrestaurants.com
Prices: $$$

Blue Ribbon stays open until the wee hours, serving somewhat simple but particularly memorable food to SoHo's stylish set. Moreover, this unaffectedly warm and *very* classic bistro boasts zero pretense and deserves all praise that comes its way. Its décor may have stayed the same through the years—think timeless—but those bar seats remain a hot ticket.

This "chef's canteen" as it is typically hailed is well-tread for masterpieces like fresh shucked oysters; smoked trout salad tossed with sour cream and zippy horseradish; or matzo ball soup—enjoyable, aromatic, and full of root vegetables. Fried chicken with mashed potatoes takes home the gold medal for comfort classics, while banana-walnut bread pudding with caramel sauce is the very essence of decadence.

Blue Ribbon Sushi

Japanese XX

B1

119 Sullivan St. (bet. Prince & Spring Sts.)

Subway: Spring St (Sixth Ave.) Lunch & dinner daily
Phone: 212-343-0404
Web: www.blueribbonrestaurants.com
Prices: $$$

Set just below street level and down the block from its eldest sibling, Blue Ribbon Sushi is an inviting spot to watch the masters at work. A sushi bar dominates the space, with colorful sake bottles and premium spirits on display. The low, wood-covered ceilings and polished tables provide an intimate setting, while the counter is a prime perch for a solo diner.

The staff may point to Americanized options, but it's best to trust the expert chefs and go with an omakase. The menu divides itself into *Taiheiyo* ("Pacific") offerings, like the *kohada* spotted sardine, or a sweet and briny giant clam; and *Taiseiyo* ("Atlantic"), perhaps featuring fluke fin or a spicy lobster knuckle. Maki tempts with the *karai kaibashire*, with spicy minced scallop and smelt roe.

Burger & Barrel

Gastropub

25 W. Houston St. (at Greene St.)

Subway: Broadway - Lafayette St — Lunch & dinner daily
Phone: 212-334-7320
Web: www.burgerandbarrel.com
Prices: $$

Comfort food becomes downright elegant at this urbane gastropub, where clubby leather booths, louvered blinds, and requisite chalked-up blackboards stay on the approachable side of chic. When the long bar and closely set tables are at capacity, conversations bouncing off the wood-paneled walls can reach a dull roar. Still, the atmosphere remains relaxed.
The modern pub menu covers all the bases with panache. The griddled Bash burger, slathered with house-made caramelized onion and bacon jam crowned with two crisp onion rings, is a memorable affair. Lighter dishes like a traditional panzanella with chewy-crusty bread cubes and translucent cucumber slices; or chilled sweet-and-tart corn soup with chunks of peekytoe crab are just as satisfying.

Café el Portal

Mexican

174 Elizabeth St. (bet. Kenmare & Spring Sts.)

Subway: Spring St (Lafayette St.) — Lunch & dinner Mon – Sat
Phone: 212-226-4642
Web: www.cafeelportal.com
Prices:

In an area paved by PR campaigns and flashy restaurants, one authentic Mexican spot trudges on, in a pocket-sized room decked out with the bright colors of a hacienda. While some may view it as kitschy (it's hardly a hipster hangout), foodies gather here for the unique cooking churned out of this genuine kitchen.
The fundamentals that distinguish authentic tacos from the Tex-Mex version are more than adequately covered in the *carnitas taco*. Tortillas, properly warmed on the comal, encase tender pulled pork and jalapeño and are topped with a complex, spicy salsa with just a pinch of cilantro—as fresh as any native could hope to taste. Foodies are equally thankful for the *flor de calabaza* quesadilla drizzled with avocado purée and filled with zucchini.

Charlie Bird

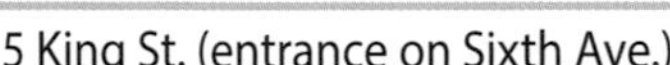

B1 — Italian XX

5 King St. (entrance on Sixth Ave.)

Subway: Houston St — Lunch & dinner daily
Phone: 212-235-7133
Web: www.charliebirdnyc.com
Prices: $$$

Of all the cool out-of-the-way restaurants that dot this stretch of SoHo, perhaps none are hipper than little Charlie Bird. You'll be greeted by a blast of music the second you hit the door, where a long bar leads to a cozy, brick-lined dining space with leather seats.

From there, things just take off: along with the clever, urbane menu, an upbeat service staff, and thoughtful wine list brimming with sweet Puglian reds and organic Catalonians, the kitchen delights long before Chef/co-owner Ryan Hardy's renowned pastas hit your plate. Think tender rigatoni with fennel-roasted suckling pig; or perfectly al dente *spaghetti alla carbonara* piled into a heavenly ball and topped with buttery spring onions, smoked bacon, and a bright yellow duck egg.

Chefs Club

C2 — Contemporary XXX

275 Mulberry St. (bet. Houston & Jersey Sts.)

Subway: Broadway - Lafayette St — Lunch Sun
Phone: 212-941-1100 — Dinner nightly
Web: www.chefsclub.com
Prices: $$$$

Like a never-ending All-Star game featuring the country's best dishes, the innovative concept behind Chefs Club (by Food & Wine) is a rotating lineup of the magazine's "Best New Chefs" honorees over the years. If that weren't exciting enough, the space itself is visually stunning, featuring a state-of-the-art open kitchen with a striking blue-tile backdrop; a sensational modern bar; and lots of loud music to set the mood.

Dinner might include a cool, creamy spring pea soup dotted with pickled pearl onions and fresh herbs; or expertly smoked and seared Hudson Valley foie gras paired with sunchoke purée, apple chips, and buttermilk-thyme jam. Squab *à la plancha* is then glazed with sage-honey and served over grilled confit leeks with a giblet ragout.

Cherche Midi

French XX

D2

282 Bowery (at Houston St.)

Subway: 2 Av Lunch & dinner daily
Phone: 212-226-3055
Web: www.cherchemidiny.com
Prices: **$$$**

Restaurateur Keith McNally went back to his bistro roots with Cherche Midi, his restaurant on a bustling SoHo epicenter of sorts. Romantic, French, and timeless, this inviting space is filled with spectacular flower arrangements, burgundy leather booths, antique mirrors, and a semi-round bar with wood stools.

A *pot de fromage* sets the tone for the meal. This luscious parmesan custard, served with toast points slathered in anchovy butter, is simple, satisfying with just the right amount of richness. At lunch, a steak sandwich with aged Gruyère and bacon marmalade on a Balthazar-baked brioche bun is a hit. At dinner, opt for elevated classics like the bone-in skate wing meunière with onion-fennel soubise. Don't forget some pencil-thin pommes frites on the side.

Ciccio 

Italian 

B1

190 Sixth Ave. (bet. Prince & Vandam Sts.)

Subway: Spring St (Sixth Ave.) Lunch & dinner daily
Phone: 646-476-9498
Web: www.ciccionyc.com
Prices: **$$**

Chef/owner Giacomo Romano defines this brilliant little restaurant as an *alimentaria*—a place where patrons can find ever-changing temptations day or night. This may mean hearty *ribollita* for lunch or satisfying pasta for dinner. The sunny space is a former antique store that fashions a raw look through whitewashed brick walls and blonde wood tables.

Simple, unpretentious food is the signature here, in dishes like *insalata di carota*, mixing sweet roasted carrots, peppery arugula, and pumpkin seeds—grab wedges of bread to soak up its citrusy vinaigrette. Fresh pasta is a must, especially the *strisce alla Chiantigiana* tossed with a reduction of wine, *guanciale*, and red onions. End with a perfect espresso or rich and oozing molten chocolate cake.

Cómodo

Latin American

58 MacDougal St. (at King St.)

Subway: Houston St — Lunch Sat – Sun
Phone: 646-370-4477 — Dinner nightly
Web: www.comodonyc.com
Prices: $$

This charming, candlelit restaurant flaunts a Latin tilt while maintaining its very American, homey feel. Away from artsy SoHo this quiet slice of the neighborhood draws locals looking for an unfussy meal with bright flavors. The small space has exposed brick, two long communal tables, a semi-open kitchen, and carefully chosen music.

Detail sets Cómodo apart, beginning with a thick, deep evergreen cilantro soup poured tableside, over a mound of fresh crab, smoky roasted poblano peppers, and tart goat cheese. The interesting and very approachable dishes go on to include lamb sliders on *pão de queijo* (Brazilian bread made with cheese and cassava) finished with a pop of chipotle cream. Coffee-rubbed slow-roasted pork shoulder shouldn't be missed.

The Dutch

American

131 Sullivan St. (at Prince St.)

Subway: Spring St (Lafayette St.) — Lunch & dinner daily
Phone: 212-677-6200
Web: www.thedutchnyc.com
Prices: $$$

Buzzy and beloved since day one, Chef Andrew Carmellini's The Dutch has quickly become a major hit and SoHo institution. Its primo corner windows open onto the sidewalk, tempting guests inside with a stocked oyster bar, cozy banquettes, and a sharply dressed service staff.

The menu is just as seductive as the space, familiar but with fresh updates. Highlights include a roundabout take on the plump fried oyster po' boy, made here with mustard-pickled okra remoulade. Tasty pastas refresh the menu consistently; you might find black *rigatini* tossed with tender squid and spicy pork sausage, finished with fiery breadcrumbs. Desserts are divine, with fresh pies made daily, such as salted lime pie with passion fruit, *nata de coco*, and coconut sorbet.

Ed's Lobster Bar

Seafood

222 Lafayette St. (bet. Kenmare & Spring Sts.)

Subway: Spring St (Lafayette St.) Lunch & dinner daily
Phone: 212-343-3236
Web: www.lobsterbarnyc.com
Prices: $$

Thanks to Ed's, there's no need to leave the city for an outstanding lobster roll. This seafood-driven favorite is a pitch-perfect encapsulation of the Northeast coast with a lively New York vibe. Inside the white-brick room, the long, gleaming marble bar is definitely the place to sit.

With a mean Bloody Mary, pristine raw bar, and freshly caught daily chalkboard specials, Ed's has amassed a loyal following; aim for off-peak times to avoid the wait.

Shareable appetizers of sweet and briny Ipswich clams are lightly fried for amazing salty-crisp contrast. Pewter caldrons of linguini bathed in olive oil with lemony-garlicky clams and toasted breadcrumbs are terrific. And that signature mayo- and butter-rich lobster roll is worth every calorie.

Emilio's Ballato

Italian

55 E. Houston St. (bet. Mott & Mulberry Sts.)

Subway: Broadway - Lafayette St Lunch & dinner daily
Phone: 212-274-8881
Web: N/A
Prices: $$

This unassuming Houston St. standard is an unsung hero, even if many walk past Emilio's gold- and red-etched window and write it off as some run-of-the-mill red sauce joint. Step inside the narrow, weathered space, where owner Emilio Vitolo offers each guest a personal welcome and a genuine Italian-American experience.

The menu is filled with pasta classics like Roman *cacio e pepe*, tossed with sharp pecorino cheese and freshly ground black pepper. Signature specialties include *pollo Emilio*, a delicately breaded chicken cutlet draped in lemon-caper sauce; and plump clams *oreganata* speckled with garlicky breadcrumbs. Crisp cannoli shells filled with vanilla- and cinnamon-tinged ricotta cream rival any other version found from Palermo to Siracusa.

Emporio

231 Mott St. (bet. Prince & Spring Sts.)

Subway: Spring St (Lafayette St.) Lunch & dinner daily
Phone: 212-966-1234
Web: www.emporiony.com
Prices: $$

Everything at Emporio has been strategically placed, from canned tomatoes by the open kitchen to the pressed-tin ceiling and reclaimed wood accents. It's this Italian-inspired café's attention to detail that has made it a local mainstay, filled with gorgeous crowds and friendly servers. Here, everyone shares conversation over sips set to go with complimentary spreads or "aperitivo" like crispy pancetta with rosemary.

Although the space is small, flavors are huge, and the same attention that went into décor goes into the food—from grass-feed beef to excellent handmade *orecchiette* with cauliflower and shrimp. For a real treat, try a Nutella calzone—its wonderfully thin dough oozing with hazelnut-chocolate and topped with fresh cream and hazelnut crumbs.

Estela

Contemporary 

47 E. Houston St. (at Mulberry St.)

Subway: Broadway - Lafayette St Lunch Sat – Sun
Phone: 212-219-7693 Dinner nightly
Web: www.estelanyc.com
Prices: $$$

Despite the fact that it's hidden in plain sight, this *muy* cozy charmer manages to attract a crowd of VIP's (ahem, President Obama). The narrow dining room is loud and cramped, boasting a kitchen that has both its eye on simplicity and an applause-worthy knack for elegant offerings.

To that end, Estela's irreverent chef turns out focused, decidedly creative, and (very) small plates. Grilled bread laden with mussels and a tangy aïoli turns into a dazzling bite when paired with pickled carrots, just as beef tartare tossed in chili oil is smartly teamed with sunchoke crisps for sweet and savory hints. And while your greeting upon entry may be less than agreeable, a quivering, bee pollen-crowned panna cotta makes for an utterly perfect goodbye.

Giorgione

Italian XX

307 Spring St. (bet. Greenwich & Hudson Sts.)

Subway: Spring St (Sixth Ave.) Lunch Mon – Fri
Phone: 212-352-2269 Dinner nightly
Web: www.giorgionenyc.com
Prices: $$

In far west SoHo, beyond Chanel and Balenciaga, find this long-time resident cherished for its quiet location where Spring Street locals enjoy a slower pace—much like Italy itself. Founded by Dean & Deluca's Giorgio Deluca, the stylish and distinctly Italian L-shaped room focuses on straightforward pizza, outstanding pastas, and serious desserts.

You can't go wrong with the handful of pastas on the menu, such as the lovingly crafted pouches of spinach and ricotta ravioli in a light tomato sauce. Delicately grilled lamb chops with *peperonata* and rosemary-roasted new potatoes are simple yet beguiling. Try one (or two) noteworthy desserts, including the flaky *crostata* filled with rich chocolate ganache and bright green *pistacchio di Bronte*.

Houseman

American XX

508 Greenwich St. (bet. Canal & Spring Sts.)

Subway: Spring St (Sixth Ave.) Dinner nightly
Phone: 212-641-0654
Web: www.housemanrestaurant.com
Prices: $$

Just around the corner form the legendary Ear Bar, you'll find this amazing new offering courtesy of Chef/owner Ned Baldwin. Sporting a small, but sharply designed interior by Louis Yoh, replete with schoolhouse chairs and reclaimed bowling alley wood tables, Houseman's seasonal menu isn't extensive, but each dish is extremely well-sourced—not to mention well-executed, with the help of co-chef, Adam Baumgart.

Kick things off with a grilled tomato salad, bursting with fresh herbs, salty feta and smoky shishito peppers. Then linger over a superbly fresh, slashed, and fried whole black sea bass, laced in a tarragon-forward herby sauce; or excellent, beer-braised sausage links, served with sweet caramelized onions and roasted banana peppers.

Hirohisa ✿

Japanese

B2

73 Thompson St. (bet. Broome & Spring Sts.)

Subway: Spring (Sixth Ave.) — Lunch Mon – Fri
Phone: 212-925-1613 — Dinner Mon – Sat
Web: www.hirohisa-nyc.com
Prices: $$$

There's nothing like a discreet entrance to raise expectations—and Hirohisa is nicely concealed on Thompson Street. When you do find it you enter into a stylish, beautifully understated and meticulously laid out room that wouldn't look out of place in the pages of "Wallpaper" magazine. It's run with considerable charm by a discreet and very courteous Japanese team.

A lack of headings makes the two-page menu a daunting document so, instead of trying to construct your own meal, you're better off letting the chefs decide by going for the balanced and seasonal dishes of the seven- or nine-course omakase. Two things will quickly become clear: the ingredients are exceptional and the technical skills of the chefs considerable. This is food that is as rewarding to eat as it is restorative; standouts will be the lingering flavor of Washu beef, perfectly grilled *anago*, and anything with uni or their homemade tofu.

There are tables available but it's so much more satisfying to sit at the counter and engage with the chefs—this way, you may even find that there are a few more dishes in their repertoire than they advertise.

Mercer Kitchen

Contemporary XX

99 Prince St. (at Mercer St.)

Subway: Prince St — Lunch & dinner daily
Phone: 212-966-5454
Web: www.themercerkitchen.com
Prices: $$$

Whether you're here to pick at a salad or up your intake of carbs, Jean-Georges' slick restaurant within the Mercer Hotel has something for you. It has been an inexorable part of the SoHo scene for over a decade and so knows what its customers want and how to keep them coming back. Those customers are quite an international bunch and the restaurant provides them with stylish surroundings and a healthy dose of glamour—the occasional sighting of someone from the sunny side of Celebrity Street helps too.

The extensive menu is an appealing document, with everything from hot dogs to pizza, seafood platters to roast chicken. Servings are reassuringly generous yet the kitchen has a commendably light touch—try the wonderful Peekytoe crab fritters.

Navy

Seafood 

137 Sullivan St. (bet. Houston & Prince Sts.)

Subway: Spring St (Sixth Ave.) — Lunch & dinner daily
Phone: 212-533-1137
Web: www.navynyc.com
Prices: $$

Only Navy could pull off a nautical-themed restaurant with repurposed WWII military duffle bags, and panels of distressed copper as well as antique sconces on the walls. Everything is beyond chic here, from the former bowling alley bench banquette, to that massive espresso machine used to serve coffee and pastries to early-to-rise SoHo-ites.

But seafood rules after breakfast, when the raw bar spouts oysters, clams, sea urchin, as well as bright Mediterranean white wine. The menu presents culinary hedonism at its finest, like mussel toast: plump mollusks, paprika, and caper aïoli spread over crunchy sourdough bread. Similarly, soft-shell crabs arrive atop a squash blossom pancake with hints of anchovy, and are accented with a dreamy blend of maple syrup.

The Musket Room ✿

D2 Contemporary XX

265 Elizabeth St. (bet. Houston & Prince Sts.)

Subway: Broadway - Lafayette St Dinner nightly
Phone: 212-219-0764
Web: www.themusketroom.com
Prices: $$$

The Musket Room is just the restaurant Nolita deserves. Service is incredibly hospitable; and whitewashed walls, raw timber, mortar-smeared brick, and modern Danish chairs fashion a farmhouse-chic interior that's as head-turning as the willowy young locals. To whet their thirst, wine bottles topping a wall-length table in the back dining room are presented and poured with panache.

Chef Matt Lambert's forte is the modern cuisine of New Zealand with a contemporary twist. While he may be a Kiwi ambassador, Chef Lambert uses his understanding of very particular ingredients to craft dishes that are seasonal, delicious, and sometimes wildly creative. A rum-cured torchon of foie gras is at once dense yet melting upon contact, accompanied by sweet dates, tart green apple gel, and buttery brioche. Provenance is clearly a high priority in the exceptional Ora king salmon; the bright and supple tranche is topped with freeze-dried Satsuma, citrus oil, and herbs to complement its delicate flavor.

For dessert, the superb carrot cake pulls together a spectrum of textures and tastes. However, the stark white, crisp pavlova filled with passion fruit curd, whipped cream, slivered strawberries, and passion fruit pulp is a true classic.

Papatzul

Mexican

B2

55 Grand St. (bet. West Broadway & Wooster St.)

Subway: Canal St (Sixth Ave.) Lunch & dinner daily
Phone: 212-274-8225
Web: www.papatzul.com
Prices: $$

Sangria and salsas rule at Papatzul, a swanky SoHo scene rife with a classically trained chef churning out delightful Mexican cuisine. On any given evening, the cozy and narrow space, decorated with masks and dark wood, is abuzz with drinking buddies getting friendly with tequila offerings and tables of friends diving into five types of salsas—each inspired by a different region in Mexico.

Great care is given to each dish, like chicken flautas made with some of the city's best tortillas, and filled with tender grilled meat, and a dab of salsa *borracha*. For a regal repast, try slow-roasted duck enchiladas featuring a rich, almond-chili *mole*. It rises well above the neighborhood norm, making this spot quite the destination for margarita-fueled fun.

Pearl & Ash

Contemporary

D2

220 Bowery (bet. Prince & Spring Sts.)

Subway: Bowery Dinner nightly
Phone: 212-837-2370
Web: www.pearlandash.com
Prices: $$

For small plates that spark contemplation, this deep, dark, and narrow restaurant delivers. Long wood tables line the room under a striking wall of boxes puzzle-pieced together to showcase collectibles like antique cameras. Shimmering subway tiles, an atmospheric soundtrack, and dim lighting lend a sultry feel.

House-smoked whole wheat bread arrives with freshly churned "chicken butter" (that's butter with chicken fat) and maple syrup. A lamb belly and *guajillo* pepper roulade rests in goat-milk yogurt, topped with crushed almonds, pea tendrils, and paper-thin slices of radish. Confit fingerling potatoes are buried under an avalanche of porcini purée with smoky chorizo over the top. The negroni ice cream sandwich has quickly risen to signature status.

Peasant

194 Elizabeth St. (bet. Prince & Spring Sts.)

Subway: Spring St (Lafayette St.) Dinner Tue – Sun
Phone: 212-965-9511
Web: www.peasantnyc.com
Prices: $$

Year after year, Peasant hits it out of the park—from the mouthwatering Italian food to the spot-on service to the utterly charming osteria spirit, Frank DeCarlo's ode to the Italian gathering spot is the essence of easy excellence. The décor is charmingly rustic—picture whitewashed walls, bare wood tables, and a bustling downstairs wine bar.

Kick things off with ricotta and otherworldly bread, fresh from the visible centerpiece hearth—which is the main method of cooking and sets this spot apart. But save room for house-made lasagna with braised rabbit ragù, creamy béchamel, and sweet root vegetables; tender razor clams in a fragrant white wine broth; succulent porchetta studded with garlic and rosemary; or stewed and perfectly chewy *trippa alla Romana*.

Raoul's

French XX

B1

180 Prince St. (bet. Sullivan & Thompson Sts.)

Subway: Spring St (Sixth Ave.) Dinner nightly
Phone: 212-966-3518
Web: www.raouls.com
Prices: $$$

It's the nature of all great cities to constantly change but that doesn't mean severing ties to the past. Raoul's has been around since the '70s—which alone qualifies it as an "institution"—but this is no museum piece living on past glories. Wander in on any given night and you'll see a crowd of all ages united in their fondness for French food and their ability to enjoy themselves.

The menu wouldn't necessarily entice the passer-by on content alone but the kitchen has a surprisingly delicate touch that raises dishes above the ordinary, whether that's tender octopus with chickpea purée or succulent rack of lamb with oyster mushrooms. In the stampede to find all that is new, shiny and hot we shouldn't ignore those whose sin is mere longevity.

Public ✿

C2

210 Elizabeth St. (bet. Prince & Spring Sts.)

Subway: Spring St (Lafayette St.) Lunch Sat – Sun
Phone: 212-343-7011 Dinner nightly
Web: www.public-nyc.com
Prices: $$$

Let the other restaurants copy each other down to the table linens: Public has always done it's own thing, and boy, does it do it right. Housed in an old loading dock in SoHo, Public still sports elevated garage doors on its exterior, but the sexy interior is pure style and grace. The décor features unique bronze mailboxes, where box-holders are delivered artisanal wines hand-selected by the chef, and private rooms contoured with billowing fabrics.

A first-come, first-serve "Sunday Supper" menu is offered every Sunday with limited seating, and almost always sells out. Chef Brad Farmerie's menu is truly innovative—fusion might be an overused descriptor, but it aptly describes his style.

Never shy to marry unique items in interesting ways (think smoked paprika oil paired with pea shoots), a sample Farmerie dinner might include house-made ricotta cavatelli tossed in a lovely carrot sauce fashioned like a Bolognese, with pickled ramps, candied sunflower seeds, and a ramp purée; or tender New Zealand venison with pickled beets, hibiscus, currants, and a quinoa-black garlic salad. End on a high with pea-and-crème fraîche ice cream with green matcha, sponge cake, ganache, and lemon tapioca.

Rebelle ✿

French XX

D3

218 Bowery (bet. Prince & Spring Sts.)

Subway: Bowery Dinner Mon – Sat
Phone: 917-639-3880
Web: www.rebellenyc.com
Prices: $$$

Heat-seeking foodies on the hunt for the next big thing have found it at this chic bistro from the owners of Pearl & Ash. The dining room is as dim as a cave—its palette of concrete and ebony brightened only by a white marble bar and gracious team of servers who know when they're needed and seem to disappear when they're not. Rebelle has an edgy vibe—the space was once a burlesque bar, after all. But, beneath that veneer is impressive talent delivered with a sexy French accent.

While Chef Daniel Eddy's streamlined presentations and foam flourishes have contemporary flair, rest assured that classic technique is at the root of every dish. Lamb tartare is perfectly balanced, boasting *piment d'Espelette*-kissed cubes of meat tossed with green chickpeas, strained yogurt, and a slice of excellent toasted bread. Then, exceptionally tender pork loin is served over a mustard-tinged sauce with wilted greens, grilled spring onions, and a delicious bite of deep-fried headcheese.

For dessert, gâteau Saint-Honoré is seasonally reimagined as crisp layers of *pâte feuilletée*, mascarpone pastry cream, and fragrant wild strawberries adorned with tiny strawberry-caramel-lacquered profiteroles.

Rouge et Blanc

B1

48 MacDougal St. (bet. Houston & Prince Sts.)

Subway: Houston St — Dinner Tue – Sun
Phone: 212-260-5757
Web: www.rougeetblancnyc.com
Prices: $$$

The lines between Vietnamese and French cuisines are blurred at Rouge et Blanc, a cozy restaurant with an Indochine-influenced décor. A burlap-covered ceiling, red lacquered chairs, handcrafted pottery, and plants add up to an intimate setting on one of SoHo's quiet side streets.

The cuisine avoids common fusion pitfalls to display a balanced approach to cooking, through dishes such as the green papaya salad enlivened with a green curry vinaigrette and crunchy-fried head-on shrimp. Excellent specials include *pho* ramped up with a lemongrass- and chili oil-laced broth and tender grilled duck breast. Braised beef cheeks showcase classic Vietnamese flavors of cloves, anise, and *nuoc cham.* A noteworthy selection of French wines complements the delectable menu.

Rubirosa

C2

235 Mulberry St. (bet. Prince & Spring Sts.)

Subway: Spring St (Lafayette St.) — Lunch & dinner daily
Phone: 212-965-0500
Web: www.rubirosanyc.com
Prices: $$

Push back the dark red velvet curtain into the dimly lit narrow dining room to find out how very cool *nonna* can be on Mulberry Street. Although it may be loud and cramped with the requisite 80's tunes blaring overhead, this adept Italian-American kitchen is bright with classic dishes and a pizza recipe, which as the menu reads, is a 55-year old Staten Island heirloom.

The classic pizza balances a cracker-thin crispy crust with tart tomato sauce and oven-browned spots of salty, melting mozzarella. Catch the pasta special like *paccheri* with subtly sweet and spicy sugo and meaty, tender roasted pork. Night owls may simply snack on the selection of alluring antipasti like mini arancini, but it's worth tasting how efficiently this kitchen can feed the crowds.

Sessanta

Italian XX

60 Thompson St. (bet. Broome & Spring Sts.)

Subway: Spring St (Sixth Ave.) — Dinner nightly
Phone: 212-219-8119
Web: www.sessantanyc.com
Prices: $$$

Restaurateur John McDonald's newest venture finds him mining the unique flavors of Sicily, with the oh-so-talented Chef Jordan Frosolone helming the kitchen. Located in the SIXTY SoHo, Sessanta's mid-century Italian décor boasts vintage chandeliers, wood paneling, and a warm, earthy palette. The overall effect is retro, urban, and gorgeous.

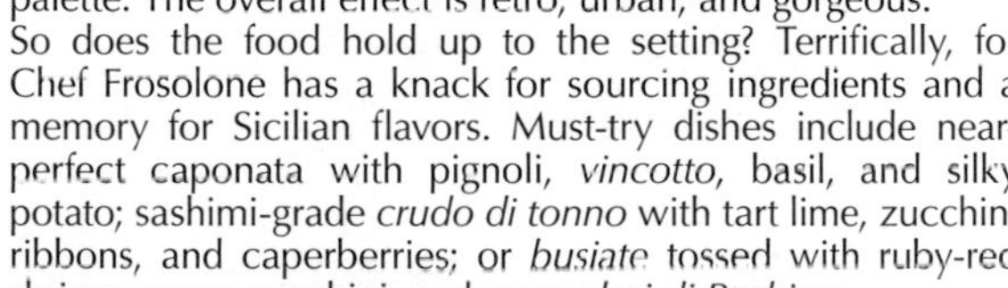

So does the food hold up to the setting? Terrifically, for Chef Frosolone has a knack for sourcing ingredients and a memory for Sicilian flavors. Must-try dishes include near-perfect caponata with pignoli, *vincotto*, basil, and silky potato; sashimi-grade *crudo di tonno* with tart lime, zucchini ribbons, and caperberries; or *busiate* tossed with ruby-red shrimp, green zucchini, and *pomodori di Pachino*.

Snack

105 Thompson St. (bet. Prince & Spring Sts.)

Subway: Spring St (Sixth Ave.) — Lunch & dinner daily
Phone: 212-925-1040
Web: www.snacksoho.com
Prices: ⊜

No need to second-guess the purpose of Snack. It's a casual spot bursting with meze, where shoppers take a break from the jewel-box boutiques that flank this miniscule storefront. Here, juice glasses double as wine goblets, sepia-toned antique photographs line the space, and starting your meal with a baklava is perfectly acceptable. It's no surprise that two sister tavernas have sprouted in the West Village and Hell's Kitchen.

The Mediterranean menu features plenty of signatures including marinated anchovies wrapped in grape leaves, garlicky *skordalia*, and earthy Macedonian wines. The chalkboard's daily specials are a great starting point, especially the *palpoutsaka*, smoky eggplant stuffed with sirloin and topped with tomatoes and béchamel.

Uncle Boons ✿

Thai

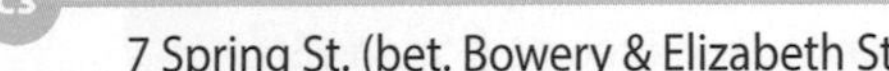
C3

7 Spring St. (bet. Bowery & Elizabeth St.)

Subway: Bowery

Dinner nightly

Phone: 646-370-6650

Web: www.uncleboons.com

Prices: $$

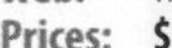

Can't afford a trip to Thailand? No problem. Head along to this whimsical and transporting den—brought to you stateside by husband-wife duo Matt Danzer and Ann Redding—and get sipping on Singha slushies among a lively crowd of downtowners. Tables are itsy-bitsy, but the kitchen feels immense in its creative vision and dilation of traditional Thai fare.

Refined techniques and top ingredients combine to produce a blend of homegrown-haute cuisine that's presented with exceptional service here. *Laab neuh gae* sets hand-chopped lamb ablaze with chilies, lime, and mint, whereas tender snails doused in a gently spiced green curry reveal a deep knowledge of nuanced savors. Funky flavors reach full bloom in *gaeng som muu krob*, crisp pork belly floating in a tart tamarind curry of sausage-stuffed squid, perfectly foiled by sweet lychees. And for a brazen show of taste and texture, tuck into the crispy duck leg (*pet palo*), served in a soy-anise broth with caramelized tangerine and a soft-cooked egg.

Dessert highlights include a coconut sundae accentuated by salty peanuts. And brioche French toast, dunked into condensed milk and caramelized to perfection, is a far cry from its "milquetoast" moniker.

PYLONES
Spring St
Station
6 Downto

DRINK AND DINE

TriBeCa is an established commercial center sprinkled with haute design stores, warehouses-turned-lavish lofts, and trendy drink-cum-dining destinations. Quite simply, this triangle below Canal is a cool place to eat, and its affluent residents can be seen splurging in restaurants whose reputations precede them. Of course that isn't to say that this area's famously wide, umbrella-shaded sidewalks aren't cramped with more modest hangouts. In fact, **Puffy's Tavern** is a favored neighborhood haunt with small bites, hearty sandwiches, and five flat-screens for the happy-hour crowds. Over on West Broadway, **Square Diner** is a local institution that takes you back in time via red vinyl booths and that diner counter cooking up the staples. Like every other Manhattan neighborhood, TriBeCa claims its own culinary treasures: **Bubby's** is a gem for comfort food; while **Zucker's Bagels & Smoked Fish** flaunts an updated décor and floors patrons with a taste of *bubbe*'s best. **Dirty Bird To Go** delivers fresh, all-natural chicken in its many glorious forms—try the buttermilk-fried or slow-roasted

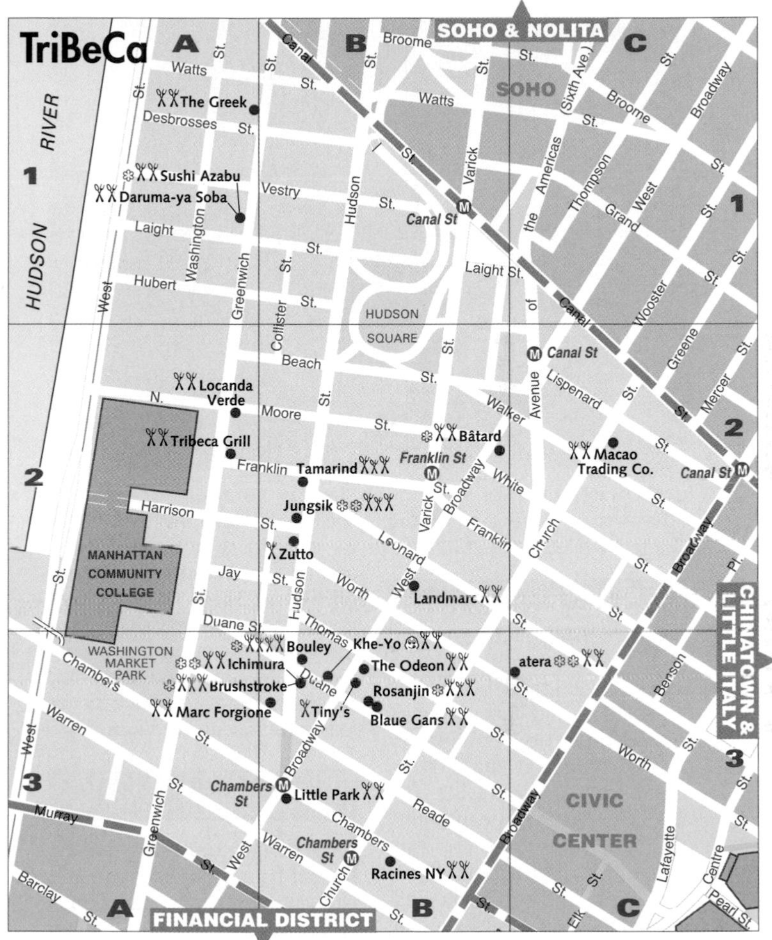

rotisserie and join its endless line of fans. And over on North Moore Street, **Smith & Mills** continues to make waves as a cocoon for fantastic eats plus spectacular drinks.

In keeping with its cutting-edge spirit, TriBeCa also offers a gourmet experience for any palate and price tag. **Grand Banks** bobs along the Hudson and is a summer special for seasonal oysters or a lobster roll, while winter calls for brunch at **Almond**, featuring delicious eggs, all things sweet, and... wait for it...homemade baby food! Here, tots can have their cake and eat it to, after which the adults can head over to **Chambers Street Wines** to keep the party going. Those looking for something to enjoy with their wine will rejoice over the events sponsored by **New York Vintners**. These include free wine and cheese tastings and cooking demonstrations on how

to decorate cupcakes with the kids—sip on a few sparkling varietals while you're at it!

BATHS & BAKERS

Work off a hangover at AIRE Ancient Baths, a luxury spa inspired by ancient civilizations and water-induced relaxation. They even offer rituals where you can soak in olive oil, cava, or red wine. The only downside? You can't drink it! Then, take your appetite to one of TriBeCa's numerous (and well-lauded) bakeries. **Sarabeth's** is an award-winning jam maker who turned this once humble retail store into the monstrous hit it is today. With its impressive array of cookies, cakes, preserves, and other sweets, this specialty store knows how to play the culinary game with such solid competitors as **Duane Park Patisserie**, known for pastries and seasonal specialties; or even **Tribeca Treats** for a plethora of decadent chocolates. Meanwhile, **Birdbath**, an integral part of the City Bakery clan, is admired for its eco-friendly philosophy as well as its unique selection of bites and bevvies. **Takahachi Bakery** on Murray Street is a modestly decorated but must-visit treasure for Japanese refreshers. While here, slurp up a *matcha* latte, but save room to snack on at least one macaron *sakura*.

AROUND THE WORLD

Korin is a culinary haven that flaunts an extensive and exquisite knife collection, plus tableware and gorgeous kitchen supplies. Not only do these products shine in many fine dining establishments, but they also bring to life the essence of food art. Chefs come here to get their blades worked on or to order a specific knife, while others may opt for the gorgeous gift sets that are sure to excite a friend or impress a colleague. From top-notch gear to fantastic grub, **Mangez Avec Moi** is a tiny Southeast Asian marvel beloved for its big and bold flavors. Skip the ubiquitous pan-Asian staples for more authentic, home-style Thai and Laotian specials—*nam kao* is a bamboo stew bobbing with mushrooms, fish, and salty anchovy sauce. Before this area became associated with top films from varying genres, director Bob Giraldi shot his mob- and food-themed movie *Dinner Rush* at famed eatery, **Gigino Trattoria**. However, thanks to the annual Tribeca Film Festival, a springtime extravaganza created by Robert DeNiro to revitalize the area after 9/11, TriBeca is now the official home of twelve days of great films and plenty of community camaraderie. Gaggles of locals, tourists, and film buffs collect here every year to see the movies and share their views and reviews at hot spots like **Nish Nush**, a sidewalk show-stopper incorporating authentic Israeli hummus and crispy falafel into sandwiches, hearty platters, and healthy salads.

From healthy eats to heavenly treats, **Baked** is another new tenant in TriBeCa. While the mothership continues to flourish in Red Hook, this considerably larger venture is loved by locals for breakfast, sandwiches, coffee, and sweet treats like cakes, brownies, and pastries. Carb junkies craving more bread (including flatbread pizza) but in a historic setting, can head on over to **Arcade Bakery** on Church Street. But, for those craving crêpes, sweet and savory selections abound at **By Suzette**—a mini counter on Chambers that is quickly gaining a major following. Speaking of laudable ventures, Chef David Bouley and team have created **Bouley Botanical**, a resourceful event space, designed to entice the senses and committed to celebrating every occasion in style. Outfitted with state-of-the-art sound and lighting equipment as well as an impressive exhibition kitchen, this greenhouse-inspired venue pledges to fit your every mood with the likes of yoga, Pilates, and other wholesome practices.

atera ✿✿

Contemporary XX

C3

77 Worth St. (bet. Broadway & Church St.)

Subway: Chambers St (Church St.) Dinner Tue – Sat
Phone: 212-226-1444
Web: www.ateranyc.com
Prices: $$$$

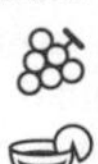

Well, hello there, Ronny Emborg—this visionary new culinary talent takes the reigns at Jodi Richard's sleek TriBeCa tasting menu restaurant, atera—and the results are nothing short of sublime.

Guests access atera by an ultra-discreet entrance; from there, a polished and attentive staff member might offer you a complimentary drink before whisking you off to a lovely, U-shaped counter with supple leather seats positioned to watch the kitchen execute its magic. Sound like a beautiful dream? It is wonderfully real, and that's *before* they ply you with their excellent wine pairing, cocktails or tea tasting (yes, tea—trust us, you'll be talking about it for days).

Chef Emborg's Danish-accented menu might begin with an exquisite chilled green tomato soup with juniper oil, before proceeding to a buttery waffle with savory mushroom cream and earthy black truffle. Then, tender snow crab in an ethereal tomato broth with rose hip cream; or sweet scallop with crisp green apple, dill fronds and horseradish ice may be tailed by springy sepia plated with tart currants and laced with a deadly delicious hazelnut fish cream. Plump razor clams in a miso-brown butter broth are topped with bitter greens and foam for added flavor.

Bâtard ✿

Contemporary XX

B2

239 West Broadway (bet. Walker & White Sts.)

Subway: Franklin St — Dinner Mon – Sat
Phone: 212-219-2777
Web: www.batardtribeca.com
Prices: $$$

239 West Broadway will be a familiar address to those who know their restaurants as it has hosted a number of seminal establishments over the years—namely Montrachet and Corton. Drew Nieporent's Bâtard restaurant is now firmly in situ and once again we have a talented chef making waves in TriBeCa.

Chef Markus Glocker's cooking is very precise and his dishes look quite delicate on the plate. But like a good featherweight they pack more of a punch than you're expecting. You'll even notice his Austrian roots in evidence in some of the dishes, such as short rib and *tafelspitz* terrine, or the Granny Smith and sweetbread strudel.

The room is comfortable and neat and the atmosphere grown-up yet animated. When it comes to service though, it appears that the restaurant has mistaken informality for indifference as it lacks coordination or direction. So you may need to remind yourself that you're here primarily for the food. But that food is very good indeed.

Blaue Gans

Austrian

139 Duane St. (bet. Church St. & West Broadway)

Subway: Chambers St (West Broadway) — Lunch & dinner daily
Phone: 212-571-8880
Web: www.kg-ny.com
Prices: $$

This sleek, unbridled Viennese-style café feels almost smoky and well-worn, but never out of touch. Its walls are papered with vintage movie posters, while banquettes and tables dominate the dining space.

Blaue Gans' strong, loyal following (an increasingly rare feat in the city) is comprised of locals engaging in familiar banter at the bar or communal table. Everyone is here for the impressive Austrian cooking, which may unveil a beautiful bibb, pumpkin seed, and shaved radish salad with a light, creamy pumpkin oil dressing. Other classic treasures include pork Jäger schnitzel with mushrooms, bacon, and herbed spätzle; or classic *kavalierspitz* accompanied by salty creamed spinach and sweet-tart apple horseradish. Delish desserts will have you at hello.

Daruma-ya Soba

Japanese

428 Greenwich St. (bet. Laight & Vestry Sts.)

Subway: Franklin St — Lunch Mon – Fri
Phone: 212-274-0428 — Dinner nightly
Web: www.darumaya-nyc.com
Prices: $$

Known for sensational soba and expert execution, Chef Shuichi Kotani crafts his renowned buckwheat noodles every 30 minutes, cooks them in a mere 20 seconds, and offers an experience as authentic as any you'd find in Japan. Cozy up in a round leather booth in the clubby front area, or take a seat in the more elegant wood and stone dining room.

To truly understand the elasticity, texture, nutty flavors, and the precision that goes into hand-cutting each strand, go for the purest expression of the complex noodles—served in a simple, delicate dashi with scallions, alongside green vegetables and *takuan* (Japanese yellow pickled daikon). Also explore small plates like fishcake with shiso and wasabi, sushi offerings, or the fixed dinner menu.

Bouley ✿

French

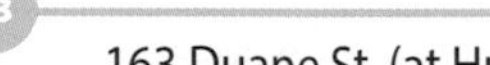

B3

163 Duane St. (at Hudson St.)

Subway: Chambers St (West Broadway)
Lunch & dinner Mon – Sat
Phone: 212-964-2525
Web: www.davidbouley.com
Prices: **$$$$**

Even from the outside, Bouley hints at the certain level of luxury that every successful TriBeCa restaurant strives to attain. Here, it begins with an industrial façade, high arches, exposed brick, and oversized windows dressed in silk. Inside, hand-painted wallpaper, bold watercolors, and a generous floral budget make for an operatic setting reminiscent of a château—maybe the same one from which they salvaged the floors (literally). An undeniable formality keeps the varied clientele muted but never hushed. The ambience may seem a bit old school, yet the cooking mixes tradition with modernity.

Meals may start with a fresh, earthy mix of wild mushrooms with sweet garlic, subtle seasoning, and grilled toro that brings unexpected dimension to the dish. Slightly smoky Alaskan salmon with corn sauce and hearts of palm is almost overshadowed by the superlative pomme purée that is buttery yet retains its pronounced potato flavor. But, remember to pace yourself as Bouley pushes one of the most serious carb chariots in town—think death by bread.

Finish with an amaretto flan piped with white chocolate, caramelized banana, and silky-smooth maple and amaretto ice cream. It's delicious and never disappoints.

Brushstroke ✿

Japanese XXX

B3

30 Hudson St. (at Duane St.)

Subway: Chambers St (West Broadway)
Phone: 212-791-3771
Web: www.davidbouley.com
Prices: **$$$$**

Lunch Tue – Sat
Dinner Mon – Sat

The name may not give too much away but as soon as you enter you just know you're in a Japanese restaurant. It's probably all that calming wood—there's enough here of assorted hues and from various sources to excite the woodsman in us all. Or it could be the L-shaped counter behind which chefs go about their work with studied determination; or more probably, it's the sight of graciously polite servers carrying bowls, boards, and cups containing delicate dishes of infinite beauty.

This joint venture between David Bouley and Yoshiki Tsuji aims to showcase the beauty, subtlety, harmony, and precision that is Japanese cuisine. This isn't the place for sushi—you go next door for that. Instead, it serves seasonally pertinent dishes that are a joy to behold, but where the art never comes at the expense of taste. The Washu beef *sukiyaki*, for example, has a wonderful depth of flavor.

Desserts, such as sake crème brûlée, have more obvious European parentage but are still light, delicate creations. Indeed, such is the nature of the food here that one can, unlike with many styles of restaurant, still engage in constructive work afterwards.

The Greek

Greek XX

A1

458 Greenwich St. (bet. Desbrosses & Watts Sts.)

Subway: Franklin St — Lunch & dinner daily
Phone: 646-476-3941
Web: www.thegreektribeca.com
Prices: $$

This upscale *ouzerie* and taverna is a cozy den of Greek hospitality. Beyond the slender mahogany bar and mounted wine barrels, the rustic-chic dining room is meticulously decorated with vine-wrapped columns to echo the wine-centric theme as well as plush sofas for sinking into the very relaxed vibe. The long bar is a lovely perch for the solo diner craving chicken souvlaki or just an afternoon frappé.

Begin with *keftedes*, tender beef meatballs slowly simmered in aromatic tomato sauce and topped with crumbled aged feta. Then move on to a thick yellow split pea purée folded with olive oil, capers, and bright lemon juice. The *mousaka* is bubbling perfection layered with potato, grilled eggplant, zucchini, and beef topped with eggy-buttery béchamel.

Khe-Yo

Lao XX

B3

157 Duane St. (bet. Hudson St. & West Broadway)

Subway: Chambers St (West Broadway) — Lunch & dinner daily
Phone: 212-587-1089
Web: www.kheyo.com
Prices: $$

This Laotian hot spot serves up vibrant family-style plates brimming with tart and spicy notes that pack a punch—make that a Bang Bang, actually, as in the house sauce of mixed chilies, cilantro, fish sauce, and garlic served to diners as a welcome along with a basket of sticky rice.

The food is worth braving the wait and decibel levels, so sip a craft brew or cocktail before digging in. Start with a plate of wide rice noodles and bits of slow-cooked pork in a coconut-rich yellow curry garnished with herbs, bean sprouts, and slivered banana blossom. Banana leaf-steamed red snapper is another beautifully prepared item, served with crisped artichoke hearts, Chinese broccoli, and more of that sauce. Bright and bitter grapefruit sorbet is a fitting finish.

Ichimura ✿✿

B3

30 Hudson St. (at Duane St.)

Subway: Chambers St (West Broadway) Dinner Tue – Sat
Phone: 212-791-3771
Web: www.davidbouley.com
Prices: $$$$

Tucked away in the bustling swirl of TriBeCa, Ichimura is an oasis of tranquility—with a bright, sun-drenched wood décor that effortlessly blends minimalist Japanese style with a modern sensibility. It's the perfect space to take a seat at the L-shaped counter, take a deep breath, and let go of that city angst. Then, give yourself over completely to the genius Chef Eiji Ichimura and his talented waitstaff.

Throughout your omakase experience, Chef Ichimura always handles the service himself—first bending over his heart-stopping creations and shaping dishes with fingers as nimble as a cellist's, then delivering it with a gracious smile.

Dinner might begin with the traditional *zensai,* or appetizer plate of cold bites; and then move on to dishes like a warm, excellent *chawan mushi* topped with Florida golden crab, truffle dashi, and confetti of chopped chives. A plate of superbly fresh and seasonal sashimi, some of it expertly cured or carrying a drop of delicious sauce, may be tailed by a mind-blowing parade of bright sushi that might include *hiramasa,* king mackerel, Japanese ocean trout, Flying fish, sea perch, or the creamiest ebi you've ever tasted, carrying a whisper of shiso and Japanese uni.

Jungsik ✿✿

Korean XXX

B2

2 Harrison St. (at Hudson St.)

Subway: Franklin St
Dinner Mon– Sat

Phone: 212-219-0900

Web: www.jungsik.kr

Prices: $$$$

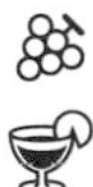

Cool, chic, and completely urbane, Jungsik is the epitome of contemporary elegance. Inside the large, neatly partitioned space, find rich browns and ivory furnishings with flattering lighting that is just bright enough to see your food clearly. The chairs are deep and tables are well spaced, but request a plush corner banquette for maximum comfort. Even the place settings show sculptural beauty through dark pottery and white porcelain. The ambience is fairly quiet and somewhat reflective.

The modern cuisine is confident, complex, and happens to be leaning much more toward Europe than Korea of late. No matter—the cooking remains profoundly enjoyable. At the same time, the most inspired dishes are the ones that retain their heritage, as in the dome of seaweed-seasoned rice with cubes of smoked and torched yellowtail, finished with slivered lettuce. Before the crispy red snapper arrives at the table, hot oil is poured overtop to cook the fish but also to yield incredibly crisped skin, served with a brunoise of hearty greens and potatoes and rich perilla vinaigrette.

Artful desserts include black raspberry and coconut sorbet with crumbles of spinach cake, yuzu meringue, and perfect berry slices.

Landmarc

Mediterranean 

B2

179 West Broadway (bet. Leonard & Worth Sts.)

Subway: Franklin St — Lunch & dinner daily
Phone: 212-343-3883
Web: www.landmarc-restaurant.com
Prices: $$

Chef/owner Marc Murphy's Landmarc is *the* TriBeCa destination for meeting friends over casual drinks and food that happens to be rib-sticking delicious. Downstairs, the bi-level space showcases thick steel cables suspending industrial art and a horseshoe bar flanking a large cooking fire that warms the soul and sizzles those lamb chops. The upstairs is more serene.

Meals may start with lighter plates of smoky and blistered shishito peppers flecked with crunchy sea salt. Then, move on to deeply satisfying (and reasonably priced) nightly pasta specials, like thick and buttery spaghetti *alla Bolognese*. "Landmarc classic" cheese plates are a reliable highlight. Miniature desserts mean that there is always room for a lemon-custard tart (or four).

Little Park

American XX

B3

85 West Broadway (at Chambers St.)

Subway: Chambers St (West Broadway) — Lunch & dinner daily
Phone: 212-220-4110
Web: www.littlepark.com
Prices: $$

Chef/owner Andrew Carmellini strikes again, this time with an inviting all-day eatery on the ground floor of the Smyth Hotel. White tiled walls, amazing artwork, and lovely fresh flowers ensure that the well-designed dining room feels cheery and comfortable. Generous space between tables promises privacy.

Local and seasonal ingredients dictate the menu, especially in the raw and cured section—Long Island fluke or Peconic Bay scallops are simple, fresh opening acts. Purple and orange carrots are roasted until tender, topped in crisp breadcrumbs, then beautifully plated with a tangy black garlic aïoli. A burgundy-hued beetroot risotto is studded with goat cheese. Brimming with cuttlefish, clams, and mussels, the spiced shellfish ragù is downright outstanding.

Locanda Verde

Italian XX

377 Greenwich St. (at N. Moore St.)

Subway: Franklin St — Lunch & dinner daily
Phone: 212-925-3797
Web: www.locandaverdenyc.com
Prices: $$$

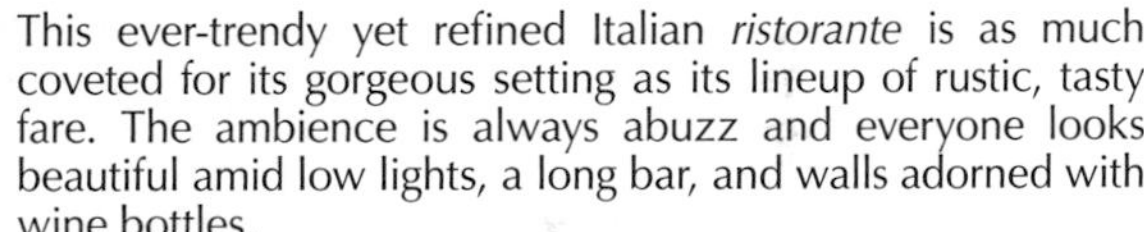

This ever-trendy yet refined Italian *ristorante* is as much coveted for its gorgeous setting as its lineup of rustic, tasty fare. The ambience is always abuzz and everyone looks beautiful amid low lights, a long bar, and walls adorned with wine bottles.

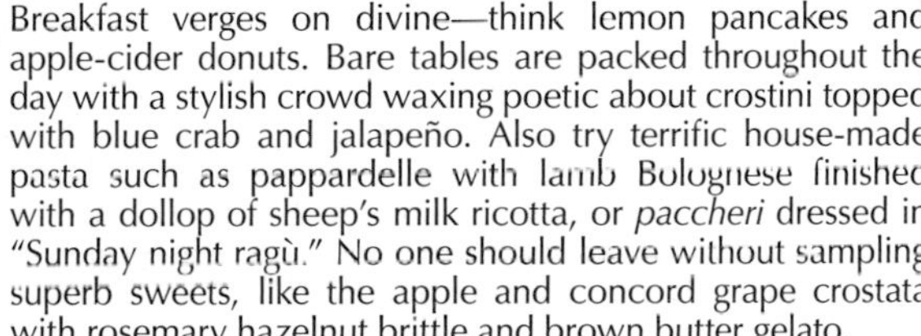

Breakfast verges on divine—think lemon pancakes and apple-cider donuts. Bare tables are packed throughout the day with a stylish crowd waxing poetic about crostini topped with blue crab and jalapeño. Also try terrific house-made pasta such as pappardelle with lamb Bolognese finished with a dollop of sheep's milk ricotta, or *paccheri* dressed in "Sunday night ragù." No one should leave without sampling superb sweets, like the apple and concord grape crostata with rosemary hazelnut brittle and brown butter gelato.

Macao Trading Co.

Macanese XX

311 Church St. (bet. Lispenard & Walker Sts.)

Subway: Canal St (Sixth Ave.) — Dinner nightly
Phone: 212-431-8750
Web: www.macaonyc.com
Prices: $$$

Droves of curious downtowners continue their love affair with this cushy mainstay for Macanese cuisine. With nothing but a red light over a dark door to mark its entrance, make your way into this bi-level beauty, accoutered with heavy velvet drapes, double-height ceilings, and a dimly lit yet sexy bar. The mien is playful, buzz palpable, and first-rate drinks are flowing.

Start with the Tuscan kale-and-romaine salad, enticingly smoky with texturally perfect potato "croutons" and paprika vinaigrette. Then, move on to a Taipa steamboat (cross between a Chinese hotpot and Portuguese paella) teeming with briny shellfish, fried chicken wings, and linguiça. Sample a slice of their chocolate *diablo* cake for an indulgent and notably decadent finish.

Marc Forgione

American

134 Reade St. (bet. Greenwich & Hudson Sts.)

Subway: Chambers St (West Broadway)
Phone: 212-941-9401
Web: www.marcforgione.com
Prices: $$$

Lunch Sun
Dinner nightly

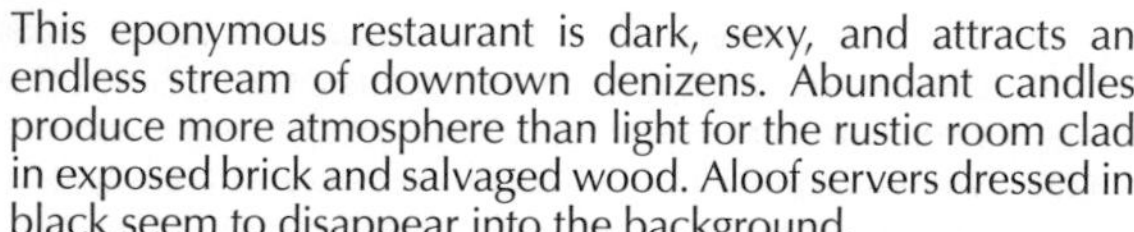

This eponymous restaurant is dark, sexy, and attracts an endless stream of downtown denizens. Abundant candles produce more atmosphere than light for the rustic room clad in exposed brick and salvaged wood. Aloof servers dressed in black seem to disappear into the background.

The innovative American fare excites with bold flavors, as in barbecued oysters sprinkled with pancetta powder. Montauk fluke *en croute*, set over roasted cauliflower, hazelnuts, and capers topped with a buttery panel of toast, is dressed with *sauce proposal*—so named because the rich brown butter and golden raisin emulsion is said to have earned the chef a few romantic offers. It is delicious, but Chef Forgione deserves equal affection for those amazing butter-glazed potato rolls.

The Odeon

American

145 West Broadway (at Thomas St.)

Subway: Chambers St (West Broadway)
Phone: 212-233-0507
Web: www.theodeonrestaurant.com
Prices: $$$

Lunch & dinner daily

It's easy to see why The Odeon has been a part of the fabric of TriBeCa life for so long. Like watching a re-run of *Seinfeld*, it is reassuringly familiar, classically New York and, even when you know what's coming next, still eminently satisfying. The menu is a roll-call of everyone's favorites, from chicken paillard to beet salad, burgers to cheesecake. Cocktails are well made and beers carefully poured. Dishes are executed with sufficient care and portions are of manageable proportions.

The room comes with an appealing art deco feel and the terrace at the front pulls in the occasional passer-by. Service is personable and willing too, although after all this time the place could probably run itself.

Racines NY

French

B3

94 Chambers St. (bet. Broadway & Church St.)

Subway: Chambers St (West Broadway) — Dinner Mon – Sat
Phone: 212-227-3400
Web: www.racinesny.com
Prices: **$$$$**

The American outpost of this popular Parisian original cuts an elegant figure, with its wide marble bar and pristine flower arrangements. Throw in romantic low lighting, brick-lined walls and a tony TriBeCa address—and you have quite the operation.

The service can be a bit off-putting, which is a shame because Racines NY has an ace, even affordable, wine list that bears discussion and recommendations. As for the food, you'll pay for all that sexy ambience a little more than the cuisine currently merits—but certain dishes, like a rich chicken liver mousse served with grilled breads, make for an elegant bar snack. Paired with one of those excellent wines by the glass and a seat at that handsome bar, you have a recipe for a glam night on the town.

Tamarind

Indian XXX

B2

99 Hudson St. (at Franklin St.)

Subway: Franklin St — Lunch & dinner daily
Phone: 212-775-9000
Web: www.tamarindrestaurantsnyc.com
Prices: **$$$**

Building Tamarind cost a cool five million, and it shows—every inch of this soaring space oozes with grandeur. With its classic TriBeCa edifice and gorgeous marble bar (an ideal perch for post-work indulgence), the glass-fronted behemoth draws a posh crowd of Wall Streeters and well-heeled locals. Most impressive of all is the sleek display kitchen, outfitted with a gleaming tandoor that turns out exceptional Mughlai food like *nawab shami kabab* (lamb patties seasoned with ginger) and *hara bhara kabab* (pearl-white paneer mingled with bright emerald-green spinach). While service is mediocre at best and the kitchen may fall behind at peak times, mains like *kolambi pola* (prawns in a coconut-and-chili curry) make up for any gaffes and guarantee a return visit.

Rosanjin ✿

B3

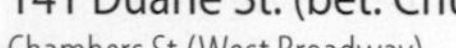

141 Duane St. (bet. Church St. & West Broadway)

Subway: Chambers St (West Broadway) — Dinner Mon – Sat
Phone: 212-346-0664
Web: www.rosanjintribeca.com
Prices: **$$$$**

From its ultra-discrete entrance to its heavily curtained windows, everything about this elegant TriBeCa Japanese restaurant spells delicious rendezvous. Should you be lucky enough to find your way into Rosanjin's barely marked entrance, you'll discover a sleek, sophisticated and oh-so-private dining room with soft jazz music that reads tranquil even when it's full.

Despite its tony address and well-heeled clientele, Rosanjin retains a sort of bonhomie from another era—it's not uncommon for the chef to hand-deliver a few of your dishes with a heartfelt thank you. It's a gesture of gratitude you're likely to return after witnessing the stunning composition on your plate.

A typical kaiseki meal here would feature a bright selection of sushi, some of it scored to deliver that perfect melt-in-your-mouth experience; and might include a delicate (and dramatic) starter of lobster and uni, suspended in a jellied dashi broth and served in a glass with a wispy cloud of orange dry ice. Then, an excellent *chawan mushi* may follow, with salty caviar, tender oyster mushrooms, fresh uni, and chives; or a delicious clear soup with a scallop mousse dumpling, mountain yam, mountain greens, and ginger.

Sushi Azabu ✿

Japanese XX

A1

428 Greenwich St. (bet. Laight & Vestry Sts.)

Subway: Franklin St — Dinner nightly
Phone: 212-274-0428
Web: www.darumaya-nyc.com
Prices: $$$$

Like a little secret tucked beneath Daruma-ya, this standout sushi den has a serene look and private feel that is intimacy incarnate. This works out well, since the subterranean room can only seat about a dozen guests.

The changing roster of Japanese chefs maintain their mystical composure beneath the dark painting of a carp behind the counter, fostering a relaxed pace to each meal even as orders pile in from upstairs. True, they may be serving the same quality fish as the spot above, but the omakase dishes here are incomparably superior.

This is immediately clear from the first bit of *otoshi*, house-made silken tofu with the bold flavors of sea urchin and salmon roe, finished with bits of crisped nori. The kitchen's seasonal influences may be reflected in a springtime bowl of bamboo shoots braised in smoky dashi, or a delicate cube of steamed Japanese red snapper in soy-ginger broth with grated turnip and a fragrant, bright green cherry leaf. The array of sushi includes an explosively briny giant clam, sea scallop with grated yuzu on perfectly cooked rice, and raw sweet shrimp that is downright knee-weakening. The miso soup is the best you've had in a long time.

Tiny's

B3 **American**

135 West Broadway (bet. Duane & Thomas Sts.)

Subway: Chambers St (West Broadway) Lunch & dinner daily
Phone: 212-374-1135
Web: www.tinysnyc.com
Prices: $$

The name says it all—Tiny's is indeed tiny, but in that old New York, wood-burning fire and pressed-tin ceiling kind of way. Enter the narrow Federal-style home (c. 1810) and sidle up to the beautiful people along the pew seats overlooking a poster of the Marlboro Man, or head on to the aptly named Bar Upstairs.

The food may be American but seamlessly weaves in Italian influences. Creamy burrata arrives over date purée, glazed in lemon-honey and sprinkled with crushed pistachios. Hake is thickly cut and enticingly flaky, drizzled in brown butter with tart capers, lemon, and parsley, then complemented with both pan-roasted fingerling potatoes and beautifully dressed frisée salad. Even their delicate California chardonnay harkens to old-world flavors.

Tribeca Grill

A2 **Contemporary**

375 Greenwich St. (at Franklin St.)

Subway: Franklin St Lunch Sun – Fri
Phone: 212-941-3900 Dinner nightly
Web: www.myriadrestaurantgroup.com
Prices: $$$

Beckoning business titans day and night, this corner restaurant is a destination for its big, bright dining room with well-spaced tables. Wall-to-wall windows overlook two quintessential TriBeCa streets, while exposed brick, moody artwork, and a spectacular bar smack in the center of the room complete the refined vibe.

Gigantone, large tubular pasta loaded with a braised short rib Bolognese beneath a dollop of fresh sheep's milk ricotta, makes a rich start to a meal. The decadence continues with seared scallops over creamy carrot risotto, topped with a truffled-Madeira vinaigrette, and brought over the top with a few fragrant shavings of black truffle. Desserts are as classic as the space; try the banana tart with malted chocolate and pecan ice cream.

Zutto

Asian

B2

77 Hudson St. (bet. Harrison & Jay Sts.)

Subway: Franklin St

Lunch & dinner daily

Phone: 212-233-3287
Web: www.zuttonyc.com
Prices: $$

Exposed filament bulbs and a red brick wall give this cozy Japanese pub an inviting, industrial feel. There is a communal wood table for groups, small sushi bar, and long wall of banquettes and tables topped with linen napkins cleverly folded, origami-style. Service is eager, efficient, and less concerned with the flow of a leisurely meal.

Unlike many Japanese restaurants with one specialty, this *izakaya's* diverse menu includes bar snacks, sushi, steamed buns, and ramen. Tangy, spicy buffalo cauliflower is a playful take on wings, replacing chicken with bright orange chunks of deep-fried cauliflower tempered by cool, creamy ranch sauce. The Zutto fried rice is another ideal drinking accompaniment, peppered with kimchi and pastrami beneath a runny egg.

Look for **red** couverts, indicating a particularly pleasant ambience.

Upper East Side

Famously expensive and particularly charming, the Upper East Side is flanked by lush Central Park on one side and the East River on the other. If watching barges and boats bob along the water from a dense metropolis doesn't sound like a perfect paradox, know that this prime area is predominantly residential and home to iconic addresses like Gracie Mansion. Closest to the park are posh spots catering to expats with expense accounts. But, walk a few steps east and discover young families filling the latest *sushi-ya,* artisanal pizzeria, or hot sidewalk spot. Carnegie Hill's **Lucy's Whey** is cheesy, but in a good way, stocked with a wide variety of cheeses and accouterments. They also have a

sit-down café where you can dig into salads, soup, and other types of gooey goodness—imagine panini-pressed ciabatta rolls stuffed with Iowa cheddar and locally sourced pickles...from Brooklyn, of course. Along First and Second avenue, classic Irish pubs are packed with raucous post-grads who keep the party alive well through happy hour and into the wee hours.

SHOPPING CENTRAL

The most upper and eastern reaches of this neighborhood were originally developed by famous families of German descent. While here, make sure to join the queue of carnivores at **Schaller & Weber** as they hover over Austro-German specialties, including wursts for winter steaming or summer grilling as well as a plethora of pungent mustards to accompany them. This area also boasts a greater concentration of gourmet markets than any other part of town. Each of these emporiums are more packed than the next and make processing long lines an art of inspired efficiency. The presence of **Fairway**, a gourmet sanctuary showcasing everything from fresh produce and glistening meats, to seafood and deli delights, has made shopping for homemade meals a complete breeze. And, with such easy access to **Agata & Valentina**, a family-owned and operated food store whose famously cramped aisles are supplied with everything Italian, residents of the Upper East can't imagine residing elsewhere in the city. Outfitted with delicious gift ideas, baskets, and recipes, this epicurean haven brings an

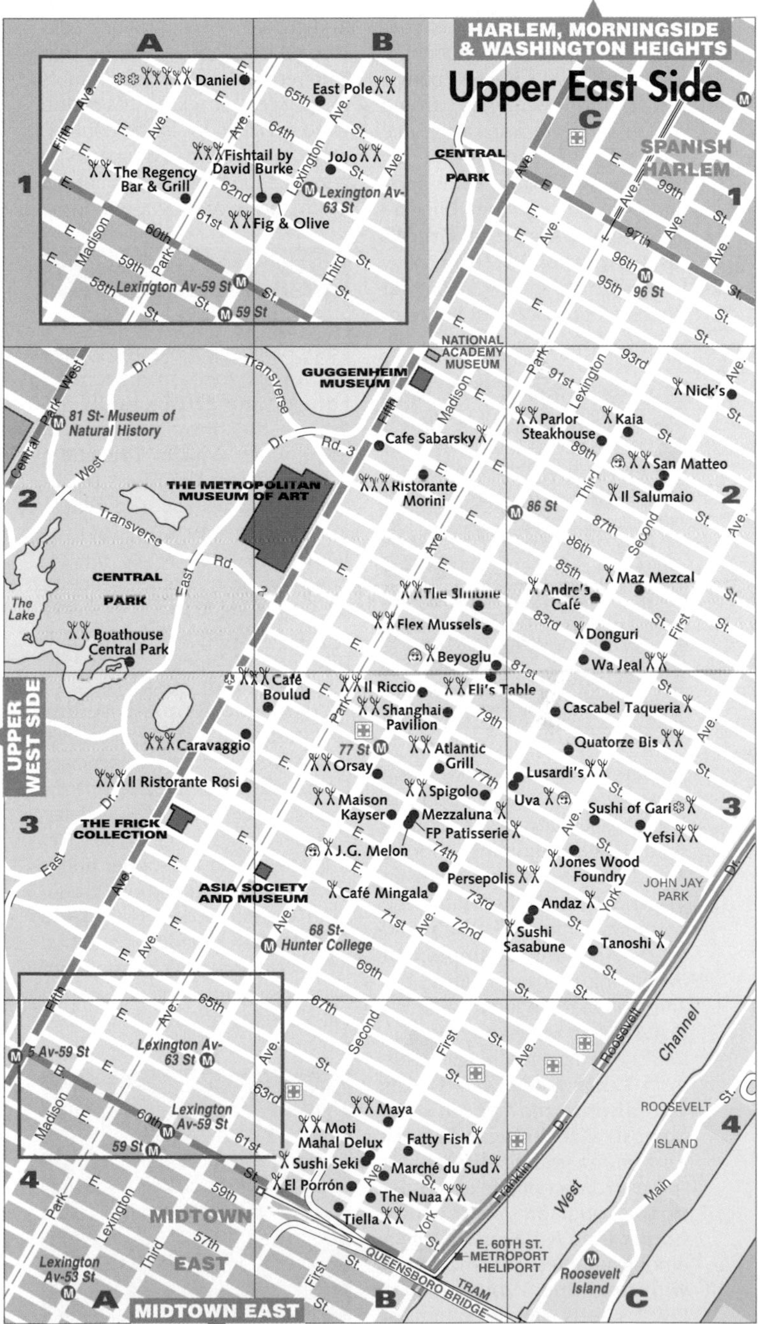

HARLEM, MORNINGSIDE & WASHINGTON HEIGHTS
Upper East Side
CENTRAL PARK
SPANISH HARLEM
Daniel
East Pole
Fishtail by David Burke
JoJo
The Regency Bar & Grill
Lexington Av-63 St
Fig & Olive
Lexington Av-59 St
59 St
96 St
NATIONAL ACADEMY MUSEUM
GUGGENHEIM MUSEUM
81 St- Museum of Natural History
Nick's
Parlor Steakhouse
Kaia
Cafe Sabarsky
San Matteo
THE METROPOLITAN MUSEUM OF ART
Ristorante Morini
Il Salumaio
86 St
The Lake
Maz Mezcal
The Simone
André's Café
Flex Mussels
Donguri
Boathouse Central Park
Beyoglu
Wa Jeal
Café Boulud
Il Riccio
Eli's Table
Cascabel Taqueria
Shanghai Pavilion
UPPER WEST SIDE
Quatorze Bis
77 St
Atlantic Grill
Caravaggio
Orsay
Lusardi's
Il Ristorante Rosi
Spigolo
Uva
Sushi of Gari
Maison Kayser
Mezzaluna
THE FRICK COLLECTION
FP Patisserie
Yefsi
J.G. Melon
Jones Wood Foundry
JOHN JAY PARK
ASIA SOCIETY AND MUSEUM
Café Mingala
Persepolis
Andaz
68 St-Hunter College
Sushi Sasabune
Tanoshi
5 Av-59 St
Lexington Av-63 St
Channel
Lexington Av-59 St
59 St
Maya
Moti Mahal Delux
Fatty Fish
ROOSEVELT ISLAND
Sushi Seki
Marché du Sud
El Porrón
The Nuaa
Tiella
MIDTOWN EAST
E. 60TH ST. METROPORT HELIPORT
QUEENSBORO BRIDGE
TRAM
Roosevelt Island
Lexington Av-53 St
MIDTOWN EAST

authentic European experience to the mean streets of Manhattan. A few steps west, **Citarella** pumps out its mouthwatering aroma of rotisserie chickens to entice passersby. Prime meats and rare produce are also on offer here, and contend with the abundant goodness available at **Grace's Marketplace**. In their new location, this beloved bazaar boasts more space, but no lesser quality, variety, or guests at the

prepared foods counter. Such a savory spectacle is bound to leave you starving, so grab a seat at their adjoining trattoria and devour some pasta or even a whole pizza. At the head of the gourmet game and celebrated as the reigning champion of everything uptown is Eli Zabar and his ever-expanding empire. **E.A.T.** is a Madison Avenue treasure selling all things edible in its casual café. Thanks to its vast offerings and appeal, other outposts (like **Vinegar Factory** and mega-mart **Eli's**) have sprouted and continue to prosper in this quarter. Meanwhile, **Corner Café & Bakery** is a gem among nannies and mommies with uniformed young'uns in tow for tasty salads, sammies, and fro-yo. Finally, every self-respecting foodie knows that **Kitchen Arts & Letters** flaunts the largest stock of food and wine publications in the country, and founder Nach Waxman is as good a source of industry insight as any book or blog around.

SUPPER, SWEETS AND SIPS

In spite of such large-scale shopping, still there are smaller purveyors to patronize here. **Lobel's** and **Ottomanelli** are among the finest butchers in town; while **William Greenberg** continues to bake moist *babka* and Gotham's favorite black-and-white cookie. Just as **Ladurée**'s rainbow of pastel-hued macarons brings a slice of the City of Lights to this exclusive enclave, **Glaser's Bake Shop** is reminiscent of everything Old World and **Lady M's** haute cakes fit right into its plush setting off Madison Avenue. Likewise, thirsty revelers will appreciate **Bemelmans Bar** or **The Jeffrey**, a railcar-like space serving stellar sips beside great pub grub. But, if in the mood for supper and a show, it doesn't get more classic than the storied hotel's, **Café Carlyle**. **Bar Pleiades** is another, more contemporary offering, but just as elegantly uptown as one would expect with its quilted walls and lacquer finishes.

Andaz

Indian

1378 First Ave. (bet. 73rd and 74th Sts.)

Subway: 77 St — Lunch and dinner daily
Phone: 212-288-0288
Web: www.andazny.com
Prices: $$

Simply stated, Andaz is one of *the* best Indian dining gems in the city's upper quarter. This demure space feels tidy and neutral beneath colorful ceiling pendants and wine shelves. A polite staff attends to the familiar coterie of neighborhood patrons.

The menu specializes in regional dishes that are spiced to your desired level. Sample rich bowls of *keema matar*, a thick and meaty stew of minced lamb and sweet peas in a spicy curry paste of dried red chilies, ginger, coriander, and cloves. Hearty vegetarian options include *paneer makhani*, brimming with cubes of diced house-made cheese in a decadent cream and butter-enriched tomato sauce; or lusciously seasoned and distinctly tart vegetable *vindaloo* stocked with cauliflower, potatoes, and sweet carrots.

Andre's Café

Eastern European 

1631 Second Ave. (bet. 84th & 85th Sts.)

Subway: 86 St (Lexington Ave.) — Lunch & dinner daily
Phone: 212-327-1105
Web: www.andrescafenewyork.com
Prices: ⊜

A glass case displaying a decadent selection of traditional pastries—everything from savory meat pies to apple strudel and Sachertorte—greets and tempts guests entering this charming Hungarian café. Purchase something to-go, or take a seat at one of the small wooden tables in the brick-walled, knickknack-filled dining room and peruse the menu. Standouts include a crisp cucumber salad, marinated in slightly sweetened vinegar and served ice-cold, and meaty stuffed cabbage, braised until silken and rustically presented in a pool of paprika-infused tomato broth.

For dessert, tuck into the *Dobos* torte, a tall stack of yellow sponge cake and chocolate buttercream topped with a thick layer of crunchy, amber-tinged caramel embedded with a whole hazelnut.

Atlantic Grill

Seafood XX

B3

1341 Third Ave. (bet. 76th & 77th Sts.)

Subway: 77 St — Lunch & dinner daily
Phone: 212-988-9200
Web: www.atlanticgrill.com
Prices: $$

This gorgeous Grill's sprawling patio is a seafood oasis in the midst of urban chaos. It seems deceivingly vast until you round the bend to a second, beachy dining room decked with a marble sushi counter and rattan chairs—a taste of tropicana on Third Avenue. Despite its name, Atlantic Grill pulls influence from the Pacific (think delicious yet unapologetically unauthentic sushi).

Hints of *sriracha* and ginger keep things bright in bigeye tuna tartare, served in a glass jar glistening with sesame oil and avocado. Soft tacos filled with spicy shrimp and pineapple *pico de gallo* or red-miso Atlantic cod are filling and light at once. Brunch is a hit with twists on traditional fare.

Some whine about the prices, but considering the neighborhood, hush up!

Beyoglu

B2

1431 Third Ave. (at 81st St.)

Subway: 77 St — Lunch & dinner daily
Phone: 212-650-0850
Web: N/A
Prices: $$

Upper East Siders can't get enough of the meze at cheerful Beyoglu and its enticing Turkish, Greek, and Lebanese cooking. Vibrant flavors enhanced by garlic and herbs start with chilled platters loaded with hummus, mashed eggplant spread (*patlican salatasi*), and salads like *kisir*, tabbouleh made with cracked wheat. The only other thing you'll need to fully enjoy the Beyoglu experience is a bowl of strained, house-made yogurt. That flatbread is pulled straight from the hot oven only to arrive on your table seconds later, gratis and absolutely gratifying.

Tile-topped tables and pistachio-green walls displaying painted flowers accent the interior. French doors separate the dining room from the sidewalk, but during warm weather both areas fill quickly.

Boathouse Central Park

American

The Lake at Central Park (E. 72nd St. & Park Dr. North)

Subway: 68 St - Hunter College — Lunch & dinner daily
Phone: 212-517-2233
Web: www.thecentralparkboathouse.com
Prices: $$$

The word "touristy" is mostly used pejoratively but there's no denying that sometimes visitors to the city know a good thing when they see one. Loeb Boathouse was built in 1954 and includes an outdoor bar and a restaurant whose glass wall folds away in the summer to give every table a great view of the lake. If you want to swap the chaos of the city and its cacophony of car horns for a couple of tranquil hours, then here's where to come.

The menu is a mix of American and European classics alongside less successful dishes of a more innovative persuasion. Try the robustly seasoned linguine with Little Neck clams or Scottish salmon with chickpea purée.

While brunch and lunch are year-long affairs, dinner is only served during warmer months.

Café Mingala

1393B Second Ave. (bet. 72nd & 73rd Sts.)

Subway: 68 St - Hunter College — Lunch & dinner daily
Phone: 212-744-8008
Web: N/A
Prices: ⊜

Café Mingala is a special destination—not simply because this is the only Burmese restaurant in all five boroughs. The cuisine itself is downright addictive and undeniably unique. This cross-cultural cuisine distills the flavors of Myanmar's neighbors—China, India, Thailand, and Malaysia—into its own luscious specialties.

The pickled green tea leaf salad combines chopped lettuce, bean sprouts, peanuts, sesame seeds, and bits of tea leaf all dressed with spiced oil and fresh lime. Follow this with *mo-goke* pork, from the "land of rubies" made with tender chunks of meat braised in a salty and sweet dark sauce. Café Mingala's signature dish is a flaky "thousand-layer" pancake, or *keema,* topped with ground beef and potatoes in a turmeric-rich curry.

Café Boulud ✿

French XXX

B3

20 E. 76th St. (bet. Fifth & Madison Aves.)

Subway: 77 St

Lunch & dinner daily

Phone: 212-772-2600

Web: www.cafeboulud.com

Prices: $$$$

Taking its cue from classic French cuisine, Daniel Boulud's refined vision of food and beverage at the Surrey hotel is comprised of two spaces: the jewel box known as Bar Pleiades and this elegant, appealingly understated restaurant.

Inside, ritzy residents and in-the-know globetrotters dine in a well-groomed, secluded room furnished with plush carpeting, rich wood accents, and mirrored surfaces. Sparkling elements atop beautifully laid tables set off the spot's conviviality, and gallant, smartly-dressed servers display unwavering competence in their presentation of uniquely constructed and superb tasting compositions. Under the watch of Chef Aaron Bludorn, the kitchen makes culinary decisions that never disappoint. Classically done *poulet rôti* showcases evenly moist, crispy skinned chicken finished with a fragrant tarragon jus, while the Crescent Farms Pekin duck, cooked to a perfect pink and sprinkled with coarse salt, is served with currant-studded kasha for wonderful depth in flavor and texture.

For dessert, intricately layered crêpe cakes are garnished with rhubarb gelée and kissed with ricotta sorbet. And warm and springy madeleines—a house signature—send satisfied diners on their way.

Cafe Sabarsky

Austrian

1048 Fifth Ave. (at 86th St.)

Subway: 86 St (Lexington Ave.)
Phone: 212-288-0665
Web: www.kg-ny.com
Prices: **$$**

Lunch Wed – Mon
Dinner Thu – Sun

This Museum Mile *kaffeehaus* is so authentic it may as well be set along Vienna's *Ringstrasse*. Instead, find in the Beaux Arts mansion—which is also home to Serge Sabarsky and Ronald Lauder's Neue Galerie rife with 20th century Austrian-cum-German art and design. Located across from Central Park, this gorgeous ground-floor den is clad in dark-stained wood with diners seated along a banquette covered in Otto Wagner fabric.

Stunning cakes and pastries are displayed on a marble-topped sideboard. But first, order one of Chef Kurt Gutenbrunner's traditional specialties, including the city's best wiener schnitzel or hearty Hungarian beef goulash with creamy, herbed spätzle. When it's time for dessert, try a wedge of the chocolate, almond, and rum *Sabarskytorte*.

Caravaggio

23 E. 74th St. (bet. Fifth & Madison Aves.)

Subway: 77 St
Phone: 212-288-1004
Web: www.caravaggioristorante.com
Prices: **$$$**

Lunch & dinner daily

Nestled among Madison Avenue boutiques and commanding a rather formal air, this highbrow Italian dining room is a good reason to dress up and splurge. The slender setting is adorned with silk-lined walls, sleek leather seating, and evocative artwork. The well-dressed staff is serious, but their hospitality is genuine.

The team of highly experienced co-chefs is equally intense in turning out their skilled cooking. Antipasti might include an elegant, warm octopus salad with baby artichoke and crispy potatoes, while heartier options may feature house-made *cavatelli* with jumbo crabmeat and sea urchin. Lunch offers a more pared-down experience, but a bowlful of velvety *pasta e fagioli* stocked with plump *borlotti* beans is a perfect post-shopping tonic.

Cascabel Taqueria

Mexican

1538 Second Ave. (at 80th St.)

Subway: 77 St — Lunch & dinner daily
Phone: 212-717-8226
Web: www.nyctacos.com
Prices:

Inexpensive tacos stuffed with skill and creativity are the reasons this taqueria has been a hit from the start. Highlights begin with the carnitas tacos, slow-roasted pork belly with *chile de arbol* piled high into two masa tortillas sprinkled with pickled onion, *culantro,* and the unorthodox but intriguing crunch from puffed rice. Other choices include burritos served with sweet potato fries, refreshing salads in crisp tostadas, and black beans with quinoa.

Meals are presented on aluminum sheet pans emphasizing the laid-back vibe here. A caddy of salsas—roasted tomato, tomatillo, and very spicy *diablo*—tops and thrills each table. The corner location features a sunny room with exposed brick, bright green accent wall, and retro-style chrome chairs.

Donguri

Japanese

309 E. 83rd St. (bet. First & Second Aves.)

Subway: 86 St (Lexington Ave.) — Dinner Tue – Sun
Phone: 212-737-5656
Web: www.donguriny.com
Prices: $$

This cozy Yorkville hideaway has endured years of non-stop construction along Second Avenue and a more recent change in ownership and chef. Yet Donguri still perseveres as a highly recommendable venue. Service has lightened up of late, reflected in the genuine smiles of the small and gracious crew, but the cuisine's ethos remains very much unaltered.

Don't expect to dine on sushi here—there's more to Japanese cuisine after all as evidenced by their home-style cooked dishes. Nightly specials posted on the wall direct your attention to options like fried soft-shell crabs so pleasingly crispy and plump they don't need anything else. Okay, a squeeze of lemon if you must. Rice bowls topped with the likes of yellowtail and scallion are yet another specialty.

Daniel 

French XXXXX

A1

60 E. 65th St. (bet. Madison & Park Aves.)

Subway: 68 St - Hunter College

Dinner Mon – Sat

Phone: 212-288-0033

Web: www.danielnyc.com

Prices: $$$$

The elegant façade, the revolving door, the sound of clinking glasses—even before you reach the dining room you feel a part of something special. This bastion of classical French cooking epitomises the "special occasion," yet even those unencumbered by fiscal considerations treat it with respect.

The dining room is dominated by the striking porcelain-tiled chandeliers hanging from the soaring ceiling. If you're on one of the raised tables you get to look down—literally rather than patronizingly—onto your fellow diners through the neo-classical arches. Yet thanks to the personable service, the grandeur of the room never stifles the animated atmosphere.

The cooking is as sophisticated as the surroundings and the ingredients come from the top drawer. The kitchen has had an obvious classical education yet you never feel it is tied by the tyranny of tradition. Just order the succulent Niman Ranch lamb chops and you'll find them accompanied with quinoa mixed with avocado. Occasionally, over-enthusiastic garnishing can overawe the dish's main ingredient but there's no doubting this is a very capable kitchen.

East Pole

B1 — Contemporary XX

133 E. 65th St. (bet. Lexington & Park Aves.)

Subway: 68 St - Hunter College — Lunch & dinner daily
Phone: 212-249-2222
Web: www.theeastpolenyc.com
Prices: $$$

Just off Park Avenue's pre-war grandeur is this hip addition to the neighborhood, courtesy of the Fat Radish team. The cozy space is on the ground floor of a brownstone, so the setting is understandably narrow. East Pole's front bar is hopping, while black leather booths in the back allow parties to sit and enjoy an eclectic menu in relative peace.

The stimulating cooking here begins with a salad of roasted heirloom carrots with *hijiki*, diced avocado, and an Asian-inspired soy-and-sesame oil vinaigrette. Then move on to explore Kiev-style chicken, stuffed with garlic butter-enriched broccoli purée, or creamy fish pie stocked with cod, lobster, and fennel. The adult ice cream sundae is a boozy combo of Scotch-chocolate ice cream and Pimm's-soaked cherries.

Eli's Table

B3 — American XX

1413 Third Ave. (at 80th St.)

Subway: 77 St — Dinner nightly
Phone: 212-717-9798
Web: www.elistablenyc.com
Prices: $$

Formerly known as Taste, Eli Zabar has redone the formal café located adjacent to his eponymous gourmet emporium. The facelift has revealed a more casual vibe—no tablecloths—but the scene is just about as casual as Upper East Siders can stomach. Inlaid geometric patterned flooring and an earthy palette remain, while a mural of the Côte d' Or is an attractive new touch signaling a more serious approach to wine.

Rooftop greens as well as bread and gelato made in-house at the market factor into the revised menu that boasts a sunny disposition in its affection for the Mediterranean. Expect to enjoy pig's ear salad with a mustard vinaigrette, plump sardines over olive oil-smashed potatoes, or fresh pappardelle twirled with wild mushrooms and a bit of cream.

El Porrón

Spanish

1123 First Ave. (bet. 61st & 62nd Sts.)

Subway: Lexington Av - 59 St — Lunch & dinner daily
Phone: 212-207-8349
Web: www.elporronnyc.com
Prices: $$

Black-and-white portraits of people pouring streams of wine into their mouths directly from *porróns*—blown glass wine vessels with long, tapered spouts—give you the idea of what this spot is all about. Dark colors give a cloistered feel to the intimate space, which is a pleasant contrast to its traffic-clogged location.

The kitchen churns out a graceful, all-encompassing array of tapas, large plates, and even paellas worth their 40-minute wait. Sample bites like canned *esparragos blancos Navarro*—their thick, tender stalks are served cool and dressed with Chardonnay vinaigrette—or *bacalao a la Vizcaina*, Basque-style salt cod with a sauce melding the flavors of roasted peppers, garlic, olives, and potatoes served in a bubbling hot *cazuela*.

Fatty Fish

International 

406 E. 64th St. (bet. First & York Aves.)

Subway: Lexington Av - 63 St — Lunch & dinner daily
Phone: 212-813-9338
Web: www.fattyfishnyc.com
Prices: $$

Beneath a distinguishing orange awning, Fatty Fish is a bright spot in Yorkville. The comfy space is downright homey with its intimate rooms, creaky wood floors, and a staff that treats everyone like regulars.

The cuisine reflects varied inspiration, but rest assured everything is tempting. From the sushi counter, experience skillfully knifed sashimi, *chirashi*, and maki. Dig into cooked fare like Japanese eggplant and wild mushroom lasagna layered with shredded pork; green curry shrimp and vegetables; or perfectly grilled filet mignon medallions dabbed with spicy Chinese-style mustard gently sweetened with honey, alongside stir-fried bok choy and a tower of crispy onion rings. End with refreshing ginger ice cream studded with strips of candied ginger.

Fig & Olive

Mediterranean XX

B1

808 Lexington Ave. (bet. 62nd & 63rd Sts.)

Subway: Lexington Av - 63 St — Lunch & dinner daily
Phone: 212-207-4555
Web: www.figandolive.com
Prices: $$$

This reliable, Mediterranean-inspired retreat is a popular post-museum (or post-shopping) pick. The sleek long bar glows beneath dangling light fixtures, while the shelf-lined walls are stocked with olive oils in verdant hues of green. Candles flicker over stone tables near plates of glistening olives.

An olive oil tasting showcases the stark nuances of different regions and makes an ideal start to a meal, served with fluffy rosemary *fougasse*. Then, move on to buttery, round tartlets of Gorgonzola dolce, caramelized figs, and chopped walnuts with a pile of arugula lending peppery spark. Nutty, truffle-infused risotto with meaty mushrooms is a high note. A shot glass of luscious chocolate mousse compensates for its paltry size with absolute decadence.

Fishtail by David Burke

Seafood XXX

B1

135 E. 62nd St. (bet. Lexington & Park Aves.)

Subway: Lexington Av - 63 St — Lunch Sat – Sun
Phone: 212-754-1300 — Dinner nightly
Web: www.fishtaildb.com
Prices: $$$

First-rate seafood served in a ritzy, residential townhouse makes Fishtail a perennial hot spot. The first floor is an oyster bar and lounge swamped by after-work crowds devouring iced shellfish towers. Upstairs, find a deep-red dining room with touches that colorfully convey the ocean theme.

Fresh-off-the-boat seafood is prepared with the eponymous chef's trademark stamp of creativity, resulting in dishes like pastrami-spiced smoked salmon. These gossamer slices are drizzled with horseradish crème fraîche and mustard oil, topped with fried capers, and accompanied by chewy slices of toasted pretzel. Entrées include an Asian-themed steamed black cod brushed with tamarind glaze and plated with turnip-*lap cheong* (Chinese sausage) cake.

Flex Mussels

Seafood

174 E. 82nd St. (bet. Lexington & Third Aves.)

Subway: 86 St (Lexington Ave.)
Phone: 212-717-7772
Web: www.flexmusselsny.com
Prices: $$

Dinner nightly

Featuring a focused menu of cleverly made, high-quality seafood, it's no surprise that this mussels haven was an immediate success. Still going strong, this setting is routinely packed to the gills, both up front where there is a bar and dining counter, as well as the proper dining room in the back, adorned with an abundance of maritime-themed artwork.

Expect to taste plenty of the namesake bivalve, hailing from Prince Edward Island. Priced by the pound and steamed in no fewer than twenty globally inspired broths, they are best with some killer hand-cut skinny fries. Mussels No. 23 refers to the nightly special, perhaps featuring a succulent bath of hot and sour soup bobbing with soft tofu, bits of pork, wood ear mushrooms, and dried red chili flakes.

FP Patisserie

French

1293 Third Ave. (at 74th St.)

Subway: 77 St
Phone: 212-717-5252
Web: www.francoispayard.com
Prices: $$

Lunch daily
Dinner Mon – Sat

This enticing emporium marks Francois Payard's return to the Upper East Side, where sophisticated sweet-tooths can either grab a box of handmade chocolates or macarons to take home, or stay for an enjoyable meal in the *salon de thé*. Popular among the ladies, this petite room carries a sunny color scheme.

Salads paired with freshly baked bread comprise their fine lighter fare; while heartier appetites will enjoy a choice of *croque monsieur*, or perhaps foie gras- and mushroom *duxelles*-stuffed chicken breast dressed with an intense mushroom jus.

It goes without saying one must save room for dessert. Walk up to the sparkling display case and select any one of the fabulous creations, like the simply stated caramel tart for a salt-flecked piece of heaven.

Il Riccio

Italian XX

B3

152 E. 79th St. (bet. Lexington & Third Aves.)

Subway: 77 St — Lunch & dinner daily
Phone: 212-639-9111
Web: N/A
Prices: $$

Long-standing and low-key, this is just the right spot to recharge after an afternoon of perusing fabulous neighborhood boutiques or meandering through the nearby museums. Il Riccio has a cozy feel with warm ochre walls, simple furnishings, and an assemblage of photographs. Regulars know to head back to the enclosed garden to enjoy their meal.

The cooking here is fuss-free, pasta-focused, and lovingly dedicated to the Amalfi Coast. Favored dishes include roasted red peppers topped with salty, marinated white anchovies; or *fedelini primavera*, a rustic presentation of thin pasta strands tossed with an assortment of fresh vegetables and well-seasoned tomato sauce. Grilled fish dressed simply with olive oil and lemon rounds out the menu.

Il Ristorante Rosi

Italian XXX

A3

903 Madison Ave. (bet. 72nd & 73rd Sts.)

Subway: 77 St — Lunch & dinner daily
Phone: 212-517-7700
Web: www.salumeriarosi.com
Prices: $$$

Madison Avenue has no shortage of shops, but none is more detrimental to your waistline (or wallet) than the Parmacotto *salumi* counter displayed at the front of Il Ristorante Rosi. Dare to indulge in more than just a snack? Venture further inside, and you'll be rewarded with a snazzy dining room complete with crimson walls, white leather furnishings, and frescoes and sculptures thrown in for dramatic effect.

Start with a plate of that paper-thin *salumi* before moving on to enjoyable cooking that includes *melanzane* roasted until silky soft, capped by grated parmesan turned golden under the broiler, and plated with diced tomatoes and chickpea purée. Non-meat eaters will be happy to find porcini risotto or a satisfying cauliflower "steak."

Il Salumaio

Italian

1731 Second Ave. (bet. 89th & 90th Sts.)

Subway: 86 St (Lexington Ave.)
Phone: 646-852-6876
Web: www.ilsalumaiony.com
Prices: $$

Lunch Fri – Sun
Dinner nightly

Yorkville residents have been doubly blessed by Fabio and Ciro Casella. First, their pizzeria San Matteo arrived on the scene with its wood-fired specialties. Now, the brothers bring more delightfully rustic fare by way of primo panini and pastas, to this underserved neighborhood.

The slender space seats only a handful, but sidewalk tables increase the accommodations. Cured meats and imported cheeses temptingly stocked in a refrigerator display case are skillfully manifested atop luscious plates like the Arthur Avenue—basically a *panino* bursting with ham, *salume*, mortadellla, and provolone. The *paccheri all'Amatriciana* or fat tubes of perfectly cooked pasta in a thick tomato ragù seasoned with onion, pancetta and *pecorino Romano*, is a delight unto itself.

J.G. Melon

American

1291 Third Ave. (at 74th St.)

Subway: 77 St
Phone: 212-744-0585
Web: N/A
Prices: $$

Lunch & dinner daily

Posterity will remember J.G. Melon as a classic and coveted New York institution. Make your way into this cave set upon a cozy Upper East corner, where the timeless vibe and cheery staff make up most of its allure. Drinks are steadily churned out at a dark wood bar, so arrive early to avoid the hordes.

The focus at this multi-generational saloon is the burger—perhaps paired with a lip-smacking Bloody Mary at brunch? The warm toasted bun topped with meat cooked on a griddle to rosy pink is coupled with onions, pickles, and crispy crinkle-cut fries. Be forewarned: you will go through the entire stack of napkins before finishing. Other simple pleasures include standards like salads, steaks, and eggs. Seal the meal with a chocolate chip-studded layer cake.

JoJo

Contemporary XX

B1

160 E. 64th St. (bet. Lexington & Third Aves.)

Subway: Lexington Av - 63 St — Lunch & dinner daily
Phone: 212-223-5656
Web: www.jojorestaurantnyc.com
Prices: $$$

Chef Jean-Georges Vongerichten's little neighborhood bistro has been serving these affluent residents for nearly a generation, offering proof that although trends may come and go, classics remain steadfast.

Within Jojo's snug townhouse quarters, ritzy locals and well-heeled tourists dine at elegantly dressed tables—think starched linens and polished silver—amid terra-cotta tile floors, plum velvet banquettes, and toile drapery.

The look isn't fresh or exciting, but the cuisine makes up for it. Lunch offers great value for three courses that have featured a salad of warm asparagus with avocado; pan-roasted hake and sautéed wild mushrooms dressed with lime segments and a ginger-scallion condiment; and a zucchini cake with pecan ice cream for dessert.

Jones Wood Foundry

Gastropub X

C3

401 E. 76th St. (bet. First & York Aves.)

Subway: 77 St — Lunch & dinner daily
Phone: 212-249-2771
Web: www.joneswoodfoundry.com
Prices: $$

Jones Wood Foundry is a stateside take on a classic public house—the kind that Chef/partner Jason Hicks frequented during his childhood in England—that serves the same style of spot-on pub grub. The front bar is a choice spot to sip and savor from the selection of drafts. The space then opens up to a seating area of marble-topped tables, handsome button-tufted brown leather banquettes, and plush red velvet chairs. Beer-battered haddock and chips with tartar sauce, hearty meat pie of the day, and coronation chicken sandwich—the classic mid-century chicken salad dressed with intensely yellow, curry-tinged mayonnaise on toasted baguette—are a few of the true-blue hits. The vibe is charming, but dinner offers much more ambience than midday service.

Kaia

South African

1614 Third Ave. (bet. 90th & 91st Sts.)

Subway: 86 St (Lexington Ave.) Dinner nightly
Phone: 212-722-0490
Web: www.kaiawinebar.com
Prices: $$

This South African wine bar takes its name from the word for shelter. It is owned by a native South African who chased her dreams of stardom to New York City, while building an impressive resume of work in some in the city's finer dining rooms. The space has a comfortable appeal, spotlighting a lively dining counter as well as high and low wood tables.
Discover a plethora of wines not just from South Africa, but also South America and New York. To accompany your glass, select from the interesting small plates like "spear and shield" of bacon-wrapped asparagus with cheddar-stuffed mushroom caps; or *vark ribbetjies en vark pensie*, a pork duo of ribs glazed with honey and *rooibos* tea plus belly braised in Indian pale ale dressed with candied kumquats.

Lusardi's

Italian

1494 Second Ave. (bet. 77th & 78th Sts.)

Subway: 77 St Lunch Mon – Fri
Phone: 212-249-2020 Dinner nightly
Web: www.lusardis.com
Prices: $$$

With its pumpkin-colored walls, dark woodwork, and vintage posters, this beloved old-school mainstay offers a menu that relishes in decadant Northern Italian cooking. Picture an array of fresh pasta and veal, richly embellished with cream, authentic cheeses, or truffle-infused olive oil.
The *insalata bianca* is a monotone-white yet delightfully refreshing composition of shaved fennel, sliced artichoke hearts, chopped endive, and slivered hearts of palm dressed with lemony vinaigrette and *Parmigiano Reggiano*, all singing with black pepper freshly ground tableside. *Paccheri* in *salsa affumicata* presents large pasta tubes draped with plum tomato sauce that has been enriched with creamy smoked mozzarella and strewn with bits of roasted eggplant.

Maison Kayser

French

B3

1294 Third Ave. (at 74th St.)

Subway: 77 St — Lunch & dinner daily
Phone: 212-744-3100
Web: www.maison-kayser-usa.com
Prices: **$$**

Maison Kayser is the US flagship of French baker extraordinaire Eric Kayser whose skill with flour and water has yielded him a collection of *boulangeries* that span the globe. Arrive to find a small retail area stocked with temptation and a bustling café that comforts guests in an oak-floored, mirror-paneled room staffed with servers sporting Breton tees. Get the ordering out of the way to speed up the arrival of the bread, made from organic New York-grown grain and studded with walnuts or dried fruit, rustically presented in a burlap sack.

From the menu, enjoy the likes of shrimp- and lump crabmeat-topped guacamole; traditional bœuf Bourguignon presented in a cocotte; or pistachio éclair. All are worthy complements to the array of bread.

Marché du Sud

French

B4

1136 First Ave. (bet. 62nd & 63rd Sts.)

Subway: Lexington Av - 59 St — Lunch & dinner daily
Phone: 212-207-4900
Web: www.marchedusud.com
Prices: **$$**

Open all day and offering everything from a morning cappuccino to a late evening digestif, Marché du Sud wears many hats—gourmet shop, wine bar, dining room—without a glitch.

Back issues of *Paris Match* (and other French-language titles) double as menu covers. Speaking of which, be sure to peruse the Alsatian *tarte flambée* offerings. *Cette cousine* of pizza features a thin, flaky crust presented with an array of toppings. Traditionalists should go for the *l'authentique* loaded with crème fraîche, lardons, onions, and Gruyère. The remainder of the menu also offers enjoyable specials like sienna-hued *soupe de poisson*, a lush coalescence of seafood, saffron, orange peel, tomato, and herbs. Follow this with roasted chicken draped in zesty mustard-cream sauce.

Maya

B4 — Mexican XX

1191 First Ave. (bet. 64th & 65th Sts.)

Subway: 68 St - Hunter College — Lunch & dinner daily
Phone: 212-585-1818
Web: www.richardsandoval.com
Prices: $$

Upscale Mexican dining thrives at Chef Richard Sandoval's *muy* popular Maya. Slick with polished dark wood furnishings, vibrant tiled flooring, and accent walls the color of a ripe mango, this is always a fun scene. Adding to the revelry is the Tequileria, Maya's bar with a serious focus on agave spirits.

Antojitos, such as squash blossom quesadillas and their trio of salsas, headline as starters. Tasty tacos are stuffed with smoked brisket and creamy chili slaw. Heartier dishes feature *huitlacoche* and wild mushroom enchiladas swathed in a creamy, fire roasted poblano chile sauce. *Especialidades* like achiote-marinated carne asada with cactus-green bean salad and bacon-wrapped jalapeños display the kitchen's contemporary flair.

Maz Mezcal

C2 — Mexican X

316 E. 86th St. (bet. First & Second Aves.)

Subway: 86 St (Lexington Ave.) — Lunch Sat – Sun, Dinner nightly
Phone: 212-472-1599
Web: www.mazmezcal.com
Prices: $$

This family-run, longtime haunt still draws its legion of neighborhood regulars for satisfying and traditional Mexican food. The front room is brightened by turquoise walls and quirkily decorated with watermelon-themed artwork; while the back room is warmer with its terra-cotta-colored backdrop. Welcomes are personalized, and the dining rooms are filled with guests chatting and quizzing the staff about their latest news.

Chips and salsas are a crunchy and colorful precursor to Maz Mescal's commendable specialties. Family-friendly combination platters are a popular option, but a glimpse and whiff of the sizzling fajita platter might be all the enticement necessary to sway your decision. For dessert, brandy and Kahlua spike their take on the classic flan.

Mezzaluna

B3

1295 Third Ave. (bet. 74th & 75th Sts.)

Subway: 77 St — Lunch & dinner daily
Phone: 212-535-9600
Web: www.mezzalunanyc.com
Prices: $$

Time and time again, this Italian idol hits the spot. Just take a look at the jubilant crowd huddled together at pink granite tables throughout the Euro-chic yet cozy room. One wall is yellow while another is completely lined with 77 depictions of the restaurant's name, beneath a sky-blue ceiling painted with clouds.

Neighborhood residents and savvy tourists know Mezzaluna's unfussy Italian cooking is guaranteed to be *delizioso*. Take for example the veal Milanese—pounded thin and delicately crunchy, simply topped with peppery wild arugula and sliced cherry tomatoes. Other hits include pizzas that emerge from a wood-burning oven unceremoniously stationed in a corner, or beef carpaccio with a choice of toppings like artichokes and *Parmigiano Reggiano*.

Moti Mahal Delux

Indian

B4

1149 First Ave. (at 63rd St.)

Subway: Lexington Av - 63 St — Lunch & dinner daily
Phone: 212-371-3535
Web: www.motimahaldelux.us
Prices: $$

This corner spot marks the first American location of a fine dining chain that began in Delhi and now boasts outposts throughout India. Here in NYC, Moti Mahal Delux offers two distinct seating areas: an earth-toned dining room and windowed sidewalk atrium.

Their Northern dominated cuisine traces back to the kitchens of the Mughal Empire, which brought Muslim influences to the Indo subcontinent. Tasty tandoori preparations factor heavily, like *anardana tikka*—grilled white meat chicken infused with a pomegranate and black pepper marinade. Delightful flavors abound through the home-style mutton curry showcasing a brick-red sauce of spiced tomato, onion, and ginger; hot *paratha* dusted with dried mint; and mustard seed- and curry leaf-infused lemon rice.

Nick's

Pizza

1814 Second Ave. (at 94th St.)

Subway: 96 St (Lexington Ave.) — Lunch & dinner daily
Phone: 212-987-5700
Web: www.nicksnyc.com
Prices:

This Manhattan outpost of the Forest Hills original named for owner Nick Angelis is a cozy setup focused on the pizza station, where dexterous *pizzaiolos* work the gas-fired oven and put on a show. Despite the continuing construction along Second Avenue, a devoted following still seeks out this favored neighborhood pizzeria.

Begin with the spinach salad slicked with hot bacon fat and red wine vinegar before enjoying a thin-crusted but tender and nicely chewy pie, decked with the likes of fennel sausage crumbles, crushed tomatoes, creamy mozzarella, and sweet basil. A delightful finish is Nick's signature cannoli, served as a freshly made *pizzelle* cookie filled upon order with satiny smooth sweetened ricotta and sprinkled with crushed pistachios.

The Nuaa

Thai

1122 First Ave. (bet. 61st & 62nd St.)

Subway: 59 St — Lunch & dinner daily
Phone: 212-888-2899
Web: N/A
Prices: $$

The Nuaa offers a certain sultry vibe to this rather blah, trafficky stretch—it's dim and moody even in the middle of the day. Shimmering gold accents pop against the room's brown leather seating, carved woodwork, and dark palette.

Fans of Thai cuisine will enjoy the pleasantly pungent notes throughout the selection of salads and noodle dishes. Crunchy curried rice salad features deep-fried nuggets strewn with Thai sausage and lemongrass served with plenty of shallots, long beans, and lettuce, and a drizzle of Kaffir lime-mint vinaigrette. The *kanom jeen* features thin rice noodles soaked in a mildly spiced coconut-rich yellow curry that is generously stocked with huge lumps of crab meat, chopped pickled mustard greens, and caper berries.

Orsay

French XX

B3

1057 Lexington Ave. (at 75th St.)

Subway: 77 St — Lunch & dinner daily
Phone: 212-517-6400
Web: www.orsayrestaurant.com
Prices: $$

With its mahogany paneling, hand-laid mosaic tiles, windows dressed with lacy café curtains, and pewter bar, this luxe brasserie is a painstakingly realized vision of art nouveau. Orsay proves its dedication to French tradition from the sidewalk seating to marble stairs leading up to a private room. Chef Antoine Camin's cheese soufflés sustain much of the well-dressed crowd here, but the classic menu brings much more. *Soupe de poisson* is a richly satisfying fusion of fish, tomatoes, fennel, and herbs; brook trout is presented *à la Grenobloise* with browned butter, capers, and finely diced croutons; and roasted pork tenderloin arrives with savoy cabbage, apples, and hard cider sauce. The soaked *baba au rhum* is as fine a rendition as any *à* Paris.

Parlor Steakhouse

Steakhouse XX

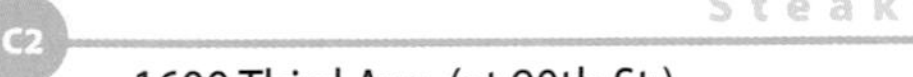

C2

1600 Third Ave. (at 90th St.)

Subway: 86 St (Lexington Ave.) — Lunch & dinner daily
Phone: 212-423-5888
Web: www.parlorsteakhouse.com
Prices: $$$

Set amid subway construction, sexy Parlor Steakhouse has sadly remained under the radar. Boasting top-shelf Belgian and American beers as well as a clubby vibe, this unpretentious steakhouse seems to have it all...including space. Dine here—there's even elbow room for the classically large portions of high-quality beef.

Meat really stands out as does the expert seasoning. Find evidence of this in hand-cut steak tartare, tossed with pickled onions, mustard, and gherkins topped with rye croutons. Served over sweet potato purée with smoked bacon and caramelized onions, the garlicky, herb-crusted Berkshire pork chop is a culmination of divine flavors. Cheesecake crowned with candied pecans and caramel sauce offers an extravagant yet excellent finale.

Persepolis

Persian

1407 Second Ave. (bet. 73rd & 74th Sts.)

Subway: 77 St — Lunch & dinner daily
Phone: 212-535-1100
Web: www.persepolisnewyork.com
Prices: **$$**

Silky-smooth spreads, homemade yogurt, grilled meats, and fragrantly spiced stews have solidified Persepolis' reputation as one of the city's finest Persian restaurants. Linen-draped tables, spacious banquettes, and big windows facing Second Avenue fashion a look that inspires dressing up (or not). Service is always gracious, if at times earnest.

The kitchen shines with its eggplant *halim*, a creamy, steaming roasted eggplant and onion dip with tender lentils and a dollop of yogurt on top. A kebab duo of saffron-tinged chicken and grilled beef are both succulent successes, served with basmati rice flecked with bits of sour cherry. For dessert, try the tart-sweet Persian lemon ice studded with bits of rice noodles and doused in deep red cherry syrup.

Quatorze Bis

French 

323 E. 79th St. (bet. First & Second Aves.)

Subway: 77 St — Lunch Tue – Sun, Dinner daily
Phone: 212-535-1414
Web: N/A
Prices: **$$**

Savoring a meal at this ever-lovely bistro is like taking a break from the constant evolution that is life in New York City, where tastes change faster than you can tweet. The red-lacquer façade, claret-velvet banquettes, and sophisticated clientele are all much the same as when Quatorze Bis opened almost 25 years ago.

Though the ambience's timeless appeal is noteworthy, the traditional French cooking is their key to success. Frilly chicory, drizzled with hot bacon fat and red wine vinegar, and pocked with lardons, croutons, and shallots makes for a very hearty, *très* French salad. Seafood sausage is plump and studded with sweet red pepper and pine nuts. Daily specials keep the menu new, with dishes like striped bass served beside a creamy sorrel sauce.

The Regency Bar & Grill

Contemporary XX

A1

540 Park Ave. (at 61st St.)

Subway: Lexington Av - 59 St

Lunch & dinner daily

Phone: 212-339-4050

Web: www.regencybarandgrill.com

Prices: $$$

The Loews Regency now serves up a contemporary vision of hotel dining that can stand entirely on its own. Fully-stocked glass-and-metal shelves at the bar invites passersby to ditch Park Avenue for a cocktail before sinking into the plush dining room, where ivory leather and sky-blue velvet seating is laid out over carpeting inspired by Italian mosaic tiles.

The setting's fresh face is a fitting home for Chef Dan Silverman's au courant cuisine in which shaved radishes and julienned snow peas are combined with pickled shiitake mushrooms and sesame dressing for an inspired salad. Grilled double-cut lamb loin chop, cooked perfectly to spec and plated with a stack of panisse- and mint-infused béarnaise sauce, is a sweet dream in the making.

Ristorante Morini

Italian XXX

B2

1167 Madison Ave. (bet. 85th & 86th Sts.)

Subway: 86 St (Lexington Ave.)

Lunch Mon – Fri
Dinner nightly

Phone: 212-249-0444

Web: www.ristorantemorini.com

Prices: $$$

Altamarea Group's prime Madison Avenue corner boasts a lively street-level lounge and second story window-lined dining room where even children in tow are properly attired for lunch. Despite the high-rent address, Ristorante Morini offers an economical lunch prix-fixe, a late-night pasta special early in the week, and family-style Sunday supper.

Slick Italian dining is the draw here, as demonstrated by the likes of bigeye tuna crudo plated with pickled onions, nettle pesto, and fried salt-cured capers with a crouton-like crunch; or veal Milanese draped with prosciutto and melted fontina. Desserts continue to be a highlight, as in a cooling *coppa* of vanilla bean gelato and strawberry sorbet, whipped cream, basil, and crunchy meringue.

San Matteo ☺

Italian XX

C2

1739 Second Ave. (at 90th St.)

Subway: 86 St (Lexington Ave.) — Lunch Fri – Sun
Phone: 212-426-6943 — Dinner nightly
Web: www.sanmatteopanuozzo.com
Prices: ⊜

This tiny pizzeria has made a big splash with its *panuozzo*, a regional specialty hailing from Campania that's a cross between a calzone and *panino*. The puffy plank of tender, salted dough emerges from San Matteo's hand-built, wood-fired oven crusty and smoke-infused before being sliced and stuffed with first-rate ingredients (highlights include the *ortolano's* fresh, house-made mozzarella, grilled eggplant, roasted sweet peppers, and baby arugula).
The room is graciously attended to and perpetually crowded with neighborhood folks stuffing their faces. In addition to the appetizing house signature, other favorites feature fresh salads such as escarole with Gaeta olives, capers, and gorgonzola; Neapolitan-style pizza; or the day's special baked pasta.

Shanghai Pavilion

Chinese XX

B3

1378 Third Ave. (bet. 78th & 79th Sts.)

Subway: 77 St — Lunch & dinner daily
Phone: 212-585-3388
Web: N/A
Prices: $$

Polished Shanghai Pavilion offers plenty of choice, but the slurp-inducing steamed juicy buns are what keeps the crowds returning time and again. Pay attention to the list of chef's picks, which should include firm chunks of grey sole braised in sweet rice wine sauce. This Shanghainese specialty is studded with crisp pea pods and plump goji berries for a memorable combination of subtle elements. Clean, simple flavors underscore every bit of the soft bean curd sheets tossed with fresh soybeans and pickled cabbage. Unique tastes are a highlight in "Hang Zhou" beef presented in a bamboo steamer lined with cabbage, topped with strips of tender beef and slivered green onions, dressed in soy sauce and spicy oil.
Service is as upscale as the attractive room.

The Simone

Contemporary XX

B2

151 E. 82nd St. (bet. Lexington & Third Aves.)

Subway: 86 St (Lexington Ave.) Dinner Mon – Sat
Phone: 212-772-8861
Web: www.thesimonerestaurant.com
Prices: $$$

Chef Chip Smith and wife Tina Vaughn prove hospitality isn't dead at their posh dining room, where genuine and forthcoming service—combined with excellent cuisine—has Upper East Siders giddy.

The bonhomie present here sets the perfect tone for astute cooking typified by intricately composed plates. A savory tart to start boasts a shell of perfect house-made *pâté feuilletée* and is luxuriously filled with Gruyère, prosciutto, and a sunny-side up egg. Braised rabbit thigh—dusted with Dijon mustard-smacked breadcrumbs, grilled loin, and fried liver—is presented with pan-fried herbed spaetzle and bacon-wrapped prunes. For an old-fashioned finish, try the Lord Baltimore: a tower of Bourbon-soaked sponge, dried fruits, pecans, and torched soft meringue.

Spigolo

Italian XX

B3

1471 Second Ave. (bet. 76th & 77th Sts.)

Subway: 77 St Dinner nightly
Phone: 212-744-1100
Web: www.spigolonyc.com
Prices: $$

This wildly popular trattoria has moved to a new address merely steps from its old location. Cozy and inviting, the larger setting offers a comfortable bar area and seating in a warm, modern room of knotty pine flooring, white stucco walls, and dark wood beams.

This good-looker's founding husband-and-wife chef team are no longer involved, but the kitchen remains steady in the hands of Chef Joseph d'Angelo, who turns out classic cuisine with a Mediterranean accent. Slices of marinated fluke dabbed with lavender-hued Kalamata olive aïoli is a bracing crudo of the day. Starters include crunchy eggplant "meatballs" nestled in tomato sauce; while chewy *cavatelli* with shredded red wine-braised lamb is just one of the most heartwarming plates on offer.

Sushi of Gari ✿

C3

402 E. 78th St. (bet. First & York Aves.)

Subway: 77 St — Dinner Tue – Sun
Phone: 212-517-5340
Web: www.sushiofgari.com
Prices: $$$$

Great things come in unassuming packages—such is the case at Sushi of Gari, where the handsome, but decidedly unflashy décor belies a transporting omakase experience.

Sold? A few insider tips from the regulars and you're on your way: make your reservation weeks in advance, as the dining room stays quite booked; score a seat only at the sushi counter, not just to enjoy those freshly scored slices of sushi straight from the chef's hand, but also because the congenial vibe at the bar surpasses the somewhat rushed experience at the tables; and do keep an eye on those prices, which can add up quicker than a trip to Target.

Sushi of Gari is Chef Masatoshi "Gari" Sugio's flagship restaurant, and the legendary chef's trademark creativity and skill shine in spades here. A night indulging in his omakase might include delicately seared kanpachi, topped with a lightly poached quail egg; wildly fresh Japanese red snapper paired with pine nuts, bright greens, and fried lotus root; tender, seared toro with garlic and ginger sauce; or perfectly poached yellowtail, laced with sesame sauce and a sprinkle of chives.

Sound too good to wait for a reservation? Sushi of Gari also offers a booming takeout service.

Sushi Sasabune

401 E. 73rd St. (at First Ave.)

Subway: 77 St — Lunch Tue – Fri
Phone: 212-249-8583 — Dinner Tue – Sat
Web: N/A
Prices: $$$$

True, Sushi Sasabune has a drab dining room with service that is best described as efficient. That said, everyone comes for their omakase-only menu of pristine fish and skillfully prepared sushi, which deserves every ounce of its high praise. For those who don't already know the drill, abandon any idea of getting a spicy tuna roll—only truly authentic Japanese cuisine is served here. And it happens to be fantastic.

The team sends out the finest from behind the counter and instructs you on exactly how to eat it, as in "soy sauce" or "no soy sauce." Cede control and delight in lean *maguro* drizzled with ponzu, *kurodai* nigiri sprinkled with crunchy sesame seeds, firm *houbou* brushed with hot ginger-soy sauce, and a creamy blue crab hand roll.

Sushi Seki

1143 First Ave. (bet. 62nd & 63rd Sts.)

Subway: Lexington Av - 59 St — Dinner Mon – Sat
Phone: 212-371-0238
Web: N/A
Prices: $$

An Upper East Side standby that doesn't actually look like much, Sushi Seki combines exceptional sushi and sashimi with a casual vibe that keeps neighborhood loyalists packed in for late-night dinners and take-out. It may seem like a simple restaurant for a very good spicy tuna roll, but their excellent and unique omakase is what put it on the map as a worthy favorite.

The quality and creativity of each bite shows the chef's training at Sushi of Gari, with added twists. Sample excellent toro chopped with ginger that is at once tender, fatty, and crunchy over rice; or a slice of fatty salmon with avocado sauce. Don't miss the signature hand roll of toasted nori surrounding juicy chopped scallop with crunchy tempura flakes, tobiko, and spicy mayo.

Tanoshi

Japanese 

1372 York Ave. (bet. 73rd & 74th Sts.)

Subway: 77 St — Dinner Tue – Sat
Phone: 917-265-8254
Web: www.tanoshisushinyc.com
Prices: $$$

For three seatings nightly Chef Toshio Oguma works his magic at this 10-seat, omakase-only Yorkville sushi haunt. The ocean's currents dictate the catch of the day, but here's what you can always expect as decreed by the chef: loosely formed body temperature rice and room temperature fish cured Edo-style.

Tanoshi's pristine piscine selection will reveal an enticing bounty. Items can be as simple as a piece of deep ocean sea bream brushed with soy sauce and touched with sea salt, or as dressed up as a salt- and vinegar-cured branzini topped with sweet pickled white kelp and marinated cherry leaf. Five-second-poached Hokkaido sea scallops and salmon roe marinated for 48-hours in soy, honey, and sake may fall somewhere in between courses and are quite excellent.

Tiella

1109 First Ave. (bet. 60th & 61st Sts.)

Subway: Lexington Av - 59 St — Lunch Tue – Sat
Phone: 212-588-0100 — Dinner nightly
Web: www.tiellanyc.com
Prices: $$

Neapolitan specialties and gracious hospitality make Tiella absolutely worth seeking out. This railcar-sized space is set along a traffic-clogged stretch, but once inside, the ambience is sweet with espresso-tinted wood furnishings set against cream walls and exposed brick.

Petite pizzas baked in the wood-fired oven arrive bearing fresh mozzarella, spicy *'nduja,* and fava beans, among other tasty combinations. Starters include *gallette,* chickpea flour fritters stacked with *stracciatella* and shaved prosciutto, drizzled with fig syrup, and stuck with a sprig of rosemary. Enjoyable *primi* include risotto studded with diced artichokes, pancetta, and showered with shaved black truffle. Desserts like the lemon-soaked *delizia al limone* are homespun delights.

Uva 

C3 · Italian 

1486 Second Ave. (bet. 77th & 78th Sts.)

Subway: 77 St — Lunch Sat – Sun
Phone: 212-472-4552 — Dinner nightly
Web: www.uvanyc.com
Prices: $$

Perpetually packed and always pleasing, this cousin of elegant Lusardi's is a rocking, rustic good time. Votive-filled nooks and fringed sconces cast a flattering light on the inviting room furnished with straw-seat chairs and wooden tables laden with wine bar-themed small plates.

Cheeses, meats, and salads are fine ways to start. The *insalata di manzo* is a tasty hybrid of all three—shaved lean beef topped by peppery young arugula, shaved parmesan, and pickled mushrooms. Join the crowds at the start of the week for Meatball Mondays offering three courses revolving around…you guessed it. Sample the hearty beef meatball ravioli garnished with sliced artichoke hearts, silky smooth tomato sauce, and a drizzle of extra virgin olive oil.

Wa Jeal

C2 · Chinese 

1588 Second Ave. (bet. 82nd & 83rd Sts.)

Subway: 86 St (Lexington Ave.) — Lunch & dinner daily
Phone: 212-396-3339
Web: www.wajealrestaurant.com
Prices: $$

This Sichuan chili house is not merely weathering the local torrent of Second Avenue subway construction; their spotless room and tasty food will make you forget that the outside world exists. The ambience is upscale and appealing, combining pale walls, prescient images of wicked-red chilies, an engaging staff, and a substantial wine list.

The chef's specialties reveal the most noteworthy cooking, as in diced fish and crispy tofu stir-fried in a reddish-brown chili sauce speckled with chili seeds and sliced green onions. Sautéed chicken with spiced miso is another pleasure, mixing crisped, boneless pieces, wok-fried with roasted red chilies and charred jalapeños. Tender baby bok choy with garlic is a refreshing contrast to such potent flavors.

Yefsi

Greek XX

C3

1481 York Ave. (bet. 78th & 79th Sts.)

Subway: 77 St
Phone: 212-535-0293
Web: www.yefsiestiatorio.com
Prices: $$

Dinner nightly

Chef Christos Christou brings a wealth of experience to the kitchen of this Yorkville standout. Having manned the stoves at some of the city's Greek stalwarts, the Cyprus-native knows his way around his Aegean and Mediterranean coastal specialties.

Begin with salads showcasing superb feta or explore the array of luscious meze including zucchini and eggplant chips with tzatziki, octopus braised in *mavrodafni* or wine-spiked tomato sauce, and grilled sausages over black-eyed peas. Entrées entice with freshness and flavor, such as the wow-inducing nightly special of grilled tiger shrimp. Served head-on and lobster-like in size and texture, they are accompanied by a mound of creamy spinach rice and squeeze of fresh lemon—the perfect embellishment.

Remember, stars (✿✿✿...✿) are awarded for cuisine only! Elements such as service and décor are not a factor.

Upper West Side

The Upper West Side is the epitome of classic New York. Proudly situated between Central Park and the Hudson River, this family-friendly neighborhood is one of the Big Apple's most distinct and upscale localities that has a near-religious belief in its own way of doing things. Whether it's because these charming streets cradle some of the best cafés in town, or that life here means constantly tripping over culture vultures destined for world-renowned Lincoln Center, area residents cannot imagine living elsewhere. On the heels of this famed institution is **Dizzy's Club Coca-Cola**—one of the better places to spend a night on the town. From its alluring vibe and exceptional jazz talent, to a stellar lineup of Southern food, audiences seem entranced by this imposing home to America's creative art form. The Upper West Side is also considered an intellectual hub—cue the distinguished presence of Columbia University to the north—and coveted real estate mecca with residential high-rises freckled amid quaint townhouses. In fact, legendary co-ops like *The Dakota* speak to the area's history, while agreeable eateries like **Épicerie Boulud** nourish its affluent tenants, hungry locals, and Ivy Leaguers on the run.

ALL IN THE FAMILY

Acknowledged for strolling, these sidewalks are stacked with charming diners and pre-war brownstones featuring polished parquet floors, intricate moldings, and bookish locals—arguing with equal gusto over the future of opera or if Barney Greengrass still prepares the best sturgeon. One is also likely to find these deep-rooted residents browsing the shelves at **Murray's** for killer cheese; while more discerning palates may seek gratification at **Cleopatra's Needle**—an old-time jazz club-cum-Middle Eastern eatery named for the monument in Central Park. However, if stirring live performances and open mic (on Sunday afternoons) served with a side of Mediterranean cuisine doesn't fit the bill, then keep it easy indoors by stocking up on a selection of simple yet tasty sandwiches from **Indie Food and Wine**. Nestled inside the Elinor Bunin Munroe Film Center, this interesting café aims to entice the palates of visitors to Lincoln Center by way of Italian sandwiches and salads, finished with American flair.

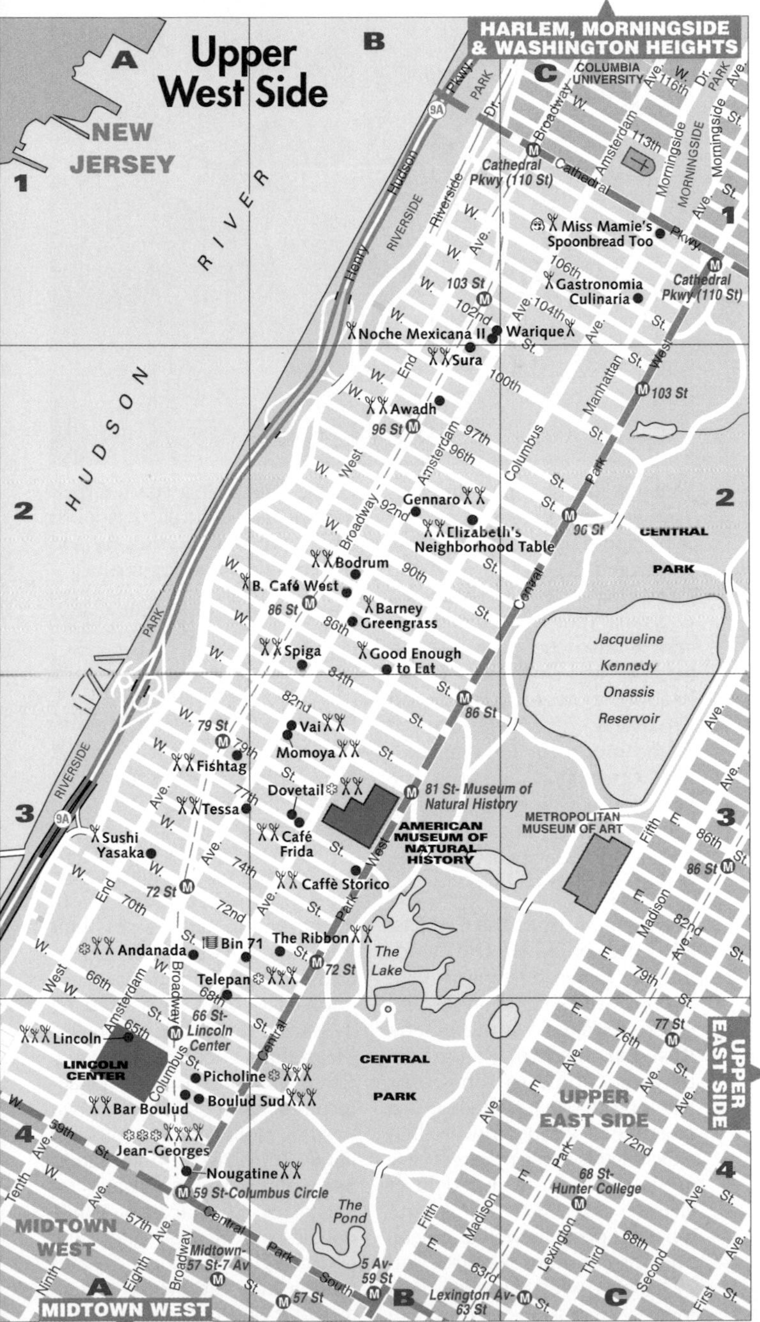
Upper West Side
HARLEM, MORNINGSIDE & WASHINGTON HEIGHTS
NEW JERSEY
HUDSON RIVER
COLUMBIA UNIVERSITY
Miss Mamie's Spoonbread Too
Gastronomia Culinaria
Noche Mexicana II
Warique
Sura
Awadh
Gennaro
Elizabeth's Neighborhood Table
Bodrum
B. Café West
Barney Greengrass
Spiga
Good Enough to Eat
Vai
Momoya
Fishtag
Dovetail
Tessa
Café Frida
Sushi Yasaka
Caffè Storico
Andanada
Bin 71
The Ribbon
Telepan
Lincoln
LINCOLN CENTER
Picholine
Boulud Sud
Bar Boulud
Jean-Georges
Nougatine
AMERICAN MUSEUM OF NATURAL HISTORY
METROPOLITAN MUSEUM OF ART
CENTRAL PARK
Jacqueline Kennedy Onassis Reservoir
The Lake
The Pond
UPPER EAST SIDE
MIDTOWN WEST
59 St-Columbus Circle
81 St- Museum of Natural History
66 St-Lincoln Center
68 St-Hunter College
Lexington Av-63 St
5 Av-59 St
Midtown-57 St-7 Av

Sitting within shouting distance, **The Tangled Vine** places fine wine and elegant eats under a warm and accessible spotlight. Presenting an extraordinary list of organic varietals, this boutique spot is also *the* perfect roost for a sip and small plate before heading south for a show...on Broadway, of course. But, if in the mood for familiar, old-time kitsch, find at seat at **The Cottage**, a Chinese-American standby serving nostalgic items late into the night for area families and caffeinated scholars.

Migrating from the Far East and back to the Med, prepare for an evening in with *nonna* by stocking up on sips and other specialties from **Salumeria Rosi Parmacotto**. Regardless of your choice to dine-in or take-out, this Italian stallion is a guaranteed good time. Wallet-watching residents may rest easy as the price is always right at **Celeste**—known for churning out a perfect pizza as well as a regal Sunday afternoon repast. And in keeping with the value-meal theme, "Recession Specials" are all the rage at legendary **Gray's Papaya**, the politically outspoken (check the window slogans) and quintessential hot dog chain.

BRUNCH AND BAKE

This dominantly residential region also jumped on the bakery-brunch bandwagon long before its counterparts; and today, its paths are rarely short on calorie-rich treats. From chocolates at **Mondel** or a trove of treasures at **Urbani Truffles**, to madeleines at **La Toulousaine**, the Upper West flaunts it all. In-the-know tenants get their sweet fix at **Levain**, where the addiction to chocolate chip cookies is only surpassed by their size. Meanwhile, not unlike **Magnolia's** cupcake following, **Grandaisy Bakery** is an Italian-inspired confectionary known to string along a coterie of sugar fiends. True to its posh surrounds, **Sugar & Plumm** is yet another master of the macaron. While cookies are also on offer here and achieve near-legend status among kids, adults remain in awe of their brunch hits and sips.

A MEDLEY OF MARKETS

Such a "spirited" sense extends to all aspects of life in the Upper West Side—particularly food. For foodies and home cooks, the **Tucker Square Greenmarket** (anchored on West 66th; open on Thursdays and Saturdays) is popular for leafy greens and Mexican provisions—*papalo* anyone? Equally storied is the original **Fairway**, a culinary shrine to well-priced gourmet treats. Intrepid shoppers should brave its famously cramped elevator to visit the exclusively organic second floor. Finally, no trip here is complete without a visit to **Zabar's**—home of all things kosher. Ogle their olives; grab some knishes to nosh on; then take the time to admire a line of exquisite kitchen supplies. Yet still rest assured that smaller purveyors reside (and reign supreme) here. In fact, **Zingone Brothers**, once a fruit and vegetable stall, is now a famous, family owned-and-operated grocer that teems with conventional goodies...and treats you like a long-lost friend.

Andanada ✿

Spanish XX

A3

141 W. 69th St. (bet. Broadway & Columbus Ave.)

Subway: 72 St (Broadway) — Lunch Sat – Sun
Phone: 646-692-8762 — Dinner nightly
Web: www.andanada141.com
Prices: **$$$**

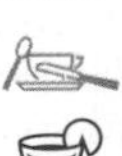

The ambience of this unselfconscious Spanish dynamo is vibrant and notably personable. Located just below street-level, Andanada is laid-back but still formal, with professional, customer-driven servers attending to your every whim. The crowd is lively yet sophisticated—whether seated at the date-friendly bar, pleasant glass atrium, or brick dining room decorated with memorable bullfighting scenes.

Like its surrounds, this noteworthy cuisine arrives much more beautiful than expected—clearly there is modern talent in Chef Manuel Berganza's kitchen. While the chef's creative expression has been met with mixed results of late, each dish can at its best be composed with an eye on innovative cooking as well as classic flavors.

Here, Catalan pork sausage is interestingly composed with shaved fennel and a fava bean casserole to elevate each bite. Then, pristine sardines are wrapped around *pan con tomate* and set over a bed of *picada*-style sauce for good flavor. Likewise, *berenjenas asada* is appealingly complex, served as cubed and puréed eggplant, balanced by a honey- and red wine-vinegar reduction. Simple-sounding mushroom croquettes combined with barely pickled mushrooms are gloriously earthy.

Awadh

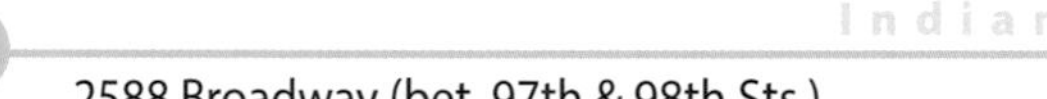

Indian XX

B2

2588 Broadway (bet. 97th & 98th Sts.)

Subway: 96 St (Broadway) — Lunch & dinner daily
Phone: 646-861-3604
Web: www.awadhnyc.com
Prices: **$$**

Awadh isn't an ordinary Indian spot, but one that advertises faithful flavors from Uttar Pradesh. This Northern Indian region excels in low- and slow-cooked *dum pukht* dishes, and the menu reads like a study in authenticity (there's no *tandoori* chicken in sight). Even the small room, polished and modern, is ideal for the city's well-traveled locals.

Top service and table settings further elevate the dining experience here that begins with *aloo chutney pulao* or basmati rice scattered with silky potatoes and spiced peas. Couple it with *nali ki nihari* (perfectly pink lamb in a creamy cardamom-infused curry) or *khaas* chicken korma rich with nuts for a profound and regal repast. Then cool down with minty *pudina* raita, and just like that, you've become a regular.

Bar Boulud

French XX

A4

1900 Broadway (bet. 63rd & 64th Sts.)

Subway: 66 St - Lincoln Center — Lunch & dinner daily
Phone: 212-595-0303
Web: www.barboulud.com
Prices: **$$$**

The restaurant that launched Chef Daniel Boulud's Upper West Side trifecta, Bar Boulud's first-class charcuterie and stellar wine list make it an idyllic prelude to any Lincoln Center show. Sit at the communal table with a hefty pour of a rare wine (ask about specials), and gaze at the tunnel-like dining room, crafted to mimic a barrel and clothed with Vik Muniz photographs of abstract wine spills. The wine-centric motif is as clear as the glassware.

While their array of sips are winning, meat and cheese boards are equally worthy, thanks to the genius of Gilles Verot. He's responsible for the award-winning *fromage de tête* (bright and clean in flavor). The rest of the menu is as infallible and includes everything from Provençal rabbit to the *Île flottante*.

Barney Greengrass

Deli

B2

541 Amsterdam Ave. (bet. 86th & 87th Sts.)

Subway: 86 St (Broadway) — Lunch Tue – Sun
Phone: 212-724-4707
Web: www.barneygreengrass.com
Prices:

Bagels and bialys reign supreme in this culinary institution, set amid a culturally rich stretch dotted with lavish synagogues and purveyors of authentic deli delights. Not all are created equal, though, and little details make all the difference inside this sturgeon king, lauded for its weathered décor featuring muraled walls, a storied past, and service that is as authentically NY as can be. It's the sort of spot families flock to for brunch—imagine a triple-decker (tongue, turkey, and Swiss cheese) on rye paired with a pickle, of course.

Whether you take-out or eat-in, chopped liver with caramelized onions and boiled egg is sure to sate. Finish with a perfect black-and-white cookie, rugelach, or rice pudding, which are all favorites and fittingly so.

B. Café West

Belgian 

B2

566 Amsterdam Ave. (bet. 87th & 88th Sts.)

Subway: 86 St (Broadway) — Lunch Sat – Sun, Dinner nightly
Phone: 212-873-0003
Web: www.bcafe.com
Prices: $$

Discover a slice of Belgium at this Upper West charmer, where the space may be narrow and deep, but the front bar is always in full swing at happy hour. The dining room is slightly elevated and very warm thanks to cozy bistro-style tables covered in white linen, a pressed-tin ceiling, and beaming waiters.

Posters and brass accents verge on cliché but all misgivings are pardoned upon tasting their fine and familiar favorites. Start with numerous *moules* options like delicious Malay *laksa* (red curry), Pamplona (chorizo), or red Duvel with hot sauce. Crunch your way through beer-battered fish and frites, before savoring a seafood *ostendaise* finished with shallots and cream.

Gaufre de Bruxelles drizzled with chocolate sauce is fit for a Belgian queen.

Bin 71

A3 Italian

237 Columbus Ave. (bet. 70th & 71st Sts.)

Subway: 72 St (Central Park West) Lunch & dinner Tue – Sun
Phone: 212-362-5446
Web: www.bin71.com
Prices: $$

An *enoteca* in the true sense of the term, Bin 71 focuses on *vino* with more than 30 varieties by the glass and over 60 by the bottle. A place to discover new blends and producers, this haunt is known to promote wine-focused conversation and amazing Italian-accented cuisine. An all-consuming U-shaped marble bar makes it easy—stay long enough and you're reaching for the menu.

Beyond excellent cheese and charcuterie, dishes feature flavorful herbs that perfume a grilled chicken, which comes on a bed of sautéed spinach with white bean ragout and sweet-sour caponata. Basil-scented North Atlantic cod soup swarming with creamy, thinly sliced potatoes hits the spot, as does dessert—maybe a fanned-out poached pear served with a scoop of *gianduja*-hazelnut gelato?

Bodrum

B2 Turkish

584 Amsterdam Ave. (bet. 88th & 89th Sts.)

Subway: 86 St (Broadway) Lunch & dinner daily
Phone: 212-799-2806
Web: www.bodrumnyc.com
Prices: $$

Like the white sandy beaches of its namesake fishing village in Turkey, Bodrum has amassed a following of area residents, who stop in for a Mediterranean escape complete with well-made food. Although nearby storefronts lack polish, this retreat breaks the mold with attentive service and charming touches like a brick-covered, wood-burning oven surrounded by blue mosaic-tiled walls.

Wines and spirits are straight out of Turkey, including the refreshing *raki*. Similarly, the menu leans towards classic plates with a few creative additions like pizza or braised leeks with rice. Regulars go for *b'stila djej*, a sweet-savory combo of cinnamon-scented chicken, almonds, and herbs wrapped in phyllo pastry; or stuffed cabbage filled with lamb, rice and dill.

Boulud Sud

Mediterranean XxX

A4

20 W. 64th St. (bet. Broadway & Central Park West)

Subway: 66 St - Lincoln Center — Lunch & dinner daily
Phone: 212-595-1313
Web: www.bouludsud.com
Prices: $$$

Far from a chichi French affair, Chef Daniel Boulud uses this ode to Mediterranean cuisine to explore all sides of the sea—from Morocco to Italy to Turkey and back again. Packed and lively, the dining room is airy with vaulted ceilings, natural lighting, and long striped banquettes. A semi-open kitchen allows a glimpse into the creation of deftly prepared delicacies.

The menu here is light yet dense with bright flavor, from the *crudo du jour* (perhaps cubes of hamachi with gently braised cauliflower, pignoli, white raisins, and herbs) to a tender octopus salad with Marcona almonds, arugula, and Jerez vinegar. Huge morsels of chicken with cous cous, wilted greens, and preserved lemons make a hearty dish, attractively served in a classic tagine vessel.

Café Frida

Mexican XX

B3

368 Columbus Ave. (bet. 77th & 78th Sts.)

Subway: 81 St - Museum of Natural History — Lunch & dinner daily
Phone: 212-712-2929
Web: www.cafefrida.com
Prices: $$

Margaritas and guacamole, the two tentpoles of any good Mexican restaurant, become the standard bearers for all others at this Columbus Avenue fiesta. Guests sample sips from the extensive tequila list at the intricately carved bar, or scoop up chipfuls of tart, chunky guacamole at tables throughout the bi-level space.

Regional specialties on the frequently changing menu let diners explore beyond the typical Mexican dishes, though traditional enchiladas simmered in deep, earthy *mole* are hearty and pleasing. Meanwhile, succulent lamb shank marinated in a *guajillo* sauce, avocado leaf, and olives is tender enough to make steak knives superfluous. Flaming dessert plantains with ice cream replace the same old *sopaipillas* for a new hot-and-cold sensation.

Caffè Storico

Italian XX

B3

170 Central Park West (in the NY Historical Society)

Subway: 81 St - Museum of Natural History — Lunch & dinner Tue – Sun
Phone: 212-485-9211
Web: www.nyhistory.org
Prices: **$$**

Gone are the days when museum food lacked character, and top Philadelphia restaurateur Stephen Starr's Caffè Storico proves it. Housed in the New York Historical Society, this marble-clad sparkler incorporates the collection into its design, with antique porcelain filling its sky-high shelves and views of the sculpture arcade.

Starr certainly knows how to please a crowd with marvelous salads and Italian-inspired dishes alongside unique wines from some of the country's emerging regions. Though *frittata del giorno* pocked with red peppers, tomato, and mozzarella, as well as panzanella with creamy burrata are eye-poppingly good, save room for a berry *crostata* whose flaky crust is perfectly accompanied by a smidge of vanilla ice cream.

Elizabeth's Neighborhood Table

American XX

B2

680 Columbus Ave. (at 93rd St.)

Subway: 96 St (Broadway) — Lunch & dinner daily
Phone: 212-280-6500
Web: www.elizabethsnyc.com
Prices: **$$**

Picket fencing, a shingled veranda, and mullioned windows might seem more at home in New England than this relatively forgotten nook of the Upper West Side, but Elizabeth's pops out from the surroundings to embrace her warm and homey name. The décor follows suit with a butcher-block table, white wainscoting, dark walls, and wide, comfortable tables. The kitchen promises a focus on carefully sourced organic and biodynamic ingredients—the kind that Granny used. (Evidently, their foremothers had access to quinoa and excellent feta.) Cobb salad is a pitch-perfect combination of grilled chicken, bacon, blue cheese, and more in a creamy dressing. End with a seasonal crumble that is tart and cinnamon-sweet with apples, berries, and vanilla ice cream.

Dovetail ✿

American 

B3

103 W. 77th St. (at Columbus Ave.)

Subway: 81 St - Museum of Natural History Dinner nightly
Phone: 212-362-3800
Web: www.dovetailnyc.com
Prices: **$$$**

Serious but never pretentious, Dovetail is a well-frequented culinary destination. Don't be duped by its slight façade, as the seriously overhauled space within now feels much more spacious, ultra-warm, and very chic. Then consider the delightfully accommodating and well-orchestrated staff only to find that it all comes together in perfect harmony.

Menus are handsomely bound in leather and highlight remarkably unique, ingredient-focused treats like a chickpea panisse coupled with garlicky aïoli; wedges of cool and tender chayote topped with crunchy pumpkin seeds and a creamy pumpkin purée; or king trumpet mushrooms coasting alongside paper-thin shavings of Asian pear, finished with an earthy and silky sunchoke paste. One large and plump potato *raviolo*, filled with creamy herb-flecked ricotta and floating in a pool of potato foam, is topped with a deep-fried sage leaf, which in turn makes for an ideal counterpoint to the rich layer beneath.

Feeling self-righteous after such a wonderfully wholesome feast? You may look forward to some good old-fashioned decadence by way of a bittersweet chocolate soufflé—very light, delightfully frothy, and enriched with just the right dab of cardamom-cocoa nib ice cream.

Fishtag

Seafood XX

A3

222 W. 79th St. (bet. Amsterdam Ave. & Broadway)

Subway: 79 St — Lunch Sat – Sun
Phone: 212-362-7470 — Dinner nightly
Web: www.michaelpsilakis.com
Prices: $$$

Slightly below street level in a classic townhouse, this charming restaurant from Chef Michael Psilakis offers the pleasures of the sea plus Mediterranean-inspired cuisine. Grab a seat at the marble-topped bar among exposed brick walls and wood panels for dishes that may be simple (grilled fish with greens, tomatoes, and olives) or inventive (headcheese-stuffed trout). A modern Greek salad—tomato, cucumber, feta, olives, and grilled kale in a simple red wine vinaigrette—is a lovely start. Excellent bruschetta-like treats may bring an assortment of ingredients over sourdough bread, such as grilled prawns, tangy feta, and red chili peppers. Save room for sheep's milk dumplings with tomato fonduta, baby spinach, braised lamb, and white anchovies.

Gastronomia Culinaria

Italian X

C1

53 W. 106th St. (bet. Columbus & Manhattan Aves.)

Subway: 103 St (Central Park West) — Dinner nightly
Phone: 212-663-1040
Web: www.gastronomiaculinaria.com
Prices: $$

From his experience in world-celebrated kitchens, Chef/owner Vincenzo Pezzilli has created this darling Italian restaurant that far exceeds the Big Apple's expectations. A native of Rome, he presides over his talented kitchen nightly, carefully watching over each sous as they transport authentic flavors to a dining room of locals and Ivy League professors. Paintings decorate exposed brick walls, and the soft lighting creates just the scene for satisfying dishes and Italian wines.

Pastas induce swoons, especially the enticingly chewy *strascinati alla norcina* with garlicky pork and porcini bathed in a delectable vegetable ragù. To close, the *tortino ai due cioccolati* (dark chocolate cake filled with white chocolate) is absolutely worth the 20-minute wait.

Gennaro

Italian

665 Amsterdam Ave. (bet. 92nd & 93rd Sts.)

Subway: 96 St (Broadway) Dinner nightly
Phone: 212-665-5348
Web: www.gennaronyc.com
Prices: $$

Despite its age, Gennaro hasn't lost its good looks or popularity—it still packs in hungry locals nightly, who aren't deterred by its borderline gritty surrounds or no-reservations policy. Come early or risk waiting, which isn't so bad considering the bar, whose by-the-glass offerings are vast and very appealing with both familiar and unusual Italian choices. The menu can be overwhelming considering its long list of pastas and daily specials, so trust your gut and you can't go wrong. Start with the polenta, served almost *quattro stagione*-style, with gorgonzola, prosciutto, and sliced portobellos; before twirling your taste buds around chewy *bucatini* showered with pecorino and pepper. The tiramisu is a light, creamy, and fluffy slam dunk.

Good Enough to Eat

American

B2

520 Columbus Ave. (at 85th St.)

Subway: 86 St (Broadway) Lunch & dinner daily
Phone: 212-496-0163
Web: www.goodenoughtoeat.com
Prices: $$

A mom-and-pop mainstay, Good Enough to Eat makes the most of its warm digs and those wide, stroller-friendly sidewalks of Columbus Avenue. Inside, the vibe is eternally homey and endearing with small, thoughtful touches like lots of cow art and a famously friendly staff, making this a primo stomping ground among residents.

The food here is unconditionally good, with a daily rotation of down home dishes like roast turkey with gravy, cornbread stuffing, and cranberry relish. The standout vegetarian Napoleon combines roasted portobellos, sweet potatoes, peppers, and summer squash cut into a perfect square alongside grilled focaccia. Be sure to sample (extensively) their made-to-order cakes and sweets—especially the sensational coconut custard pie.

Jean-Georges ✿✿✿

A4 Contemporary XXXX

1 Central Park West (bet. 60th & 61st Sts.)

Subway: 59 St - Columbus Circle Lunch & dinner daily
Phone: 212-299-3900
Web: www.jean-georgesrestaurant.com
Prices: $$$$

The crown-jewel restaurant of a crown-jewel Trump hotel, Jean-Georges reigns supreme over the Central Park dining scene. Facing its lush grounds and mighty Columbus himself, the restaurant's separate entrance can be something of a whirlwind as guests must pass through buzzing Nougatine to arrive at this silver-gray dining room. Still, those immense windows, columns, and twinkling skyline views make this a very special place.

On weekdays, the feel is formal and business-driven, while weekends hum with affluent tourists, local socialites, and an easier vibe. The highly professional service staff is one well-oiled and smooth machine.

While the contemporary menu is fixed, options are numerous and particularly appealing. Let the fascinating interplay of flavors begin with sea trout and oyster tartare merged with horseradish cream, lemon, and chive oil. Simple but lavish elegance underscores a perfectly cooked Maine lobster accompanied by roasted chili paste. Composed with Asian flavors and French technique, this is a standout worthy of a special occasion.

And in place of a single, haunting finale, desserts are served as a "sampler" focused on one ingredient—say caramel—in all its outrageous glory.

Lincoln

Italian

142 W. 65th St. (bet. Amsterdam Ave. & Broadway

Subway: 66 St - Lincoln Centerw — Lunch Wed – Sun
Phone: 212-359-6500 — Dinner nightly
Web: www.lincolnristorante.com
Prices: $$$$

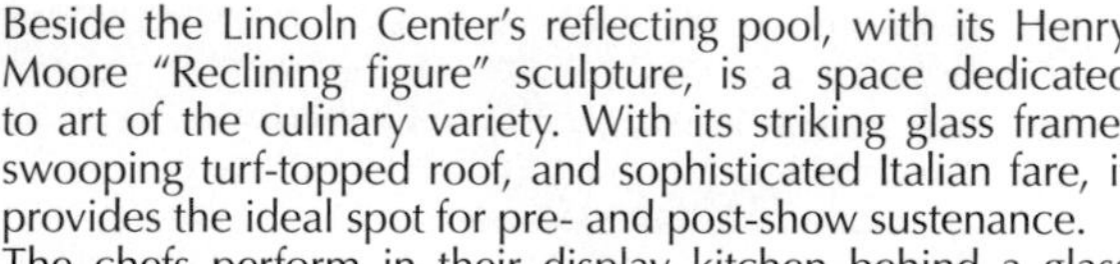

Beside the Lincoln Center's reflecting pool, with its Henry Moore "Reclining figure" sculpture, is a space dedicated to art of the culinary variety. With its striking glass frame, swooping turf-topped roof, and sophisticated Italian fare, it provides the ideal spot for pre- and post-show sustenance.

The chefs perform in their display kitchen behind a glass screen, but instead of offering a generic menu they choose a different region each month and then showcase its specialities and best known ingredients. So come in, say, May and it could be Sardinia when you can have *malloreddus* as a pasta course or some *mosciame* with your linguine. The cooking is robust and generously proportioned, although the care and craftsmanship of previous years is no longer evident.

Miss Mamie's Spoonbread Too

Southern

366 W. 110th St./Cathedral Pkwy. (bet. Columbus & Manhattan Aves.)

Subway: Cathedral Pkwy/110 St (Central Park West) — Lunch & dinner daily
Phone: 212-865-6744
Web: www.spoonbreadinc.com
Prices:

Come to Miss Mamie's and plan to indulge, Southern style. This tiny institution recently got a makeover in the bright, clean dining room—think comfier wicker chairs, roomier tables, and lots of flowers. Despite its more sophisticated appearance, the kitchen still embraces such tried and true classics as fried chicken thighs with black-eyed peas and collard greens, Louisiana catfish, and a creamy red velvet cake for dessert. Grab a fresh-squeezed lemonade and dive into the sampler, stocked with deep-fried shrimp, fall-off-the-bone beef short ribs, more fried chicken, and probably too many sides of cornbread stuffing and hop 'n John.
End with a cinnamon-scented coffee and start planning a stop by Miss Maude's, the second location in Hamilton Heights.

Momoya

Japanese XX

427 Amsterdam Ave. (bet. 80th & 81st Sts.)

Subway: 79 St — Lunch & dinner daily
Phone: 212-580-0007
Web: www.momoyanyc.com
Prices: $$$

A beguilingly simple aesthetic flows through handsome Momoya. The dining room is outfitted in floor-to-ceiling blonde wood, slate floors, and leather booths that exude a subdued masculinity. The front is dedicated to a bar where the drinks flow like a river and the sushi is always tasty.

Appetizers here can be showstoppers, starting with small plates like piping-hot grilled shishitos with yuzu salt, black cod with spinach and kabocha purée, or grilled eggplant with sweet miso. The small sushi counter's strength lies in its creative maki, like a namesake roll combining shiso, cucumber, and ginger topped with beautifully grilled black cod, spicy miso, and sweet potato crisp. Sake offerings are balanced, smooth, and enjoyable to the very last sip.

Noche Mexicana II

842 Amsterdam Ave. (at 101st St.)

Subway: 103 St (Broadway) — Lunch & dinner daily
Phone: 212-662-6900
Web: N/A
Prices: ©©

If you had a Mexican *tía*, you'd want her to be one of the lovely chefs pounding masa and wrapping tamales at Noche Mexicana II. The tasty corner is dominated by two veranda doors that open onto the sidewalk—a perfect setting for the specialties this talented kitchen sends out routinely.

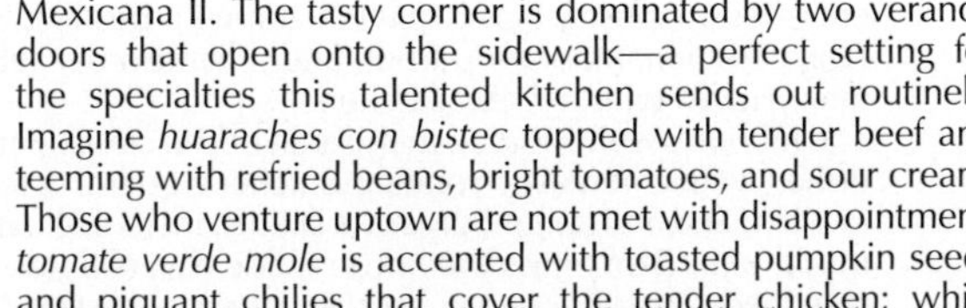

Imagine *huaraches con bistec* topped with tender beef and teeming with refried beans, bright tomatoes, and sour cream. Those who venture uptown are not met with disappointment: *tomate verde mole* is accented with toasted pumpkin seeds and piquant chilies that cover the tender chicken; while brick-red *chilate* boasts plump shrimp swimming in a spicy *guajillo* broth with a sprinkling of cilantro and *queso fresco*. A fresh flan, the only dessert on the menu, is simply excellent.

Nougatine

Contemporary

A4

1 Central Park West (at 60th St.)

Subway: 59 St - Columbus Circle — Lunch & dinner daily
Phone: 212-299-3900
Web: www.jean-georgesrestaurant.com
Prices: $$

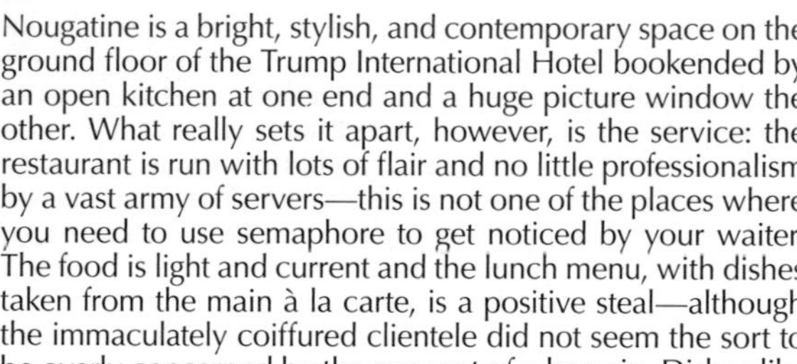

Nougatine is a bright, stylish, and contemporary space on the ground floor of the Trump International Hotel bookended by an open kitchen at one end and a huge picture window the other. What really sets it apart, however, is the service: the restaurant is run with lots of flair and no little professionalism by a vast army of servers—this is not one of the places where you need to use semaphore to get noticed by your waiter. The food is light and current and the lunch menu, with dishes taken from the main à la carte, is a positive steal—although the immaculately coiffured clientele did not seem the sort to be overly concerned by the concept of a bargain. Dishes like veal Milanese are confidently executed and it's worth leaving room for desserts, like apple tart.

The Ribbon

XX

American

B3

20 W. 72nd St. (bet. Central Park West & Columbus Ave.)

Subway: 72 St (Central Park West) — Dinner nightly
Phone: 646-416-9080
Web: www.theribbonnyc.com
Prices: $$$

Eric and Bruce Bromberg, the talented brothers behind the city's Blue Ribbon empire, strike again—this time in an enormous, industrial-chic space featuring a bustling bar and long communal tables up front; and a handsome, light-filled dining room with a visible kitchen.

The Ribbon's well-sourced menu is an ode to classic American dishes, with a fantastic rotating butcher's board; a tempting raw bar; and a roster of burger variations, including oxtail and mushroom. Don't miss the house-made cavatelli tossed with shredded chicken, creamy artichoke hearts, blistered cherry tomatoes, and tender wilted spinach. The juicy, spit-roasted Amish chicken marinated in sage and Riesling, and served with spicy mustard and crispy sage leaves, is yet another delight.

Picholine ✿

Mediterranean XXX

A4

35 W. 64th St. (bet. Broadway & Central Park West)

Subway: 66 St - Lincoln Center — Dinner Tue – Sat
Phone: 212-724-8585
Web: www.picholinenyc.com
Prices: $$$$

With a longstanding reputation for old-world elegance, Picholine remains as swank as it is discreet, stationed just steps from Lincoln Center. Most of the area's fine dining scene seems contemporary in comparison to this rather grande-dame, but that's ok. This space, with its dusty rose silks, silver candleholders, and crystal aplenty, is as suitably formal as the theater-goers of a certain age who populate it. Service can be brusque, as if the notably adept kitchen has stolen all the finesse from the room.

The menu may offer à la carte options, but dining here is designed to be a prix-fixe experience. Start with precisely made pasta that combine intense flavors, such as agnolotti filled with creamy ricotta, balanced by chopped morsels of soft artichoke, basil, and rich tomato. Brightly colored wild king salmon paired with dabs of black garlic paste, charred cucumber, and tender squid floats in a pool of squid-infused dashi.

Desserts may veer from classic with a nonetheless delicious vacherin, served as an elemental presentation of beautifully ripe strawberries and coulis, balsamic vinegar ice cream, strawberry sorbet with crunchy little meringues, and crystal-clear rhubarb soup.

Spiga

Italian

B2

200 W. 84th St. (bet. Amsterdam Ave. & Broadway)

Subway: 86 St (Broadway)
Dinner nightly
Phone: 212-362-5506
Web: www.spiganyc.com
Prices: $$$

Located among classic brownstones, Spiga presents a setting and cuisine that is unrivaled in this neighborhood. Its style sets the scene for a romantic, relaxed meal and suits the area through exposed brick walls and wine bottles lining wood shelves. Servers charm with their thick, Italian accents and candles flicker on tightly packed, dark-wood tables.

A rotating list of Italian cheeses and cured meats makes a fine appetizer and prelude to a pasta course that shifts with the seasons. Soft, light potato and spinach gnocchi are executed precisely, with mascarpone cheese, asparagus, and cherry tomatoes. Save room for the entrées, such as pan-seared halibut fillet with clams and mussels in a tomato broth over a crispy polenta cake.

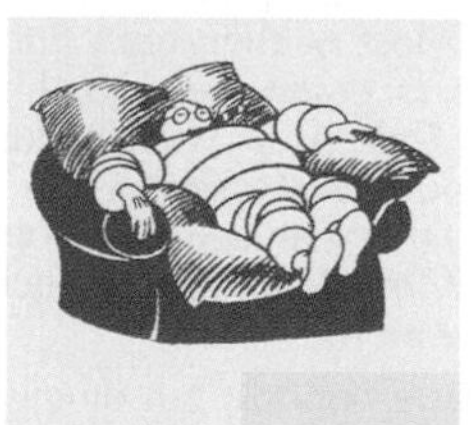

Couverts (X... XXXXX) indicate the level of comfort found at a restaurant. The more X's, the more upscale a restaurant will be.

Sushi Yasaka

Japanese

251 W. 72nd St. (bet. Broadway & West End Ave.)

Subway: 72 St (Broadway) — Lunch & dinner daily
Phone: 212-496-8466
Web: www.sushiyasaka.com
Prices: $$

There are no decorative distractions at this efficient if spare *sushi-ya* located a few steps below street level. The simple space offers three rows of tables, unadorned white walls, and a well-lit counter in the rear, and is warmed up by enthusiastic servers. Devoted customers know the draw here is not atmosphere, but the quality and excellent value omakase.
Fish can be surprisingly luscious, especially the salmon, which has a remarkably clean finish and great salty note. The medium fatty tuna needs nothing more than a kiss of soy sauce. A 12-course omakase might also include giant clam, uni, sea eel, fluke, smelt roe, and for dessert, tamago. The *kanto* soba is excellent too, with a rich soy-bonito broth with scallions, seaweed, and a fish cake.

Tessa

Mediterranean

349 Amsterdam Ave. (bet. 76th & 77th Sts.)

Subway: 79 St — Lunch Sat – Sun
Phone: 212-390-1974 — Dinner nightly
Web: www.tessanyc.com
Prices: $$$

An industrial-inspired *enoteca,* Tessa makes a huge, packed room feel intimate enough for a date—a feat in New York. A wine rack made of steel cables, metal security gates across the ceiling, and exposed brick complete the modern *vineria* look that is simply smart and very unique.
Gorgeous French walnut boards holding cheese and *salumi* makes the food even more enticing. Pasta here can be at once luxurious and comforting, as in the *cavatelli* topped with rabbit and pancetta ragù with smoky-sweet cipollini. Grilled entrées may include a swordfish steak with a slightly tangy white wine-artichoke *barigoule* and citrusy caper *gremolata.* For dessert, don't miss the thick, cool coffee *pot de crème* topped with cardamom sablé and sweet date purée.

Telepan ✿

American 

A3

72 W. 69th St. (bet. Central Park West & Columbus Ave.)

Subway: 66 St - Lincoln Center
Phone: 212-580-4300
Web: www.telepan-ny.com
Prices: $$$

Lunch Wed – Sun
Dinner nightly

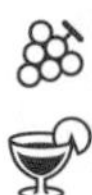

There is a reason why we all wish that a Telepan would appear in our own neighborhood—this is among the city's most solid restaurants. With its brownstone charm firmly in place, the impeccable interior has an equally New York feel with cozy rooms, brick, and food-centric artwork decorating the light walls. Every element feels as though it is in smart proportion and lends an airy feel to the space, from the contemporary plates to the petite wood tables. The waitstaff is professional, not overly formal, and genuinely interested in each guest.

Classic American elegance shines in a menu that effortlessly balances technique, ingredients, and flavor in perfect measure, while remaining creative and never predictable. Don't miss signature dishes like the lobster Bolognese, served as a whole tail or claws over a massive twirl of beautifully cooked spaghetti with finely chopped lobster meat in a light shallot-garlic-tomato broth that ensures the sauce melds with each bite. A gorgeous fillet of butter-poached turbot, which arrives alongside roasted winter squash made fragrant and sweet with allspice, is then finished with a decadent touch of caviar.

The peanut butter and chocolate-gianduja crémeux is a perennial highlight.

Vai

B3

429 Amsterdam Ave. (bet. 80th & 81st Sts.)

Subway: 79 St — Lunch Fri – Sun
Phone: 212-362-4500 — Dinner nightly
Web: www.vairestaurant.com
Prices: $$

Warm, cozy, and strikingly attractive, Vai is a casual yet sultry choice for tasty food and wine. The entire space seems to be illuminated by flickering votives bouncing light off cream-colored walls, brown leather seating, and bare wood tables. The small marble bar is superb for solo dining and offers the complete menu, as well as a full view into the hectic kitchen, where Chef Vincent Chirico is at the helm.

On the menu, sample delightful dishes that focus on Mediterranean flavors, as in charred Portuguese octopus with watercress, crisp potato nuggets, and jalapeño "pesto." Then, move on to plump ravioli filled with silky burrata and sweet ricotta, dressed in truffle cream, topped with feathery *parmigiano* and cracked pepper, set over hon shimeji mushrooms.

Warique

Peruvian

B1

852 Amsterdam Ave. (bet. 101st & 102nd Sts.)

Subway: 103 St (Broadway) — Lunch & dinner daily
Phone: 212-865-0101
Web: www.wariquenyc.com
Prices: $$

The façade may not seem to stand out against the neighborhood, but their food is straightforward delicious. Two narrow dining rooms flank the semi-visible kitchen at the heart of this restaurant, where the serious yet rib-sticking cuisine is prepared. The staff is helpful and welcoming.

Warique knows how to please its guests with dishes that they come to savor time and again. Start with *causa Peruana* or cold, smashed potatoes dressed with mashed avocado, *aji amarillo* (a hellfire-breathing sauce), and then studded with shrimp. Or, try the *papa rellena,* a generous ensemble of potatoes stuffed with tender ground ribeye, chopped egg, raisins, olives, and a smattering of peppers. This may be accompanied by yet another *aji* crafted from jalapeños and black mint.

The Bronx

The Bronx

The only borough attached to the island of Manhattan, the Bronx boasts such awe-inspiring sights as the Bronx Zoo, Hall of Fame for Great Americans, as well as Yankee Stadium. However, it is also revered as a hotbed of culinary treasures. For instance, The New York Botanical Garden is devoted to education and hosts many garden- and food-related classes. In fact, the Botanical Garden's **Bronx Green-Up** is an acclaimed program aimed at improving inner-city areas by offering them agricultural advice and practical training. Located along the west side, Belmont is a residential quarter marked by various ethnic and religious groups. Once an Italian hub, its population is now comprised of Hispanics (primarily Puerto Ricans), African-Americans, West Indians, and Albanians. Much of the Bronx today consists of parkland, like Pelham Bay Park with its sandy Orchard Beach. And since a day at the beach is never complete without salty eats, you'll want to step into pizza paradise—**Louie & Ernie's**—for a slice of bliss. Home cooks and haute chefs alike stock up on spices, herbs, and seeds that are directly flown in from Mexico and featured on the shelves of **El Atoradero**; while thirsty travelers pop into **Gun Hill Brewing Co.** for an impressive bevy and more. Beyond, City Island is a gem of a coastal community teeming with seafood spots. **The Black Whale** is a local fixture frequented for its classic-meets-contemporary cuisine and quenching cocktails. Savor their offerings, either inside the quirky dining room or out in the garden. When the sun beats down, pop into **Lickety**

Split for a cooling scoop of sorbet or ice cream, or both! Belmont's most renowned street, Arthur Avenue, is home to Italian food paradise—**The Arthur Avenue Retail Market.** This enclosed oasis is a culinary emporium overrun with self-proclaimed foodies as well as famed epicureans, who can be seen prowling for quality pasta, homemade sausages, extra virgin olive oil, notorious heroes, heirloom seeds, and such. Some begin by diving into a ball of rich, gooey mozzarella at **Joe's Deli** (open on Sundays!). Others may grab them to go, along with pistachio-studded mortadella from **Teitel Brothers** or *salumi* from **Calabria Pork Store**.

Beyond this venerable marketplace, find early-risers ravenously tearing into freshly baked breads from either **Terranova** or **Addeo**—the choices are plenty. Come lunchtime, find a myriad of Eastern European eats. At **Tony & Tina's Pizzeria** skip the signatures and opt for Albanian or Kosovar *burek* (flaky rolls with sweet pumpkin purée). Just as **Xochimilco Restaurant** is a playground for families with tots, South Bronxite singles revel in Ecuadorian delights like *bollon de verde* at **Ricuras Panderia**. Then strolling south east where **Gustiamo's** warehouse continues to flourish as a city-wide favorite for regional Italian specialties including olive oils, pastas, and San Marzano tomatoes. Likewise, the butchers at **Honeywell Meat Market** can be seen teaching newbies a thing or two about breaking down a side of beef, which always reigns as king. But, over on Willis Avenue, Mott Haven's main drag, bright awnings designate a plethora of Puerto Rican diners and Mexican bodegas.

YANKEE STADIUM

Home to the "sultans of swat" (AKA the "Bronx Bombers"), **Yankee Stadium** is *the* spot for world-champion baseball. And what goes best with baseball? Big and bold bites of course, all of which may be found at the stadium's own food court—**Lobel's**, the ultimate butcher, is one such tenant and crafts perfectly marbled steak sandwiches to order. Even the Carbone-Torrisi boys have set up shop here at

Parm, hooking fans with hearty sammies and heavenly sweets. The bro-mance continues at **Brother Jimmy's**, one of New York's best-selling barbecue chains, cooking up the staples —think pulled pork, fried pickles, baked beans, and more. Refined palates will relish the farm-fresh produce from **Melissa's Farmers Market**, just as the cool kids are sure to swoon over the sips at **Tommy Bahama Bar**.

COMFORT FOODS

Eastchester, Wakefield, and Williamsbridge are home to diverse cultures, and ergo, each of their unique eats. Still, there are everyday vendors to be frequented here. **Astor Prime Meats** proudly presents premium grade meats for every type of holiday feast, while **G & R Deli** pays homage to the neighborhood's deep Italian roots by delivering authentic flavors in sausages and meat sauce sold by the quart. Then there's **Sal & Dom's** who stick with this line of duty by serving deliciously flaky *sfogliatelle*. Over on Grand Concourse, **Bate** and **Papaye** cook up a buffet of fresh, pungent Ghanian goodies for the surrounding West African community. Indulge in this savory, smoky spread, before closing over a treat at **Kingston Tropical Bakery**. **Valencia Bakery** is yet another sweet marvel among the borough's mighty Puerto Rican masses.

It is important to note that Asian food has officially arrived in the Bronx, with **Phnom Penh-Nha Trang Market** bragging a variety of important Vietnamese ingredients necessary for a Southeast Asian-themed dinner party. **Sabrosura** offers an excellent blend of Spanish and Chinese inspiration, and even purists can't help but crave their crispy yuca chips paired with sweet crabmeat. But, bringing it back to the basics, the hamburger craze rages on uptown at **Bronx Alehouse**, pouring a litany of beers. Bronx beer you say? You bet. And, there is an equally thrilling selection to be relished at **Jonas Bronck's**

Beer Co. or **Bronx Brewery** over on East 136th Street. Hosts keep the house party hoppin' and stoves turning by stocking up on pantry staples for late-night snacking from **Palm Tree Marketplace**. Also, find everything you may need here for a Jamaican-themed evening. **Hunts Point Food Distribution Center** is another epicurean wonder, vital to NYC's food services. This expansive 329-acre complex of wholesalers, distributors, and food-processing vendors is also home to the **Hunts Point Meat Market** that sells every imaginable cut under the sun. Also housed within these grounds is the **Hunts Point Terminal Produce Market** supplying patrons with fantastic variety, as well as the famous **Fulton Fish Market**. This formidable network of stores caters to the city's most celebrated chefs, restaurateurs, and wholesale suppliers. Such mouthwatering cruising is bound to result in voracious cravings, all of which may be gratified at **Mo Gridder's BBQ**, a classic joint oozing with potent doses of Bronx flavor.

RIVERDALE

Riverdale is not known for its culinary distinction. However, its winning location as the northernmost tip of the city affords it incredible views, and as a result, lavish mansions. Moneyed residents mingle with curious visitors over the aromatic offerings at **S&S Cheesecake**, or freshly baked babkas at the always-primped **Mother's Bake Shop**. From here, those in need of sips may head to **Skyview Wines** for an exceptional display of kosher varietals. Then, finish with style and flair at **Lloyd's Carrot Cake**, which has been doling out divine slices of red velvet or German chocolate cake to the community for over a quarter-century.

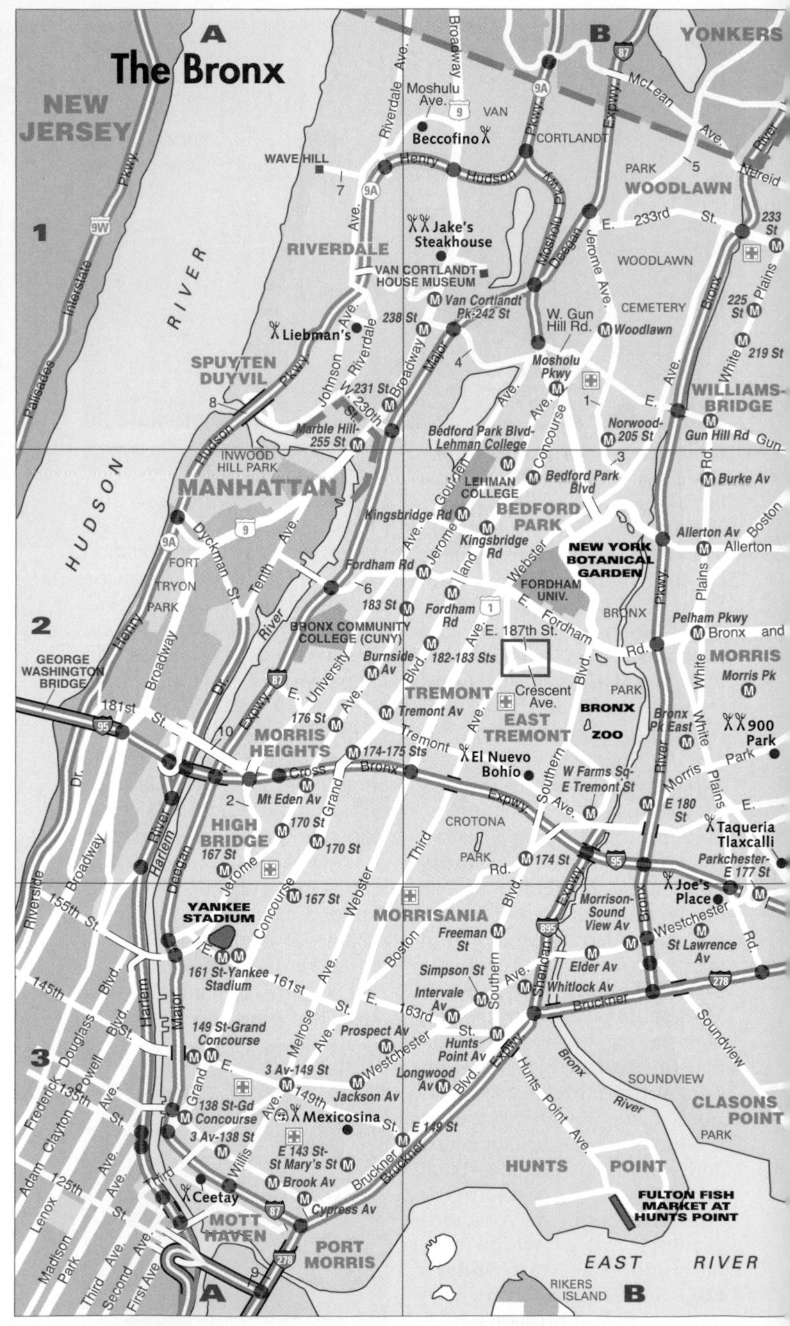
The Bronx
A
B
1
2
3
NEW JERSEY
YONKERS
HUDSON
RIVER
Palisades
Interstate
Pkwy.
9W
WAVE HILL
RIVERDALE
Beccofino
Jake's Steakhouse
VAN CORTLANDT HOUSE MUSEUM
Liebman's
SPUYTEN DUYVIL
INWOOD HILL PARK
MANHATTAN
FORT TRYON PARK
GEORGE WASHINGTON BRIDGE
VAN CORTLANDT
PARK
WOODLAWN
WOODLAWN CEMETERY
WILLIAMS-BRIDGE
Moshulu Ave.
McLean Ave.
Nereid
E. 233rd St.
Van Cortlandt Pk-242 St
238 St
W. Gun Hill Rd.
Woodlawn
Mosholu Pkwy
Norwood-205 St
Gun Hill Rd
Burke Av
Allerton Av
Allerton
Marble Hill-255 St
W 231 St
W. 230th St.
Bedford Park Blvd-Lehman College
LEHMAN COLLEGE
Bedford Park Blvd
BEDFORD PARK
Kingsbridge Rd
NEW YORK BOTANICAL GARDEN
FORDHAM UNIV.
Fordham Rd
183 St
E. 187th St.
Crescent Ave.
Pelham Pkwy
Bronx and
MORRIS
Morris Pk
BRONX COMMUNITY COLLEGE (CUNY)
Burnside Av
182-183 Sts
TREMONT
Tremont Av
EAST TREMONT
BRONX ZOO
Bronx Pk East
900 Park
176 St
MORRIS HEIGHTS
174-175 Sts
El Nuevo Bohío
W Farms Sq-E Tremont St
E 180 St
Taqueria Tlaxcalli
Cross Bronx Expwy.
Mt Eden Av
HIGH BRIDGE
170 St
167 St
CROTONA PARK
174 St
Parkchester-E 177 St
Joe's Place
YANKEE STADIUM
161 St-Yankee Stadium
MORRISANIA
Freeman St
Morrison-Sound View Av
St Lawrence Av
Elder Av
Whitlock Av
Simpson St
Intervale Av
149 St-Grand Concourse
Prospect Av
Hunts Point Av
3 Av-149 St
Longwood Av
Jackson Av
138 St-Gd Concourse
Mexicosina
E 149 St
3 Av-138 St
E 143 St-St Mary's St
Brook Av
Cypress Av
Ceetay
MOTT HAVEN
PORT MORRIS
SOUNDVIEW
CLASONS POINT
PARK
HUNTS POINT
FULTON FISH MARKET AT HUNTS POINT
EAST RIVER
RIKERS ISLAND
Bruckner Expwy.
Soundview
Bronx River
Hunts Point Ave.
Harlem River
Major Deegan
Grand Concourse
155th St.
145th St.
135th St.
125th St.
181st St.
Dyckman St.
Broadway
Riverside Dr.
Henry Hudson Pkwy.
Frederick Douglass Blvd.
Adam Clayton Powell Ave.
Lenox Ave.
Madison Ave.
Park Ave.
Third Ave.
Second Ave.
First Ave.
Webster Ave.
Jerome Ave.
Boston Rd.
Southern Blvd.
Melrose Ave.
Willis Ave.
Westchester Ave.
Sheridan Expwy.
White Plains Rd.
Bronx River Pkwy.
Morris Park Ave.
161st St.
163rd St.
Third Ave.
University Ave.

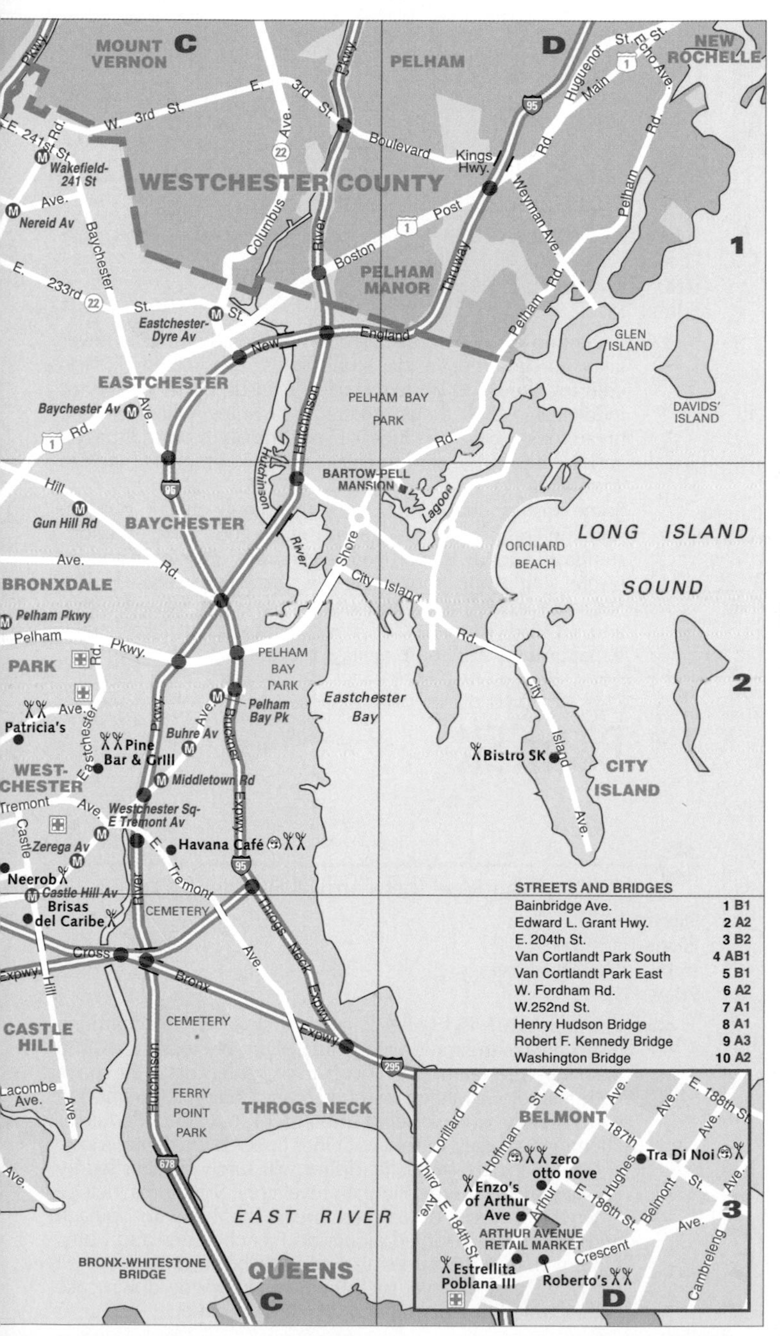

STREETS AND BRIDGES

Bainbridge Ave.	1 B1
Edward L. Grant Hwy.	2 A2
E. 204th St.	3 B2
Van Cortlandt Park South	4 AB1
Van Cortlandt Park East	5 B1
W. Fordham Rd.	6 A2
W.252nd St.	7 A1
Henry Hudson Bridge	8 A1
Robert F. Kennedy Bridge	9 A3
Washington Bridge	10 A2

Beccofino

Italian

B1

5704 Mosholu Ave. (at Fieldston Rd.)

Subway: Van Cortlandt Park-242 St — Dinner nightly
Phone: 718-432-2604
Web: www.beccofinorestaurant.com
Prices: $$

Beccofino is an earnest neighborhood darling that is never taken for granted. Inside, string lights, exposed brick, and colorful, life-sized posters fashion a rustic bistro setting for indulging in their Italian-American favorites (with plenty of bread for sopping up sauces). Expect meals to be well-paced and the dedicated staff to ensure that everything is made to your liking.

Some dishes stray from being genuinely Italian but are nonetheless popular and surprisingly good, like seafood-stuffed manicotti topped with a generous amount of shrimp bisque and mild mozzarella. A crowd-pleasing chicken Milanese arrives as an insanely savory cutlet, pounded thin and sautéed, topped with broccoli rabe, chili flakes, spicy tomato sauce, and more melting mozzarella.

Bistro SK

French

D2

273 City Island Ave. (bet. Carroll & Hawkins Sts.)

Subway: N/A — Lunch Sun
Phone: 718-885-1670 — Dinner Tue – Sun
Web: www.bistrosk.com
Prices: $$

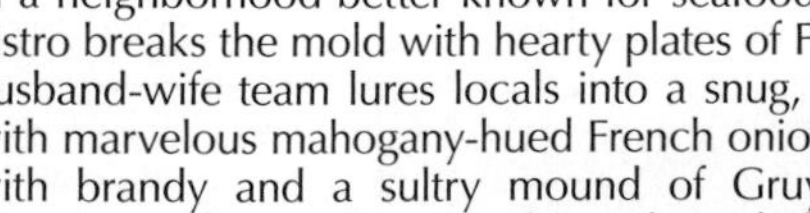

In a neighborhood better known for seafood, this charming bistro breaks the mold with hearty plates of French fare. The husband-wife team lures locals into a snug, dimly lit space with marvelous mahogany-hued French onion soup finished with brandy and a sultry mound of Gruyère. Particular attention to the art of service shines through the dining room.

A craving for classic Gallic dishes will surely be satisfied by cooking that is more solid than revelatory. Signatures include a tender roulade of chicken breast stuffed with spinach and mushrooms, served alongside French beans and fluffy, buttery mashed potatoes tucked with black olive for a bit of "wow!" For a finale, try the pineapple upside-down cake with a grilled ring of fruit and drizzle of caramel.

Brisas del Caribe

Latin American

1207 Castle Hill Ave. (bet. Ellis & Gleason Aves.)

Subway: Castle Hill Av
Lunch & dinner daily
Phone: 718-794-9710
Web: www.brisasdelcaribe.net
Prices: ©©

Thanks to a major exterior facelift, Brisas del Caribe is looking finer than ever. The interior is still adorned with frescos of Caribbean beach scenes and benches to ease the wait for tables, but everyone's eyes are drawn to the piles of food, *sopas*, and counters laden with freshly made cakes sold by the slice. No matter the time of day, this place is packed with large families and groups of locals enjoying copious amounts of hot, tasty, ridiculously affordable comfort food.

Start with a hearty Dominican treat like *sancocho*, or go for *relleno de papa*, deep-fried mashed potatoes stuffed with gooey cheese and aromatic ground meat. Don't miss the superb *patitas de cerdo*, a stew of pig's feet with cassava, potatoes, herbs, and strips of tripe.

Ceetay

Asian

129 Alexander Ave. (at Bruckner Blvd.)

Subway: 3 Av - 138 St
Lunch Mon – Fri
Phone: 718-618-7020
Dinner nightly
Web: www.ceetay.com
Prices: $$

Its location near Hunts Point and the burgeoning South Bronx art community may have put it on the foodie trail, but Ceetay has become known for inventive Asian cooking at its best. The open kitchen offers diners a view of the race among cooks cutting, washing, and packing up an endless number of takeout orders. The tiny dining room features Mason jar fixtures, a handcrafted bar, and a wall papered with yellowing Asian newspapers.

Creative specials include a seared square of sesame-studded rice "bruschetta" topped with avocado purée, tuna tartare, and frizzled onions. Don't miss such highflying maki as the Kawasaki roll with a mishmash of crab, scallion, sweet glaze, and more. Traditional sushi here stands equally strong, with very nice *maguro*, *ebi*, and uni.

El Nuevo Bohío

791 E. Tremont Ave. (at Mapes Ave.)

Subway: West Farms Sq - E Tremont Av — Lunch & dinner daily
Phone: 718-294-3905
Web: www.elnuevobohiorestaurant.com
Prices:

On a prominent corner, windows filled with *lechòn* lure in passersby with mouthwatering visions of shiny-skinned roast pork. Beloved by the local Puerto Rican community, the front room is minimally adorned and often filled with lines of those waiting for to-go orders. Snag a seat in the back—where bright walls are flooded with photos—for friendly table service.

Begin with *morcilla,* a thick blood sausage bright with chili peppers, cilantro, and garlic before moving on to the succulent *pernil,* pork shoulder roasted to a luxuriously crisp exterior and served with stinging garlic sauce, rice and beans, and plantains. Don't miss an array of complex *sopas*—from rich cow's feet soup with yucca and sweet potato to *asopado de carmarones,* a hearty combo of rice and shrimp.

Enzo's of Arthur Ave

D3

2339 Arthur Ave. (bet. Crescent Ave. & 186th St.)

Subway: Fordham Rd (Grand Concourse) — Lunch Mon– Sat
Phone: 718-733-4455 — Dinner nightly
Web: N/A
Prices: $$

It's easy to love Enzo's, a quaint red-sauce throwback on Arthur Avenue. In an area once dominated by Italian-American culture, including a library full of Italian literature, Enzo's sits among longstanding favorites and clearly is welcomed as part of the family. The popular bar invites local business owners and faculty from nearby Fordham University for casual conversation, while the kitchen churns out steaming plates of glistening clams oreganata and rich pastas delivered by a careful service team.

The nostalgic Sunday special—pillow-soft gnocchi topped with tomato gravy and slow-braised pork *braciola* tucked with garlic, parsley, and cheese—is worth an end-of-weekend quest. So is the fresh swordfish steak with wonderfully assertive Livornese sauce.

Estrellita Poblana III

Mexican 

2328 Arthur Ave. (bet. Crescent Ave. & 186th St.)

Subway: Fordham Rd (Grand Concourse) Lunch & dinner daily
Phone: 718-220-7641
Web: www.estrellitapoblanaiii.com
Prices: ⊜

The Arthur Avenue area may be known as the artery of the Little Italy of the Bronx, but a Mexican restaurant shines here with its fluffy tamales loaded with tender, fragrant corn, and much more. The small interior is brightened with gold walls, a fuchsia ceiling, and three stars set in the fuchsia coffered ceiling. Exposed brick and a semi-open kitchen complete the comfortable scene.

Conversation is common between the pleasant servers and other diners, as searing hot *sopa* with shredded chicken and a nest of *fideos*, is placed on an immaculate table. The *bistec Estrellita* is served with a fiery habanero sauce, topped with *pico de gallo*, and flanked by a side of rice and beans. Flan is a lovely finish—though that generous steak may fulfill even the heartiest appetite.

Havana Café

Latin American 

3151 E. Tremont Ave. (at LaSalle Ave.)

Subway: N/A Lunch & dinner daily
Phone: 718-518-1800
Web: www.bronxhavanacafe.com
Prices: **$$**

The Schuylerville area of the Bronx has seen an influx of Latin restaurants, but this longstanding stucco façade still commands a presence. With bright yellow walls, tropical décor, and lazy ceiling fans, Havana Café feels straight out of Cuba, run by three Latin friends who understand the formula for success.

Drinkers and diners pack the U-shaped bar nightly for sports games on the TV's and chewy Cuban *pan de agua*. The dishes range from Caribbean to South American; this cooking is more concerned with taste than authenticity. Try the crispy green plantain *tostones* topped with *ropa vieja* and lime-spiked sour cream, mortar-mashed yucca, or the battered "Pargo" red snapper bathed in garlic, tomato and ever-present pork cracklings.

Jake's Steakhouse

Steakhouse XX

B1

6031 Broadway (bet. Manhattan College Pkwy. & 251st St.)

Subway: Van Cortlandt Park-242 St — Lunch & dinner daily
Phone: 718-581-0182
Web: www.jakessteakhouse.com
Prices: $$$

Lodged across the way from the expansive Van Cortlandt Park, Jake's has claimed its place among the city's finer steakhouses. This multi-floor arena, with its pretty price tags, clubby décor, and a well-stocked bar, is one of the Bronx's better-kept secrets. Servers are personable and very professional.

Mussels *fra diavolo* features meaty mollusks tossed in spicy marinara and paired with crunchy garlic crostini. Porterhouse for two is tender, perfectly marbled, cooked to exact specification, and even better when accompanied by creamy mashed cauliflower flecked with cracked pepper, cheddar, and crispy bacon bits.

Jake's Boston cream pie gilds this robust meal with an addictive layering of moist cake, vanilla pastry cream, and rich chocolate ganache.

Joe's Place

Puerto Rican 

B3

1841 Westchester Ave. (at Thieriot Ave.)

Subway: Parkchester — Lunch & dinner daily
Phone: 718-918-2947
Web: www.joesplacebronx.com
Prices: $$

From *abuelas* to *niños*, locals know to come to this "place" for solid Puerto Rican food. A glance at the wall of politicos and celebrities who have dined here proves how well-loved it truly is. The space is divided into two very different areas: a classic lunch counter also serving takeout, and a dark wood dining room.

A wonderful Nuyerican accent can be heard at gathering family tables and tasted in classic dishes like *mofongo al pilon de bistec* (savory shredded beef over mashed plantains) or *pernil con arroz y gandules* (roasted pork with pigeon peas and rice). Prices become even more reasonable when you realize that dishes are big enough to be split three ways. Daily *sopa* specials are a highlight, but end meals with hot and flaky cheese-filled *pastelito*.

Liebman's

Deli

552 W. 235th St. (bet. Johnson & Oxford Aves.)

Subway: 231 St
Lunch & dinner daily
Phone: 718-548-4534
Web: www.liebmansdeli.com
Prices: $$

Some things never change (phew!) and thankfully this iconic kosher deli is still stuffing sandwiches and ladling matzoh ball soup (reputed for its healing powers), just as it has for over 50 years. Residents wax poetic about the place: a true-blue deli with a neon sign in the front window, the grill slowly roasting hot dogs, and meat-slicing machines churning out endless piles of pastrami.

Soulful classics include stuffed veal breast, potato latkes, and tongue sandwiches with tangy pickles. Some order to-go, but it's better to slide into a booth with a Reuben, stacked with mounds of hot corned beef, sauerkraut, and Russian dressing, when it's freshly plated. End with a perfect little rugelach filled with chocolate and ground nuts.

Mexicosina 

Mexican

503 Jackson Ave. (at E. 147th St.)

Subway: E 149 St
Lunch & dinner daily
Phone: 347-498-1339
Web: www.mexicosina.com
Prices: $$

The light-filled interior of this Mexican powerhouse sitting on a quiet corner is a busy amalgam of rustic artifacts, wolf taxidermy, and the Virgin in all her glory with flowers and votives at her feet. And those huge jars of *jamaica, horchata,* and the *agua fresca del dia* are just as tasty and refreshing as they are decorative.

If they have the *tlayuda,* order it. Its crunchy paper-thin base is smothered in a veritable fiesta of refried black beans, *chicharrón,* lettuce, *queso Oaxaca, crema* and much, much more. Other equally terrific specials have included *chivo,* a rich goat stew in an intense habanero-spiked consommé, or tender and fatty lamb barbacoa tacos. Cold accompanying salsas are so divine one could skip the chips and just eat them—with a spoon.

Neerob

Bangladeshi

C2

2109 Starling Ave. (bet. Odell St. & Olmstead Ave.)

Subway: Castle Hill Av — Lunch & dinner daily
Phone: 718-904-7061
Web: N/A
Prices: ⊜

Short on atmosphere but saturated in fiery flavor, this Bronx restaurant dishes out some of the best Bangladeshi fare this side of South Asia. Though harsh lighting, steam tables, and a cash register give the main room the feel of a fast food joint, none of that will matter after that first bite of sultry, explosively spicy cuisine.

Shingara, vegetable pakoras, and samosas are always available. This is in addition to a parade of daily specials: *chandal*, yellow lentils, is seasoned with garlic, ginger, and cumin; jumbo prawns or *golda chingri* are simmered in a thick sauce of spiced coconut milk; and gura mas, pan-fried small fish, swim in a tangy purée of greens and mustard oil. Order plenty of buttery, multi-layered *paratha* to scoop up the curries.

900 Park

Italian

B2

900 Morris Park Ave. (at Bronxdale Ave.)

Subway: Bronx Park East — Lunch & dinner daily
Phone: 718-892-3830
Web: www.900park.com
Prices: $$

Neither fancy nor innovative, there is a certain heartwarming quality that makes this an easy place to return to time and again. Couples often settle in the lounge near the fireplace while larger groups gather in the elevated dining room for platters of hot antipasti. White leather chairs, cotton panels, and rustic tables lend a breezy feel.

Italian and Italian-American classics span the wide menu, from grilled calamari with a mild tomato sauce topped with peppers and black olives, to ridged tubes of manicotti stuffed with ricotta and pecorino, cooked in a meaty Bolognese and finished with a rich béchamel. Brick-oven pizzas are always worthy orders, especially the *Calabrese* decked with spicy *soppressata* and a few dollops of mozzarella.

Patricia's

C2 **Italian** XX

1082 Morris Park Ave. (bet. Haight & Lurting Aves.)

Subway: Morris Park (& bus Bx8) Lunch & dinner daily
Phone: 718-409-9069
Web: www.patriciasnyc.com
Prices: $$

Much more than a neighborhood staple, Patricia's is an elegant restaurant committed to the convivial spirit of Southern Italy. Its seasonal fare is served in a gracious, brick-lined dining room among white tablecloths, chandeliers, and the warmth of a wood-burning oven.

That brick oven churns out pleasing pizzas with lightly charred crusts, like the Regina simply adorned in buffalo mozzarella, torn basil, and a drizzle of excellent olive oil. Spaghetti Frank Sinatra is a stain-making bowl of slippery pasta loaded with shrimp, clams, olives, and capers in chunky tomato sauce. A light touch is seen in the grilled vegetables, topped with paper-thin cremini mushrooms. Don't miss the flaky and gently poached *baccalà alla Livornese* in a sharp, tangy sauce.

Pine Bar & Grill

C2 **Italian** XX

1634 Eastchester Rd. (at Blondell Ave.)

Subway: Westchester Sq - Tremont Av Lunch & dinner daily
Phone: 718-319-0900
Web: www.pinebargrill.com
Prices: $$

Between this outpost and their popular sister restaurant, Pine Tavern, the Bastone family has become a fixture on the Bronx restaurant scene, and their eateries thrive for good reason. Pine Bar & Grill, with its lovely muted yellow walls and black-and-white photos depicting the hometown borough, is, at heart, a red sauce joint of the old school variety—yet the menu reflects the neighborhood's sizable Latin-American population in dishes like pernil and coconut shrimp paella; or a tender trio of empanadas.

Don't miss the mouthwatering *pizzette* (especially good when Frankie's around); eggplant *rollatini*, stewed in a fragrant tomato sauce and drizzled with basil aïoli; or a juicy center-cut pork chop, finished with sweet and hot cherry peppers.

Roberto's

Italian 

603 Crescent Ave. (at Hughes Ave.)

Subway: Fordham Rd (Grand Concourse) Lunch & dinner Mon – Sat
Phone: 718-733-9503
Web: www.roberto089.com
Prices: $$

You can't miss Roberto's, whose distinctive design falls somewhere between a cozy, welcoming farmhouse and a Mediterranean villa complete with a coral-hued façade and wrought-iron balcony. One of the most highly regarded restaurants in the borough, this storied Italian-American is the kind of charmer that makes groups feel right at home.

It's also the kind of place that piles on the pasta and takes espresso seriously, whether it's the fettuccine special that features fresh shaved truffle, the soft-shell crabs finished in a butter-white wine sauce, or the ricotta cream that fills an insanely good cannoli. For a real taste of what makes Roberto's shine, let the hearty *tubettini con polipo e fave,* folded with grilled octopus, fava beans, and baby clams speak for itself.

Taqueria Tlaxcalli

Mexican

2103 Starling Ave. (bet. Odell St. & Olmstead Ave.)

Subway: Castle Hill Av Lunch & dinner daily
Phone: 347-851-3085
Web: N/A
Prices: ©

What this sweet little Mexican spot lacks in looks it makes up for in personality—plus a warm, inviting atmosphere that draws a constant stream of locals. Behind the counter, a smiling staff prepares each order with machine gun speed, and professional servers are quick to help anyone not fluent in Spanish.

Daily specials could include anything from a complex *mole* to slow-braised goat with broth, though the menu is rife with options. Begin with a *torta,* stuffed with steak, layers of beans, avocado, onions, lettuce, and a bright chipotle mayo. In the *molcajetes,* grilled cactus strips, Mexican sausage, and tortillas are sautéed and then buried under a spicy green sauce and sprinkled with *queso.* A nice end is found in a cool disk of coconut flan.

Tra Di Noi

Italian

622 E. 187th St. (bet. Belmont & Hughes Aves.)

Subway: Fordham Rd (Grand Concourse) — Lunch & dinner Tue – Sun
Phone: 718-295-1784
Web: www.tradinoi.com
Prices: $$

Decked out with crimson walls and red checkered tablecloths, this is the kind of place where diners feel like they're in on a delicious secret—and that's no coincidence, as Tra Di Noi is Italian for "between us." Responsible for the success behind this tiny spot is Chef/owner Marco Coletta, who directs the front and back of house with the precision of an air traffic controller and the passion of an Italian *nonno*.

This sincerity shines through in the cooking, from the ethereally light *gnocchi di patate* in a rich lamb ragù to the quickly pan-fried fillet of sole *francese* nestled in a creamy lemon sauce with shrimp, parsley, and white wine. Only a few desserts are on offer, and all are made in house. For a classic finale, go with the ricotta cheesecake.

zero otto nove

2357 Arthur Ave. (at 186th St.)

Subway: Fordham Rd (Grand Concourse) — Lunch Tue - Sat
Phone: 718-220-1027 — Dinner Tue – Sun
Web: www.roberto089.com
Prices: $$

This Arthur Avenue favorite is easily recognized by the powder-blue FIAT parked outside, but is better appreciated for the wood-burning dome oven. Brick and cement archways, high ceilings, and a second-floor dining terrace strive to keep that oven—and its wares—within each table's line of vision.

The menu showcases Salerno-style cooking with pizzas, baked pastas, and wood-fired entrées. In fact any dish that is "al cartoccio" (in parchment) is sure to please. Open up this pouch to try the pitch-perfect al dente *radiatori* baked with porcini, cherry tomatoes, breadcrumbs, and loads of deliciously spicy sausage. The ragù Salernitano is a gut-busting triumph of stewed braciole, sausage, and tender meatballs. The Nutella calzone makes a sweet, rich finish.

Brooklyn

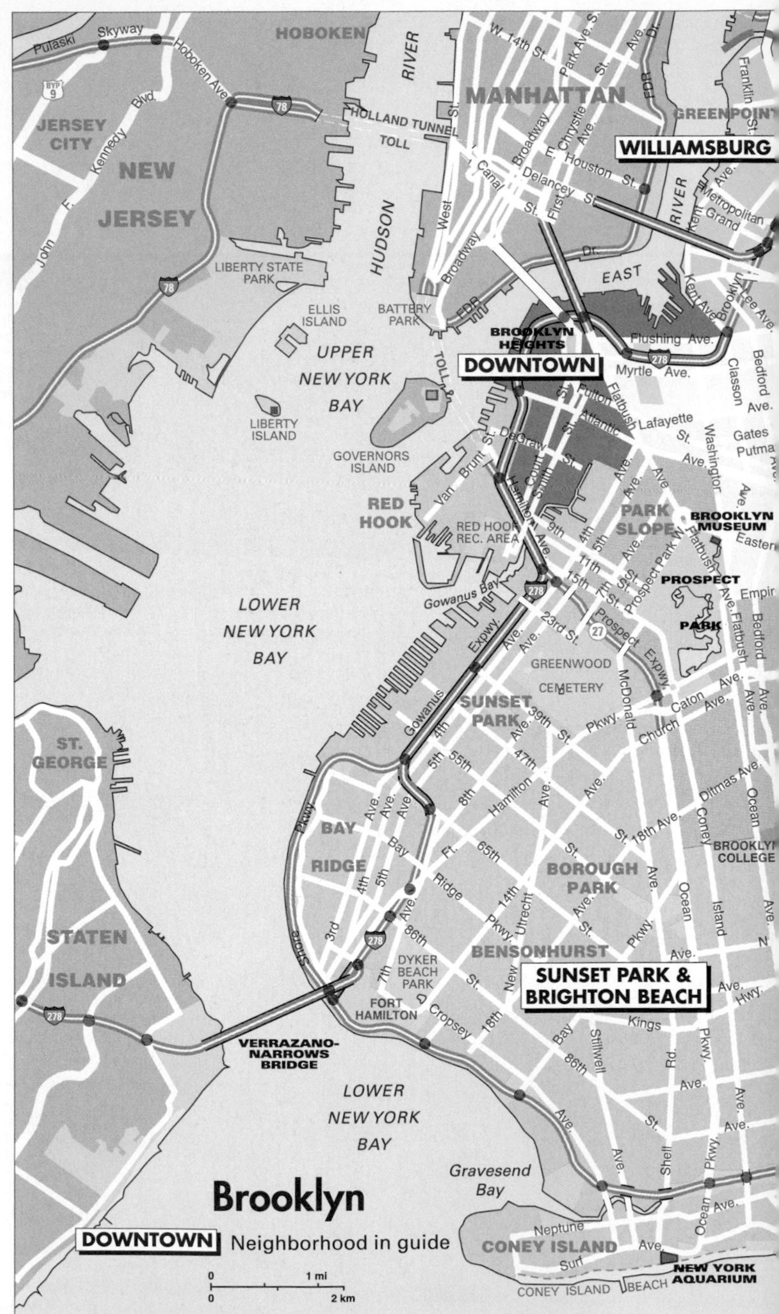
Brooklyn
DOWNTOWN
Neighborhood in guide
WILLIAMSBURG
BROOKLYN HEIGHTS
DOWNTOWN
SUNSET PARK & BRIGHTON BEACH
HOBOKEN
MANHATTAN
GREENPOINT
JERSEY CITY
NEW JERSEY
LIBERTY STATE PARK
ELLIS ISLAND
BATTERY PARK
UPPER NEW YORK BAY
LIBERTY ISLAND
GOVERNORS ISLAND
HUDSON RIVER
EAST RIVER
HOLLAND TUNNEL
TOLL
RED HOOK
RED HOOK REC. AREA
PARK SLOPE
BROOKLYN MUSEUM
PROSPECT PARK
LOWER NEW YORK BAY
Gowanus Bay
GREENWOOD CEMETERY
SUNSET PARK
ST. GEORGE
BAY RIDGE
BOROUGH PARK
STATEN ISLAND
BENSONHURST
DYKER BEACH PARK
FORT HAMILTON
VERRAZANO-NARROWS BRIDGE
BROOKLYN COLLEGE
Gravesend Bay
CONEY ISLAND
NEW YORK AQUARIUM
CONEY ISLAND BEACH
Pulaski Skyway
Hoboken Ave.
John F. Kennedy Blvd.
Flushing Ave.
Myrtle Ave.
Lafayette St.
Prospect Expwy.
Gowanus Expwy.
Shore Pkwy.
Ocean Pkwy.
Neptune Ave.
Surf Ave.
Kings Hwy.
Cropsey Ave.
Caton Ave.
Church Ave.
Ditmas Ave.
18th Ave.
0 1 mi
0 2 km

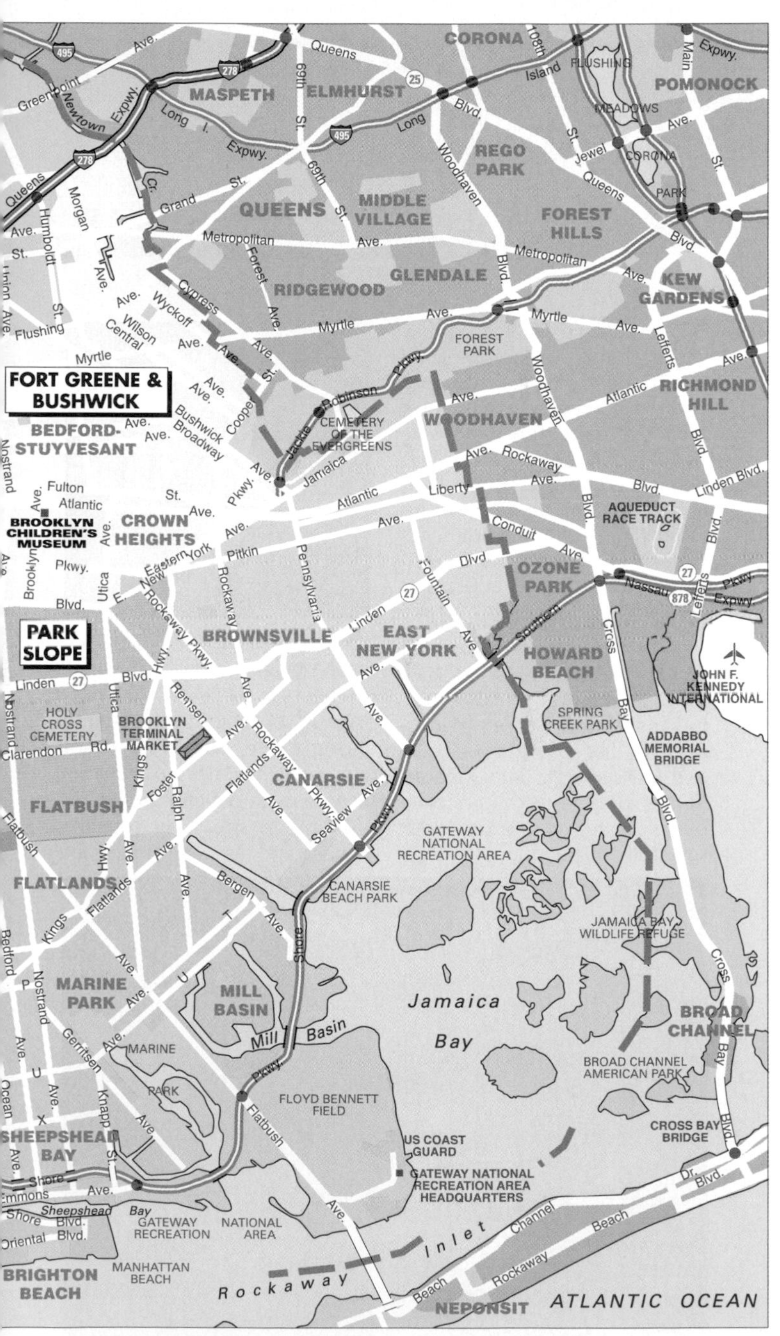
FORT GREENE & BUSHWICK
PARK SLOPE
CORONA
MASPETH
ELMHURST
POMONOCK
FLUSHING MEADOWS CORONA PARK
REGO PARK
QUEENS
MIDDLE VILLAGE
FOREST HILLS
GLENDALE
RIDGEWOOD
KEW GARDENS
FOREST PARK
RICHMOND HILL
CEMETERY OF THE EVERGREENS
WOODHAVEN
BEDFORD-STUYVESANT
BROOKLYN CHILDREN'S MUSEUM
CROWN HEIGHTS
AQUEDUCT RACE TRACK
OZONE PARK
BROWNSVILLE
EAST NEW YORK
HOWARD BEACH
JOHN F. KENNEDY INTERNATIONAL
HOLY CROSS CEMETERY
BROOKLYN TERMINAL MARKET
SPRING CREEK PARK
ADDABBO MEMORIAL BRIDGE
CANARSIE
FLATBUSH
GATEWAY NATIONAL RECREATION AREA
FLATLANDS
CANARSIE BEACH PARK
JAMAICA BAY WILDLIFE REFUGE
MARINE PARK
MILL BASIN
Jamaica Bay
BROAD CHANNEL
BROAD CHANNEL AMERICAN PARK
FLOYD BENNETT FIELD
MARINE PARK
SHEEPSHEAD BAY
US COAST GUARD
CROSS BAY BRIDGE
GATEWAY NATIONAL RECREATION AREA HEADQUARTERS
GATEWAY NATIONAL RECREATION AREA
MANHATTAN BEACH
BRIGHTON BEACH
Rockaway Inlet
NEPONSIT
ATLANTIC OCEAN

Downtown

BROOKLYN HEIGHTS · CARROLL GARDENS · COBBLE HILL

The Brooklyn Navy Yard may be a hub for commercial business and houses over 200 vendors, but the most impressive tenant remains the expansive **Brooklyn Grange Farm**. This leading green-roof consultant and urban farm is responsible for promoting healthy communities by providing them with fresh and locally sourced vegetables and herbs.

After admiring DUMBO's stellar views, stroll down cobblestoned Water Street. Then do like every proud local and walk straight into **Jacques Torres** for a taste of chocolate bliss. If savory is more your speed, then spend an afternoon in Caroll Gardens, a historically Italian neighborhood that offers shoppers a spectrum of family-owned butchers and bakers along Court Street. Also set along this shopper's paradise is **D'Amico**, an old-time institution dealing in specialty roasted coffees and teas. Step inside for

a rewarding whiff, before heading over to **Caputo's Fine Foods** for more substantial sustenance—think *salumi*-packed sandwiches, lard bread, and fresh mozz. Folks also favor **G. Esposito & Sons** for sausages, *sopressata,* arancini, and other Italian-American fun. Otherwise, rest your weary heels at **Ferdinando's Focacceria**, an age-old haunt famous for cooking up the classics, which taste as if they were transported straight from *nonna's* kitchen in Palermo and onto your palate. For the perfect finale, stop by **Court Pastry** for such sweets as cannoli, rainbow cookies, Italian ice, and the like. As Court Street blends into family-friendly Cobble Hill, find **Staubitz Market**, the most sociable butcher in town that blends the best of the old with the new by way of meticulously cut, top-quality chops, cheeses, and charcuterie. But, those with tots in tow or groups looking for a change in mood (and food) may shift "hills" from Cobble to Boerum to feast on Middle Eastern hits at **Sahadi's** or **Damascus Bakery**, each lauded for outrageously good pitas, spreads, and pastries.

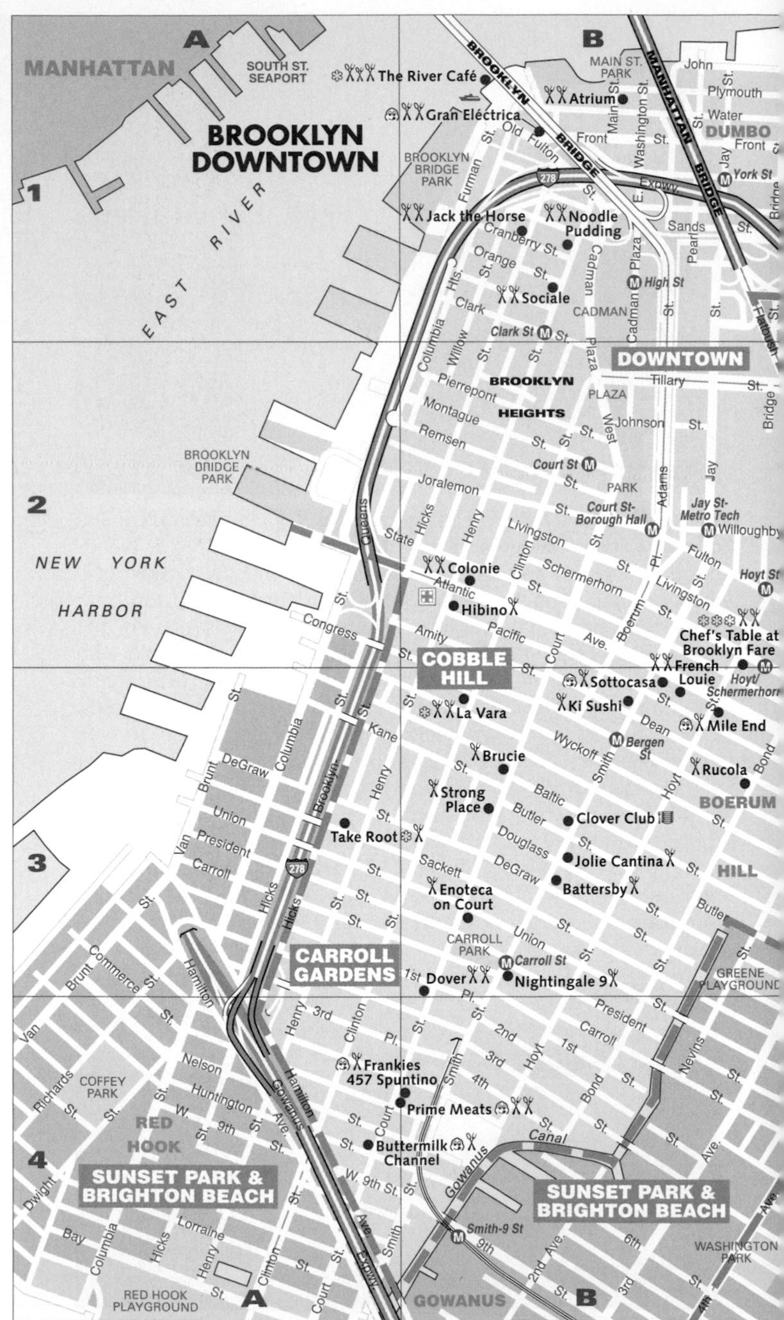
BROOKLYN
DOWNTOWN
MANHATTAN
SOUTH ST. SEAPORT
The River Café
Gran Eléctrica
Atrium
Jack the Horse
Noodle Pudding
Sociale
BROOKLYN BRIDGE PARK
EAST RIVER
BROOKLYN BRIDGE
MANHATTAN BRIDGE
MAIN ST. PARK
DUMBO
York St
High St
Clark St
Court St
CADMAN PLAZA
DOWNTOWN
BROOKLYN HEIGHTS
Court St-Borough Hall
Jay St-Metro Tech
Hoyt St
NEW YORK HARBOR
Colonie
Hibino
COBBLE HILL
Chef's Table at Brooklyn Fare
French Louie
Hoyt/Schermerhorn
Sottocasa
Ki Sushi
La Vara
Mile End
Bergen St
Brucie
Rucola
BOERUM HILL
Strong Place
Clover Club
Take Root
Jolie Cantina
Battersby
Enoteca on Court
CARROLL PARK
Carroll St
CARROLL GARDENS
Dover
Nightingale 9
GREENE PLAYGROUND
Frankies 457 Spuntino
Prime Meats
Buttermilk Channel
COFFEY PARK
RED HOOK
SUNSET PARK & BRIGHTON BEACH
Smith-9 St
WASHINGTON PARK
RED HOOK PLAYGROUND
GOWANUS
A
B
1
2
3
4

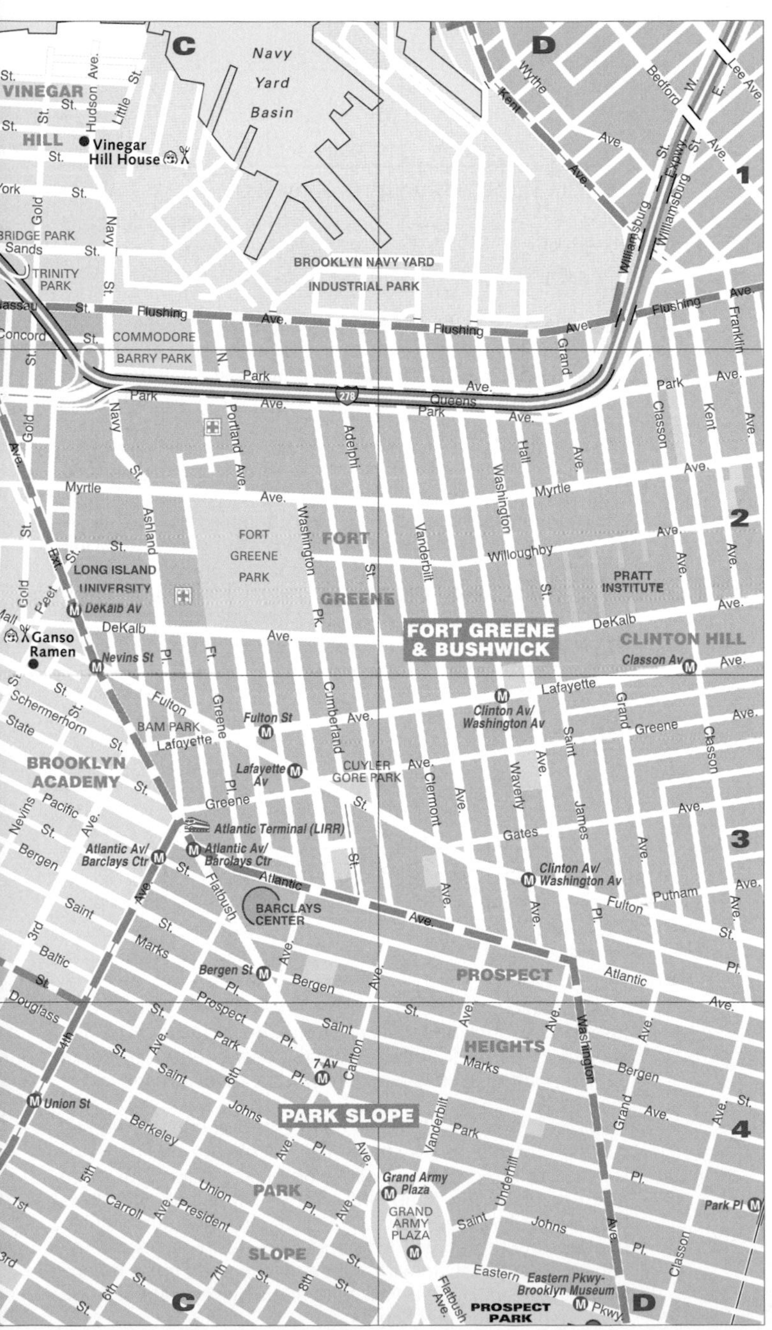
FORT GREENE & BUSHWICK
Navy Yard Basin
BROOKLYN NAVY YARD INDUSTRIAL PARK
VINEGAR HILL
Vinegar Hill House
TRINITY PARK
COMMODORE BARRY PARK
FORT GREENE PARK
FORT GREENE
LONG ISLAND UNIVERSITY
PRATT INSTITUTE
CLINTON HILL
Ganso Ramen
BAM PARK
BROOKLYN ACADEMY
CUYLER GORE PARK
Atlantic Terminal (LIRR)
BARCLAYS CENTER
PROSPECT HEIGHTS
PARK SLOPE
GRAND ARMY PLAZA
Eastern Pkwy-Brooklyn Museum
PROSPECT PARK
DeKalb Av
Nevins St
Fulton St
Lafayette Av
Atlantic Av/Barclays Ctr
Clinton Av/Washington Av
Classon Av
Bergen St
7 Av
Union St
Grand Army Plaza
Park Pl

Atrium

Contemporary

15 Main St. (bet. Plymouth & Water Sts.)

Subway: York St — Lunch & dinner daily
Phone: 718-858-1095
Web: www.atriumdumbo.com
Prices: **$$$**

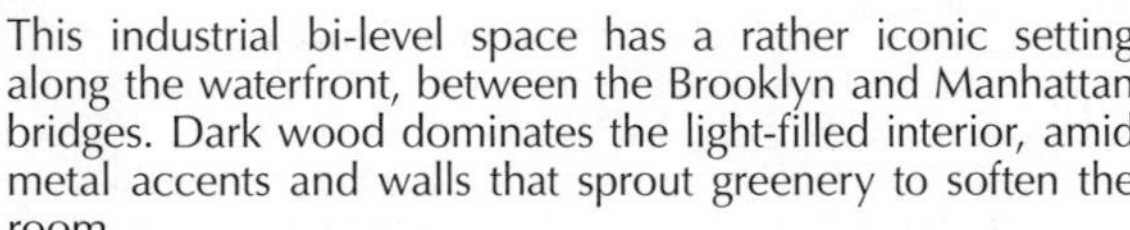

This industrial bi-level space has a rather iconic setting along the waterfront, between the Brooklyn and Manhattan bridges. Dark wood dominates the light-filled interior, amid metal accents and walls that sprout greenery to soften the room.

The food may have a farm-to-table focus, but a contemporary tilt is clear in everything that emerges from Atrium's bustling open kitchen. Elegant "baby greens" arrive as enticingly charred root vegetables over peppery arugula coulis; whereas crisply seared red snapper served over wild rice with dashi-simmered baby turnips, meaty mushrooms, and finished with a rich fumet makes the chef's (Laurent Kalkotour) French heritage abundantly clear. The chocolate-dipped crème fraîche and quark cheesecake is deservedly popular.

Battersby

Contemporary

B3

255 Smith St. (bet. Degraw & Douglas Sts.)

Subway: Bergen St (Smith St.) — Dinner nightly
Phone: 718-852-8321
Web: www.battersbybrooklyn.com
Prices: **$$**

This intimate Smith Street stunner is the domain of Co-chefs Joseph Ogrodnek and Walker Stern, also of Dover. The tiny kitchen at the back of the minimally decorated room belies the abundance of brilliance delivered by the short and sweet menu.

Caserecci tossed with petite, al dente cauliflower florets, capers, currants, and a showering of crunchy breadcrumbs is a treat. Choosing the smaller portion size allows for more room to enjoy the lamb duo—rare seared loin and slow-braised belly—composed with a chickpea-and-piquillo pepper stew slicked with gorgeous lamb jus. For dessert, the chocolate mille-feuille with mint ganache and Fernet Branca whipped cream is like a Thin Mint made by very talented and very sophisticated Girl Scouts.

Brucie

Italian

B3

234 Court St. (bet. Baltic & Kane Sts.)

Subway: Bergen St (Smith St.) — Lunch Sat – Sun
Phone: 347-987-4961 — Dinner Tue – Sun
Web: www.brucienyc.com
Prices: $$

Despite the tough guy name, this local canteen proudly claims the distinctly female touch of Chef/owner Zahra Tangorra. The pleasantly thrown-together space seats a diverse selection of patrons, many with kids in tow. Step in to find a smattering of tables, copper-topped dining counter, and shelves lined with canned products, jars, and bottles.

Old-world inspiration combines with new-world sensibility and results in product-driven, mostly Italian creations like *tagliatelle* with Brussels sprouts, tomato butter, and house-made *burrata*. Then, savor the brined and barbecued chicken basted with earthy stout- and maple syrup-enriched sauce. Try the chef's signature lasagna service: drop off your empty pan and pick it up filled and ready to feed a crowd.

Buttermilk Channel 

American

A4

524 Court St. (at Huntington St.)

Subway: Smith - 9 Sts. — Lunch Sat – Sun
Phone: 718-852-8490 — Dinner nightly
Web: www.buttermilkchannelnyc.com
Prices: $$

Doug Crowell and Chef Ryan Angulo run the sort of joint we'd all like to have at the end of our street. It's warm and relaxed, run with care and attention, offers an appealing menu for all occasions—and has prices that encourage regular attendance. The name may refer to the tidal strait but also evokes feelings of comfort and cheer in a place that's already cute and where the close-set tables and large bar both add to the animated atmosphere.

The kitchen seeks out worthy suppliers and with no little skill imbues each dish with that little extra something, be it the cod with Littleneck clams, the fresh linguini with beets or indeed the buttermilk-fried chicken. This care is even evident at weekend brunches on standouts like short rib hash.

Chef's Table at Brooklyn Fare ✿✿✿

Contemporary XX

B2

200 Schermerhorn St. (bet. Bond & Hoyt Sts.)

Subway: Hoyt-Schermerhorn — Dinner Tue – Sat
Phone: 718-243-0050
Web: www.brooklynfare.com
Prices: **$$$$**

At 7:00 P.M. this storefront attached to a gourmet grocer turns into something conceptual and remarkable. Here, Chef César Ramirez—the bespectacled authoritarian—stands center stage, surrounded by sous chefs and state-of-the-art everything. He personally welcomes every guest to his "table" which is actually a gleaming steel counter surrounding his kitchen, where each copper pot is watched-over and every porcelain vessel is cooled or warmed to match the temperature of the food it holds. The bar for painstaking detail seems to rise with each dish.

Expect a bang of flavor to open your meal, perhaps with a tart layering briny sea trout roe. Signatures like sea urchin piled over toasted brioche with a round of Périgord truffle never lose their impact. However, what was once an endless parade of seafood bites from faraway shores has grown and refined into equally lush mini-entrées. A square of Miyagi beef is *whoa*-inducing. Tiny wild strawberries, yogurt ice cream, and sake gelée balance each element with wondrous intensity.

The menu changes every night, but Chef Ramirez never veers from his brilliant melding of French and Japanese cuisines with modern style that keeps pleasure at the forefront.

Clover Club

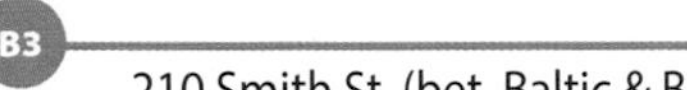

American

B3

210 Smith St. (bet. Baltic & Butler Sts.)

Subway: Bergen St (Smith St.) — Lunch Sat – Sun
Phone: 718-855-7939 — Dinner nightly
Web: www.cloverclubny.com
Prices: $$

A former shoe store is now an atmospheric rest stop that fashions a spot-on vintage vibe with mosaic-tiled floors, glove-soft leather banquettes, and pressed-tin ceilings dangling etched-glass pendants that glow as warmly as single malt. The glossy mahogany bar (furnished with leather-upholstered bar stools) is overseen by natty bartenders artfully shaking and pouring a stellar selection of libations like the namesake Clover Club—a mixture of gin, dry vermouth, lemon, and raspberry syrup.

An excellent savory carte is a perfect counterpoint to such liquid indulgences. Highlights may include herb-marinated hanger steak over toasted baguette spread with horseradish cream; duck fat-fried potato crisps; oysters on the half-shell; and American caviar service.

Colonie

Contemporary XX

B2

127 Atlantic Ave. (bet. Clinton & Henry Sts.)

Subway: Borough Hall — Lunch Sat – Sun
Phone: 718-855-7500 — Dinner nightly
Web: www.colonienyc.com
Prices: $$

Hip and lively (both the crowd and the green wall of lush plants that is), this is a buzzing retreat for taking in all that makes Brooklyn so enticing. There is the exposed brick dining room and the ceilings of distressed wood, of course, along with the requisite long bar and perhaps most important, a sharp crowd who give Colonie its measured dose of cool.

Start with crostini, perhaps laden with egg salad, a ribbon of lardo and drizzle of veal jus. A deeply nutty rye berry ragout brings together crispy mushrooms, cabbage, and a perfectly fried duck egg. Opt for the whole market fish, served deboned with tart and herbaceous salsa verde, crisp garlic, and roasted lemon. Be sure to save room for warm, yeasty sugar donuts stuffed with Chantilly cream.

Dover

B3 — **Contemporary** XX

412 Court St. (at 1st Pl.)

Subway: Carroll St — Lunch Sat – Sun
Phone: 347-987-3545 — Dinner nightly
Web: www.doverbrooklyn.com
Prices: **$$$**

Creative global accents are the guiding force behind the enticing lineup of plates at this tastefully spare candlelit bistro. Chefs Walker Stern and Joe Ogrodnek (the duo behind Battersby) prove the world is their oyster—raw or broiled and seasonally embellished to kick things off—so settle in and expect to be impressed.

Sweet watermelon *aguachile* is boldly dressed with fresh lime juice, spicy green chiles, blistered shisito peppers and a hit of feta; while house-made links of merguez are nestled in a thick and creamy chickpea purée dotted with plumped golden raisins and accompanied by perfectly puffy wedges of hot pita. Dessert is delicious and seasonal: picture a summery olive oil cake plated with white peach semifreddo and verjus gelée.

Enoteca on Court

B3 — **Italian** 

347 Court St. (bet. President & Union Sts.)

Subway: Carroll St — Lunch & dinner daily
Phone: 718-243-1000
Web: www.enotecaoncourt.com
Prices:

This Carroll Gardens wine bar is a fresh-faced take on *la Cucina Italiana*, almost in spite of its location next to the old-school stalwart Marco Polo. Slim, spare, and dishing out wood and brick details, the cozy spot accommodates neighborhood crowds at its L-shaped bar leading to the open kitchen and on to a handful of tables in the back.

A wood-burning oven brings a distinct personality to a range of specialties here like pizzas, baked pastas, and *spiedini* (skewered meat or seafood). The piping-hot panini are always a treat, made from a slab of fresh pizza dough that's crusty yet moist within, stuffed with sweet sausage, melted fresh mozzarella, a drizzle of olive oil, and tender broccoli rabe. The possibilities and tempting combinations are endless.

Frankies 457 Spuntino

Italian

457 Court St. (bet. 4th Pl. & Luquer St.)

Subway: Smith - 9 Sts — Lunch & dinner daily
Phone: 718-403-0033
Web: www.frankiesspuntino.com
Prices: **$$**

Frank Castronovo and Frank Falcinelli (collectively known as the Franks) have built a small empire for themselves based on delicious, seasonal Italian fare served in rustic little haunts. Frankies 457 Spuntino, a charming, brick-lined space with bare wood tables and a quiet, shady backyard strung with twinkling bistro lights, is a classic example of their easy Brooklyn style.

Seem familiar by now? Well, these guys wrote the book. Service is laid-back and unpretentious, perhaps because they know the food does the talking here: a wildly fresh fennel, celery root, and parsley salad arrives with aged pecorino and a delicate lemon vinaigrette; while a tender tangle of linguini is laced with a fresh tomato broth studded with fava beans and garlic.

French Louie

Mediterranean

320 Atlantic Ave. (bet. Smith & Hoyt Sts.)

Subway: Hoyt-Schermerhorn — Lunch & dinner daily
Phone: 718-935-1200
Web: www.frenchlouienyc.com
Prices: **$$**

From the team behind Buttermilk Channel, French Louie combines a candlelit vibe with rustic touches and a dominantly Mediterranean menu in a welcoming setting that's become *the* neighborhood hideaway. Whether you perch at the mahogany bar or in the spacious backyard, be sure to come hungry for the splurge-worthy cheese plate and profiteroles—golden, puffy and encapsulating a fennel pollen-flavored ice cream.

For a dish to share, try the *Le Grand Socca*, not normally found outside Liguria (where's it's called *farinata*) or the South of France. A bit thicker than the traditional, this pizza-sized crêpe arrives topped with a shelled-bean stew, charred asparagus, *freekeh*, and spiced lemon yogurt, with just the right amount of smokiness from the skillet.

Ganso Ramen

C2 — Japanese

25 Bond St. (bet. Fulton & Livingston Sts.)

Subway: Nevins St — Lunch & dinner daily
Phone: 718-403-0900
Web: www.gansonyc.com
Prices:

A welcome sight amid the sneaker stores and pizza joints of commercial Fulton Mall, this friendly, comforting *ramen-ya* is a sure sign that things are changing in downtown Brooklyn. Inside, wood booths and tables sit atop stone floors while buzzing chefs are visible through encased glass. The same team has opened an equally appealing spot, Ganso Yaki, in Boerum Hill.

Cookbook author and owner Harris Salat ensures that these steaming bowls of springy noodles remain a notch above those slurp shops opening throughout the city. Nightly specials are deftly executed, including a Mongolian lamb ramen in chili-sansho broth topped with slices of lamb, fried onions, garlic chives, and *ajitama* egg. Try pillowy steamed buns stuffed with pork belly or tangy duck.

Gran Eléctrica

B1 — Mexican

5 Front St. (bet. Dock & Old Fulton Sts.)

Subway: High St — Lunch Sat – Sun
Phone: 718-852-2700 — Dinner nightly
Web: www.granelectrica.com
Prices: $$

Looking to market ingredients and a California-style approach to Mexican cuisine, this chic yet comfortable restaurant impresses with its lovely décor and lively vibe. Servers are engaged and enthusiastic about the menu's pleasures. An ideal visit starts with a margarita at the bar and moves to the garden as strings of lights flicker to life.

Mexico and Brooklyn are in balance on a menu that includes small plates such as *memelitas de frijoles,* a masa disc topped with mashed black beans, spicy salsa verde, *queso fresco,* and *crema*. Flavor is bright in the deliciously untraditional poblano *chile relleno* stuffed with Havarti, roasted tomato-jalapeño salsa, and tortillas. Try the *frijoles de la olla* (black beans topped with avocado) on the side.

Hibino

Japanese

333 Henry St. (at Pacific St.)

Subway: Borough Hall — Lunch Mon – Fri
Phone: 718-260-8052 — Dinner nightly
Web: www.hibino-brooklyn.com
Prices: ⓈⓈ

The team at this demure retreat isn't constrained by a menu. Instead, diners are greeted by servers bearing blackboards that list the day's offerings. The list of *obanzai* (Kyoto-style tapas) are enticing and include marinated, fried chicken thigh with tartar sauce, grilled pork sausage, or roasted oysters with spicy gazpacho. The kitchen's regional dedication is also evident in its offering of Osaka's traditional *hako* sushi. This box-pressed preparation might be served as a layering of quality rice, shiso, *kanpyo* (preserved gourd), and salmon. Meanwhile, lunch is a concise affair that reveals either a bento box or platter of nigiri accompanied by a neatly stuffed *futomaki*.

Of course, if lunch seems limited, come back for dinner when the kitchen truly shines.

Jack the Horse

American

66 Hicks St. (at Cranberry St.)

Subway: High St — Lunch Sun
Phone: 718-852-5084 — Dinner nightly
Web: www.jackthehorse.com
Prices: $$

A Brooklyn Heights favorite, this sleepy American tavern is a consistent spot in a neighborhood that lacks a variety of serious eats. Exposed brick walls covered with old-fashioned clocks set a cozy tone, and regulars return for the well-stocked bar with myriad bitters and a bargain three-course prix-fixe.

Slurp a few bivalves at the Oyster Room next door before settling into a table, or if thirst beckons, sip an Old Fashioned with barrel strength Bourbon while perusing the menu. Some locals head straight for the burger—focaccia layered with Gruyère, caramelized Bourbon onions, and a juicy beef patty. Though ricotta and butternut squash ravioli, tossed in sweet brown butter and topped with crumbled smoky bacon, is a fine alternative.

Jolie Cantina

Fusion 

B3

241 Smith St. (at Douglass St.)

Subway: Bergen St (Smith St.)
Phone: 718-488-0777
Web: www.joliecantina.com
Prices: $$

Lunch Tue – Sun
Dinner nightly

A marriage of French and Mexican sensibilities is the guiding force behind Jolie Cantina's novel cuisine. The kitchen sates diners all-day with spins on the classics like a hot *croque señor* made with roasted poblanos, chorizo, melting Comté, and (*bien-sûr*) accompanied by excellent fries. The range of fascinating creations also includes Mexican steak tartare dressed with pickled jalapeños, tequila, and capers; as well as the Cantina cassoulet comprised of black beans and *chicharrónes*.

The walls of this Cobble Hill corner spot feature whimsical artwork like a red-and-blue mural of roosters and piñatas, in a room furnished with bright red and yellow enameled chairs. Reiterating its French leaning, the bar hangs a sign that reads: "Hecho en France."

Ki Sushi

Japanese 

B3

122 Smith St. (bet. Dean & Pacific Sts.)

Subway: Bergen St (Smith St.)
Phone: 718-935-0575
Web: N/A
Prices: $$

Lunch Mon – Sat
Dinner nightly

Smith Street offers plenty of dining options to choose from, but Ki is this strip's sushi standout. Low-key and proffering good value, it is also a neighborhood favorite. At lunch, find downtown Brooklyn professionals taking a respite from the day's proceedings. At night, young couples and families routinely pack the room that brandishes a dim and earthy mien.

Sample an array of cold and hot appetizers like yellowtail tartare with yuzu-ginger vinaigrette or rock shrimp tempura with creamy-spicy sauce. Follow this with creative maki, or better yet, the sushi deluxe platter. The skillfully constructed nigiri lineup features an array of fluke, sea bream, amberjack, and mackerel, as well as a roll stuffed with lean and deliciously unadulterated tuna.

La Vara ✿

Spanish ✕✕

B3

268 Clinton St. (at Verandah Pl.)

Subway: Carroll St
Phone: 718-422-0065
Web: www.lavarany.com
Prices: $$

Lunch Sat – Sun
Dinner nightly

Set in quiet and charming Cobble Hill, La Vara is as alluring as its surrounds. Inside, hip urbanites get down to business around the sleek marble bar; while stroller-rolling parents might migrate to curved leather booths or nestle in the wooden alcoves up front. In the main dining room, white tables set with contemporary crockery offer just the right contrast to rustic brick walls.

From soft lighting and personable service, to countrified food and inventive presentations, this convivial respite never misses a beat. Embark on a journey to culinary heights with the visually strange but wonderful tasting *remojón* featuring a scoop of house-cured salt cod mingled with orange segments, pistachios, and sliced green olives. Then, sail on to *fideuà* or Valencian-style noodle paella tossed with fresh, briny clams, tender squid, and a creamy aïoli.

With luck on your side, *cochinillo* (slow-cooked, amber-hued suckling pig with crackling skin and rose-quince sauce) or *tortillita de gambas* accompanied by a pale pink shrimp pâté may star on the menu. If not, rest easy as you can still have your cake (or in this case an orange blossom-scented walnut tart finished with lemon curd and cream) and eat it too.

Mile End

Deli 

B3

97A Hoyt St. (bet. Atlantic Ave. & Pacific St.)

Subway: Hoyt-Schermerhorn — Lunch & dinner daily
Phone: 718-852-7510
Web: www.mileendbrooklyn.com
Prices:

Boerum Hill's most bodacious deli serves up killer smoked meat and so much more. The tiny space gets lots of traffic, and those who can't find a seat along the counter or trio of communal tables can feast at home with takeout procured from the sidewalk window. Now for the food: a cured and smoked brisket sandwich, stacked onto soft rye bread and smacked with mustard, is the stuff that dreams are made of. Eclectic and vegetarian-friendly, the menu also reveals poutine (owner Noah Bernamoff is a Montreal native), roasted eggplant *brik* dotted with briny capers, pine nuts, and sweet raisins; as well as fresh-baked desserts like almond cake with house-made vanilla ice cream.

Manhattanites take heed: there's a location now on Bond Street.

Nightingale 9

Vietnamese 

B3

329 Smith St. (bet. Carroll & President Sts.)

Subway: Carroll St — Lunch & dinner Tue – Sun
Phone: 347-689-4699
Web: www.nightingale9.com
Prices: $$

Smith Street's fresh take on Vietnamese cuisine is the brainchild of Chef Robert Newton. Nightingale 9's home is the old Seersucker space, and the larger digs better accommodate the stream of neighborhood families out for something different. Its curious name refers to the old Brooklyn telephone exchange.

Meanwhile, the ingredient-driven menu offers a subtle take on shredded green papaya salad that is accented by nuggets of house-dried beef, mint, and crispy shallots. Grilled beef meatballs are wonderfully chewy, flavorful, and fun in your mouth. They are in turn accompanied by sheets of rice paper and water; diners moisten these sheets until they become soft, pliable, and ready to roll with meat and herbs, before being dunked in spicy *nuoc cham*.

Noodle Pudding

Italian

38 Henry St. (bet. Cranberry & Middagh Sts.)

Subway: High St — Dinner Tue – Sun
Phone: 718-625-3737
Web: N/A
Prices: **$$**

With Dean Martin and Frank Sinatra rotating on the playlist and a dark wood bar full of regulars, Noodle Pudding embodies all the essential qualities of a winning neighborhood spot. It's the type of place to kick back and relax, dine on consistently good food, and even sit solo but never feel "alone."

The kitchen has mastered Italian-American classics, with honest ingredients and great preparation, like the balance of acidic and sweet components in the gently poached cod *Livornese*. The tantalizing eggy-cheesy, slightly smoky-sweet, and creamy carbonara that bathes toothsome mezze rigatoni, fava beans, and tiny pork sausage meatballs is "dyno-mite." Top it all off with the exemplary (and shareable) house-made cheesecake and a perfect shot of espresso.

Prime Meats

European

465 Court St. (at Luquer St.)

Subway: Smith - 9 Sts. — Lunch & dinner daily
Phone: 718-254-0327
Web: www.frankspm.com
Prices: **$$**

Prime Meats stands tall and proud as a true original and local gem for German eats set to American beats. The booths in front are bright and snug, while bentwood chairs and net curtains tied into a knot add to that brasserie feel. A warm vibe and cheery servers complete the picture.

Hand-crafted sausages and burgers are all the rage here. Nibble away on homemade pretzels while perusing the lunch menu, which may be simple and sandwich-focused, but always showcases a gutsy edge. Bold flavors shine through in a creamy roasted squash soup; *jagerwurst*, a lightly charred, delicately smoky, and meaty sausage with red cabbage casserole; or Jen's German potato salad tossing waxy potato slices, chopped herbs, and thick bacon lardons in a pickled dressing.

The River Café ✿

B1 **Contemporary** XXX

1 Water St. (bet. Furman & Old Fulton Sts.)

Subway: High St — Lunch Sat – Sun
Phone: 718-522-5200 — Dinner nightly
Web: www.therivercafe.com
Prices: **$$$$**

Thanks to its enviable location and stunning skyline vistas, this waterside favorite more than lives up to its reputation as one of the dreamiest escapes in town. Delicate details like fresh, fragrant flowers, beautifully set tables, and cozy rattan chairs make for romantic environs—and though the tight space has a way of turning intimate whispers into public displays of affection, all will be forgiven after a bite or two of Chef Brad Steelman's solid-as-ever cuisine.

Launch into plump wild shrimp smothered in creamy Hollandaise and served with crunchy white asparagus for added texture; or the perfectly crisped crab cake arranged with creamy uni, avocado, and a light herb salad. Pearly white halibut with roasted maitakes is a testament to the kitchen's focus on simplicity and supreme freshness, while a glistening rack of mint- and mustard seed-glazed lamb—charred on the outside with an evenly pink interior—exemplifies its artistry.

Enjoy dessert, as the mouthwatering offerings (think milk chocolate soufflé with melted marshmallow, or dark chocolate marquise topped with a replica of the nearby Brooklyn Bridge) are a veritable education in soigné presentations and sumptuous flavors.

Rucola

Contemporary X

B3

190 Dean St. (at Bond St.)

Subway: Bergen St (Smith St.) Lunch & dinner daily
Phone: 718-576-3209
Web: www.rucolabrooklyn.com
Prices: **$$**

Nestled among the brownstone-lined streets of beautiful Boerum Hill, this inviting trattoria is open all day. Rucola's attractive interior rocks that prototypical rusticity of reclaimed wood and aged mirrors, while tables are set with sprigs of fresh wild flowers.

Yogurt and granola with local honey is part of the kitchen's repertoire, but the restaurant's Northern Italian influence fully comes into focus in the evenings. Vegetable antipasti, like spicy spears of pickled fennel, are offered alongside cured meats and imported cheeses. Arugula (that's *rucola in Italiano*) is tossed with shaved radish and a celery seed vinaigrette. Enjoyable entrées include a neat block of lasagna layering pasta sheets and hearty pork ragù with a creamy béchamel sauce.

Sociale

Italian 

B1

72 Henry St. (at Orange St)

Subway: High St Lunch & dinner daily
Phone: 718-576-3588
Web: www.socialebk.com
Prices: **$$**

Although the name evokes a swinging place with cocktails and conversation, Sociale proves much more than a neighborhood social club. With true Italian hospitality and a cozy corner location across from a throw-back cinema, Sociale has become the Brooklyn Heights spot to spend a lively Friday night. Regulars wedge up to the bar for glasses of mineral-rich Italian whites or crowd into a charming, lair-like dining room, where the table inches away from yours may host your newest companion.

The menu sticks to classics, with perfectly cooked spaghetti in fresh and chunky *pomodoro* sauce; or veal loin wrapped in pancetta and drizzled with great veal jus. Come dessert, the banana and date bread pudding with Guinness gelato is absolutely delicious.

Sottocasa

B3 — Pizza

298 Atlantic Ave. (bet. Hoyt & Smith Sts.)

Subway: Hoyt-Schermerhorn — Lunch Sat – Sun
Phone: 718-852-8758 — Dinner nightly
Web: www.sottocasanyc.com
Prices: $$

Located just below street level on frenetic Atlantic Avenue, a nondescript façade holds a quiet den of serious Neapolitan pizza magic. Enter and you'll find a simple, narrow, wood-paneled room with whitewashed brick walls; a little bar showcasing a handful of wines; an enormous, two-ton clay oven (imported directly from Naples); and a little patio out back for alfresco dining.

The mood is decidedly relaxed, and while there are delicious salads, antipasti, and desserts to be tried at Sottocasa, the name of the game here is undoubtedly their wickedly good pizza, served folded, *blanche* or *rosse* (with—hurrah!—a gluten-free option as well). Regulars adore the *Diavola* pie, which comes laced with excellent mozzarella, fresh basil, black olives, and hot sopressata.

Strong Place

B3 — Gastropub 

270 Court St. (bet. Butler & Douglass Sts.)

Subway: Bergen St (Smith St.) — Lunch Fri – Sun
Phone: 718-855-2105 — Dinner nightly
Web: www.strong-place.com
Prices: $$

Strong Place is a Cobble Hill favorite for its epic beer list, which offers more than 20 brews on tap plus over ten bottled options. Kick back, unwind, and drink up; the vibe is chill, and chunky tables with metal seating render a comfortable, vaguely industrial look.

The snacks pair perfectly with their frosty pints—imagine spicy duck fat edamame, Cajun boiled peanuts, or a platter of iced shellfish from the raw bar. Stay on for dinner, because the menu offers plenty of proper options. Smooth asparagus and fennel soup sprinkled with crushed bacon gains its silken texture from puréed red bliss potatoes; while the thick, juicy lamb burger is topped with creamy feta cheese and accompanied by sun-dried tomato ketchup and rosemary salt-tossed French fries.

Take Root ✿

A3 — Contemporary

187 Sackett St. (bet. Henry & Hicks Sts.)

Subway: Carroll St — Dinner Thu – Sat
Phone: 347-227-7116
Web: www.take-root.com
Prices: **$$$$**

If you're lucky enough to score one of the precious few seats here, make it your mission to arrive on time. The tasting menu's procession begins promptly, so stragglers run the risk of missing out on its first luscious bites—and to deprive yourself of a crunchy fennel pollen-dusted potato croquette would be nothing short of a culinary crime.

Since this is strictly a two-woman operation, the military-like precision is easily forgiven. Chef Elise Kornack single-handedly runs the immaculate kitchen while her wife, Anna Hieronimus, congenially attends to the tranquil, intimate dining room. But, the team works in tandem when it comes to presenting the uniquely composed plates.

Substitutes are not offered, but there's little chance you won't be happy with what's to come. Black garlic-glazed lamb's tongue *anticucho* is a stimulating opening act for a refreshing summertime composition of slivered snap peas, intensely flavorful tomato pulp, wild ginger, and a creamy drizzle of chocolate mint purée. The chef's style is a fresh and light approach to quality product as seen in asparagus dressed with oysters whipped into a froth or roasted local pork plated with diced celtuce and wild strawberries.

Vinegar Hill House

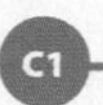

American

C1

72 Hudson Ave. (near Water St.)

Subway: York St
Phone: 718-522-1018
Web: www.vinegarhillhouse.com
Prices: $$

Lunch Sat – Sun
Dinner nightly

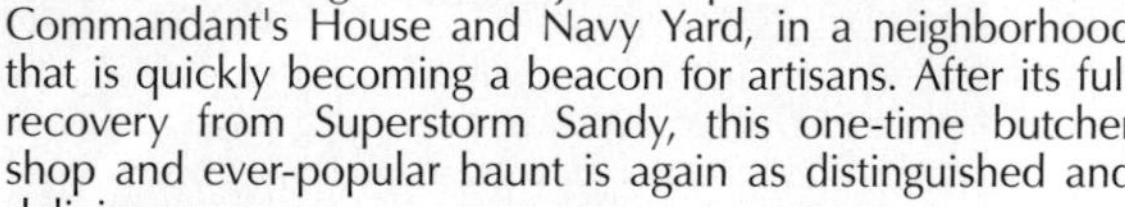

Find this carriage house just steps from the historic Commandant's House and Navy Yard, in a neighborhood that is quickly becoming a beacon for artisans. After its full recovery from Superstorm Sandy, this one-time butcher shop and ever-popular haunt is again as distinguished and delicious as ever.

Packed to the rafters with locals, this "house" boasts quality, sustainable products prepared in a wood-burning oven. A wonderfully broiled grapefruit topped with puffed rice mixed with shrimp paste, or liver pâté topped with pistachios display an inventive mix of global ingredients. Favorites like pappardelle with shad roe and lemon zest, or caramelized pork chops with creamy grits are flooded with flavor; while most everything that comes from that prominent oven is a big hit.

Bib Gourmand indicates our inspectors' favorites for good value.

Fort Greene & Bushwick

BEDFORD-STUYVESANT · CLINTON HILL · CROWN HEIGHTS

Brooklyn is big on international cuisine, and its every nook overflows with enticing eats. Set in the northwest corner and right across from Lower Manhattan lies Fort Greene, famous for West Indian and African communinities (and cuisines). **Bati** is a traditional retreat for Ethiopean home food with a focus on vegetarian options. Since 1999, **Madiba** (named for the late-great Nelson Mandela) has amassed a cult-like following for faithfully conceived South African dishes. But, if good 'ole Caribbean food is what you're in the mood for, then get in line at **Gloria's Caribbean** for excellent roti, oxtail, jerk chicken, and more. Otherwise, simply imbibe the vibe and feel the love at the annual West Indian Day parade—a veritable riot of color and flavor.

Follow the culinary trail further east to Bedford-Stuyvesant. Here in Bed-Stuy (as locals commonly refer to it), carb-junkies gather at **SCRATCHbread** for its nostalgic scene and

addictive eats. You can also preorder from their unique selection of "Bourbon wheat," "Focaccia rolls," "Peasant sour," and "Stuyvesant sour" to impress your dinner guests back home. Others who wish to plan a Southen-themed evening should stock up on wares from **Carolina Country Store**. Bringing crave-worthy signatures straight from the namesake states, this food truck sensation is every carnivores fantasy. Meanwhile, Mexico makes its presence known at old-timey **Tortilleria Mexicana Los Hermanos**, a bona fide factory turning out tortillas in Bushwick. Likewise, **Caesar's Empanada Truck** is mobbed for cheesy renditions of the eponymous treat. And, if all's well that ends well, then be sure to sample the 200-plus flavors found at **Dun-Well Doughnuts**. Speaking of bliss, **Berg'n** in Crown Heights is a big and boisterous beer hall pouring myriad drafts or popping bottles of beer that pair perfectly with bites from **Asia Dog** or **Ramen Burger** (also housed within).

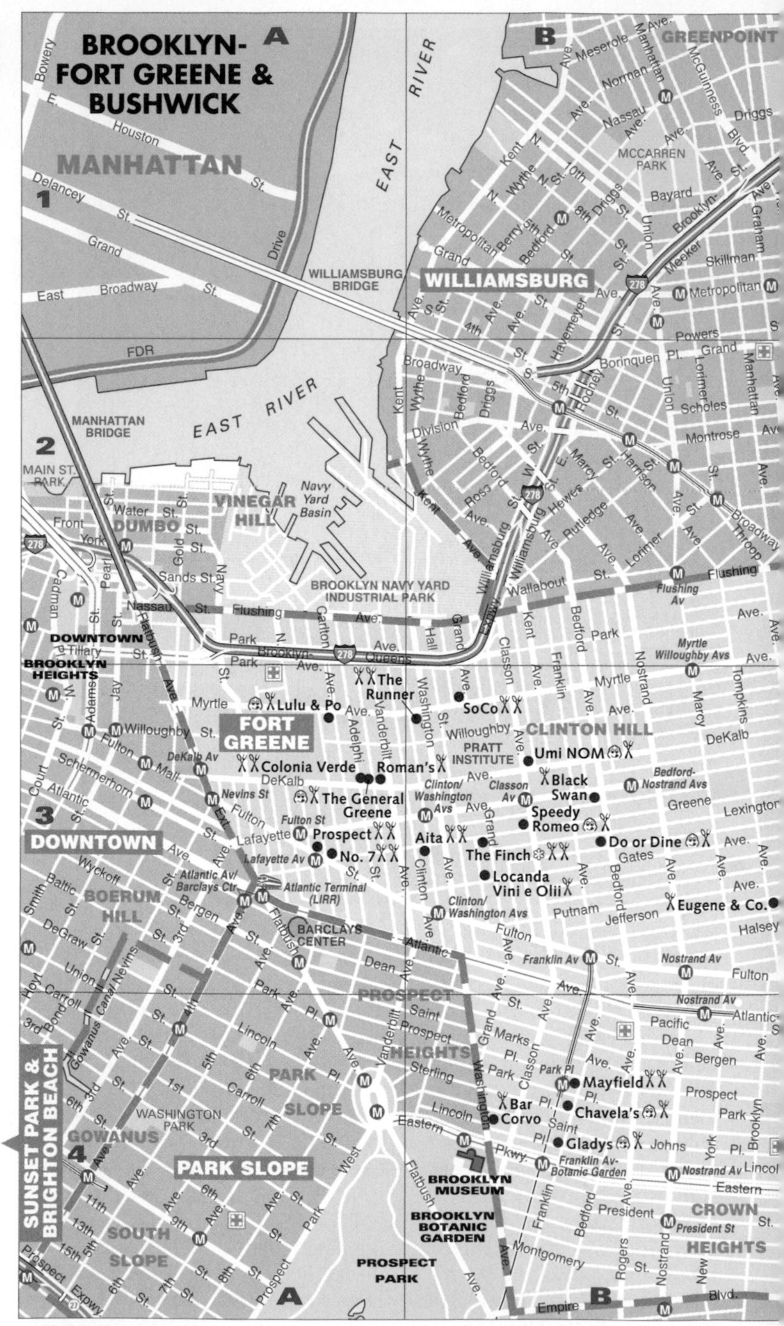
BROOKLYN-
FORT GREENE &
BUSHWICK
MANHATTAN
WILLIAMSBURG
GREENPOINT
MCCARREN PARK
WILLIAMSBURG BRIDGE
MANHATTAN BRIDGE
EAST RIVER
MAIN ST. PARK
VINEGAR HILL
DUMBO
BROOKLYN NAVY YARD INDUSTRIAL PARK
DOWNTOWN BROOKLYN
BROOKLYN HEIGHTS
FORT GREENE
CLINTON HILL
PRATT INSTITUTE
DOWNTOWN
BOERUM HILL
BARCLAYS CENTER
PROSPECT HEIGHTS
PARK SLOPE
WASHINGTON PARK
GOWANUS
SOUTH SLOPE
BROOKLYN MUSEUM
BROOKLYN BOTANIC GARDEN
PROSPECT PARK
CROWN HEIGHTS
SUNSET PARK & BRIGHTON BEACH
The Runner
Lulu & Po
SoCo
Umi NOM
Colonia Verde
Roman's
Black Swan
The General Greene
Speedy Romeo
Prospect
Aita
Do or Dine
No. 7
The Finch
Locanda Vini e Olii
Eugene & Co.
Mayfield
Bar Corvo
Chavela's
Gladys

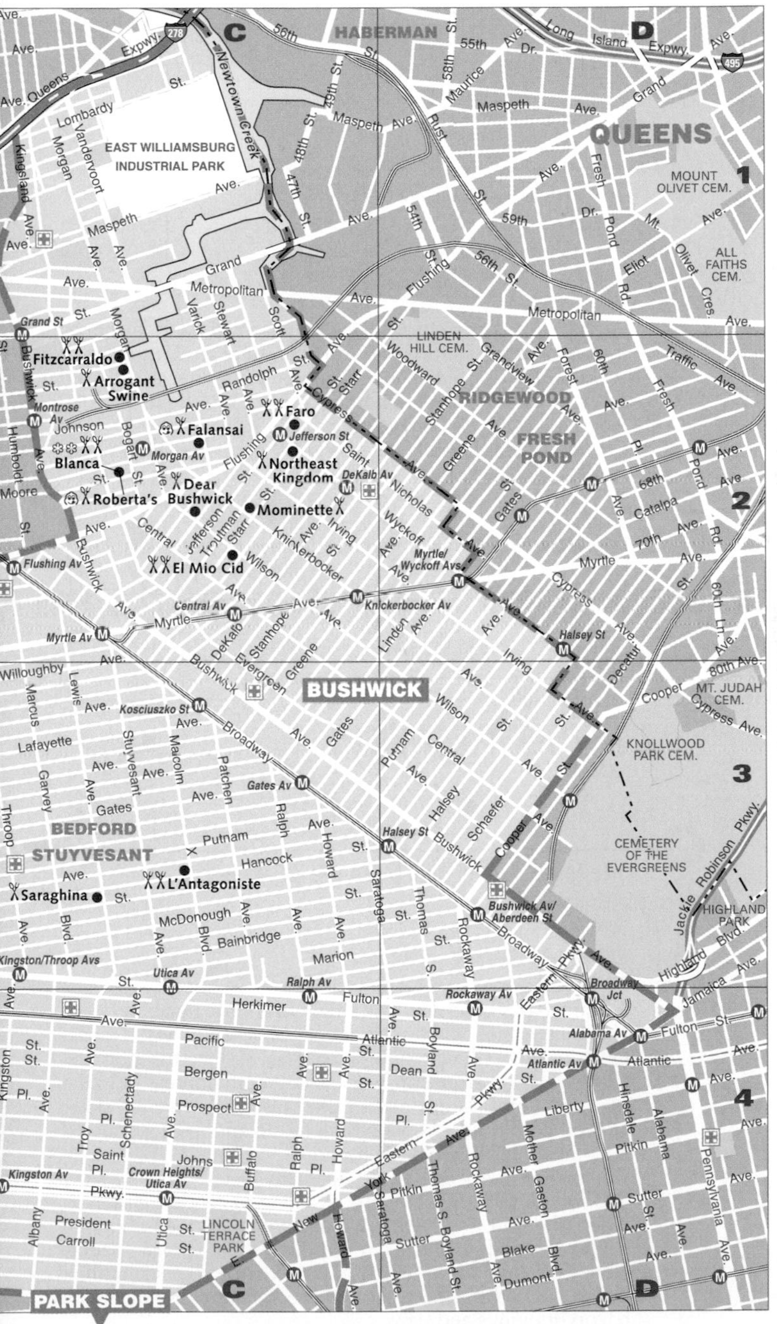

C
D
HABERMAN
QUEENS
EAST WILLIAMSBURG INDUSTRIAL PARK
MOUNT OLIVET CEM.
ALL FAITHS CEM.
LINDEN HILL CEM.
RIDGEWOOD
FRESH POND
BUSHWICK
MT. JUDAH CEM.
KNOLLWOOD PARK CEM.
CEMETERY OF THE EVERGREENS
HIGHLAND PARK
BEDFORD STUYVESANT
LINCOLN TERRACE PARK
PARK SLOPE
1
2
3
4
Fitzcarraldo
Arrogant Swine
Falansai
Faro
Northeast Kingdom
Blanca
Roberta's
Dear Bushwick
Mominette
El Mio Cid
L'Antagoniste
Saraghina
Grand St
Montrose Av
Morgan Av
Jefferson St
DeKalb Av
Flushing Av
Myrtle/Wyckoff Avs
Central Av
Knickerbocker Av
Myrtle Av
Halsey St
Kosciuszko St
Gates Av
Bushwick Av/Aberdeen St
Kingston/Throop Avs
Utica Av
Ralph Av
Rockaway Av
Broadway Jct
Alabama Av
Atlantic Av
Kingston Av
Crown Heights/Utica Av
Long Island Expwy.
Queens Expwy.
Newtown Creek
Metropolitan Ave.
Grand Ave.
Flushing Ave.
Myrtle Ave.
Broadway
Bushwick Ave.
Eastern Pkwy.
Jackie Robinson Pkwy.
Atlantic Ave.
Fulton St.

Aita

Italian XX

B3

132 Greene Ave. (at Waverly Ave.)

Subway: Clinton - Washington Avs — Lunch Fri – Sun
Phone: 718-576-3584 — Dinner Tue – Sun
Web: www.aitarestaurant.com
Prices: $$

Tucked into a cozy corner, this quintessential trattoria echoes the beauty and charm of Clinton Hill. Amid a robust culinary scene, Aita finds a niche with its warm (never effusive) service and equally comforting décor of antique mirrors, wood paneling, and lacy curtains.

Chef/co-owner Roberto Aita certainly has a way with pasta, crafting thick, homemade noodles twirled with flavorful sauces, such as the *taglierini* with buttery clam broth that is slightly sweet with melted leeks and strewn with irresistibly briny littlenecks. Italian tradition echoes through beguilingly simple desserts, like a bowl of plump fresh berries with nothing more than a dollop of cream and end-of-meal biscotti.

The wines are as deliciously approachable as the cooking itself.

Arrogant Swine

Barbecue X

C2

173 Morgan Ave. (bet. Meserole & Scholes Sts.)

Subway: Morgan Av — Dinner nightly
Phone: 347-328-5595
Web: www.arrogantswine.com
Prices:

A boon to this otherwise industrial warehouse neighborhood, Arrogant Swine's whitewashed brick walls and rows of picnic tables steadily fill with hungry patrons. Striking exterior wall murals and the aroma of sweet smoke both impress from the approach. Heat lamps extend the season for savoring slow-cooked pork outdoors, with rock music and a smoke-fueled barbecue buzz in the background.

Whole hog barbecue is the specialty here—smoked slow and whole over live embers, resulting in tender, glistening meat. The loin, shoulder, jowl, and more are then chopped or pulled and tossed with Carolina-style vinegar sauce. Sides complete the downhome experience, especially their traditional cornpone (savory cornbread in an iron skillet with bacon drippings and slaw).

Bar Corvo

Italian

791 Washington Ave. (bet. Lincoln & St John's Pls.)

Subway: Eastern Pkwy - Brooklyn Museum — Lunch Sat – Sun
Phone: 718-230-0940 — Dinner nightly
Web: www.barcorvo.com
Prices: $$

Walk by Bar Corvo and sense the goodness that awaits inside. A pane of glass provides a sneak peek at the large marble bar, communal table, penny-tile flooring, and cheerfully retro décor. Its eclectic vibe and artistic touches lead to a spacious garden, perfect for groups, and a culinary experience that keeps lines spilling onto the sidewalk.

Here, a house-made aïoli adds a horseradish kick to sublimely tender beef tongue fries—braised in a chicken stock, tossed in a beer and rice-flour batter, and finally fried to perfection. The savory *pesce al forno* starts with a base of fingerling potatoes and continues with a lightly breaded fillet of hake, baked with cherry tomatoes, black olives, and finished with garlic and herb *salmoriglio*.

Black Swan

American 

1048 Bedford Ave. (bet. Clifton Pl. & Lafayette Ave.)

Subway: Bedford - Nostrand Avs — Lunch & dinner daily
Phone: 718-783-4744
Web: www.blackswannyc.com
Prices: $$

You can't go wrong at Black Swan, so slide into a dark wooden booth, order a craft beer, and strike up a conversation with the other diners crammed into the deep, long space. As young as this American gastropub is, it feels as comfortable and rustic as a well-worn pair of jeans—just right for settling into a fast-paced match on TV.

True to its pub spirit, the food keeps pace with the ample beer list with a crackling, tender, and moist crab cake, fried until golden and topped with a deeply spiced remoulade. Deep bowls of turkey chili are rich and hearty, with loads of ground turkey, cumin, and bits of smoky bacon served with fluffy white rice and cornbread. Sea bass with wild mushroom ragout, cilantro, and grapefruit is effortlessly enjoyable.

Blanca ✿✿

Contemporary XX

C2

261 Moore St. (bet. Bogart & White Sts.)

Subway: Morgan Av — Dinner Wed – Sat
Phone: 347-799-2807
Web: www.blancanyc.com
Prices: $$$$

Tucked deep into the Roberta's compound—that den of restaurant cool that helped elevate seedy Bushwick into a legitimately haute food 'hood—lays this gleaming warehouse kitchen aimed at the serious eater. If you're lucky enough to snag a seat at Blanca, you'll make your way first into Roberta's lively, corrugated metal-facade, past the delicious smell of their wood-burning pizza oven and sound of vinyl records playing the blues, and through the buzzing outdoor garden. Can this many tattooed urbanites and Millennials know something you don't? Indeed.

Blanca's interior is sleek and minimal, with a pristine white counter lined with cognac leather stools positioned to watch the chefs create each dish. Chef Carlo Mirarchi's nightly 20-course menu is never published beforehand, nor does the restaurant take any dietary accommodations into account. The message is loud and clear: trust us and we'll delight your senses.

And delight it does as dinner might begin with deep orange lobes of sea urchin dusted with coarse sea salt and a tiny dollop of warm polenta. Then move on to impeccably fresh sliced fluke in almond water and plum vinegar, topped with fennel fronds; or tender ravioli fat with spicy *'nduja* and laced with zesty grated orange.

Chavela's 

Mexican

B4

736 Franklin Ave. (at Sterling Pl.)

Subway: Franklin St — Lunch & dinner daily
Phone: 718-622-3100
Web: www.chavelasnyc.com
Prices: 

Look for the light blue dome and wrought-iron doors to enter Chavela's and discover an absolute riot of color inside. From the bar's Mexican tiles to the wall of ceramic butterflies, the room is an explosion of artistic sensibilities.

Guacamole is just as pleasing as the setting, whether going for a traditional or creative version mixed with flaky smoked trout, *pico de gallo*, and *morita chile* salsa. Small, crisp *taquitos de cangrego* filled with the perfect balance of sweet crabmeat, salsa verde, white cheese, and *crema Mexicana* arc irresistible. *Costilla en salsa verde* (deliciously tender, mild pork short rib stew) is studded with nopales swimming in a thick, verdant sauce, and served with a delectable mountain of yellow rice and refried black beans.

Colonia Verde

Latin American 

A3

219 DeKalb Ave. (bet. Adelphi St. & Clermont Ave.)

Subway: Clinton - Washington Avs — Lunch Sat – Sun
Phone: 347-689-4287 — Dinner Tue – Sun
Web: www.coloniaverdenyc.com
Prices: $$

The historic blocks with row homes on Fort Greene's DeKalb Ave. make for an equally appealing restaurant row. Thanks to a sunken front room that flanks the open kitchen's wood-fired oven, plus a glassed-in "greenhouse" that transitions to a pebbled outdoor garden, locals stroll into Colonia Verde no matter the time of year. And why not? The banter is lively and meals rewarding.

Its menu is a Brazilian-esque expression of the owners of Cómodo in SoHo. Curiously named dishes like poblano pepper fettuccine stars pasta tossed with a spicy, satisfying ragù made from roasted poblanos, pecans, and ground beef. For dessert, the Brooklyn Mess sweetens the deal: three scoops of coffee ice cream topped with mango, dulce de leche syrup, and toasted manioc flour.

Dear Bushwick

Contemporary

41 Wilson Ave. (bet. George & Melrose Sts.)

Subway: Morgan Av — Lunch Sat – Sun
Phone: 929-234-2344 — Dinner nightly
Web: www.dearbushwick.com
Prices: $$

Paying homage to the UK with a distinctly edgy spirit, Dear Bushwick is a slim, snug favorite for deliciously hearty cooking that is mingled with contemporary inflections. A handsome curving copper bar is beloved by solo diners, while hanging birdcages, a pressed-tin ceiling, and vintage portraits of sheep, kings, and churches keep the overall vibe groovy.

The English-inspired menu features such devourable delights as braised ox tongue set atop navy beans and a beet green salad, but vegetarian dishes like cauliflower hash with silky potatoes, crisp granny smith apples, and a spiced curry yogurt are equally robust. Finish, of course, with a perfect Yorkshire pudding, topped with chocolate sauce, crumbled walnuts, and candied orange peel.

Do or Dine

Contemporary

1108 Bedford Ave. (bet. Lexington Ave. & Quincy St.)

Subway: Bedford - Nostrand Avs — Lunch Sat – Sun
Phone: 718-684-2290 — Dinner nightly
Web: www.doordinebk.com
Prices: $$

Under a yellow awning advertising Caribbean takeout lies Do or Dine, a groovy, psychedelic trip into fine dining under a disco ball. Teacups serve as lampshades next to graffiti art in this hodgepodge chic, Bed-Stuy restaurant, started by four chef-friends who wanted more for this neighborhood.

Leave inhibitions behind when digging into the Nippon nachos, a cross of Japanese and Tex-Mex that tops crisp *gyoza* with cheddar cheese, *pico de gallo*, and *masago*-infused sour cream. "You've got quail" and truffle polenta primes you for more cheeky dishes, such as habanero chicken and "woffals" (waffles enriched with chicken liver) or a deep-fried foie gras doughnut. Get "drank" at the bustling bar with George and Gingers, the signature Bourbon mule.

El Mio Cid

Spanish

50 Starr St. (at Wilson Ave.)

Subway: Jefferson St — Lunch & dinner daily
Phone: 718-628-8300
Web: www.elmiocidrestaurant.com
Prices: $$

In contrast to popular tapas spots sweeping the city, this is an old-guard Iberian stalwart, deep in the heart of Bushwick. The interior bears a Mediterranean sensibility, with idyllic murals of the Spanish countryside, dark wood tables, and huge vessels of refreshing sangria. It has the feel of a relic from another time, when attentive service and a polished dining room were standard.

Familiar flavors abound, as in sardinas *a la plancha*, two fat Portuguese sardines simply grilled and served with a wedge of lemon. The hearty *paella Valenciana* sees lobster claws, mussels, smoky chicken, chorizo, clams, and roasted peppers folded into a mound of sultry rice. For dessert, opt for *torrejas*, bread soaked in spiced red wine and served with vanilla ice cream.

Eugene & Co.

American

397 Tompkins Ave. (at Jefferson Ave.)

Subway: Kingston-Throop Avs — Lunch & dinner Tue – Sun
Phone: 718-443-2223
Web: www.eugeneandcompany.com
Prices: $$

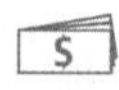

Straddling a corner of Brooklyn's increasingly trendy Bed-Stuy, you'll spot homey little Eugene & Co. by its sweet hanging planters and soft light emanating from its large windows. It's the kind of rustic, farm-to-table restaurant you might find tucked away in a small town in California; its exposed brick walls lined with artwork and hand-tufted banquettes.

Cheerful waiters, clearly invested in the evening's menu, meander from table to table, discussing the food and dropping dishes like a ripe stone fruit and prosciutto salad with salted honey Cloumage cheese; or a tower of savory fried green tomatoes laced with buttermilk dressing; or moist meatloaf tucked into a soft roll and dressed with fresh cabbage, pickles, and barbecue sauce.

Falansai

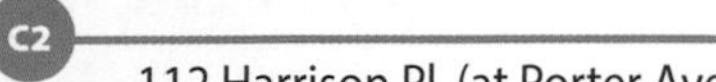

C2

Vietnamese

112 Harrison Pl. (at Porter Ave.)

Subway: Morgan Av — Lunch Tue – Fri
Phone: 347-599-1190 — Dinner Tue – Sun
Web: www.falansai.com
Prices: $$

Just say yes should someone invite you to sample the amazing food at Falansai. Bay Area food enthusiasts might recognize Chef/owner Henry Trieu from his days cooking at the popular Slanted Door; here at Falansai, a pretty little nook that feels miles from the gritty streets surrounding it, Trieu elevates the already complex Vietnamese cuisine to the next level. The results will knock your socks off—honestly, you might never look at a *bánh mì* the same way again.

Don't miss the tender shrimp fritters, enveloped in mashed cassava and chilies; fresh papaya salad laced with mint leaves, sweet poached shrimp, and crushed toasted peanuts; or a surprisingly complex and special coconut curry bobbing with sweet kabocha squash, Thai eggplant, and tender carrots.

Faro

C2

American

436 Jefferson St. (bet. St Nicholas & Wyckoff Aves.)

Subway: Jefferson St — Dinner nightly
Phone: 718-381-8201
Web: www.farobk.com
Prices: $$

The dining scene along this industrial corridor where East Williamsburg meets Bushwick is on fire—possibly spurred by the talented chefs who now call this area home. The husband-and-wife behind Faro have years of restaurant experience between them, so it's not surprising that this casual, dependable restaurant serves dishes carefully crafted from well-sourced ingredients.

If the goal at Faro is comfort food with integrity, they more than succeed in this mission by pushing out dishes like sweet pea porridge studded with fresh morel mushrooms; and light, chewy gnocchi Sardi dotted with sweet ricotta, braised goat, artichokes, and tomatoes. Round out the repast with an ebony tangle of squid ink *chitarra* tossed with olive oil, roasted garlic, clams, and mussels.

The Finch ✿

American XX

B3

212 Greene Ave. (bet. Cambridge Pl. & Grand Ave.)

Subway: Classon Av — Dinner Wed– Sun
Phone: 718-218-4444
Web: www.thefinchnyc.com
Prices: $$

Chef Gabe McMackin has nailed the definition of the perfect neighborhood restaurant, making it well worth a trip to this charming Brooklyn quarter no matter where you live. Step through the bright blue façade to find a welcoming vibe, contemporary rustic décor—complete with wood beam ceilings and farmhouse chairs—and *seriously* enjoyable food.

Having incorporated a former tattoo parlor and storefront, The Finch sprawls out into a series of cozy nooks. At the heart of the operation is an open kitchen where the chef, a Roberta's alum, guides his team to excellence before an audience of diners seated at a Carrara marble counter.

Modern yet comforting, the beautiful creations to be enjoyed here are a show of skill and personality. Asparagus is the very symbol of spring when slashed into matchsticks and thrown over a quivering orb of burrata accurately brought to room temperature and accompanied by charred young onions. Chicken is rescued from the mundane as crispy-skinned white meat partnered with a poached egg and smoked bread pudding, all ringed by an intense consommé. Unsurprisingly, dessert is divine, revealing crumbly shortcake filled with sour cherry compote and dabbed with whipped cream.

Fitzcarraldo

Italian XX

C2

195 Morgan Ave. (bet. Meadow & Stagg Sts.)

Subway: Grand St — Lunch Sat – Sun
Phone: 718-233-2566 — Dinner nightly
Web: www.fitzbk.com
Prices: $$

Nestled into a remote web of Brooklyn where hip East Williamsburg meets even hipper Bushwick, it was almost guaranteed that the new Fitzcarraldo (brought to you by Rucola partners, Henry Rich and Julian Brizzi) would deliver on style. And that it does—welcoming diners with a lazy string of bistro lights, an enormous picture window, rustic bare wood tables, and a thumping open kitchen.

It's a sexy, clandestine little nook, perfected with industrial style. Luckily, the delicious food is given equal attention, with a sharp-as-tacks service staff pushing out creative fare like the warm, crispy *farinata,* served in a cast iron skillet and humming with fragrant pesto and a chunky tomato sauce; or tender orecchiette bathed in creamy *cacio e pepe*.

The General Greene

American X

A3

229 DeKalb Ave. (at Clermont Ave.)

Subway: Lafayette Av — Lunch & dinner daily
Phone: 718-222-1510
Web: www.thegeneralgreene.com
Prices: $$

Despite the fact that this sounds like Grandpa's pet-name for his antique tractor, The General Greene is a space that nicely straddles rusticity and hipness while serving three satisfying meals a day. Everything seems cool here, if perhaps a bit aloof, from the perfectly ambient lighting, comfy banquettes, and leather bar stools to that highly prized espresso machine and free WiFi for your iPad.

The menu has a playful Southern slant, as seen in a warm haricot vert salad tossed with dates, almonds, and orange segments with a chive-buttermilk biscuit; or mac and cheese melting Vermont cheddar, Gruyère, and parmesan folded with *cavatelli.* Ham-and-Gruyère bread pudding is custard-like and brutally addictive. Homemade cookies seem to fly out the door.

Gladys

Caribbean

788 Franklin Ave. (at Lincoln Pl.)

Subway: Franklin Av
Phone: 718-622-0249
Web: www.gladysnyc.com
Prices: $$

Lunch Sat – Sun
Dinner nightly

A popular sandwich shop turned Caribbean joint, Gladys makes it possible to sip a custom cocktail and live the Caribbean dream without leaving Crown Heights. Chef/owner Michael Jacober has transformed this corner location into a festive, turquoise destination, with a kitchen full of cooks roasting, grilling, and pan-frying jerk specialties, including fresh lobster.

It's no surprise that the wood-fired, whole porgy makes for a delicious and generous dish, with its smoky notes and accents like refreshing cucumber, pickled onion, and mango. Whale-sized, unshelled, and peppered shrimp arrive head-on with traditional Jamaican garlic, habanero, and a flirtatious dash of allspice. Dishes are remarkably luscious and flavor-packed at budget prices.

L'Antagoniste

French 

238 Malcom X Blvd. (at Hancock St.)

Subway: Utica Av
Phone: 917-966-5300
Web: www.lantagoniste.com
Prices: $$$

Lunch Sat – Sun
Dinner Tue – Sun

From the razor-sharp service and charming décor (think elegantly set wood tables and banquettes), to the killer but traditional French menu, everything about this newbie in burgeoning Bed-Stuy is bang-on. The fact that it's surrounded by bodegas and a fast food joint simply adds to the overall intrigue.

Owner Amadeus Broger also co-owns the popular Nolita restaurant, Le Philosophe, and here he relies on the same formula that made the latter such a hit: serious food in a fun, casual setting. Don't miss the *soufflé au fromage*, rendered light and frothy with nutty Comté; the *tournedos Rossini*, tender filet mignon over a potato pancake, topped with foie gras medallions and finished with Madeira; or the perfectly executed duck *a l'orange*.

Locanda Vini e Olii

Italian

129 Gates Ave. (at Cambridge Pl.)

Subway: Clinton - Washington Avs — Lunch Sun
Phone: 718-622-9202 — Dinner nightly
Web: www.locandany.com
Prices: $$

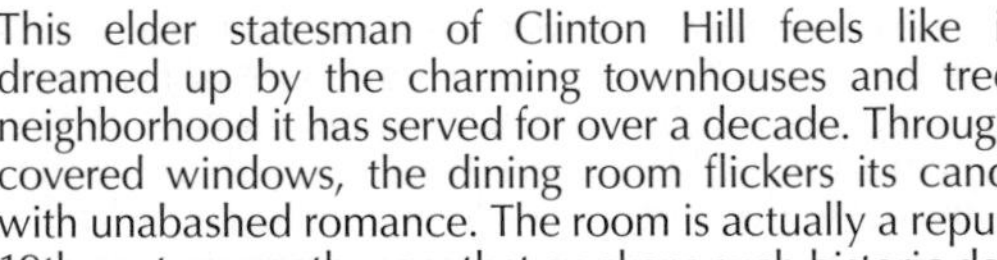

This elder statesman of Clinton Hill feels like it was dreamed up by the charming townhouses and tree-lined neighborhood it has served for over a decade. Through lace-covered windows, the dining room flickers its candlelight with unabashed romance. The room is actually a repurposed 19th century apothecary that awakens such historic details as rolling ladders and small wooden drawers.

Begin with diverse antipasti, including custardy cauliflower *sformato di cavolfiore* set atop puréed spinach. Unusual *paste* include tiny house-made *gnocchetti* tossed with clams, mussels, and tender shrimp over perfectly braised broccoli rabe. Move on to a restrained and luscious Hudson Valley duck breast, then finish with a warm chocolate torte topped with caramel sauce.

Lulu & Po

American

154 Carlton Ave. (at Myrtle Ave.)

Subway: DeKalb Av — Dinner nightly
Phone: 917-435-3745
Web: www.luluandpo.com
Prices: $$

Nestled around the corner of an otherwise forgettable street lined with bodegas, somewhere between Fort Greene and Clinton Hill, the Lilliputian Lulu & Po carries a sweet name but a big foodie punch. For that reason alone, you'll battle neighborhood regulars for a table or spot at the bar, but you'll probably have a grand time doing it.

For the uninitiated, the setup is simple: you walk in, wait for a seat at one of the few tables that run the length of the room, and order from an ever-changing menu filled with delights. Try the creamy chicken liver pâté punched up with savory pancetta; tender grilled octopus with minty cilantro-jalapeño sauce; or a juicy half-chicken marinated with bright spices, then seared to perfection under the weight of a cast-iron pan.

Mayfield

American XX

688 Franklin Ave. (bet. Park & Prospect Pls.)

Subway: Park Pl — Lunch Tue – Sun
Phone: 347-318-3643 — Dinner nightly
Web: www.mayfieldbk.com
Prices: $$

Managing to be rustic yet hip, and dark yet welcoming, this Crown Heights hideaway has won the hearts of *nouveau* locals with its feel-good soundtrack and crave-worthy comfort food. A mix of distressed brick walls and sleek tiles fill the dining room, while brass mermaid door handles give the look a playful edge. Art deco-inspired fixtures hang over the inviting bar.

Tasso ham lends a smoky hint of the South to chewy mounds of hand-rolled linguini and tender coins of braised octopus tossed with a chunky *puttanesca* sauce of tomato, olives, capers, and garlic. Silky, organic chicken liver mousse is served alongside a stack of toasted baguette slices and fennel-apple salad. A *pot de crème* spiked with chilies is a welcome twist on the classic dessert.

Mominette

French 

221 Knickerbocker Ave. (bet. Starr & Troutman Sts.)

Subway: Jefferson St — Lunch & dinner daily
Phone: 929-234-2941
Web: www.mominette.com
Prices: $$

Enter through the swinging wooden doors to discover that the less-than-glitzy surroundings seem a world away. Inside, Mominette's highly romanticized glow is impossible to ignore—picture wallpaper crafted from sepia-toned newspapers along with risqué photos of women amid vintage chandeliers. Add to that a familial staff and fantastic food...*et voilà*...a fun, energetic, instant favorite!

There is a reason why each newcomer becomes a regular: the food is surprisingly delicious and very authentic. The menu focuses on classics like escargots deliciously baked with tomatoes and garlic; a fresh kerchief of puff pastry filled with tender roast duck infused with wine and tart cranberries; followed by braised pork tenderloin set atop nutty lentils.

Northeast Kingdom

C2 — American

18 Wyckoff Ave. (at Troutman St.)

Subway: Jefferson St — Lunch & dinner daily
Phone: 718-386-3864
Web: www.north-eastkingdom.com
Prices: $$

Deer camps and farming communities of Vermont inspire Northeast Kingdom's wonderfully playful food and seasonal menu. Vintage chairs surround bare tables beneath a wood planked ceiling in the pleasantly simple but tight dining room—still popular after all these years. The downstairs area has been transformed into a wine and cocktail bar.

Parsnip, carrots, and tender chickpeas feature in a restorative bone soup of clear and beefy broth sprinkled with fresh herbs. A focus on rich, meaty flavors continues in the NEK burger, made with properly seasoned and grilled beef topped with onions, mushroom duxelles, and Vermont cheddar with a side of duck fat fries and tots. Chewy cavatelli is beautifully dressed with a lamb ragù enlivened by shiitakes and kale.

No. 7

American

7 Greene Ave. (bet. Cumberland & Fulton Sts.)

Subway: Lafayette Av — Lunch Sat – Sun
Phone: 718-522-6370 — Dinner Tue – Sun
Web: www.no7restaurant.com
Prices: $$

This is the type of place where you sit down, look at the menu, and say, "Does that really work?" And it does—most of the time—as far as No. 7 is concerned. With its worn-in good looks, casual vibe, and horseshoe-shaped banquettes, this perpetually packed spot screams group dinners.

Feast your eyes on the open kitchen, where the talented team crafts obsession-worthy dishes like the double-decker broccoli tacos. The exemplary combination of flavors and textures is simply brilliant: both a soft and a crisp taco shell (with just the right grease-tinged crunch) hold a mixture of cooked broccoli, salty feta, creamy beans, and fried shallots. To balance the earthy flavors, sink into the salted chocolate and corn puff tart, served with peanut butter ice cream.

Prospect

American 

773 Fulton St. (bet. Oxford & Portland Aves.)

Subway: Lafayette Av — Dinner Mon – Sat
Phone: 718-596-6826
Web: www.prospectbk.com
Prices: **$$**

This Fort Greene standout offers delicious cooking and just so happens to be pretty cool, too. Barrel-aged negronis are among the offerings from a white marble bar that provides much needed real estate. Walls are lined with reclaimed planks of the Coney Island boardwalk, and genuinely hospitable service tames the perpetually packed house.

Quality trumps quantity in the streamlined selection of product-driven creations. Silken strands of house-made fettucine twirled with lemon beurre blanc and finely grated parmesan make an enticing starter, while pan-seared skate garnished tableside with coconut milk broth redolent of lemongrass and Persian lime is an inspired entrée. Finish off with a *tres leches* cake topped with salted sugar cookie crumbs.

Roberta's

Contemporary 

261 Moore St. (bet. Bogart & White Sts.)

Subway: Morgan Av — Lunch & dinner daily
Phone: 718-417-1118
Web: www.robertaspizza.com
Prices: **$$**

Entering through this (now) iconic red door is like a trip through the looking glass and into Bushwick's foodie wonderland. The city's love affair with Roberta's seems stronger each year, and for good reason. Everything from the industrial space to the underground Bohemian vibe epitomizes Brooklyn-chic. A new takeaway option has been added to the compound, so when the wait for a table is too long, snag a porchetta sandwich to-go.

Queens native Carlo Mirarchi leads a talented kitchen and its menu of beautifully prepared pasta, vegetables, and more. Many diners stick to the creatively named, less than purely Italian pizza, like the Speckenwolf: freshly dried oregano, house-made mozzarella, thinly sliced speck, red onion, and roasted cremini mushrooms.

Roman's

Italian 

243 DeKalb Ave. (bet. Clermont & Vanderbilt Aves.)

Subway: Lafayette Av — Lunch Sat – Sun
Phone: 718-622-5300 — Dinner nightly
Web: www.romansnyc.com
Prices: $$

Candlelight bounces off white-tiled walls and a colorful mosaic throughout this cozy hideaway's small, tasteful dining room. Locals return for the two daily cocktails (one bitter, one sour) along with the short, none-too-complicated menu that is a study in the strength of focus. This is the type of inviting neighborhood joint that calls for a glass of wine and soulful pasta at the bar.

Dishes are straightforward but satisfy in their careful execution. A squid salad with cannellini beans, tomato, herbs, and fantastic olive oil is elevated by seasoning and texture from toasted breadcrumbs. Tortelli stuffed with fluffy ricotta find a succulent home in pork ragù. A wonderfully rich and almost chocolate-hued braised beef rib tops buttery whipped potatoes.

The Runner

American 

B3

458 Myrtle Ave. (bet. Washington & Waverly Aves.)

Subway: Clinton - Washington Avs — Lunch & dinner daily
Phone: 718-643-6500
Web: www.therunnerbk.com
Prices: $$

Part cocktail bar, part farm-to-table restaurant, The Runner has that low-lit industrial cool look that draws in passersby both day and night. With a rustic aesthetic and modern touches, it's a lovely spot to cozy up with a craft beer at the bar, where the bartender is on a first-name basis with regulars.

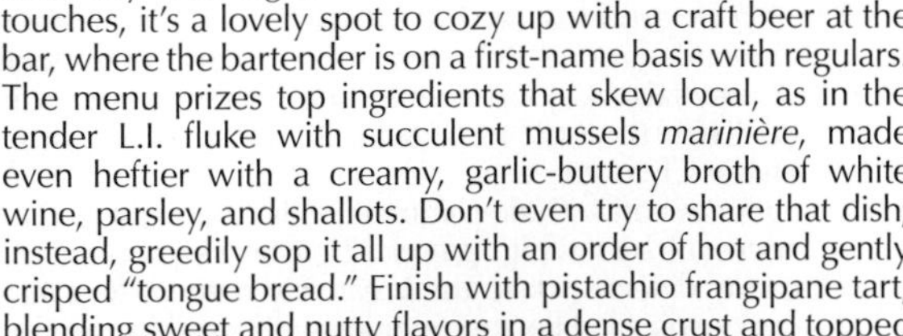

The menu prizes top ingredients that skew local, as in the tender L.I. fluke with succulent mussels *marinière*, made even heftier with a creamy, garlic-buttery broth of white wine, parsley, and shallots. Don't even try to share that dish; instead, greedily sop it all up with an order of hot and gently crisped "tongue bread." Finish with pistachio frangipane tart, blending sweet and nutty flavors in a dense crust and topped with a scoop of vanilla ice cream.

Saraghina

Italian 

C3

435 Halsey St. (at Lewis Ave.)

Subway: Utica Av — Lunch & dinner daily
Phone: 718-574-0010
Web: www.saraghinabrooklyn.com
Prices: $$

If you build it, they will come: and sure enough, from the moment Saraghina opened its doors to a just-burgeoning Bed-Stuy, diners have flooded this cool, multi-room, restaurant decorated in garage sale knickknacks, old butcher signs, and marmalade jars. It's downright adorable. But, it's the delicious food that fills the seats.

Still best known for their irresistible pizzas, blistered to puffy perfection, the menu offers all kinds of heavenly dishes not to miss, like the fried calamari and shrimp, served with tangy lemon and aïoli; or a wood-fire roasted side of cauliflower mixed with creamy mascarpone, tart *labneh* cheese, and Marcona almonds.

Just around the corner, at 433 Halsey, a sister bakery serves up fresh pastries and a mean espresso all day.

SoCo

Southern 

B3

509 Myrtle Ave. (bet. Grand Ave. & Reyerson St.)

Subway: Classon Av — Lunch Fri – Sun
Phone: 718-783-1936 — Dinner Tue – Sun
Web: www.socobk.com
Prices: $$

Southern food meets bohemian city life at SoCo, an urbane, industrial-chic restaurant where guests are greeted at the door with a splash of wonderful jazz. The gracious, hospitable staff manages to meander through the young professionals and artsy Pratt students with ease, and if the cool charm of SoCo doesn't woo you, the outstanding Southern fare will certainly do the trick: organic buttermilk-fried chicken arrives crispy and tender, and served over a delicious red velvet waffle; while fall-off-the-bone short ribs are braised in an irresistible coconut-molasses-ginger sauce, and served with creamy garlic mashed potatoes and tender okra. Then a soft peach cobbler is spiced to perfection.

Brunch is especially popular, so arrive early.

Speedy Romeo

American

B3

376 Classon Ave. (at Greene Ave.)

Subway: Classon Av

Phone: 718-230-0061

Web: www.speedyromeo.com

Prices: $$

Lunch & dinner daily

Named for a racehorse and just as focused and quick, Speedy Romeo is in for a successful run. Part tavern, part roadside grill, its kitschy décor and modern touches transform this former automotive shop into a surprisingly attractive spot.

The owner benefited from years at Jean-Georges' empire, and that intelligence and experience is conveyed through the smart accents and whimsical menu that begins with Italian ingredients. Look to the wood-burning oven for smoky, meaty artichoke halves topped with lemon aïoli, sourdough crumbs, mint, and peppery arugula. Take a chance on the non-traditional but utterly fantastic pizza combinations, such as the St. Louis, layering a proper crust with meats, pickled chillies, and Midwestern Provel cheese.

Umi NOM

Asian 

B3

433 DeKalb Ave. (bet. Classon Ave. & Taaffe Pl.)

Subway: Classon Av

Phone: 718-789-8806

Web: www.uminom.com

Prices: $$

Lunch Sat
Dinner Mon – Sat

Discerning Pratt students likely inspired the team behind Umi NOM, a fun and adventurous area standout. Outfitted in wood paneling and pew-like benches, the narrow space incorporates intriguing design elements and bamboo ornaments to keep the eyes as pleased as the palate—and rises well above the typical takeout joints that line this unremarkable block.

The lack of a liquor license is all but forgotten with a sip of the thirst-quenching calamansi juice to pair with fusion tacos stuffed with strips of pig's ear, pickled onions, smoked spicy salsa, and more. Don't miss the *pad krapow* made with ground beef, long beans, Thai chilies, and clove-like holy basil. Pork belly adobo, braised for three hours in coconut milk and spices, is a thing of beauty.

Park Slope

DITMAS PARK · PROSPECT HEIGHTS

Bordering Prospect Park, historic Park Slope brags of fancy trattorias and chic cafés perpetually crammed with stroller-rolling parents. Set in the heart of the 'hood, **The Park Slope Food Coop** is a veteran member-operated and owned purveyor of locally farmed produce, grass-fed meat, and free-range poultry. Lauded as the largest of its kind in the country, membership is offered to anyone willing to pay a small fee and work a shift of less than three hours each month. The like-minded **Grand Army Plaza Greenmarket**, held every Saturday at Prospect Park, is a shopping haven among area residents craving organic, farm-fresh produce as well as cooking programs and demonstrations to boot.

Close at hand on Flatbush Avenue, **Bklyn Larder** is an artisanal provisions store that sells every imaginable type of cheese, meat, snack, beverage, and sweet. Devoted locals line up outside **The Ploughman**—a South Slope boutique—for an impressive bevy of beers, even more cheese, and over 20 varieties of cured meats. Favoring something sweet? Find it at **The Chocolate Room** where desserts are exclusively hand-crafted and composed of pure, all-natural ingredients. From myriad boxes and bars of chocolate, to cakes, cocoa, coffees, and teas, this is every sugar fiend's reverie. Over in Windsor Terrace, **Brancaccio's Food Shop** is a serious dine-in and take-out treat that keeps the crowds returning for Italian-American signatures (think caponota and meatballs) or even breakfast specials featuring eggs, potatoes, cheese and meats. Ramen is another wildly popular comfort food. So, on those cold, wintry days, head to **Chuko's** in Prospect Heights for an enormous selection with vegetarian options that are bound to stun. Further south, Ditmas Park residents make the pilgrimage to **Olympic Pita** for fresh, handmade bread or arguably the most perfect falafel in town. Finally, go big or go home—with a bold cup of tea (or coffee) at **Qathra Cafe**.

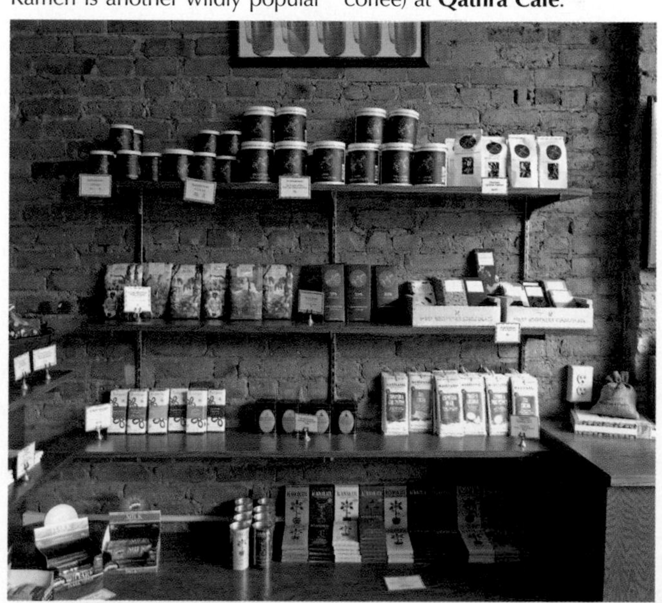

BROOKLYN-PARK SLOPE
DOWNTOWN
SUNSET PARK & BRIGHTON BEACH
BOERUM HILL
GOWANUS
PARK SLOPE
SOUTH SLOPE
PROSPECT HEIGHTS
WINDSOR TERRACE
PROSPECT PARK SOUTH
KENSINGTON
DITMAS PARK
FISKE TERRACE
SUNSET PARK
BOROUGH PARK
GREENWOOD CEMETERY
PROSPECT PARK
Prospect Park Lake
PROSPECT PARK PARADE GROUND
BROOKLYN MUSEUM
BROOKLYN BOTANIC GARDEN
BARCLAYS CENTER
WASHINGTON PARK
Atlantic Terminal (LIRR)
Atlantic Av/ Barclays Ctr
Bergen St
Union St
7 Av
Grand Army Plaza
Eastern Pkwy-Brooklyn Museum
4 Av-9 St
15 St/ Prospect Park
Prospect Av
Prospect Park
Parkside Av
Church Av
Fort Hamilton Pkwy
Beverley Rd
Cortelyou Rd
Newkirk Plaza
Avenue H
Morgan's BBQ
Bricolage
James
Elberta
Cooklyn
Palo Santo
Franny's
Al di Là
Stone Park Cafe
Juventino
Al Seabu
Sushi Katsuei
Applewood
Café Steinhof
Talde
Fonda
Java
Thistle Hill Tavern
Krupa Grocery
Mimi's Hummus
Purple Yam
The Farm on Adderly
Lea

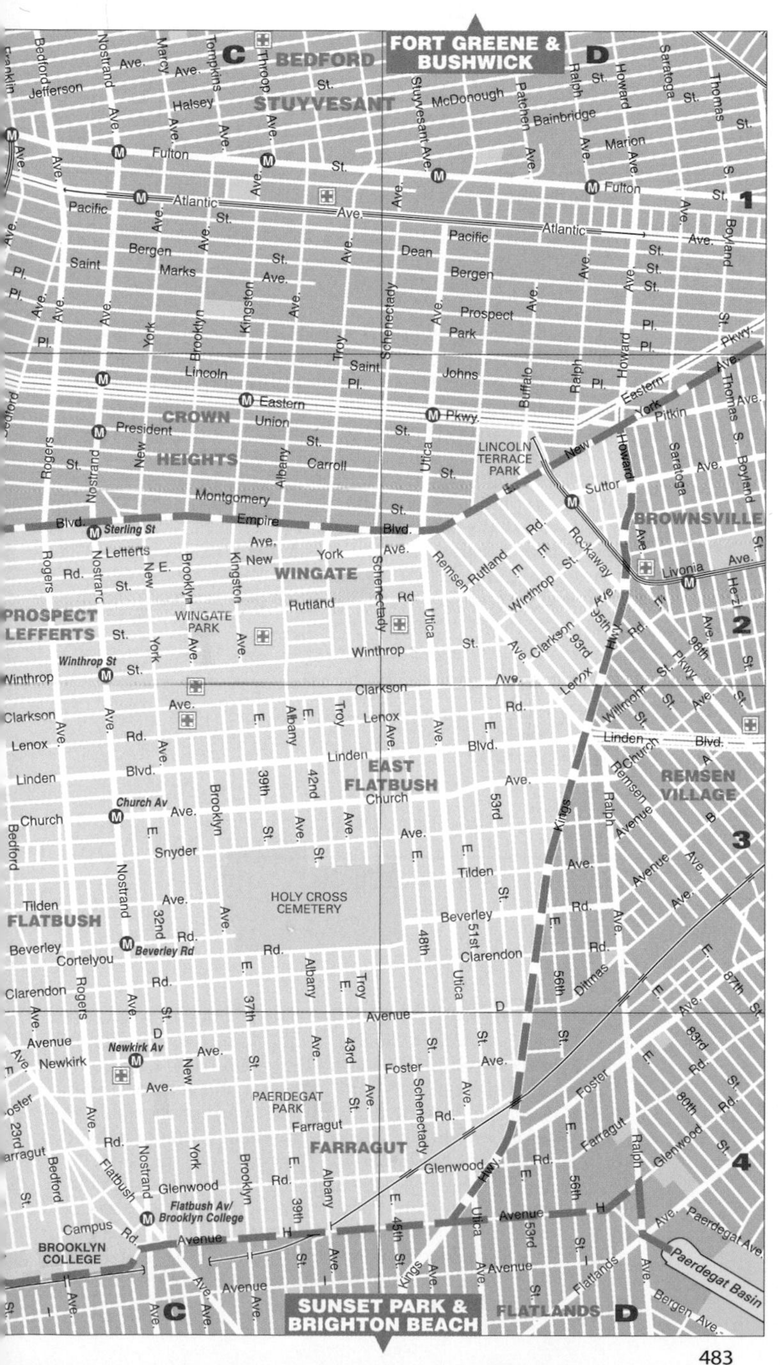
FORT GREENE &
BUSHWICK
C
D
BEDFORD
STUYVESANT
CROWN
HEIGHTS
LINCOLN
TERRACE
PARK
BROWNSVILLE
WINGATE
WINGATE
PARK
PROSPECT
LEFFERTS
EAST
FLATBUSH
REMSEN
VILLAGE
HOLY CROSS
CEMETERY
FLATBUSH
PAERDEGAT
PARK
FARRAGUT
BROOKLYN
COLLEGE
FLATLANDS
Paerdegat Basin
SUNSET PARK &
BRIGHTON BEACH
1
2
3
4
Sterling St
Winthrop St
Church Av
Beverley Rd
Newkirk Av
Flatbush Av/
Brooklyn College
Fulton
Atlantic
Ave.
Pacific
Dean
Bergen
Prospect
Park
Eastern
Pkwy.
Empire
Blvd.
Livonia
Linden
Church
Kings
Hwy.
Avenue
H
Nostrand
Utica
Schenectady

Al di Là

Italian

A1

248 Fifth Ave. (at Carroll St.)

Subway: Union St — Lunch & dinner daily
Phone: 718-783-4565
Web: www.aldilatrattoria.com
Prices: $$

This long-loved Park Slope gem from husband-and-wife team Emiliano Coppa and Chef Anna Klinger (of the Crown Heights café Lincoln Station) has been deliciously consistent over the years. Inviting and lived-in with wooden pew seating, dainty wallpaper, and a blown glass chandelier, it's both comfortable and chic enough for a romantic dinner *a due*.

Al di Là's Italian delights are northern in spirit and include enticing preparations. A salad of roughly chopped escarole is tossed with thinly shaved Jerusalem artichokes, slivers of red onion, diced crisped pancetta, toasted walnuts, and a warm sherry vinaigrette. When offered, the *lasagna alla Bolognese*, fashioned from sheets of fresh pasta and served hot from the oven with crisped edges, is a must.

Al Seabu

Malaysian 

383 Fifth Ave. (bet. 6th & 7th Sts.)

Subway: 4 Av - 9 St — Lunch Fri – Sun
Phone: 718-369-0309 — Dinner nightly
Web: N/A
Prices: ⊜

The already impressive Park Slope dining scene gets another notch in its belt with Al Seabu, a little family-run restaurant with a seafood-centric menu and big personality. Decorated in cheerful sea-blue walls and industrial shelves lined with charming seashells, Al Seabu also boasts a friendly staff and fun, contemporary music. The overall effect is one of relaxed charm—and that's before the food knocks your socks off.

Don't miss the grilled *pulut panggang*, little cigars of sticky rice dabbed with coconut and shrimp paste; or fork-tender *nyonya* beef *rendang* served with a pile of fluffy white rice and cool slices of cucumber and tomato to cut the heat. Fried *mantou*, hot sweet buns served with creamy condensed milk for dipping, makes for a dreamy finish.

Applewood

American

A2

501 11th St. (bet. Seventh & Eighth Aves.)

Subway: 7 Av (9th St.)
Phone: 718-788-1810
Web: www.applewoodny.com
Prices: $$

Lunch Sun
Dinner Tue – Sat

A rustic counterpoint to the common hip Brooklyn restaurant, find Applewood in a quaint corner townhouse with wrought-iron fencing, box planters, and wooden park benches out front. The inside may appear cramped at first, but perception shifts once seated as the fireplace, exposed brick walls, pressed-tin ceiling, and shelves lined with books work their cozy magic.

Dishes are layered with flavor, including chewy herb spaetzle and wilted greens topped with grilled lamb sausage and mustard seeds. Pickled red cabbage tops a pork chop sliced off the bone, with a light yet delish potato gratin on the side. High minded desserts may include a warm carrot cake with fragrant cardamom syrup. A reasonably priced three-course prix-fixe turns locals into regulars.

Bricolage

Vietnamese

A1

162 Fifth Ave. (bet. Degraw & Douglass Sts.)

Subway: Union St
Phone: 718-230-1835
Web: www.bricolage.nyc
Prices: $$

Dinner Wed – Sun

This delicious and fresh-faced Vietnamese gem arrives courtesy of the team behind San Francisco's popular Slanted Door. Tucked into a simple, wood-and-exposed-brick space in family-friendly Park Slope, the restaurant's open kitchen bustles with energy as diners huddle in lively conversation. Bricolage bills itself as a gastropub (and the creative cocktails are certainly fantastic), but make no mistake—this is modern, next-level Vietnamese bar fare.

Crispy, golden imperial rolls arrive stuffed with shiny glass noodles, crunchy cabbage, earthy mushrooms, and minced pork; while a dish of "Unshaking Beef" is laced in a light, salty-sweet marinade and seared to tender, juicy perfection alongside a peppery watercress salad.

Café Steinhof

Austrian

A2

422 Seventh Ave. (at 14th St.)

Subway: 7 Av (9th St.) — Lunch Tue – Sun
Phone: 718-369-7776 — Dinner nightly
Web: www.cafesteinhof.com
Prices: ⊜

Austrian flavors abound at this eccentric Park Slope café. The space is anchored by a large, wooden bar where a selection of beers on draught, generously measured libations, and fruit brandies are poured. Vintage posters hang on the walls and oldies play nostalgically in the background. Sturdy wood tables alongside large windows provide a cozy spot to feast on Austrian comfort food.

Old-world classics are executed with care; the expertly fried Wiener schnitzel is brightened with a few wedges of lemon and a side of thin, pickled cucumbers. Texture is also nailed in a side of pan-fried, golden-brown spaetzle that showcases chewy, butter-coated noodles. Linzer torte is the final Austrian flourish, satisfying with sour cherry jam and a flaky crust.

Cooklyn

Contemporary

B1

659 Vanderbilt Ave. (bet. Park & Prospect Pls.)

Subway: 7 Av (Flatbush Ave.) — Lunch Sat – Sun
Phone: 347-915-0721 — Dinner Tue – Sun
Web: www.cooklyn-nyc.com
Prices: $$

Work from local artists, a smattering of reclaimed objects, and whitewashed exposed brick walls set a cozy, inviting scene at Cooklyn. The vibe is warm and homey, and a variety of wines—poured by both the glass and quartino—encourage lingering in the clean, uncluttered dining room with its white marble-topped bar, semi-exposed kitchen, and bare wood tables.

Slices of fluke, topped with a whisper of yuzu, maple, basil purée, and a sprinkle of sea salt is a delicate start, while the lamb bun is slathered with feta cream and stuffed with tender meat, fresh dill, and pickled onion. Flavors are just as intense in the entrées, from the sea urchin fusilli with lump crabmeat to the seared duck breast over cous cous with a tart fennel-and-pomegranate salad.

Elberta

Southern

335 Flatbush Ave. (bet. Park & Prospect Pls.)

Subway: 7 Av (Flatbush Ave.) Lunch Sat – Sun
Phone: 718-638-1936 Dinner Tue – Sun
Web: www.elbertarestaurant.com
Prices: $$

Elberta has certainly found her groove. This soulful speakeasy that pays homage to a jazz singer and the fuzzy Elberta peach drink, also dedicates nights to live music and creative cocktails. Her approachable vibe leads right into a Southern-inspired menu, featuring elegant interpretations of the usual suspects, including dessert: fantastic brioche doughnuts stuffed with sweet potato, caramel, and chocolate sauce.

But before the sweet tooth kicks in, try curry goat-stuffed ravioli in a creamy, cauliflower-based sauce; or Creole fisherman's stew dominated by whole prawns, scallops, mussels, and octopus. Use toasted sourdough or dirty rice loaded with gizzards and chicken liver to sop up the cherry-red tomato base, spiked with peppers, herbs, and spices.

The Farm on Adderley

American

1108 Cortelyou Rd. (bet. Stratford & Westminster Rds.)

Subway: Cortelyou Rd Lunch & dinner daily
Phone: 718-287-3101
Web: www.thefarmonadderley.com
Prices: $$

This hot spot perfectly exemplifies its diverse neighborhood, where eco-conscious residents refurbish old Victorian homes and support the most profitable food co-op in the city. Kid-friendly and cocktail-ready with rustic exposed brick walls, this farm-to-table respite creates seasonal dishes that are both delicious and healthy. Surprise yourself by digging into nourishing roasted spaghetti squash with aged goat feta and pumpkin seeds; or thinly pounded and crispy fried beef heart slices set atop a knoll of cheesy grits. Otherwise, stick to the classics with a poached farm egg over quinoa pocked with almonds.

This "Farm" is so popular that it spun off the Sycamore and set up an expanded bakery on Church Ave., proffering a variety of loaves.

Fonda

Mexican 

A2

434 Seventh Ave. (bet. 14th & 15th Sts.)

Subway: 7 Av (9th St.)
Lunch Sat – Sun
Phone: 718-369-3144
Dinner nightly
Web: www.fondarestaurant.com
Prices: $$

A lively retreat set in a quiet neighborhood, Fonda is a local darling for creative Mexican food. Tiny tables are tightly packed into the dim room, where blood-red walls, a black ceiling, and paintings hanging over exposed brick create an intimate feel. Metal fans spin overhead and soft Mexican tunes are almost drowned out by animated conversations.

Looking for tacos? Go elsewhere. This menu is more nuanced with such appetizing items as duck *zarape*, a mound of tender, shredded duck between warm, flaky tortillas and blanketed in a roasted tomato-habanero sauce. *Pescado en chile atole* is equally layered with flavor, featuring ancho-rubbed red snapper over creamy fingerling potatoes and tender poblanos.

Outposts also reside in Chelsea and the East Village.

Franny's

Italian 

B1

348 Flatbush Ave. (bet. Sterling & St. John's Pls.)

Subway: Grand Army Plaza
Lunch & dinner daily
Phone: 718-230-0221
Web: www.frannysbrooklyn.com
Prices: $$

This timeless neighborhood staple keeps its crowds happy with two wood-burning ovens that churn out lovely thin-crust pizzas. The long bar will likely be your first stop with excellent cocktails that help pass the wait time. The warm space has colorful patterned floor tiles and neatly stacked cords of wood for those crackling ovens.

The open kitchen provides a bit of theater as pies are plucked from the oven—that delicate pizza topped with tomato, sausage, and mozzarella is simple and satisfying. True Italian spirit shines in the carefully executed bucatini with garlic, anchovies, chilies, and toasted breadcrumbs, even if portions are a bit shy. Thankfully there may be more room for dessert, so go for the crunchy cannolo filled with lemon ricotta.

James

American

B1

605 Carlton Ave. (at St. Marks Ave.)

Subway: 7 Av (Flatbush Ave.) — Lunch Sat – Sun
Phone: 718-942-4255 — Dinner nightly
Web: www.jamesrestaurantny.com
Prices: **$$**

This phenomenal little jewel of a restaurant feels as though it has been presiding over this corner for a hundred years. Pressed-tin ceilings and creaky wood floors make it a nostalgic spot, with modern touches like the Dutch Lucite chandelier lending a chic, romantic vibe.

The owners take every detail seriously, from the herb garden on the roof to that wonderful "Cecil & Merl" cheesecake they sell online. The contemporary American cooking highlights top ingredients handled with great care, as in delicate celery root soup topped with silky smoked trout and sharp wasabi sprouts. Generous pastas include enticingly chewy *trofie* enrobed in a pale sauce of puréed greens balancing tart Meyer lemon, earthy sautéed mushrooms, and sharp *Pecorino sardo* shavings.

Java

Indonesian 

455 Seventh Ave. (at 16th St.)

Subway: 7 Av (9th St.) — Dinner nightly
Phone: 718-832-4583
Web: N/A
Prices: ⊜

Java's corner in Park Slope has been an enduring first choice for the exotic eats of Indonesia since 1992. Tiny yet tidy, this dark wood-furnished space is brightened by tall windows covered in golden drapery, native artwork, and the smiles of a friendly staff wearing batik aprons.

A nibble from the bevy of fried appetizers is certainly recommended. Begin with *bakwan* or golden-fried corn fritters, but don't forget about the mouthwatering *sate*—charred skewers of chicken, beef, or seafood brushed with *kecap manis* and topped with diced tomato and crispy fried shallots. The array of saucy, simmered options includes *sambal goring udang*: excellent batter-fried shrimp doused in turmeric-tinted coconut milk infused with lemongrass, ginger, and basil.

Juventino

Contemporary XX

A1

370 Fifth Ave. (bet. 5th & 6th Sts.)

Subway: 4 Av - 9 St — Lunch daily
Phone: 718-360-8469 — Dinner Tue – Sun
Web: www.juventinonyc.com
Prices: $$

A lovely storefront opens into this airy restaurant with distressed wood details and whitewashed walls lending a rustic farmhouse vibe. Tables are lined with pages from old cookbooks and the walls have vintage mirrors and shelves stocked with an impressive selection of cookbooks. This Latin-influenced neighborhood spot also has a seasonal back patio for alfresco dining.

Daily brunch makes the most of the bright, sunny eggs that enhance many dishes, especially the lush yolks that ooze into the herbaceous pumpkin seed *mole* over potato hash with thinly sliced chunks of tender *lengua*. A deliciously chewy grain salad popping with quinoa, barley, and tender beluga lentils in a tart, lemony vinaigrette is a healthy, tasty pick—and an easy favorite.

Krupa Grocery

American XX

A2

231 Prospect Park West (bet. 16th St. & Windsor Pl.)

Subway: 15 St - Prospect Park — Lunch Wed – Mon
Phone: 718-709-7098 — Dinner nightly
Web: www.krupagrocery.com
Prices: $$

Though it only recently opened its doors, Krupa Grocery makes you want to become a regular right out of the gate. Chef Domenick Gianfrancesco's food is so simple, fresh, and perfectly calibrated, it's hard to miss here. Get things started with a selection of country toast, served with delicious spreads like one of smashed pea and fava bean with pecorino, tarragon vinaigrette, and pea leaves; or whipped *lardo* with crisp radish, caper salad, and parsley. For dinner, try the buttermilk-fried skate, served over a bed of cracked hominy with basil seeds and salsa verde.

Designed with a long industrial bar that's perfect for solo eating or lingering couples, the interior is effortlessly cool, but the place to be come summer is undoubtedly the gorgeous backyard.

Lea

Italian XX

1022 Cortelyou Rd. (at Stratford Rd.)

Subway: Cortelyou Rd — Lunch & dinner daily
Phone: 718-928-7100
Web: www.leabrooklyn.com
Prices: $$

From its prime corner location with sidewalk seating to its all-glass façade, Lea is quite the looker. But its substance lives up to the pretty face, with a breezy vibe and eccentric accents like reclaimed wood and dismantled water tower segments that cover the ceiling.

The food is an equally lovely collection of Italian dishes made with a degree of deference to the country's regional cuisines. Don't miss the expert cannelloni served Neapolitan-style: stuffed with ricotta and braised lamb, covered with a sensational *ragù di pomodoro,* and baked to the perfect texture in a wood-burning oven. On the lighter side, try the smartly made panzanella that pairs braised squid with root vegetables and a fragrant, herb-laced sheep's milk yogurt dressing.

Mimi's Hummus

Mediterranean 

1209 Cortelyou Rd. (bet. Argyle & Westminster Rds.)

Subway: Cortelyou Rd — Lunch & dinner daily
Phone: 718-284-4444
Web: www.mimishummus.com
Prices: 

Think meze and you have the right idea behind this heavenly destination for extra-delicious hummus. Though the space is teeny-tiny, a wise, thoughtful design and large windows ferrying swaths of natural light into the dining room make it very inviting. The open kitchen encourages a cheerful vibe and plenty of playful banter between the warm staff and upbeat patrons.

Oven-hot pitas arrive ready for scooping up the rich, creamy hummus (a mix of chickpeas, tahini, onion, and cumin). A variety of garnishes are also available, including meaty mushrooms, which are a worthy companion to the silky signature dish. Pickles are a necessary side with an Iraqi sandwich stuffed with hardboiled egg, fried eggplant slices, boiled potato...and yes...more hummus.

Morgan's BBQ

Barbecue

B1

267 Flatbush Ave. (at St. Marks Ave.)

Subway: Bergen St (Flatbush Ave.) — Lunch & dinner daily
Phone: 718-622-2224
Web: www.morgansbrooklynbarbecue.com
Prices: $$

Barbecue has been having a New York moment, mixing up sauces ranging from the vinegar-heavy Eastern NC-style to sweeter Tennessee renditions. At Morgan's, it's all about Texas, where there is an unparalleled emphasis on the quality of meat and smoke. The bare wood tables, plastic bottles, and industrial rolls of paper towels provide no dining frills—not that they are missed.

Come hungry for slow-smoked brisket with a spicy and inspired rub that's straight out of Austin. Hard to find outside the state, the Hill Country specialty of deep-fried turkey tails is especially tender, served over porky collard greens and salty-sweet cornbread with pepper jelly. Sides are to die for; same goes for the signature pecan "cutie pie" made with Widow Jane Bourbon.

Palo Santo

Latin American 

A1

652 Union St. (bet. Fourth & Fifth Aves.)

Subway: Union St — Lunch Sat – Sun
Phone: 718-636-6311 — Dinner nightly
Web: www.palosantorestaurant.com
Prices: $$

Jacques Gautier is the artiste behind this snug den cooking Latin and Caribbean cuisine. Nestled at the base of a townhouse, the dimly lit room makes for a lively (cue the salsa beats) yet intimate dining experience. Service can be slow, but nobody's in a hurry, so play along and make a night to remember.

Closely set tables make privacy a challenge, but the arrival of crave-worthy pork tacos topped with creamy avocado, crunchy radish, and cilantro will keep your eyes on the prize. Find equal appeal in a fillet of roasted fluke set atop pickled purple cabbage, paired with a pineapple-habanero sauce that will make you singe with abandon, and scattered with tart tomatillo salsa. Still have room for more? Continue the feast across the street at Taco Santo.

Purple Yam

Asian 

1314 Cortelyou Rd. (bet. Argyle & Rugby Rds.)

Subway: Cortelyou Rd — Lunch Sat – Sun
Phone: 718-940-8188 — Dinner nightly
Web: www.purpleyamnyc.com
Prices: $$

Filipino food authorities Amy Besa and Romy Dorotan serve up a deliciously freewheeling array of Southeast Asian treats at this inviting café, named for their homeland's adored tuber. Located in lovely Ditmas Park, a neighborhood extoled for its Victorian homes, the interior charms with soothing colors and a view of the kitchen at work.

Filipino favorites abound, as in chicken *adobo*—the bone-in pieces are browned and braised in a complex-tasting sauce of coconut sap vinegar, coconut milk, and soy sauce. Standouts might include *pancit bihon* made with rice vermicelli stir-fried with roast pork, bok choy, and bean sprouts. Other tasty options depart from the Philippines, such as sweetly spiced goat curry with fresh mango chutney.

Stone Park Cafe

Contemporary 

324 Fifth Ave. (at 3rd St.)

Subway: Union St — Lunch Tue – Sun
Phone: 718-369-0082 — Dinner nightly
Web: www.stoneparkcafe.com
Prices: $$

A true neighborhood place that feels fuss-free, laidback, and just right for lingering, this little corner eatery makes the most of its large windows peering onto Park Slope's vibrant thoroughfare and small nearby park. The airy interior has exposed brick walls, a long bar near the entrance for pre-dinner cocktails, and a candlelit, sunken dining room scattered with linen-topped tables.

Satisfying light fare includes grilled baby octopus with chorizo and fingerling potatoes, or grilled lacinato kale served over a frisée salad with tangy buttermilk dressing. Mains like pork loin over Brussels sprouts and rainbow carrots are hearty, and may be tailed by such inventive treats as a mini ravioli-shaped puff pastry baked atop a nutty and crumbly apple cookie.

Sushi Katsuei

Japanese

B2

210 Seventh Ave. (at Third St.)

Subway: 7 Av (9th St.)
Phone: 718-788-5338
Web: www.sushikatsuei.com
Prices: $$

Lunch Sat – Sun
Dinner nightly

Park Slope's serious sushi den is the kind of place where the *itamae* will adamantly decline requests for soy sauce. But rest assured it comes from a place of love, because that beautiful piece of nigiri has already been brushed with soy sauce, sprinkled with yuzu and sea salt, or dabbed with *yuzu kosho*. In other words, it's fantastic as is.

A handful of straightforward cooked items like free-range chicken teriyaki or tempura udon are great if the kids are in tow, but the real focus is sushi best enjoyed in an omakase that won't break the bank. Be sure to choose the option that includes sashimi and begin this repast with velvety slices of medium fatty tuna and sparkling sea bass, followed by a maki of mackerel, slivered cucumber and pickled ginger.

Talde

Asian 

A2

369 Seventh Ave. (at 11th St.)

Subway: 7 Av (9th St.)
Phone: 347-916-0031
Web: www.taldebrooklyn.com
Prices: $$

Lunch Sat – Sun
Dinner nightly

This corner of Park Slope is the domain of Chef Dale Talde, whose forte for cooking creative pan-Asian delights at glitzy hot spots has been astutely translated. Carved woodwork and figurines define this sexy venue that, by virtue of its location, is also family-friendly.

His menu invokes the flavors of China, Japan, Thailand, Korea, as well as the Philippines. Wonton noodle soup is not to be missed: pork-and-chive dumplings poached in a rich, cloudy broth stocked with springy noodles, tender pork shoulder, wilted greens, and a six-minute egg. Miso-marinated salmon is plated with puffed bulgur, pickled plums, and *salsa verde*; while local corn is tossed with long beans and lemongrass-Kaffir lime butter for a light yet delightful bite.

Thistle Hill Tavern

A2 — American

441 Seventh Ave. (at 15th St.)

Subway: 15 St - Prospect Park
Phone: 347-599-1262
Web: www.thistlehillbrooklyn.com
Prices: $$

Lunch Sat – Sun
Dinner nightly

At this offshoot from the team behind Talde, you can also expect highly creative cooking, but this time the accent is decidedly American. Set along a corner, this is a fine spot for dining alfresco; inside, find a charming assemblage of sports memorabilia and servers flitting around.

Locals head to this South Slope tavern to fill up on hearty cooking that hints of the Mediterranean but is best typified by the likes of pulled pork sliders tucked between a bun, stuffed with pickled ramp and spicy mayonnaise; or crunchy fried chicken, drizzled with black pepper country gravy and sided by a cheddar biscuit. Wrap up the contemporary flavors offered here with apple pie. The deep fried pocket is accompanied by a buttery apple cider sauce and cinnamon gelato.

Your opinions are important to us. Please write to us directly at: michelin.guides@us.michelin.com

Sunset Park & Brighton Beach

BAY RIDGE · RED HOOK

Red Hook rests on Brooklyn's waterfront, where diligent locals and responsible residents have transformed the area's aged piers and deserted warehouses into cool breweries, bakeries, and bistros. Following suit, the **Red Hook Lobster Pound** is a popular haunt for seafood fans, but if sugar is what you favor, then **Baked** is best, followed by **Steve's Authentic Key Lime Pie**. Close the deal at **Cacao Prieto**, widely cherished for family farm-sourced chocolates and spirits. Just as **Red Hook Village Farmers' Market** (open on Saturdays) brings pristine produce from its Community Farm to the locality, trucks and tents in Red Hook Ball Fields cater to natives in the know with *delicioso* Central American and Caribbean cuisine. Dining destinations in their own right, these diners-on-wheels may only be parked on weekends from May through October, but leave an impression that lasts through the year. Meanwhile, carnivores on a mission venture west to Gowanus where **Fletcher's Brooklyn Barbecue** proffers tons of variety and quality; while Bensonhurst best-seller **Bari Pork Store** sticks to perfecting the pig. Foodies can also be found scouring the shelves of **G & S Salumeria and Pork Store** for cold cuts to be stuffed into delicious sandwiches. But, even flesh fiends need a break—

perhaps at **Four & Twenty Blackbirds**—a bakeshop with *the* best black bottom oatmeal pie in town. Or, look for **Raaka Chocolate** showcasing beans in all their glory, while ensuring a healthy relationship with the environment. Pair these sweets with cherries from **Dell's Maraschino** and know you're in for a serious treat. An afternoon in Sunset Park is a must, especially for mouthwatering Mexican flavors. Then cool off with an original ice pop (*paleta*) at **Sley Deli**—an authentic grocer booming with business in Borough Park. Inventor of the "Nutelasagna," **Robicelli's Bakery** may have started out as a cupcake shop, but today it is a full-fledged storefront with interestingly flavored cupcakes, cookies, whoopie pies, and more. Of course, die-hard butter cookie fans can't imagine going a day without a whiff from **St. Anthony's Bakery**. Across from Maimonides Medical Center, **Fei Long Market** is a giant emporium flooded with Asian foodies in search of dried squid, eel, and all things exotic. Slightly south, where Mexico meets China, sidewalks teem with vendors steaming tofu; and fishmongers purveying wonderfully offbeat eats—bullfrog anyone? More mainstream but equally tasty is **Ba Xuyên**, a modest storefront revered for deliciously crusty *bánh mì*. Moving from the Far East to a flock of kosher restaurants, **Di Fara** is a popular pizzeria with a mini offshoot (**MD Kitchen**) in Midwood. **Totonno's Pizza** is another sought-after haunt for Neapolitan-style pies; and **Joe's of Avenue U** is divine for crispy chickpea panelle.

At the southernmost end of Brooklyn is Brighton Beach, best known for its borscht and blintzes. This dominantly Russian nook is also home to Ukranian hot spot **Café Glechik**, churning out staples for its patrons packed within. But for a true alfresco snack to tote, **Gold Label International Food** remains unrivaled. Bakery buffs take a time out at **Toné Café**, where an ancient tandoor-like oven turns out impeccable Georgian bread (*shoti*). Couple these killer carbs with juicy kielbasa from **Jubilat Provisions** for a real deal treat. Customs, traditions, and cuisine come alive in culinary bastion **Moldova**, while over at **Octopus Garden** the nostalgic scene is never-ending with Italian regulars stocking up on goods for the Christmas Feast of the Seven Fishes. Also set within this Eastern European enclave is **Mansoura**, a Syrian institution proudly preparing savories and pastries. **Le Sajj** dishes up Lebanese food with live classical tunes (on Saturdays); and across the way, local sensation, **Lindenwood Diner** is loved for liberally spiced Cajun food. And while there is no confusing the Chesapeake with Sheepshead Bay, **Randazzo's Clam Bar** promises to provide you with a superior seafood experience. However, never forget that beef is always king here, and there are big flavors to be had at **Brennan & Carr**—where the menu doesn't change, but NY'ers love it all the same.

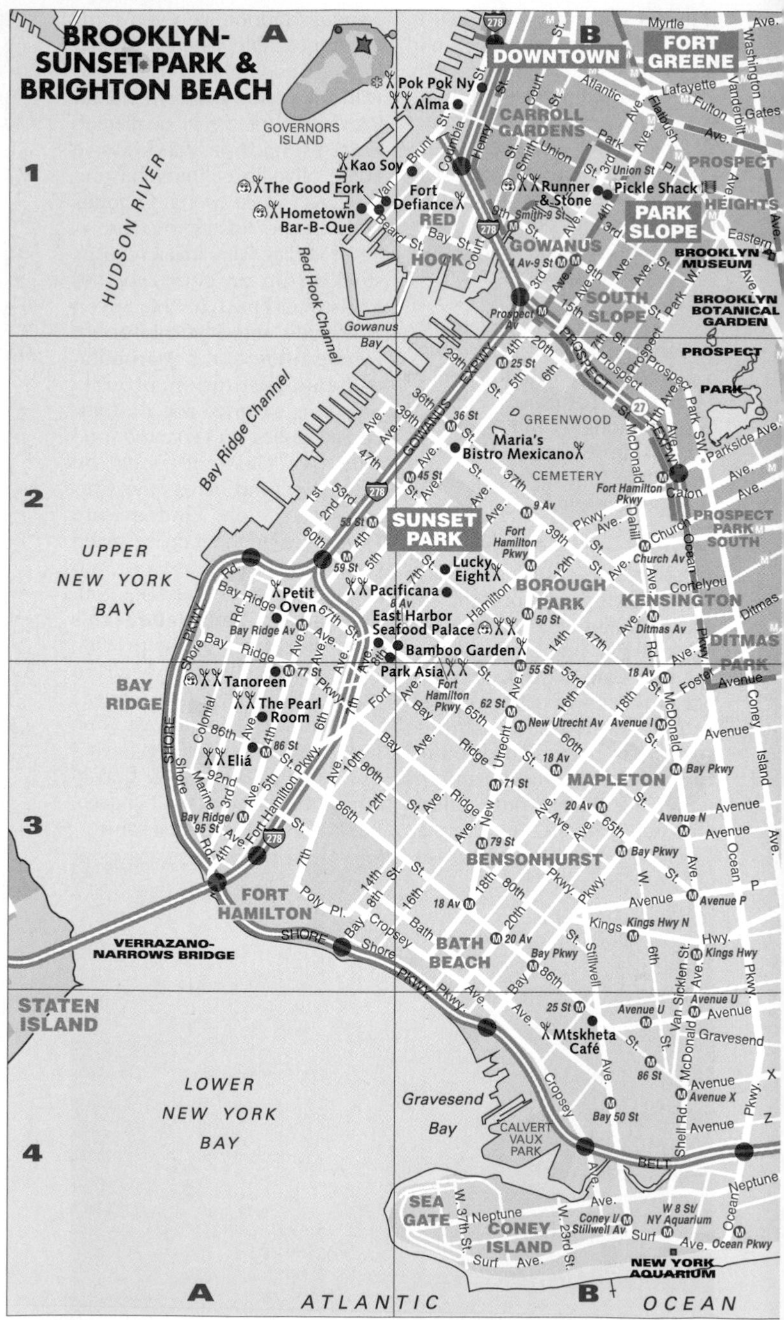
BROOKLYN-
SUNSET PARK &
BRIGHTON BEACH
Pok Pok Ny
Alma
GOVERNORS ISLAND
Kao Soy
The Good Fork
Hometown Bar-B-Que
Fort Defiance
Runner & Stone
Pickle Shack
DOWNTOWN
FORT GREENE
CARROLL GARDENS
PROSPECT HEIGHTS
PARK SLOPE
RED HOOK
GOWANUS
SOUTH SLOPE
BROOKLYN MUSEUM
BROOKLYN BOTANICAL GARDEN
PROSPECT PARK
HUDSON RIVER
Red Hook Channel
Gowanus Bay
Bay Ridge Channel
GREENWOOD CEMETERY
Maria's Bistro Mexicano
SUNSET PARK
UPPER NEW YORK BAY
Petit Oven
Pacificana
Lucky Eight
East Harbor Seafood Palace
Bamboo Garden
Park Asia
BOROUGH PARK
KENSINGTON
DITMAS PARK
PROSPECT PARK SOUTH
BAY RIDGE
Tanoreen
The Pearl Room
Eliá
MAPLETON
BENSONHURST
FORT HAMILTON
VERRAZANO-NARROWS BRIDGE
BATH BEACH
STATEN ISLAND
Mtskheta Café
LOWER NEW YORK BAY
Gravesend Bay
CALVERT VAUX PARK
SEA GATE
CONEY ISLAND
NEW YORK AQUARIUM
ATLANTIC OCEAN

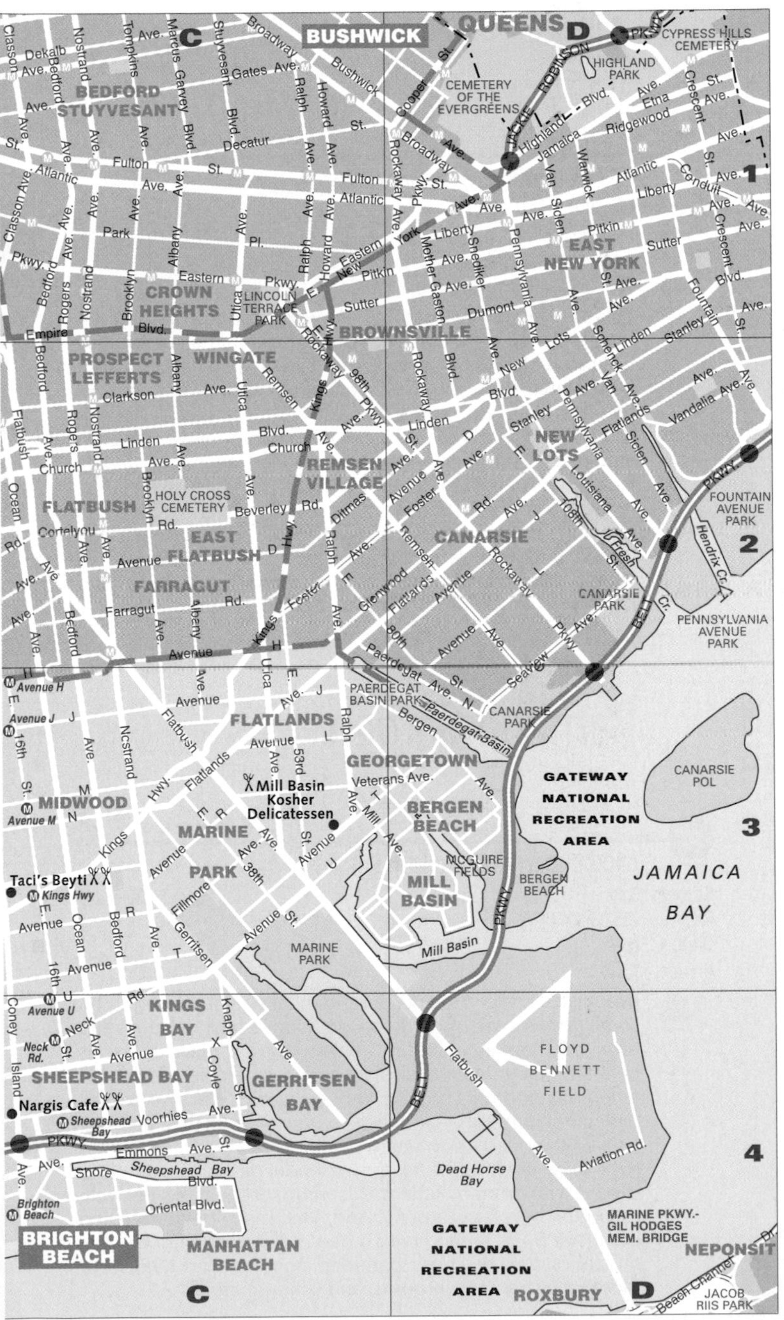
BUSHWICK
QUEENS
C
D
CYPRESS HILLS CEMETERY
HIGHLAND PARK
CEMETERY OF THE EVERGREENS
JACKIE ROBINSON PKWY.
BEDFORD STUYVESANT
CROWN HEIGHTS
LINCOLN TERRACE PARK
BROWNSVILLE
EAST NEW YORK
PROSPECT LEFFERTS
WINGATE
REMSEN VILLAGE
NEW LOTS
FLATBUSH
HOLY CROSS CEMETERY
EAST FLATBUSH
FARRAGUT
CANARSIE
FOUNTAIN AVENUE PARK
CANARSIE PARK
PENNSYLVANIA AVENUE PARK
PAERDEGAT BASIN PARK
FLATLANDS
GEORGETOWN
GATEWAY NATIONAL RECREATION AREA
CANARSIE POL
MIDWOOD
Mill Basin Kosher Delicatessen
BERGEN BEACH
MARINE PARK
MCGUIRE FIELDS
MILL BASIN
JAMAICA BAY
Taci's Beyti
Kings Hwy
KINGS BAY
FLOYD BENNETT FIELD
SHEEPSHEAD BAY
GERRITSEN BAY
Nargis Cafe
Sheepshead Bay
Dead Horse Bay
Brighton Beach
BRIGHTON BEACH
MANHATTAN BEACH
MARINE PKWY.-GIL HODGES MEM. BRIDGE
NEPONSIT
GATEWAY NATIONAL RECREATION AREA
ROXBURY
JACOB RIIS PARK
1
2
3
4

Alma

Mexican XX

187 Columbia St. (at Degraw St.)

Subway: Carroll St
Phone: 718-643-5400
Web: www.almarestaurant.com
Prices: $$

Lunch Sat – Sun
Dinner nightly

This festive stalwart with a renowned rooftop has come a long way since its early days along this rather unromantic waterfront. Mexican artifacts and mirrors line the brick walls of this multi-story spot with a margarita-fueled vibe and food that puts a smile on every face.

Alma's pleasing Mexican cooking focuses on good, clean ingredient combinations in a nuanced menu of simple, flavorful dishes. Go for a delicious standard like plump, tender short rib enchiladas in soft, flour tortillas with roasted *ranchero*, Gouda cheese, and pumpkin seed sauces. Be sure to add on baked *arroz con queso*, a decadent side of rice with tomato, poblano, and sharp cheddar. The classic palate-cooling flan is topped with an enticingly sticky mantel of caramel.

Bamboo Garden

Chinese 

6409 Eighth Ave. (at 64th St.)

Subway: 8 Av
Phone: 718-238-1122
Web: N/A
Prices: ⊜

Lunch & dinner daily

Brooklyn's Dyker Heights, a residential neighborhood in the southwest corner of the borough, is awash in delicious dim sum, but Bamboo Garden holds a special place in locals' hearts. An impressive display of roasted meats is the key differentiator of this bright and bustling gem that also proffers piping hot dim sum—and the servers are more than happy to explain their cart's content to newbies.

Kick things off with the *har gow*, a tender quartet of dumplings stuffed with crunchy little rock shrimp; or the flaky, perfectly savory barbecue pork puffs. And, then move on to succulent barbecue pork, fanned over a bed of fluffy white rice with a drizzle of soy; or crispy pan-fried noodles with tender stir-fried beef, straw mushrooms, and Chinese greens.

East Harbor Seafood Palace

Chinese XX

A2

714-726 65th St. (bet. Seventh & Eighth Aves.)

Subway: 8 Av — Lunch & dinner daily
Phone: 718-765-0098
Web: N/A
Prices: **$$**

Dim sum is a well-orchestrated dance at this boisterous hall, where small crowds wait for a spot at one of the large round tables for an indulgent weekend brunch. Steaming carts roll by and waiters ferry trays briskly into the red dining room with shiny gold accents. Service is quick but helpful; the constant clatter of chopsticks and rollicking groups are part of the fun. Eyes can guide the ordering when it comes to the dim sum carts, stocked with authentically prepared bites. Try the plump shrimp *siu mai* followed by rice noodles wrapped around crunchy whole shrimp and doused in a salty-sweet soy sauce. Snappy, stir-fried green beans are addictively crunchy. Don't miss the Singapore *mei fun*, a mound of vermicelli noodles with shrimp, pork, and scallions.

Eliá

Greek XX

A3

8611 Third Ave. (bet. 86th & 87th Sts.)

Subway: 86 St — Dinner Tue – Sun
Phone: 718-748-9891
Web: www.eliarestaurant.com
Prices: **$$**

This sliver of Mykonos in Bay Ridge evokes the Greek island spirit with its white walls, baby-blue accents, and rustic wood-beamed ceilings. Choose between the charming backyard patio, the small bar, or a table surrounded by woven chairs. Then, tuck into a menu of Greek classics, beginning with the deliciously familiar flavors of spanakopita, elegantly presented as small triangles of buttery filo filled with earthy spinach, tender leeks, and a whisper of salty feta. Slightly charred and nicely crunchy grilled shrimp arrive on a bed of plump Israeli couscous tinted pink with pomegranate syrup. Crowd-pleasing options include house-made ravioli filled with shredded braised lamb. *Rizogalo* (rice pudding) is topped with preserved cherries and crunchy granola.

Fort Defiance

American

365 Van Brunt St. (at Dikeman St.)

Subway: Smith - 9 Sts (& bus B61)
Phone: 347-453-6672
Web: www.fortdefiancebrooklyn.com
Prices: $$

Lunch daily
Dinner Wed – Mon

Surprisingly mellow for a restaurant named after a Revolutionary War fort, this Southern tavern (of sorts) is a warm and inviting space where one meal can easily bleed into the next. With a reputation for cocktails, a classic wood bar, and tables covered in colorful oilcloths depicting flora and fauna, this is a lively but not-too-crowded watering hole with solid cooking and heaps of character. A meal could start with crostini topped with local ricotta, shiitake mushrooms, kale, and parmesan. On a blustery day in windswept Red Hook, perhaps the smoky lentil soup will do.

Locals return time and again for classics like faultless deviled eggs dusted with paprika. A lean towards the South is seen in the hearty muffuletta of New Orleans fame.

The Good Fork

Contemporary

391 Van Brunt St. (bet. Coffey & Van Dyke Sts.)

Subway: Smith - 9 Sts (& bus B61)
Phone: 718-643-6636
Web: www.goodfork.com
Prices: $$

Lunch Sat – Sun
Dinner Tue – Sun

The Good Fork is a destination restaurant, and foodies know that it's well worth the journey. Located on the food-centric Van Brunt Street near the Red Hook Waterfront, this inviting spot swaps New York pretense for pure passion—it's the dream of a married couple who built the restaurant from scratch, literally. Co-owner Ben Schneider crafted the space, while his classically trained wife, Chef Sohui Kim, helms the kitchen.

Her cuisine reflects the team's commitment to the locality, as seen in such original dishes as pan-seared cod reclining on squid rings braised in a spicy kimchi broth; or hot and crisp manchego *arancini* cooled with yogurt and a fennel-tomato marmalade. A *tres leches* cake with fresh berry compote is a crowning way to close this meal.

Hometown Bar-B-Que

Barbecue

A1

454 Van Brunt St. (entrance on Reed St.)

Subway: Smith - 9 Sts (& bus B61) Lunch & dinner Tue – Sun
Phone: 347-294-4644
Web: www.hometownbarbque.com
Prices: $$

Texas-style barbecue has come to Brooklyn, even if this 'cue begins in an 18-foot smoke pit located a few blocks away, thereby keeping its on-site kitchen free from wood smoke. Instead, it remains focused on creamy mac n' cheese, whiskey sour pickles, and mayo-mustardy potato salad. Meats arrive sweet and tender enough to have a caramel crunch, while smoky sausages snap and explode with juice and chili-spiced bite—each is sold by the plump quarter-pound link. Ribs are cooked until the moment before they fall off the bone; and desserts feature Steve's Key lime pie locally made in Red Hook.

The warehouse-like space is clad in repurposed wood with communal picnic tables lending an intimate and friendly vibe. Water Taxi is the easiest way here from Manhattan.

Kao Soy

Thai

B1

283 Van Brunt St. (bet. Pioneer St. & Visitation Pl.)

Subway: Smith - 9 Sts (& bus B61) Lunch & dinner daily
Phone: 718-875-1155
Web: N/A
Prices:

The flavors of Northern Thailand are sparkling and alive at this Red Hook hangout, featuring a bright, basic, and brick-walled dining room. Inside, tables loaded with vibrant dishes flaunting heightened levels of fire are bound to tingle palates and tempt passersby.

Kao soy, the famous curry from Chiang Mai, is a signature for fitting reason. Topped with crispy egg noodles, this combo unites dark meat chicken, egg noodles, crushed peanut, and lime. A tart green mango salad mingled with crispy anchovies and sweet cashew nuts is a delight on its own; while banana blossom fritters should be dunked in thick peanut-chili sauce for more flavor. Bitter melon soup served with a whole deep-fried red snapper is yet another intriguing offering.

Lucky Eight

B2 **Chinese**

5204 Eighth Ave. (bet. 52nd & 53rd Sts.)

Subway: 8 Av
Lunch & dinner daily
Phone: 718-851-8862
Web: N/A
Prices: ⊜

For an intimate alternative to the nearby Eighth Avenue banquet halls, this cozy restaurant is a reliable spot for Cantonese specialties from quick stir-fries to roasted meats. Beyond the bustling takeaway counter, turquoise fish tanks, and butchers at work, the mellow dining room houses small tables. English-speaking waiters can help maneuver through the menu against a soundtrack of clinking plates and bowls from the nearby kitchen.

The expertly cooked noodle soups are a must—springy egg noodles swim in piping-hot chicken broth, studded with generous chunks of tender roasted duck. The roast barbecue pork platter contains juicy, thin layers of pork with just the right whisper of fat. Greens like *choy sum* are steamed to a vibrant emerald-green.

Maria's Bistro Mexicano

B2 **Mexican**

886 Fifth Ave. (bet. 38th & 39th Sts.)

Subway: 36 St
Lunch & dinner daily
Phone: 718-438-1608
Web: N/A
Prices: **$$**

In a vibrant pocket of Brooklyn, locals flock to this timeworn façade for generous portions of fresh, well-priced, and tasty Mexican cuisine. Complete with a backyard, the décor of this quirky neighborhood staple is distinctly Mexican, from its bright woven textiles and vibrant pink walls, to lava rock *molcajetes* that top each table.

Start your meal with a delicious and filling chorizo taco topped with onion, tomato, and cilantro. *Crepas de elote* are stuffed with bits of tender onion, juicy corn, and poblano peppers. The chile poblano is a house specialty that satisfies with its one-two punch: the first is plumped with a savory combination of cheeses, while the other is stuffed with a beguiling mixture of chicken, almonds, diced plantain, and crunchy apple.

Mill Basin Kosher Delicatessen

Deli

5823 Ave. T (bet. 58th & 59th Sts.)

Subway: N/A
Lunch & dinner daily
Phone: 718-241-4910
Web: www.millbasindeli.com
Prices: $$

This middle-aged Brooklyn treasure is as old-school as it gets, and though it's a bit of a trek to Mill Basin, anyone looking for a real Jewish deli won't think twice. Part deli counter, part artsy dining room, and part party hall, Mark Schachner's beloved spot serves up all the classics from beef tongue sandwiches to gefilte fish.

The wildly overstuffed sandwiches (all served with homemade pickles and coleslaw) are a home run, as in the pastrami, which is steamed not once but twice, leaving the meat juicy yet hardly fatty. Dive into a Rueben—an open-face and intense pile of juicy corned beef, Swiss cheese, and tart sauerkraut on toasted rye bread, topped with Russian dressing. The pastrami eggroll is a serious, cultish favorite.

Mtskheta Café

Central Asian 

2568 86th St. (bet. Bay 41st St. & Stillwell Ave.)

Subway: 25 Av
Lunch & dinner Thu – Tue
Phone: 718-676-1868
Web: N/A
Prices:

Deep in the heart of Brooklyn bordering Bath Beach, Mtskheta Café pumps out Georgian classics in a green-hued, faux-brick dining room complete with paper napkins, a campy jungle mural, and television looping foreign music videos. While the décor may lack, the service and food excel, setting this impossible-to-pronounce restaurant apart from the nearby bodegas and elevated subway tracks.

Whether or not you can deduce what's on the Cyrillic menu, friendly servers standby, directing guests to native dishes like *badrijani*, an almost overwhelming helping of eggplant stuffed with fluffy walnut purée. It's light compared to the mutton *bozbashi*, though—a heady soup of tarragon, cilantro and lamb fat that adds a layer to any blustery day.

Nargis Cafe

Central Asian XX

C4

2818 Coney Island Ave. (bet. Kathleen Pl. & Ave. Z)

Subway: Sheepshead Bay Lunch & dinner daily
Phone: 718-872-7888
Web: www.nargiscafe.com
Prices: **$$**

This industrial strip is ground zero for Central Asian hot spots, where Nargis Cafe endures as a real treat. Composed of a front bar area and larger, brighter dining room, the entire space is brought together with marvelous Persian rugs and exotic pierced-metal sconces.

Nargis hits a strong stride among the locals for its convivial vibe and unique repertoire of dishes that may include a *bojon* salad of smoky eggplant tossed with garlic, peppers, carrots, and cucumber. Kebabs are taken seriously here, so try the succulent lamb with chopped onion and dill. Uzbek *plov* studded with chickpeas, lamb, and raisins is simple but imperative. For dessert, the honey-sweet *chak-chach* is fried but surprisingly light and exquisitely indulgent.

Pacificana

Chinese XX

B2

813 55th St. (at Eighth Ave.)

Subway: 8 Av Lunch & dinner daily
Phone: 718-871-2880
Web: N/A
Prices: **$$**

Among the best of the superior Chinese options in this far-flung pocket of Brooklyn, Pacificana is a bustling, airy second-floor jewel. After getting a number (which will be called out in Mandarin, Cantonese, and finally English) and waiting in the inevitable line, settle into a large, circular table along with other diners and prepare for a feast. The fun begins when silver dim sum carts start to roll by, hauling delicacies from the open kitchen.

Service is curt as signature temptations such as plump pork dumplings and shrimp rice noodle rolls are plopped onto the table. Chicken with crunchy mustard greens, paired with preserved black beans and a steaming bowl of fluffy white rice is nothing short of heavenly so plan to linger here a while.

Park Asia

Chinese XX

6521 Eighth Ave. (bet. 65th & 66th Sts.)

Subway: 8 Av — Lunch & dinner daily
Phone: 718-833-1688
Web: N/A
Prices: ☺☺

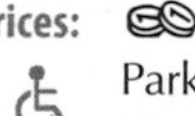

Park Asia's recent design overhaul is giving Dyker Heights' popular Dim Sum Row a jolt of style these days, wowing new and old customers with its floor-to-ceiling windows, soaring ceilings, sparkling chandelier, and light-flooding sky lights. If it all seems a bit showy for your average weekend dim sum rush, not to worry: Park Asia takes its food just as seriously. Servers are well-mannered and friendly, delivering delicious, well-executed Chinese dishes like plump shrimp paired with crispy bacon, as well as succulent minced beef wrapped in glutinous rice noodles and drizzled with a sweet-savory sauce. A pile of snappy *choy sum* is dusted with fried garlic chips; and warm fried crullers wrapped in rice noodles are topped with sweet soy for a saucy finish.

The Pearl Room

Contemporary XX

8201 Third Ave. (at 82nd St.)

Subway: 86 St — Lunch & dinner daily
Phone: 718-833-6666
Web: www.thepearlroom.net
Prices: **$$**

With its jumbo garden and bright, sun-streaked dining room, this Brooklyn steady is a solid choice year-round. Most days you'll catch a glimpse of the charming Chef/owner Anthony Rinaldi, working his magic both in the kitchen and out in the cozy dining room.

Every meal begins with a bread basket, served with a creamy dip of cannellini beans, roasted red peppers, and garlic. The Pearl Room earns its reputation for a vast seafood spread (and generous portions) with dishes like pine nut-crusted lemon sole or lobster stuffed ravioli. Meat dishes are just as satisfying, so try the shell steak au poivre—a juicy cut paired with creamed spinach and a luscious potato gratin. End with tongue-wagging desserts, such as spiced carrot cake with a caramel drizzle.

Petit Oven

French

276 Bay Ridge Ave. (bet. Ridge Blvd. & Third Ave.)

Subway: Bay Ridge Av — Dinner Wed– Sun
Phone: 718-833-3443
Web: www.petit-oven.com
Prices: $$

Unassuming but worth your attention, this little Bay Ridge site offers a petite, tidy room that is simply done and fills quickly. The ambience here brings a gracious welcome, and the air wears a palpable note of authenticity.

Chef/owner Katarzyna Ploszaj styles her agreeable and refreshingly relaxed cuisine through a classic French lens. Appetizers may include a novel riff on Greek salad composed of thinly shaved Brussels sprouts mingled with diced feta, a handful of black olives, sliced red onion, and a sprig of fragrant oregano all licked with olive oil and a bright hit of lemon juice. Expect equally impressive entreés like a cooked duck breast, crisped and rosy, with red onion-ginger marmalade, and duck fat-roasted potatoes scented with thyme.

Pickle Shack

Gastropub 

B1

256 Fourth Ave. (bet. Carroll & President Sts.)

Subway: Union St — Lunch & dinner daily
Phone: 347-763-2127
Web: www.pickleshacknyc.com
Prices: ☺☺

Start with a menu that highlights the small-batch handiwork of Brooklyn Brine Co., then add an extensive assortment of beers from Dogfish Head Craft Brewery. Toss in wood tables, inviting counter seating, and dusky blue walls, and you have this enticing pub.

Chef Neal Harden has put together a menu of suds-friendly food consisting of vegetarian snacks (think fried hop pickles with preserved lemon aïoli), and salads such as grilled romaine and Tuscan black kale with beluga lentils. Pickle Shack's lighter fare is rounded out by hearty, imaginative sandwiches crafted from local ingredients and purveyors. To that end, order the crusty artisan baguette filled with warm cannellini bean purée, grilled asparagus, and fennel-pickled beets.

Pok Pok Ny

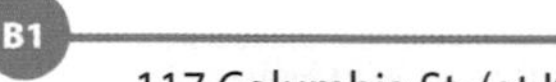

Thai

B1

117 Columbia St. (at Kane St.)

Subway: Carroll St
Phone: 718-923-9322
Web: www.pokpokny.com
Prices: $$

Lunch Sat – Sun
Dinner nightly

Foodies flock to this penultimate scene not for the vibe, but for a profound understanding of Isaan culinary traditions. If *pok pok* means "mortar and pestle" then Chef Andy Ricker makes this utensil the foundation of his trademark cooking, which takes excellent local product and imparts it with American flair.

The spacious room, outfitted with salvaged wood and exposed brick walls, is filled with a Brooklyn crowd. The kitchen has struggled with turnover and while some dishes remain solid as ever, others can disappoint.

Top-quality boar collar coated in a flavorful rub of soy sauce, sugar, and spice is seared to chewy perfection before being coupled with cool mustard greens. Superb execution and pronounced flavors are clear in *khanom jiin kaeng khiaw waan luuk chin plae,* a tart and texturally exquisite green coconut curry floating with delicate fish balls and garnished with fried anchovies for unbeatable texture; and *sai ua samun phrai* or grilled Thai sausage accompanied by a spicy eggplant sauce, crispy pork cracklings, and a bouquet of long beans. Seal the deal with *affogato*—a shot of espresso poured over decadent condensed milk ice cream, which ensures nothing but sweet dreams.

Runner & Stone 

B1 — Contemporary XX

285 Third Ave. (bet. Carroll & President Sts.)

Subway: Union St — Lunch & dinner daily
Phone: 718-576-3360
Web: www.runnerandstone.com
Prices: $$

An innate sense of purpose pervades this ambitious Gowanus operation. The name refers to the two stones used to grind grain; the location is just blocks away from where the city's first tide-water grist mill once stood; and the dining room is backed by a fantastic bakery headed by an alum of Per Se. Inside, the theme continues with walls constructed out of flour sack-formed concrete blocks.

For lunch, sandwiches on mouthwatering bread include grilled cheddar with roasted and pickled peppers on whole wheat *pain au lait,* or falafel-inspired broccoli fritters swaddled in a warm pita with shots of *harissa* and walnut-yogurt sauce. Impressive house-made pastas and the likes of roasted chicken with soft buckwheat dumplings are crowd-pleasers at dinnertime.

Taci's Beyti

C3 — Turkish XX

1953-55 Coney Island Ave. (bet. Ave. P & Quentin Rd.)

Subway: Kings Hwy (16th St.) — Lunch & dinner daily
Phone: 718-627-5750
Web: www.tacisbeyti.com
Prices: $$

Find safety from the evil eye at Taci's Beyti, a bright Turkish spot tucked into a busy thoroughfare in Midwood, where smiling strangers chat at communal tables amid dozens of *nazar boncugu* amulets. Homey and cozy, families dig into rustic dishes as servers spring to and fro with platters of golden, fresh, fragrant food and pile tables high with *pide, tabuli,* grape leaves, and almond-stuffed apricots.

Turkish options are few and far between in this predominately Orthodox neighborhood, and dishes here reflect this mergence of ethnicities, as in the unexpected but appealing combination of hummus topped with pastrami. Indulge in dishes that focus on vivid Aegean flavors, like the artichoke heart salad with potatoes and sweet peas (a meal unto itself).

Tanoreen

Middle Eastern

7523 Third Ave. (at 76th St.)

Subway: 77 St

Lunch & dinner Tue – Sun

Phone: 718-748-5600

Web: www.tanoreen.com

Prices: **$$**

One of the city's finest Middle Eastern experiences is tucked into an unassuming Bay Ridge corner and run by Chef/owner Rawia Bishara and her daughter.

Meals graciously commence with pickled vegetables and *za'atar*-dusted flatbread and are followed by a tableful of unique plates brimming with flavors and colors. Turkish salad is actually a bright red tomato spread shot with *harissa* and dressed with bits of diced cucumber and a drizzle of excellent olive oil. Appetizers are numerous, but try to fit in the chicken *fetti*: an entrée of basmati rice pilaf studded with toasted, broken vermicelli and topped with spicy bits of chicken, slivered toasted almonds, a generous drizzle of yogurt-tahini sauce, and chopped parsley for a fresh, final note.

Look for our category small plates.

Williamsburg
GREENPOINT

Williamsburg—traditionally an Italian, Hispanic, and Hasidic hub—is now a mecca for hipsters and artists. Here in Billyburg, creative culinary endeavors abound and include several, small-scale stores preparing terrific eats—imagine the artisan chocolate line crafted at **Mast Brothers Chocolate** and you'll start to get the picture. Bring an appetite or posse of friends to **Smorgasburg**, where sharing is crucial for a true gustatory thrill. This open-air market is held on the waterfront from spring through fall and headlines beef sliders and brisket, to *bulgogi* and *chana masala*. Less interested in

eating and more so in cooking? Sign up for a class at *Brooklyn Kitchen*, where home cooks can keep up with haute chefs by learning how to pickle, bake, and ferment...even kombucha! Over on Metropolitan Avenue, cute takeout shop **Saltie** serves a

small but tempting list of sammies and sweets; while **Pies 'n' Thighs** soothes the soul with down-home goodness. And, there's no going wrong with a cup of joe from **Toby's Estate** or **Blue Bottle Coffee Co.** on Berry Street. In need of a different type of pick-me-up? **Maison Premiere** is perfect. The vague signage out front is of little help, but the line out the door is enough of a clue that this boîte is *the* spot for stellar sips. Within its distressed walls, freshly shucked oysters are washed down with absinthe, icy juleps, and other skillfully made libations. Inspired by the art of butchery, **Marlow & Daughters** is adored for regionally sourced meat, house-made sausages, and dry goods. Locals who live and breathe by meat and cheese make routine trips to **Best Pizza**, a destination that delivers on what its name proclaims. In keeping with the vibe of the 'hood, the interior is disheveled by design; but, that doesn't keep peeps from coming for a slice of "white." Tried and true **Fette Sau** brings rudimentary comfort with roadhouse-style barbecue to area residents; and **BrisketTown** on Bedford has been winning over hearts and palates for a while now.

Greenpoint bakeries offers stacks of traditional Polish pastries, but for a change of pace head to **Ovenly**, just steps away from WNYC Transmitter Park,for a slice of pitch-dark Brooklyn blackout cake.

BROOKLYN-WILLIAMSBURG
MANHATTAN
EAST RIVER
WILLIAMSBURG BRIDGE
WILLIAMSBURG
VINEGAR HILL
DOWNTOWN
FORT GREENE & BUSHWICK
BROOKLYN NAVY YARD INDUSTRIAL PARK
Navy Yard Basin
MCCARREN PARK
COMMODORE BARRY PARK
Anella
River Styx
Paulie Gee's
Karczma
Le Fond
Krolewskie Jadlo
El Born
Luksus at Tørst
Reynard
Miranda
Allswell
Zenkichi
Ramen Yebisu
Egg
El Almacen
Delaware and Hudson
Aurora
1 or 8
Salt + Charcoal
Samurai Mama
Roebling Tea Room
St. Anselm
Baci & Abbracci
La Superior
M Shanghai
Tabaré
Bozu
Rye
Zizi Limona
Marlow & Sons
Diner
Traif
Semilla
Xixa
Meadowsweet
Peter Luger
Shalom Japan
Greenpoint Av
Bedford Av
Metropolitan Av
Marcy Av
Hewes St
Broadway
FDR Drive
Brooklyn-Queens Expwy

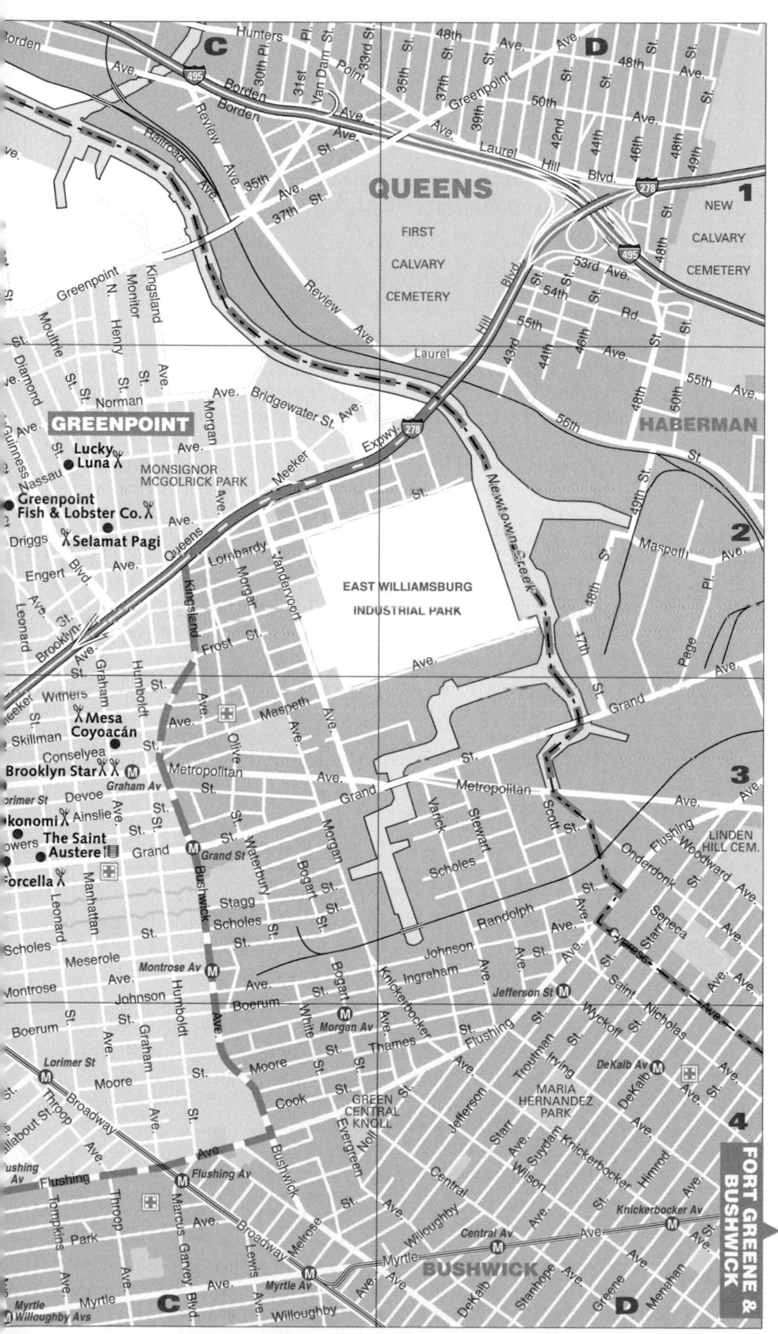
QUEENS
FIRST CALVARY CEMETERY
NEW CALVARY CEMETERY
GREENPOINT
HABERMAN
MONSIGNOR MCGOLRICK PARK
EAST WILLIAMSBURG INDUSTRIAL PARK
LINDEN HILL CEM.
GREEN CENTRAL KNOLL
MARIA HERNANDEZ PARK
BUSHWICK
Lucky Luna
Greenpoint Fish & Lobster Co.
Selamat Pagi
Mesa Coyoacán
Brooklyn Star
Okonomi
The Saint Austere
Forcella
Graham Av
Grand St
Montrose Av
Morgan Av
Jefferson St
DeKalb Av
Lorimer St
Flushing Av
Myrtle Av
Central Av
Knickerbocker Av
Myrtle Willoughby Avs
FORT GREENE & BUSHWICK

Allswell

Gastropub

B2

124 Bedford Ave. (at N. 10th St.)

Subway: Bedford Av — Lunch & dinner daily
Phone: 347-799-2743
Web: www.allswellnyc.com
Prices: $$

It's all good at this all-day Williamsburg tavern, where the vibe is welcoming and the setting is comfortable. Come as you are for friendly service amidst a patchwork of vintage wallpaper, then settle in to choose from the enjoyable selection listed on the wall-mounted blackboard.

In keeping with the cozy atmosphere, brunch is served every day of the week. Offerings include eye-opening chorizo and beans with poached eggs; and smoked whitefish toast—house-baked brioche topped with fresh ricotta and large chunks of infused fish, sided by a perfect boiled egg and parsley salad. Dinner brings yet more comfort fare like orecchiette with lamb ragù and fava beans; grilled chicken with lentils; or divine sweets like a tall wedge of seed-crusted cinnamon cake.

Anella

Contemporary

B1

222 Franklin St. (bet. Green & Huron Sts.)

Subway: Greenpoint Av — Lunch & dinner daily
Phone: 718-389-8100
Web: www.anellabrooklyn.com
Prices: $$

Tucked away in Greenpoint, just a few blocks from the East River, Anella hosts diners in an intimate rough and tumble space boasting a sliver of a dining room, charming back patio, and welcoming bar fashioned out of a reclaimed work bench from the Steinway & Sons piano factory.

The kitchen is on display and sends forth a menu of ambitious creations, beginning with a loaf of bread freshly baked and served in a clay flowerpot. Smoke was a recent inspiration as seen in a slice of brisket afloat in a lusciously fluid risotto of spinach and garlic. Other preparations have included seared striped bass paired with lentils and cauliflower that was roasted and whirled into a purée; and a finale of apple *crémeux* atop almond cake sided by rum ice cream.

Aurora

Italian

70 Grand St. (at Wythe Ave.)

Subway: Bedford Av — Lunch & dinner daily
Phone: 718-388-5100
Web: www.aurorabk.com
Prices: $$

This charming trattoria has long been a popular dining choice for residents of this dynamic stretch of Williamsburg. Stocked with wood furnishings, the rustic brick and plaster room is dressed up with vintage knickknacks and features a pretty ivy-covered outdoor area that doubles the seating capacity of the corner setting.

Aurora's enjoyable Italian cuisine speaks to the power of simplicity with minimally dressed market greens, expertly prepared pastas, and roasted meats. One can't go wrong with a meal of plump house-made sausage with lightly sautéed broccoli rabe and pickled Calabrian pepper; silky agnolotti stuffed with ricotta, spring peas, and fresh mint; or *affogato* with chocolate crumb-coated vanilla gelato, all offered at impressive value.

Baci & Abbracci

Italian

204 Grand St. (bet. Bedford & Driggs Sts.)

Subway: Bedford Av — Lunch Sat – Sun
Phone: 718-599-6599 — Dinner nightly
Web: www.baciny.com
Prices: $$

This upbeat Williamsburg eatery features Italian cuisine with a wholehearted emphasis on pizza. With more than twenty permutations of pies baked in their wood-burning oven from Naples, these smoky-chewy crusts may be the foundation for sauce and freshly made mozzarella, or even *focaccia tartufata*—two thin layers filled with *robiola* cheese and topped with truffle oil. Beyond this, the adept kitchen also boasts homemade bread, enjoyable pastas, and an impressive short list of *secondi* like juicy lamb chops with a crisp potato-rosemary crust.

The intimate space sports a contemporary design framed by a concrete floor, sleek furnishings, and glazed-tile accents. A charming little patch of backyard makes an especially popular setting for weekend brunch.

Bozu

B3

296 Grand St. (bet. Havemeyer & Roebling Sts.)

Subway: Bedford Av — Dinner nightly
Phone: 718-384-7770
Web: www.oibozu.com
Prices: ⚭

An enticing selection of Japanese tapas—with many pleasing vegetarian options—is buttressed by a gracious staff and laid-back vibe at this upbeat, hip, and tasty spot. The slim wood and brick space is dressed in grey and installed with an L-shaped counter, a row of tables, and back patio. Bring friends and order a lot.

The sushi bar tempts with the *yakko* roll filled with silken house-made tofu and green onion; spicy mushroom roll dabbed with tomatillo purée; and *gunkanzushi* topped with sweet sea scallop and plump salmon roe alongside soy sauce pre-seasoned with wasabi. Cooked dishes bring on the likes of deep-fried *gyoza* filled with tomato, and fantastically intense nuggets of fried chicken thigh marinated for 48 hours in garlic and soy sauce.

Brooklyn Star

American XX

C3

593 Lorimer St. (at Conselyea St.)

Subway: Lorimer St - Metropolitan Av — Lunch Sat – Sun, Dinner nightly
Phone: 718-599-9899
Web: www.thebrooklynstar.com
Prices: $$

Chef Joaquin Baca's handiwork at Brooklyn Star displays a fun and creative streak that yields admirable results. Pork chops are brined with molasses, striped bass is poached in duck fat, and roasted chicken is glazed with sweet tea and plated with dirty rice. Gluttony will convince you to bolster a meal here with bacon-jalapeño cornbread or buttermilk biscuits. But, let restraint chime in with a tasty raw kale salad; starring golden raisins, toasted peanuts, lemon vinaigrette, and a lacy cheddar crisp on top, it's pleasure on a plate.

Though the focus is on the eats, the room is comfortably outfitted with brick red terrazzo floors and grey-trimmed walls. Blonde wood tables are set with bottles of hot sauce, pepper vinegar, and wild flowers.

Delaware and Hudson ✿

American XX

B3

135 N. 5th St. (bet. Bedford Ave. & Berry St.)

Subway: Bedford Av — Lunch & dinner Tue – Sun
Phone: 718-218-8191
Web: www.delawareandhudson.com
Prices: **$$$**

This small Williamsburg gem arrives courtesy of Chef/owner Patti Jackson, who marries her Northeastern Pennsylvania upbringing (sourcing her ingredients from the wonderful farms that dot the Mid-Atlantic) with her lengthy culinary resume (I Trulli, for starters). The results are, as you'd expect, delightful.

In summer months, there's a small outdoor patio with a handful of seats overlooking the sidewalk. Inside the restaurant, you'll find a long, narrow dining space with exposed wood beams; bare wooden tables; and photographs on the walls depicting farm life. The overall effect is one of rustic, folksy ease—with a genuinely warm and knowledgeable service staff adding to the appeal.

Diners are offered a rotating, four-course dinner at an excellent value, where a collection of seasonal, farm-fresh small plates kick off the meal, followed by a pasta course, choice of entrée, and, finally, the day's dessert. Each dish is more delicious than the last: a mouthwatering plate of hand-rolled *macaroni alla pettine* arrives with tender grilled zucchini, salty farmer's cheese, and mint; while a flaky fillet of Long Island fluke is paired with smooth polenta, ripe Sun Gold tomatoes, and a cascade of chopped eggplant.

Diner

American

B3

85 Broadway (at Berry St.)

Subway: Marcy Av — Lunch & dinner daily
Phone: 718-486-3077
Web: www.dinernyc.com
Prices: $$

Williamsburg's restored 1920s-era diner is a modern day hipster hangout complete with swivel stools lining the counter and wood-slat booths in the dining room. In lieu of a menu, the cool-looking servers handwrite Diner's concise carte directly onto paper-topped tables, all the while explaining each item in detail.

A fried chicken sandwich or grass-fed burger are thoroughly appropriate fare for the setting, but it's the less expected plates that really wow. Take for example the grilled chicory, served charred and wilted, and plated with a fluffy dollop of ricotta cheese, crispy bacon lardons, and toasted walnuts. An equally impressive fillet of pan-seared trout boasts caramelized cipollini onions, poached currants, and a smear of strained yogurt.

Egg

American

B3

109 N. Third St. (bet. Berry St. & Wythe Ave.)

Subway: Bedford Av — Lunch daily
Phone: 718-302-5151
Web: www.eggrestaurant.com
Prices: (coins symbol)

It was only a matter of time before owner George Weld would have to find larger digs for his home of the city's best biscuits. Egg's ravenous following is now accommodated in a much larger location that's light and bright with seating at a number of counters and ample table space; yet it's still common to be faced with a queue.

Breakfast is served all day, every day, and stars those fantastic buttermilk biscuits. The fresh-baked beauties are split open and smothered with pork sausage-studded sawmill gravy, stacked with country ham, house-made fig jam, and Vermont cheddar cheese; or simply accompanied by molasses, honey, or jelly. Lunchtime brings savory fare like Carolina kale wilted in a spicy tomato broth poured over a wedge of crumbly cornbread.

El Almacen

B3 **Argentinian**

557 Driggs Ave. (bet. N. 6th & N. 7th Sts.)

Subway: Bedford Av — Lunch Sat – Sun
Phone: 718-218-7284 — Dinner nightly
Web: www.elalmacennyc.com
Prices: $$

This Argentinian grill is a carnivore's delight with its menu of meaty entrées from the grill (*de la parrilla*) like the *parrillada* featuring hearty ribeye and chorizo with truffle fries; or the "kitchen" offerings (*de la cocina*) which might include malbec-braised short ribs with sweet potato purée and Brussels sprouts. These hearty creations are best followed by *dulce de leche* in one of its several guises.

El Almacen, which means general store in Spanish, boasts a dark, rustic, and atmospheric setting replete with creaking wood furnishings, shelves of bric-a-brac, and cast iron skillets mounted on a brick wall. The bar is inviting, amply stocked with wine bottles, and set against a backdrop of creamy white tiles warmed by the candlelit room.

El Born

B2 **Spanish**

651 Manhattan Ave. (bet. Nassau & Norman Aves.)

Subway: Nassau Av — Lunch Sat – Sun
Phone: 347-844-9295 — Dinner nightly
Web: www.elbornnyc.com
Prices: $$

Hip and happening Greenpoint is a highly appropriate location for this tapas den named after the equally trendy Barcelona district of El Born. The slender expanse of red brick and concrete is brightened by a neon squiggle suspended from the ceiling, red Shaker-style chairs, and a kitchen-fronting wall clad with encaustic cement tile.

A tray of crostini, simmered tomato, and garlic cloves is served gratis, for a do-it-yourself *pan con tomate* to stimulate the palate for what's to come. Enjoy *croquetes* oozing goat cheese and served with apple compote; or shaved summer squash with *ibérico* ham, blueberries, and padrón pepper vinaigrette. Stone-grilled octopus seasoned with olive oil, thyme, and paprika is a pretty plate packed with big flavors.

Forcella

Pizza

485 Lorimer St. (bet. Grand & Powers Sts.)

Subway: Lorimer St - Metropolitan Av — Lunch Fri – Sun
Phone: 718-388-8820 — Dinner nightly
Web: www.forcellaeatery.com
Prices: ⊜

This favored pizzeria offers a convivial vibe in a quaint setting that is simply decorated with white stucco walls and brass sconces.

The wood-burning domed pizza oven, encrusted with shards of black tile, is the heart of Forcella. It pumps out a listing of signature pies built upon disks of moist chewy dough that is charred in all the right places, like the *pignasecca*. A sauce-less pizza *Bianca*, it's strewn with bits of caramelized onions, crumbles of fennel sausage, and gobs of fresh mozzarella and fontina. Also try the *montanara*, a house specialty crust that's fried before being decked and then baked as a traditional Margherita. If that doesn't do the trick, create your own pie with any combination from their wide selection of toppings.

Greenpoint Fish & Lobster Co.

Seafood 

114 Nassau Ave. (at Eckford St.)

Subway: Nassau Av — Lunch & dinner daily
Phone: 718-349-0400
Web: www.greenpointfish.com
Prices: $$

Fronted by green awnings, and flooded with light, this corner gem is equal parts sustainably sourced fish market and fantastic eat-in spot. Walk past iced specimens to claim a seat at the white marble counter; then dig into the day's catch dressed-up with global influences.

New England clam chowder is given the classic treatment, while grilled sea bass skewers are accompanied by a Thai coconut-and-peanut dipping sauce. Local fluke touched by extra virgin olive oil, a squeeze of Meyer lemon, and Maldon sea salt is an example of the first-rate crudo of the day; while Baja-style fish tacos feature tortillas stuffed with fried pollack, shredded cabbage, and chipotle-lime mayonnaise. For the fish-free, a raw vegan kelp noodle-pad Thai is remarkably satisfying.

Karczma

Polish

136 Greenpoint Ave. (bet. Franklin St. & Manhattan Ave.)

Subway: Greenpoint Av — Lunch & dinner daily
Phone: 718-349-1744
Web: www.karczmabrooklyn.com
Prices: $$

Located in a slice of Greenpoint that still boasts a sizeable Polish population, Karczma offers a lovely old-world ambience that may belie its age (opened for five-plus years) but perfectly matches its very traditional, budget-friendly menu. Hearty offerings may include peasant-style lard mixed with bacon and spices, or a plate of Polish specialties piled high with pierogies (three varieties, steamed or fried, topped with sliced onions and butter), kielbasa, potato pancakes, hunter's stew, and stuffed cabbage. Grilled plates can be prepared for two or three, while others, like the roasted hocks in beer, could easily feed an army.

The quaint, farmhouse-inspired interior is efficiently staffed with smiling servers in floral skirts and embroidered vests.

Krolewskie Jadlo

Polish

694 Manhattan Ave. (bet. Nassau & Norman Aves.)

Subway: Nassau Av — Lunch & dinner daily
Phone: 718-383-8993
Web: www.krolewskiejadlo.com
Prices: $$

Krolewskie Jadlo ("king's feast" in Polish) sits in a Greenpoint enclave that was once home to a large number of Polish immigrants. Although the size of the community has decreased through the years, the area still thrives with a distinct Eastern European soul.

The room is pleasant and routinely packed with crowds basking in the enjoyable authenticity. The Polish plate brings all one could hope for in a hearty old-world platter: cabbage rolls stuffed with ground beef and braised in tart tomato sauce; pan-fried potato pierogis; and a link of smoky kielbasa. Other items are just as tasty, like the pounded pork shoulder steak, grilled and brushed with honey, and served with pickled cabbage and beets.

A second outpost is located in Ridgewood, Queens.

La Superior

B3 **Mexican**

295 Berry St. (bet. S. 2nd & S. 3rd Sts.)

Subway: Bedford Av — Lunch & dinner daily
Phone: 718-388-5988
Web: www.lasuperiornyc.com
Prices: ◎◎

This south Williamsburg taqueria is as loved for its lip-smacking selection of tacos as it is for its budget-friendly prices and rock star vibe. A handful of tables add seating beyond the tiny bar, decorated with vintage wallpaper, brightly painted chili-red walls, and a mounted Mexican flag. Tacos anchor La Superior's menu, and include *lengua*, creamy *rajas*, or *carne asada* to be wrapped in excellent tortillas. However, other options also tempt like the *torta ahogada*—a "drowned" sandwich served as toasted sourdough bread stuffed with roasted pork drenched in *chile de arbol* and tomato sauce. A specialty of Guadalajara, the *cebollitas cambray* is a great side dish made with fat scallions that have been grilled until blistered, tender, and sweet.

Le Fond

B2 **French**

105 Norman Ave. (at Leonard St.)

Subway: Nassau Av — Lunch Sat – Sun
Phone: 718-389-6859 — Dinner Tue – Sun
Web: www.lefondbk.com
Prices: $$

Chef-owner Jake Eberle's cute corner restaurant shows us that not every dish needs reimagining and not every recipe requires reinterpretation. He's a French-trained chef whose cooking is crisp, clean, and comfortingly classic—and his well-balanced menu includes words like "roulade" and "blancmange" that here seem curiously reassuring. That's not to say his food doesn't pack a punch: the rich, meaty cassoulet could keep an army on the march for days.

Globe lights hang from the ceiling to illuminate a sea-blue room with bespoke wooden furniture. The acoustics can be bouncy and those lacking the necessary padding will find the seating a little numbing. But, there is honest toil and earnest endeavor happening here and it deserves support.

Lucky Luna

Fusion

167 Nassau Ave. (at Diamond St.)

Subway: Nassau Av — Lunch Wed – Sun
Phone: 718-383-6038 — Dinner Tue – Sun
Web: www.luckyluna-ny.com
Prices: ⊜

There's no other restaurant around like Lucky Luna. Seriously. Their delicious menu is a hybrid of Taiwanese and Mexican cuisine. The pizzazz on the plate is served in a simple yet tidy assemblage of glossy black tables, and an ambitious beverage program makes the small bar a total draw.

Mom's sweet-and-sour cucumber salad, flavored with ginger and garlic, is a bracing start for Peking duck confit *bao* spread with hoisin mayonnaise, garnished with crispy duck *chicharrònes* and duck fat popcorn dusted with Chinese five spice. Another hit: the taco of "reverse" carnitas is a pile of succulent pork shoulder that's been seared *then* braised in a broth of beer, oranges, and tomatoes, and finally topped with crunchy bits of radish and spicy pickles.

Marlow & Sons

Gastropub

81 Broadway (bet. Berry St. & Wythe Ave.)

Subway: Marcy Av — Lunch & dinner daily
Phone: 718-384-1441
Web: www.marlowandsons.com
Prices: $$

This enticing den is manna for the dozens of Williamsburg's gastronomes who come for a taste of Marlow & Sons' deliciously fuss-free fare at breakfast, lunch and dinner. In the front, find strong coffee and sweet treats as well as some interesting sundries. The back room presents a minimally worded carte that offers lunchtime sustenance like a refreshingly chilled yellow squash purée revved up with curry powder and a swirl of yogurt—the perfect antidote to a hot summer afternoon. Smoked trout, a salad-y composition of silken fish with warm potato wedges and creamy dill dressing, is another cooling classic.

Dinner features the succulent, bronze-skinned brick chicken, a menu mainstay, as well as oysters, cheeses, and an oft-changing list of specials.

Luksus at Tørst ✿

Contemporary XX

B2

615 Manhattan Ave. (bet. Driggs & Nassau Aves.)

Subway: Nassau Av — Dinner Tue – Sun
Phone: 718-389-6034
Web: www.luksusnyc.com
Prices: $$$$

Enter through Tørst, wander to the back, and find Luksus—it's like unearthing a little boudoir behind a beer bar. The small, highly Instagrammable room has a Scandinavia-via-Brooklyn look, with a choice marble dining counter for chef viewing and a smattering of tables. Sure, the crowd is heavily tattooed and tight-shirted, but this is no place for poseurs. Luksus has an artsy edge that cements Greenpoint's status as the current hotbed of NY cool. Cue the *Girls* location scouts.

The young staff may be hipsters, but everyone is passionate, friendly, and can recite beer history like it's their catechism. Absolutely go for the pairing.

The cuisine is firmly rooted in Scandinavian techniques and ingredients, with inspiration from afar and unfussy flashes of tinkered modernism. Simple staples add drama through spears of crusty sourdough with mouthwatering salty cultured butter. This may lead to barely smoked bluefish set over sunchoke salad, finished tableside in warm broth. Humble palate cleansers more than serve a purpose in the tart, tangy sea buckthorn sorbet with carrot sauce. Clever desserts include the sandy-brown malt granita over parsnip purée dotted with little kisses of cranberry meringue.

Meadowsweet ✿

B3 — Mediterranean XX

149 Broadway (bet. Bedford & Driggs Aves.)

Subway: Marcy Av — Lunch Sat – Sun
Phone: 718-384-0673 — Dinner nightly
Web: www.meadowsweetnyc.com
Prices: $$

One of Brooklyn's most beloved venues, this chill yet sophisticated destination is illuminated by a soaring glass-fronted façade, whitewashed brick walls, and reclaimed pine furnishings. While the original mosaic-tiled floors lend a stunning, old-timey accent that hearkens back to the building's former life as a printer's shop built in the late 19th century, Meadowsweet is clearly rooted in the present day thanks to Chef Polo Dobkin and his skilled team.

Best described as enticingly familiar and temptingly novel Americana with whiffs of the Mediterranean woven throughout, the menu is a delight every time. Each composition is beautifully plated, as in a bowlful of egg-rich *tajarin* slicked with intoxicating black truffle butter and served with frilly bits of sautéed hen-of-the-woods mushrooms as well as a showering of grated parmesan. A meaty block of wild halibut is expertly seared, presented cracker-crisp skin side up, and adorned with morels, asparagus, and pea shoots—or whatever the season's finest produce happens to be.

Desserts are equally impressive, like the homespun but sophisticated cylinder of warm blueberry crumble presented with lemon curd and ice cream.

Mesa Coyoacán

Mexican

C3

372 Graham Ave. (bet. Conselyea St. & Skillman Ave.)

Subway: Graham Av — Lunch Wed – Sun
Phone: 718-782-8171 — Dinner nightly
Web: www.mesacoyoacan.com
Prices: $$

Mexico City native, Chef Ivan Garcia has settled into this Brooklyn hot spot, where wolfish appetites are sated with richly flavored fare. Fronted by windows that open up to bustling Graham Avenue, the long space is outfitted with patterned wallpaper, snug banquettes, and communal tables. The kitchen's spirited cooking is simply a joy. Partake in tacos featuring hand-crafted tortillas, like the *suadero* stuffed with beef brisket and avocado salsa; or *torta tinga de pollo,* packed with shredded chipotle-braised chicken, mashed black beans, pickled jalapeños, and a toasted roll to sop up that delish sauce. Reposado and diced mango enhances the *pastel tres leches*—and to keep the tequila flowing, hit up nearby Zona Rosa, Chef Garcia's latest venture.

Miranda

Fusion

B2

80 Berry St. (at N. 9th St.)

Subway: Bedford Av — Lunch Fri – Sun
Phone: 718-387-0711 — Dinner Wed – Mon
Web: www.mirandarestaurant.com
Prices: $$

The cuisines of Latin America and Italy join for a splendid union at this Williamsburg trattoria, run by husband-wife team Sasha and Mauricio Miranda. The pretty space is illuminated with jewel-toned votives and boasts a cement floor inlaid with oak, straw seat chairs, and exposed brick. Beyond this, the chef puts her impressive experience to work in the open kitchen.

The house-made *pappardelle* is a perfect example of Miranda's unique approach: the wide delicate strands of pasta clutch on to bits of slow-cooked lamb in a dark, earthy, *mole* tasting of dried chilies, sweet spices, and bitter chocolate. Other items may include grilled baby octopus with avocado and jalapeño, or roasted pork tenderloin with tomato and cumin-scented Arborio rice.

M Shanghai

Chinese

292 Grand St. (bet. Havermeyer & Roebling Sts.)

Subway: Bedford Av — Lunch & dinner daily
Phone: 718-384-9300
Web: www.newmshanghai.com
Prices: ⊜

Look at the steamer full of luscious soup dumplings on just about every table in this notable Williamsburg Chinese café, and there should be little doubt of the best way to begin a meal here. Plump full of hot pork broth magically encased in scalloped wonton wrappers, they are sheer pleasure. Vegan and vegetarian treats include fried tofu with sweet peppers and black bean sauce; or cool, silken batons of eggplant salad dressed with plenty of garlic, soy, and a hint of sweetness. The scallion pancakes are fantastically large, hot, and shatteringly crisp wedges accompanied by a dipping sauce prepared tableside.

The low-key room is accented by whitewashed brick walls, honey-toned bamboo slats, and ceiling lights fashioned out of birdcages.

Okonomi

Japanese

150 Ainslie St. (bet. Leonard & Lorimer Sts.)

Subway: Lorimer St - Metropolitan Av — Lunch daily
Phone: N/A — Dinner Mon – Fri
Web: www.okonomibk.com
Prices: ⊜

A small counter and a handful of tables is the extent of this tiny café headed by Chef Yuji Haraguchi, famous for his ramen pop-ups. Regardless of the time of day, Okonomi's delightfully unconstrained Japanese cuisine is a compelling reason to visit.

Locally grown produce and domestic fish are the foundation of the high-quality *ichiju sansei*, a set lunch of *shioyaki* (salt-grilled) or miso-marinated broiled fish, rice, miso soup, and *shira-ae* (wilted greens with a tofu dressing). Come evening, the focus shifts to ramen, with each steaming bowl bearing the distinctive hand of the skilled chef. A surf-and-turf broth stocked with thin, straight noodles and roasted fish is just one example; while broth-less *mazeman* is dressed for the season.

1 or 8

Japanese XX

B3

66 S. 2nd St. (at Wythe Ave.)

Subway: Bedford Av Dinner Tue – Sun
Phone: 718-384-2152
Web: www.oneoreightbk.com
Prices: $$

Step inside this chic Williamsburg hideaway to find a lofty and dramatically appointed room. A stark white palette complements the setting's industrial bones, which even made an appearance in an episode of *The Good Wife*.

1 or 8's kitchen turns out impressive cooked food organized as small plate appetizers. It's an ideal destination for group dining, but smaller parties should make a beeline to the impressive sushi counter. Score a seat, request the omakase, and revel in the pieces Chef Kazuo Yoshida sets before you. Soy-marinated bluefin tuna, wild Alaskan sockeye salmon, and sea scallop sprinkled with yuzu and sea salt are but a few of the piscine delights to be enjoyed. Dark miso soup poured over house-made tofu concludes the admirable meal.

Paulie Gee's

Pizza 

B2

60 Greenpoint Ave. (bet. Franklin & West Sts.)

Subway: Greenpoint Av Dinner nightly
Phone: 347-987-3747
Web: www.pauliegee.com
Prices:

Owner Paul Giannone, aka Paulie Gee, channeled a lifelong love of pizza into this charmingly delicious spot that feels as if it has been around forever. Rustic in appearance, the room's cool concrete and brick are warmed by the glow of the wood-burning oven imported from Naples. From here, Giannone and his son work their magic.

The addictive crust is beguilingly moist and chewy, perfumed with smoke, and adroitly salted. Killer wood-fired pies dominate the menu with tempting combinations, excellent ingredients, and whimsical names. Offerings may include the Harry Belafontina—fontina, tomatoes, beefy meatballs, cremini mushrooms, and golden raisins. Vegans get equal respect here, with an added menu of vegan cheese and house-made vegan sausage.

Peter Luger ✿

Steakhouse

178 Broadway (at Driggs Ave.)

Subway: Marcy Av — Lunch & dinner daily
Phone: 718-387-7400
Web: www.peterluger.com
Prices: **$$$$**

Venerated Peter Luger resides in an expansive space reminiscent of old New York and early German ale houses—an endless line of visitors only serves to reiterate how special a place this truly is. Add to that a series of imposing pane windows, wood-paneled walls, and decorative old steins, and find yourself utterly smitten.

Begin with thrillingly fatty, thick-cut bacon nearly sweet on the outside, or shrimp cocktail in a rich tomato dressing. But, what truly leaves diners speechless is that delightfully succulent Porterhouse for two, three, or four. These slabs of beautifully naked meat are simple but their marbling is a thing of complexity and perfection, sizzling in drippings. The wedge salad sets a new standard: it is an enormous and crisp slice of iceberg drowned in blue cheese dressing, chopped tomato, and more bacon. The carnivorous feast is complete when sanctified by crispy French fries or excellent creamed spinach. Properly prepped servers are cordial, yet informal and never chatty.

A hunk of NY cheesecake, creamy, tart, and served with *schlag*, is every bit as classic as one imagines. Equally marvelous and dressed to the nines is a "Holy cow sundae"—the title speaks for itself.

Ramen Yebisu

Japanese

B3

126 N. 6th St. (bet. Bedford Ave. & Berry St.)

Subway: Bedford Av — Lunch & dinner daily
Phone: 718-782-1444
Web: www.ramenyebisu.com
Prices: ⊜

At this popular Williamsburg *ramen-ya*, Chef and Hokkaido native Akira Hiratsuka ladles signature bowlfuls of Sapporo-style ramen, characterized by its seafood-infused broth and wavy noodles aged for 48-hours. The results are distinct and delicious. Among the host of options to be tried are *shoyu* (soy-based), *shio* (salt-based), or the special house ramen brimming with a bounty of shellfish. A recent unique offering featured a fiery broth infused with a blend of 12 spices and fish sauce and filled with bone-in pork rib, cabbage, and red chilies.

Slurp your soup at one of two seating options in the moody, dark-walled space: perched atop tall tables or at a counter looking into the kitchen, where a refrigerator unit is stocked with custom-made noodles.

Reynard

American

B2

80 Wythe Ave. (at N. 11th St.)

Subway: Bedford Av — Lunch & dinner daily
Phone: 718-460-8004
Web: www.reynardsnyc.com
Prices: $$

Inside the Wythe hotel, find this fun and *très* Brooklyn-chic dining room, thanks to restaurateur Andrew Tarlow (of Diner and Marlow & Sons). The setting's former life as a century-old cooperage is proudly honored in myriad details like original masonry and cast iron columns. Parchment-colored walls and mosaic-tile floors enhance the throwback mien. Even in the cool light of day, over a bowl of strained house-made yogurt drizzled with golden honey and topped with granola, Reynard feels sexy.

The kitchen—equipped with a wood-burning oven—produces intriguing creations such as warm olives or red kale tossed with smoked Caesar dressing to snack on while awaiting hake chowder. Hearty entrées include oyster stew or rabbit with whole grain mustard.

River Styx

Contemporary

21 Greenpoint Ave. (near West St.)

Subway: Greenpoint Av
Phone: 718-383-8833
Web: www.riverstyxny.com
Prices: $$

Lunch Sat – Sun
Dinner nightly

Walk down Greenpoint Avenue and keep walking until you almost hit the East River to reach this newly launched venture. The setting is an undeniably cool combination of raw edges like rough timber ceiling beams, tables embedded with shards of glazed ceramic tile, and an open kitchen installed with a wood-burning oven.

Take a look at the menu and find items like hake with raw almond butter. Sound familiar? This is the handiwork of Chef Dennis Spina, also of Roebling Tea Room. Choose from a tempting lineup and enjoy anchovies sitting by a fire; *raviolo* stuffed with Taleggio afloat in a bright green nettle broth; or morsels of braised pork dabbed with spicy tomatillo salsa. Vanilla panna cotta with blueberry and black vinegar compote is a lovely finish.

Roebling Tea Room

Contemporary

143 Roebling St. (at Metropolitan Ave.)

Subway: Lorimer St - Metropolitan Av
Phone: 718-963-0760
Web: www.roeblingtearoom.com
Prices: $$

Lunch & dinner daily

Cuisine that bristles with creativity keeps the foodie crowd coming to this rough-hewn Williamsburg café. A popular bar anchors the room's layout, which is rustically appointed with absinthe-green ceramic tiles, rusted window frames, and pale beige painted-over brick accented by vintage wallpaper.

Lunch starts early and includes eye-opening options like the big pancake. Really, it's huge—baked in a cast iron skillet, laden with thinly sliced apples, and accompanied by warm maple syrup. Steak tartare with fried chickpeas and Kewpie mayonnaise satisfies savory cravings; and creamy grits- and egg yolk-stuffed ravioli, slicked with shrimp-infused "flamingo butter" sauce, is a specialty that successfully sums up the kitchen's distinct personality.

Rye 

American 

B3

247 S. 1st St. (bet. Havemeyer & Roebling Sts.)

Subway: Marcy Av — Lunch Sat – Sun
Phone: 718-218-8047 — Dinner nightly
Web: www.ryerestaurant.com
Prices: $$

Rye's Classic Old Fashioned—a carefully crafted swirl of liquid amber—is the perfect personification of Chef Cal Elliott's beloved gastropub: strong, satisfying, and comforting. Anchored by a reclaimed mahogany bar, the Brooklyn speakeasy is accented accordingly with creaky plank flooring, a pressed-tin ceiling, and exposed filament bulbs overhead. For even more reasons to imbibe, climb down to the basement offshoot, The Bar Below Rye.

Bar snacks such as oysters, cheeses, and duck rillettes with pickled watermelon lead to a succinct lineup of cooking that includes crispy skin seared Scottish salmon dressed with seasonal vegetables and preserved lemon. For dessert, the warm and fudgy molten chocolate cake is another classic Rye gets just right.

The Saint Austere

Contemporary 

C3

613 Grand St. (bet. Leonard & Lorimer Sts.)

Subway: Lorimer St - Metropolitan Av — Dinner Mon – Sat
Phone: 718-388-0012
Web: www.thesaintaustere.com
Prices: 

Sometimes all one needs is a fine glass of wine and a little snack (or three). For this, The Saint Austere fits the bill nicely. Platings bring on far-flung influences—as in the *bánh Mi(lano)*, pork terrine, thinly shaved mortadella, and house-pickled vegetables sandwiched into a toasted baguette moistened by a chili-flecked dressing. However, the menu's truest muse is a general coupling of Italian and Spanish flavors, such as pork belly *croquetas* accompanied by a dipping sauce of crushed chicken livers; or slow-cooked polenta topped with sweet onions caramelized in sausage drippings.

The spartanly adorned room offers a hospitable bar in addition to three communal tables. And the wine list proffers a gently priced selection of mostly European labels.

Salt + Charcoal

Japanese

B3

171 Grand St. (at Bedford Ave.)

Subway: Bedford Av — Lunch & dinner daily
Phone: 718-782-2087
Web: www.saltandcharcoal.com
Prices: $$

The attention-grabbing, mouthwatering name says it all: this place is all about *robata* items, cooked over Japanese charcoal and dressed with a selection of salts. Inside the tiny corner space, minimal seating is amplified by a counter accented with black-glazed brick and mid-century modern chairs. And, highly-coveted sidewalk tables serve as a front row for Bedford Avenue's hipster parade.

Skewers and small plates of charred nibbles include sweet miso-glazed *goma fu*, fish collar of the day, or strips of boneless Kurobuta pork short rib. Even the flame-free items are enticing, including soba, *hako* sushi, house-made chilled tofu accompanied by a trio of salts, as well as a refreshing salad comprised of four different varieties of seaweed.

Samurai Mama

Japanese 

B3

205 Grand St. (bet. Bedford & Driggs Aves.)

Subway: Bedford Av — Lunch & dinner daily
Phone: 718-599-6161
Web: www.samuraimama.com
Prices: ¢¢

For an authentic taste of Japan in Williamsburg, Chef Makoto Suzuki's cozy den is the place to be. Save for a handful of seats and high-backed wooden booths, a communal table touched by seasonal flora hosts the majority of its occupants. Raw offerings include taco-style sushi, the fish cradled by a sheet of toasted nori, but the menu's crux is on cooked bites—think handmade pork gyoza, kabocha squash simmered in dashi, and nicely done tempura. A truly special treat here is the udon, a tangle of plump, chewy house-made noodles crafted from California-milled flour and filtered water bobbing in luscious broths. Try the seafood curry variation—a rich, bonito and curry powder-spiked broth stocked with sweet shrimp, mussels, and scallops.

Selamat Pagi

Indonesian 

C2

152 Driggs Ave. (bet. Humboldt & Russell Sts.)

Subway: Nassau Av — Lunch Sat – Sun
Phone: 718-701-4333 — Dinner Tue – Sun
Web: www.selamatpagibrooklyn.com
Prices: ©©

This curious little café in the far reaches of Greenpoint is owned by the folks behind Van Leeuwen artisanal ice cream. The whitewashed room has limited seating between the wood plank banquette and metal chairs. Dining here is utterly charming, unique, and cheap.

Selamat Pagi means "good morning" in Balinese and it greets the 'hood with brunch on the weekend. The concise menu of fragrant and flavorful cooking keeps people coming back for luscious compositions like *nasi campur*—chopped long bean *lawar* dressed in lime juice, galangal, and toasted coconut, served with prawn crackers plus shaved red chili. A Bali fish salad seasoned with turmeric and shallot is yet another favored treat. And for dessert, choose a scoop of sticky black rice or lemongrass ice cream.

Shalom Japan

Fusion 

B3

301 S. 4th St. (at Rodney St.)

Subway: Marcy Av — Lunch Sat – Sun
Phone: 718-388-4012 — Dinner Tue – Sun
Web: www.shalomjapannyc.com
Prices: $$

The curious moniker of this sweet spot refers to the backgrounds of its husband-and-wife team, Chefs Aaron Israel and Sawako Okochi. Each has an impressive resume, and together the result is a unique labor of love. Nightly specials are displayed via a wall-mounted blackboard with small plates progressing to a handful of entrées.

Monkfish hot pot features *ankimo*-enriched miso broth, ground shrimp balls, glass noodles, and a heap of fragrant fresh herbs. The house-baked sake *kasu* challah with raisin butter is a highly recommended start. But, it may also turn up as toro toast smeared with scallion and wasabi cream cheese and topped with finely chopped, smoked lean tuna belly. Still craving more? Experience it once again in the warm chocolate bread pudding.

Semilla ✿

160 Havemeyer St., No. 5 (bet. S. 2nd & S. 3rd Sts.)

Subway: Marcy Av — Dinner Tue – Sat
Phone: 718-782-3474
Web: www.semillabk.com
Prices: $$$

Vegetables bask in the spotlight at this stellar South Williamsburg counter, where the formidable team of Chefs José Ramírez-Ruiz and Pamela Yung apply their fine dining aptitude to produce an improvisational feast out of the season's bounty.

Turning the notion of service on its head, members of the kitchen step away from their stations to deliver their intricate compositions—each of them plated on hand thrown pottery. The briefest of descriptions is offered upon presentation, which means that a mouthful of "grilled squash," for example, might also deliver raw slivers of pattypan, creamy peanut sauce, and a dusting of dried mint. Embellishments like foie gras and trout roe are used sparingly and to splendid effect, never outshining the true flavor of the produce. Semilla's bread is house-made, excellent, and used to accentuate the menu; as seen in a wedge of flax seed-barley sourdough with cultured butter to accompany a roasted carrot "mille-feuille," alongside smoked potato purée and fava-greens sauce.

Although the duo of sweets to finish may include options that disappoint, dessert can also be an electrifying success as in the egg yolk-saffron sorbet, cloud of smoked cream, and passion fruit.

St. Anselm

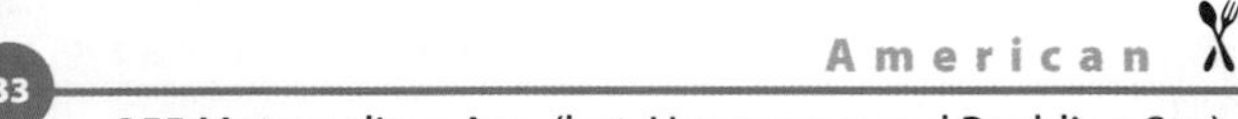

American

B3

355 Metropolitan Ave. (bet. Havemeyer and Roebling Sts.)

Subway: Bedford Av — Lunch Sat – Sun
Phone: 718-384-5054 — Dinner nightly
Web: N/A
Prices: $$

Look to this roughhewn yet charming café for a meal of grilled, meaty satisfaction. Loud and proud carnivores, this one's for you.

The perpetually rollicking kitchen embraces grilling as its preferred method of cooking to turn out a commendable bill of fare. Razor clams, sardines, artichokes, or *haloumi* comprise the offering of sizzling "smalls," while "bigs" are founded on cuts of hormone-free meats procured from small ranches, and have included a dinner plate-sized lamb blade steak—scorched, enjoyably fatty, and deliciously salted—topped with a coin of mint-gremolata butter. Other options can include a sweet tea-brined chicken; sides like decadent spinach gratin; or a Mason jar of chocolate *pot de crème* topped with *fleur de sel* and whipped cream.

Tabaré

Latin American

B3

221 S. 1st St. (bet. Driggs Ave. & Roebling St.)

Subway: Bedford Av — Lunch Sat – Sun
Phone: 347-335-0187 — Dinner nightly
Web: N/A
Prices: $$

Spanish tuna and black olive empanadas, homemade pastas, and the market-driven likes of a summery chilled soup made of Cubanelle peppers all deliciously co-exist at the charming Tabaré, where the cuisine of Uruguay headlines the delightful roster. Attractively rustic, the compact dining room is lined by slats of unpolished wood, and provides seating along a colorful fabric-covered banquette. The bar—like the back patio—is an inviting roost.

Tabaré's cooking uses local product and represents the Italian-Spanish influences that color the kitchen's creations. This includes *malfatti,* luscious ricotta dumplings adorned with squash blossoms wilted under a drizzle of hot butter and white truffle oil; or grass-fed skirt steak sided by savory *chimichurri.*

Traif

Contemporary 

229 S. 4th St. (bet. Havemeyer & Roebling Sts.)

Subway: Marcy Av — Dinner Tue – Sun
Phone: 347-844-9578
Web: www.traifny.com
Prices: $$

Small plates smacked with flavor are the dishes du jour at this rollicking eatery. The moniker translates to "forbidden" in Yiddish, and the renegade menu displays an affinity for pork and shellfish. From the open kitchen, Chef Jason Marcus and his team send a steady stream of solid creations like cornmeal-dusted fried green tomatoes with Old Bay aïoli and Tabasco sauce. Head-on prawns, pan roasted in foie gras fat with wild mushrooms and spring onion, are served on a slice of toast thick enough to absorb all the savory drippings. For dessert, try the butterscotch *budino* layered with rosemary ice cream and chopped hazelnuts.

The narrow space is muted with pale grey walls but enhanced by a mural of cartoon colors and an especially pleasant back patio.

Xixa

Mexican 

241 S. 4th St. (bet. Havemeyer & Roebling Sts.)

Subway: Marcy Av — Dinner Tue – Sun
Phone: 718-388-8860
Web: www.xixany.com
Prices: $$

Flaunting the trademark style of Chef Jason Marcus, this Mexican romp packs Williamsburg denizens into a slender space set aglow by etched brass ceiling pendants.

A delicious alchemy is at work here, as evidenced in the crabmeat-topped tamale flan sauced with fava bean-poblano purée; baked lamb meatballs in chipotle cream accompanied by grilled garlic and cheese sprinkled Texas toast; or strawberry *tres leches* with fragrant cilantro ice cream.

Like the menu, the beverage listing is loads of fun. Wines are whimsically arranged under headings of iconic women (Rieslings listed in the Helen Mirren section are described as concentrated and transcendent), and deconstructed margaritas feature a shot of tequila poured over frozen cubes of fruit juices.

Zenkichi

Japanese

77 N. 6th St. (at Wythe Ave.)

Subway: Bedford Av
Phone: 718-388-8985
Web: www.zenkichi.com
Prices: **$$**

Dinner nightly

This exceptional Japanese brasserie bears an utterly unique setting. Pay attention, or you'll miss the entry—the wood-armored façade is a sly indication of its existence. Step inside and receive warm greetings all around, followed by an escorted journey to your private dining booth on one of the floors above. Each booth is sequestered by cooling bamboo shades, while dark wood and minimal lighting further elevate the sense of intimacy. When you need assistance, ring the tabletop buzzer.

Zenkichi's omakase is a big draw, but items may also be ordered à la carte. These may highlight house-made tofu drizzled with chilled dashi; *maguro* carpaccio arranged over shredded carrots and dressed with a ginger sauce; or grilled *jidori* chicken with *yuzu kosho*.

Zizi Limona

Mediterranean

129 Havemeyer St. (at S. 1st St.)

Subway: Lorimer St - Metropolitan Av
Phone: 347-763-1463
Web: www.zizilimona.com
Prices: **$$**

Lunch Fri – Sun
Dinner nightly

A trio of skilled partners have come together at this low-key Williamsburg café to offer up some of the finest Mediterranean cooking around. A home-style spin on Israeli and Moroccan cooking reveals amazing hummus; plus treats like a warm grilled cauliflower and artichoke hearts salad dressed with strained yogurt and mouth-coatingly rich raw tahini. The menu possesses whimsy and a wink, as in kosher (not really?) octopus with garlic purée and a white bean salad. The *basbousa*—crumbles of semolina cake with floss halva, creamy cardamom sauce, and date syrup—provides a decadent finish.

Hummus Kitchen, the adjacent take-out shop is stocked with fragrant staples of the Mediterranean kitchen to peruse while waiting for your order of chicken couscous.

MetLife

Queens

Queens

Nearly as large as Manhattan, the Bronx, and Staten Island combined, Queens covers 120 square miles on the western end of Long Island. Reputedly the most ethnically varied district in the world, its diversified nature is reflected in the numerous immigrants who arrive here each year for its affordable housing, strong sense of community, and cultural explosion. Such a unique convergence of cultures results in this stately borough's predominantly global and very distinctive flavor. Though Superstorm Sandy was especially damaging to the Rockaways, these streets continue to prosper with amazing and affordable international eats even today.

GLOBE-TROTTING

Begin your around-the-world feast in Astoria, a charming quarter of old-world brick row houses and Mediterranean groceries. Discover grilled octopus bookended by baklava at one of the many terrific Greek joints. Then, prolong your culinary spree over juicy kebabs at **Little Egypt** on Steinway Street; or chow on equally hearty Czech *tlačenka* at the-popular **Bohemian Hall & Beer Garden**. On lazy days, brew buffs can be found at Astoria's hottest beer havens—**Sweet Afton**—for an intimate setting with a serious selection, or equally sublime **Studio Square** for the ultimate alfresco experience. Showcasing equally exquisite beverages alongside beautifully baked goods, **Leli's Bakery** may be a relatively young member of Astoria's dining scene, but hooks its troops with age-old roots—their commercial kitchen in the Bronx has been supplying fine dining establishments with

a wealth of sweetness since time immemorial. Founded in 1937, **La Guli** is an Italian *pasticceria* whose expert talent has been feeding families with rich and creamy cakes and cookies. Staying true to tradition, **The Lemon Ice King of Corona**, brought to you by Family Benfaremo, is a nostalgic ode to Italian ice complete with sugar-free selections for health-embattled hordes. But, for an unapologetically potent treat, **Laiko** is the area's favorite for a delicious frappe.

Sojourning south and then to the east, **La Boulangerie** brings a slice of France to Forest Hills by means of fresh-baked loaves of white bread and crusty baguettes. Of course, cheese couples best with bread, and the choices are also abundant at **Leo's Latticini** in Corona. Surprisingly, eating in **Terminal C** at La Guardia Airport is now considered a gastronomic delight with wonderful food and beverage outposts churned out by star chefs like Andrew Carmellini and Michael Lomonaco. Hopping airports, JFK's **Delta Terminal 4** is also becoming known as a culinary emporium replete with such acclaimed offerings as **Shake Shack** courtesy of restaurateur Danny Meyer, and **Uptown Brasserie** from the much raved about Marcus Samuelsson. Frequent flyers with refined palates will appreciate Dave Cook's *Eating in Translation*, a daily newsletter citing fantastic food finds at unusual locations—including airports! Speaking of outposts, **Syliva's**—once a Harlem landmark—has also set up shop here (in Jamaica) and cooks up generous portions of its Southern comfort food. And, **M. Wells Dinette** housed inside MoMA PS 1 delivers insanely inventive offerings to curious visitors and the lucky locals of Long Island City. Offering an imaginative blend of diner signatures, Quebecois favorites, and "are you serious!?" combos, this sequel to the original, outstanding diner continues to charm crowds by simply doing their thing. While in this 'hood, feel the sass and spirit at PS 1's "Warm Up"—one of Gotham's greatest summer soirées featuring a DJ, turntables, and all that jazz. And housed in the historic Falchi Building, **Doughnut Plant** boasts an outré selection, crafted from the best ingredients in town—tres leches doughnuts anyone? And, what goes best with dessert? Coffee of course,

with a crowning range of roasted beans available at **Vassilaros and Sons**. Enhancing this quarter's global repute is **Güllüoglu**, a Turkish bakery and café whose elegant space and tasty bites bring Istanbul to life. But, if Pakistani flavors are a particular fave, then **Bundu Khan** is worth a trip, for every type of grilled delight. Close out these global eats at cozy **Café Norma**—a hot spot for homey, comfort fare.

ASIA MEETS THE AMERICAS

Flushing still reigns as Queens' most vibrant Asian haven and NYers are always dropping in for dim sum, Henan specialties, or a savory bowl of *pho* like you'd find street side in Saigon. Food vendors at Flushing's mini-malls offer feasts from far flung corners of China that are light on the pockets but big on flavor. Of both local note and city-wide acclaim, **New World Mall Food Court** is a clean, airy space serving excellent Asian food. You'll find everything at these inviting stalls from hand-pulled noodles (at **Lanzhou**) and fiery Sichuan dishes at **Chengdu Snacks**, to Taiwanese shaved ice for the end of the night. And the offerings don't stop here. Over on Main Street, vegans feel the love and care at **New Bodai Vegetarian** where such kosher-friendly dishes as vegetarian duck and seaweed sesame rolls keep the crowds returning time and again. These same health food fans as well as epicureans from all walks may then trek east to arrive at **Queens County Farm Museum**, considered one of the largest working farms in the city that supports sustainable farming, farm-to-table meals, and is rife with livestock, a greenhouse, and educational programs. Speaking of livestock, **Chand Halal Meat** is a specialty market where the butchers know your name and game: beef, goat, or lamb. From Flushing to Floral Park, **Real Usha Sweets & Snacks** cooks India's favorite street eats, which also make for excellent dinner party treats. Think *chana chor*, *papadi*, and banana chips—a Kerala specialty. Also reminiscent of flavors from the sub-continent, **Singh's Roti Shop and Bar** prepares Caribbean delicacies like curry chicken, saltfish, and *aloo pie* to gratify its contiguous community. Shifting gears from south to Central Asia, as many as 40,000 immigrants travelled to New York after the fall of the Soviet Union. They staked their claim in Forest Hills, and **King David Kosher Restaurant** remains a paragon among these elder statesmen and their large families for Bukharian specialties.

Energy and variety personify Elmhurst, the thriving hearth of settlers primarily from Latin America, China, and Southeast Asia. **The Royal Kathin**, a celebration that occurs at the end of Thailand's rainy season, pays homage to the spirit of Buddhist monks. While Elmhurst's adaptation of this festival may lack the floods, it certainly proffers a bounty of authentic Thai bites. Whitney Avenue is home to a booming restaurant row with an array of small Southeast Asian storefronts. Indulge your *gado gado* yearning at **Upi Jaya** before getting your *laksa* on at **Taste Good**. Elmhurst spans the globe, so if the pungent flavors of Southeast Asia don't fit the bill, relocate from Asia to the Americas by way of thick, creamy Greek yogurt at **Kesso Foods**. This mini shop is a gem among locals, while **Cannelle Patisserie**'s carb-o-licious goodies keep the entire borough abuzz.

Jackson Heights is home to a large South Asian community. Take in the bhangra beats blaring from cars rolling along 74th Street. This dynamic commercial stretch is dotted with numerous Indian markets, Bengali sweet shops, and Himalayan-style eateries serving all types of *tandoori* specialties and steaming Tibetan *momos*. In keeping with the fact that Latin Americans also make up a large part of the demographic here, Roosevelt Avenue swarms with authentic taquerias, aromatic Colombian coffee shops, and sweet Argentinean spots to sate this vast range of assorted tastes.

WANDERING THROUGH WOODSIDE

Take this thriving thoroughfare west to Woodside, where Irish bars mingle with spicy Thai spots. Once home to an enormous Irish population, Woodside now shares its streets with Thai and Filipino communities—even if kelly green awnings of decade-old pubs continue to scatter these blocks and clover-covered doors advertise in Gaelic. Positioned alongside **Donovan's**, an age-old Irish respite grilling up one of the best burgers in town, is **Little Manila**—an eight-block stretch of Roosevelt Avenue where you can stock up on Filipino groceries galore. Find these folks join the line outside **Jollibee**, an ultra-popular fast-food chain serving up flavors from home. If Filipino sounds too funky, rest assured as **Piemonte Ravioli** carries every choice of fresh-made pasta for an Italian *cena con la famiglia*. Down south in Sunnyside, you may also eat your way through Korea, Romania, China, Turkey, Mexico, and more.

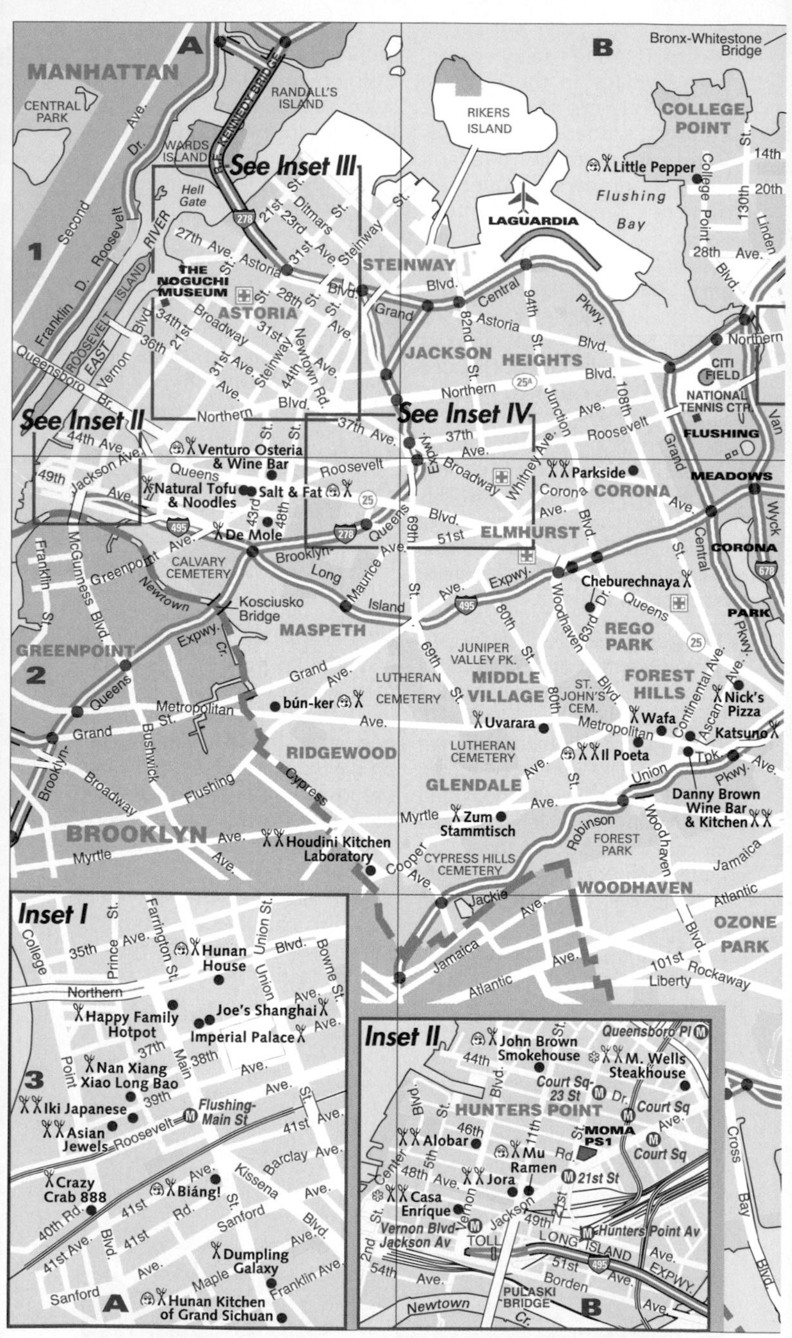

Inset I
Hunan House
Happy Family Hotpot
Joe's Shanghai
Imperial Palace
Nan Xiang Xiao Long Bao
Iki Japanese
Asian Jewels
Flushing-Main St
Crazy Crab 888
Biáng!
Dumpling Galaxy
Hunan Kitchen of Grand Sichuan
Inset II
John Brown Smokehouse
M. Wells Steakhouse
Queensboro Pl
Court Sq-23 St
Court Sq
HUNTERS POINT
MOMA PS1
Alobar
Mu Ramen
Jora
21st St
Casa Enríque
Vernon Blvd-Jackson Av
Hunters Point Av
PULASKI BRIDGE
MANHATTAN
RANDALL'S ISLAND
WARDS ISLAND
RIKERS ISLAND
COLLEGE POINT
Little Pepper
Flushing Bay
LAGUARDIA
See Inset III
See Inset II
See Inset IV
THE NOGUCHI MUSEUM
ASTORIA
STEINWAY
JACKSON HEIGHTS
CITI FIELD
NATIONAL TENNIS CTR.
FLUSHING MEADOWS CORONA PARK
Venturo Osteria & Wine Bar
Natural Tofu & Noodles
Salt & Fat
De Mole
Parkside
CORONA
ELMHURST
CALVARY CEMETERY
Kosciusko Bridge
MASPETH
Cheburechnaya
REGO PARK
GREENPOINT
JUNIPER VALLEY PK.
MIDDLE VILLAGE
LUTHERAN CEMETERY
ST. JOHN'S CEM.
FOREST HILLS
Nick's Pizza
Wafa
Katsuno
bún-ker
Uvarara
RIDGEWOOD
Il Poeta
GLENDALE
Danny Brown Wine Bar & Kitchen
Zum Stammtisch
BROOKLYN
Houdini Kitchen Laboratory
CYPRESS HILLS CEMETERY
FOREST PARK
WOODHAVEN
OZONE PARK

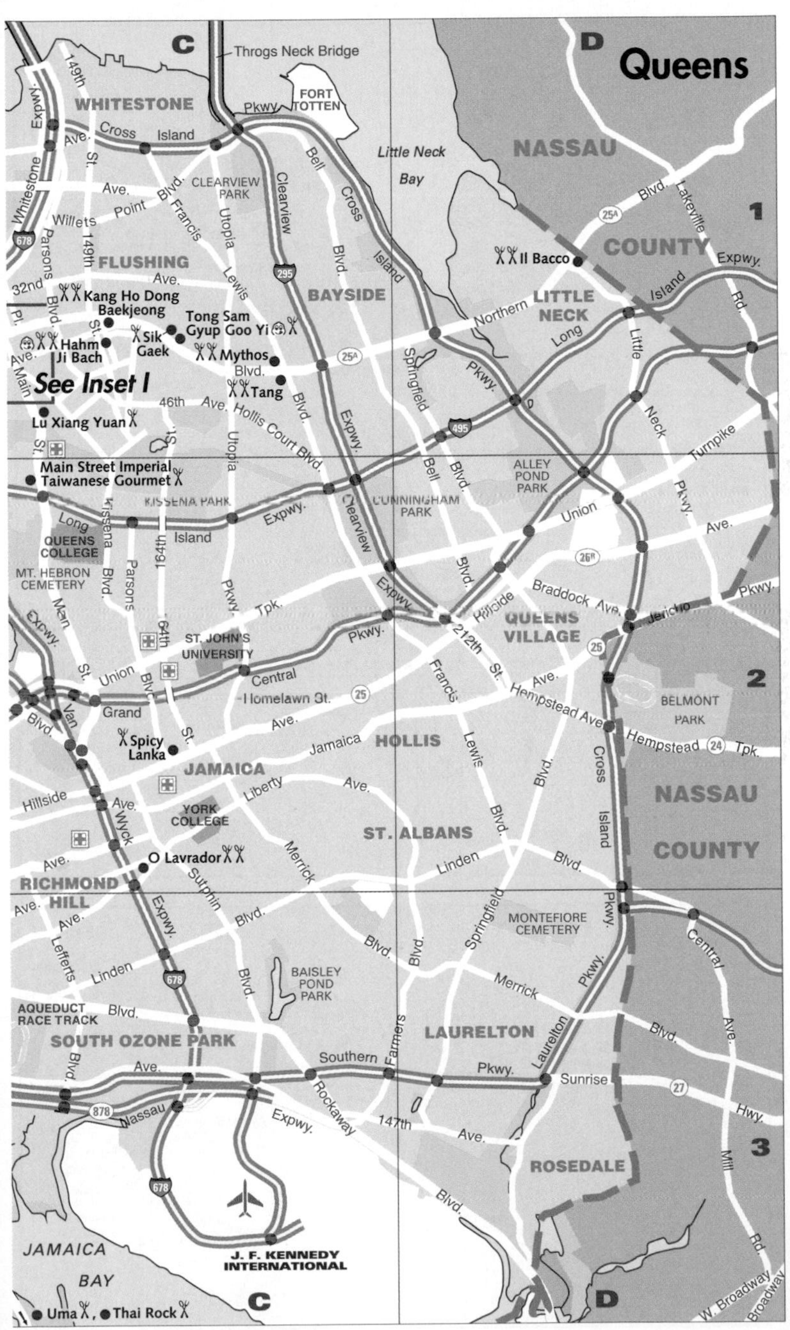
Queens
C
D
1
2
3
Throgs Neck Bridge
FORT TOTTEN
WHITESTONE
FLUSHING
BAYSIDE
LITTLE NECK
NASSAU
COUNTY
Little Neck Bay
CLEARVIEW PARK
Il Bacco
Kang Ho Dong Baekjeong
Tong Sam Gyup Goo Yi
Hahm Ji Bach
Sik Gaek
Mythos
Tang
See Inset I
Lu Xiang Yuan
Main Street Imperial Taiwanese Gourmet
KISSENA PARK
CUNNINGHAM PARK
ALLEY POND PARK
QUEENS COLLEGE
MT. HEBRON CEMETERY
ST. JOHN'S UNIVERSITY
QUEENS VILLAGE
BELMONT PARK
HOLLIS
JAMAICA
Spicy Lanka
YORK COLLEGE
ST. ALBANS
O Lavrador
RICHMOND HILL
MONTEFIORE CEMETERY
BAISLEY POND PARK
AQUEDUCT RACE TRACK
SOUTH OZONE PARK
LAURELTON
ROSEDALE
J. F. KENNEDY INTERNATIONAL
JAMAICA BAY
Uma, Thai Rock
Cross Island Pkwy.
Clearview Expwy.
Long Island Expwy.
Northern Blvd.
Union Tpk.
Hempstead Ave.
Jamaica Ave.
Linden Blvd.
Merrick Blvd.
Southern Pkwy.
Sunrise Hwy.
Nassau Expwy.
Rockaway Blvd.
Van Wyck Expwy.
Grand Central Pkwy.
Hillside Ave.
Jericho Tpk.
Francis Lewis Blvd.
Springfield Blvd.
Farmers Blvd.
Laurelton Pkwy.
Cross Island Pkwy.
Little Neck Pkwy.
Lakeville Rd.
Mill Rd.
Central Ave.
W. Broadway
Broadway
Sutphin Blvd.
Lefferts Blvd.
Liberty Ave.
Homelawn St.
147th Ave.
Braddock Ave.
Utopia Pkwy.
Bell Blvd.
Main St.
Parsons Blvd.
Kissena Blvd.
164th St.
212th St.
Whitestone Expwy.
Willets Point Blvd.
149th St.
46th Ave.
32nd Ave.
Hollis Court Blvd.

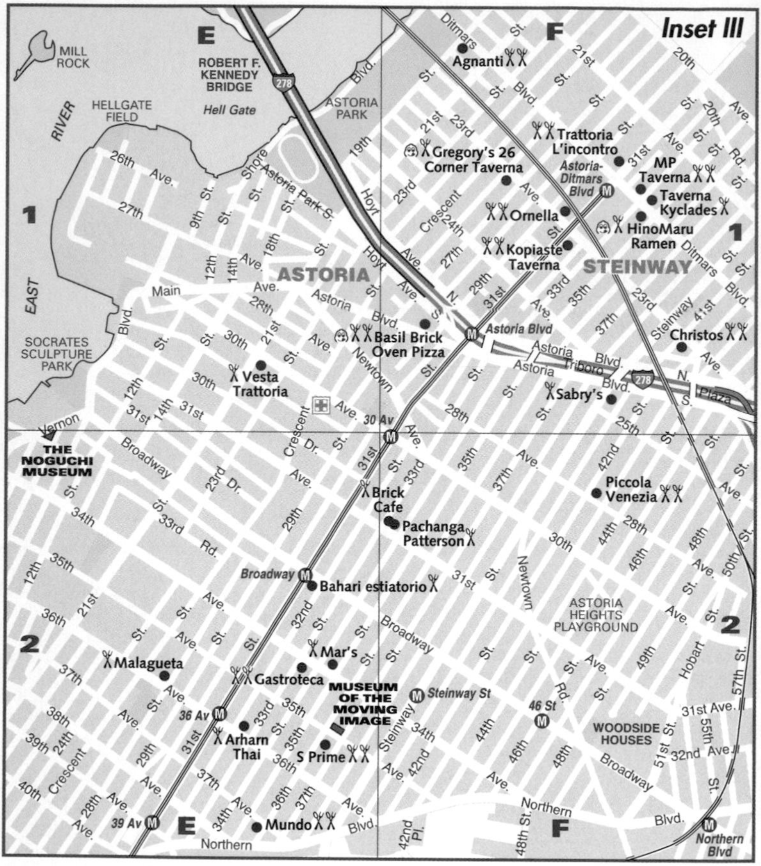

Inset III
E
F
1
2
MILL ROCK
ROBERT F. KENNEDY BRIDGE
Hell Gate
HELLGATE FIELD
EAST RIVER
ASTORIA PARK
ASTORIA
STEINWAY
SOCRATES SCULPTURE PARK
THE NOGUCHI MUSEUM
MUSEUM OF THE MOVING IMAGE
ASTORIA HEIGHTS PLAYGROUND
WOODSIDE HOUSES
Agnanti
Trattoria L'incontro
Gregory's 26 Corner Taverna
MP Taverna
Taverna Kyclades
Ornella
HinoMaru Ramen
Kopiaste Taverna
Basil Brick Oven Pizza
Christos
Vesta Trattoria
Sabry's
Brick Cafe
Pachanga Patterson
Piccola Venezia
Bahari estiatorio
Mar's
Malagueta
Gastroteca
Arharn Thai
S Prime
Mundo
Astoria-Ditmars Blvd
Astoria Blvd
30 Av
Broadway
36 Av
39 Av
Steinway St
46 St
Northern Blvd
Ditmars Blvd.
Astoria Park S.
Shore Blvd.
Hoyt Ave.
Crescent St.
Main Ave.
Astoria Blvd.
Newtown Ave.
Triboro Plaza
Broadway
Northern Blvd.
Vernon Blvd.
31st Ave.
32nd Ave.
278

Inset IV
E
F
3
WOODSIDE
ELMHURST
BIG BUSH PARK
NEW CALVARY CEMETERY
NATHAN WEIDENBAUM PARK
Urubamba
Samudra
Kitchen 79
Casa del Chef Bistro
Himalayan Yak
Zabb Elee
Engeline's
Payag
Ayada
Paet Rio
Sweet Yummy House
Tito Rad's Grill
Nusara
Uncle Zhou
Taiwanese Gourmet
82 St-Jackson Hts
90 St-Elmhurst Av
Jackson Hts-Roosevelt Av
Woodside-61 St
Elmhurst Av
Grand Av-Newtown
Roosevelt Ave.
Queens Blvd.
Broadway
Barnett Ave.
Woodside Ave.
Brooklyn Queens Expwy.
Hampton St.
Judge St.
Baxter Ave.
Britton Ave.
Elmhurst Ave.
Kneeland Ave.
Codwise Pl.
Grand Ave.
278

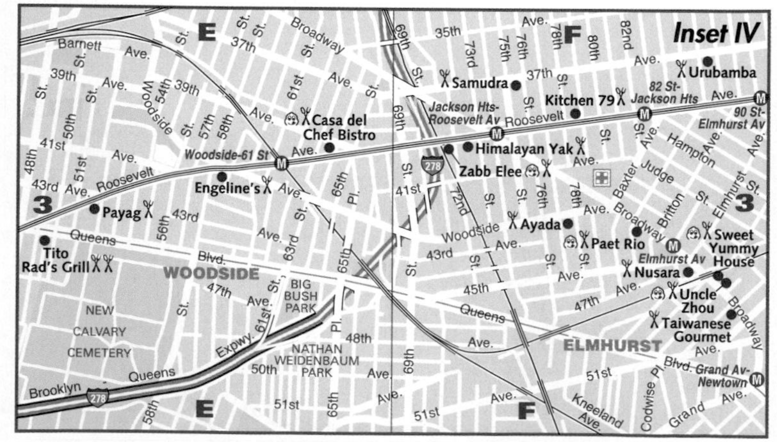

Agnanti

Greek XX

F1

19-06 Ditmars Blvd. (at 19th St.)

Subway: Astoria - Ditmars Blvd
Lunch & dinner daily
Phone: 718-545-4554
Web: N/A
Prices: **$$**

Situated on a corner lot, this taverna offers stunning panoramas of midtown, the Queensboro Bridge, and Astoria Park; on sunny days, outdoor tables speckle the front area. The view alone sets this darling apart from the host of Greek restaurants that popularized Astoria as a dining destination. Yet the food offers its own view of Greek cuisine. Here, East meets West in a menu section reserved for Turkish classics with a unique spin, such as *midia dolma* or mussels with pine-nut studded rice. Other usual suspects also make an appearance including tzatziki with cucumber, lemon, and garlic—a marvelous accompaniment to zucchini-and-cheese croquettes. But don't fill up until you've sampled smoky swordfish kabobs basted with rosemary and lemon sauce.

Alobar

American 

46-42 Vernon Blvd. (bet. 46th Rd. and 47th Ave.)

Subway: Vernon Blvd - Jackson Av
Lunch Sat – Sun
Phone: 718-752-6000
Dinner Tue – Sun
Web: www.alobarnyc.com
Prices: **$$**

This leisurely gastropub radiates old-world appeal through the red brick exterior and dining room adorned with antiques, copper-rimmed architect lamps, and rustic wood tables. From the softly lit, stocked bar to the cozy banquettes, this space has an attention to design that enhances each meal. Most everyone here begins with a selection from the pickled menu—curried apples, mushrooms—perhaps to pair with the house chicken liver or country pâté (sadly, most of the charcuterie is no longer made in-house). From there, the inventive pleasures range from half chicken with roasted sweet yellow corn and chipotle honey to the bacon-chocolate bread pudding oozing with chunks of chocolate, served with salted caramel, crème anglaise, and a satisfying crust.

Arharn Thai

E2 — Thai

32-05 36th Ave. (bet. 32nd & 33rd Sts.)

Subway: 36 Av — Lunch & dinner daily
Phone: 718-728-5563
Web: www.thaiastoria.com
Prices:

Dishes burst with delightfully refreshing flavor here at Arharn Thai. The small space is bright and clean, arranged with glass-topped tables, decked with artifacts from the motherland, and equipped with two flat screen TVs.

An organized kitchen spins out goodies like *khaum jep*: steamed dumplings stuffed with ground chicken, shrimp, crabmeat, and meaty mushrooms, served with a wonderfully sticky- garlicky- and salty-dipping sauce. The exquisitely tender *gob kra prow* (frog legs) are marinated and fried until golden, then cooked with garlic, chili peppers, onions, coconut milk, and Penang curry paste. Roasted eggplant arrives white, silky, and sublime, tossed in a light and vibrant salad with citrus-lime dressing, then crowned with flaky dried shrimp.

Asian Jewels

A3 — Seafood

133-30 39th Ave. (bet. College Point Blvd. & Prince St.)

Subway: Flushing - Main St — Lunch & dinner daily
Phone: 718-359-8600
Web: www.tunseng.com
Prices: $$

Arguably the best dim sum in Flushing, this spectacular gem is an absolute must for anyone seeking serious seafood and very authentic Cantonese cooking. A longtime resident of 39th Avenue, the expansive dining room is outfitted with round, banquet-style tables, bamboo plants, and ornate chandeliers.

Let the feasting begin with memorable crab-and-pork soup dumplings, before moving on to the thrill-inducing dim sum carts. Taste the likes of steamed rice rolls with honey-roast pork; pork spareribs with rice starch and black beans; chicken and ham wrapped in yuba; and poached jellyfish with scallions and sesame. The signature Dungeness crab—steamed and stir-fried with ginger and green onions, served with Japanese eggplant and garlic—is simply outstanding.

Ayada

Thai

77-08 Woodside Ave. (bet. 77th & 78th Sts.)

Subway: Elmhurst Av
Phone: 718-424-0844
Web: N/A
Prices: $$

Lunch Mon – Fri
Dinner nightly

A bright green sign leads the way to little Ayada, where the décor's a bit plain but the food is anything but. Inside the popular Thai restaurant, guests are greeted with a smattering of tables; a simple, but homey setting; and a warm, family-focused staff to walk them through the menu.

And what a menu it is, with dishes like the crispy catfish salad, paired with green mango and laced with a perfectly balanced lime dressing; a whole, deep-fried snapper, served with shredded green mango and tamarind sauce; a bowl of chewy drunken noodles sporting crisp green beans and tender chicken in a fragrant chili-garlic sauce; or fresh ripe mango and sticky rice, steamed to pearly, translucent perfection and carrying flavors of of sweetened coconut milk.

Bahari estiatorio

Greek

31-14 Broadway (bet. 31st & 32nd Sts.)

Subway: Broadway
Phone: 718-204-8968
Web: www.bahariestiatorio.com
Prices: $$

Lunch & dinner daily

Go hungry to Bahari estiatorio, a classic Greek-American restaurant where families gather for solid dishes with a hint of rusticity. Not trying to be anything more, the simple décor—featuring dozens of shutters hanging on bright blue walls—is refreshing rather than indifferent, as clear thought went into making the two open rooms feel embracing.

Head straight to the *Mageirefta* portion of the menu, a collection of traditional casserole dishes showcased at the front the restaurant. Though pre-prepared, glorious kabobs and plates like *gemista me kima*-stuffed tomatoes with rice, herbs, and beef can make for an entire meal. Daily dessert specials like a custardy *galaktoboureko* pie provide the perfect ending to this big, fat, Greek feast.

Basil Brick Oven Pizza 

Italian

F1

28-17 Astoria Blvd. (bet. 28th & 29th Sts.)

Subway: Astoria Blvd — Lunch & dinner daily
Phone: 718-204-1205
Web: www.basilbrickoven.com
Prices: $$

In an area crying out for a reliable neighborhood Italian joint, Basil's was an instant hit upon opening. The tiny front room is dominated by a dome wood burning pizza oven, but down a long and narrow hallway there's a larger dining room with dark wood floors, exposed brick walls, and lantern-like light fixtures that is a cozy spot for devouring pizza or daily specials.

Meals here must include thin-crust pizza crafted from well-salted dough. If you can look beyond the classic *Margherita,* the *Napoletana* with black olives or the *salsiccia* with caramelized onions both delight. Specials might reveal oven-roasted swordfish, tender and served with oven-roasted root vegetables. Thick, fluffy squares of tiramisu have earned their own loyal following.

Biáng! 

A3

41-10 Main St. (bet. 41st Ave. & 41st Rd.)

Subway: Flushing - Main St — Lunch & dinner daily
Phone: 718-888-7713
Web: www.biang-nyc.com
Prices: $$

Biáng! isn't exotic by accident. In fact, Chef/owner Jason Wang's cuisine interplays contrasts and textures with the intention to excite. Tucked into Flushing's main artery, the setting is boisterous and tables are busy, but shabby-chic details like a plate-glass exterior are the first sign that you're in for an unencumbered and unique treat. Dark walls and floors cover the inside, but gentle lighting and lofty ceilings add dimension to the narrow space.

Strong flavors and fiery oils star in dishes like crispy lotus root tossed in an earthy sesame vinaigrette; fresh buckwheat noodles mingled with cucumber, soy, and mustard oil; and *chang,* hot, creamy tofu with pickled vegetables. Lamb burgers seasoned with jalapeños and cumin are a fitting signature.

Brick Cafe

Mediterranean

30-95 33rd St. (at 31st Ave.)

Subway: Broadway — Lunch & dinner daily
Phone: 718-267-2735
Web: www.brickcafe.com
Prices: $$

This neighborhood *bijou* is beloved for its big flavors and small, rustic space. From lace curtains and weathered floors, to a yellow façade with a "stained" glass pane, everything at Brick Cafe invokes the charming French countryside including its olive-tinted walls set beneath a hand-crafted tin ceiling. It's all very quaint to the point of being precious, but nonetheless appealing.

To match a lovely wine list, the menu highlights such well-made items as cucumber salad tossed with tomatoes, olives, and yogurt; or specials like goat cheese and asparagus-stuffed chicken wrapped in speck, roasted until crisp, and poured with a parmesan cream set over mashed potatoes. Light and fluffy crêpes filled with berries offer the perfect end to such decadence.

bún-ker

Vietnamese

46-63 Metropolitan Ave. (at Woodward Ave.)

Subway: Grand St (& bus Q54) — Lunch Sat – Sun
Phone: 718-386-4282 — Dinner Tue – Sun
Web: www.bunkervietnamese.com
Prices: 

Located along an industrial stretch of Ridgewood, this charismatic Vietnamese restaurant doesn't offer much in the way of location—which is even more reason to suspect the throngs of people clamoring for it to open on a Saturday are here for something special. It's the food, of course, though the funky hipster surf shack interior and warm staff certainly add to the appeal.

You really can't miss on bún-ker's menu, a whirlwind of Vietnamese dishes sporting a California-like freshness. But, highlights include the bang-on *bánh xèo*, a crispy crêpe featuring tender shrimp, bacon, bean sprouts, and fresh herbs; the excellent *pho ga* bobbing with tender poached chicken, chewy rice noodles, sprouts, lime, and jalapeño; or any of the mouthwatering daily specials.

Casa del Chef Bistro

Contemporary

E3

39-06 64th St. (bet. 39th & Roosevelt Aves.)

Subway: 69 St — Dinner Tue – Sun
Phone: 718-457-9000
Web: www.casadelchefny.com
Prices: $$

Heart, passion, and skill—this inviting bistro embodies the spirit of its dedicated owners. Chef Alfonso Zhicay earned his stripes at some of New York's finest, including Blue Hill at Stone Barns; his daughter is the one-woman show behind personal, warm service. In a cozy room with large glass windows, elegant (and often vegetable-driven) dishes comfort and surprise.

The four-course prix-fixe is a remarkable value, perhaps beginning with a mushroom confit tart showcasing meaty strips of portobellos, mushroom purée, and truffle oil. Move on to savory pasta courses like orzo folded with seasonal vegetable ragout, topped with parmesan foam. Chocolate-hued braised short ribs sit among braised savoy cabbage, buttery potatoes, and a hit of citrus-horseradish.

Cheburechnaya

Central Asian

B2

92-09 63rd Dr. (at Austin St.)

Subway: 63 Dr - Rego Park — Lunch Sun – Fri
Phone: 718-897-9080 — Dinner Sun – Thu
Web: N/A
Prices:

This may be a kosher spot with no bagel in sight, but one look at its counter loaded with layers of bowl-shaped *noni toki* bread and you quickly realize that a meal here is a dining adventure. Specializing in Bukharian (Central Asian) cuisine, longstanding Cheburechnaya has been a neighborhood pioneer.

The focused menu is more engrossing than the décor, and it's easy to want every cumin- and paprika-laced item on it. Bring your own vodka and start with the house specialty, *chebureki*, an empanada-like deep-fried wrap stuffed with either hand-cut lamb seasoned with cumin, chili, cilantro, and paprika; or fennel-sparked cabbage. It may serve as the perfect complement to smoky lamb fat, tender quail, veal heart, and seared beef sweetbread kebabs.

Casa Enríque ✿

Mexican XX

5-48 49th Ave. (bet. 5th St. & Vernon Blvd.)

Subway: Vernon Blvd - Jackson Av — Lunch Sat – Sun
Phone: 347-448-6040 — Dinner nightly
Web: www.henrinyc.com
Prices: $$

Chiapas. Puebla. San Luis Potosí. One can literally taste the regions and cities that Chef Cosme Aguilar's amazingly complex menu explores—including his own childhood recipes to honor his mother's memory. A steady stream of hungry diners seeks out this rather small, tasteful dining room for friendly yet professional service and soul-warming fare. Aim for the large, fantastic communal table.

Start your meal with hearty *rajas con crema*, combining none-too-spicy poblanos with sweet, fresh corn, Mexican sour cream, and cheese served alongside a stack of fresh and slightly toasty tortillas. This kitchen's tender chicken enchiladas with *mole de Piaxtala* may induce swooning, thanks to a sauce that is unexpectedly sweet yet heady with bitter chocolate, raisins, almonds, cloves, cinnamon, chilies, garlic, sesame, and so much more, with incomparable results. It's the kind of food that thrills palates (and tempts wanton thoughts). Expect the *chamarros de borrego al huaxamole* to arrive falling off the bone and redolent of epazote, allspice, and *pulla* chilies. Its fruity-spicy broth is drinkable.

Every bit of every spongy and buttery layer of the cow and goat's milk *pastel tres leches* is absolutely worth the indulgence.

Christos

Steakhouse XX

F1

41-08 23rd Ave. (at 41st St.)

Subway: Astoria - Ditmars Blvd — Dinner nightly
Phone: 718-777-8400
Web: www.christossteakhouse.com
Prices: $$$

This beloved Astoria steakhouse has a lot going for it, but its cause for celebration is that authentic Greek accent that imbues everything here. Excellent quality beef, as in the signature prime "wedge" for two, is dry-aged in-house, charbroiled to exact specification, and finished with sea salt and dried oregano. Vibrant starters and sides underscore the Aegean spirit at play with pan-fried *vlahotyri* cheese, charred octopus with roasted peppers and red wine dressing, and smoked feta mashed potatoes.

Christos has a commanding presence on a quiet tree-shaded corner just off of bustling Ditmars Blvd. Mixing shades of brown, the cozy and elegant dining room has a separate bar area and is lined with fish tanks stocked with live lobsters.

Crazy Crab 888

Burmese X

A3

40-42 College Point Blvd. (bet. 40th Rd. & 41st Ave.)

Subway: Flushing - Main St — Lunch & dinner daily
Phone: 718-353-8188
Web: www.crazycrab888.com
Prices: $$

You may second-guess your arrival to Crazy Crab 888 when you see the tarred-over landscape and auto body shops, but one step inside this downright delicious gem dispels any and all reservations. A sort of Burmese-Chinese seafood shack with influences from India and Thailand, the food offers recognizable ingredients in creative combos worthy of its wacky title—in Chinese culture, the number 8 is known to bring much good luck.

The pickled ginger salad packs a punch-crunch of fried garlic with cilantro, and makes for a cooling lead into the seafood 888 platter of Dungeness crab and crawfish—complete with a bib! For more spice, Yunnan sliced pork, straight from the face of a pig, combines fleshy meat with peanuts and chilies for a funky, must-try delight.

Danny Brown Wine Bar & Kitchen

Mediterranean

104-02 Metropolitan Ave. (at 71st Dr.)

Subway: Forest Hills - 71 Av — Dinner Tue – Sun
Phone: 718-261-2144
Web: www.dannybrownwinekitchen.com
Prices: $$

Tucked within the enclave of Forest Hills, Chef Danny Brown's tony bistro proves that Manhattan and Brooklyn aren't the only boroughs worth dining in. Ever the consummate and creative professional, the chef and his team reward diners with a memorable experience and serious cuisine that never misses the mark. Inside, the well-appointed dining room bursts with conviviality as devoted fans line the bar and fill every table.

The kitchen is on display in the back, allowing a view of the cadre of cooks at work as they prepare European-inspired cuisine that makes this space special. Roasted quail finished with bacon jus and a New York strip steak plated with potato strudel, creamed kale, and cumin-spiced carrots are just two enticing recommendations.

De Mole

Mexican

45-02 48th Ave. (at 45th St.)

Subway: 46 St - Bliss St — Lunch & dinner daily
Phone: 718-392-2161
Web: www.demolenyc.com
Prices: ⊜

If the words sweet, competent, clean, and authentic come to mind, you're most likely thinking of this heart-warming haunt for delightful Mexican. Albeit a tad small, with a second dining room in the back, rest assured that De Mole's flavors are mighty, both in their staples (burritos and tacos) and unique specials—seitan fajitas anyone?

This delightful pearl rests on a corner of low-rise buildings where Woodside meets Sunnyside, yet far from the disharmony of Queens Boulevard. Fans gather here for hearty *enchiladas verdes con pollo,* corn tortillas smeared with tomatillo sauce and *queso blanco.* Crispy chicken *taquitos* are topped with rich sour cream; steamed corn tamales are surprisingly light but filled with flavor; and the namesake *mole* is a must.

Queens

Dumpling Galaxy

Chinese

42-35 Main St. (in Arcadia Mall)

Subway: Flushing - Main St — Lunch & dinner daily
Phone: 718-461-0808
Web: www.dumplinggalaxy.com
Prices: ©©

Neon bounces off all the new, shiny surfaces at Dumpling Galaxy, inside the Arcadia Mall. Navigate beyond the phone retailers and stalls to find this huge, modern space full of red booths and hanging red lights. Spiffy and inviting, the newcomer is already lauded for crafting scores of dumpling variations, plus comforting entrées that shouldn't be ignored. Fill your table with a dumpling feast, stuffed chock-full of duck and mushroom, spicy-sour squash, or lamb and celery redolent of lemongrass and spices. Larger dishes are equally memorable; those cold, thick, slurp-inducing green bean noodles soaked in heady, tart black vinegar with raw white sesame seeds, cilantro, cucumbers, and wood-ear mushrooms will have you coming back for more...and then some more.

Engeline's

Filipino 

58-28 Roosevelt Ave. (at 59th St.)

Subway: Woodside - 61 St — Lunch & dinner daily
Phone: 718-898-7878
Web: N/A
Prices: ©©

This may be the place for your local Filipino gossip. A breakfast, lunch, and dinner hangout for the area's growing Filipino population, this bakery-restaurant invites conviviality. A taste of the soft, flan-like cassava cake alone is worth the visit. Head to the well-maintained dining room for a more thorough introduction.

Discerning just what's in each dish can prove challenging for novices, but find straightforward pleasure in the *sarsiadong bangus,* fried milkfish steaks simmered in garlic, tomatoes, green onion, a subtle yet flavorful fish sauce, and then topped with scrambled eggs. The *chicharon bulaklak* and the accompanying house-made *suka* (coconut-sugarcane vinegar steeped with bird chilies) gives quite the kick to sinfully crispy fried chicken skin.

Gastroteca

Italian XX

E2

33-02 34th Ave. (at 33rd St.)

Subway: 36 Av — Lunch & dinner daily
Phone: 718-729-9080
Web: www.gastrotecaastoria.com
Prices: $$

Astoria gets a much-needed jolt of rustic Italian cooking with Gastroteca, a charming new restaurant courtesy of Chef/owner John Parlatore. Tucked into a lovely corner location with enormous framed windows, exposed brick, and movies being projected onto the wall behind the bar, this is a fun spot but with a serious menu—the latter brought to life by a technically talented culinary team.

The ingredient-driven menu offers a wonderful selection of crostini to start. Don't miss the one with Sicilian pineapple, mascarpone, chili flakes, or the avocado—before diving into the likes of *linguini al limone* with a poached egg and grated lemon zest; or fragrant, oven-roasted rosemary chicken, paired with creamy mashed potatoes and chicken gravy.

Gregory's 26 Corner Taverna

Greek X

F1

26-02 23rd Ave. (at 26th St.)

Subway: Astoria - Ditmars Blvd — Lunch & dinner daily
Phone: 718-777-5511
Web: N/A
Prices: $$

Judge a book by its cover and miss the rustic pleasures found within this old-fashioned Greek taverna. Disheveled charm fills the tiny two-room interior, festooned with Greek flags, bunches of artificial grapes, and framed countryside scenes. The bare tables are topped with butcher paper and the service is slow as molasses, but the cooking is honest and intensely flavorful.

Begin with *tirokafteri*, a spicy, satisfying spread of thick feta blended with pickled red chili peppers and served with hot pita points. A stuffed green horn pepper might be next, over a bed of fried squash slices and a well of garlicky *scordalia*. The seafood combo offers the simple pleasures of stuffed clams, mussels, lobster, and shrimp with lots of butter, lemon, and parsley...Greek style!

Hahm Ji Bach

Korean XX

C1

40-11 149th Pl. (bet. Barclay & 41st Aves.)

Subway: Flushing - Main St
Lunch & dinner daily
Phone: 718-460-9289
Web: N/A
Prices: $$

This beloved Queens institution enjoys fine digs where they serve popular and praise-worthy Korean food. The contemporary dining room is spacious and airy, with the warm, always informative, staff buzzing from table to table. It's not uncommon for the manager to roll up her own sleeves when the pace elevates—and elevate it does, for this is not your average Korean barbecue.

It's hard to go wrong on Hahm Ji Bach's delightful menu, but don't miss the *samgyeopsal*, tender slabs of well-marinated pork belly sizzled to crispy perfection tableside for you to swaddle in crisp lettuce with paper-thin daikon radish, spicy kimchi, and bright scallions; or the *mit bachan*, a hot clay pot with soft steamed eggs, kimchi, tofu, pickled cucumbers, and spicy mackerel.

Happy Family Hotpot

Chinese X

A3

36-35 Main St. (bet. 37th Ave. & Northern Blvd.)

Subway: Flushing - Main St
Lunch & dinner daily
Phone: 718-358-6667
Web: www.happyfamilyhotpot.com
Prices:

You'll think you've died and gone to Hong Kong. Every table at this popular Flushing hot pot spot is fitted out with iPads and a square cooker, and the interior is ultra sleek. Think tufted white leather walls and flat-screen televisions dangling over the tables.

It's a stylish place to cool your heels but the real star of the show exists within the kitchen's authentic hot pot selection—pork brain, anyone? You can build your own, choosing from 70+ dunkables like tender pork belly that cooks in a flash; paper-thin taro root; tender baby greens; flavorful head-on shrimp; or chewy udon noodles. From there, choose either the mild white broth or an irresistibly spicy red one bobbing with peppercorns. Better yet, get both, also known as a half and half.

Queens

Himalayan Yak

F3 — Tibetan

72-20 Roosevelt Ave. (bet. 72nd & 73rd Sts.)

Subway: 74 St - Broadway — Lunch & dinner daily
Phone: 718-779-1119
Web: www.himalayanyak.com
Prices: $$

Broadly appealing yet truly unique, Himalayan Yak transports diners to a fantastical world of intricately carved wooden doors, mask-covered walls, and miniature stuffed yaks. It reflects an area of Central Asia where a hybrid cuisine of Nepalese, Tibetan, and Indian specialties rules.

Lassi here is made from scratch and an absolute highlight of any meal. Start with an order of tender steamed dumplings filled with ground pork, scallions, cilantro, ginger, and cabbage. For an exotic array of tastes, try the *phaparko dhendo* combination platter with buckwheat flour roti used to scoop up Nepali-style goat curry; or dig into the mound of *tse shogo ngopa* (sautéed potatoes, spinach, mushrooms and bell pepper) with grated radish pickles and tart yogurt sauce.

HinoMaru Ramen

F1 — Japanese 

33-18 Ditmars Blvd. (bet. 33rd & 34th Sts.)

Subway: Astoria - Ditmars Blvd — Lunch & dinner daily
Phone: 718-777-0228
Web: www.hinomaruramen.com
Prices: $$

A trip to this Japanese "tapas" and ramen bar doesn't take much convincing. The simple spot forgoes fussy décor for a chalkboard menu, friendly service, and energetic open kitchen. Grab a Sapporo on tap or cold jasmine tea, and dig into a collection of small plates, including seriously crispy strips of pig ears; wonderfully juicy and spicy chicken wings (*nagoya tebasaki*); as well as *buta kimchi*—pork belly with sautéed kimchi and bonito flakes. The other real focus here is a big, slurp-worthy bowl of ramen. In addition to superbly traditional pork and miso stocks, HinoMaru also offers an excellent vegetarian ramen showcasing a soy milk base and teeming with carrots, ginger, and broccoli.

Midtown residents: Lucky Cat, an offshoot, sits on busy East 53rd.

Houdini Kitchen Laboratory

Pizza XX

A2

15-63 Decatur St. (at Wyckoff Ave.)

Subway: Halsey St — Lunch & dinner daily
Phone: 718-456-3770
Web: N/A
Prices: $$

Houdini's Kitchen Laboratory rests in an industrial neighborhood near Queens' massive cemeteries. But despite its character-less setting, the inventive restaurant more than lives up to its creative name. A large, airy space complete with an impressive cement dome oven, Houdini's whips up a small but selective menu of excellent pastas and unique pizzas with daily specials.

The generous spirals of tagliatelle bathed in a meat ragù make for a very satisfying start. Sure, it's carb-heavy, but when in Rome—right? Follow that up with the popular, 18-month-old Monte Poro pecorino, or go all in with the sensational *habanera* pizza: crazy spicy peppers and strips of spicy pork loin in one fiery mozzarella- and tomato sauce-topped pie. Who says Queens isn't hot?

Hunan House

Chinese

137-40 Northern Blvd. (bet. Main & Union Sts.)

Subway: Flushing - Main St — Lunch & dinner daily
Phone: 718-353-1808
Web: www.hunanhouseflushing.com
Prices: $$

Located along quiet Northern Boulevard in Flushing, Hunan House offers a delicious reprieve from the street. The interior is crisp and sophisticated, with dark, ornately carved wood and thick linen tablecloths. But, the real draw here is the wonderfully authentic Hunanese fare, with its myriad fresh river fish; flavorful preserved meats; complex profiles; and mouth-puckering spice.

Hunan House's menu is filled with exotic delights, but don't miss the wonderful starter of sautéed sour string beans featuring minced pork, chilies, ginger, and garlic; smoky dried bean curd with the same preserved meat; or spicy sliced fish-Hunan style, perfectly cooked and served in a delicious pool of fiery red sauce and plated with tender bulbs of bok choy.

Hunan Kitchen of Grand Sichuan

Chinese

42-47 Main Street (bet. Blossom & Franklin Aves.)

Subway: Flushing - Main St — Lunch & dinner daily
Phone: 718-888-0553
Web: N/A
Prices: ⊖⊖

As New York's Sichuan renaissance continues apace, this pleasant and unpretentious Hunanese spot has popped up on Flushing's Main Street. The look here is tasteful and uncomplicated; the cooking is fiery and excellent.

The extensive menu of Hunan specialties includes the likes of the classic regional dish, pork "Mao's Style" simmered in soy sauce, Shaoxing wine, oil, and stock, then braised to tender perfection. Boasting heat and meat in equal amounts, the spicy-sour string beans with pork expertly combines rich and savory aromatics, vinegary beans, and fragrant pork with tongue-numbing peppercorns. The barbecue fish Hunan-style is a brilliant menu standout.

Smaller dishes, like winter melon with seafood soup, round out an expertly prepared meal.

Iki Japanese

Japanese

133-42 39th Ave. (bet. College Point Blvd. & Prince St.)

Subway: Flushing - Main St — Lunch & dinner daily
Phone: 718-939-3388
Web: www.ikicuisine.com
Prices: $$$

This upscale Japanese restaurant tucked into the newly constructed Hyatt Place Hotel is a lovely addition to the Queens dining scene. Duck inside the modern glass façade and you're greeted with curving leather booths; thick wood tables; and beautiful blonde flooring. You've seen this before, you think to yourself, but only in Brooklyn or Manhattan. This is Queens in high heels.

Diners can opt for traditional omakase or à la carte: the former might begin with silky house-made tofu, topped with caviar and cool dashi. Then move on to a fresh Dungeness crab salad with yuzu jelly and crab roe; soft shell crab and zucchini flower tempura; soft Wagyu carpaccio dusted with sea salt and truffles; or a bright, rainbow-assortment of fresh sushi.

Il Bacco

Italian 

D1

253-24 Northern Blvd. (bet. Little Neck Pkwy & Westmoreland St.)

Subway: N/A
Lunch & dinner daily
Phone: 718-224-7657
Web: www.ilbaccoristorante.com
Prices: $$

With its striking Mediterranean façade, crimson awnings, and rooftop garden, Il Bacco is hard to miss. This local favorite offers a stylish Little Neck-by-way-of-Tuscany setting for enjoying thoughtfully crafted classics with top-notch ingredients. A seasoned staff guides patrons through the many menu temptations.

The kitchen dutifully honors Italian-American staples with skill. The pizza oven is a beauty, churning out perfect pies, while tables pile up with salads of fennel, red radicchio, pitted olives, and orange, as well as pastas like house-made spinach fettuccine with peas, cream, mushrooms, and parmesan. Portions are generous but do not sacrifice quality, which is clear in the hefty rack of lamb with brandy sauce and simple roasted potatoes.

Il Poeta

Italian

B2

98-04 Metropolitan Ave. (at 69th Rd.)

Subway: Forest Hills - 71 Av
Lunch Mon – Fri
Phone: 718-544-4223
Dinner nightly
Web: www.ilpoetarestaurant.com
Prices: $$

Queens is teeming with family-owned Italian restaurants dishing up the red sauce, and yet Il Poeta manages to carve out a unique place among its competitors by cooking real classics that locals can't help but enjoy. Perched on a quaint corner of Forest Hills, the refreshed décor is simple but elegant, with a suited staff and vibrant pieces of art lining the walls.

Chef Mario di Chiara knows a thing—or ten—about Italian fare: you can't miss with items like *cannelloni gratinati al profumo di tartufo*, a homemade pasta plump with veal and carrot, baked in buttery béchamel, and kissed with truffle oil; or *pollo spezzatino alla pizzaiola con salsiccia*, a rustic chicken stewed in a light-as-air tomato sauce pocked with sweet porky sausage and roasted peppers.

Imperial Palace

A3 — Chinese

136-13 37th Ave. (bet. Main & Union Sts.)

Subway: Flushing - Main St — Lunch & dinner daily
Phone: 718-939-3501
Web: N/A
Prices: $$

You might mistake Imperial Palace for one of those red awning-covered restaurants on this strip of Chinese eateries—but don't. While it may share the same lettered signage, wide windows, and nondescript facade, inside find some of the best sticky rice and Dungeness crab Flushing has to offer.

Seafood is front and center, with servers promptly presenting everything from deep-fried jumbo shrimp tossed with candied sesame walnuts to shrimp-stuffed tofu with slices of conch. It's easy to plow through all the fresh shellfish dishes with a chilled beer and sweet rice, but try to leave room for the clam casserole: a spicy broth full of Cantonese flavors, loads of onions, and small, briny clams, finished with a sprinkling of crisp coriander stems.

Joe's Shanghai

A3 — Chinese

136-21 37th Ave. (bet. Main & Union Sts.)

Subway: Flushing - Main St — Lunch & dinner daily
Phone: 718-539-3838
Web: www.joeshanghairestaurants.com
Prices: $$

Patience is a virtue at Joe's Shanghai, where a hectic rush to snag a table precedes a visit for the soup dumplings. As with most Flushing restaurants, flavor outdoes the interior decoration, with walls in need of fresh paint and dated furnishings.

What the atmosphere lacks, the food fulfills as the kitchen swiftly prepares delicate *xiao long bao*, that despite stiff competition, still stand a head above the rest. The chefs have perfected the art of wrapping hot liquid into these soft, thin pouches, complete with spiraled shoulders. To bite into a soup dumpling is so sensual that diners don't even bother to glance at the flat-screens hanging in the dining room. While the menu offers fried bean curd and smoked fish, nothing sticks like the dumplings.

John Brown Smokehouse

Barbecue

B3

10-43 44th Dr. (bet. 10th & 11th Sts.)

Subway: Court Sq - 23 St
Phone: 347-617-1120
Web: www.johnbrownseriousbbq.com
Prices: $$

Lunch & dinner daily

Regional barbecue has arrived in the city, but John Brown continues his reign as the true "bawss" for Kansas-style bites. The décor is minimal with a front area plating infinite orders, but find a seat in the back and settle in for a serious shindig. Amid sepia-toned photos and a flat-screen showing football (a religion here), find famished city folk ordering perfectly done proteins served with a thick and rich barbecue sauce.

Rib tips and burnt ends are juicy, tender, and sumptuous when paired with tart, spicy kimchi. And, sandwiches like seasoned ground beef piled high on a brioche with pickles are as hearty and warming as plates of *pollo gregorio* slathered with still more of that sweet and signature barbecue sauce. Finger-licking is an inevitable end.

Jora

Peruvian

B3

47-46 11th St. (at 48th Ave.)

Subway: Vernon Blvd - Jackson Av
Phone: 718-392-2033
Web: N/A
Prices: $$

Lunch Fri – Sun
Dinner nightly

Peruvian pottery and tapestries set a casually elegant scene at this newcomer, which is quickly earning a loyal following for frothy pisco sours and spicy dishes full of fresh flavor. Beyond the pale limestone façade, the deep, narrow dining room is filled with light from arched windows and boasts a wall covered in river stones as well as a relaxed bar with striking artwork.

The diversity of Peruvian cuisine is on tasty display here, from classic dishes like *ceviche mixto* with slices of crunchy red onion, oversized kernels of corn and sweet potato, to *chupe de camarones*—a thick, restorative soup of rice, seafood, and gently poached eggs. A juicy skirt steak with sautéed onions, peppers, cilantro, and sweet plantains on the side will satisfy carnivores.

Kang Ho Dong Baekjeong

C1 Korean XX

152-12 Northern Blvd. (bet. 153rd & Murray Sts.)

Subway: Flushing - Main St (& bus Q13) Lunch & dinner daily
Phone: 718-886-8645
Web: N/A
Prices: **$$**

The Korean barbecue of the moment is a short LIRR trip away, and well worth the ride. This was the first East Coast branch of (Korean wrestler and TV personality) Kang Ho Dong's growing empire—and it is already among the best in the city. A younger sib now resides in midtown.

The menu is focused, the space is enormous, the air is clean, and the service is friendly. Start your grill off with steamed egg, corn, cheese, and more to cook along the sides while marbled pork belly or deeply flavorful marinated skirt steak strips sizzle at the center. *Bibimbap* is a classic rendition, mixing beef seasoned with *gochujang*, vegetables, sesame, nori, and crisp sprouts in a hot stone bowl—so hot that it sears the bottom rice to golden while cooking the raw egg on top.

Katsuno

Japanese X

103-01 Metropolitan Ave. (at 71st Rd.)

Subway: Forest Hills - 71 Av Dinner Tue – Sun
Phone: 718-575-4033
Web: www.katsunorestaurant.com
Prices: **$$**

To find Katsuno, look for the white lantern and those traditional *noren* curtains. Featuring less than ten tables, what this Japanese jewel lacks in size it makes up for in flavor and attitude. The owner's wife greets each guest at the door, while Chef Katsuyuki Seo dances around the miniscule kitchen crafting precise Japanese dishes from top-quality ingredients. His elegant plating of sashimi may reveal the likes of amberjack topped with a chiffonade of shiso, luxurious sea urchin, translucent squid crested with needle-thin yuzu zest, as well as supremely fresh fluke, tuna, and mackerel. Meanwhile, carb fans will enjoy a warm bowl of soba in duck broth with tender duck breast; or the fantastically brothy *inaniwa udon*, served only on special nights.

Kitchen 79

Thai

F3

37-70 79th St. (bet. Roosevelt & 37th Aves.)

Subway: 82 St - Jackson Hts — Lunch & dinner daily
Phone: 718-803-6227
Web: www.kitchen79nyc.com
Prices:

Shiny black subway tiles and glowing fixtures set a date-worthy tone at this new Thai standout. Patient, helpful servers assist in exploring the menu, focused mainly on dishes of southern Thailand. Patrons can choose to be as adventurous as the sometimes familiar yet authentic and funky menu allows.

Thick green curry (*gaeng kiew warn*) is packed with tender shrimp, bamboo shoots, eggplant, Chinese long beans, and holy basil simmered in coconut milk with pleasantly restrained spicing. A whole flounder (*pla neung ma nao*) is brilliant, distinct, and steamed to perfection with sour and spicy notes from garlic, minced ginger, and a Thai hot sauce. Flat noodles (*ka nom jeen gang tai pla*) with pumpkin, mackerel, and curry paste is a powerful, spicy dish.

Kopiaste Taverna

Greek

F1

23-15 31st St. (bet. 23rd Ave. & 23rd Rd.)

Subway: Astoria - Ditmars Blvd — Lunch Sun – Fri, Dinner nightly
Phone: 718-932-3220
Web: www.kopiastetaverna.com
Prices: $$

While there's no dearth of Greek food in town, Cypriot cuisine is a singular treat. Tinged with Turkish and Syrian accents, delicacies are served with finesse and twists at this warm, comfy iteration of the tiny island. Make your way up the marble stairs (away from the jarring side of subway central) to arrive inside a room adorned with beautiful silk curtains, lush planters, and walls draped with traditional garb. If the ambience alone doesn't transport you to the Medi, your first bite most certainly will. The meze is a parade led by marinated olives, *pantzaria*, tzatziki, *taramasalata*, and hummus, which may be followed by morsels of meat from *keftedes* to *koupepia*. A starter of fried calamari is every bit as as obligatory as baklava to round out the meal.

Little Pepper ☺

Chinese

18-24 College Point Blvd. (bet. 18th & 20th Aves.)

Subway: Flushing - Main St (& bus Q20A) — Lunch & dinner Fri – Wed
Phone: 718-939-7788
Web: N/A
Prices: ⊜

Set on an ordinary block of residences and businesses is Little Pepper, a tiny yet extraordinary rendition of Sichuan cooking. The room wears a delicate vibe with hand-painted murals, marble-tiled floors, and a cozy service bar. But, the real focus remains on the food, which is honest, bold, and always on-point.

Sample soft and yielding *mapo* tofu, sweet with minced pork, fiery with chilies, and smoky with ground peppercorns sinking into a thick, oily gravy; or shredded pork tossed with potato strands and pickled cabbage to truly appreciate their excellent (if occasionally) underrated food. Pine nuts sautéed with corn and snow pea leaves are marvelous for mellow palates, while chicken stir-fried with dried red chilies is a hit among those on a spice trip.

Lu Xiang Yuan

Chinese

42-87 Main St. (bet. Blossom & Cherry Aves.)

Subway: Flushing - Main St — Lunch & dinner daily
Phone: 718-359-2108
Web: N/A
Prices: ⊜

The ambience appears unassuming and ordinary, but Lu Xiang Yuan is an outstanding choice for tasty, affordable, regional Qingdao fare. The crowds have calmed, so tables are often available at peak meal times.

This is the place to hit for deep bowlfuls of restorative Chinese noodle soups that could carry you through the day—picture translucent bean threads, long slices of dried tofu, and morsels of lamb bobbing among fragrant cilantro, Chinese wolfberries, and black tree mushrooms in a broth enhanced with smoky chili paste. Other intriguing dishes unveil delicate kingfish steaks that have been subtly smoked, gently spiced, and served chilled. The black bone chicken and *ginseng* soup showcases the dark flesh and deep flavor of its ingredients.

Main Street Imperial Taiwanese Gourmet

Chinese 

C2

59-14A Main St. (bet. 59th & 60th Aves.)

Subway: Flushing - Main St (& bus Q44) Lunch & dinner daily
Phone: 718-886-8788
Web: N/A
Prices: 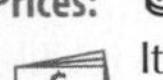

It's a real journey to this Taiwanese treasure—not only in its trek from the closest subway stop, but more importantly, in the experience. Here, the staff speaks their mother tongue for the most part, incense wafts from an altar, and the food is otherworldly.

Dishes present dazzling, authentic flavors, easily savored in the peaceful atmosphere. Sweet, head-on shrimp arrive steamed and still in the shell, housing juice that accentuates the concentrated flavor when dipped in soy sauce. Likewise, the stinky tofu (a traditional delicacy) gets its flavor from a light sauté and a finish of kimchi-style pickles. And if you're any sort of fan of the famed oyster pancake, this outstanding version will remain in your memory long after the lengthy ride home.

Malagueta

Brazilian 

E2

25-35 36th Ave. (at 28th St.)

Subway: 36 Av Lunch & dinner daily
Phone: 718-937-4821
Web: www.malaguetany.com
Prices: **$$**

A longstanding spot for authentic Northeastern Brazilian fare, Malagueta's pop of color and spice stands out from its residential surroundings. From its personable and dedicated staff to the warm and unassuming setting, this culturally rich retreat keeps locals and destination diners returning to the tiny spot and settling into a bistro chair.

The kitchen plays with smoky, sour, hot, and salty flavors stewed to mellowness to strike just the right balance. Even the humble *arroz y feijao* is a deeply satisfying blend of tender beans with pearly white rice. *Picanha* features grilled slices of sirloin topped with *farofa* (toasted manioc flour), enhanced by a citrus-herb vinaigrette, and accompanied by rice and beans. Finish with an excellent coconut flan.

Mar's

Seafood 

334-21 34th Ave. (at 35th St.)

Subway: Steinway St
Phone: 718-685-2480
Web: www.lifeatmars.com
Prices: $$$

Lunch Sat – Sun
Dinner nightly

Oh, Astoria, fine—you're finally the coolest kid on the culinary block. Mar's, a charming oyster bar plucked out of another century, is a good example of why: with its weathered seaside tavern décor, whitewashed walls, and curving bar, you'll feel dropped into a sun-bleached, turn-of-the-century photo.

Most of the menu is given over to raw seafood and New England classics; part, to Mediterranean tavern small plates like sweetbreads and steak tartare. Kick things off with the excellent Mar's chowder, bobbing with briny clams, tender potatoes, bacon, and thyme. Then move on to the same sautéed sweetbreads with buttery fingerlings, pickled onion, and a swirl of balsamic reduction; or the house lobster roll kicked up with salty batons of Granny Smith apple.

MP Taverna

Greek 

31-29 Ditmars Blvd. (at 33rd St.)

Subway: Astoria - Ditmars Blvd
Phone: 718-777-2187
Web: www.michaelpsilakis.com
Prices: $$

Lunch & dinner daily

Just in case you still weren't convinced of Astoria's hopping dining scene, enter MP Taverna—courtesy of Greek food God, Michael Psilakis. No one owns the modern Greek kitchen like this beloved author, chef, and local who manages to keep his food authentic and uniquely refined. And here he does it again, this time in a fun, tri-level space boasting a cool, industrial feel with wood paneling, iron chairs, and an impressive patio for warmer months.

For a more intimate feel, head to the second floor decked with leather chairs and chandeliers, or better yet, the rooftop terrace. Any place you land, be prepared for delicious fare: a perfectly cooked fillet of sole arrives stuffed with spinach, feta, and dill, and is finished in a wine-caper sauce.

Mundo

E2

37-06 36th St. (at 37th Ave.)

Subway: 36 St — Dinner nightly
Phone: 718-706-8636
Web: www.mundonewyork.com
Prices: $$

The Mediterranean hot spot that turned the city on to "Red Sonja"—a popular Turkish dish of red lentil and bulgur wheat—has relocated to larger digs. Mundo's new space is tucked into Queens' trendy Paper Factory Hotel, and both are a stunning addition to this industrial stretch of Long Island City. The interior is now a sexy, bi-level affair, complete with a spiral staircase and lounge.

Kick things off with the *cuatro sabores*, a medley of dips (think caramelized carrot or fava and dill) served with warm naan. Then move on to the Argentinian baked empanadas, with braised short ribs or Swiss chard and feta; feather-light Turkish meatballs, paired with spicy cilantro tzatziki; or the Egyptian artichoke "Nile's Flower" with a verdant dill-fava mousse.

Mu Ramen

Japanese

B3

12-09 Jackson Ave. (bet. 47th Rd. & 48th Ave.)

Subway: Vernon Blvd - Jackson Av — Lunch Mon – Fri
Phone: 917-868-8903 — Dinner nightly
Web: N/A
Prices: $$

What began as a pop-up found an insanely popular home behind an unmarked door in this industrial yet residential nook of Long Island City. Lines never cease; arrive early if possible. A thick wood block serves as a communal table in the dining room, where slurpers can witness the focus and dedication of chefs working within an open kitchen in the back.

The kitchen's methodical devotion results in a superior bowl of ramen. In the spicy miso ramen, springy noodles (from Sun Noodle) are nested in a red miso and pork based soup of rich bone broth that slowly simmers for over 24 hours. Topped with scallion, ground pork, sesame, and chili oil, it is one of many rewarding bowls. *Okonomiyaki* are ethereally light, with smoked trout and shaved bonito.

M. Wells Steakhouse ✿

Gastropub XX

B3

43-15 Crescent St. (bet. 43rd Ave & 44th Rd.)

Subway: Court Sq - 23 St — Dinner Wed – Mon
Phone: 718-786-9060
Web: www.magasinwells.com
Prices: $$$$

At this ultra-hip gastropub in Long Island City, first impressions can be wildly deceiving. At first, you'll wonder if you got the right address: from the outside, M. Wells Steakhouse looks like the old auto body garage it's housed in, but step inside and wow—the interior is all gloss and swagger, from its gold-and-black wallpapered ceiling and dripping crystal chandeliers, to its sexy red walls, stunning bar area, and open, wood-burning kitchen.

Service is friendly and just as polished and charming as the design; though mercifully more earnest than hip. They seem refreshingly invested in your experience, dropping dishes with explanations; checking in regularly; and genuinely thanking you for your patronage. Don't miss the opportunity to drill them on wine pairing ideas. Their answers are thoughtful and spot-on.

M. Wells may bill itself as a steakhouse, but the excellent raw bar, fresh fish entrées, and unique appetizers are up for some serious best supporting nods. Don't miss the bone marrow onion soup, a rich, delicious take on the French classic; rabbit terrine studded with candied fruit, truffle, and served *en croute*; and decadent *Paris-Brest*, a crispy pastry piped with hazelnut cream.

Mythos

Greek XX

C1

196-29 Northern Blvd. (bet. 196th St. & Francis Lewis Blvd.)

Subway: N/A — Lunch & dinner daily
Phone: 718-357-6596
Web: www.mythosnyc.com
Prices: $$

A gathering place for Greeks and non-Greeks alike, this family-run and friendly restaurant tempts with impeccably fresh fish, cooked over charcoal and basted simply with olive oil, lemon juice, and herbs. Beyond the whitewashed exterior and dark blue awning is a large dining room with rows of neat tables for indulging in Hellenic pleasures, from zesty appetizers to boisterous conversations.

Settle into an array of *pikilia*; cold appetizers such as *melitzansalata*, eggplant whipped with herbs and olive oil. Chargrilled fish, priced by the pound, has a delightfully smoky essence and moist flesh. Whole smelts are a rare and traditional treat, simply pan-fried with a lemony herb dressing. Finish with a choice of authentic, nutty, and syrup-soaked pastries.

Nan Xiang Xiao Long Bao

Chinese X

A3

38-12 Prince St. (bet. 38th & 39th Aves.)

Subway: Flushing - Main St — Lunch & dinner daily
Phone: 718-321-3838
Web: N/A
Prices: ©©

Also known as Nan Xiang Dumpling House, it is easily found among a strip of restaurants reflecting the diversity of Flushing's dominant Asian population. Simply decorated, the comfortable dining room features rows of closely set tables and a mirrored wall that successfully gives the illusion of space.

The enjoyable and interesting menu focuses on noodle-filled soups, toothsome stir-fried rice cakes, and the house specialty, juicy dumplings. These are made in-house and have a delicate, silky wrapper encasing a flavorful meatball of ground pork or crab with rich tasting broth. Eating the specialties may take some practice, but take your cue from the slurping crowd: puncture the casing on your spoon to cool the dumplings and avoid scalding your mouth.

Natural Tofu & Noodles

Korean

40-06 Queens Blvd. (bet. 40th & 41st Sts.)

Subway: 40 St

Lunch & dinner daily

Phone: 718-706-0899

Web: N/A

Prices: $$

This is the sort of place you've walked by a hundred times and never noticed. But it's time to look up, because the house-made tofu here is unrivaled. The space may be more functional than cozy, but this staff knows how to treat its customers, from happily adjusting a dish's spice level to presenting the bill with melon-flavored Haitai gum.

They also clearly know the many secrets of tofu—the kitchen makes its own, then deploys it in a series of silken *soondubu* (soft bean curd stews) like the funky Korean favorite "kimchi soft tofu." The fragrant and rich "seafood tofu" arrives in a small cauldron of bubbling broth with steel tongs for serving oysters, shrimp, clams, mushrooms, and scallions with the most custardy tofu on this side of Queens Boulevard.

Nick's Pizza

Pizza

108-26 Ascan Ave. (off Austin St.)

Subway: 75 Av

Lunch & dinner daily

Phone: 718-263-1126

Web: N/A

Prices: 

For all the historic touches and architectural details at Nick's Pizza, this 20-plus-year-old spot has the feel of a '50s diner that happens to live among the Tudor-style homes of Forest Hills. The clientele comes for the pie but also the cannolis, *tartufo*, and a *caffè* from the antique brass espresso machine. Wearing an old-school New York pizza attitude, Nick's shuttles pies to and from the oven at unbelievable speeds, keeping each table loaded. The terrific crust delivers a deliciously smoky flavor that's heightened by the crisp texture and any number of toppings—from salty anchovies to tender meatballs. The signature calzone is also worth a bite, with tangy mozzarella and ricotta oozing like slow lava and a cup of red sauce on the side for dipping.

Nusara

Thai

82-80 Broadway (at Whitney Ave.)

Subway: Elmhurst Av — Lunch & dinner daily
Phone: 718-898-7996
Web: www.nusarathaikitchen.com
Prices: $$

Tucked between an array of eateries and a sprawling supermarket, little Nusara's excellent Thai dishes make it a welcoming spot for a satisfying meal. The exterior looks more like a shop than a restaurant, but inside, the attractive yet simple décor and colorful sketches that line the walls are trumped by your dive into the extensive two-page menu.

Begin with the pork strips soaked in fish sauce and lime marinade, deep-fried for perfect salty-sweet contrast, and served with a chili dipping sauce. The *khao mon gai* is a Thai take on Haianese chicken, where the remarkably tender and pale white meat is poached in ginger and rice wine, set over fragrant rice, and eaten with a spicy ginger-chili dipping sauce and a bowl of marvelous chicken broth.

O Lavrador

Portuguese 

138-40 101st Ave. (bet. Cresskill & Sanders Pls.)

Subway: Sutphin Blvd - Archer Av - JFK Airport — Lunch & dinner daily
Phone: 718-526-1526
Web: www.olavradorrestaurant.com
Prices: $$

This throwback pleases with rib-sticking Portuguese fare and an attention to hospitality. Choose between two experiences: the long, well-worn bar (which may be rowdy with soccer fans) or the spacious dining room, reached through lovely arches. Seasoned servers know how to charm and keep customers patient, as dishes are made to order and can take time.

Zoom in on anything with *bacalhau* here, a superior air-dried fish (not salt-cured) with excellent flavor and texture. The *bacalhau à pescador* sates with a stew of clams, mussels, shrimp, calamari, and potatoes. Another appealing soup is *caldo verde* full of meaty collards and smoky chorizo. Round out this elaborate feast with *feijoada de mariscos*, a slurry of white beans, seafood, and of course, more chorizo.

Ornella

Italian XX

29-17 23rd Ave. (bet. 29th & 31st Sts.)

Subway: Astoria - Ditmars Blvd — Lunch & dinner daily
Phone: 718-777-9477
Web: www.ornellatrattoria.com
Prices: $$

Ornella and Giuseppe Viterale are always at home in their small and warm trattoria, settled in the middle of vibrant Astoria. The friendly service here includes Giuseppe swinging by tables and talking about the farmhouse event space he runs upstate. Ornella's orange-striped awning, stained glass sconces, and mural-lined walls give it a kitschy, fairy-tale feel that mirrors the Italian-American menu.

Here, you'll find tasty and popular duck meatballs in an orange-brandy reduction (think duck *à l'orange* in Italian) or braised short ribs with Madeira sauce. For a filling treat, try the *imbustata*, pasta filled with ground veal, chicken mushroom, mascarpone, and a knob of mozzarella that's drenched in a chunky sauce of tomatoes, onions, and fresh basil.

Pachanga Patterson

Mexican 

33-17 31st Ave. (at 34th St.)

Subway: 30 Av — Lunch Sat – Sun, Dinner nightly
Phone: 718-554-0525
Web: www.pachangapatterson.com
Prices: $$

This unassuming spot for tasty Mexican food with a twist has been a smash from the start. The vibe inside is always a feel-good one, with floor-to-ceiling windows, fairy lights, and quirky artifacts adorning the space. While the décor is subtle, the fuchsia-painted kitchen brims with bold flavors and superb textures as seen in soft tortillas folded with sweet grilled pineapple, spicy habanero salsa, and adobo-marinated shrimp. In a salad of red beets, salty crumbled *cotija* deliciously offsets those tangy chunks of pickled watermelon; and empanadas are a particular treat, filled with meaty portobellos and creamy potatoes.

End with crispy sweetbreads *con mole coloradito*, redolent of cumin, *guajillo*, and chocolate, and find yourself thinking—dessert what?

Queens

Parkside

Italian XX

B2

107-01 Corona Ave. (at 51st Ave.)

Subway: 103 St - Corona Plaza — Lunch & dinner daily
Phone: 718-271-9871
Web: www.parksiderestaurantny.com
Prices: $$$

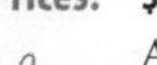

A veteran on the Corona dining scene, Parkside carries that old-fashioned kind of New York energy—back when waiters donned tuxedos, hosts boomed hello, and walls boasted classic photos of city elite. And though the neighborhood has changed much since Parkside first opened its doors, the fantastic Italian-American food they dole out stands the test of time. Join in the celebratory mood and make some new friends (no one really dines alone here) while tucking into tender ribbons of savory fettuccini Alfredo; tender veal *pizzaiola* laced with a delectable marinara; or cannoli freshly piped with ricotta and studded with candied fruit.

The irresistible desserts are wheeled around to guests on a rolling tray, of course. Old school or no school, right?

Paet Rio

Thai X

F3

81-10 Broadway (bet. 81st & 82nd Sts.)

Subway: Elmhurst Av — Lunch & dinner daily
Phone: 917-832-6672
Web: N/A
Prices: ⊜

With so many Thai places around, it's easy to get lost in this exceptional concentration; just be sure to find yourself at Paet Rio. The design of this long and inviting room may elevate the experience, but it is their spicy and unusual cooking that makes everything shine.

The menu here is a dance of sensations—tart, spicy, sour, fresh—as seen in Chinese broccoli leaves (*miang kha-na*) with pork, chilies, peanuts, garlic, and lime. Grilled squid (*pla muek yang*) has an addictive fiery sauce, while fermented pork and sticky rice sausage (*sai krok Isan*) is pleasurably sour with cabbage, chili, and peanuts. End this steamy affair over noodles sautéed with pork, squid, and soy sauce (*kua gai*); or *khao phat pla kem* featuring a tasty twist on the tired fried rice.

Payag

Filipino

51-34 Roosevelt Ave. (at 52nd St.)

Subway: 52 St — Lunch & dinner daily
Phone: 347-935-3192
Web: www.payagrestaurant.com
Prices: $$

Thoughtfully crafted with ingenuity and spirit, Payag is intended to feel like a home. From the open and light design that evokes a *bahay kubo* (Tagalog for "house") to the chatty and knowledgeable servers, this restaurant brings a welcoming air to this quiet corner. With bamboo touches and live Filipino music on the weekends, Payag strives to preserve a cultural identity both on and off the menu.

The dishes showcase a regional approach to the multi-island nation's cuisine. National favorite *kinilaw na isda*, a sour ceviche of delicate white fish, ginger, and cucumber, is a refreshing start to the meal. Then move on to the beautiful *bulalo*, a tender beef shank specialty from Batangas, gently simmered in a broth with yellow corn, cabbage, and baby bok choy.

Piccola Venezia

Italian 

42-01 28th Ave. (at 42nd St.)

Subway: 30 Av — Lunch Mon – Fri
Phone: 718-721-8470 — Dinner nightly
Web: www.piccola-venezia.com
Prices: $$$$

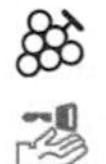

This old-time idol deserves its landmark status as it has been going strong since opening in 1973. With Italian-American cooking so rampant in the city, it's wholly refreshing to happen upon a classic of such welcoming comfort. The décor is outdated, but white tablecloths are clean and crisp, and glasses gleam at the prospect of great wine varietals.

With a trio of pasta, you needn't choose between *fusi* swirled in a grappa- mushroom- and Grana-sauce; squid ink *taglierini*; or *maltagliati* in a roasted tomato and basil sauce with a touch of cream. *Spiedini alla Romana* sees thick slabs of focaccia and mozzarella dredged and fried, served with an anchovy and caper sauce, and pork osso buco is of the falling-apart-tender variety—perfect with the velvety polenta.

Sabry's

Seafood 

F1

24-25 Steinway St. (bet. Astoria Blvd. & 25th Ave.)

Subway: Astoria Blvd — Lunch & dinner daily
Phone: 718-721-9010
Web: N/A
Prices: $$

Among the hookah lounges of Astoria's Steinway St., Sabry's offers authentic Egyptian seafood and friendly service. A strictly Muslim (no alcohol) establishment, the focus here is on tradition—one bite of the complimentary hot, puffy, deliciously chewy, and totally enjoyable Egyptian pita with sesame dipping sauce proves the team attends to every detail. Take a seat near wood-framed doors that open to the street for people-watching, or by the open kitchen for chef-watching. Then, prepare for hearty items beginning with impossibly tender and smoky grilled octopus. An icebox labeled "Day's Catch" features a daily roster of whole fish, cooked-to-order and served with lemon and rice. *Taojine* with scallops laden in a fragrant tomato sauce is a savory thrill.

Salt & Fat 

Contemporary 

A2

41-16 Queens Blvd. (bet. 41st & 42nd Sts.)

Subway: 40 St — Dinner Tue – Sun
Phone: 718-433-3702
Web: www.saltandfatny.com
Prices: $$

An ode to the pleasures of the pig, this is the pleasantly casual and unpretentious home to Sunnyside-rasied Chef/owner Daniel Yi. Dark woods, playful pig motifs, and soft lighting decorate the simple space, known for its friendly, personal service

Yet more renowned are the beloved bao and beer pairings that change frequently. Options may include the *Cubano*, served on a flattened bun and ready to be folded with a thick slice of smoky pork, mayo, mustard, pickles, and Swiss cheese, and matched with a smoky, malty local Porter, all for one affordable price. The Korean barbecue wraps are equally irresistible, with strips of spicy and funky marinated and grilled hanger steak, jalapeño, pickled daikon, and fried shallots combining in crisp Boston lettuce.

Samudra

Indian

F3

75-18 37th Ave. (bet. 75th & 76th Sts.)

Subway: 74 St - Broadway — Lunch & dinner daily
Phone: 718-255-1757
Web: N/A
Prices: ⊜

Excellent and affordable Southern Indian food arrives via this humble little gem in Jackson Heights. Guests are greeted by a long and simply decorated room laced with a few hand-woven textiles from India; and Samudra's owner (a personable presence when he's in-house) certainly adds to the cozy ambience by smiling and greeting guests upon entry. Of course, the real star of the show here is the vegetarian menu, which features 16 different kinds of dosas, including a perfectly crispy Mysore masala version stuffed with turmeric-tinged mashed potato. South Indian fermented dough specialties, like an *idli-vada* combo, arrive on a silver tray with sides of tangy tomato- and coconut-chutney—and is just another sample of the delicacies on offer here.

Sik Gaek

161-29 Crocheron Ave. (bet. 161st & 162nd Sts.)

Subway: Flushing - Main St (& bus Q12) — Dinner nightly
Phone: 718-321-7770
Web: N/A
Prices: $$

There may be glitzier Korean spots in town, but insanely delicious, exceedingly simple Sik Gaek assures a good time, every time. Dressed in silly costumes, the staff is always having a blast in this seasonally decorated shack-like dining room featuring corrugated metal roofs, street lights, buckets for shells, and walls papered in dollar bills. Booths along the edge are filled with noisy regulars.

The kitchen serves the ocean's bounty, starting with a deliciously crisp and gargantuan pancake, *pajeon*, studded with seafood and kimchi begging to be dipped in enticingly salty soy-sesame sauce. A cloudy soup bobbing with tofu arrives piping hot, boasting that sharp, nutty, telltale flavor of fermented bean curd, and seems to have its own restorative powers.

Spicy Lanka

Sri Lankan

C2

159-23 Hillside Ave. (bet. 160th St. & Parsons Blvd.)

Bus: Parsons Blvd
Lunch & dinner daily
Phone: 718-487-4499
Web: N/A
Prices: ⊜

Walk through the door at Spicy Lanka, and—BAM!—the heady aroma of spice might just knock you off your feet. It's worth the trek to this far-out Jamaica restaurant, full of hip-hop music, brightly colored murals of palm trees, and an unbridled enthusiasm for heat and colliding Sri Lankan flavors.

The biryani is steamed for hours in a bubbling blend of cardamom, nutmeg, paprika, bay leaves, and star anise, then tossed with garlic- and ginger-marinated chicken and okra—a blast of flavor on the palate. Further rock your world with the string hopper *kothu*, mutton curry filled with noodles and a fistful of herbs and spices—think cardamom, cloves, and turmeric. To cool off, treat your tongue to the *watalappam* coconut custard, spiked with bits of buttery cashew.

S Prime

Steakhouse

35-15 36th St. (bet. 35th & 36th Aves.)

Subway: 36 Av
Dinner Tue – Sat
Phone: 718-707-0660
Web: www.sprimenyc.com
Prices: $$$$

You can take the steakhouse out of Manhattan, but you can't take Manhattan out of the steakhouse. At this slick Astoria joint, beef rules and the same New York service applies: rough around the edges but not without its charm. Here, a neighborhood crowd packs into the loud bar and industrial-style dining room, toasting to another happy hour or date-night.

While the menu offers some contemporary dishes beyond the classics, aficionados know to stick to the solid sides and aged cuts of meat. That ribeye is dry-aged with Himalayan sea salt onsite for 60 days, which results in heavily flavored beef that pairs excellently with classic accompaniments. Imagine traditionally prepared béarnaise sauce, creamy spinach, and a crispy pancake of grated hashbrowns.

Sweet Yummy House 

Chinese

83-13 Broadway (bet. Cornish & Dongan Aves.)

Subway: Elmhurst Av
Lunch & dinner daily
Phone: 718-699-2888
Web: N/A
Prices: $$

This tiny, impeccably clean dining room is drawing diners left and right to Elmhurst these days. But wait, you argue—isn't this just another Chinese joint along a stretch of Broadway filled with such Chinese joints? Not quite. In fact, Sweet Yummy House is a diamond in the rough for those hunting down authentic spice levels and Taiwanese specialties they've never heard of.

A meal might kick off with a duo of sautéed cabbages, one cooked in a delicate Taiwanese style, the other in the Shanghai tradition, sporting fiery oil. Then move on to tender, crispy chicken and pickled turnips in a nose-twitching spicy sauce; before lingering over deep and dark cold jelly, rendered Chengdu-style, with slippery mung bean noodles and lip-numbing Sichuan peppercorns.

Taiwanese Gourmet

Chinese

84-02 Broadway (at St. James Ave.)

Subway: Elmhurst Av
Lunch & dinner daily
Phone: 718-429-4818
Web: N/A
Prices: ⊜

A truly local spot, Taiwanese Gourmet puts diners in the mood with its semi-open kitchen (a rarity for Chinese restaurants) and tasty food. Natural light floods the walls, which showcase an impressive collection of ancient warrior gear, all beautifully framed as if museum-ready. Menu descriptions are minimal but the staff is happy to elaborate.

Excellent technique shines through the Taiwanese specialties, notably in strips of "shredded beef" sautéed in a dark, meaty paste, and tossed with dried tofu that balances complex flavors with fresh Chinese celery—a hands down winner on the menu. Likewise, the stir-fry of wonderfully briny clams and basil offers a perfect balance of sweet and salty flavors with oyster sauce, soy, rice wine, and red chilies.

Tang

C1

196-50 Northern Blvd. (at Francis Lewis Blvd.)

Subway: N/A — Lunch & dinner daily
Phone: 718-279-7080
Web: N/A
Prices: $$

When craving authentic Korean specialties, Tang is an absolute must-visit. The restaurant's impeccably cool style extends from its angled exterior ablaze in beams of yellow light to its sleek interior with exposed brick walls and bare wood tables. The attractive art gallery next door is attached and doubles as a private dining space.

Meals begin with an unending supply of wonderfully crisp and mild house kimchi. Also try the hearty *bibimbap* of marinated beef strips, root vegetables, and mushrooms alongside a bowl of ox-bone broth. The main attraction is the sensational *jeon*, traditional Korean pancakes grilled to order (weekend dinners, only). Round out the meal with steamed pigs feet accompanied by Tang's special fiery, salty, shrimp-based dipping sauce.

Taverna Kyclades

Greek 

33-07 Ditmars Blvd. (bet. 33rd & 35th Sts.)

Subway: Astoria - Ditmars Blvd — Lunch & dinner daily
Phone: 718-545-8666
Web: www.tavernakyclades.com
Prices: 💲

Forget the no-frills surroundings and focus instead on the fantastically fresh fish. This beloved Greek spot has folks happily dining elbow to elbow in a tiny yet lively space where the bustling kitchen is in view and seafaring scenes paint the walls. Quick, straightforward servers may address you in Greek if you look the part—that's just how local it gets here. Grab a seat on the enclosed patio for some serenity and get things going with garlicky and bubbling hot crab-stuffed clams; or the cold, classic trio of powerful *skordalia*, cooling tzatziki, and briny *taramosalata* served with toasted pita triangles. Order a side of *horta* (steamed escarole and dandelion) to accompany a plate of sweet and delicate mullets, served with a side of lemon potatoes.

Thai Rock

Thai 

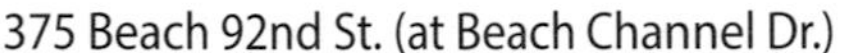

375 Beach 92nd St. (at Beach Channel Dr.)

Subway: Beach 90 St — Lunch & dinner daily
Phone: 718-945-5111
Web: www.thairock.us
Prices: $$

The "rock" in Thai Rock is not just a reference to the restaurant's location in the beachside Rockaways, but a nod to the live music that takes over after the sun dips down. Inside, you'll find tightly packed wooden tables and comfortable high-backed chairs, but the large uncovered patio overlooking the bay is certainly the place to be come summer.

The menu covers the usual Thai standards—think pad Thai, curries and various stir fries—as well as a few Northern Thai specialties, with aplomb. Don't miss the plump and tender dumplings stuffed with crunchy turnips, peanuts, and fragrant garlic; refreshing chicken *larb gai*, laced with a bright and zesty lime sauce featuring mint and scallion; or the delicious and very savory Issan sausage.

Tito Rad's Grill

Filipino XX

49-10 Queens Blvd. (bet. 49th & 50th Sts.)

Subway: 46 St - Bliss St — Lunch & dinner daily
Phone: 718-205-7299
Web: www.titorads.com
Prices:

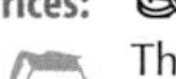

This eclectic grill's move to bigger digs gives it that much more space to seduce with its innovative fusion yet hearty flavors. The new dining room, clad in rough white marble and dark wood, includes several cozy touches including a framed photo of the original Tito's and white butcher paper atop the tables. The décor is just the right balance between contemporary and familiar, one that perfectly encapsulates the unique Malay- Spanish- Chinese- and Japanese-inspired menu.

Intensity abounds in every dish, from the fiery kick of the spicy *laing taro* leaves with pork and chicken, to the *lechon kawali*'s crispy pork belly skin. If it's available, be sure to try the *tortang dilis*, a puffball-like torta that's stuffed with tiny silver anchovies called *dulong*.

Tong Sam Gyup Goo Yi 

Korean 

C1

162-23 Depot Rd. (bet. Northern Blvd. & 164th St.)

Subway: Flushing - Main St (& bus Q13) Lunch & dinner daily
Phone: 718-359-4583
Web: N/A
Prices: $$

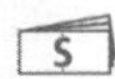

Murray Hill is no stranger to Korean food, but this prized, pig-loving barbecue destination is always packed. Inside, the bright room's décor forgoes all frills to focus on regional specialties. Smiling servers are earnest and hospitable.

Begin with the usual but very exquisite *banchan* like pickled turnips, fermented bean paste soup, and specially aged house kimchi—funky, garlicky, and a total pleasure. Bowls of glassy *naengmyun* noodles dancing in a chilled broth with kimchi are just as popular. Yet what makes this place unique is that barbecue grill on each table, used for sizzling slices of flavorful duck with miso, garlic cloves, and bean sprouts; spicy, tender bits of octopus; and sweet, fatty pork with soy sauce, red chili paste, and scallions.

Trattoria L'incontro

Italian

F1

21-76 31st St. (at Ditmars Blvd.)

Subway: Astoria - Ditmars Blvd Lunch & dinner Tue – Sun
Phone: 718-721-3532
Web: www.trattorialincontro.com
Prices: $$

A litany of delights sets the stage for an entertaining evening at this beloved institution of Italian-American pleasure. Frescoes of tranquil Italian scenes adorn coral walls in the unfussy dining room, complete with white-clothed tables spread at an ample distance. Service is relaxed, professional, and even theatrical in their performance of reciting special upon special.

Flavors are classic and robust, from eggplant rollatini stuffed with ricotta and herbs to the ravioli *golosi*, filled with both ground filet and veal, then topped with a sauce of mushrooms and sausage. Tender veal scaloppini is gently dredged and pan-fried, then bathed in a silky sauce of wine, butter, garlic, and lemon. Crunching through crisp cannoli is a divine finale.

Uma

Central Asian

92-07 Rockaway Beach Blvd. (bet. Beach 92nd & 94th Sts.)

Subway: Beach 90 St
Lunch & dinner daily
Phone: 718-318-9100
Web: N/A
Prices: $$

Rockaway Beach boasts a number of surfer-style hangouts with a laid-back vibe, one that extends to the hospitable Uma. Here, time is relative, and a chef's break is truly relished, but that doesn't mean he isn't working hard.

Behind a rusty brick façade, this Central Asian gem is packed to the gills by folks craving such delightful and generous specialties as *moshova,* a vegetarian soup with mung beans, rice, and finished with tart yogurt. Since many dishes err on the heavy side, start with a light yet filling signature salad tossing red peppers, cubes of fried eggplant, herbs, and feta. Then continue with butternut squash *manti*. Typically filled with meat, this delightful vegetarian version comes in a thin wrapper and is topped with a caramelized onion sauce.

Uncle Zhou 

Chinese

83-29 Broadway (at Dongan Ave.)

Subway: Elmhurst Av
Lunch & dinner daily
Phone: 718-393-0888
Web: N/A
Prices: 

Gifted cooks have been setting up in Elmhurst to show off their skills, but the chef/visionary of this modestly decked, massively popular Henanese gem has been a fixture from the start. Seat yourself inside the butterscotch-hued room, surrender to the affable staff, and await a memorable feast.

Opening this culinary show are pickled cucumbers and briny bamboo shoots with mushrooms, followed by pan-seared lamb dumplings or hugely fortifying "Dial oil" noodles sautéed with dried red chilies. For the consummate finale, pre-order "Taosibao," an impressive showpiece of rice-stuffed quail inside a squab, inside a chicken, inside a duck. Not only is this trumped-up version of *turducken* technically superb, but every element is flavored by an aromatic broth.

Urubamba

Peruvian

F3

86-20 37th Ave. (at 86th St.)

Subway: 82 St - Jackson Hts　Lunch & dinner daily
Phone: 718-672-2224
Web: N/A
Prices: $$

Named for Peru's intensely beautiful river, the Rio Urubamba, this hacienda-inspired space features indigenous paintings and artifacts that echo the rustic fare pouring out of the kitchen.

On weekends, the eatery serves traditional *desayuno*, a gut-bursting feast of *chanfainita* beef stew, and other hearty favorites. Here, tamales are a broad and flat banana leaf wrapped and stuffed with chicken and olives—a tasty contrast to the familiar Meso-American counterpart. For ultimate comfort, go for the *seco de cabrito*, a fantastically tender lamb and *ají panca* stew served with chunks of cassava and extra sauce in a tiny clay kettle. The dense *alfajor* cookie sandwich filled with dulce de leche and *crema volteada* flan is a perfectly decadent ending.

Uvarara

Italian

B2

79-28 Metropolitan Ave. (at 80th St.)

Subway: Middle Village - Metropolitan Av (& bus Q54)　Dinner Wed – Sun
Phone: 718-894-0052
Web: www.uvararany.com
Prices: $$

Tucked away in the quaint, residential neighborhood of Middle Village, Uvarara is an intimate, homey restaurant with quirky mismatched chairs and a curtain created from strings of wine corks. All this is the work of the Iadicicco family, who hail from Caserta, and have succeeded in creating an atmosphere akin to the *osterie* of their native Italy.

The kitchen consistently spins out a short menu of favorites (plus daily specials) including large *gnocchi alla Romana* simply adorned with butter, parmesan, and sage. Stuffed mushroom caps are a classic dish here, and an oven roasted chicken breast stuffed with mozzarella and spinach satisfies every time. Sweet fiends know not to skip the *affogato*, topped with a shot of hot, hearty, and wicked espresso.

Venturo Osteria & Wine Bar 

Italian

A2

44-07 Queens Blvd. (bet. 44th & 45th Sts.)

Subway: 46 St - Bliss St — Lunch & dinner daily
Phone: 718-406-9363
Web: www.venturovino.com
Prices: $$

From the moment it opened its doors, this delicious osteria has amassed a loyal following of Italian food fiends in Queens. Original canvas paintings dress the Aegean-blue walls and distressed wood accents reinforce the calm Mediterranean vibe—even at peak times.

Chef Michelle Vido helms a dedicated kitchen that surprises with excellence and generosity. House-made defines every dish, from freshly baked focaccia to the honey yogurt drizzled upon a lemon tart. Plump P.E.I. mussels in a fiery, serrano-tomato broth make for a great snack. But, for a fuller meal, try chewy ribbons of whole-wheat fettuccine tossed with hedgehog mushrooms, leeks, and pancetta; or a roasted leg of lamb stuffed with garlicky herbs over braised chickpeas and escarole.

Vesta Trattoria

Italian

E1

21-02 30th Ave. (at 21st St.)

Subway: 30 Av — Lunch Sat – Sun
Phone: 718-545-5550 — Dinner nightly
Web: www.vestavino.com
Prices: $$

Astoria favorite, Vesta Trattoria, still attracts neighborhood foodies to its postage stamp-sized room—modestly dressed with sage-green banquettes—for a respectable wine list and ever-changing daily specials. Not only does this Italian idol walk the line between classic and contemporary cooking with seasonal ingredients, but it also boasts a wine on tap program.

The extremely appetizing menu includes light bites like sugar snap peas tossed with brown butter yogurt. Keeping it in the "pea" family is a chilled English pea soup topped with spiced *labneh*, perfectly tailed by pappardelle laced with a luscious veal-and-tomato sauce and Grana Padano. It screams for more forkfuls, not unlike a spiced Baby Jesus Cake—light, spongy, and covered in caramel sauce.

Wafa

Middle Eastern

100-05 Metropolitan Ave. (bet. 70th Ave. & 70th Rd.)

Subway: Forest Hills - 71 Av
Lunch & dinner Wed – Mon
Phone: 718-880-2055
Web: www.wafasfood.com
Prices: $$

One cannot know the sheer joy and passion that goes into homemade Lebanese food without a visit to Wafa. Nestled among the mom-and-pop shops of Forest Hills' main strip, this pocket-sized spot appears shy on décor but bold on authenticity.

The smiling owner, Wafa Chami, runs the kitchen and her falafel still ranks among the best in town—these perfect orbs of chickpeas and "secret Wafa spices" are stuffed in a fluffy pita with hummus, pickled turnips, and *har* hot sauce. Primo specials range from stuffed eggplant and zucchini, to ground lamb steeped in garlicky tomato sauce. Meat pies sound pedestrian but should be sampled—these light-as-air flatbreads are topped with minced beef, sautéed with onions, tomatoes, and her infamous spice mix.

Zabb Elee

Thai

71-28 Roosevelt Ave. (bet. 70th & 72nd Sts.)

Subway: 74 St - Broadway
Lunch & dinner daily
Phone: 718-426-7992
Web: N/A
Prices:

This popular Isaan Thai restaurant, which focuses on hard-to-find Northeastern Thai fare, doesn't look like much from the simple façade. But once inside, you'll find a sweetly decorated space furnished with shiny metal tables that are in turn attended to by somewhat spaced out servers.

The crowd here is mixed, and if you request your dinner be spiced authentically, they will indeed bring the heat. Unfortunately, the once spectacular menu has been reduced, and a few of the fan favorites no longer exist. Still, you can't miss with the *yum moo krob*, a delicious, crispy pork salad laced in a dressing featuring lime, fish sauce, crushed chilies, and scallion; or the *larb ped*, a lovely minced duck salad sporting pickled onions, Thai basil, and mint.

Zum Stammtisch

German

B2

69-46 Myrtle Ave. (bet. 69th Pl. & 70th St.)

Subway: N/A

Lunch & dinner daily

Phone: 718-386-3014

Web: www.zumstammtisch.com

Prices: $$

Family owned and operated since 1972, this unrelenting success story has expanded over the years and welcomed Stammtisch Pork Store & Imports next door.

Zum Stammtisch hosts a crowded house in a Bavarian country inn setting where old-world flavor is relished with wholehearted enthusiasm. The goulash is thick and hearty, stocked with potatoes and beans, but that's just for starters. Save room for *sauerbraten*, *jägerschnitzel*, or a platter of succulent grilled sausages that includes *bratwurst*, *knockwurst*, and hickory-smoked *krainerwurst* served with sauerkraut and potato salad. The *Schwarzwälder Kirschtorte* (classic Black Forest cake) layers dense chocolate sponge with Kirsch soaked cherries and cream, and is absolutely worth the indulgence.

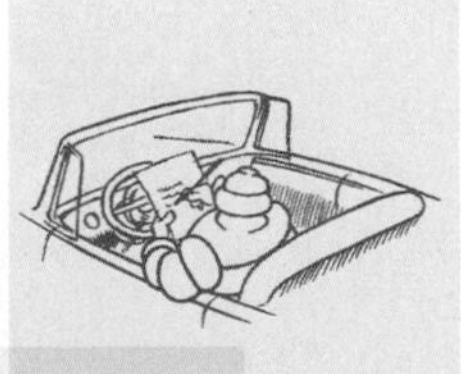

Avoid the search for parking. Look for 🅿.

DEPT. OF TRANSPORTATION
Staten

Staten Island

Staten Island

Staten Island may be the least populated borough of NYC, but the building of the Verrazano-Narrows Bridge ended its once bucolic existence. This fact is especially apt because one of the strongest, most accurate simplifications is that this "island" is home to a large Italian-American population, and no self-respecting foodie visits here without picking up a *scungilli* pizza from **Joe & Pat's**, or slice from **Nunzio** and **Denino's**. These shores, marinas, and waterfronts, once in shambles thanks to Superstorm Sandy, are slowly but surely recovering. In fact, **Skippy's**, originally a famous food truck, is back in (big) business with its hot dogs prepared in various regional styles for the residents of Mariner's Harbor right on Richmond Terrace. In fact, anyone with preconceived notions about this "forgotten borough," can leave them at the ferry door. Though deemed at one time the largest landfill in the world, Staten Island is currently being transformed into a verdant and very vast public park.

CULINARY CORNUCOPIA

While it is revered as an Italian-American hub, Staten Island continues to surprise visitors with its ethnically diverse enclaves. Take a culinary tour of the Mediterranean and Balkans at **Dinora**, proffering an abundance of olives, cheeses, and halal-butchered meat. Or, stop by those popular old-time Polish delis, which seem to comfortably thrive on their takeout business and homemade jams alone. It may not have **Cangiano's** bread recipe missed by many around here, but **Giuliano's Prodotti Italiani** continues to keep patrons happy with homey, old country classics like handmade pizzas, pastas, calzones, and more.

Spice heads will rejoice at the fantastic Sri Lankan food finds in the area surrounding Victory Boulevard. A spectrum of restaurants (think storefronts) reside here, including **New Asha** serving this country's fiery cuisine. Of course, **Lanka Grocery** is an epicurean's dream featuring a riot of colorful, authentic ingredients Staying within South Asia—its cuisine and culture—this borough is also home to Jacques Marchais Museum of Tibetan Art, an institution aimed at advancing Tibetan and Himalayan art. Steps from these subcontinent gems, discover authentic taquerias and a large Liberian outdoor market in the vicinity of Grasmere, where a small but special selection of

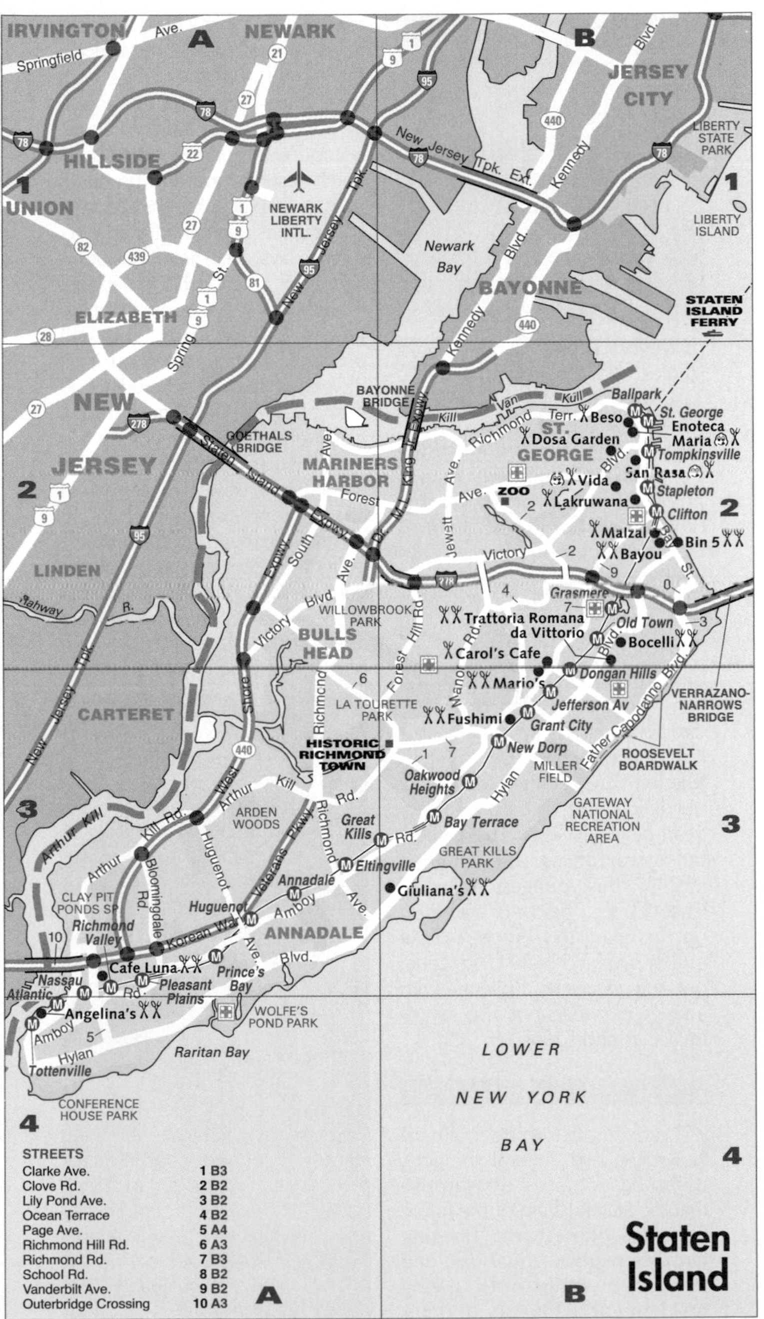
IRVINGTON
NEWARK
JERSEY CITY
LIBERTY STATE PARK
LIBERTY ISLAND
HILLSIDE
UNION
NEWARK LIBERTY INTL.
Newark Bay
BAYONNE
STATEN ISLAND FERRY
ELIZABETH
NEW JERSEY
BAYONNE BRIDGE
GOETHALS BRIDGE
MARINERS HARBOR
ST. GEORGE
ZOO
Beso
St. George
Enoteca Maria
Dosa Garden
Tompkinsville
San Rasa
Vida
Stapleton
Lakruwana
Clifton
Malzai
Bin 5
Bayou
LINDEN
WILLOWBROOK PARK
BULLS HEAD
Grasmere
Trattoria Romana da Vittorio
Old Town
Bocelli
Carol's Cafe
Dongan Hills
Mario's
Jefferson Av
VERRAZANO-NARROWS BRIDGE
CARTERET
LA TOURETTE PARK
Fushimi
Grant City
HISTORIC RICHMOND TOWN
New Dorp
ROOSEVELT BOARDWALK
MILLER FIELD
Oakwood Heights
ARDEN WOODS
Great Kills
Bay Terrace
GATEWAY NATIONAL RECREATION AREA
GREAT KILLS PARK
Eltingville
Annadale
Giuliana's
CLAY PIT PONDS SP
Huguenot
ANNADALE
Richmond Valley
Cafe Luna
Prince's Bay
Pleasant Plains
Atlantic
Nassau
Angelina's
WOLFE'S POND PARK
Tottenville
Raritan Bay
CONFERENCE HOUSE PARK
LOWER NEW YORK BAY
STREETS
Clarke Ave. 1 B3
Clove Rd. 2 B2
Lily Pond Ave. 3 B2
Ocean Terrace 4 B2
Page Ave. 5 A4
Richmond Hill Rd. 6 A3
Richmond Rd. 7 B3
School Rd. 8 B2
Vanderbilt Ave. 9 B2
Outerbridge Crossing 10 A3
Staten Island

purveyors supply West African staples and other regional eats. Take these to enjoy at home; or cook up a globally inspired feast with locally farmed produce from **Gerardi's** farmer's market in New Brighton or **St. George Greenmarket**, open on Saturdays. Historic Richmond Town pays homage to the sustainable food movement here by organizing the family-focused festival **Uncorked!**, which features the best in homemade cuisine and wine. They even offer recipes for traditional American classics. For rare and more mature varietals, **Mission Fine Wines** is top-notch, but if in need of calorie-heavy (read heavenly) eats, **The Cookie Jar** is way above par. Opened in 2007, this youngest sibling of **Cake Chef**, a beloved bakeshop up the road and **Piece-A-Cake** further south on New Dorp Lane, not only incites its audience with a range of sweets but also savory focaccias and soups.

FOOD, FUN & FROLIC

Given its booming culinary scene and cultural merging, it should come as no surprise that the Staten Island of the future includes plans for a floating farmer's market, aquarium, and revamped waterfronts, giving residents and tourists another reason to sit back and savor a drink at one of the bars along Bay Street. Tail these sips with small plates, which can be found in abundance at **Adobe Blues**, a cantina preparing sumptuous Southwestern food and prettified with a fireplace, clay walls, and collectables depicting the island's rodeo days…yee-haw! Residents adore this neighborhood hangout for its modest demeanor coupled with gratifying grub, and will probably continue to flood it till the end of time. After dawdling on Lafayette Avenue, drive through some of the city's wealthiest zip codes starring mansions with magnificent views of Manhattan and beyond. Whether here to glimpse the world's only complete collection of rattlesnakes at the zoo; or seek out the birthplaces of such divas as Christina Aguilera and Joan Baez, a visit to Staten Island is nothing if not interesting.

Angelina's

Italian XX

399 Ellis St. (at Main St.)

Bus: N/A — Lunch & dinner Tue– Sun
Phone: 718-227-2900
Web: www.angelinasristorante.com
Prices: **$$$**

It's no secret that Angelina's is Staten Island's place to celebrate Italian-American culture. Packed by 7:00 P.M. and boasting stunning river sunset views, it also offers live music and a massive atrium attracting revelers from near and far.

The multi-level Victorian may conjure New Orleans, but Angelina's keeps the focus clearly on Italian-American cooking with excellent pastas and plush red wines. The classic baked clams oreganata have that idyllic blend of butter and garlic. *Spaghettini al pomodoro* is as lovely as it sounds, with long-simmered tomato ragù, basil, and a sprinkling of Parmigiano. The popular *trenette nere con frutti di mare* piles a mountain of shrimp, clams, mussels, and scallops on thick squid ink pasta bathed in chunky tomato sauce.

Bayou

Cajun XX

1072 Bay St. (bet. Chestnut & St. Marys Aves.)

Bus: 51, 81 — Lunch & dinner daily
Phone: 718-273-4383
Web: www.bayounyc.com
Prices: **$$**

Southern food isn't novel to the city, but Cajun cuisine on Staten Island is a whole new realm. Bayou delivers with its veritable setting and spread. The space is a bit bawdy with gold and green accents, but linen-covered tables, luminous mirrors, and chandeliers lend refinement. Live music on occasion also to the lure.

Kitchen offerings begin with wonderfully decadent nachos featuring crawfish tails and crispy tortilla chips smothered in red beans, cheese, *pico de gallo,* and pickled jalapeños. Follow this up with a soul-satisfying and deliciously fragrant chicken-andouille sausage gumbo kicked up a notch with celery and peppers. Banana-chocolate bread pudding with vanilla ice cream turns heavenly when kissed with a boozy Bourbon cream sauce.

Beso

Spanish

B2

11 Schuyler St. (bet. Richmond Tr. & Stuyvesant Pl.)

Bus: N/A — Lunch & dinner daily
Phone: 718-816-8162
Web: www.besonyc.com
Prices: **$$**

Well-located? Yes, just by the Richmond County Courthouse. Good food and helpful staff? Of course. Great for groups or solo diners? You know it. Beso seems to have it all, including an interior that spotlights quaint accents like beautiful antique sideboards.

Grazing menus are all the rage, so it's worth exploring their vibrant tapas, which includes *empanada de res* stuffed with sautéed beef and served with a yucca-tomato sauce. *Pan y cerdo* or garlic-infused shredded roast pork slathered over a crostini and topped with melted Mahon along with avocado-*pico de gallo* is a savory treat, while *bistek Cubano* reveals a sherry wine- and garlic-marinated skirt steak grilled until tender and garnished with mojito sauce. Finish with a classic, ultra-smooth coconut flan.

Bin 5

Contemporary

B2

1233 Bay St. (bet. Maryland & Scarboro Aves.)

Bus: 51, 81 — Dinner Tue – Sun
Phone: 718-448-7275
Web: www.bin5nyc.com
Prices: **$$**

At this intimate bistro in Rosebank, dinner comes with a view of the twinkling Manhattan skyline. Complete with teardrop chandeliers, exposed brick, and a walled, outdoor garden, Bin 5's romantic setting has for long drawn locals seeking consistently good food and quiet conversation (plus that fantastic panorama!).

The playful menu—complete with solid daily specials—ranges from the perfectly chilled crab martini to a ceviche of top-notch crabmeat, avocado, cilantro, and mango. Fluffy knobs of ricotta gnocchi are tossed with a sweet pear sauce, caramelized onions, and toasted pignoli nuts. Then, try the grilled pork loin, a truly fantastic dish which is cooked to medium, cut into three slices, and drizzled with a hoisin-ginger- and sweet chili-barbecue sauce.

Bocelli

Italian XX

B2

1250 Hylan Blvd. (bet. Parkinson Ave. & Quintard St.)

Bus: 78 — Lunch & dinner daily
Phone: 718-420-6150
Web: www.bocellirest.com
Prices: **$$$**

Tucked into a workaday shopping mall, Bocelli doesn't make much of an impression at first glance. But, make your way past the simple façade, and wow, behold a gorgeous sloping staircase as well as a vast, theatrical dining room with polished dark wood, stunning light fixtures, and well-spaced tables that are luxuriously set. Could the delicious looking Italian menu be just as special?

The answer is most delightedly yes. An appetizer of *spiedini alla Romana* arrives topped with a delicious lemon, anchovy, and caper sauce; while a generous bowl of *rigatoni ripieni alla Sangiovese* is stuffed with savory beef tenderloin tips that have been braised in Sangiovese. At the end, a decadent chocolate three-layer cake gets a luscious hit from salty peanut butter.

Cafe Luna

Italian XX

A3

31 Page Ave. (bet. Boscombe Ave. & Richmond Valley Rd.)

Bus: 74 — Lunch Mon – Fri
Phone: 718-227-8582 — Dinner nightly
Web: www.cafelunanyc.com
Prices: **$$**

This well-run local institution proves that one should never judge a restaurant by its strip mall cover. With its Italian-American cooking, romantic fireplace, enclosed wine room, and covered veranda, Cafe Luna has a friendly, warm, and familial air thanks to the Sicilian owners who hail from Palermo.

Their perfectly prepared pastas mean the standards are taken care of, and it's easy to leave here satisfied. Start with short little corkscrews of fresh fusilli *puttanesca* in a strong, plum tomato sauce enhanced by anchovies, red chili flakes, garlic, basil, and black olives. Deliciously fresh red snapper *marechiaro* combines briny clams and sweet mussels with a fresh fish fillet and light tomato sauce with hints of chili flakes and lots of fresh parsley.

Carol's Cafe

American

B2

1571 Richmond Rd. (at Four Corners Rd. & Seaview Ave.)

Bus: 74, 76, 84, 86 — Dinner Wed – Sat
Phone: 718-979-5600
Web: www.carolscafe.com
Prices: $$

Dining here is like dining in Chef/owner Carol Frazzetta's kitchen—almost literally, because she lives on the premises. Her delightful personality fills the space, from the fresh flowers and pink linens, to shareable dishes and that homemade chocolate stout triple layer cake.

Not only has Frazzetta owned the building since the 1970s, but she clearly knows her neighbors, many of whom flock to the café for a roster of daily specials (top hits include "wild game of the day" like grilled buffalo ribeye and a marvelous prosciutto- and tomato-stuffed bread). The chef's slow-cooked *spaghetti al pomodoro* is another fan fave, topped with a chiffonade of basil and peppered with parmesan, before serving. Like everything else, it's simple, well-made, and *delizioso*.

Dosa Garden

Indian

B2

323 Victory Blvd. (bet. Cebra Ave. & Jersey St.)

Bus: 46, 48, 61, 66 — Lunch Tue – Sun
Phone: 718-420-0919 — Dinner nightly
Web: N/A
Prices:

The spicy, complex, and fragrant *dosas* of Dosa Garden make this casual stop a thoroughly impressive hidden gem. The ambience feels more storefront eatery than sit-down restaurant, with just a few hints of South Asian décor, but the warm, made-to-order dishes and aromas from the kitchen are transporting.

The kitchen boasts a tandoor oven but also churns out an array of elaborate *dosas*, like the tantalizingly crisp Mysore masala served with a sour yogurt sauce, spread with spicy chutney, and folded with potatoes, peppercorns, curry leaves, chili, and cumin. Don't miss the unique *rasa vada*, crunchy lentil doughnuts soaked in a deliciously spicy *rasam*. Curries are amazingly delish, like the shockingly deep brown Chettinadu fish, accented with mustard seeds.

Enoteca Maria 

Italian

B2

27 Hyatt St. (bet. Central Ave. & St. Marks Pl.)

Bus: N/A — Dinner Wed – Sun
Phone: 718-447-2777
Web: www.enotecamaria.com
Prices: **$$**

No need to venture far on Staten Island for excellent Italian food—Enoteca Maria is just two blocks from the ferry terminal. With its Carrara marble and lively vibe, this tiny spot could easily be wedged into Greenwich Village. Thankfully, it's not—anywhere else its certain authenticity would be sacrificed.

Each night, the menu changes depending on which *nonna* is presiding over the kitchen, as in Teresa from Sicily, who might serve an oxtail ragù or grilled artichokes glistening with excellent olive oil and a squeeze of lemon over spicy greens. *Coniglio alla cacciatora* arrives as diverse cuts of tender rabbit swimming in an inspired sauce of braised tomatoes, root vegetables, herbs, and a sweet-wine reduction with rosemary and garlic.

Fushimi

Fusion 

B3

2110 Richmond Rd. (bet. Colfax & Lincoln Aves.)

Bus: 51, 81 — Lunch & dinner daily
Phone: 718-980-5300
Web: www.fushimigroup.com
Prices: **$$$**

Fushimi is the ultimate spot for hungry locals in search of a dependable club scene sans commute. On any given night, its cozy booths are packed with islanders slinging back colorful cocktails and digging into architecturally designed sushi and sashimi from the Asian-fusion menu. Presentations are a knockout here, and the creativity and precision extends to the quality and combination of ingredients as well. Case in point: the aptly named Staten Island, a shrimp tempura roll topped with thin slices of seared filet mignon and dollops of mint-honey mustard and spicy aïoli.

Sink your teeth into the long-braised short ribs, which are fall-off-the-bone tender and served with Korean *galbi* sauce and "pee wee" potato chips made from those adorably tiny tubers.

Giuliana's

Italian

4105 Hylan Blvd. (at Osborn Ave.)

Bus: 54, 78, 79 — Lunch & dinner Tue – Sun
Phone: 718-317-8507
Web: www.giulianassi.com
Prices: $$

Staten Island may swarm with Italian-American eateries, but this festive classic does a masterful job in keeping its kitchen distinct and the patrons loyal. Guiliana's is the queen bee amid shops, catering halls, and ample competition. The interior is modest and charming, with framed pictures of smiling patrons and a fully stocked bar.

Hearty *stracciatella* is loaded with spinach and a comforting sauce of eggy parmesan, finished with a generous shower of black pepper. Seek out the *perciatelle con sarde*, a Sicilian-style pasta tossed in a powerful blend of fennel, saffron, raisins, sardines, anchovy paste, and crunch of toasted breadcrumbs. A trio of gelatos—pistachio, chocolate, and bitter almond, served with biscotti—is a divine ending.

Lakruwana

Sri Lankan

668 Bay St. (at Broad St.)

Bus: 51, 76 — Lunch & dinner Tue – Sun
Phone: 347-857-6619
Web: www.lakruwana.com
Prices:

Prepare for a sensory overload the moment you set foot into Lakruwana—the Sri Lankan hot spot is covered from floor-to-ceiling in murals, sculptures, flags, and more. The bright kaleidoscope of textures and colors is a welcome sight in an otherwise downtrodden part of the borough, as is the energetic owner who drifts from table to table.

Those familiar with Indian food will love Lakruwana's abundance of curries, green chili-spiked *kuttu roti*, as well as refreshingly salty-and-sour *lassi*. But their flavorful fare is considerably spicier, packing heat into everything from fiery red chili *lunu miris* chutney to devilled chicken. Loaded with ginger and garlic, this stellar tomato-based chicken specialty comes with cooling *raita* and tangy vegetable curry.

Maizal

990 Bay St. (bet. Lynhurst & Willow Sts.)

Bus: 51, 76 — Lunch Sun
Phone: 347-825-3776 — Dinner nightly
Web: www.maizalrestaurant.com
Prices: $$

This lovely, festive, and downright delicious Mexican restaurant is the perfect reprieve should you need a night off from Staten Island's endless stream of Italian fare. Featuring bright artwork, rustic wood tables, a well-stocked bar and semi-open kitchen, the mood at Maizal is fun and informal, with live music offered on weekends.

Kick things off with the house-made guacamole, mashed to order in a *molcajete* and spiced to request. Then tuck into tender chicken enchiladas rolled in warm handmade corn tortillas and laced with a smoky chile-ancho sauce; or one of the authentic house specials like *tikin xic* grouper, a subtle Mayan dish where citrus- and annatto-marinated fish is steamed to delicate and mouthwatering perfection in a banana leaf.

Mario's

Italian XX

1657 Richmond Rd. (bet. Buel & Liberty Aves.)

Bus: N/A — Lunch Tue – Sat
Phone: 718-979-1075 — Dinner Tue – Sunw
Web: www.mariossiny.com
Prices: $$

Does Staten Island really need another Italian-American restaurant? A fair question, but Chef/owner Mario Gentile confirms the answer is a yes. And, after a bite or two of his delicious red sauce food, you might be inclined to agree. Sprawled on a stretch of Richmond Road dotted with florists and bridal shops, Mario's offers big windows for people watching, leather banquettes, and oversized artwork.

It's practically law in this borough to start your meal with calamari, and this respite doesn't disappoint—it's refreshingly light and served with a scrumptious, herby lemon sauce. Move on to a tender poached pear salad with crushed walnuts, creamy Gorgonzola, and crispy prosciutto; or fall-off-the-bone osso buco plated with a soft pile of saffron risotto.

San Rasa

Sri Lankan

19 Corson Ave. (bet. Daniel Low Ter. & Monroe Ave.)

Subway: 51 — Lunch & dinner Wed – Mon
Phone: 718-420-0027
Web: www.sanrasa.com
Prices:

A little excursion to Staten Island is a must for knock-your-socks-off Sri Lankan food? Life is short, and honestly—so is that charming ferry ride, which deposits you on this local island destination for the best Sri Lankan food. Inside the bright, large dining space, you'll find wood accents and vessels lined up for their popular Sunday lunch buffet.

San Rasa's food is prepared fresh to order, offering the perfect excuse to nurse a cold, salty lassi while you wait. Dinner may begin with a starter of string hoppers or crispy little pancakes laced in a rich fish curry carrying hints of clove, fennel, and cardamom; and then move on to the *lampri*, a succulent little bundle of beef curry wrapped in banana leaf with nutty yellow rice, eggplant, and cashews.

Trattoria Romana da Vittorio

Italian

B2

1476 Hylan Blvd. (at Benton Ave.)

Bus: 54, 78, 79 — Lunch & dinner Mon – Sat
Phone: 718-980-3113
Web: www.trattoriaromanasi.com
Prices: $$

This delicious Staten Island via Lazio trattoria serves up heaping platters of al dente pasta and irresistible nightly specials, alongside bubbling pizzas that roll out of its brick oven in the back. Owned and guided by local personality and beloved chef, Vittorio Asoli (his cooking classes are televised on a local community channel), Trattoria Romana da Vittorio offers a cozy reprieve from the busy avenue outside, with diners huddling over snug tables or gathering at a communal table to chat up their neighbors.

Don't miss the juicy chicken *scarpariello*, caramelized to perfection and simmered in a delicate white wine sauce with rosemary and garlic; or tender *trippa alla Romana*, served in a fresh tomato sauce with a hunk of crusty bread for dipping.

Vida

American

B2

381 Van Duzer St. (bet. Beach & Wright Sts.)

Bus: 78 Dinner Tue – Sat
Phone: 718-720-1501
Web: www.vidany.com
Prices: **$$**

All the locals love Vida, where popular Chef/owner Silva Popaz has created a cozy little restaurant with a firm commitment to simple, but well-executed, dishes. Inside the café-like atmosphere, you'll find unique artwork lining brightly painted walls, and a smattering of tables surrounding a long communal wood table in the center.

The charming Popaz travels quite often, and the flavors she picks up along her journeys tend to make their way back into her menu at Vida. The "Mexican Duo"—her most popular dish—features pulled pork- and chicken-stuffed tortillas, topped with a vibrant Chimayo chile and tangy cheese sauce, and paired with tender stewed beans sporting bright green onion; while a delicate bread pudding arrives puddled in creamy vanilla ice cream.

The sun is out – let's eat alfresco! Look for .

Indexes

Where to **Eat**

Alphabetical List of Restaurants 612
Restaurants by Cuisine 622
Cuisines by Neighborhood 633
Starred Restaurants 648
Bib Gourmand 651
Under $25 653
Brunch 655

Alphabetical List of Restaurants

A

Restaurant	Distinction	Comfort	Page
ABC Cocina	☺	XX	102
ABC Kitchen		XX	102
Aburiya Kinnosuke		XX	228
ABV		X	190
A Casa Fox		XX	208
Acme		XX	140
Agnanti		XX	551
Ai Fiori	✿	XXX	266
Aita		XX	462
al Bustan	☺	XX	228
Alcala		XX	229
Aldea	✿	XX	103
Al di Là		X	484
Aldo Sohm Wine Bar		≡	267
All'onda		XX	140
Allswell		X	516
Alma		XX	500
Almayass		XX	104
Alobar		XX	551
Al Seabu		X	484
Alta		XX	141
Amma		XX	229
Anassa Taverna		XX	230
Andanada	✿	XX	396
Andaz		X	363
Andre's Café		X	363
Añejo		X	267
Anella		X	516
Angelina's		XX	600
Anjappar		X	104
annisa		XX	141
Antique Garage		X	319
Applewood		X	485
Aquagrill		XX	319
Aquavit	✿✿	XXX	231
Ardesia		≡	268
Arharn Thai		X	552
Armani Ristorante		XX	230
Aroma Kitchen & Wine Bar	☺	X	142
Arrogant Swine		X	462
Asian Jewels		XX	552
atera	✿✿	XX	344
Atlantic Grill		XX	364
Atrium		XX	440
Aureole	✿	XXX	269
Aurora		X	517
Au Za'atar		X	52
A Voce Madison		XX	105
Awadh		XX	397
A-Wah		X	35
Ayada		X	553

B

Restaurant	Distinction	Comfort	Page
Babbalucci		X	190
Babbo	✿	XX	143
Bacaro		X	208
Bacchanal		X	35
Baci & Abbracci	☺	X	517
Bahari estiatorio		X	553
Baker & Co.	☺	XX	142
Balaboosta		XX	320
Balade		XX	52
Balthazar		XX	320
Balvanera		X	209
Bamboo Garden		X	500
Bao (The)		X	53
Barawine		XX	191
Barbetta		XXX	268
Bar Boulud		XX	397
Barbounia		XX	105
Barbuto		XX	144
Bar Corvo		X	463
Bar Masa		XX	270
Barney Greengrass		X	398
Bar Primi	☺	XX	53
Barraca		XX	144
Basil Brick Oven Pizza	☺	XX	554
Bâtard	✿	XX	345
Battersby		X	440
Bayou		XX	600
B. Café West		X	398
Becco		XX	270
Beccofino		X	422
Benares		XX	271

Restaurant	Award	Comfort	Page
Benoit		XX	271
Beso		X	601
Betony	✿	XXX	272
Bettolona		X	191
Beyoglu	☺	X	364
BG		X	273
Bhatti		X	106
Bianca	☺	X	145
Biáng!	☺	X	554
Bin 5		XX	601
Bin 71		≣	399
Bistro SK		X	422
Bistro Vendôme		XX	232
Black Ant (The)		XX	54
Black Swan		X	463
Blanca	✿✿	XX	464
Blaue Gans		XX	346
Blenheim		XX	145
Blossom		XX	18
BLT Prime		XX	106
BLT Steak		XXX	232
Blue Hill	✿	XX	146
Blue Ribbon		XX	321
Blue Ribbon Bakery		XX	147
Blue Ribbon Sushi		XX	321
Blue Water Grill		XX	107
BLVD Bistro		X	192
Boathouse Central Park		XX	365
Bobby Van's		XX	233
Bocca		XX	107
Bocelli		XX	602
Bodrum		XX	399
Bo Ky		X	36
BONDST		XX	147
Boqueria	☺	XX	108
Bottega del Vino		XX	233
Bouley	✿	XXXX	347
Boulud Sud		XXX	400
Bowery Meat Company		XX	54
Bozu		X	518
Braai		XX	273
Brasserie 8 1/2		XXX	274
Brasserie Ruhlmann		XX	274
Bread & Tulips	☺	XX	108
Breslin (The)	✿	X	109
Brick Cafe		X	555
Bricolage		X	485
Brinkley's		X	36
Brisas del Caribe		X	423
Brooklyn Star		XX	518
Brucie		X	441
Brushstroke	✿	XXX	348
Bukhara Grill		XX	234
bún-ker	☺	X	555
Burger & Barrel		XX	322
Buttermilk Channel	☺	X	441
Buvette		X	148

C

Restaurant	Award	Comfort	Page
Cacio e Pepe		X	55
Café Boulud	✿	XXX	366
Café China	✿	XX	235
Cafe Cluny		XX	148
Café el Portal		X	322
Cafe El Presidente		X	110
Café Frida		XX	400
Cafe Katja		X	209
Cafe Luna		XX	602
Café Mingala		X	365
Café Mogador		X	55
Cafe Sabarsky		X	367
Café Steinhof		X	486
Caffè Storico		XX	401
Cagen	✿	XX	56
Caravaggio		XXX	367
Carbone	✿	XX	149
Carol's Cafe		X	603
Casa del Chef Bistro	☺	X	556
Casa Enríque	✿	XX	557
Casa Lever		XXX	234
Casa Mono	✿	XX	111
Casa Nonna		XX	275
Cascabel Taqueria		X	368
Casellula		≣	275
Cata		XX	210
Caviar Russe	✿	XXX	236

Restaurant	Distinction	Comfort	Page
Cecil (The)		XX	192
Cédric		XX	193
Ceetay		X	423
Charlie Bird		XX	323
Chavela's	☺	X	465
Cheburechnaya		X	556
Chefs Club		XXX	323
Chef's Table at Brooklyn Fare	✿✿✿	XX	442
Cherche Midi		XX	324
Chevalier		XXX	276
Chez Napoléon		X	276
ChikaLicious		▤	57
Cho Dang Gol	☺	X	277
Chop-Shop		X	18
Christos		XX	558
Ciccio	☺	X	324
Clement		XXX	277
Clinton St. Baking Company		X	210
Clocktower (The)		XXX	110
Clover Club		▤	443
Co.		X	19
cocoron		X	211
Colicchio & Sons		XXX	19
Colonia Verde		XX	465
Colonie		XX	443
Community Food & Juice		XX	193
Cómodo		XX	325
Congee Village	☺	X	211
Contra		XX	212
Cooklyn		XX	486
Cookshop		XX	20
Coppelia	☺	X	20
Copper Chimney		XX	112
Corner Social		XX	194
Cosme		XX	112
Craft		XX	113
Craftbar		XX	113
Crave Fishbar		XX	237
Crazy Crab 888		X	558
Crema		XX	21
Crispo	☺	XX	150
Cull & Pistol		XX	21
Curry-Ya		X	57

D

Restaurant	Distinction	Comfort	Page
Daniel	✿✿	XXXXX	369
Danji		X	278
Danny Brown Wine Bar & Kitchen		XX	559
Daruma-ya Soba		XX	346
da Umberto		XX	22
db Bistro Moderne		XX	278
DBGB Kitchen & Bar	☺	XX	58
Dear Bushwick		X	466
Degustation		XX	58
Delaware and Hudson	✿	XX	519
Del Frisco's		XXX	279
Del Posto	✿	XXXX	23
De Mole		X	559
Dieci		▤	59
Dim Sum Go Go	☺	X	37
Diner	☺	X	520
Dinosaur Bar-B-Que		X	194
Dirt Candy		XX	212
Dirty French		XX	213
Dojo Izakaya		▤	59
Don Antonio by Starita	☺	XX	279
Donguri		X	368
Donostia	☺	X	60
Don's Bogam		XX	237
Do or Dine	☺	X	466
Dosa Garden		X	603
Dover		XX	444
Dovetail	✿	XX	402
Dumpling Galaxy		X	560
Dutch (The)		XX	325

E

Restaurant	Distinction	Comfort	Page
East 12th Osteria		XX	60
East Harbor Seafood Palace	☺	XX	501
East Pole		XX	370
Eddy (The)		XX	61
Edi & The Wolf		X	61
Ed's Lobster Bar	☺	X	326
Egg	☺	X	520
El Almacen		X	521
élan		XX	114
Elberta	☺	XX	487
El Born		XX	521
Eleven Madison Park	✿✿✿	XXXX	115
Eliá		XX	501
Eli's Table		XX	370
Elizabeth's Neighborhood Table		XX	401
El Mio Cid		XX	467

Restaurant			Page
El Nuevo Bohío		X	424
El Parador	☺	XX	238
El Paso		X	195
El Porrón		X	371
El Quinto Pino		XX	22
Emilio's Ballato		XX	326
Empellón Taqueria		XX	150
Emporio		XX	327
Engeline's		X	560
EN Japanese Brasserie		XXX	151
Enoteca Maria	☺	X	604
Enoteca on Court		X	444
Enzo's of Arthur Ave		X	424
Esca		XX	280
Estela		XX	327
Estiatorio Milos		XXX	280
Estrellita Poblana III		X	425
Eugene & Co.		X	467
Extra Virgin		XX	151

F

Restaurant			Page
Falansai	☺	X	468
Farm on Adderley (The)		XX	487
Faro	☺	XX	468
Fat Radish (The)		XX	213
Fatty Fish		X	371
Feast		X	62
Fedora		XX	152
Felidia		XXX	238
15 East		XX	114
Fig & Olive		XX	372
Finch (The)	✿	XX	469
Fishtag		XX	403
Fishtail by David Burke		XXX	372
Fitzcarraldo		XX	470
Flat Top		X	195
Flex Mussels		XX	373
Flinders Lane		X	62
Fonda		X	488
Foragers City Table		XX	24
Forcella		X	522
Fort Defiance		X	502
44 & X Hell's Kitchen		XX	281
Four Seasons (The)		XXXX	239
FP Patisserie		X	373
Frankie & Johnnie's		XX	281
Frankies 457 Spuntino	☺	X	445
Franny's		XX	488
French Louie		XX	445
Fung Tu		XX	214
Fushimi		XX	604

G

Restaurant			Page
Gabriel Kreuther	✿	XXX	282
Gallagher's		XX	283
Gander (The)		XX	116
Ganso Ramen	☺	X	446
Gastronomia Culinaria		X	403
Gastroteca		XX	561
Gato		XX	152
General Greene (The)	☺	X	470
Gennaro		XX	404
Gigino at Wagner Park		XX	92
Giorgione		XX	328
Giuliana's		XX	605
Gladys	☺	X	471
Gnocco		X	63
Golden Unicorn		X	37
Good		XX	153
Good Enough to Eat		X	404
Good Fork (The)	☺	X	502
Gotham Bar and Grill	✿	XXX	154
Gradisca		XX	153
Graffiti		▤	63
Gramercy Tavern	✿	XXX	117
Grand Harmony		X	38
Gran Eléctrica	☺	XX	446
Great N.Y. Noodletown		X	38
Greek (The)		XX	349
Greenpoint Fish & Lobster Co.		X	522
Gregory's 26 Corner Taverna	☺	X	561

H

Restaurant			Page
Hahm Ji Bach	☺	XX	562
Hakata Tonton		X	155
Hakkasan		XXX	283
Haldi		X	116
HanGawi	☺	XX	239
Hanjan		XX	118
Happy Family Hotpot		X	562
Harry's Cafe & Steak		XX	92
Hasaki		X	64
Hatsuhana		XX	240
Havana Café	☺	XX	425

Restaurant			Page
Hearth		XX	64
Hecho en Dumbo	☺	X	155
Hell's Kitchen		XX	284
Hibino		X	447
Hide-Chan Ramen	☺	X	240
Hill Country		X	118
Hill Country Chicken	☺	X	119
Himalayan Yak		X	563
HinoMaru Ramen	☺	X	563
Hirohisa	✿	XX	329
Hometown Bar-B-Que	☺	X	503
Hot Kitchen		X	65
Houdini Kitchen Laboratory		XX	564
Houseman		XX	328
Huertas		XX	65
Hunan House	☺	X	564
Hunan Kitchen of Grand Sichuan	☺	X	565
I			
Ichimura	✿✿	XX	350
Iki Japanese		XX	565
Il Bacco		XX	566
Il Buco		X	156
Il Buco Alimentari e Vineria	☺	XX	156
Il Cortile		XX	39
Il Gattopardo		XX	284
Il Poeta	☺	XX	566
Il Riccio		XX	374
Il Ristorante Rosi		XXX	374
Il Salumaio		X	375
Imperial Palace		X	567
Inatteso Pizzabar Casano		XX	93
I Sodi		XX	157
I Trulli		XX	119
Ivan Ramen		X	214
J			
Jack the Horse		XX	447
Jake's Steakhouse		XX	426
James		XX	489
Java		X	489
Jean-Georges	✿✿✿	XXXX	405
Jewel Bako	✿	X	66
J.G. Melon	☺	X	375
Jin Ramen	☺	X	196
Joe & MissesDoe		X	67
Joe's Place		X	426
Joe's Shanghai		X	567
John Brown Smokehouse	☺	X	568
John Dory Oyster Bar (The)		X	120
JoJo		XX	376
Jolie Cantina		X	448
Jones Wood Foundry		X	376
Jora		XX	568
Joseph Leonard		X	157
J. Restaurant Chez Asta	☺	X	196
Jubilee		XX	241
Jukai		XX	241
Jungsik	✿✿	XXX	351
Juni	✿	XXX	242
Junoon	✿	XXX	121
Juventino		XX	490
K			
Kafana		X	67
Kaia		X	377
Kajitsu	✿	XX	243
Kang Ho Dong Baekjeong		XX	569
Kang Suh		XX	285
Kanoyama		X	68
Kao Soy		X	503
Karczma		X	523
Katsuno		X	569
Katz's	☺	X	215
Keens		XX	285
Kesté Pizza & Vino	☺	X	158
Khe-Yo	☺	XX	349
Kiin Thai	☺	XX	158
Kirakuya		▤	286
Ki Sushi		X	448
Kitchen 79		X	570
Kokum		X	120
Kopiaste Taverna		XX	570
Kristalbelli		XX	286
Krolewskie Jadlo		X	523
Krupa Grocery		XX	490
Kung Fu Little Steamed Buns Ramen	☺	X	287
Kunjip		X	287
Kura		X	68
Kurumazushi		XX	244
Kyo Ya	✿	XX	69
L			
La Esquina		X	39
Lafayette		XX	159

Restaurant			Page
La Grenouille		XXX	244
Lakruwana		X	605
La Masseria		XX	288
Lambs Club (The)		XX	288
Landmarc		XX	352
Land of Plenty	☻	XX	245
Lan Sheng		X	289
L'Antagoniste		XX	471
L'Apicio		XX	70
Larb Ubol	☻	X	289
L'Artusi		XX	159
Las Ramblas		≣	160
La Superior		X	524
Laut	☻	X	122
Lavagna		X	70
La Vara	✽	XX	449
Lea	☻	XX	491
Le Bernardin	✽✽✽	XXXX	290
Le Cirque		XXXX	245
Le Fond		X	524
Left Bank		XX	160
Legend Bar & Restaurant		XX	24
Le Gigot		X	161
Le Philosophe		XX	161
Le Relais de Venise (L'Entrecôte)		XX	246
Les Halles		X	122
Liebman's		X	427
Lil' Frankie's	☻	X	71
Limani		XXX	291
Lincoln		XXX	406
Little Beet Table (The)		XX	123
Little Owl (The)		X	162
Little Park		XX	352
Little Pepper	☻	X	571
Locanda Verde		XX	353
Locanda Vini e Olii		X	472
Loi Estiatorio		XX	291
Louie and Chan		X	215
Lucky Eight		X	504
Lucky Luna		X	525
Lugo		XX	292
Luksus at Tørst	✽	XX	526
Lulu & Po	☻	X	472
Lupa	☻	XX	162
Lupulo		XX	25
Lusardi's		XX	377
Lu Xiang Yuan		X	571
Luzzo's		X	71

M

Restaurant			Page
Macao Trading Co.		XX	353
Macondo		XX	216
Madangsui		XX	292
Maialino		XX	123
Main Street Imperial Taiwanese Gourmet		X	572
Maison Harlem		X	197
Maison Kayser		XX	378
Maizal		X	606
Malagueta		X	572
Malai Marke		XX	72
Malaparte		X	163
Malaysian Kitchen		XX	93
Mandoo Bar		X	293
Manzo		XX	124
Má Pêche		XX	293
Mapo Tofu	☻	X	246
Marc Forgione		XX	354
Marcha Cocina		X	197
Marche du Sud		X	378
Marea	✽✽	XXX	294
Margaux		XX	163
Marla's Bistro Mexicano		X	504
Mario's		XX	606
Mari Vanna		XX	124
Market Table		XX	164
MarkJoseph		XX	94
Marlow & Sons	☻	X	525
Mar's		X	573
Marta		XX	125
Mary's Fish Camp		X	164
Mas (farmhouse)		XXX	165
Masa	✽✽✽	XX	295
Maya		XX	379
Mayfield		XX	473
Maysville		XX	125
Maz Mezcal		X	379
Meadowsweet	✽	XX	527
Melba's		X	198
Mercato		X	296
Mercer Kitchen		XX	330
Mermaid Inn (The)		X	72
Mesa Coyoacán		X	528
Mexicosina	☻	X	427
Mezzaluna		X	380
Mighty Quinn's		X	73
Mile End	☻	X	450

Restaurant	Award	Comfort	Page
Mill Basin Kosher Delicatessen		X	505
Mimi's Hummus		≣	491
Minetta Tavern	✿	X	166
Minton's		XXX	198
Miranda		XX	528
Miss Korea		XX	296
Miss Lily's		X	165
Miss Mamie's Spoonbread Too	☺	X	406
Modern (The)	✿✿	XXX	297
Molyvos		XX	298
Mominette		X	473
Momofuku Ko	✿✿	XX	74
Momofuku Noodle Bar	☺	X	73
Momofuku Ssäm Bar	☺	X	75
Momokawa	☺	X	126
Momoya		XX	407
Montmartre		XX	25
Morandi		XX	167
Morgan's BBQ		X	492
Moti Mahal Delux		XX	380
Motorino		X	75
Mozzarella & Vino		XX	298
MP Taverna		XX	573
Mr Chow		XX	247
M Shanghai		X	529
Mtskheta Café		X	505
Mundo		XX	574
Mu Ramen	☺	X	574
Murray's Cheese Bar		XX	167
Musket Room (The)	✿	XX	331
M. Wells Steakhouse	✿	XX	575
Mythos		XX	576

N

Restaurant	Award	Comfort	Page
Naka Naka		X	26
Nan Xiang Xiao Long Bao		X	576
Narcissa		XX	76
Nargis Cafe		XX	506
Natural Tofu & Noodles		X	577
Navy		X	330
Naya		XX	247
Nebraska Steakhouse		XX	94
Neerob		X	428
Nerai		XX	248
New Leaf Café		XX	199
New Malaysia	☺	X	40
New Wonjo		XX	299
Nick's		X	381
Nick's Pizza		X	577
Nightingale 9		X	450
900 Park		XX	428
No. 7		XX	474
Nocciola		XX	199
Noche Mexicana II		X	407
NoMad	✿	XX	127
Nom Wah Tea Parlor	☺	X	40
Noodle Pudding		XX	451
Noreetuh		X	76
Norma's		XX	299
Northeast Kingdom		X	474
North End Grill		XXX	95
Northern Spy Food Co.		X	77
Nougatine		XX	408
Novitá		XX	126
Nuaa (The)		XX	381
Nusara		X	578
Nyonya	☺	X	41

O

Restaurant	Award	Comfort	Page
Obikà		XX	248
Oceana		XXX	300
Oda House		X	77
Odeon (The)		XX	354
Oiji	☺	X	78
Okonomi		X	529
O Lavrador		XX	578
1 or 8		XX	530
Ootoya		XX	128
Oriental Garden		X	41
Ornella		XX	579
Orsay		XX	382
Osteria al Doge		XX	300
Osteria del Circo		XX	301
Osteria Laguna		XX	249
O Ya		XX	128

P

Restaurant	Award	Comfort	Page
Pachanga Patterson		X	579
Pacificana		XX	506
Paet Rio	☺	X	580
Pagani		XX	168
Palo Santo		X	492
Pampano		XX	249
Panca		X	168

Restaurant			Page
Papatzul		X	332
Paradou		X	169
Parigot		XX	42
Park Asia		XX	507
Park Avenue		XX	129
Parkside		XX	580
Parlor Steakhouse		XX	382
Pastai		XX	26
Patricia's		XX	429
Patroon		XXX	250
Paulie Gee's	☺	X	530
Payag		X	581
Pearl & Ash	☺	XX	332
Pearl Oyster Bar		X	169
Pearl Room (The)		XX	507
Peasant		XX	333
Peking Duck House		XX	42
Pera		XX	250
Perilla		XX	170
Periyali		XX	129
Perla		XX	170
Perry Street		XX	171
Per Se	✿✿✿	XXXXX	302
Persepolis		XX	383
Peter Luger	✿	X	531
Petit Oven		X	508
Petrossian		XXX	301
Phoenix Garden	☺	X	251
Piccola Venezia		XX	581
Picholine	✿	XXX	409
Pickle Shack		≡	508
Pier A		XX	95
Pine Bar & Grill		XX	429
Piora	✿	XX	172
Pippali	☺	XX	130
pizzArte		XX	303
P.J. Clarke's		X	251
Place (The)		XX	171
Pó		XX	173
Pok Pok Ny	✿	X	509
Porsena	☺	XX	78
Porter House		XXX	303
Prime & Beyond New York		X	79
Prime Meats	☺	XX	451
Print		XX	304
Prospect		XX	475
Prova	☺	XX	27
Prune	☺	X	79
Public	✿	XX	334
Purple Yam	☺	X	493
Pylos		XX	80

Q

Restaurant			Page
Quatorze Bis		XX	383

R

Restaurant			Page
Racines NY		XX	355
Radiance Tea House		X	304
Rai Rai Ken		X	80
Ramen Misoya		X	81
Ramen Yebisu		X	532
Raoul's		XX	333
Rebelle	✿	XX	335
Recette		XX	173
Red Cat (The)		XX	27
RedFarm		X	174
Red Rooster		XX	200
Regency Bar & Grill (The)		XX	384
Remi		XXX	305
Resto		X	130
Reynard		XX	532
Ribbon (The)		XX	408
Ricardo Steakhouse		XX	200
Risotteria Melotti		XX	81
Ristorante Morini		XXX	384
River Café (The)	✿	XXX	452
River Styx		X	533
Robataya		XX	82
Roberta's	☺	X	475
Roberto's		XX	430
Rocking Horse Cafe		XX	28
Rockmeisha		≡	174
Roebling Tea Room		X	533
Roman's		X	476
Root & Bone		X	82
Rosanjin	✿	XXX	356
Rouge et Blanc		XX	336
Royal Seafood		X	43
Rubirosa	☺	XX	336
Rucola		X	453
Runner (The)		XX	476
Runner & Stone	☺	XX	510
Russ & Daughters Cafe	☺	XX	216
Russian Samovar		XX	305
Rye	☺	X	534

S

Restaurant			Page
Sabry's		X	582
Saint Austere (The)		≣	534
Sakagura		XX	252
SakaMai		XX	217
Sake Bar Hagi		X	306
Salinas		XX	28
Salt + Charcoal		X	535
Salt & Fat	☺	X	582
Samudra		X	583
Samurai Mama		X	535
San Matteo	☺	XX	385
San Rasa	☺	X	607
Santina		XX	175
Saraghina		X	477
Saravanaas		X	131
Sauce		X	217
Saxon + Parole		XX	175
Scarlatto		XX	306
Schiller's Liquor Bar		XX	218
Sea Grill (The)		XXX	307
2nd Avenue Deli		X	252
Selamat Pagi		X	536
Semilla	✿	X	537
Sessanta		XX	337
Settepani		XX	201
Sevilla		X	176
Shalom Japan	☺	X	536
Shanghai Café	☺	X	43
Shanghai Heping		XX	44
Shanghai Pavilion		XX	385
Shuko		XX	176
Sigiri		X	83
Sik Gaek		X	583
Simone (The)		XX	386
Sip Sak		XX	253
Smith & Wollensky		XX	253
Snack	☺	X	337
Snack EOS		X	307
Sobakoh		X	83
Soba Totto		XX	254
Soba-Ya	☺	XX	84
Socarrat		XX	29
Sociale		XX	453
SoCo		XX	477
Somtum Der	✿	X	85
Soto	✿✿	XX	177
Sottocasa	☺	X	454
Spasso		XX	178
Speedy Romeo	☺	X	478
Spicy Lanka		X	584
Spiga		XX	410
Spigolo		XX	386
Spitzer's Corner		X	218
Spotted Pig	✿	X	179
S Prime		XX	584
Standard Grill		XX	178
St. Anselm		X	538
Stanton Social (The)		XX	219
Stella 34		XX	308
Stone Park Cafe		X	493
Streetbird Rotisserie	☺	X	201
Strong Place		X	454
Supper	☺	XX	84
SushiAnn		XX	254
Sushi Azabu	✿	XX	357
Sushi Dojo		X	86
Sushi Katsuei		X	494
Sushi Nakazawa		XX	180
Sushi of Gari	✿	X	387
Sushi Sasabune		X	388
Sushi Seki		X	388
Sushi Yasaka		X	411
Sushi Yasuda	✿	XX	255
Sushi Zen		XX	308
Sweet Yummy House	☺	X	585
Szechuan Gourmet	☺	X	309

T

Restaurant			Page
Tabaré		X	538
Taboon		XX	309
Taci's Beyti		XX	510
Taiwanese Gourmet		X	585
Takashi		X	180
Take Root	✿	X	455
Talde		XX	494
Tamarind		XXX	355
Tamba		X	131
Tang		XX	586
Tang Pavilion		XX	310
Tanoreen	☺	XX	511
Tanoshi		X	389
Taqueria Tlaxcalli		X	430
Taverna Kyclades		X	586
Tavola		X	310
Telepan	✿	XXX	412

Restaurant			Page
Tempura Matsui	✿	XX	256
Tertulia	☺	XX	181
Tessa		XX	411
Thai Rock		X	587
Thái Sơn		X	44
Thelma on Clinton	☺	XX	219
Thistle Hill Tavern		X	495
Tía Pol		≣	29
Tiella		XX	389
Tiny's		X	358
Tipsy Parson		XX	30
Tito Rad's Grill		XX	587
Tocqueville		XX	132
Toloache		XX	311
Tong Sam Gyup Goo Yi	☺	X	588
Tori Shin	✿	XX	312
Toro		XX	30
Trading Post		XX	96
Tra Di Noi	☺	X	431
Traif	☺	X	539
Trattoria L'incontro		XX	588
Trattoria Romana da Vittorio		XX	607
Tre Otto		XX	202
Trestle on Tenth		XX	31
Tribeca Grill		XX	358
Tsushima		XX	257
Tulsi	✿	XX	258
Tuome		X	86
Turkish Kitchen	☺	XX	132
21 Club		XX	311
Txikito		XX	31

U

Restaurant			Page
Uma		X	589
Umi NOM	☺	X	478
Uncle Boons	✿	XX	338
Uncle Zhou	☺	X	589
Union Square Cafe		XX	133
Untitled	☺	XX	181
Upland		XX	133
Urubamba		X	590
Utsav		XX	313
Uva	☺	X	390
Uvarara		X	590

V

Restaurant			Page
Vai		XX	413
Venturo Osteria & Wine Bar	☺	X	591
Vesta Trattoria		X	591
Via Carota		XX	182
Vics		XX	182
Vida	☺	X	608
Vinatería		XX	202
Vinegar Hill House	☺	X	456
Virginia's		XX	87
Vitae		XXX	257

W

Restaurant			Page
Wafa		X	592
Wa Jeal		XX	390
Wallflower		XX	183
Wallsé	✿	XX	184
Warique		X	413
Wasan		X	87
Wassail		XX	220
Wild Edibles	☺	XX	259
Wolfgang's		XX	259

X

Restaurant			Page
Xe Lua		X	45
Xixa	☺	X	539

Y

Restaurant			Page
Yakitori Totto		X	313
Yefsi		XX	391
Yerba Buena Perry		XX	183
Yopparai		XX	220
Yunnan Kitchen	☺	XX	221
Yuzu		X	203

Z

Restaurant			Page
Zabb Elee	☺	X	592
Zenkichi		X	540
zero otto nove	☺	XX	431
Zizi Limona	☺	X	540
Zoma	☺	X	203
Zum Stammtisch		X	593
Zutto		X	359
ZZ's Clam Bar	✿	X	185

Restaurants by Cuisine

American

Restaurant			Page
Alobar		XX	551
Applewood		X	485
Barbuto		XX	144
BG		X	273
Black Swan		X	463
Blenheim		XX	145
Blue Hill	✿	XX	146
Boathouse Central Park		XX	365
Bobby Van's		XX	233
Brooklyn Star		XX	518
Buttermilk Channel	☺	X	441
Carol's Cafe		X	603
Casellula		🍽	275
Clinton St. Baking Company		X	210
Clover Club		🍽	443
Colicchio & Sons		XXX	19
Community Food & Juice		XX	193
Cookshop		XX	20
Corner Social		XX	194
Craft		XX	113
Delaware and Hudson	✿	XX	519
Diner	☺	X	520
Dovetail	✿	XX	402
Dutch (The)		XX	325
Egg	☺	X	520
Eli's Table		XX	370
Elizabeth's Neighborhood Table		XX	401
Eugene & Co.		X	467
Farm on Adderley (The)		XX	487
Faro	☺	XX	468
Finch (The)	✿	XX	469
Fort Defiance		X	502
44 & X Hell's Kitchen		XX	281
Four Seasons (The)		XXXX	239
General Greene (The)	☺	X	470
Good		XX	153
Good Enough to Eat		X	404
Gotham Bar and Grill	✿	XXX	154
Harry's Cafe & Steak		XX	92
Hill Country Chicken	☺	X	119
Houseman		XX	328
Jack the Horse		XX	447
James		XX	489
J.G. Melon	☺	X	375
Krupa Grocery		XX	490
Lambs Club (The)		XX	288
Little Beet Table (The)		XX	123
Little Owl (The)		X	162
Little Park		XX	352
Lulu & Po	☺	X	472
Marc Forgione		XX	354
Market Table		XX	164
Mayfield		XX	473
Maysville		XX	125
Minton's		XXX	198
Murray's Cheese Bar		XX	167
New Leaf Café		XX	199
No. 7		XX	474
Norma's		XX	299
Northeast Kingdom		X	474
North End Grill		XXX	95
Northern Spy Food Co.		X	77
Odeon (The)		XX	354
Patroon		XXX	250
Pier A		XX	95
Place (The)		XX	171
Print		XX	304
Prospect		XX	475
Prune	☺	X	79
Red Cat (The)		XX	27
Red Rooster		XX	200
Reynard		XX	532
Ribbon (The)		XX	408
Root & Bone		X	82
Runner (The)		XX	476
Rye	☺	X	534
Schiller's Liquor Bar		XX	218
Speedy Romeo	☺	X	478
St. Anselm		X	538
Telepan	✿	XXX	412
Thelma on Clinton	☺	XX	219

Thistle Hill Tavern		X	495
Tiny's		X	358
Tipsy Parson		XX	30
Trading Post		XX	96
21 Club		XX	311
Union Square Cafe		XX	133
Untitled	☺	XX	181
Vida	☺	X	608
Vinegar Hill House	☺	X	456

Argentinian

Balvanera		X	209
El Almacen		X	521

Asian

Ceetay		X	423
Chop-Shop		X	18
Fung Tu		XX	214
Laut	☺	X	122
Momofuku Noodle Bar	☺	X	73
Purple Yam	☺	X	493
Radiance Tea House		X	304
RedFarm		X	174
Talde		XX	494
Umi NOM	☺	X	478
Zutto		X	359

Austrian

Blaue Gans		XX	346
Cafe Katja		X	209
Cafe Sabarsky		X	367
Café Steinhof		X	486
Edi & The Wolf		X	61
Trestle on Tenth		XX	31
Wallsé	✿	XX	184

Bangladeshi

Neerob		X	428

Barbecue

Arrogant Swine		X	462
Dinosaur Bar-B-Que		X	194
Hill Country		X	118
Hometown Bar-B-Que	☺	X	503
John Brown Smokehouse	☺	X	568
Mighty Quinn's		X	73
Morgan's BBQ		X	492

Belgian

B. Café West		X	398

Brazilian

Malagueta		X	572

Burmese

Café Mingala		X	365
Crazy Crab 888		X	558

Cajun

Bayou		XX	600

Caribbean

Gladys	☺	X	471

Central Asian

Cheburechnaya		X	556
Mtskheta Café		X	505
Nargis Cafe		XX	506
Uma		X	589

Chinese

A-Wah		X	35
Bamboo Garden		X	500
Bao (The)		X	53
Biáng!	☺	X	554
Bo Ky		X	36
Café China	✿	XX	235
Congee Village	☺	X	211
Dim Sum Go Go	☺	X	37
Dumpling Galaxy		X	560
East Harbor Seafood Palace	☺	XX	501
Golden Unicorn		X	37
Grand Harmony		X	38
Great N.Y. Noodletown		X	38
Hakkasan		XXX	283
Happy Family Hotpot		X	562
Hot Kitchen		X	65
Hunan House	☺	X	564

Restaurant	Distinction	Comfort	Page
Hunan Kitchen of Grand Sichuan	Bib	X	565
Imperial Palace		X	567
Joe's Shanghai		X	567
Kung Fu Little Steamed Buns Ramen	Bib	X	287
Land of Plenty	Bib	XX	245
Lan Sheng		X	289
Legend Bar & Restaurant		XX	24
Little Pepper	Bib	X	571
Lucky Eight		X	504
Lu Xiang Yuan		X	571
Main Street Imperial Taiwanese Gourmet		X	572
Mapo Tofu	Bib	X	246
Mr Chow		XX	247
M Shanghai		X	529
Nan Xiang Xiao Long Bao		X	576
Nom Wah Tea Parlor	Bib	X	40
Oriental Garden		X	41
Pacificana		XX	506
Park Asia		XX	507
Peking Duck House		XX	42
Phoenix Garden	Bib	X	251
Royal Seafood		X	43
Shanghai Café	Bib	X	43
Shanghai Heping		XX	44
Shanghai Pavilion		XX	385
Sweet Yummy House	Bib	X	585
Szechuan Gourmet	Bib	X	309
Taiwanese Gourmet		X	585
Tang Pavilion		XX	310
Uncle Zhou	Bib	X	589
Wa Jeal		XX	390
Yunnan Kitchen	Bib	XX	221

Contemporary

Restaurant	Distinction	Comfort	Page
ABC Kitchen		XX	102
Acme		XX	140
Aldo Sohm Wine Bar		small plates	267
Alta		XX	141
Anella		X	516
Ardesia		small plates	268
atera	✿✿	XX	344
Atrium		XX	440
Aureole	✿	XXX	269
Bacchanal		X	35
Barawine		XX	191
Bâtard	✿	XX	345
Battersby		X	440
Betony	✿	XXX	272
Bin 5		XX	601
Blanca	✿✿	XX	464
Blue Ribbon		XX	321
Blue Ribbon Bakery		XX	147
Cafe Cluny		XX	148
Casa del Chef Bistro	Bib	X	556
Caviar Russe	✿	XXX	236
Chefs Club		XXX	323
Chef's Table at Brooklyn Fare	✿✿✿	XX	442
Chevalier		XXX	276
ChikaLicious		small plates	57
Clement		XXX	277
Clocktower (The)		XXX	110
Colonie		XX	443
Contra		XX	212
Cooklyn		XX	486
Craftbar		XX	113
db Bistro Moderne		XX	278
Dear Bushwick		X	466
Do or Dine	Bib	X	466
Dover		XX	444
East Pole		XX	370
Eddy (The)		XX	61
élan		XX	114
Eleven Madison Park	✿✿✿	XXXX	115
Estela		XX	327
Fat Radish (The)		XX	213
Feast		X	62
Fedora		XX	152
Flat Top		X	195
Foragers City Table		XX	24
Gabriel Kreuther	✿	XXX	282
Gander (The)		XX	116
Good Fork (The)	Bib	X	502
Graffiti		small plates	63
Gramercy Tavern	✿	XXX	117
Jean-Georges	✿✿✿	XXXX	405
Joe & MissesDoe		X	67
JoJo		XX	376
Joseph Leonard		X	157
Juni	✿	XXX	242
Juventino		XX	490
Left Bank		XX	160
Luksus at Tørst	✿	XX	526
Mas (farmhouse)		XXX	165

Restaurant			Page
Mercer Kitchen		XX	330
Modern (The)	✿✿	XXX	297
Momofuku Ko	✿✿	XX	74
Momofuku Ssäm Bar	☺	X	75
Musket Room (The)	✿	XX	331
Narcissa		XX	76
NoMad	✿	XX	127
Nougatine		XX	408
Park Avenue		XX	129
Pearl & Ash	☺	XX	332
Pearl Room (The)		XX	507
Perilla		XX	170
Perry Street		XX	171
Per Se	✿✿✿	XXXXX	302
Piora	✿	XX	172
Recette		XX	173
Regency Bar & Grill (The)		XX	384
Resto		X	130
River Café (The)	✿	XXX	452
River Styx		X	533
Roberta's	☺	X	475
Roebling Tea Room		X	533
Rouge et Blanc		XX	336
Rucola		X	453
Runner & Stone	☺	XX	510
Saint Austere (The)		≣	534
Salt & Fat	☺	X	582
Saxon + Parole		XX	175
Semilla	✿	X	537
Simone (The)		XX	386
Standard Grill		XX	178
Stone Park Café		X	493
Take Root	✿	X	455
Tocqueville		XX	132
Traif	☺	X	539
Tribeca Grill		XX	358
Upland		XX	133
Virginia's		XX	87
Vitae		XXX	257

Deli

Restaurant			Page
Barney Greengrass		X	398
Katz's	☺	X	215
Liebman's		X	427
Mile End	☺	X	450
Mill Basin Kosher Delicatessen		X	505
Russ & Daughters Cafe	☺	XX	216
2nd Avenue Deli		X	252

Eastern European

Restaurant			Page
Andre's Café		X	363
Kafana		X	67
Oda House		X	77

Ethiopian

Restaurant			Page
Zoma	☺	X	203

European

Restaurant			Page
Le Cirque		XXXX	245
Prime Meats	☺	XX	451

Filipino

Restaurant			Page
Engeline's		X	560
Payag		X	581
Tito Rad's Grill		XX	587

French

Restaurant			Page
Balthazar		XX	320
Bar Boulud		XX	397
Benoit		XX	271
Bistro SK		X	422
Bistro Vendôme		XX	232
Bouley	✿	XXXX	347
Brasserie 8 1/2		XXX	274
Brasserie Ruhlmann		XX	274
Buvette		X	148
Café Boulud	✿	XXX	366
Cédric		XX	193
Cherche Midi		XX	324
Chez Napoléon		X	276
Daniel	✿✿	XXXXX	369
DBGB Kitchen & Bar	☺	XX	58
Dirty French		XX	213
FP Patisserie		X	373
Jubilee		XX	241
Lafayette		XX	159
La Grenouille		XXX	244
L'Antagoniste		XX	471
Le Fond		X	524
Le Gigot		X	161
Le Philosophe		XX	161
Les Halles		X	122

Maison Harlem		X	197
Maison Kayser		XX	378
Marché du Sud		X	378
Mominette		X	473
Montmartre		XX	25
Orsay		XX	382
Paradou		X	169
Parigot		XX	42
Petit Oven		X	508
Petrossian		XXX	301
Quatorze Bis		XX	383
Racines NY		XX	355
Raoul's		XX	333
Rebelle	✿	XX	335
Wallflower		XX	183

Fusion

annisa		XX	141
Dieci		🍽	59
Fushimi		XX	604
Jolie Cantina		X	448
Lucky Luna		X	525
Má Pêche		XX	293
Miranda		XX	528
Noreetuh		X	76
Public	✿	XX	334
Shalom Japan	☺	X	536
Stanton Social (The)		XX	219
Streetbird Rotisserie	☺	X	201
Tuome		X	86

Gastropub

ABV		X	190
Allswell		X	516
Breslin (The)	✿	X	109
Brinkley's		X	36
Burger & Barrel		XX	322
Jones Wood Foundry		X	376
Marlow & Sons	☺	X	525
Minetta Tavern	✿	X	166
M. Wells Steakhouse	✿	XX	575
Pickle Shack		🍽	508
P.J. Clarke's		X	251
Spitzer's Corner		X	218
Spotted Pig	✿	X	179
Strong Place		X	454
Wassail		XX	220

German

Zum Stammtisch		X	593

Greek

Agnanti		XX	551
Anassa Taverna		XX	230
Bahari estiatorio		X	553
Eliá		XX	501
Estiatorio Milos		XXX	280
Greek (The)		XX	349
Gregory's 26 Corner Taverna	☺	X	561
Kopiaste Taverna		XX	570
Limani		XXX	291
Loi Estiatorio		XX	291
Molyvos		XX	298
MP Taverna		XX	573
Mythos		XX	576
Nerai		XX	248
Periyali		XX	129
Pylos		XX	80
Snack	☺	X	337
Snack EOS		X	307
Taverna Kyclades		X	586
Yefsi		XX	391

Indian

Amma		XX	229
Andaz		X	363
Anjappar		X	104
Awadh		XX	397
Benares		XX	271
Bhatti		X	106
Bukhara Grill		XX	234
Copper Chimney		XX	112
Dosa Garden		X	603
Haldi		X	116
Junoon	✿	XXX	121
Kokum		X	120
Malai Marke		XX	72
Moti Mahal Delux		XX	380
Pippali	☺	XX	130
Samudra		X	583
Saravanaas		X	131
Tamarind		XXX	355
Tamba		X	131
Tulsi	✿	XX	258
Utsav		XX	313

Indonesian

Restaurant		Comfort	Page
Java		X	489
Selamat Pagi		X	536

International

Restaurant		Comfort	Page
ABC Cocina	㊂	XX	102
Cecil (The)		XX	192
Fatty Fish		X	371
Flinders Lane		X	62
Mundo		XX	574

Italian

Restaurant		Comfort	Page
Ai Fiori	✿	XXX	266
Aita		XX	462
Al di Là		X	484
All'onda		XX	140
Angelina's		XX	600
Armani Ristorante		XX	230
Aroma Kitchen & Wine Bar	㊂	X	142
Aurora		X	517
A Voce Madison		XX	105
Babbalucci		X	190
Babbo	✿	XX	143
Bacaro		X	208
Baci & Abbracci	㊂	X	517
Baker & Co.	㊂	XX	142
Barbetta		XXX	268
Bar Corvo		X	463
Bar Primi	㊂	XX	53
Basil Brick Oven Pizza	㊂	XX	554
Becco		XX	270
Beccofino		X	422
Bettolona		X	191
Bianca	㊂	X	145
Bin 71		🍷	399
Bocca		XX	107
Bocelli		XX	602
Bottega del Vino		XX	233
Bread & Tulips	㊂	XX	108
Brucie		X	441
Cacio e Pepe		X	55
Cafe Luna		XX	602
Caffè Storico		XX	401
Caravaggio		XXX	367
Carbone	✿	XX	149
Casa Lever		XXX	234
Casa Nonna		XX	275
Charlie Bird		XX	323
Ciccio	㊂	X	324
Crispo	㊂	XX	150
da Umberto		XX	22
Del Posto	✿	XXXX	23
East 12th Osteria		XX	60
Emilio's Ballato		XX	326
Emporio		XX	327
Enoteca Maria	㊂	X	604
Enoteca on Court		X	444
Enzo's of Arthur Ave		X	424
Felidia		XXX	238
Fitzcarraldo		XX	470
Frankies 457 Spuntino	㊂	X	445
Franny's		XX	488
Gastronomia Culinaria		X	403
Gastroteca		XX	561
Gennaro		XX	404
Gigino at Wagner Park		XX	92
Giorgione		XX	328
Giuliana's		XX	605
Gnocco		X	63
Gradisca		XX	153
Il Bacco		XX	566
Il Buco		X	156
Il Buco Alimentari e Vineria	㊂	XX	156
Il Cortile		XX	39
Il Gattopardo		XX	284
Il Poeta	㊂	XX	566
Il Riccio		XX	374
Il Ristorante Rosi		XXX	374
Il Salumaio		X	375
Inatteso Pizzabar Casano		XX	93
I Sodi		XX	157
I Trulli		XX	119
La Masseria		XX	288
L'Apicio		XX	70
L'Artusi		XX	159
Lavagna		X	70
Lea	㊂	XX	491
Lil' Frankie's	㊂	X	71
Lincoln		XXX	406
Locanda Verde		XX	353
Locanda Vini e Olii		X	472
Louie and Chan		X	215
Lugo		XX	292
Lupa	㊂	XX	162
Lusardi's		XX	377

Restaurant			Page
Maialino		XX	123
Malaparte		X	163
Manzo		XX	124
Mario's		XX	606
Marta		XX	125
Mercato		X	296
Mezzaluna		X	380
Morandi		XX	167
Mozzarella & Vino		XX	298
900 Park		XX	428
Nocciola		XX	199
Noodle Pudding		XX	451
Novitá		XX	126
Obikà		XX	248
Ornella		XX	579
Osteria al Doge		XX	300
Osteria del Circo		XX	301
Osteria Laguna		XX	249
Pagani		XX	168
Parkside		XX	580
Pastai		XX	26
Patricia's		XX	429
Peasant		XX	333
Perla		XX	170
Piccola Venezia		XX	581
Pine Bar & Grill		XX	429
pizzArte		XX	303
Pó		XX	173
Porsena	☺	XX	78
Prova	☺	XX	27
Remi		XXX	305
Risotteria Melotti		XX	81
Ristorante Morini		XXX	384
Roberto's		XX	430
Roman's		X	476
Rubirosa	☺	XX	336
San Matteo	☺	XX	385
Saraghina		X	477
Sauce		X	217
Scarlatto		XX	306
Sessanta		XX	337
Settepani		XX	201
Sociale		XX	453
Spasso		XX	178
Spiga		XX	410
Spigolo		XX	386
Stella 34		XX	308
Supper	☺	XX	84
Tavola		X	310
Tiella		XX	389
Tra Di Noi	☺	X	431
Trattoria L'incontro		XX	588
Trattoria Romana da Vittorio		XX	607
Tre Otto		XX	202
Uva	☺	X	390
Uvarara		X	590
Venturo Osteria & Wine Bar	☺	X	591
Vesta Trattoria		X	591
Via Carota		XX	182
Vics		XX	182
Vinatería		XX	202
zero otto nove	☺	XX	431

Jamaican

Restaurant			Page
Miss Lily's		X	165

Japanese

Restaurant			Page
Aburiya Kinnosuke		XX	228
Bar Masa		XX	270
Blue Ribbon Sushi		XX	321
BONDST		XX	147
Bozu		X	518
Brushstroke	✿	XXX	348
Cagen	✿	XX	56
cocoron		X	211
Curry-Ya		X	57
Daruma-ya Soba		XX	346
Dojo Izakaya		≡	59
Donguri		X	368
EN Japanese Brasserie		XXX	151
15 East		XX	114
Ganso Ramen	☺	X	446
Hakata Tonton		X	155
Hasaki		X	64
Hatsuhana		XX	240
Hibino		X	447
Hide-Chan Ramen	☺	X	240
HinoMaru Ramen	☺	X	563
Hirohisa	✿	XX	329
Ichimura	✿✿	XX	350
Iki Japanese		XX	565
Ivan Ramen		X	214
Jewel Bako	✿	X	66
Jin Ramen	☺	X	196
Jukai		XX	241
Kajitsu	✿	XX	243

Kanoyama		X	68
Katsuno		X	569
Kirakuya		≣	286
Ki Sushi		X	448
Kura		X	68
Kurumazushi		XX	244
Kyo Ya	✿	XX	69
Masa	✿✿✿	XX	295
Momokawa	☺	X	126
Momoya		XX	407
Mu Ramen	☺	X	574
Naka Naka		X	26
Okonomi		X	529
1 or 8		XX	530
Ootoya		XX	128
Rai Rai Ken		X	80
Ramen Misoya		X	81
Ramen Yebisu		X	532
Robataya		XX	82
Rockmeisha		≣	174
Rosanjin	✿	XXX	356
Sakagura		XX	252
SakaMai		XX	217
Sake Bar Hagi		X	306
Salt + Charcoal		X	535
Samurai Mama		X	535
Shuko		XX	176
Sobakoh		X	83
Soba Totto		XX	254
Soba-Ya	☺	XX	84
Soto	✿✿	XX	177
SushiAnn		XX	254
Sushi Azabu	✿	XX	357
Sushi Dojo		X	86
Sushi Katsuei		X	494
Sushi Nakazawa		XX	180
Sushi of Gari	✿	X	387
Sushi Sasabune		X	388
Sushi Seki		X	388
Sushi Yasaka		X	411
Sushi Yasuda	✿	XX	255
Sushi Zen		XX	308
Takashi		X	180
Tanoshi		X	389
Tempura Matsui	✿	XX	256
Tori Shin	✿	XX	312
Tsushima		XX	257
Wasan		X	87
Yakitori Totto		X	313
Yopparai		XX	220
Yuzu		X	203
Zenkichi		X	540

Korean

Cho Dang Gol	☺	X	277
Danji		X	278
Don's Bogam		XX	237
Hahm Ji Bach	☺	XX	562
HanGawi	☺	XX	239
Hanjan		XX	118
Jungsik	✿✿	XXX	351
Kang Ho Dong Baekjeong		XX	569
Kang Suh		XX	285
Kristalbelli		XX	286
Kunjip		X	287
Madangsul		XX	292
Mandoo Bar		X	293
Miss Korea		XX	296
Natural Tofu & Noodles		X	577
New Wonjo		XX	299
Oiji	☺	X	78
Sik Gaek		X	583
Tang		XX	586
Tong Sam Gyup Goo Yi	☺	X	588

Lao

Khe-Yo	☺	XX	349

Latin American

A Casa Fox		XX	208
Brisas del Caribe		X	423
Colonia Verde		XX	465
Cómodo		XX	325
Coppelia	☺	X	20
Havana Café	☺	XX	425
Macondo		XX	216
Marcha Cocina		X	197
Palo Santo		X	492
Tabaré		X	538
Yerba Buena Perry		XX	183

Lebanese

al Bustan	☺	XX	228
Almayass		XX	104
Balade		XX	52

Naya		XX	247

Macanese

Macao Trading Co.		XX	353

Malaysian

Al Seabu		X	484
Malaysian Kitchen		XX	93
New Malaysia	☺	X	40
Nyonya	☺	X	41

Mediterranean

Aldea	✿	XX	103
Balaboosta		XX	320
Barbounia		XX	105
Boulud Sud		XXX	400
Brick Cafe		X	555
Danny Brown Wine Bar & Kitchen		XX	559
Extra Virgin		XX	151
Fig & Olive		XX	372
French Louie		XX	445
Gato		XX	152
Hearth		XX	64
Landmarc		XX	352
Margaux		XX	163
Meadowsweet	✿	XX	527
Mimi's Hummus		☰	491
Picholine	✿	XXX	409
Tessa		XX	411
Vai		XX	413
Zizi Limona	☺	X	540

Mexican

Alma		XX	500
Añejo		X	267
Black Ant (The)		XX	54
Café el Portal		X	322
Cafe El Presidente		X	110
Café Frida		XX	400
Casa Enríque	✿	XX	557
Cascabel Taqueria		X	368
Chavela's	☺	X	465
Cosme		XX	112
Crema		XX	21
De Mole		X	559
El Parador	☺	XX	238
El Paso		X	195
Empellón Taqueria		XX	150
Estrellita Poblana III		X	425
Fonda		X	488
Gran Eléctrica	☺	XX	446
Hecho en Dumbo	☺	X	155
Hell's Kitchen		XX	284
La Esquina		X	39
La Superior		X	524
Maizal		X	606
Maria's Bistro Mexicano		X	504
Maya		XX	379
Maz Mezcal		X	379
Mesa Coyoacán		X	528
Mexicosina	☺	X	427
Noche Mexicana II		X	407
Pachanga Patterson		X	579
Pampano		XX	249
Papatzul		X	332
Rocking Horse Cafe		XX	28
Taqueria Tlaxcalli		X	430
Toloache		XX	311
Xixa	☺	X	539

Middle Eastern

Au Za'atar		X	52
Taboon		XX	309
Tanoreen	☺	XX	511
Wafa		X	592

Moroccan

Café Mogador		X	55

Persian

Persepolis		XX	383

Peruvian

Jora		XX	568
Panca		X	168
Urubamba		X	590
Warique		X	413

Pizza

Co.		X	19
Don Antonio by Starita	☺	XX	279

Forcella		X	522
Houdini Kitchen Laboratory		XX	564
Kesté Pizza & Vino	☺	X	158
Luzzo's		X	71
Motorino		X	75
Nick's		X	381
Nick's Pizza		X	577
Paulie Gee's	☺	X	530
Sottocasa	☺	X	454

Polish

Karczma		X	523
Krolewskie Jadlo		X	523

Portuguese

Lupulo		XX	25
O Lavrador		XX	578

Puerto Rican

El Nuevo Bohío		X	424
Joe's Place		X	426

Russian

Mari Vanna		XX	124
Russian Samovar		XX	305

Scandinavian

Aquavit	✿✿	XXX	231

Seafood

Aquagrill		XX	319
Asian Jewels		XX	552
Atlantic Grill		XX	364
Blue Water Grill		XX	107
Crave Fishbar		XX	237
Cull & Pistol		XX	21
Ed's Lobster Bar	☺	X	326
Esca		XX	280
Fishtag		XX	403
Fishtail by David Burke		XXX	372
Flex Mussels		XX	373
Greenpoint Fish & Lobster Co.		X	522
John Dory Oyster Bar (The)		X	120
Le Bernardin	✿✿✿	XXXX	290
Marea	✿✿	XXX	294
Mar's		X	573
Mary's Fish Camp		X	164
Mermaid Inn (The)		X	72
Navy		X	330
Oceana		XXX	300
O Ya		XX	128
Pearl Oyster Bar		X	169
Sabry's		X	582
Santina		XX	175
Sea Grill (The)		XXX	307
Wild Edibles	☺	XX	259
ZZ's Clam Bar	✿	X	185

Senegalese

J. Restaurant Chez Asta	☺	X	196

South African

Braai		XX	273
Kaia		X	377

Southern

BLVD Bistro		X	192
Elberta	☺	XX	487
Melba's		X	198
Miss Mamie's Spoonbread Too	☺	X	406
SoCo		XX	477

Spanish

Alcala		XX	229
Andanada	✿	XX	396
Barraca		XX	144
Beso		X	601
Boqueria	☺	XX	108
Casa Mono	✿	XX	111
Cata		XX	210
Degustation		XX	58
Donostia	☺	X	60
El Born		XX	521
El Mio Cid		XX	467
El Porrón		X	371
El Quinto Pino		XX	22
Huertas		XX	65

Las Ramblas		🍽	160
La Vara	✿	XX	449
Salinas		XX	28
Sevilla		X	176
Socarrat		XX	29
Tertulia	☺	XX	181
Tía Pol		🍽	29
Toro		XX	30
Txikito		XX	31

Sri Lankan

Lakruwana		X	605
San Rasa	☺	X	607
Sigiri		X	83
Spicy Lanka		X	584

Steakhouse

BLT Prime		XX	106
BLT Steak		XXX	232
Bowery Meat Company		XX	54
Christos		XX	558
Del Frisco's		XXX	279
Frankie & Johnnie's		XX	281
Gallagher's		XX	283
Jake's Steakhouse		XX	426
Keens		XX	285
Le Relais de Venise (L'Entrecôte)		XX	246
MarkJoseph		XX	94
Nebraska Steakhouse		XX	94
Parlor Steakhouse		XX	382
Peter Luger	✿	X	531
Porter House		XXX	303
Prime & Beyond New York		X	79
Ricardo Steakhouse		XX	200
Smith & Wollensky		XX	253
S Prime		XX	584
Wolfgang's		XX	259

Thai

Arharn Thai		X	552
Ayada		X	553
Kao Soy		X	503
Kiin Thai	☺	XX	158
Kitchen 79		X	570
Larb Ubol	☺	X	289
Nuaa (The)		XX	381
Nusara		X	578
Paet Rio	☺	X	580
Pok Pok Ny	✿	X	509
Somtum Der	✿	X	85
Thai Rock		X	587
Uncle Boons	✿	XX	338
Zabb Elee	☺	X	592

Tibetan

Himalayan Yak		X	563

Turkish

Antique Garage		X	319
Beyoglu	☺	X	364
Bodrum		XX	399
Pera		XX	250
Sip Sak		XX	253
Taci's Beyti		XX	510
Turkish Kitchen	☺	XX	132

Vegan

Blossom		XX	18

Vegetarian

Dirt Candy		XX	212

Vietnamese

Bricolage		X	485
bún-ker	☺	X	555
Falansai	☺	X	468
Nightingale 9		X	450
Thái So'n		X	44
Xe Lua		X	45

Cuisines by Neighborhood

MANHATTAN

Chelsea

American
Colicchio & Sons XXX 19
Cookshop XX 20
Red Cat (The) XX 27
Tipsy Parson XX 30

Asian
Chop-Shop X 18

Austrian
Trestle on Tenth XX 31

Chinese
Legend Bar & Restaurant XX 24

Contemporary
Foragers City Table XX 24

French
Montmartre XX 25

Italian
da Umberto XX 22
Del Posto ✿ XXXX 23
Pastai XX 26
Prova ☺ XX 27

Japanese
Naka Naka X 26

Latin American
Coppelia ☺ X 20

Mexican
Crema XX 21
Rocking Horse Cafe XX 28

Pizza
Co. X 19

Portuguese
Lupulo XX 25

Seafood
Cull & Pistol XX 21

Spanish
El Quinto Pino XX 22
Salinas XX 28
Socarrat XX 29
Tía Pol ≣ 29
Toro XX 30
Txikito XX 31

Vegan
Blossom XX 18

Chinatown & Little Italy

Chinese
A-Wah X 35
Bo Ky X 36
Dim Sum Go Go ☺ X 37
Golden Unicorn X 37
Grand Harmony X 38
Great N.Y. Noodletown X 38
Nom Wah Tea Parlor ☺ X 40
Oriental Garden X 41
Peking Duck House XX 42
Royal Seafood X 43
Shanghai Café ☺ X 43
Shanghai Heping XX 44

Contemporary
Bacchanal X 35

French
Parigot XX 42

Gastropub
Brinkley's X 36

Italian
Il Cortile XX 39

Malaysian
New Malaysia ☺ X 40
Nyonya ☺ X 41

Mexican
La Esquina X 39

Vietnamese

Thái Sơn		X	44
Xe Lua		X	45

East Village

American

Northern Spy Food Co.		X	77
Prune	☺	X	79
Root & Bone		X	82

Asian

Momofuku Noodle Bar	☺	X	73

Austrian

Edi & The Wolf		X	61

Barbecue

Mighty Quinn's		X	73

Chinese

Bao (The)		X	53
Hot Kitchen		X	65

Contemporary

ChikaLicious		≣	57
Eddy (The)		XX	61
Feast		X	62
Graffiti		≣	63
Joe & MissesDoe		X	67
Momofuku Ko	✿✿	XX	74
Momofuku Ssäm Bar	☺	X	75
Narcissa		XX	76
Virginia's		XX	87

Eastern European

Kafana		X	67
Oda House		X	77

French

DBGB Kitchen & Bar	☺	XX	58

Fusion

Dieci		≣	59
Noreetuh		X	76
Tuome		X	86

Greek

Pylos		XX	80

Indian

Malai Marke		XX	72

International

Flinders Lane		X	62

Italian

Bar Primi	☺	XX	53
Cacio e Pepe		X	55
East 12th Osteria		XX	60
Gnocco		X	63
L'Apicio		XX	70
Lavagna		X	70
Lil' Frankie's	☺	X	71
Porsena	☺	XX	78
Risotteria Melotti		XX	81
Supper	☺	XX	84

Japanese

Cagen	✿	XX	56
Curry-Ya		X	57
Dojo Izakaya		≣	59
Hasaki		X	64
Jewel Bako	✿	X	66
Kanoyama		X	68
Kura		X	68
Kyo Ya	✿	XX	69
Rai Rai Ken		X	80
Ramen Misoya		X	81
Robataya		XX	82
Sobakoh		X	83
Soba-Ya	☺	XX	84
Sushi Dojo		X	86
Wasan		X	87

Korean

Oiji	☺	X	78

Lebanese

Balade		XX	52

Mediterranean

Hearth		XX	64

Mexican

Black Ant (The)		XX	54

Middle Eastern

Au Za'atar		X	52

Moroccan

Café Mogador		X	55

Pizza

Luzzo's		X	71
Motorino		X	75

Seafood

Mermaid Inn (The)		X	72

Spanish

Degustation		XX	58
Donostia	☺	X	60
Huertas		XX	65

Sri Lankan

Sigiri		X	83

Steakhouse

Bowery Meat Company		XX	54
Prime & Beyond New York		X	79

Thai

Somtum Der	✿	X	85

Financial District

American

Harry's Cafe & Steak		XX	92
North End Grill		XXX	95
Pier A		XX	95
Trading Post		XX	96

Italian

Gigino at Wagner Park		XX	92
Inatteso Pizzabar Casano		XX	93

Malaysian

Malaysian Kitchen		XX	93

Steakhouse

MarkJoseph		XX	94
Nebraska Steakhouse		XX	94

Gramercy, Flatiron & Union Square

American

Craft		XX	113
Hill Country Chicken	☺	X	119
Little Beet Table (The)		XX	123
Maysville		XX	125
Union Square Cafe		XX	133

Asian

Laut	☺	X	122

Barbecue

Hill Country		X	118

Contemporary

ABC Kitchen		XX	102
Clocktower (The)		XXX	110
Craftbar		XX	113
élan		XX	114
Eleven Madison Park	✿✿✿	XXXX	115
Gander (The)		XX	116
Gramercy Tavern	✿	XXX	117
NoMad	✿	XX	127
Park Avenue		XX	129
Resto		X	130
Tocqueville		XX	132
Upland		XX	133

French

Les Halles		X	122

Gastropub

Breslin (The)	✿	X	109

Greek

Periyali		XX	129

Indian

Anjappar		X	104
Bhatti		X	106
Copper Chimney		XX	112
Haldi		X	116
Junoon	✿	XXX	121
Kokum		X	120
Pippali	☺	XX	130
Saravanaas		X	131
Tamba		X	131

International

ABC Cocina	☺	XX	102

Italian

A Voce Madison		XX	105
Bocca		XX	107
Bread & Tulips	☺	XX	108
I Trulli		XX	119
Maialino		XX	123
Manzo		XX	124
Marta		XX	125
Novitá		XX	126

Japanese

15 East		XX	114
Momokawa	☺	X	126
Ootoya		XX	128

Korean

Hanjan		XX	118

Lebanese

Almayass		XX	104

Mediterranean
Aldea ✿ XX 103
Barbounia XX 105

Mexican
Cafe El Presidente X 110
Cosme XX 112

Russian
Mari Vanna XX 124

Seafood
Blue Water Grill XX 107
John Dory Oyster Bar (The) X 120
O Ya XX 128

Spanish
Boqueria ☺ XX 108
Casa Mono ✿ XX 111

Steakhouse
BLT Prime XX 106

Turkish
Turkish Kitchen ☺ XX 132

Greenwich & West Village

American
Barbuto XX 144
Blenheim XX 145
Blue Hill ✿ XX 146
Good XX 153
Gotham Bar and Grill ✿ XXX 154
Little Owl (The) X 162
Market Table XX 164
Murray's Cheese Bar XX 167
Place (The) XX 171
Untitled ☺ XX 181

Asian
RedFarm X 174

Austrian
Wallsé ✿ XX 184

Contemporary
Acme XX 140
Alta XX 141
Blue Ribbon Bakery XX 147
Cafe Cluny XX 148
Fedora XX 152
Joseph Leonard X 157
Left Bank XX 160
Mas (farmhouse) XXX 165
Perilla XX 170
Perry Street XX 171
Piora ✿ XX 172
Recette XX 173
Saxon + Parole XX 175
Standard Grill XX 178

French
Buvette X 148
Lafayette XX 159
Le Gigot X 161
Le Philosophe XX 161
Paradou X 169
Wallflower XX 183

Fusion
annisa XX 141

Gastropub
Minetta Tavern ✿ X 166
Spotted Pig ✿ X 179

Italian
All'onda XX 140
Aroma Kitchen & Wine Bar ☺ X 142
Babbo ✿ XX 143
Baker & Co. ☺ XX 142
Bianca ☺ X 145
Carbone ✿ XX 149
Crispo ☺ XX 150
Gradisca XX 153
Il Buco X 156
Il Buco Alimentari e Vineria ☺ XX 156
I Sodi XX 157
L'Artusi XX 159
Lupa ☺ XX 162
Malaparte X 163
Morandi XX 167
Pagani XX 168
Perla XX 170
Pó XX 173
Spasso XX 178
Via Carota XX 182
Vics XX 182

Jamaican
Miss Lily's X 165

Japanese
BONDST XX 147
EN Japanese Brasserie XxX 151
Hakata Tonton X 155
Rockmeisha ≡ 174
Shuko XX 176
Soto ✿✿ XX 177
Sushi Nakazawa XX 180
Takashi X 180

Latin American
Yerba Buena Perry XX 183

Mediterranean
Extra Virgin XX 151
Gato XX 152
Margaux XX 163

Mexican
Empellón Taqueria XX 150
Hecho en Dumbo ☺ X 155

Peruvian
Panca X 168

Pizza
Kesté Pizza & Vino ☺ X 158

Seafood
Mary's Fish Camp X 164
Pearl Oyster Bar X 169
Santina XX 175
ZZ's Clam Bar ✿ X 185

Spanish
Barraca XX 144
Las Ramblas ≡ 160
Sevilla X 176
Tertulia ☺ XX 181

Thai
Kiin Thai ☺ XX 158

Harlem, Morningside & Washington Heights

American
Community Food & Juice XX 193
Corner Social XX 194
Minton's XxX 198
New Leaf Café XX 199
Red Rooster XX 200

Barbecue
Dinosaur Bar-B-Que X 194

Contemporary
Barawine XX 191
Flat Top X 195

Ethiopian
Zoma ☺ X 203

French
Cédric XX 193
Maison Harlem X 197

Fusion
Streetbird Rotisserie ☺ X 201

Gastropub
ABV X 190

International
Cecil (The) XX 192

Italian
Babbalucci X 190
Bettolona X 191
Nocciola XX 199
Settepani XX 201
Tre Otto XX 202
Vinatería XX 202

Japanese
Jin Ramen ☺ X 196
Yuzu X 203

Latin American
Marcha Cocina X 197

Mexican
El Paso X 195

Senegalese
J. Restaurant Chez Asta ☺ X 196

Southern
BLVD Bistro X 192
Melba's X 198

Steakhouse
Ricardo Steakhouse XX 200

Lower East Side

American
Clinton St. Baking Company X 210
Schiller's Liquor Bar XX 218
Thelma on Clinton ☺ XX 219

Argentinian
Balvanera X 209

Asian
Fung Tu XX 214

Austrian
Cafe Katja X 209

Chinese
Congee Village ☺ X 211
Yunnan Kitchen ☺ XX 221

Contemporary
Contra XX 212
Fat Radish (The) XX 213

Deli
Katz's ☺ X 215
Russ & Daughters Cafe ☺ XX 216

French
Dirty French XX 213

Fusion
Stanton Social (The) XX 219

Gastropub
Spitzer's Corner X 218
Wassail XX 220

Italian
Bacaro X 208
Louie and Chan X 215
Sauce X 217

Japanese
cocoron X 211
Ivan Ramen X 214
SakaMai XX 217
Yopparai XX 220

Latin American
A Casa Fox XX 208
Macondo XX 216

Spanish
Cata XX 210

Vegetarian
Dirt Candy XX 212

Midtown East

American
Bobby Van's XX 233
Four Seasons (The) XXXX 239
Patroon XXX 250

Chinese
Café China ✿ XX 235
Land of Plenty ☺ XX 245
Mapo Tofu ☺ X 246
Mr Chow XX 247
Phoenix Garden ☺ X 251

Contemporary
Caviar Russe ✿ XXX 236
Juni ✿ XXX 242
Vitae XXX 257

Deli
2nd Avenue Deli X 252

European
Le Cirque XXXX 245

French
Bistro Vendôme XX 232
Jubilee XX 241
La Grenouille XXX 244

Gastropub
P.J. Clarke's X 251

Greek
Anassa Taverna XX 230
Nerai XX 248

Indian
Amma XX 229
Bukhara Grill XX 234
Tulsi ✿ XX 258

Italian
Armani Ristorante XX 230
Bottega del Vino XX 233
Casa Lever XXX 234
Felidia XXX 238
Obikà XX 248
Osteria Laguna XX 249

Japanese
Aburiya Kinnosuke XX 228
Hatsuhana XX 240
Hide-Chan Ramen ☺ X 240
Jukai XX 241
Kajitsu ✿ XX 243
Kurumazushi XX 244
Sakagura XX 252
Soba Totto XX 254
SushiAnn XX 254

Sushi Yasuda ✿ XX 255
Tempura Matsui ✿ XX 256
Tsushima XX 257

Korean
Don's Bogam XX 237
HanGawi ☺ XX 239

Lebanese
al Bustan ☺ XX 228
Naya XX 247

Mexican
El Parador ☺ XX 238
Pampano XX 249

Scandinavian
Aquavit ✿✿ XXX 231

Seafood
Crave Fishbar XX 237
Wild Edibles ☺ XX 259

Spanish
Alcala XX 229

Steakhouse
BLT Steak XXX 232
Le Relais de Venise (L'Entrecôte) XX 246
Smith & Wollensky XX 253
Wolfgang's XX 259

Turkish
Pera XX 250
Sip Sak XX 253

Midtown West

American
BG X 273
Casellula ≣ 275
44 & X Hell's Kitchen XX 281
Lambs Club (The) XX 288
Norma's XX 299
Print XX 304
21 Club XX 311

Asian
Radiance Tea House X 304

Chinese
Hakkasan XXX 283
Kung Fu Little Steamed Buns Ramen ☺ X 287
Lan Sheng X 289
Szechuan Gourmet ☺ X 309
Tang Pavilion XX 310

Contemporary
Aldo Sohm Wine Bar ≣ 267
Ardesia ≣ 268
Aureole ✿ XXX 269
Betony ✿ XXX 272
Chevalier XXX 276
Clement XXX 277
db Bistro Moderne XX 278
Gabriel Kreuther ✿ XXX 282
Modern (The) ✿✿ XXX 297
Per Se ✿✿✿ XXXXX 302

French
Benoit XX 271
Brasserie 8 1/2 XXX 274
Brasserie Ruhlmann XX 274
Chez Napoléon X 276
Petrossian XXX 301

Fusion
Má Pêche XX 293

Greek
Estiatorio Milos XXX 280
Limani XXX 291
Loi Estiatorio XX 291
Molyvos XX 298
Snack EOS X 307

Indian
Benares XX 271
Utsav XX 313

Italian
Ai Fiori ✿ XXX 266
Barbetta XXX 268
Becco XX 270
Casa Nonna XX 275
Il Gattopardo XX 284
La Masseria XX 288
Lugo XX 292
Mercato X 296
Mozzarella & Vino XX 298
Osteria al Doge XX 300
Osteria del Circo XX 301
pizzArte XX 303

Remi XXX 305
Scarlatto XX 306
Stella 34 XX 308
Tavola X 310

Japanese

Bar Masa XX 270
Kirakuya 🍶 286
Masa ✿✿✿ XX 295
Sake Bar Hagi X 306
Sushi Zen XX 308
Tori Shin ✿ XX 312
Yakitori Totto X 313

Korean

Cho Dang Gol ㊂ X 277
Danji X 278
Kang Suh XX 285
Kristalbelli XX 286
Kunjip X 287
Madangsui XX 292
Mandoo Bar X 293
Miss Korea XX 296
New Wonjo XX 299

Mexican

Añejo X 267
Hell's Kitchen XX 284
Toloache XX 311

Middle Eastern

Taboon XX 309

Pizza

Don Antonio by Starita ㊂ XX 279

Russian

Russian Samovar XX 305

Seafood

Esca XX 280
Le Bernardin ✿✿✿ XXXX 290
Marea ✿✿ XXX 294
Oceana XXX 300
Sea Grill (The) XXX 307

South African

Braai XX 273

Steakhouse

Del Frisco's XXX 279
Frankie & Johnnie's XX 281
Gallagher's XX 283
Keens XX 285
Porter House XXX 303

Thai

Larb Ubol ㊂ X 289

SoHo & Nolita

American

Dutch (The) XX 325
Houseman XX 328

Contemporary

Blue Ribbon XX 321
Chefs Club XXX 323
Estela XX 327
Mercer Kitchen XX 330
Musket Room (The) ✿ XX 331
Pearl & Ash ㊂ XX 332
Rouge et Blanc XX 336

French

Balthazar XX 320
Cherche Midi XX 324
Raoul's XX 333
Rebelle ✿ XX 335

Fusion

Public ✿ XX 334

Gastropub

Burger & Barrel XX 322

Greek

Snack ㊂ X 337

Italian

Charlie Bird XX 323
Ciccio ㊂ X 324
Emilio's Ballato XX 326
Emporio XX 327
Giorgione XX 328
Peasant XX 333
Rubirosa ㊂ XX 336
Sessanta XX 337

Japanese

Blue Ribbon Sushi XX 321
Hirohisa ✿ XX 329

Latin American

Cómodo XX 325

Mediterranean

Balaboosta XX 320

Mexican

Restaurant		Comfort	Page
Café el Portal		X	322
Papatzul		X	332

Seafood

Restaurant		Comfort	Page
Aquagrill		XX	319
Ed's Lobster Bar	☺	X	326
Navy		X	330

Thai

Restaurant		Comfort	Page
Uncle Boons	✿	XX	338

Turkish

Restaurant		Comfort	Page
Antique Garage		X	319

TriBeCa

American

Restaurant		Comfort	Page
Little Park		XX	352
Marc Forgione		XX	354
Odeon (The)		XX	354
Tiny's		X	358

Asian

Restaurant		Comfort	Page
Zutto		X	359

Austrian

Restaurant		Comfort	Page
Blaue Gans		XX	346

Contemporary

Restaurant		Comfort	Page
atera	✿✿	XX	344
Bâtard	✿	XX	345
Tribeca Grill		XX	358

French

Restaurant		Comfort	Page
Bouley	✿	XXXX	347
Racines NY		XX	355

Greek

Restaurant		Comfort	Page
Greek (The)		XX	349

Indian

Restaurant		Comfort	Page
Tamarind		XXX	355

Italian

Restaurant		Comfort	Page
Locanda Verde		XX	353

Japanese

Restaurant		Comfort	Page
Brushstroke	✿	XXX	348
Daruma-ya Soba		XX	346
Ichimura	✿✿	XX	350
Rosanjin	✿	XXX	356
Sushi Azabu	✿	XX	357

Korean

Restaurant		Comfort	Page
Jungsik	✿✿	XXX	351

Lao

Restaurant		Comfort	Page
Khe-Yo	☺	XX	349

Macanese

Restaurant		Comfort	Page
Macao Trading Co.		XX	353

Mediterranean

Restaurant		Comfort	Page
Landmarc		XX	352

Upper East Side

American

Restaurant		Comfort	Page
Boathouse Central Park		XX	365
Eli's Table		XX	370
J.G. Melon	☺	X	375

Austrian

Restaurant		Comfort	Page
Cafe Sabarsky		X	367

Burmese

Restaurant		Comfort	Page
Café Mingala		X	365

Chinese

Restaurant		Comfort	Page
Shanghai Pavilion		XX	385
Wa Jeal		XX	390

Contemporary

Restaurant		Comfort	Page
East Pole		XX	370
JoJo		XX	376
Regency Bar & Grill (The)		XX	384
Simone (The)		XX	386

Eastern European

Restaurant		Comfort	Page
Andre's Café		X	363

French

Restaurant		Comfort	Page
Café Boulud	✿	XXX	366
Daniel	✿✿	XXXXX	369
FP Patisserie		X	373
Maison Kayser		XX	378
Marché du Sud		X	378
Orsay		XX	382
Quatorze Bis		XX	383

Gastropub

Restaurant		Comfort	Page
Jones Wood Foundry		X	376

Greek

Restaurant		Comfort	Page
Yefsi		XX	391

Indian

Restaurant		Comfort	Page
Andaz		X	363
Moti Mahal Delux		XX	380

International

Restaurant		Comfort	Page
Fatty Fish		X	371

Italian
Caravaggio XXX 367
Il Riccio XX 374
Il Ristorante Rosi XXX 374
Il Salumaio X 375
Lusardi's XX 377
Mezzaluna X 380
Ristorante Morini XXX 384
San Matteo (Bib) XX 385
Spigolo XX 386
Tiella XX 389
Uva (Bib) X 390

Japanese
Donguri X 368
Sushi of Gari ✿ X 387
Sushi Sasabune X 388
Sushi Seki X 388
Tanoshi X 389

Mediterranean
Fig & Olive XX 372

Mexican
Cascabel Taqueria X 368
Maya XX 379
Maz Mezcal X 379

Persian
Persepolis XX 383

Pizza
Nick's X 381

Seafood
Atlantic Grill XX 364
Fishtail by David Burke XXX 372
Flex Mussels XX 373

South African
Kaia X 377

Spanish
El Porrón X 371

Steakhouse
Parlor Steakhouse XX 382

Thai
Nuaa (The) XX 381

Turkish
Beyoglu (Bib) X 364

Upper West Side

American
Dovetail ✿ XX 402
Elizabeth's Neighborhood Table XX 401
Good Enough to Eat X 404
Ribbon (The) XX 408
Telepan ✿ XXX 412

Belgian
B. Café West X 398

Contemporary
Jean-Georges ✿✿✿ XXXX 405
Nougatine XX 408

Deli
Barney Greengrass X 398

French
Bar Boulud XX 397

Indian
Awadh XX 397

Italian
Bin 71 (Wine bar) 399
Caffè Storico XX 401
Gastronomia Culinaria X 403
Gennaro XX 404
Lincoln XXX 406
Spiga XX 410

Japanese
Momoya XX 407
Sushi Yasaka X 411

Mediterranean
Boulud Sud XXX 400
Picholine ✿ XXX 409
Tessa XX 411
Vai XX 413

Mexican
Café Frida XX 400
Noche Mexicana II X 407

Peruvian
Warique X 413

Seafood
Fishtag XX 403

Southern
Miss Mamie's Spoonbread Too (Bib) X 406

Spanish
Andanada ✿ XX 396

Turkish
Bodrum XX 399

THE BRONX

Asian
Ceetay X 423

Bangladeshi
Neerob X 428

Deli
Liebman's X 427

French
Bistro SK X 422

Italian
Beccofino X 422
Enzo's of Arthur Ave X 424
900 Park XX 428
Patricia's XX 429
Pine Bar & Grill XX 429
Roberto's XX 430
Tra Di Noi ☺ X 431
zero otto nove ☺ XX 431

Latin American
Brisas del Caribe X 423
Havana Café ☺ XX 425

Mexican
Estrellita Poblana III X 425
Mexicosina ☺ X 427
Taqueria Tlaxcalli X 430

Puerto Rican
El Nuevo Bohío X 424
Joe's Place X 426

Steakhouse
Jake's Steakhouse XX 426

BROOKLYN

Downtown

American
Buttermilk Channel ☺ X 441
Clover Club ≡ 443
Jack the Horse XX 447
Vinegar Hill House ☺ X 456

Contemporary
Atrium XX 440
Battersby X 440
Chef's Table at Brooklyn Fare ✿✿✿ XX 442
Colonie XX 443
Dover XX 444
River Café (The) ✿ XXX 452
Rucola X 453
Take Root ✿ X 455

Deli
Mile End ☺ X 450

European
Prime Meats ☺ XX 451

Fusion
Jolie Cantina X 448

Gastropub
Strong Place X 454

Italian
Brucie X 441
Enoteca on Court X 444
Frankies 457 Spuntino ☺ X 445
Noodle Pudding XX 451
Sociale XX 453

Japanese
Ganso Ramen ☺ X 446
Hibino X 447
Ki Sushi X 448

Mediterranean
French Louie XX 445

Mexican
Gran Eléctrica ☺ XX 446

Pizza
Sottocasa ☺ X 454

Spanish
La Vara ✿ XX 449

Vietnamese
Nightingale 9 X 450

Fort Greene & Bushwick

American

Restaurant			Page
Black Swan		X	463
Eugene & Co.		X	467
Faro	Bib	XX	468
Finch (The)	✿	XX	469
General Greene (The)	Bib	X	470
Lulu & Po	Bib	X	472
Mayfield		XX	473
No. 7		XX	474
Northeast Kingdom		X	474
Prospect		XX	475
Runner (The)		XX	476
Speedy Romeo	Bib	X	478

Asian

Restaurant			Page
Umi NOM	Bib	X	478

Barbecue

Restaurant			Page
Arrogant Swine		X	462

Caribbean

Restaurant			Page
Gladys	Bib	X	471

Contemporary

Restaurant			Page
Blanca	✿✿	XX	464
Dear Bushwick		X	466
Do or Dine	Bib	X	466
Roberta's	Bib	X	475

French

Restaurant			Page
L'Antagoniste		XX	471
Mominette		X	473

Italian

Restaurant			Page
Aita		XX	462
Bar Corvo		X	463
Fitzcarraldo		XX	470
Locanda Vini e Olii		X	472
Roman's		X	476
Saraghina		X	477

Latin American

Restaurant			Page
Colonia Verde		XX	465

Mexican

Restaurant			Page
Chavela's	Bib	X	465

Southern

Restaurant			Page
SoCo		XX	477

Spanish

Restaurant			Page
El Mio Cid		XX	467

Vietnamese

Restaurant			Page
Falansai	Bib	X	468

Park Slope

American

Restaurant			Page
Applewood		X	485
Farm on Adderley (The)		XX	487
James		XX	489
Krupa Grocery		XX	490
Thistle Hill Tavern		X	495

Asian

Restaurant			Page
Purple Yam	Bib	X	493
Talde		XX	494

Austrian

Restaurant			Page
Café Steinhof		X	486

Barbecue

Restaurant			Page
Morgan's BBQ		X	492

Contemporary

Restaurant			Page
Cooklyn		XX	486
Juventino		XX	490
Stone Park Cafe		X	493

Indonesian

Restaurant			Page
Java		X	489

Italian

Restaurant			Page
Al di Là		X	484
Franny's		XX	488
Lea	Bib	XX	491

Japanese

Restaurant			Page
Sushi Katsuei		X	494

Latin American

Restaurant			Page
Palo Santo		X	492

Malaysian

Restaurant			Page
Al Seabu		X	484

Mediterranean

Restaurant			Page
Mimi's Hummus		[small plates]	491

Mexican

Restaurant			Page
Fonda		X	488

Southern

Restaurant			Page
Elberta	Bib	XX	487

Vietnamese

Restaurant			Page
Bricolage		X	485

Sunset Park & Brighton Beach

American
Fort Defiance X 502

Barbecue
Hometown Bar-B-Que ☺ X 503

Central Asian
Mtskheta Café X 505
Nargis Cafe XX 506

Chinese
Bamboo Garden X 500
East Harbor Seafood Palace ☺ XX 501
Lucky Eight X 504
Pacificana XX 506
Park Asia XX 507

Contemporary
Good Fork (The) ☺ X 502
Pearl Room (The) XX 507
Runner & Stone ☺ XX 510

Deli
Mill Basin Kosher Delicatessen X 505

French
Petit Oven X 508

Gastropub
Pickle Shack ≣ 508

Greek
Eliá XX 501

Mexican
Alma XX 500
Maria's Bistro Mexicano X 504

Middle Eastern
Tanoreen ☺ XX 511

Thai
Kao Soy X 503
Pok Pok Ny ✿ X 509

Turkish
Taci's Beyti XX 510

Williamsburg

American
Brooklyn Star XX 518
Delaware and Hudson ✿ XX 519
Diner ☺ X 520
Egg ☺ X 520
Reynard XX 532
Rye ☺ X 534
St. Anselm X 538

Argentinian
El Almacen X 521

Chinese
M Shanghai X 529

Contemporary
Anella X 516
Luksus at Tørst ✿ XX 526
River Styx X 533
Roebling Tea Room X 533
Saint Austere (The) ≣ 534
Semilla ✿ X 537
Traif ☺ X 539

French
Le Fond X 524

Fusion
Lucky Luna X 525
Miranda XX 528
Shalom Japan ☺ X 536

Gastropub
Allswell X 516
Marlow & Sons ☺ X 525

Indonesian
Selamat Pagi X 536

Italian
Aurora X 517
Baci & Abbracci ☺ X 517

Japanese
Bozu X 518
Okonomi X 529
1 or 8 XX 530
Ramen Yebisu X 532
Salt + Charcoal X 535
Samurai Mama X 535
Zenkichi X 540

Latin American
Tabaré X 538

Mediterranean
Meadowsweet ✿ XX 527

Zizi Limona ☺ X 540

Mexican

La Superior X 524
Mesa Coyoacán X 528
Xixa ☺ X 539

Pizza

Forcella X 522
Paulie Gee's ☺ X 530

Polish

Karczma X 523
Krolewskie Jadlo X 523

Seafood

Greenpoint Fish & Lobster Co. X 522

Spanish

El Born XX 521

Steakhouse

Peter Luger ✿ X 531

QUEENS

American

Alobar XX 551

Barbecue

John Brown Smokehouse ☺ X 568

Brazilian

Malagueta X 572

Burmese

Crazy Crab 888 X 558

Central Asian

Cheburechnaya X 556
Uma X 589

Chinese

Biáng! ☺ X 554
Dumpling Galaxy X 560
Happy Family Hotpot X 562
Hunan House ☺ X 564
Hunan Kitchen of Grand Sichuan ☺ X 565
Imperial Palace X 567
Joe's Shanghai X 567
Little Pepper ☺ X 571
Lu Xiang Yuan X 571
Main Street Imperial Taiwanese Gourmet X 572
Nan Xiang Xiao Long Bao X 576
Sweet Yummy House ☺ X 585
Taiwanese Gourmet X 585
Uncle Zhou ☺ X 589

Contemporary

Casa del Chef Bistro ☺ X 556
Salt & Fat ☺ X 582

Filipino

Engeline's X 560
Payag X 581
Tito Rad's Grill XX 587

Gastropub

M. Wells Steakhouse ✿ XX 575

German

Zum Stammtisch X 593

Greek

Agnanti XX 551
Bahari estiatorio X 553
Gregory's 26 Corner Taverna ☺ X 561
Kopiaste Taverna XX 570
MP Taverna XX 573
Mythos XX 576
Taverna Kyclades X 586

Indian

Samudra X 583

International

Mundo XX 574

Italian

Basil Brick Oven Pizza ☺ XX 554
Gastroteca XX 561
Il Bacco XX 566
Il Poeta ☺ XX 566
Ornella XX 579
Parkside XX 580
Piccola Venezia XX 581
Trattoria L'incontro XX 588
Uvarara X 590
Venturo Osteria & Wine Bar ☺ X 591
Vesta Trattoria X 591

Japanese

HinoMaru Ramen ☺ X 563
Iki Japanese XX 565
Katsuno X 569

Mu Ramen ☺ X 574

Korean
Hahm Ji Bach ☺ XX 562
Kang Ho Dong Baekjeong XX 569
Natural Tofu & Noodles X 577
Sik Gaek X 583
Tang XX 586
Tong Sam Gyup Goo Yi ☺ X 588

Mediterranean
Brick Cafe X 555
Danny Brown Wine Bar & Kitchen XX 559

Mexican
Casa Enríque ✿ XX 557
De Mole X 559
Pachanga Patterson X 579

Middle Eastern
Wafa X 592

Peruvian
Jora XX 568
Urubamba X 590

Pizza
Houdini Kitchen Laboratory XX 564
Nick's Pizza X 577

Portuguese
O Lavrador XX 578

Seafood
Asian Jewels XX 552
Mar's X 573
Sabry's X 582

Sri Lankan
Spicy Lanka X 584

Steakhouse
Christos XX 558
S Prime XX 584

Thai
Arharn Thai X 552
Ayada X 553
Kitchen 79 X 570
Nusara X 578
Paet Rio ☺ X 580
Thai Rock X 587
Zabb Elee ☺ X 592

Tibetan
Himalayan Yak X 563

Vietnamese
bún-ker ☺ X 555

Staten Island

American
Carol's Cafe X 603
Vida ☺ X 608

Cajun
Bayou XX 600

Contemporary
Bin 5 XX 601

Fusion
FushImI XX 604

Indian
Dosa Garden X 603

Italian
Angelina's XX 600
Bocelli XX 602
Cafe Luna XX 602
Enoteca Maria ☺ X 604
Giuliana's XX 605
Mario's XX 606
Trattoria Romana da Vittorio XX 607

Mexican
Maizal X 606

Spanish
Beso X 601

Sri Lankan
Lakruwana X 605
San Rasa ☺ X 607

Starred Restaurants

Within the selection we offer you, some restaurants deserve to be highlighted for their particularly good cuisine. When giving one, two, or three Michelin stars, there are a number of elements that we consider including the quality of the ingredients, the technical skill and flair that goes into their preparation, the blend and clarity of flavours, and the balance of the menu. Just as important is the ability to produce excellent cooking time and again. We make as many visits as we need, so that our readers may be assured of quality and consistency.

A two or three-star restaurant has to offer something very special in its cuisine; a real element of creativity, originality, or "personality" that sets it apart from the rest. Three stars – our highest award – are given to the choicest restaurants, where the whole dining experience is superb.

Cuisine in any style, modern or traditional, may be eligible for a star. Due to the fact we apply the same independent standards everywhere, the awards have become benchmarks of reliability and excellence in over 20 countries in Europe and Asia, particularly in France, where we have awarded stars for 100 years, and where the phrase "Now that's real three-star quality!" has entered into the language.

The awarding of a star is based solely on the quality of the cuisine.

✿✿✿

Exceptional cuisine, worth a special journey

One always eats here extremely well, sometimes superbly. Distinctive dishes are precisely executed, using superlative ingredients.

Restaurant	Comfort	Page
Chef's Table at Brooklyn Fare	XX	442
Eleven Madison Park	XXXX	115
Jean-Georges	XXXX	405
Le Bernardin	XXXX	290
Masa	XX	295
Per Se	XXXXX	302

✿✿

Excellent cuisine, worth a detour

Skillfully and carefully crafted dishes of outstanding quality.

Restaurant	Comfort	Page
Aquavit	XXX	231
atera	XX	344
Blanca	XX	464
Daniel	XXXXX	369
Ichimura	XX	350
Jungsik	XXX	351
Marea	XXX	294
Modern (The)	XXX	297
Momofuku Ko	XX	74
Soto	XX	177

A very good restaurant in its category

A place offering cuisine prepared to a consistently high standard.

Restaurant	Comfort	Page
Ai Fiori	XXX	266
Aldea	XX	103
Andanada	XX	396
Aureole	XXX	269
Babbo	XX	143
Bâtard	XX	345
Betony	XXX	272
Blue Hill	XX	146
Bouley	XXXX	347
Breslin (The)	X	109
Brushstroke	XXX	348
Café Boulud	XXX	366
Café China	XX	235
Cagen	XX	56
Carbone	XX	149
Casa Enríque	XX	557
Casa Mono	XX	111
Caviar Russe	XXX	236
Delaware and Hudson	XX	519
Del Posto	XXXX	23
Dovetail	XX	402
Finch (The)	XX	469
Gabriel Kreuther	XXX	282
Gotham Bar and Grill	XXX	154
Gramercy Tavern	XXX	117
Hirohisa	XX	329
Jewel Bako	X	66
Juni	XXX	242
Junoon	XXX	121
Kajitsu	XX	243

Restaurant	Comfort	Page
Kyo Ya	XX	69
La Vara	XX	449
Luksus at Tørst	XX	526
Meadowsweet	XX	527
Minetta Tavern	X	166
Musket Room (The)	XX	331
M. Wells Steakhouse	XX	575
NoMad	XX	127
Peter Luger	X	531
Picholine	XXX	409
Piora	XX	172
Pok Pok Ny	X	509
Public	XX	334
Rebelle	XX	335
River Café (The)	XXX	452
Rosanjin	XXX	356
Semilla	X	537
Somtum Der	X	85
Spotted Pig	X	179
Sushi Azabu	XX	357
Sushi of Gari	X	387
Sushi Yasuda	XX	255
Take Root	X	455
Telepan	XXX	412
Tempura Matsui	XX	256
Tori Shin	XX	312
Tulsi	XX	258
Uncle Boons	XX	338
Wallsé	XX	184
ZZ's Clam Bar	X	185

Bib Gourmand

This symbol indicates our inspectors' favorites for good value. For $40 or less, you can enjoy two courses and a glass of wine or a dessert (not including tax or gratuity).

ABC Cocina	XX	102
al Bustan	XX	228
Aroma Kitchen & Wine Bar	X	142
Baci & Abbracci	X	517
Baker & Co.	XX	142
Bar Primi	XX	53
Basil Brick Oven Pizza	XX	554
Beyoglu	X	364
Bianca	X	145
Biáng!	X	554
Boqueria	XX	108
Bread & Tulips	XX	108
bún-ker	X	555
Buttermilk Channel	X	441
Casa del Chef Bistro	X	556
Chavela's	X	465
Cho Dang Gol	X	277
Ciccio	X	324
Congee Village	X	211
Coppelia	X	20
Crispo	XX	150
DBGB Kitchen & Bar	XX	58
Dim Sum Go Go	X	37
Diner	X	520
Don Antonio by Starita	XX	279
Donostia	X	60
Do or Dine	X	466
East Harbor Seafood Palace	XX	501
Ed's Lobster Bar	X	326
Egg	X	520
Elberta	XX	487
El Parador	XX	238
Enoteca Maria	X	604
Falansai	X	468
Faro	XX	468
Frankies 457 Spuntino	X	445
Ganso Ramen	X	446
General Greene (The)	X	470
Gladys	X	471
Good Fork (The)	X	502
Gran Eléctrica	XX	446
Gregory's 26 Corner Taverna	X	561
Hahm Ji Bach	XX	562
HanGawi	XX	239
Havana Café	XX	425
Hecho en Dumbo	X	155
Hide-Chan Ramen	X	240
Hill Country Chicken	X	119
HinoMaru Ramen	X	563
Hometown Bar-B-Que	X	503
Hunan House	X	564
Hunan Kitchen of Grand Sichuan	X	565
Il Buco Alimentari e Vineria	XX	156
Il Poeta	XX	566
J.G. Melon	X	375
Jin Ramen	X	196
John Brown Smokehouse	X	568
J. Restaurant Chez Asta	X	196
Katz's	X	215
Kesté Pizza & Vino	X	158
Khe-Yo	XX	349
Kiin Thai	XX	158
Kung Fu Little Steamed Buns Ramen	X	287
Land of Plenty	XX	245
Larb Ubol	X	289
Laut	X	122
Lea	XX	491
Lil' Frankie's	X	71
Little Pepper	X	571
Lulu & Po	X	472
Lupa	XX	162
Mapo Tofu	X	246
Marlow & Sons	X	525
Mexicosina	X	427

Name	Comfort	Page
Mile End	X	450
Miss Mamie's Spoonbread Too	X	406
Momofuku Noodle Bar	X	73
Momofuku Ssäm Bar	X	75
Momokawa	X	126
Mu Ramen	X	574
New Malaysia	X	40
Nom Wah Tea Parlor	X	40
Nyonya	X	41
Oiji	X	78
Paet Rio	X	580
Paulie Gee's	X	530
Pearl & Ash	XX	332
Phoenix Garden	X	251
Pippali	XX	130
Porsena	XX	78
Prime Meats	XX	451
Prova	XX	27
Prune	X	79
Purple Yam	X	493
Roberta's	X	475
Rubirosa	XX	336
Runner & Stone	XX	510
Russ & Daughters Cafe	XX	216
Rye	X	534
Salt & Fat	X	582
San Matteo	XX	385
San Rasa	X	607
Shalom Japan	X	536
Shanghai Café	X	43
Snack	X	337
Soba-Ya	XX	84
Sottocasa	X	454
Speedy Romeo	X	478
Streetbird Rotisserie	X	201
Supper	XX	84
Sweet Yummy House	X	585
Szechuan Gourmet	X	309
Tanoreen	XX	511
Tertulia	XX	181
Thelma on Clinton	XX	219
Tong Sam Gyup Goo Yi	X	588
Tra Di Noi	X	431
Traif	X	539
Turkish Kitchen	XX	132
Umi NOM	X	478
Uncle Zhou	X	589
Untitled	XX	181
Uva	X	390
Venturo Osteria & Wine Bar	X	591
Vida	X	608
Vinegar Hill House	X	456
Wild Edibles	XX	259
Xixa	X	539
Yunnan Kitchen	XX	221
Zabb Elee	X	592
zero otto nove	XX	431
Zizi Limona	X	540
Zoma	X	203

Under $25

Restaurant	Page
Al Seabu	484
Andre's Café	363
Arharn Thai	552
Arrogant Swine	462
A-Wah	35
Balade	52
Bamboo Garden	500
Barney Greengrass	398
Bhatti	106
Bo Ky	36
Bozu	518
Brisas del Caribe	423
bún-ker	555
Café el Portal	322
Cafe El Presidente	110
Café Mingala	365
Café Mogador	55
Café Steinhof	486
Cascabel Taqueria	368
Chavela's	465
Cheburechnaya	556
ChikaLicious	57
Cho Dang Gol	277
Clinton St. Baking Company	210
cocoron	211
Congee Village	211
Curry-Ya	57
De Mole	559
Dojo Izakaya	59
Donostia	60
Dosa Garden	603
Dumpling Galaxy	560
Egg	520
El Nuevo Bohío	424
Engeline's	560
Enoteca on Court	444
Estrellita Poblana III	425
Forcella	522
Ganso Ramen	446
Grand Harmony	38
Great N.Y. Noodletown	38
Happy Family Hotpot	562
Hibino	447
Hide-Chan Ramen	240
Hill Country Chicken	119
Houdini Kitchen Laboratory	564
Hunan House	564
Hunan Kitchen of Grand Sichuan	565
Il Salumaio	375
Java	489
J.G. Melon	375
Jin Ramen	196
J. Restaurant Chez Asta	196
Kao Soy	503
Karczma	523
Katz's	215
Kesté Pizza & Vino	158
Kitchen 79	570
Krolewskie Jadlo	523
Kung Fu Little Steamed Buns Ramen	287
Kunjip	287
Lakruwana	605
Larb Ubol	289
Las Ramblas	160
La Superior	524
Legend Bar & Restaurant	24
Liebman's	427
Lil' Frankie's	71
Little Pepper	571
Lucky Eight	504
Lucky Luna	525
Lu Xiang Yuan	571
Main Street Imperial Taiwanese Gourmet	572
Mandoo Bar	293
Mapo Tofu	246
Mexicosina	427
Mighty Quinn's	73
Mile End	450
Mimi's Hummus	491

Restaurant		Page
Miss Mamie's Spoonbread Too	X	406
Motorino	X	75
M Shanghai	X	529
Mtskheta Café	X	505
Nan Xiang Xiao Long Bao	X	576
Neerob	X	428
New Malaysia	X	40
Nick's	X	381
Nick's Pizza	X	577
Noche Mexicana II	X	407
Nom Wah Tea Parlor	X	40
Okonomi	X	529
Paet Rio	X	580
Park Asia	XX	507
Paulie Gee's	X	530
Pickle Shack		508
Rai Rai Ken	X	80
Ramen Misoya	X	81
Ramen Yebisu	X	532
Rockmeisha		174
Royal Seafood	X	43
Saint Austere (The)		534
Sake Bar Hagi	X	306
Samudra	X	583
Samurai Mama	X	535
San Matteo	XX	385
San Rasa	X	607
Saravanaas	X	131
Sauce	X	217
2nd Avenue Deli	X	252
Selamat Pagi	X	536
Shanghai Café	X	43
Sigiri	X	83
Snack	X	337
Sobakoh	X	83
Soba-Ya	XX	84
Spicy Lanka	X	584
Taiwanese Gourmet	X	585
Taqueria Tlaxcalli	X	430
Taverna Kyclades	X	586
Thái Sơn	X	44
Tía Pol		29
Tito Rad's Grill	XX	587
Uncle Zhou	X	589
Xe Lua	X	45
Zabb Elee	X	592
Zoma	X	203

Brunch

Restaurant			Page
ABC Cocina	☺	XX	102
ABC Kitchen		XX	102
ABV		X	190
Acme		XX	140
Aita		XX	462
Al di Là		X	484
All'onda		XX	140
Allswell		X	516
Alma		XX	500
Alobar		XX	551
Anassa Taverna		XX	230
Andanada	✿	XX	396
Añejo		X	267
Anella		X	516
Antique Garage		X	319
Applewood		X	485
Aquagrill		XX	319
Armani Ristorante		XX	230
Aroma Kitchen & Wine Bar	☺	X	142
Atlantic Grill		XX	364
Atrium		XX	440
Aurora		X	517
Au Za'atar		X	52
Bacchanal		X	35
Baci & Abbracci	☺	X	517
Baker & Co.	☺	XX	142
Balaboosta		XX	320
Balade		XX	52
Balthazar		XX	320
Balvanera		X	209
Barawine		XX	191
Bar Boulud		XX	397
Barbounia		XX	105
Barbuto		XX	144
Bar Corvo		X	463
Bar Primi	☺	XX	53
Barraca		XX	144
Bayou		XX	600
B. Café West		X	398
Benoit		XX	271
Beso		X	601
Bettolona		X	191
Bin 71		🍷	399
Bistro SK		X	422
Bistro Vendôme		XX	232
Black Ant (The)		XX	54
Black Swan		X	463
Blaue Gans		XX	346
Blenheim		XX	145
Blue Ribbon Bakery		XX	147
Blue Water Grill		XX	107
BLVD Bistro		X	192
Boathouse Central Park		XX	365
Bodrum		XX	399
Boqueria	☺	XX	108
Bottega del Vino		XX	233
Boulud Sud		XXX	400
Braai		XX	273
Brasserie 8 1/2		XXX	274
Brasserie Ruhlmann		XX	274
Breslin (The)	✿	X	109
Brick Cafe		X	555
Brinkley's		X	36
Brooklyn Star		XX	518
Brucie		X	441
Burger & Barrel		XX	322
Buttermilk Channel	☺	X	441
Buvette		X	148
Café Boulud	✿	XXX	366
Cafe Cluny		XX	148
Café Frida		XX	400
Cafe Katja		X	209
Café Mogador		X	55
Café Steinhof		X	486
Caffè Storico		XX	401
Casa Enríque	✿	XX	557
Cascabel Taqueria		X	368
Cecil (The)		XX	192
Cédric		XX	193
Chavela's	☺	X	465
Chefs Club		XXX	323
Cherche Midi		XX	324
Ciccio	☺	X	324
Clement		XXX	277

Restaurant	Distinction	Comfort	Page
Clinton St. Baking Company		X	210
Clocktower (The)		XXX	110
Clover Club		≣	443
Co.		X	19
Colicchio & Sons		XXX	19
Colonia Verde		XX	465
Colonie		XX	443
Community Food & Juice		XX	193
Cómodo		XX	325
Cooklyn		XX	486
Cookshop		XX	20
Coppelia	Ⓑ	X	20
Corner Social		XX	194
Cosme		XX	112
Craftbar		XX	113
Crave Fishbar		XX	237
Crema		XX	21
db Bistro Moderne		XX	278
DBGB Kitchen & Bar	Ⓑ	XX	58
Dear Bushwick		X	466
Delaware and Hudson	✿	XX	519
Diner	Ⓑ	X	520
Dirty French		XX	213
Do or Dine	Ⓑ	X	466
Dover		XX	444
Dovetail	✿	XX	402
Dutch (The)		XX	325
East 12th Osteria		XX	60
East Pole		XX	370
Edi & The Wolf		X	61
Egg	Ⓑ	X	520
El Almacen		X	521
élan		XX	114
Elberta	Ⓑ	XX	487
El Born		XX	521
Eli's Table		XX	370
Elizabeth's Neighborhood Table		XX	401
El Paso		X	195
El Quinto Pino		XX	22
Empellón Taqueria		XX	150
Emporio		XX	327
EN Japanese Brasserie		XXX	151
Estela		XX	327
Eugene & Co.		X	467
Extra Virgin		XX	151
Farm on Adderley (The)		XX	487
Fat Radish (The)		XX	213
Fatty Fish		X	371
Feast		X	62
Fig & Olive		XX	372
Fishtag		XX	403
Fishtail by David Burke		XXX	372
Fitzcarraldo		XX	470
Flat Top		X	195
Flinders Lane		X	62
Fonda		X	488
Foragers City Table		XX	24
Forcella		X	522
Fort Defiance		X	502
44 & X Hell's Kitchen		XX	281
FP Patisserie		X	373
Frankies 457 Spuntino	Ⓑ	X	445
French Louie		XX	445
Gander (The)		XX	116
Gastroteca		XX	561
General Greene (The)	Ⓑ	X	470
Gladys	Ⓑ	X	471
Gnocco		X	63
Good		XX	153
Good Fork (The)	Ⓑ	X	502
Gran Eléctrica	Ⓑ	XX	446
Greek (The)		XX	349
Harry's Cafe & Steak		XX	92
Havana Café	Ⓑ	XX	425
Hearth		XX	64
Hecho en Dumbo	Ⓑ	X	155
Huertas		XX	65
Il Buco Alimentari e Vineria	Ⓑ	XX	156
Il Gattopardo		XX	284
Il Ristorante Rosi		XXX	374
Jack the Horse		XX	447
James		XX	489
Joe & MissesDoe		X	67
John Dory Oyster Bar (The)		X	120
JoJo		XX	376
Jolie Cantina		X	448
Jones Wood Foundry		X	376
Joseph Leonard		X	157
Jubilee		XX	241
Juventino		XX	490
Khe-Yo	Ⓑ	XX	349
Krupa Grocery		XX	490
La Esquina		X	39
Lafayette		XX	159
Lambs Club (The)		XX	288
Landmarc		XX	352
L'Antagoniste		XX	471

Restaurant			Page
L'Apicio		XX	70
L'Artusi		XX	159
Las Ramblas		≣	160
La Superior		X	524
Lavagna		X	70
La Vara	❀	XX	449
Lea	☺	XX	491
Le Fond		X	524
Le Gigot		X	161
Le Philosophe		XX	161
Les Halles		X	122
Lil' Frankie's	☺	X	71
Lincoln		XXX	406
Little Beet Table (The)		XX	123
Little Owl (The)		X	162
Little Park		XX	352
Locanda Verde		XX	353
Locanda Vini e Olii		X	472
Loi Estiatorio		XX	291
Louie and Chan		X	215
Macondo		XX	216
Maialino		XX	123
Maison Harlem		X	197
Maison Kayser		XX	378
Maizal		X	606
Malaparte		X	163
Marc Forgione		XX	354
Marché du Sud		X	378
Margaux		XX	163
Maria's Bistro Mexicano		X	504
Mari Vanna		XX	124
Market Table		XX	164
Marlow & Sons	☺	X	525
Mar's		X	573
Marta		XX	125
Maya		XX	379
Mayfield		XX	473
Maysville		XX	125
Maz Mezcal		X	379
Meadowsweet	❀	XX	527
Melba's		X	198
Mercer Kitchen		XX	330
Mesa Coyoacán		X	528
Mile End	☺	X	450
Mimi's Hummus		≣	491
Minetta Tavern	❀	X	166
Miranda		XX	528
Miss Lily's		X	165
Mominette		X	473
Momofuku Ssäm Bar	☺	X	75
Montmartre		XX	25
Morandi		XX	167
Morgan's BBQ		X	492
MP Taverna		XX	573
Mundo		XX	574
Murray's Cheese Bar		XX	167
M. Wells Steakhouse	❀	XX	575
Narcissa		XX	76
Navy		X	330
New Leaf Café		XX	199
Nightingale 9		X	450
900 Park		XX	428
No. 7		XX	474
Nocciola		XX	199
NoMad	❀	XX	127
Norma's		XX	299
Northeast Kingdom		X	474
North End Grill		XXX	95
Northern Spy Food Co.		X	77
Nougatine		XX	408
Odeon (The)		XX	354
Orsay		XX	382
Osteria al Doge		XX	300
Osteria Laguna		XX	249
Pachanga Patterson		X	579
Pagani		XX	168
Palo Santo		X	492
Pampano		XX	249
Papatzul		X	332
Paradou		X	169
Parigot		XX	42
Park Avenue		XX	129
Parkside		XX	580
Parlor Steakhouse		XX	382
Pastai		XX	26
Pearl Room (The)		XX	507
Pera		XX	250
Perilla		XX	170
Perry Street		XX	171
Petrossian		XXX	301
Pier A		XX	95
Pine Bar & Grill		XX	429
Place (The)		XX	171
Porsena	☺	XX	78
Prime Meats	☺	XX	451
Print		XX	304
Prune	☺	X	79
Public	❀	XX	334

Restaurant			Page
Purple Yam	☺	X	493
Pylos		XX	80
Quatorze Bis		XX	383
Recette		XX	173
Red Cat (The)		XX	27
RedFarm		X	174
Red Rooster		XX	200
Regency Bar & Grill (The)		XX	384
Resto		X	130
Reynard		XX	532
Ristorante Morini		XXX	384
River Café (The)	✿	XXX	452
River Styx		X	533
Roberta's	☺	X	475
Rocking Horse Cafe		XX	28
Roebling Tea Room		X	533
Root & Bone		X	82
Rubirosa	☺	XX	336
Rucola		X	453
Runner (The)		XX	476
Runner & Stone	☺	XX	510
Russ & Daughters Cafe	☺	XX	216
Rye	☺	X	534
Santina		XX	175
Saraghina		X	477
Sauce		X	217
Saxon + Parole		XX	175
Scarlatto		XX	306
Schiller's Liquor Bar		XX	218
Selamat Pagi		X	536
Sessanta		XX	337
Settepani		XX	201
Shalom Japan	☺	X	536
Sip Sak		XX	253
Snack	☺	X	337
Snack EOS		X	307
Socarrat		XX	29
Sociale		XX	453
SoCo		XX	477
Spasso		XX	178
Speedy Romeo	☺	X	478
Spigolo		XX	386
Spitzer's Corner		X	218
Spotted Pig	✿	X	179
Standard Grill		XX	178
Stanton Social (The)		XX	219
Stella 34		XX	308
Stone Park Cafe		X	493
Supper	☺	XX	84
Sushi Katsuei		X	494
Tabaré		X	538
Taboon		XX	309
Talde		XX	494
Telepan	✿	XXX	412
Tertulia	☺	XX	181
Tessa		XX	411
Thelma on Clinton	☺	XX	219
Thistle Hill Tavern		X	495
Tía Pol		≣	29
Tiny's		X	358
Tipsy Parson		XX	30
Toloache		XX	311
Trestle on Tenth		XX	31
Tribeca Grill		XX	358
Turkish Kitchen	☺	XX	132
Umi NOM	☺	X	478
Union Square Cafe		XX	133
Untitled	☺	XX	181
Upland		XX	133
Uva	☺	X	390
Venturo Osteria & Wine Bar	☺	X	591
Vesta Trattoria		X	591
Vics		XX	182
Vinatería		XX	202
Vinegar Hill House	☺	X	456
Wassail		XX	220
Yefsi		XX	391
Yerba Buena Perry		XX	183
Zizi Limona	☺	X	540

Credits

Page 4: MICHELIN
Page 5: Ivo M. Vermeulen/The New York Botanical Garden
Page 9: David Buffington/Getty Images
Pages 12-14, 16-17: MICHELIN
Page 23: Del Posto
Pages 32, 34, 46-49, 56: MICHELIN
Page 66: Swee Phuah
Page 69: Mayumi Ando
Page 74: Gabriele Stabile
Page 85: Somtum Der
Pages 88, 90-91, 97, 98-99: MICHELIN
Page 103: Jerry Errico
Page 109: Melissa Hom
Page 111: Kelly Campbell
Page 115: Francesco Tonelli
Page 117: Daniel Krieger
Page 121. Ronnie Bhardwaj
Page 127: Daniel Krieger
Pages 134-137, 143: MICHELIN
Page 146: Ben Alsop
Page 149: Daniel Krieger
Page 154: David Cavallo
Page 166: Sylvia Paret
Page 172: Nicole Franzen
Page 177: Tokio Kuniyoshi
Page 179: The Spotted Pig
Page 184: KG-NY
Page 185: Dylan + Jenni
Pages 186-187, 204, 206-207: MICHELIN
Pages 222-225: MICHELIN
Page 231: Signe Birck
Page 235: Yiming Wang
Page 236: Caviar Russe
Page 242: Juni
Page 243: Chihiro Kimura
Page 255: Shinya Nakamura
Page 256: Tempura Matsui
Page 258: Eric McCarthy/Tulsi
Pages 260-263: MICHELIN
Page 266: Anthony Jackson
Page 269: Eric Laignel
Page 272: Signe Birck
Page 282: Paul Wagtouicz
Page 290: Francesco Tonelli
Page 294: Ted Axelrod
Page 295: Patrick Crawford/ Blackletter
Page 297: Ellen Silverman
Page 302: Deborah Jones
Pages 312, 316-318: MICHELIN
Page 329: Naoko Takagi
Page 331: Emily Andrews
Page 334: Michael Weber
Page 335: Evan Sung
Page 338: Oleg March
Pages 339, 340, 342-343: MICHELIN
Page 344: Nathan Rawlinson
Page 345: Daniel Krieger
Page 347: Nicole Bartelme
Page 348: Nicole Bartelme/Brushstroke
Page 350: MICHELIN
Page 351: Jungsik
Page 356: Peter Dressel
Page 357: Sushi Azabu
Pages 360, 362: MICHELIN
Page 366: Melissa Hom
Page 369: B. Milne
Page 387: Sushi of Gari
Pages 392, 394-395: MICHELIN
Page 396: Andanada
Page 402: Nick Solares
Page 405: Francesco Tonelli
Page 409: Picholine
Page 412: Luke Leonard
Pages 414-415: Ivo M. Vermeulen/The New York Botanical Garden
Page 416: Robert Benson/The New York Botanical Garden
Pages 417, 418-419: MICHELIN
Pages 432-433, 436-437: MICHELIN
Page 442: Annie Gonzalez
Page 449: Lauren Volo
Page 452: VivaVioletaPhotography.com
Page 455: Signe Birck
Pages 457, 458-459: MICHELIN
Page 464: Anthony Falco
Page 469: Gabe McMackin
Pages 479, 480-481: MICHELIN
Page 496-497: MICHELIN
Page 509: Evan Sung
Pages 512-513: MICHELIN
Page 519: John Taggart
Page 526: Signe Brick
Page 527: Evan Sung
Page 531: Peter Luger
Page 537: Melissa Hom
Pages 541, 542-547: MICHELIN
Page 557: Paloma Cacho-Sousa
Page 575: Jesse Winter/Ten10 Studios
Pages 594-596, 598-599, 609: MICHELIN

Notes

Michelin

Notes

Michelin

Notes

Michelin

Michelin is committed to improving the mobility of travellers

ON EVERY ROAD AND BY EVERY MEANS

Since the company came into being – over a century ago – Michelin has had a single objective: to offer people a better way forward. A technological challenge first, to create increasingly efficient tires, but also an ongoing commitment to travelers, to help them travel in the best way. This is why Michelin is developing a whole collection of products and services: from maps, atlases, travel guides and auto accessories, to mobile apps, route planners and online assistance: Michelin is doing everything it can to make traveling more pleasurable!

France
Tourist & Motoring Atlas
40 town plans
Safety Warnings
Sights and scenic routes indicated
Route planner with major itineraries
RESTAURANTS
2014
Itinéraires
FRANCE
2014
Michelin Apps
Because the notions of comfort and security are essential, both for you and for us, Michelin has created a package of six free mobile applications—a comprehensive collection to make driving a pleasure!
MICHELIN
Michelin MyCar • To get the best from your tires; services and information for carefree travel preparation.
MICHELIN
Michelin Navigation • A new approach to navigation: traffic in real time with a new connected guidance feature.
MICHELIN
ViaMichelin • Calculates routes and map data: a must for traveling in the most efficient way.
MICHELIN
Michelin Restaurants • Because driving should be enjoyable: find a wide choice of restaurants, in France and Germany, including the MICHELIN Guide's complete listings.
MICHELIN
Michelin Hotels • To book hotel rooms at the best rates, all over the world!
MICHELIN
Michelin Voyage • 85 countries and 30, 000 tourist sites selected by the Michelin Green Guide, plus a tool for creating your own travel book.
DUBLIN
MADRID
Plano e índice
More than 40 countries
des vignobles
en France
Stadtplan und Reg

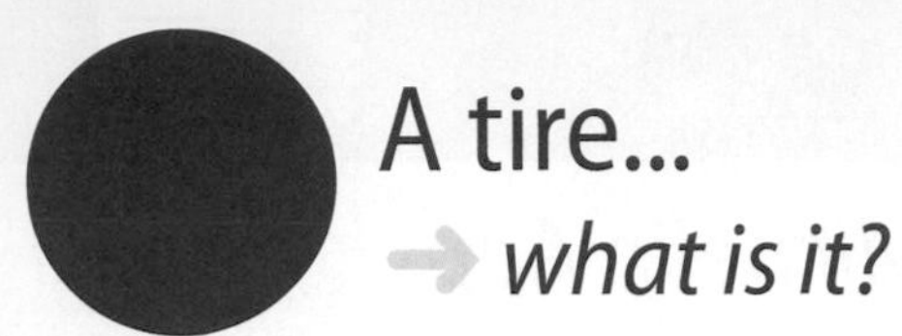

A tire...
→ what is it?

Round, black, supple yet solid, the tire is to the wheel what the shoe is to the foot. But what is it made of? First and foremost, rubber, but also various textile and/or metallic materials... and then it's filled with air! It is the skilful assembly of all these components that ensures tires have the qualities they should: grip to the road, shock absorption, in two words: 'comfort' and 'safety.'

1 *TREAD*
The tread ensures the tire performs correctly, by dispersing water, providing grip and increasing longevity.

2 *CROWN PLIES*
This reinforced double or triple belt combines vertical suppleness with transversal rigidity, enabling the tire to remain flat to the road.

3 *SIDEWALLS*
These link all the component parts and provide symmetry. They enable the tire to absorb shock, thus giving a smooth ride.

4 *BEADS*
The bead wires ensure that the tire is fixed securely to the wheel to ensure safety.

5 *INNER LINER*
The inner liner creates an airtight seal between the wheel rim and the tire.

Michelin

→ *innovation in movement*

Created and patented by Michelin in 1946, the belted radial-ply tire revolutionized the world of tires. But Michelin did not stop there: over the years other new and original solutions came out, confirming Michelin's position as a leader in research and innovation.

→ *the right pressure!*

One of Michelin's priorities is safer mobility. In short, innovating for a better way forward. This is the challenge for researchers, who are working to perfect tires capable of shorter braking distances and offering the best possible traction to the road. To support motorists, Michelin organizes road safety awareness campaigns all over the world: "Fill up with air" initiatives remind everyone that the right tire pressure is a crucial factor in safety and fuel economy.

The Michelin strategy:
→ *multi-performance tires*

Michelin is synonymous with safety, fuel saving and the capacity to cover thousands of miles. A MICHELIN tire is the embodiment of all these things – thanks to our engineers, who work with the very latest technology.

Their challenge: to equip every tire – whatever the vehicle (car, truck, tractor, bulldozer, plane, motorbike, bicycle or train!) – with the best possible combination of qualities, for optimal overall performance.

Slowing down wear, reducing energy expenditure (and therefore CO_2 emissions), improving safety through enhanced road handling and braking: there are so many qualities in just one tire – that's Michelin Total Performance.

Every day, **Michelin** is working towards sustainable mobility

OVER TIME, WHILE RESPECTING THE PLANET

Sustainable mobility

is clean mobility... and mobility for everyone

Sustainable mobility means enabling people to get around in a way that is cleaner, safer, more economical and more accessible to everyone, wherever they might live. Every day, Michelin's 113,000 employees worldwide are innovating:

- by creating tires and services that meet society's new needs.
- by raising young people's awareness of road safety.
- by inventing new transport solutions that consume less energy and emit less CO_2.

Michelin Challenge Bibendum

Sustainable mobility means allowing the transport of goods and people to continue, while promoting responsible economic, social and societal development. Faced with the increasing scarcity of raw materials and global warming, Michelin is standing up for the environment and public health. Michelin regularly organizes 'Michelin Challenge Bibendum', the only event in the world which focuses on sustainable road travel.

MICHELIN
CHALLENGE
BIBENDUM

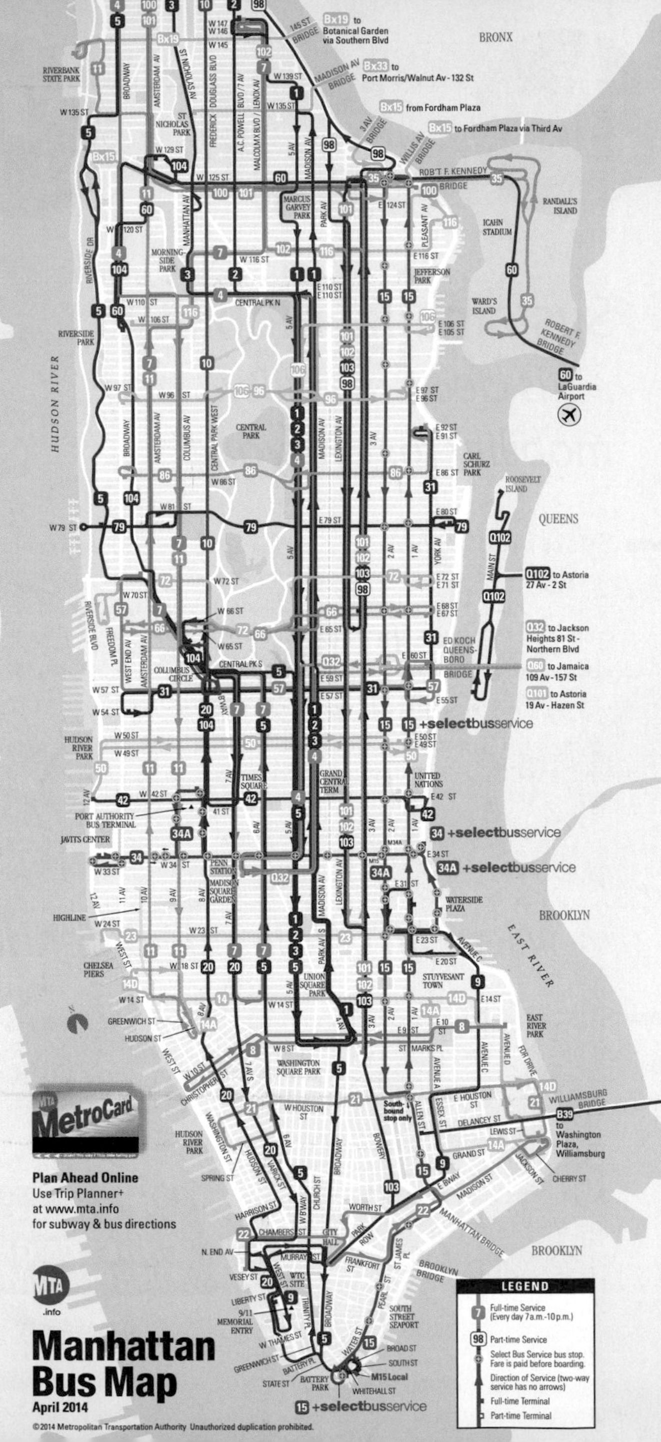
Manhattan
Bus Map
April 2014
Plan Ahead Online
Use Trip Planner+
at www.mta.info
for subway & bus directions
MetroCard
MTA
.info
LEGEND
Full-time Service (Every day 7 a.m.-10 p.m.)
Part-time Service
Select Bus Service bus stop. Fare is paid before boarding.
Direction of Service (two-way service has no arrows)
Full-time Terminal
Part-time Terminal
15 +selectbusservice
34 +selectbusservice
34A +selectbusservice
Bx19 to Botanical Garden via Southern Blvd
Bx33 to Port Morris/Walnut Av - 132 St
Bx15 from Fordham Plaza
Bx15 to Fordham Plaza via Third Av
60 to LaGuardia Airport
Q102 to Astoria 27 Av - 2 St
Q32 to Jackson Heights 81 St - Northern Blvd
Q60 to Jamaica 109 Av - 157 St
Q101 to Astoria 19 Av - Hazen St
B39 to Washington Plaza, Williamsburg
HUDSON RIVER
EAST RIVER
BRONX
QUEENS
BROOKLYN
CENTRAL PARK
©2014 Metropolitan Transportation Authority Unauthorized duplication prohibited.